Contemporary Rorschach
Interpretation

The LEA Series in
Personality and Clinical Psychology
Irving B. Weiner, Editor

Contemporary Rorschach Interpretation

Edited by

J. Reid Meloy

Marvin W. Acklin

Carl B. Gacono

James F. Murray

Charles A. Peterson

LEA LAWRENCE ERLBAUM ASSOCIATES, PUBLISHERS
1997 Mahwah, New Jersey

Lawrence Erlbaum Associates, Inc., Publishers
10 Industrial Avenue
Mahwah, New Jersey 07430

Cover design by Kathryn Houghtaling
Cover photo by Reid Meloy

Library of Congress Cataloging-in-Publication Data

Contemporary Rorschach interpretation / edited by
J. Reid Meloy . . . [et al.].
p. cm.
Includes bibliographical references and index.
ISBN 0-8058-1920-7 (cloth : alk. paper)
1. Rorschach Test—Interpretation—Case studies.
I. Meloy, J. Reid.
[DNLM: 1. Rorschach Test. 2. Psychotic Disor-
ders—diagnosis—case studies. 3. Borderline Person-
ality Disorder—diagnosis—case studies. 4. Neurotic
Disorders—diagnosis—case studies. WM 145.5.R7
C761 1997]
RC473.R6C66   1997
616.89'075—dc21
DNLM/DLC
for Library of Congress   96–49872
                                                      CIP

Printed in the United States of America
10   9   8   7   6   5   4   3   2   1

So I walk the shores of this summer world. There is no winter here, amazing, yes, no winter of discontent it would almost seem, and death a rumor beyond the dunes. I walk along in my own time and way and come on people and let the wind flap my great sailcloth shirt now veering north, south, or south-by-west and watch their eyes pop, glide, leer, squint, wonder. And when a certain person says a certain word about my ink-slashed cotton colors I give pause. I chat. I walk with them awhile. We peer into the great glass of the sea. I sidewise peer into their soul. Sometimes we stroll for hours, a longish session with the weather. Usually it takes but that one day and, not knowing with whom they walked, scot-free, they are discharged all unwitting patients. They walk on down the dusky shore toward a fairer brighter eve. Behind their backs, the deaf-blind man waves them bon voyage and trots home there to devour happy suppers, brisk with fine work done.

—Ray Bradbury, "The Man in the Rorschach Shirt"

The editors (left to right): Charles A. Peterson, Carl B. Gacono, Marvin W. Acklin, James F. Murray, J. Reid Meloy.

Contents

III. Neurotic Personality Organization

IV. Special Applications

Foreword

The editors of this volume have assembled a book that runs long and deep in the best traditions of the Rorschach Inkblot Method. First among these traditions is the long-recognized fact that the Rorschach is a complex and multifaceted assessment instrument in which both perceptual features of how subjects structure their responses and associational features of the thematic imagery they produce contribute valuable information about personality functioning. Adequate Rorschach interpretation can proceed only in the context of both empirical data to validate conclusions based on the perceptual features of the instrument, and theoretical formulations to guide hypotheses derived from its associational features.

With this in mind, Drs. Meloy, Acklin, Gacono, Murray, and Peterson have designed *Contemporary Rorschach Interpretation* to stand tall on two sturdy legs. One of these legs is the rich tradition of empirical approaches to the Rorschach, beginning with Hermann Rorschach and culminating in Exner's Comprehensive System. The other leg is the equally rich tradition of psychoanalytic approaches to the Rorschach, as pioneered by Klopfer, Rapaport, Schafer, and Schachtel and carried on in the contemporary work of such object relations theorists as Blatt and Lerner. The editors' introduction to this volume and each of the chapters that follow exemplify a firm and commendable commitment to thoughtful integration of these empirical and theoretical perspectives in Rorschach interpretation.

In their previous journal publications and in the present book, the editors have resurrected the Rorschach tradition of formal case presentation. Present-day commentaries on Rorschach's original *Psychodiagnostics* seldom note that he included 28 case illustrations in this monograph, each with a fully scored protocol and a set of interpretive comments. The scoring and comments in these cases are sketchy by today's standards, but they represent as much as Rorschach was able to say about his instrument in 1921 and established the important place of detailed case studies in the Rorschach literature. Most of the classic texts subsequently published on the Rorschach included numerous case examples accompanied by complete protocols and detailed interpretations.

However, as the editors note in their introduction, there has been little attention in the journal literature to case studies in which experienced clinicians present and analyze Rorschach protocols to demonstrate the utility of the instrument for assessing various types of persons and conditions. The editors' awareness of this gap in the literature, and their recognition of how instructive case studies can be, led them to publish a series of such reports in the *Journal of Personality Assessment*. These journal articles are reprinted in the present volume, along with several additional case studies prepared by the five editors and numerous invited contributions by other experienced and well-known Rorschach clinicians.

The third tradition embraced by the editors is the role of the mentor in the teaching and learning of Rorschach assessment. As they elaborate in their introduction, psychologists cannot become able Rorschach clinicians solely by studying textbooks and reading the research literature. To use the inkblot method effectively in providing personality descriptions and delineating the inner world of individual people, psychologists need the experience of conducting examinations in a clinical setting under the tutelage of mentors who can impart their knowledge of how to interpret a Rorschach protocol.

The editors acknowledge the mentors who have helped them become skillful Rorschach clinicians, and in preparing this volume they have signified a passing of the torch. Now they and the other contributors who speak in these pages are the mentors, and there is much for their colleagues and students to learn from what they have to say about Rorschach interpretation. As these observations imply, psychologists learning the Rorschach should take advantage of whatever opportunities they have to work with experienced and informed Rorschach clinicians and to listen to gifted teachers who describe how they use the instrument.

The particular case studies that constitute the chapters of this book cover a broad range of personality styles and problems. The cases are grouped around the three levels of personality organization formulated by Kernberg (psychotic, borderline, and neurotic), and they also address such special problems as eating disorders, deviant sexual behavior, chronic fatigue syndrome, and neuropsychological impairment. The protocols presented include some given by famous and infamous people (Linus Pauling, Sirhan Sirhan, and Baldur von Schirach) and child and adolescent as well as adult records. In each case presentation, the Rorschach protocols are carefully analyzed in light of relevant empirical and theoretical foundations and also with respect to the implications of the findings for events in the subjects' lives.

For accomplished and aspiring Rorschach examiners alike, the contents of this impressive volume will provide an entertaining and informative tour through the process of transforming Rorschach data into vibrant and meaningful pictures of people.

—Irving B. Weiner

Contributors

Marvin W. Acklin is in the full time independent practice of clinical and forensic psychology, and is affiliated with the Clinical Studies Program, University of Hawaii at Manoa, Honolulu, Hawaii.

Virginia Brabender is an associate professor and director of internship training at Widener University.

Arnold R. Bruhn is a clinical psychologist in private practice in Bethesda, Maryland.

Cynthia A. Claassen is an instructor, Division of Psychology, Department of Psychiatry, University of Texas Southwestern Medical Center.

Susan Colligan is a neuropsychologist at John Muir Medical Center and is on the faculty of Rorschach Workshops.

Clifford M. DeCato is a professor and associate director of the Institute for Graduate Clinical Psychology at Widener University.

Carl B. Gacono is with the U.S. Department of Justice and a fellow of the Society for Personality Assessment.

Ted G. Goertzel is a professor of sociology and director of the Forum for Policy Research, Rutgers University.

Leonard Handler is professor, associate director of clinical training, and director of the psychology clinic at the University of Tennessee, Knoxville.

Mark J. Hilsenroth is assistant professor, Department of Psychology, University of Arkansas, and research consultant, Austen Riggs Center and the VAMC at Mountain Home, Tennessee.

Janet Kates is a clinical psychologist in independent practice in Oklahoma City, Oklahoma.

James H. Kleiger is director of psychology training at the Menninger Clinic and an advanced candidate at the Topeka Institute for Psychoanalysis.

Robert Lovitt is an associate professor, Division of Psychology, Department of Psychiatry, University of Texas Southwestern Medical Center.

J. Reid Meloy is associate clinical professor of psychiatry at the University of California, San Diego and adjunct professor at the University of San Diego School of Law.

James F. Murray is a founding member and past president of the Appalachian Psychoanalytic Society and is in the private practice of clinical and forensic psychology in Knoxville, Tennessee.

William Perry is assistant professor of psychiatry at the University of California, San Diego, and associate director of inpatient psychiatry at the UCSD Medical Center.

Charles A. Peterson is director of training in psychology at the VA Minneapolis Medical Center and in the independent practice of psychoanalytic psychotherapy and psychodiagnosis.

Cynthia Lindman Port is a graduate student at the University of Minnesota and is an intern in counseling psychology at the Department of Veterans Affairs, Minneapolis Medical Center.

Eric Potterat is a graduate student at the California School of Professional Psychology in San Diego and an intern in clinical psychology at Balboa Naval Hospital.

Rebecca E. Rieger is affiliated with Chestnut Lodge Hospital and is clinical professor of psychiatry and pediatrics at George Washington University School of Medicine.

Barry Ritzler is a professor of psychology at Long Island University, and is on the faculty of Rorschach Workshops.

Bruce L. Smith is in the independent practice of psychoanalytic psychotherapy and psychodiagnosis and is assistant clinical professor at the University of California, Berkeley and San Francisco.

Donald J. Viglione, Jr.   is professor of psychology, California School of Professional Psychology, San Diego, and is on the faculty of Rorschach Workshops.

Diana Wright   is a clinical psychologist in Mammoth Lakes, California.

1

Introduction

J. Reid Meloy
James F. Murray

Hamlet. Do you see yonder cloud that's almost in shape of a camel?
Polonius. By the mass, and 'tis like a camel, indeed.
Hamlet. Methinks it is like a weasel.
Polonius. It is back'd like a weasel.
Hamlet. Or like a whale?
Polonius. Very like a whale.

—*Shakespeare, Hamlet, Act 3, Scene 2*

The dilemma of Polonius was that with each of his empathic comments, Hamlet produced another different response. Such is the beauty and complexity of the human mind when perceiving an ambiguous stimulus, an insight that led Hermann Rorschach to develop his scientific method 80 years ago.

We are full of gratitude for his brief life and work, and we hope this book will stand as an idiographic testament to his brilliance for those Rorschach students who come after us. But what of the origins of this particular project? Although the paternity status of this book is multiple, the maternity lies within the fecundity of the Society for Personality Assessment (SPA). The Society has nurtured, cajoled, and inspired the professional growth and development of each of the editors, most notably through the annual pilgrimage to our Mecca—the various cities selected for the SPA Midwinter Meeting each year.

As young psychologists, Meloy, Acklin, Gacono, Murray, and Peterson would attend various presentations at the meetings, retreat to their often shared hotel rooms, commiserate over the seminar content and familial dynamics of SPA, and gratify their senses in the evening with the ambience of a blues bar, selected by Peterson, and the elixir of the moment. Henry V was often bonded with us in spirit: "We few, we happy few, we band of brothers."

But something intellectual also happened. We noticed a shared view emerging that defined how we worked with the Rorschach. We were empiricists, but we also thought from within a psychoanalytic frame. Our data confirmed or disconfirmed theory, but theory gave flesh to the bone.

In those days, only a mindful decade ago, Rorschach work was fundamentally divided into two often fractious and occasionally warring camps: those adamant proponents of Exner's Comprehensive System, and their opponents, the psychoanalytic disciples of Rorschach interpretation. Each side would offer what to us were often valid critiques of the other side, but to our astonishment, remained painfully blind to the opposing camp's assets. Background checks of these individuals revealed a certain pedigree. Often, the Comprehensive System purists had worked closely and trained with John Exner, Jr., and the psychoanalytic Rorschach clinicians had been bred at the Menninger Clinic, Austen Riggs Center, or Yale University. If one paid close attention, the pungent aroma of East Coast Ivy League intellectual elitism wafted through the air, blanketing the crusty exterior of Midwest dustbowl empiricism. Balkanization of the Rorschach, we were afraid, was at hand.

From our clinical and research perspective, the combination of Comprehensive System empirical data and psychoanalytic theory concerning the Rorschach had a synergistic strength, each ameliorated by the other. We were also cognizant of the paper trail that these two avenues of Rorschach work were leaving behind—the Comprehensive System was rooted in the published volumes of Exner (1969, 1974, 1986, 1991), and the psychoanalytic research methods were defined in a series of books by different authors of the same ilk (Kissen, 1986; Kwawer, Lerner, Lerner, & Sugarman, 1980; Lerner, 1991; Lerner & Lerner, 1988). We could not help but notice historical parallels with the Anna Freud and Melanie Klein controversies a half-century earlier, and perhaps the need for a Rorschach analogue to the so-called "British School" of independent psychoanalysts that bore such luminaries as Fairbairn, Winnicott, and Guntrip. Or maybe we were just swept up in the psychohistorical pull of a Hegelian synthesis.

We observed another curious phenomenon, most eloquently captured by Peterson (1994) in his comments on the absence of "idiographic cartographers" among the authors of published Rorschach research. In other words, nomothetic (group) Rorschach studies were ubiquitous in the journals; but where were the Rorschach clinicians willing to score, analyze, and interpret a single Rorschach case for publication? And if no one was willing to do this (with a few notable exceptions; e.g., Viglione, 1990), how could we even pretend to mentor the next generation of Rorschach clinicians beyond our own doctoral students whom we personally trained?

These concerns are what motivated us to plan a 3-year series of presentations (1991–1993) at the SPA meetings titled, "Through the Looking Glass." With the trepidation and excitement that accompanies any intellectual risk, particularly one that will be contemporaneously scrutinized by our colleagues, we decided to present three cases illustrating a level of personality organization each year, beginning with psychotic personality organization, each framed by a theoretical and empirical introduction by Marvin Acklin. Needless to say, the symposiums were enjoyable, well-attended, and cordially received as scholarly attempts to conduct idiographic research with the Rorschach. The papers were published as a series in the *Journal of Personality Assessment* each subsequent year, expertly tooled by the editor, Irving Weiner, and are reprinted in full in this book.

Our understanding of the power of integrating the Comprehensive System with psychoanalytic approaches still leaves us with the question of how to best present this perspective to others. Any formal codification seems almost impossible given the daunting complexity of the issues at hand; to say nothing of the hard-headed, or at least highly individualistic, nature of each of us when dealing with the small details (*Dd*) of our own approaches to Rorschach data. Thus, largely without knowing it, we have stumbled on two truths about learning the Rorschach. First, the Rorschach can only be learned in a clinical setting. To use the Rorschach with any degree of sophistication, one must be able to weave the Rorschach within the warp and weft of developmental theory and research, theories of psychopathology, personality theory (particularly psychoanalysis), and knowledge of psychotherapy and psychopharmacology. The individual under study comes alive only in the fabric of this tapestry.

The demands imposed by such a sophisticated weave bring us to the second truth. Rorschach interpretation is the only activity in psychology that can even approach psychoanalysis in providing a deep psychological understanding of the individual. Consequently, it is best learned from a mentor through the process by which one can see how someone who knows more than you goes about analyzing and interpreting a Rorschach protocol, and integrates the findings with theory, research, and real-world behavior. It is only after several "good enough mentorings" that one has a chance to become competent with the Rorschach. Inevitably, the mentoring stage is accompanied by idealization and imitation. But after a period of time maturation occurs, and the student acquires his or her own unique style.

This book is in large part an effort to provide this mentoring to fellow students of the Rorschach, and to thank those who sheparded us. Although assimilation of one's mentor's knowledge with the student's own insights, in a true Piagetian sense, takes one beyond mere imitation, there is an indelible mark left by the experience of one's teachers. Each of us would like to thank our own teachers through a recounting of our own Rorschach genealogies, and offer this book as a token of gratitude for their patience and wisdom.

Reid Meloy was originally taught the Rorschach by Sidney Smith during his graduate studies, utilizing the methodology of Rapaport, Gill, and Schafer and the form-level scoring of Martin Mayman. He got a "B" on his first interpreted protocol, and regrets that he was never administered the Rorschach before he learned what it meant; therefore an accurate count of his reflection responses is impossible. Sidney Smith has since died, but for years made his home, and left his mark, at the Menninger Clinic. Meloy was subsequently trained in the Comprehensive System through Rorschach Workshops, his principal teachers being Phil Erdberg, John Exner, and Irving Weiner. To all these men he is grateful, but when an original mentor becomes, through the years, a close personal friend, as Phil Erdberg has become, a true gift has been received. Meloy's body of Rorschach work, moreover, is deeply influenced by psychoanalytic theory, and no one person has been more central to his grounding of analytic thought in personal experience than his psychoanalyst, James Morris, a true archaeologist of the mind.

A number of mentors have played a role in Marvin Acklin's interest and skills in the Rorschach, most notably Ray Craddick, who first taught him the Rorschach in 1980, and John Exner, whose Comprehensive System has been the matrix of his development as a clinical psychologist. Craddick taught projectives with a spirit that inspired and excited his students. He introduced Acklin to John Exner at one of the 5-day basic tutorials that Exner used to do a long time ago. Others too, less directly, but not less influentially, include Sidney Blatt, though he may never have known it; his students, Barry Ritzler and Howard Lerner; and Irving Weiner, former editor of the *Journal of Personality Assessment*. Acklin's colleagues in the SPA have been a continuing influence in recent years, including Paul Lerner, Jim Murray, Reid Meloy, Carl Gacono, Jim Kleiger, Martin Leichtman, Don Viglione, and others. Finally, he could not encompass his genealogy without mentioning his good friend and colleague, Charles Peterson. A consummate scholar and blues man, he exemplifies the analytic attitude and virtues of loyal friendship to the highest degree.

Carl Gacono's graduate studies included training with James Madero, utilizing the Comprehensive System; Jay Kwawer's primitive modes of relating; and Paul and Howard Lerner's defense scales. Subsequently, he trained and consulted with Phil Erdberg, Paul Lerner, Irving Weiner, and John Exner. Strongly influenced by the work of David Rapaport, Roy Schafer, Martin Mayman, and others, Gacono's early training set the stage for an integrative approach to Rorschach interpretation.

James Murray initially trained in the Rorschach at Case Western Reserve University with Sandra Russ and Irving Weiner. Their work has served as a source of inspiration throughout the years. He also had the privilege of serving as a teaching assistant to Marguerite Hertz for her 2-week Rorschach seminar. In this role his responsibilities included keeping Dr. Hertz in her cigarillos and coffee, and being available to be pointed at when she referred to "those Exner people" (a position she softened on over the years). While a postdoctoral fellow at Yale Psychiatric Institute, he had the delightful opportunity to study with Sidney Blatt.

Charles Peterson was first taught the Comprehensive System by Karen Maitland Schilling, a student of Molly Harrower, who studied with Bruno Klopfer, who studied with Oberholzer, who studied with Rorschach. His understanding of the Rorschach deepened and was inspired by the writings of David Rapaport, Ernest Schachtel, and Roy Schafer, and by the supervision of Gus Crivolio, Steve Gryll, Murray Tieger, and Robert Tureen.

We have organized this book into four sections; the first three—psychotic, borderline, and neurotic levels of personality organization—are literary analogues for the horizontally demarcated levels of personality organization most recently advanced by Kernberg (1975, 1976, 1980, 1984). Within each section the editors and invited authors have contributed a Rorschach case study that vertically cuts a character pathology, personality disorder, or clinical diagnosis through that particular level of personality organization. The last section we have labeled "special" because it charts the enormously varied course that Rorschach work can navigate—from the understanding of a Nobel laureate, the pain of trauma and transvestism, and the Nazi perversion of youth, to the consensus Rorschach in couples' therapy and cutting-edge work in neuropsychology.

We are especially indebted to our contributors, and want them to know, for the first time, why they were invited. We perused the Rorschach research for individuals who had shown an interest and skill in idiographic research, and who did not shrink from the task. We also wanted individuals who were pragmatic enough—as both Comprehensive System empiricists and theorists—to not let fealty get in the way of science. We were delighted with the response to our invitations, and as you will see, they did not fail us. Our contributors are clearly the most notable Rorschach clinicians in practice, and their work should both delight and stimulate the reader. Parenthetically, the number of contributors to this book who invited a student to coauthor their chapter is emblematic of their generosity.

The integration of the Rorschach and psychoanalysis is not solely a one-way street in which the Rorschach approach is enhanced by the richness and depth of psychoanalytic insight. The Rorschach gives back to psychoanalysis almost as much as it receives. There exists a long and worthy tradition involving the use of the Rorschach to operationally define, test out, and refine psychoanalytic concepts and formulations; it stretches from Holt (1960) through the contributions of Paul and Howard Lerner and their associates (Kwawer et al., 1980; Lerner & Lerner, 1988) to Gacono and Meloy's (1994) use of the Rorschach to reformulate the psychodynamics and psychopathology of aggression and violence.

As contemporary psychoanalytic theory threatens to break through the intellectual stratosphere under the expansive influence of hermeneutics, gender politics, and deconstructionism, the Rorschach allows us to grab psychoanalysis by the toe and drag one foot back to the *terra firma* proffered by the natural science tradition. The Rorschach, with its unique window into the depth and complexity of the individual, is unrivaled in its capacity to offer a level of insight that does justice to psychoanalytic conceptualizations, while still being amenable to the more quotidian world of statistics and science. It is this close-to-magical intersection of nomothetic and idiographic that is the heart and soul of contemporary Rorschach understanding, and hopefully the heart and soul of this book.

Finally, as senior editor, Reid Meloy cannot resist a forensic comment. Several of the chapters have arisen from forensic cases, and illustrate the depth and range of Rorschach data in contributing to the resolution of legal questions. However, skepticism is still heard concerning the use of the Rorschach in court. There are a number of published articles that empirically document the wide clinical and research use of the test (Piotrowski, 1996; Piotrowski & Keller, 1989, 1992; Piotrowski, Sherry, & Keller, 1985); but most germane to the legal arena, the Rorschach continues to leave an indelible stamp (Meloy, 1991). In a research study in progress we searched the federal, state, and military case laws in the United States between 1945 and 1995 for references to the Rorschach. Almost 200 legal citations were found in which the Rorschach was discussed by the courts in substantive, if not foundational, terms (T. Hansen, personal communication, August 1, 1996). Despite the esoteric nature of the Rorschach, or maybe because of it, the courts continue to find it a reliable and valid probe into the mind of the subject (Meloy, Hansen, & Weiner, in press).

Contemporary Rorschach Interpretation is written for both students and experienced practitioners of the Rorschach. It has become a large, complex, and sophisticated book, and we hope it will be especially useful to teachers of the Rorschach to show advanced students how the method can be used in many different clinical cases. We welcome your comments.

$W + Ma.FC.FT + 2 H,Sc$ 4.0 COP

REFERENCES

Exner, J. E., Jr. (1969). *The Rorschach systems*. New York: Grune & Stratton.

Exner, J. E., Jr. (1974). *The Rorschach: A comprehensive system: Vol. 1*. New York: Wiley.

Exner, J. E., Jr. (1986). *The Rorschach: A comprehensive system: Vol. 1: Basic foundations* (2nd ed.). New York: Wiley.

Exner, J. E., Jr. (1991). *The Rorschach: A comprehensive system: Vol. 2: Interpretation*. (2nd ed.). New York: Wiley.

Gacono, C., & Meloy, J. R. (1994). *The Rorschach assessment of aggressive and psychopathic personalities*. Hillsdale, NJ: Lawrence Erlbaum Associates.

Holt, R. (1960). A method for assessing primary process-manifestations and their control in Rorschach responses. In M. Rickers-Ovsiankina (Ed.), *Rorschach psychology* (pp. 375–420). Huntington, NY: Krieger.

Kernberg, O. (1975). *Borderline conditions and pathological narcissism*. New York: Aronson.

Kernberg, O. (1976). *Object relations theory and clinical psychoanalysis*. New York: Aronson.

Kernberg, O. (1980). *Internal world and external reality*. New York: Aronson.

Kernberg, O. (1984). *Severe personality disorders*. New Haven, CT: Yale University Press.

Kissen, M. (Ed.). (1986). *Assessing object relations phenomena*. New York: International Universities Press.

Kwawer, J., Lerner, H., Lerner, P., & Sugarman, A. (Eds.). (1980). *Borderline phenomena and the Rorschach test*. New York: International Universities Press.

Lerner, H., & Lerner, P. (Ed.). (1988). *Primitive mental states and the Rorschach*. Madison, CT: International Universities Press.

Lerner, P. (1991). *Psychoanalytic theory and the Rorschach*. Hillsdale, NJ: The Analytic Press.

Meloy, J. R. (1991). Rorschach testimony. *Journal of Psychiatry and Law, 19*, 221–235.

Meloy, J. R., Hansen, T., & Weiner, I. B. (in press). The authority of the Rorschach: Legal citations during the past 50 years. *Journal of Personality Assessment*.

Peterson, C. (1994). A neurotic lawyer: AIDS or Oedipus? *Journal of Personality Assessment, 63*, 10–26.

Piotrowski, C. (1996). The status of Exner's Comprehensive System in contemporary research. *Perceptual and Motor Skills, 82*, 1341–1342.

Piotrowski, C., & Keller, J. W. (1989). Use of assessment in mental health clinics and services. *Psychological Reports, 64*, 1298.

Piotrowski, C., & Keller, J. W. (1992). Psychological testing in applied settings: A literature review from 1982–1992. *Journal of Training and Practice in Professional Psychology, 6*, 74–82.

Piotrowski, C., Sherry, D., & Keller, J. W. (1985). Psychodiagnostic test usage: a survey of the Society for Personality Assessment. *Journal of Personality Assessment, 49*, 115–119.

Viglione, D. (1990). Severe psychopathology versus stress induced adaptive reaction: A Rorschach child case study. *Journal of Personality Assessment, 55*, 281–295.

I

PSYCHOTIC PERSONALITY ORGANIZATION

2

Psychodiagnosis of Personality Structure: Psychotic Personality Organization

Marvin W. Acklin
University of Hawaii, Honolulu

The last 20 years have witnessed dramatic developments in clinical theory and practice, both within and outside of Rorschach psychology. Developments in Rorschach reflect the emerging rapprochement of two divergent and sometimes antagonistic philosophies of Rorschach interpretation: (a) the nomothetic approach, represented by the work of John Exner; and (b) idiographic and content analytic approaches, deriving from psychoanalytic theory.

Exner's empirically driven, atheoretical, score-based approach has done much to strengthen the psychometric foundations of the Rorschach and to revive the test's respectability and popularity. Rorschach psychology, as a consequence, may be stronger today in the U.S. than ever before. Exner's Comprehensive System, however, is not the only development in Rorschach psychology in the last 20 years. Parallel developments in clinical psychoanalysis and applications to Rorschach theory and practice, especially in structural-developmental and object relations theories, have exercised a significant influence. The work of Mayman, Blatt and his colleagues, P. and H. Lerner, Urist, and others is noteworthy. The confluence of these traditions of inquiry—score-based and content-based Rorschach psychology—provides the contemporary Rorschach clinician with a powerful interpretive methodology.

The structural diagnosis of personality organization was proposed by Kernberg in the mid-1970s as a supplement to descriptive and genetic approaches to diagnosis (Kernberg, 1975, 1976). Kernberg's psychostructural theory—his view that personality organization can be classified into three broad levels of functioning: Psychotic, borderline, and neurotic—represents a further stage in the development of psychoanalytic metapsychology (Stone, 1980). The psychodiagnosis of psychotic personality organization, sometimes baffling and perhaps the most dramatic clinical phenomena, is our central interest here.

The concept of mental structure has occupied a central position in psychological theory. Structural models refer to an overall intrapsychic organization that has stability, continuity, and sameness across time (Kernberg, 1980). Psychological functioning stabilizes and fluctuates in terms of structure that forms the intrapsychic matrix from which behavior emerges. That mental structures undergo developmental vicissitudes—progression and regression—is now a widely accepted and investigated notion. Structural-developmental theories (Loevinger, 1976; Mahler, 1968; Werner, 1957) stress the relation between mental structures, stages of development, mental functioning, and psychopathology.

In differentiating level of personality organization, the psychodiagnostician has a large number of theoretically derived indices reflecting various developmental lines (Freud, 1965), including ego functions, stages of defensive organization, affect development, and self and object concepts. Figure 2.1 illustrates a schema deriving from ego psychology (Blanck & Blanck, 1975).

Figure 2.2 illustrates the presumptive relationships between various stages of development, including Freud's psychosexual stages, Mahler's stages of separation-individuation, object relations, and psychopathological entities. Fixations along these developmental lines are presumed to be linked to various psychopathological entities. Although the empirical linkage between stage or phase concepts and clinical syndromes has not been demonstrated (Willick, 1990), the model has ample heuristic value for the psychodiagnostician.

Kernberg, in discussing differential diagnosis of personality organization, relied on a combination of ego psychological and object relations criteria. In a well-known formulation, Kernberg (1984) wrote:

> Neurotic, borderline, and psychotic types of organization are reflected in the patient's overriding characteristics, particularly with regard to (1) his degree of identity integration, (2) the types of defenses he habitually employs, and (3) his capacity for reality testing. I propose that neurotic personality structure, in contrast to borderline and psychotic personality structures, implies an integrated identity. Neurotic personality structure presents a defensive organization centering on repression and other advanced or high level defensive operations. In contrast, borderline and psychotic structures are found in patients showing a predominance of primitive defensive operations centering on the mechanism of splitting. Reality testing is maintained in neurotic and borderline organization but is severely impaired in psychotic organization. These structural criteria can supplement the ordinary behavioral or phenomenological descriptions of patients and sharpen the accuracy of the differential diagnosis of mental illness, especially in cases that are difficult to classify. (pp. 5–6)

Table 2.1 presents a schema illustrating Kernberg's criteria for the differential diagnosis of personality organization.

In discriminating between borderline and psychotic levels of personality functioning, Kernberg emphasized three primary criteria: identity integration versus identity diffusion and the related overall quality of internalized object

PSYCHO-SEXUAL MATURA-TION	DRIVE TAMING PROCESSES	OBJECT RELATIONS		ADAPTIVE FUNCTION		ANXIETY LEVEL
Genital	Ambivalence resolved		Postoedipal	Fitting together		Fear of superego
	Neutralized libido serves narcissism and also the capacity to maintain constant relations with an object	the capacity to maintain constant relations with an object	Object constancy	Synthetic and integrative functions	S e c o n d a r y P r o c e s s	
Phallic		Cathexis of object representations with value		Abstract thought		Fear of castration
	Neutralized aggression serves identity formation	Beginning endowment of object representations with value		Speech		
Anal	Neutralization of aggressive drive serves establishment of defense mechanisms	Diacritic perception brings awareness of need-fulfilling function of object	Semantic communication, a new level of object relations	Object comprehension		Fear of loss of love of the object
			Eight-month anxiety	Locomotion		Signal anxiety achieved
	Libido and aggression fuse		Fusion of "good" and "bad" object representations	Reality testing	P r i m a r y P r o c e s s	Fear of loss of the object
	Drives differentiate into libido and aggression	Awareness of need gratification	Smiling response, beginning of psychological relations	Intentionality		
Oral				Motility		
				Perception		
	Neutralization begins	Coenesthetic receptivity	Nondifferentiated stage, biological need gratification, objectless stage	Delay		Fear of annihilation
				Memory traces		

U N D I F F E R E N T I A T E D
Birth · Undifferentiated Drives and Apparatuses of Primary Autonomy including Motility, Memory, Intentionality.

ID   E G O

FIG. 2.1. Developmental lines pertinent to psychodiagnosis of personality organization. From *Ego Psychology: Theory and Practice* (pp. 114–115) by G. Blanck and R. Blanck. Copyright © 1975 by Columbia University Press. Reprinted with permission of the publisher. *(Continued)*

relations, constellation of advanced versus primitive defensive operations, and capacity for reality testing.

Contemporary psychodiagnosis, consequently, has three dimensions: the Axis I diagnosis based on a descriptive picture of clinical symptomatology; a

DEFENSIVE FUNCTION	IDENTITY FORMATION	PROCESSES OF INTERNALIZATION			
Secondary autonomy. Defenses change in function and become adaptive	Constant cathexis of differentiated self and object representations	Superego is structured			
Repression	Increasing internalization by means of ego and superego identifications lead to establishment of identity	Resolution of oedipus by means of identification with parent of the same sex	Ego ideal		
Regression					
Intellectualization	Separation-individuation completed, object constancy attained	Identification with phallic prowess			
Isolation	Gender identity				
Reaction formation	Rapprochement subphase	Toilet training initiates identification with strength and cleanliness			Grandiose
Undoing	Practicing subphase		Gradual disillusionment with omnipotent objects	ideal	self
Identification Displacement Reversal Turning against the self	Differentiation subphase	Selective identifications begin	object		Self
		Imitation			
Projection Introjection Denial	Merged self and object representations				
	Autistic stage	Primary narcissism			

(vertical: Separation/individuation Subphony / Symbiosis)

M A T R I X

Intelligence, Perception, Thinking, and Others

S U P E R E G O

FIG. 2.1. Continued.

diagnosis of the broad, underlying level of personality organization (psychotic, borderline, or neurotic); and a characterological or personality diagnosis (Axis II in terms used in the *Diagnostic and Statistical Manual of Mental Disorders*, 3rd ed., rev. [*DSM–III–R*]; American Psychiatric Association, 1987), which captures engrained patterns of thinking, feeling, and social interaction. A complete diagnosis, for example, might be a dysthymic disorder or a major depression in an individual with a mixed personality disorder with compulsive and dependent features organized at a neurotic level of personality organiza-

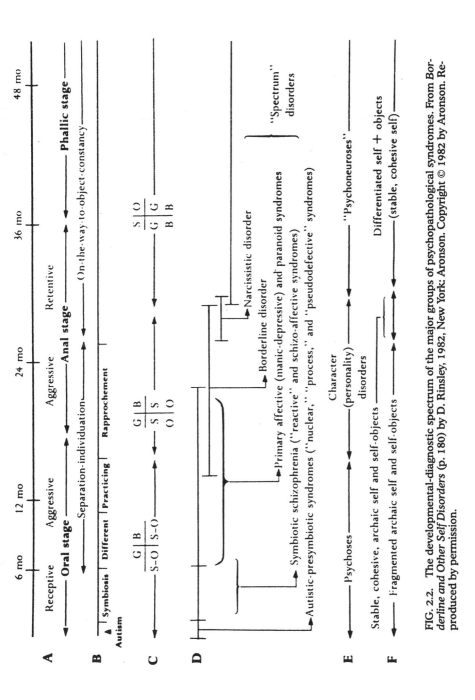

FIG. 2.2. The developmental-diagnostic spectrum of the major groups of psychopathological syndromes. From *Borderline and Other Self Disorders* (p. 180) by D. Rinsley, 1982, New York: Aronson. Copyright © 1982 by Aronson. Reproduced by permission.

15

TABLE 2.1
Kernberg's Differential Diagnosis of Personality Organization

Area	Neurosis	Borderline	Psychosis	Diff
Ego development	High	Moderate	Low	N/B/P
Reality testing	Generally intact	Good in distant relations, poor in intimate relations	Generally poor	N/B/P
Defenses	Predominantly high level	Predominantly low level	Predominantly low level	N/B
Affect	Modulated, stable, appropriate	Unmodulated, intense, unstable, inappropriate	Unmodulated, intense, unstable, inappropriate	N/B
Impulsivity	Highly selective, infrequent	Moderately selective, frequent	Unselective, frequent	N/B/P
Anxiety tolerance	High	Low	Low	N/B
Sublimatory channels	Yes	No	No	N/B
Superego integration	Contemporary, integrated, depersonified	Archaic, personified, unintegrated	Archaic, personified, unintegrated	N/B
Dynamics	Oral, anal, phallic, genital	Oral aggressive	Oral aggressive	N/B
Object relations	Contemporary, depersonified, abstract	Archaic, personified, concrete	Archaic, personified, concrete	N/B
Object constancy	Constant	Inconstant	Inconstant	N/B
Self–other differentiation	Good in most relations	Good in superficial relations	Poor in most relations	N/B/P
Identity	Intact	Diffusion likely	Diffusion	N/B
Interpersonal relationships	Stable with symptoms, anxiety inhibitions	Superficially stable, intimate relations chaotic	Unstable in all relations	N/B/P

Note. Quoted in Kernberg (1975, 1976, 1980). Diff = relevant differential diagnosis. N/B/P = neurotic, borderline, and psychotic personality organization, respectively.

tion, a narcissistic personality disorder organized at a borderline level of personality organization, or a schizoaffective disorder with psychotic structure and hysteroid character traits.

As was mentioned, the last 20 years have witnessed significant developments in clinical psychoanalytic theory and respective applications to Rorschach psychology (H. Lerner & P. Lerner, 1987; P. Lerner, 1991). Translated into a contemporary Rorschach psychology, which integrates nomothetic and idiographic approaches, the psychodiagnostician examining an individual with suspected psychotic personality organization might expect to find the following Rorschach characteristics: loading up of Special Scores, especially Level 2 special scores; a heavily Weighted Sum 6; and the Schizophrenia Index at a 4 or 5 (Exner, 1978); disturbances and oddities of syntax and representation indicative of thought disorder (Johnston & Holzman, 1979); deterioration of Form level (Exner, 1978; Rapaport, Gill, & Schafer, 1968); disturbances in the structural features of percepts (Blatt & Ritzler, 1974; Blatt, Wild, & Ritzler, 1975; Quinlan & Harrow, 1974), especially human percepts (Blatt, Brenneis, Schimek, & Glick, 1976a); failure of defensive operations and utilization of primitive defenses (Cooper & Arnow, 1986; Kwawer, 1980); expression of raw, drive-laden, primary process material (Holt & Havel, 1960; Meloy, 1986); and themes of barrenness, emptiness, and malevolent interaction (Urist, 1977). One might expect fragmented, chaotic, or merged internalized representations of self and others (Blatt, Brenneis, Schimek, & Glick, 1976b). In a classic article with broad implications for Rorschach psychology, Mahler (1960) stressed the "perceptual de-differentiation" that accompanies psychotic regression, including the "de-animation of the human object world with concomitant animation of the inanimate environment. Between these two groups of cathectic derangements there seem to exist fluent transitions" (p. 549). Athey (1986) provided an extremely useful theoretical "levels" taxonomy, using Rapaport's binary view of thought organization (representational and associational process) for understanding the impact of psychotic regression on the Rorschach response process.

The psychodiagnosis of personality organization, especially psychotic personality organization, is assisted and facilitated by the use of the Rorschach (Bychowski, 1953; Weiner, 1966). The importance of a careful clinical examination, including a battery of psychological tests, cannot be overemphasized. Discriminating between psychotic and borderline personality organization using psychological tests is not a simple matter. Rorschach (1921/1942) himself noted that "It is impossible to determine from the record of a test in some cases whether a schizophrenic reaction is manifest, latent, or dormant for the time being" (p. 121). Individuals may exhibit florid psychotic functioning on the Rorschach and, yet, upon interview or on structured psychological tests like the Wechsler Adult Intelligence Scale–Revised (WAIS–R), they may not be clinically psychotic (see Weiner, 1966, chap. 16, pp. 398–430, for a full discussion of the distinction between overt and nonovert psychosis).

The role of "structure" during the psychological evaluation has assumed considerable diagnostic importance (Gunderson & Singer, 1975; Singer, 1977). Relatively intact performance on structured tests, such as the WAIS–R, and dramatically deviant performance on unstructured measures, such as the Rorschach, have become an "almost axiomatic diagnostic rule" for borderline psychopathology (Edell, 1987). A study of structure in psychological testing confirmed the finding that *DSM–III–R* borderline personality disorders demonstrated significantly greater thought disorder on Johnston and Holzman's (1979) Thought Disorder Index (TDI) than nonpsychiatric controls (Edell, 1987). On the other hand, and somewhat troubling for the differential diagnosis of psychotic and borderline structure, is the fact that the same borderlines were indistinguishable from patients with schizophrenic disorders of relatively recent origin. Borderline cases, referred to in earlier decades as schizophrenic characters or ambulatory schizophrenics (Schafer, 1948), latent psychotics (Bychowski, 1953), or psychotic characters (Frosch, 1964) illustrate the notion that thought disorder or the distinction between primary and secondary process thinking may best be thought of as a continuous rather than categorical phenomenon (Athey, 1986; Urist, 1980). With respect to differentiating psychotic from borderline structures, Kernberg noted that, upon interpretation, the reality testing of borderlines improves, while that of psychotics deteriorates (Kernberg, 1975). Suffice to say that, when thought disorder is apparent on both unstructured (Rorschach) and structured (WAIS–R) psychological tests, this is strong putative evidence for psychotic personality organization.

Recent developments both within and outside of Rorschach psychology provide potent resources for contemporary Rorschach assessment. The convergence of nomothetic and idiographic Rorschach traditions and interpretive approaches make a truly integrated Rorschach psychology possible, strengthening the role and power of the test in psychodiagnostic practice. The differential diagnosis of personality organization, in addition to identification of the major syndrome and characterological diagnosis, is an essential link to a fuller understanding of the patient.

ACKNOWLEDGMENTS

This chapter was the introduction to a symposium entitled "Psychotic Personality Organization: Through the Looking Glass" presented at the midwinter meetings of the Society for Personality Assessment in New Orleans on March 9, 1991.

Special thanks to Charles A. Peterson for his editorial comments and inspiration over the years and to Irving B. Weiner for his support and encouragement.

REFERENCES

American Psychiatric Association. (1987). *Diagnostic and statistical manual of mental disorders* (3rd ed., rev.). Washington, DC: Author.

Athey, G. (1986). Rorschach thought organization and transference enactment in the patient–examiner relationship. In M. Kissen (Ed.), *Assessing object relations phenomena* (pp. 19–50). New York: International Universities Press.

Blatt, S., Brenneis, B., Schimek, J., & Glick, M. (1976a). *A developmental analysis of the concept of the object on the Rorschach*. Unpublished manuscript, Yale University, New Haven, CT.

Blatt, S., Brenneis, B., Schimek, J., & Glick, M. (1976b). Normal development and psychopathological impairment of the concept of the object on the Rorschach. *Journal of Abnormal Psychology, 85,* 364–373.

Blatt, S., & Ritzler, B. (1974). Thought disorder and boundary disturbances in psychosis. *Journal of Consulting and Clinical Psychology, 42*, 370–381.

Blatt, S., Wild, C., & Ritzler, B. (1975). Disturbances of object relations in schizophrenia. *Psychoanalysis and Contemporary Science, 4*, 235–288.

Blanck, G., & Blanck, R. (1975). *Ego psychology: Theory and practice.* New York: Columbia University Press.

Bychowski, G. (1953). The problem of latent psychosis. *Journal of the American Psychoanalytic Association, 4*, 484–503.

Cooper, S., & Arnow, D. (1986). An object relations view of the borderline defenses: A Rorschach analysis. In M. Kissen (Ed.), *Assessing object relations phenomena* (pp. 143–174). New York: International Universities Press.

Edell, W. (1987). Role of structure in disordered thinking in borderline and schizophrenic disorders. *Journal of Personality Assessment, 51*, 23–41.

Exner, J. (1978). *The Rorschach: A comprehensive system. Vol. 2: Current research and advanced interpretations.* New York: Wiley.

Freud, A. (1965). *Normality and pathology in childhood.* New York: International Universities Press.

Frosch, J. (1964). The psychotic character: Clinical psychiatric considerations. *Psychiatric Quarterly, 38*, 81–96.

Gunderson, J., & Singer, M. (1975). Defining borderline patients: An overview. *American Journal of Psychiatry, 132*, 1–10.

Holt, R., & Havel, J. (1960). A method for assessing primary and secondary process in the Rorschach. In M. A. Rickers-Ovsianskina (Ed.), *Rorschach psychology* (pp. 255–297). New York: Wiley.

Johnston, M., & Holzman, P. (1979). *Assessing schizophrenic thought.* San Francisco: Jossey-Bass.

Kernberg, O. (1975). *Borderline conditions and pathological narcissism.* New York: Aronson.

Kernberg, O. (1976). *Object relations theory and clinical psychoanalysis.* New York: Aronson.

Kernberg, O. (1980). Neurosis, psychosis, and the borderline states. In A. M. Freedman, H. I. Kaplan, & B. J. Sadock (Eds.), *Comprehensive textbook of psychiatry, Vol. III.* Baltimore: Williams & Wilkins.

Kernberg, O. (1984). *Severe personality disorders: Psychotherapeutic strategies.* New Haven, CT: Yale University Press.

Kwawer, J. (1980). Primitive interpersonal modes, borderline phenomena and Rorschach content. In J. Kwawer, A. Sugarman, P. Lerner, & H. Lerner (Eds.), *Borderline phenomena and the Rorschach test* (pp. 89–105). New York: International Universities Press.

Lerner, H., & Lerner, P. (1987). Rorschach Inkblot Test. In D. Keyser & R. Sweetland (Eds.), *Tests critiques compendium: Reviews of major tests from the test critiques series.* Kansas City, MO: Test Corporation of America.

Lerner, P. (1991). *Psychoanalytic theory and the Rorschach.* Hillsdale, NJ: The Analytic Press.

Loevinger, J. (1976). *Ego development: Conceptions and theories.* San Francisco: Jossey-Bass.

Mahler, M. (1960). Symposium on psychotic object relationships. III. Perceptual de-differentiation and psychotic 'object relationship.' *International Journal of Psycho-Analysis, 41*, 548–553.

Mahler, M. (1968). *On symbiosis and the vicissitudes of human individuation.* New York: International Universities Press.

Meloy, J. R. (1986). On the relationship between primary process and thought disorder. *Journal of the American Academy of Psychoanalysis, 14*, 47–56.

Quinlan, D., & Harrow, M. (1974). Boundary disturbances in schizophrenia. *Journal of Abnormal Psychology, 83*, 533–541.

Rapaport, D., Gill, M., & Schafer, R. (1968). *Diagnostic psychological testing.* New York: International Universities Press.

Rinsley, D. (1982). *Borderline and other self-disorders.* New York: Aronson.

Rorschach, H. (1942). *Psychodiagnostics* (P. Lemkau & B. Kronenberg, Eds. & Trans.). New York: Grune & Stratton. (Original work published 1921)

Schafer, R. (1948). *The clinical application of psychological tests: Diagnostic summaries and case studies.* New York: International Universities Press.

Singer, M. (1977). The borderline diagnosis and psychological tests: Review and research. In P. Hartocollis (Ed.), *Borderline personality disorders: The concept, the syndrome, the patient* (pp. 193–212). New York: International Universities Press.

Stone, M. (1980). *The borderline syndromes: Constitution, personality, and adaptation.* New York: McGraw-Hill.

Urist, J. (1977). The Rorschach test and the assessment of object relations. *Journal of Personality Assessment, 41,* 3–9.

Urist, J. (1980). The continuum between primary and secondary process thinking: Toward a concept of borderline thought. In J. Kwawer, H. Lerner, P. Lerner, & A. Sugarman (Eds.), *Borderline phenomena and the Rorschach test* (pp. 133–154). New York: International Universities Press.

Weiner, I. (1966). *Psychodiagnosis of schizophrenia.* New York: Wiley.

Werner, H. (1957). *Comparative psychology of mental development.* New York: International Universities Press.

Willick, M. S. (1990). Psychoanalytic concepts of the etiology of severe mental illness. *Journal of the American Psychoanalytic Association, 38,* 1049–1081.

3

A Psychotic Gynemimetic: "I just had a pregnant thought . . ."

Charles A. Peterson
Department of Veterans Affairs, Minneapolis
Medical Center, and University of Minnesota

Philosophers have concluded that our thoughts are proof that we exist: *Cogito ergo sum* (I think, therefore I exist). Psychologists, however, take this one step further: The nature of our thoughts reveals the level of development at which we exist (e.g., Piaget, 1937; Rapaport, 1951; Werner, 1940). Over the course of expectable development, a child's thought will evolve from primitive sensorimotor processes to more sophisticated reversible operations. The primary process becomes subordinated to the secondary process. Thought becomes less concrete; abstraction and symbol deployment become possible. Inner and outer are untangled, each increasingly differentiated and articulated: Concepts and percepts become incrementally separate and accurate. Ideas that once dominated and controlled the mind become tentative hypotheses, testing internal and external worlds. Adaptation is served by the progressive evolution and maturation of thinking (Hartmann, 1939).

These experience-distant notions become incarnate in the psychotherapeutic and psychodiagnostic situations. The clinician (Eissler, 1953; Rapaport, 1952) experiences and observes the level of the patient's thought process, resulting in a diagnostic assignment. Level of personality organization, whether neurotic, borderline, or psychotic, is reflected in the patient's level of ego development, reality testing, identity integration, impulsivity, and self–other differentiation (Kernberg, 1980, 1981). Grossly oversimplified (bordering on condensation), the more peculiar the thought (process), the more primitive the personality organization: The neurotic has troublesome ideas and is conflicted about self, other, and reality; the borderline has absent or horrific ideas and too fluidly mingles self, other, and reality; the psychotic has bizarre ideas and often does not know the difference between self, other, and reality. In other words, the level of thought is virtually synonymous with the level at which the personality is organized and psychopathology is displayed (Blatt &

Ritzler, 1974). If ideation is testimony to existence, then the nature of that thought is divinatory of (the diagnostic) level of existence.

THE PSYCHOTIC PERSONALITY: A PSYCHOTIC GYNEMIMETIC

The psychotic level of personality organization may represent one of the more compelling examples of how thought process determines the differential diagnosis. According to Kernberg (1975, 1976, 1980, 1981, 1984), the psychotic personality will show low ego strength, a preponderance of primary process function, failed reality testing, primitive defensive operations, inade-₁uate self–other differentiation, and an identity organized around one or more chaotic and delusional thoughts. This article presents such a case, a man who had a pregnant thought, one that filled the emptiness of his self: "I am a woman trapped inside a man's body." Mr. Q's psychotic personality organization is explored with a clinically familiar blend of empirical–nomothetic (score-based) and psychoanalytic–idiosyncratic (content-based) approaches, viewing the Rorschach as both a test of perception and a sample of internal representation. Other test data are presented to serve a comprehensive view and to illustrate the singular power of the Rorschach to illuminate personality structure.

Mr. Q is a right-handed, English-speaking, 11th-grade educated, sporadically employed, never-married, 37-year-old White male. Despite evidence to the contrary (he was anatomically and biologically normal), Mr. Q was convinced he was a woman—ready and willing to bear children—and sought the sex change surgery that would sculpt the outer flesh to forcibly conform with the inner thought. Mr. Q had been receiving female hormone shots but had been unable to afford the sex reassignment surgery. A self-proclaimed beautician, he had been cross-dressing for many years, working as a prostitute, buttressing his gender identity ("They think I'm a woman") by deceiving the men he fellated. Mr. Q used transitional objects (e.g., female clothes) and part–object relations (e.g., fellating strange men) to allay separation anxiety and promote the illusion of femaleness. These measures were doomed to failure: The illusion was shattered every time he urinated, shaved his face and legs, failed to menstruate, or could not have vaginal sex. The aloneness panic continued to escalate, giving rise to the wish to become a woman and achieve symbiotic fusion with his mother. This thought had become omnipresent and tyrannized him intrapsychically as a psychotic fixed idea. This testing occurred while he was hospitalized for depression and a suicide attempt (head in a gas oven) after a break up with a lover and the theft of his illusion-promoting female costumes. He received no psychotropic medication at the time of testing. He had no prior psychiatric history, which is not to say that he had no psychiatric troubles.

A mental status exam on admission revealed no sign of any psychotic process. His intelligence was average (Wechsler Adult Intelligence Scale [WAIS] Full Scale IQ = 98). The psychiatric diagnosis was dysthymic disorder in a borderline personality disorder. This descriptive diagnosis did not calm the troubled waters in the milieu. Although not stated in so many words, additional testing was requested because the ward staff was confused and anxious: A man dressed as a woman? A man who believed he was a woman? A depressed patient whose anaclitic needs might prompt the diatrophic response? Or a disgusting pervert whose invitations to collusion might prompt hostility and rejection? The testing might serve as a beachhead in a sea of uncertainty. In particular, a psychoanalytically informed psychodiagnosis might function as an integrative or organizing medium, not only among bits of test data, but disspelling confusion and restoring meaning between staff and patient, restoring the ward staff's will to empathically connect with the patient.

TESTING AND ITS INTERPRETATION

Weiner (1972, 1977) insisted that a conceptual approach separates the expert diagnostic consultant from the mental tester. Personality theory, research, and experience in the psychotherapeutic situation converge to guide the vision of the psychodiagnostician. Knowing in advance that Mr. Q believed he was "a woman trapped in a man's body," what does theory and clinical research suggest to the receptive tester? The male transsexual (Person & Ovesey, 1974a, 1974b; Socarides, 1970; Stoller, 1973, 1974) voices severe gender dysphoria based on the underlying disturbance in gender identity: That is, the host believes he is female and evidences a female or chaotic/ambiguous gender identity on closer analysis (exploratory psychotherapy or projective testing). Insufficiently differentiated from the earliest mother–child matrix, there is insufficient symbiosis anxiety to promote a comfortable separation; this is juxtaposed with profound separation anxiety, promoting the wish for fusion with mother, enacted in the sex reassignment surgery. By becoming a woman, he becomes his mother, no longer anxiously separate from mother. Various parental constellations are associated with this disorder, typically involving a symbiosis engendering incorporative mother and a passive–distant father whose masculinity is a violent caricature, a figure unworthy of identification. Imagine a busty man wearing a gaping house dress, with a swarthy five-o-clock shadow, heavy pancake make-up, little pink sponge rollers in flaming red hair, all animated with flamboyant histrionic behavior. He was, in brief, a definite challenge to the tester's equidistance from ego, id, and superego (cf. Lothstein, 1977, for a discussion of how the transsexual's bizarre thought [Imagine a patient telling a surgeon "I'm a Chinaman trapped inside a Caucasian's body"] and imposture expose the tester to powerful forces in the countertransference). Reflecting his capacity for imposture, his Bender-Gestalt Test and WAIS showed little leakage of psychopathology. The instances of the occasional bleed through were, of course, ore-laden carriers of psychopathology. While commenting on his rendition of Card #3 of the Bender-Gestalt Test, he expressed his disturbance in gender identity: "Yours is an arrow, mine's a fan." We witness a lack of neutralization in his definition of *regular* on the WAIS; he said, "You're gonna think it's crazy. I was thinking of bowel movements, to make sure [you're regular]." Cognitive slippage lurked beneath the surface of the WAIS: He defined *cavern* as "Think of Carlsbad cavern, cave, think of stalactite, galactite, malactite." Incorporative modes of relatedness appeared in his definition of *consume*: "Consume somebody's love, that's an intake, emotional intake." Gender ambiguity was displayed on Object Assembly when he commented on the "mannikin": "She's all together, or he is; it looks like a little girl with short hair" (cf. Blatt, Allison, & Baker, 1965). His first human figure drawing (Appendix A—Fig. A.1) was female and stereotypically hyperfeminine, betraying the underlying gender disturbance (Fleming, Koocher, & Nathans, 1979). He commented on the drawing: "She has a nose job. She's seen a plastic surgeon and has had too much of her nose taken off." Parenthetically, this certainly should warn any surgeon willing to collude with his psychosis (Kubie, 1974, p. 382n, spoke of surgical "alchemy"; Meerloo, 1967, p. 263, spoke of physicians failing to treat the disease but "the fantasy a patient develops about his disease"). In response to his very masculine drawing #2 (Appendix A—Fig. A.2), which he also addressed as "she," he again displayed issues of body boundary disturbance, magical, surgical reconstruction, and the fluidity of gender, noting "Oh, I don't have room for her legs! If you give me another piece of paper to stick on, I'll draw her legs on." Is this poor planning or a partial human representation? The level of Mr. Q's ego development is more consistent with the latter. Ignoring the obvious stimulus demand, reality was clearly flaunted (this is autism) when he referred to both drawings as "she" (many male transsexuals had an unmistakably feminine nickname as children). The sentence completion (Appendix B) shows inadequate differentiation between men and women (#s 20, 81), a symbiosis sponsoring mother (#s 35, 94, 99), a distant father (#s 33, 70), the promise of the fusion fantasy gratified by a sex change (#s 79, 83, 87), and a psychotic parapraxis involving both emptiness and fusion (#53).

Now we turn dutifully toward the structural summary, then the free associations and inquiry (Appendices C and D), using theory-based content analytic approaches to enrich our understanding of the patient's concept of the object and its enactment in primitive interpersonal modes. Although the record is brief, and may warrant some interpretive caution, it is likely valid, given the very low Lambda and the tester's experience of animation and intensity within the testing alliance, both suggesting good involvement with the test stimuli. If it is true that the ratios should be used cautiously, then this may be further justification to use additional theory driven resources for our understanding of this patient's psychotic organization.

Turning to Mr. Q's structural summary (Appendix D), there is good evidence of a psychotic level of development: Among others, a schizophrenia (*SCZI*) Index of 5, the weighted sum of six special scores (*WSUM6*) of 57, a good form level (*X*+%) of 54%, a poor form level (*X*–%) of 38%, and three human movement responses with poor form level (*M*–). Deficient reality testing, a thought disturbance, a psychotic fantasy, and a preponderance of primary process material all are present. The 5 populars (*P*) suggest the capacity to respond to banal, consensually compelling reality, but because 4 of 5 Ps are accompanied by special scores, it is clear that significant disturbance lurks beneath the surface. But can psychoanalytic clinical theory, when applied through content analysis, say more about this patient's psychotic object world, in particular, the representations of self and other, in order to place him on the continuum from primary narcissism to empathic object relatedness? Because the test was administered according to the Comprehensive System (Exner, 1974), the responses were not formally analyzed according to Blatt and Lerner's (1983) developmental analysis of the object. More systematic use is made of Kwawer's (1980) classification of Primitive Interpersonal Modes, Urist's (1977) Mutuality of Autonomy Scale (MOA), and Schafer's (1954) themes. A look at some of the responses illustrative of the psychotic level of personality organization follows.

Card I, Response 1

"Two eagles guarding the nest." This is an adequate initial response, built on analysis, synthesis, and form congruence. Although this response might seem like a good beginning (a thin veneer of social relatedness?), the response deteriorates upon inquiry, signaling a patient with regressive potential. What began as two eagles, becomes two heads and one body, indicating the tendency toward regression and blurred boundaries—the two bodies becoming one in the area often perceived as a woman's body. The eagles carry his fierce aggression, yet they are protecting something vulnerable, perhaps the masculine overlaying the feminine, both ultimately fused. Although there is no human content (*H, Hd*) in this response, Urist's (1977) MOA addresses his experience of relatedness. This response depicts "parallel activity," without reciprocal acknowledgment of each figure's individuality. Kwawer's (1980) Primitive Interpersonal Modes classify this as a birth response, revealing fairly directly Mr. Q's psychic involvement with early stages of self-development. Responses 2 and 3 show adequate form, but a boundary disturbance is more apparent, as Mr. Q progressively unravels, producing an incongruous combination (INCOM) on 2 and a contamination (CONTAM) on 3. Following Schafer (1954), Response 2 involves phallic, masculine imagery, then suddenly and fluidly becomes feminine, protective, and containing. Response 3 involves empty, receptive feminine imagery, a potential fecundity inside a masculine veneer, the kind of self statement often seen in the central axis of the blot

(Schachtel, 1966). The sequence of Responses 2 and 3 culminate in a *CONTAM*, a fusing of feminine and masculine imagery.

Card II, Response 4

"Two clowns." Even though this is not a scorable reflection response according to the Comprehensive System, the Urist (1977) and Kwawer (1980) systems capture the primitive quality of this self–object response: The narcissistic mirroring is obvious; the object exists as an extension or reflection of the rudimentary self. It is as if Mr. Q is projecting/saying "My happiness depends on your mirroring my happiness." The object interaction is benevolent, but the differentiation is minimal; the affective feel of the "faces blurred in laughter" is reminiscent of the coenesthetic perception that Spitz (1965) identified as preceding the establishment of the first organizer of the psyche, the smiling response, when the self begins to shift from pleasure–unpleasure of the interior to diacritic perception of external reality, a step that is an essential precursor of object relations proper.

Card III, Response 5

"Two showgirls on the shoulders of a man wearing a bowtie." The scoring of this response, namely the *M*– and the special scores, clearly indicates that this is a psychotic response. Although the interaction is benevolent, it occurs between quasi-(miniature) humans and a partial human. The oral content establishes the psychosexual level as primitive, a view reaffirmed by other complementary perspectives. Kwawer (1980) referred to this as a "boundary disturbance response," addressing the fluidity, weakness, and permeability of the ego boundaries. Urist's (1977) perspective underlines the primitive de-pendency, reflected in the figures leaning on and supporting one another, shown here as two miniature women holding up a giant man, which is probably a reversal of the infant dwarfed and held by the giantess–mother.

Card IV, Response 6

"Bigfoot" standing on and viewed from underneath some "crystal clear ice." This near-popular good form response involves a quasi-human, potentially malevolent creature. The blend of animal movement, form texture, and form dimension suggests painful awareness of isolation from and unmet dependency needs, possibly from a labile, explosive, distant father. The response also witnesses malevolence and its denial and, per Kwawer (1980), unconscious conflict and ambivalence about separation and reunion. Urist's (1977) MOA captures the omnipotence of one figure and the helplessness of the other, a Lilliputian impotence before a gigantic fearsome awe-inspiring phallus.

Card VI, Response 8

"A jellyfish eating an insect." The determinants tell us little about the status of the object here. The special scores do point to a fluidity of boundaries and an inability to manage and neutralize the raw aggression. Mr. Q's boundaries are overrun as he wonders who might eat him. Kwawer's (1980) perspective captures the primitive, incorporative modes of relatedness. The food content on a card receptive to sexual representations might argue that sex may be misused in the service of unmet dependency needs. Unable to identify with a distant father and be drawn away from the original symbiosis, he succumbs to malevolent incorporation: The vagina devours the phallus, and the gender identity becomes female.

Card VII, Response 9

A "volcano." Powerful forces are unleashed here, acting on Mr. Q, the second successive minus form H content. This is a grossly psychotic response; there is a loss of distance from the card; the ego boundaries are again breached. Urist's (1977) MOA highlights the malevolent control to which objects are subjected, here ejected by mother nature's all-powerful forces. Kwawer (1980) would have coded this as a violent separation response, for which separation is unconsciously equivalent with death. This response may tap the patient's fantasies about his birth, imagined to be an explosion and a fragmentation after the primal unity with mother had been shattered.

Card VII, Response 10

The M– response speaks to the primitive, psychotic nature of this response, suggesting that his interpersonal relations are, somewhat generically, poor and distorted according to his needs. The psychoanalytic clinical content tradition can complement and enrich the understanding of this psychotic response. Drawing on Kwawer's (1980) schema, this is a "symbiotic merging" response (i.e., the belly buttons are touching) with a secondary "birth" theme. After the violent separation on the previous response, we see that he cannot tolerate the experience of separateness: He succumbs to the lure of the symbiosis and yields to a blissful reunion with a mother ready to hold, nurse, and soothe him. After the explosion and fragmentation, there is reconstitution through linking and symbiosis. Significantly, the CONTAM places the woman's breasts in the area usually attributed to the face. This is reminiscent of Spitz's (1965) observations that the infant feels the nipple in his mouth at the same time he or she views the mother's face; contact perception blends with distance perception. This primitive response surely reveals the intrapsychic substrate of Mr. Q's marginal differentiation from original object. On another level, there is something startling about this response: Despite the special scores and the symbiotic mode of relatedness, this response would receive the highest level of relatedness, according to Urist's (1977) schema for assessing object relations, in that the figures are interacting in a way that acknowledges some individuality and mutuality. They are talking; they are friends. This paradox may suggest that Mr. Q's delusional identity (a fusion fantasy) as "a woman trapped inside a man's body" is compelling enough to function as a significant, transitional organizer, containing the bulk of the psychosis in psychotic restitution.

Space does not permit a microscopic analysis of each response in the record, which closes with themes of fecundity, the feminine aggressively triumphing over the masculine, frenzied denial of the phallus, and an intolerance of depressive affect. As per Holt (1977), libidinal content is primarily oral, with some fairly direct oral aggressive, some indirect oral receptive imagery, and some indirect sexual imagery. The aggressive content is the socially tolerated variety. Perhaps the implication here is that Mr. Q is balanced on the cusp of individuation and has insufficient aggression to help propel him from the symbiosis. In closing, the patient's last words on the inquiry to his response to Card X may be considered an unconscious summation of the transsexual self and a testimonial to the power of the Rorschach to sample the representational world: Mr. Q stated, "you can't see the details til you get up close." In this case, getting up close revealed an individual with a predominance of id over ego, a psychotic level of ego boundaries, thought processes dominated by the primary process, drives penetrating the repression barrier, marginal neutralization of libidinal and neutralization of aggressive drives, a delusional adaptation, an incompletely individuated self having difficulty maintaining a separation between independent events, self and the poorly articulated object world centered on separation, and the fantasy of the male being devoured and absorbed within the female. The Rorschach was able to detect Mr. Q's psychosis, best illuminated in the atheoretical nomothetic contributions of the structural summary. Using the complementary perspective of a theory saturated, idiographic, content analytic approach derived from clinical psychoanalysis, the Rorschach was able to describe the object world and interpersonal modes of this psychotic personality.

Paraphrasing Blatt and Ritzler's (1974) trenchant insight, diagnoses made using the nomothetic structural summary can be enriched by idiographic content analytic approaches devoted to the concepts of self and other. Although Mr. Q will remain barren, a marriage between the psychometric and the clinical psychoanalytic traditions will ensure that the Rorschach remains fecund.

ACKNOWLEDGMENTS

This chapter was initially part of a symposium entitled "Psychotic Personality Organization: Through the Looking Glass" presented at the midwinter meeting of the Society for Personality Assessment in New Orleans on March 9, 1991.

I thank Dr. Gus Crivolio who first guided the understanding of this case, the other members of this symposium for their mutual stimulation, and the Department of Veterans Affairs for supporting this research.

REFERENCES

Blatt, S. J., Allison, J., & Baker, B. L. (1965). The Wechsler Object Assembly subtest and bodily concerns. *Journal of Consulting Psychology, 29,* 223–230.

Blatt, S. J., & Lerner, H. (1983). The psychological assessment of object representation. *Journal of Personality Assessment, 47,* 7–28.

Blatt, S. J., & Ritzler, R. A. (1974). Thought disorder and boundary disturbance in psychosis. *Journal of Consulting and Clinical Psychology, 42,* 370–381.

Eissler, K. R. (1953). The effect of the structure of the ego on psychoanalytic techniques. *Journal of the American Psychoanalytic Association, 1,* 104–143.

Exner, J. (1974). *The Rorschach: A comprehensive system.* New York: Wiley.

Fleming, M., Koocher, G., & Nathans, J. (1979). Draw-A-Person Test: Implications for gender identification. *Archives of Sexual Behavior, 8,* 55–61.

Hartmann, H. (1939). *Ego psychology and the problem of adaptation.* New York: International Universities Press.

Holt, R. R. (1977). A method for assessing primary process manifestations and their control in Rorschach responses. In M. A. Rickers-Ovsiankina (Ed.), *Rorschach psychology* (2nd ed., pp. 375–420). Huntington, NY: Krieger.

Kernberg, O. (1975). *Borderline conditions and pathological narcissism.* New York: Aronson.

Kernberg, O. (1976). *Object relations theory and clinical psychoanalysis.* New York: Aronson.

Kernberg, O. (1980). Neurosis, psychosis, and the borderline states. In A. M. Freedman, H. I. Kaplan, & B. J. Saddock (Eds.), *Comprehensive textbook of psychiatry, Vol. III* (3rd ed., pp. 1079–1092). Baltimore: Williams & Wilkins.

Kernberg, O. (1981). Structural interviewing. *Psychiatric Clinics of North America, 4,* 169–195.

Kernberg, O. (1984). *Severe personality disorders: Psychotherapeutic strategies.* New Haven, CT: Yale University Press.

Kubie, L. S. (1974). The drive to become both sexes. *Psychoanalytic Quarterly, 43,* 349–326.

Kwawer, J. S. (1980). Primitive interpersonal modes, borderline phenomena and Rorschach content. In J. Kwawer, H. Lerner, P. Lerner, & A. Sugarman (Eds.), *Borderline phenomena and the Rorschach test* (pp. 89–105). New York: International Universities Press.

Lothstein, L. M. (1977). Countertransference reactions to gender dysphoric patients: Implications for psychotherapy. *Psychotherapy: Theory, Research and Practice, 14,* 21–31.

Meerloo, J. A. M. (1967). Change of sex and collaboration with the psychosis. *American Journal of Psychiatry, 124,* 263–264.

Person, E., & Ovesey, L. (1974a). The transsexual syndrome in males. I: Primary transsexualism. *American Journal of Psychotherapy, 28,* 4–20.

Person, E., & Ovesey, L. (1974b). The transsexual syndrome in males. II. Secondary transsexualism. *American Journal of Psychotherapy, 28,* 174–193.

Piaget, J. (1937). *The construction of reality in the child.* New York: Basic Books.

Rapaport, D. (1951). *The organization and pathology of thought.* New York: Columbia University Press.

Rapaport, D. (1952). Projective techniques and the theory of thinking. *Journal of Projective Techniques, 16,* 269–275.

Schachtel, E. G. (1966). *Experiential foundations of Rorschach's test.* New York: Basic Books.

Schafer, R. (1954). *Psychoanalytic interpretation in Rorschach testing.* New York: Grune & Stratton.

Socarides, C. M. (1970). A psychoanalytic study of the desire for sexual transformation ("transsexualism"): The plaster-of-Paris man. *International Journal of Psycho-Analysis, 51,* 341–349.

Spitz, R. A. (1965). *The first year of life.* New York: International Universities Press.

Stoller, R. J. (1973). The male transsexual as "experiment." *International Journal of Psycho-Analysis, 54,* 215–225.

Stoller, R. J. (1974). Symbiosis anxiety and the development of masculinity. *Archives of General Psychiatry, 30,* 164–172.

Urist, J. (1977). The Rorschach test and the assessment of object relations. *Journal of Personality Assessment, 41,* 3–9.

Weiner, I. B. (1972). Does psychodiagnosis have a future? *Journal of Personality Assessment, 36,* 534–546.

Weiner, I. B. (1977). Approaches to Rorschach validation. In M. A. Rickers-Ovsiankina (Ed.), *Rorschach psychology* (2nd ed., pp. 575–608). Huntington, NY: Krieger.

Werner, H. (1940). *Comparative psychology of mental development.* New York: Harper.

APPENDIX A: DRAW-A-PERSON

FIG. A.1

FIG. A.2

Sentence Completion Test

Instruction: complete the following sentences as rapidly as possible. Write down the *first thing* you think of.

1. WHEN SHE WAS COMPLETELY ON HER OWN, SHE worried.
2. SHE OFTEN WISHED SHE COULD Find a Better Life.
3. IT LOOKED IMPOSSIBLE, SO SHE asked for help.
4. SHE FELT BLAME WHEN she broke up with her Lover.
5. WHEN HE REFUSED HER, SHE got Hurt.
6. I USED TO FEEL I WAS BEING HELD BACK BY my sex.
7. SHE FELT PROUD THAT SHE had come this far.
8. AS A CHILD MY GREATEST FEAR WAS getting enough love.
9. HER FATHER ALWAYS let my mother be the Boss.
10. MEN are very attractive and Sometimes Egotistical.
11. A PERSON WHO FALLS IN LOVE is a very fortunate Person.
12. I WAS MOST DEPRESSED WHEN I broke up with my Lover.
13. MY FIRST REACTION WAS we belong Together.
14. WHEN HE TURNED ME DOWN, I cried.
15. HER NEW NEIGHBORS WERE very nice people.
16. MOST FATHERS don't have enough guts.
17. SOMETIMES SHE WISHED SHE could die.
18. USUALLY SHE FELT THAT SEX was a bother and over rated.
19. I COULD HATE A PERSON WHO hurt other nice people.
20. HER EARLIEST MEMORY OF HER MOTHER WAS where was my father.
21. WHEN I MEET A WOMAN, I liked, I admired her.
22. WHEN PEOPLE MADE FUN OF HER SHE was hurt and angry.
23. WHEN SHE MET HER BOSS, SHE tried to please Him.
24. WHEN I THINK BACK, I AM ASHAMED THAT I could have been more understanding.
25. IF I THINK THE JOB IS TOO HARD FOR ME, I ask for help.
26. SISTERS are very special friends.
27. SHE FELT HER LACK OF SUCCESS WAS DUE TO her sex Change.
28. WHEN THEY TALKED ABOUT SEX, I lisend and Learned.
29. I USED TO DAYDREAM ABOUT a new and peaceful world.
30. MOST MEN are ridicules.
31. WHEN I HAVE TO MAKE A DECISION, I look at both sides.
32. LOVE IS a gift to be Cherrihed.
33. MY EARLIEST MEMORY OF MY FATHER was a blur.
34. I WAS MOST ANNOYED WHEN my life went down Hill.
35. MOST MOTHERS are overly Protective.
36. TAKING ORDERS are easy, if the Person knows what they are talking about.
37. I DISLIKE TO argue with people.
38. I FEEL THAT PEOPLE are bascly good.
39. MOST WOMEN don't take Care of themselves.
40. AFTER SHE MADE LOVE TO HIM, SHE held him Close to Her.
41. IF I CAN'T GET WHAT I WANT, I wait until I Can get it.
42. WHEN I AM CRITICIZED I lisson, If it is Constructive.
43. SHE FELT SHE HAD DONE WRONG WHEN SHE let her lover go.
44. SHE FELT SHE COULDN'T SUCCEED UNLESS she had Sex Change.
45. I USED TO FEEL "DOWN IN THE DUMPS" WHEN I needed love.
46. WHEN THEY DIDN'T INVITE ME, I was hurt.
47. SHE WAS MOST ANXIOUS ABOUT her Sex Change.
48. WHEN SHE FOUND SHE HAD FAILED THE EXAMINATION, SHE tried again.

49. A LOT OF OTHER PEOPLE don't have Consideration for other people.
50. BROTHERS are Protectice.
51. AFTER THEY KNOCKED HER DOWN, SHE got back up again.
52. MOST OF ALL I WANT someone to love and my Sex Change.
53. MY SEXUAL DESIRES to be a hole Person.
54. HER CONSCIENCE BOTHERED HER MOST WHEN she broke up with her lover.
55. SHE FELT SHE COULD MURDER A MAN WHO never.[a]
56. AT TIMES SHE WORRIED ABOUT the Basics of Live.
57. SHE DID A POOR JOB BECAUSE She Had a lot on her mind.
58. MOST MARRIAGES don't work for one reason or another.
59. WHILE HE WAS SPEAKING TO ME, l lisend, with much Care.
60. MY MOTHER is Basicley a good woman.
61. SEXUAL INTERCOURSE with a person you love, is Beautiful.
62. RESPONSIBILITY helps build Charicture.
63. WHENEVER SHE DOES AVERAGE WORK SHE trys again.
64. I FELT MOST DISSATISFED WHEN my life when down Hill.
66. WHEN I FIRST MEET PEOPLE, I GENERALLY FEEL Cheerful.
67. MY FIRST REACTION TO HER WAS I want her to be My Friend.
68. WHEN THEY PUT ME IN CHARGE, I did a good job.
69. I FEEL GUILTY ABOUT nothing.
70. WHEN MY FATHER CAME HOME I felt he was a stranger.
71. AS SHE SPOKE TO HER, SHE held her hand.
72. WHEN SHE WAS PUNISHED BY HER MOTHER SHE Cried.
73. PEOPLE IN AUTHORITY ARE and should be Compashonate.
74. I FEEL HAPPIEST WHEN I'm loving someone and have a home.
75. SHE BOILED UP WHEN her lover Cheated on her.
76. WHEN MY MOTHER CAME HOME, I had dinner Cooked.
77. WHEN THEY TOLD HER WHAT TO DO, SHE did it.
78. AFTER A YEAR OF MARRIAGE SHE was happy.
79. HER GREATEST MEMORY WAS Sex Change and Love.
80. WHEN SHE GOT THE SPANKING FROM HER FATHER, SHE hated him.
81. MOST WOMEN ACT AS THOUGH as men.
82. WHEN I FEEL THAT OTHERS DON'T LIKE ME, I ask why.
83. MORE THAN ANYTHING ELSE SHE NEEDED Love and a Sex Change.
84. MOST PEOPLE ARE afraid of each other and themselves.
85. WHEN HER TURN CAME TO SPEAK SHE said it all.
86. I COULD LOSE MY TEMPER IF I was pushed to far.
87. I AM AFRAID OF not having Love or my Sex Change.
88. WHENEVER SHE WAS WITH HER FATHER SHE FELT uneasy.
89. A MAN WOULD BE JUSTIFED IN BEATING A WOMAN WHO not at all.[a]
90. WHEN THEY TOLD HER TO GET OUT, SHE Cried and left.
91. SOMETIMES I FEEL THAT MY BOSS needs me alot.
92. WHEN I THINK OF MARRIAGE I think of Loove and contment.
93. WHENEVER SHE IS INTRODUCED TO PEOPLE, SHE is grachis.
94. WHEN SHE WAS WITH HER MOTHER, SHE FELT smothered.
95. MOST MEN ACT AS THOUGH as they think they should be.
96. FATHERS should have more to say.
97. SHE FELT INFERIOR WHEN she thought about her Sex Change.
98. IF I WERE QUEEN, I would Rule Wisely and with Love.
99. MOTHERS are overly proctive.
100. I FEEL SAD ABOUT my being Lonley.

Note. The stems are in upper case; the completions are in lower case. The responses verbatim.
[a]Indicates the patient crossed out these stems.

I.

1. Looks like two eagles guarding the nest.

Here's the nest, here, the eggs, the wings, the body, the bills and the heads up here, really not the body though.

2. Looks like those lions that have wings, guarding a steeple on a chapel, like gargoyles or a bell.

Here's the bell, the wings; gargoyles have different shapes; the heads, little tail, the chapel.

3. Some how I see a chalice.

This is the emblem, like from King Arthur's days, on an imaginary chalice or cup.

II.

4. Looks like two clowns with their hands together, sitting knee to knee, laughing; maybe the clown is looking at a mirror. No, unless it's a wall to wall mirror. No, the one is saying you look like a reflection of me.

He're the clown hats. The faces are blurred in laughter. Clown collar, very baggy suits, the frills, the ruffles of their cuffs. Faces blurred in laughter cause they find each other so funny. (?) Just look like clowns.

III.

5. Really strange, two showgirls, real small, like Las Vegas showgirls, small like fairies, sitting on the shoulders of a man wearing a bow tie and they're kissing him on the cheeks, on both sides simultaneously. Make sure they're miniature otherwise he couldn't take it no matter how cute they are. Do you have more with color? It makes them more interesting.

Here are the faces of the miniature showgirls kissing the man very lovingly on the cheeks. Here are their breasts. Here are their arms down there holding, caressing his chin. There's their hips, body. Everything's connected, legs, little high-heeled shoes. Each girl has a headdress of ostrich boa feathers shaped like a huge.... Man had a bow tie right under his chin. Do they still wear them there? Here's the lapels on his tux. He's in a classy place, in New York or Paris, like the Lido.

IV.

6. (laughs) Looking up at a version of Bigfoot, a hairy gorilla, prehistoric, the missing link, bushy, huge feet, long tail, a mean look but he's not really mean.

Underneath his legs; looks like looking under crystal clear ice and he's standing over you. Here's his feet; see his big feet, Bigfoot. Coming from between his, you can't see the whole tail cause it's flipping up. Here's his body, legs, big, fat, furry. These paws look limp. Not mean; just because he's different from you, just because he's big, doesn't mean he's big. (?) This looks furry, bushy (touches card), long nose.

V.

7. A bat.

Legs, wings, it's in flight. The head, these look like radar-things, bat tentacles. Could be a moth, insect. (?) Shape of the legs, insects don't have legs or claws. Wings are really huge. Only thing that makes him look like an insect is these things. They don't interest me, but another bat might be interested.

VI.

8. Some kind of jellyfish eating some kind of insect. The insect is trying to get away. The jellyfish is devouring it. Everybody's got to eat. Wonder who eats us.

Body of jellyfish, a blob, no real shape. Here's the insect. The mouth of the jellyfish. Here's the body, the wings, like a dragonfly, large insect. (?) This is one of them that weren't very interesting. I don't find them very attractive.

34

VII.

9. Looks like the insides coming out of a volcano, like the person himself or herself would be the lava coming out of the volcano.

10. Or I'm seeing two pregnant ladies sitting together belly to belly, and their great big tits hanging out full of milk, just a gossiping.

VIII.

11. The colors are prettier. They're very balancing. 1 see two's. 1 see two polar bears crawling up the side of an iceberg. It's just not the weather they're used to, but it looks like a fire down below. They're stepping out of the fire cooling their heels. It's so pretty because there's a mountain behind the iceberg. A green forest, cool crisp air, a very livable climate for the polar bears.

IX.

12. I'm seeing two's of everything. 1 see many different things. Looks like two very pretty prize winning hens that are full of eggs and jealousy, bitching at each other. Like one says I'm the prize winning hen and the other one says it's me. The poor rooster's all worn out. That's an after thought. 1 don't see him there. He's probably passed out somewhere, trying to please the old biddies.

X.

13. Love the colors. It looks like France at night with all the lights lit up and in the background is the Eifel tower. You can see all the people coming out at night in their bright colored clothes, happy colors, drinking champagne, good clean fun, singing, dancing, all around the Eifel tower. Most people don't know that the Eifel tower is from France, a gift.

Because I was in a angry mood. You really can't see it unless you're in my mind. Here you are the object, ready to explode, coming out of the top. Here's the rim or edge of the volcano.

Here are the bellies. Here are the belly buttons touching. They're good friends. Here are the breasts, the nipples, the rest of the body, the faces up there somewhere. (?) Feeding the babies of course. Most women's breasts enlarge and fill during 9 months of pregnancy.

Here's the fire, not a bad roaring fire. They're used to colder weather. Here's the legs, leg, paw, bodies, the heads, the ice, icebergs. In the background is the mountain, forests, green trees, growing like iceberg lettuce. (?) Just looks like the fire, hot rolling flames, the colors, oranges, reds.

Here are the plumage with the prize winning feathers, cuffs of feathers on the feet. This is their bodies. These are the plumage, feathery mane around their necks. Like puffed up with ego, their breasts all puffed up. Manes, combs, the part that sticks out at each other is their beaks, going buck-buck, chattering old hens, like they're spoiled. (?) They couldn't just be happy both being pretty. One has to be prettier.

This is obviously the Eifel tower because everybody's dancing around it. 1 don't see the faces, mostly the costumes, the colors that are reflected from the costumes, prints, colors, flowers. 1 see yellow roses opening up. This is some kind of collage, because you're looking at it from a distance. (?) You can see the colors, but you can't see the details till you get up close.

Q: What is your most favorite card?
A: Love 'em all for certain reasons, like saying to a child, you're my favorite; you wouldn't throw 'em out; you love 'em all fine.
Q: But what is your most favorite?
A: X.
Q: What is your least favorite?
A: VI.

35

Rorschach: Structural Summary

LOCATION FEATURES	DETERMINANTS BLENDS	SINGLE	CONTENTS	S-CONSTELLATION
			H = 4,1	NO..FV + VF = V + FD > 2
				NO..Col-Shd Bl>0
Zf = 13	FM.FT.FD	M = 3	(H) = 0,0	YES..Ego<.31,>.44
ZSum = 49.0	FM.CF	FM = 5	Hd = 0,0	NO..MOR>3
ZEst = 41.5	M.CF	m = 1	(Hd) = 0,0	YES..Zd > ± 3.5
		FC = 0	Hx = 0,0	YES..es>EA
W = 12		CF = 0	A = 5,0	YES..CF+C>FC
(Wv = 0)		C = 0	(A) = 2,0	YES..X+%<.70
D = 0		Cn = 0	Ad = 0,0	NO..S>3
Dd = 1		FC' = 0	(Ad) = 0,0	NO..P<3 or >8
S = 2		C'F = 0	An = 0,0	NO..Pure H <2
		C' = 0	Art = 0,0	YES..R<17

DQ

	(FQ-)	FT = 0	Ay = 0,0	6.....TOTAL
+ = 4(1)		TF = 0	Bl = 0,0	
o = 5(2)		T = 0	Bt = 0,0	SPECIAL SCORINGS
v/+ = 4(2)		FV = 0	Cg = 0,1	Lv1 Lv2
v = 0(0)		VF = 0	Cl = 0,0	DV = 1x1 0x2
		V = 0	Ex = 1,0	INC = 2x2 0x4
		FY = 0	Fd = 0,1	DR = 4x3 0x6
		YF = 0	Fi = 0,1	FAB = 4x4 0x7
		Y = 0	Ge = 0,0	ALOG = 2x5
		Fr = 0	Hh = 1,0	CON = 2x7
		rF = 0	Ls = 0,1	SUM6 = 15

FORM QUALITY

	FQx	FQf	MQual	SQx				WSUM6 = 57
					FD = 0	Na = 0,0		
+	= 0	0	0	0	F = 1	Sc = 0,0		
o	= 7	1	1	0		Sx = 0,1	AB =0	CP = 0
u	= 1	0	0	0		Xy = 0,0	AG =1	MOR = 0
–	= 5	0	3	2		Id = 0,2	CFB =0	PER = 3
none	= 0	–	0	0	(2) = 7		COP =0	PSV = 0

This is a short record and may not be interpretively valid.

RATIOS, PERCENTAGES, AND DERIVATIONS

R = 13	L = 0.08		FC:CF+C =0:2	COP = 0	AG =1
			Pure C =0	Food	=1

EB = 4: 2.0	EA = 6.0	EBPer = 2.0	Afr =0.30	Isolate/R	= 0.08
eb = 8:1	es = 9	D = -1	S =2	H:(H)Hd(Hd)	= 5:0
	Adj es = 9	Adj D = -1	Blends:R =3:13	(HHd):(AAd)	= 0:2
			CP =0	H+A:Hd + Ad	= 12:0

FM = 7	C' = 0	T = 1			
m = 1	V = 0	Y = 0			

			P = 5	Zf =13	3r+(2)/R = 0.54
a:p	= 11.1	Sum6 =15	X+% = 0.54	Zd =7.5	Fr+rF = 0
Ma:Mp	= 4:0	Lv2 = 0	F+% = 1.00	W:D:Dd =12:0:1	FD = 1
2AB+Art+Ay	= 0	WSum6 = 57	X-% = 0.38	W:M =12:4	An + Xy = 0
M-	= 3	Mnone = 0	S-% = 0.40	DQ+ =4	MOR = 0
			Xu% = 0.08	DQv =0	

SCZI = 5*	DEPI = 3	CDI = 4*	S-CON = 6	HVI = No	OBS = No

4

A Psychotic (Sexual) Psychopath:
"I just had a violent thought . . ."

J. Reid Meloy
University of California, San Diego

Carl B. Gacono
U.S. Department of Justice

The ways in which level of personality organization and character formation are interdependent have been theoretically advanced by Kernberg's (1984) work. Empirical research to test such theory, however, has been virtually absent. Specific character pathologies and their relationship to psychotic personality organization have likewise received little attention (Frosch, 1983; Meloy, 1988). In fact, it was not until the *Diagnostic and Statistical Manual of Mental Disorders* (3rd ed., rev. [*DSM–III–R*]; American Psychiatric Association, 1987) that the diagnoses of schizophrenia and antisocial personality disorder, for instance, could be applied to the same patient at the same time.

In this study, we present a case of a young man who is organized at a psychotic level of personality and is also a psychopathic character. Rorschach findings are used empirically to understand the nature of the relationship between these two dimensions of personality and to provide concurrent validity for the psychopathology suggested by his overt behavior. Our approach to the Rorschach data is both psychostructural and psychodynamic.

CASE STUDY

Huntley is a 33-year-old White male, born and raised in an intact family with one older sister. His father is an electrician, and his mother is a homemaker. He and others describe him as a loner while growing up. His mother confirms a history of enuresis, multiple runaways from home, stealing money from his parents, and lying: behaviors that are consistent with a diagnosis of conduct disorder. He also had marked developmental delays in such activities as shoe tying, telling time, bike riding, and knot tying. There is no evidence of cruelty toward animals or firesetting and truancy or vandalism. His classmates, however, nicknamed him "blondie the animal."

His sexual history is significant; at the age of 5, he remembers "falling in love with Olive Oyl" while watching a Popeye cartoon on television. He was attracted to her because of her brightly polished toenails and probably because she was the love object of two strong and powerful men. He also remembers being sexually aroused while rubbing his mother's feet at her request. His foot fetish has been consistently present throughout his childhood, adolescence, and adulthood.

Huntley was first diagnosed with a grand mal seizure disorder by a neurologist when he was 14. It was well controlled with primidone. He was 16 when he first visited a psychiatrist. His major complaint was intense fears of losing control of his sexual and aggressive impulses due to constant rejections by girls. He also began to think about rape fantasies after viewing the television movie, "A Case of Rape," starring Elizabeth Montgomery.

Self-report indicates that he assaulted two acquaintances in late adolescence. These incidents were never reported to the police. The first involved a 17-year-old girl who refused to let him kiss her. He stated that he heard a voice at the time telling him, "Hey, look at her. Wouldn't you like her?" He also grabbed a male friend by the collar and said, "You know who I am?" He delusionally believed at the time that he was possessed by Satan and he "had no control over it." He reported auditory hallucinations of "both God and Satan. God gives me directions. Satan probes into my head telling me about killing people." He continued to seek psychiatric help, but refused medications. He dropped out of military school at age 17.

By the age of 20, Huntley was spending most of his time away from home, riding buses around the city as, in his own words, "a weird pervert," seeking opportunities to run his hands across the exposed feet of women. If he "was lucky," he would slide his fingers between their toes and "grab one if I could." He reported this compulsion as ego dystonic at the time.

In fantasy, these encounters went further. "I would move my hand as far as I can. I would feel under their blouses and go all the way." These sexually sadistic fantasies would consistently involve carrying a knife to frighten the female into submission and then kill her, "so that she couldn't tell anybody, and no one would know." Actual heterosexual experience was completely absent in Huntley's life. He also described in detail plunging a knife into a pillow at home, rape fantasies during masturbation, and a sadistic homicidal fantasy: He would nail a person to a wall in a crucified position, severely cut the individual, gather the blood, mix it with gasoline, pour it over the victim, set it on fire, and then paint a sign on the wall, "Love is Death." The gender of this victim was unclear.

Five months before his criminal offense, a psychiatrist wrote, "he is bordering on a psychotic regression which would be imminent without therapeutic intervention." Several days before Huntley's crime, he contacted his fourth psychiatrist and reported he was having "horrible problems" coping with his frustrations and impulses. He also felt he might need hospitalization. The psychiatrist requested that his mother drive him to the local mental health hospital, which she did. He refused to go in.

He was now having constant fantasies and impulses to rape and murder a 36-year-old mother of two whom he had met during church. He was "impressed with her body, particularly her boobs." He asked her for a ride home from her house one day, and she let him sit in the back seat. He suddenly grabbed her around the neck with a knife to her throat and told her he was going to rape her. She struggled and escaped, but was seriously injured with a stab wound to the neck. Huntley was found guilty for attempted rape and murder, and not guilty by reason of insanity. He was 21 years old.

During the evaluations to determine his sanity he said, "I've got a split personality, some form of schizophrenia. I have a Dr. Jekyll and Mr. Hyde complex. Hyde is dirty, perverted, deranged. He makes me think of doing things that I've never considered in my life; all sorts of shit, about pulling a knife on someone in a car where they can't stop because then I have full control." He was subsequently committed to a regional forensic hospital.

Nine years later, Huntley was conditionally released to an involuntary outpatient program (Meloy, Haroun, & Schiller, 1990) with a diagnosis of schizophrenia, paranoid type, chronic; fetishism; mixed personality disorder with borderline and schizotypal traits; a history of grand mal seizures; enuresis; peptic ulcer; and intermittent impotence. He moved into a residential home and remained somewhat stable for 3 years.

When he was 33, however, things began to fall apart. He had a mentally ill girlfriend, but she ended the relationship. He had a pet kitten, with which he masturbated, but another kitten arrived at the residence and played with his. The new animal was found with its neck broken, buried in the back yard several weeks later. Huntley was then observed blocking the passage of a female staff person in the hallway and teasingly putting his hands around the neck of another. He was also harassing his former girlfriend. The day he was brought back into custody as a preventive measure, he told a clinician, "I am suicidal, homicidal, and cannot be responsible for my actions."

Huntley was administered the Wechsler Adult Intelligence Scale-Revised, Multiphasic Sex Inventory (MSI) and Rorschach within several weeks of his incarceration. His Full-Scale IQ was 84 (Verbal IQ 90, Performance IQ 80). On the MSI, he responded true to Question 296, "I have fantasized about killing someone during sex," and Question 53, "I have used a weapon to scare a person into having sex." He was receiving the following medications at the time of this Rorschach: fluphenazine decanoate, 1 cc every 2 weeks; lithium carbonate, 1500 mg each day; chlorpromazine, 200 mg each day; and imipramine, 100 mg at bedtime.

RESULTS

Appendix A is the Rorschach protocol. Appendix B is the sequence of scores, and Appendix C is the structural summary, both generated by Rorschach Interpretation Assistance Program: Version 2 (Exner, 1990).

DISCUSSION

Huntley's Rorschach suggests both psychotic personality organization (Kernberg, 1984) and psychopathic character (Meloy, 1988). An analysis of both the psychostructural (Exner, 1986) and psychodynamic aspects of the protocol underscores ways in which a primitive level of personality and a particular character formation interact with and shape each other.

Psychostructure

Structural characteristics (Exner, 1986) of severe psychopathy have been identified in various groups of antisocial personality disordered males (Gacono & Meloy, 1991, 1992; Gacono, Meloy, & Berg, 1992; Gacono, Meloy, & Heaven, 1990). Huntley's protocol is consistent with psychopathic character in his omnipotence and identification with the aggressor ($Personals$ = 4); reduced interest in others as whole, real, and meaningful human beings (H = 2; $H{:}Hd$ = 2:3); unmodulated affect ($FC{:}CF + C$ = 0:3); emotional constraint while incarcerated (C' = 9); chronic anger (S = 4); perceptual unconventionality ($X+\%$ = 42); and severely impaired reality testing ($X-\%$ = 21).

A psychotic level of personality organization, however, is suggested by structural aspects that differentiate Huntley from higher developmental level psychopaths and predict global impairments. This individual's stress tolerance and controls, both state and trait, are very poor (D = –4, $Adjusted\ D$ = –3). Coupled with his unmodulated affect, repetitive loss of impulse control would be expected. He experiences dysphoria to a profound degree ($DEPI$ = 5, eb = 10:11), and a major mood disorder, perhaps a psychotic one, is probable. Although not suicidal, one would consider aggressive behavior (Ag = 1) in this angry man with a possible loss of reality testing ($S-\%$ = 25). These psychotic outbursts would likely occur in the midst of sexual preoccupation (Sx = 2; Responses 3, 13) and feelings of rage.

Cognitive problems, particularly ideation, are most pathognomonic of Huntley's psychotic organization. Formal thought disorder is pervasive and severe ($WSum6$ = 52, $Level\ 2$ = 5). Although formal thought disorder is expected in psychopathy, Level 2 special scores are not. Huntley's cognitive processing deficits, coupled with his affective disorder, would warrant consideration of a schizoaffective diagnosis despite the clinical absence of overt delusions and hallucinations at the time of testing, probably due to aggressive pharmacotherapy. Other ideational concerns are apparent ($M-$ = 1, $S-$ = 1). Abuse of fantasy is likely ($Ma:Mp$ = 2:4), and in the context of sexual aggression, may indicate rehearsal fantasy in the planning of predatory violence (Meloy, 1988; Prentky et al., 1989). Although no $Mp-$ responses are evident, suggesting delusion, two Mpu responses (2, 18) linked to formal thought disorder, DR, probably indicate overvalued ideas and Huntley's vulnerability to delusion when not medicated (Meloy & Singer, 1991).

The three FD responses are unexpected (4, 8, 11). This determinant can be considered a subset of M (P. Erdberg, personal communication, November 11, 1991) and in normals is considered a positive and balanced capacity to think about the self. In this case, however, Huntley used his insight into himself to create discomfort in others, usually clinicians, by verbalizing his most bizarre and sadistic thoughts in an unexpected and quiet manner. On one occasion, he said to his psychotherapist, "I'm just imagining what you'd look like with a noose around your neck." He would use introspection in an interpersonally sadistic manner.

Huntley's interpersonal and affective world is isolative ($Isolate/R$ = .47) and avoidant (Afr = .19). Despite this, and unlike most severe psychopaths, he normatively seeks affectional bonds (T = 1, COP = 3) but is highly ambivalent about them. Part objects, rather than whole objects ($H:Hd$ = 2:3) provide the structural templates for his internal representations. Huntley's self-perception of not being damaged (MOR = 1) is surprising in light of his mental illness and may suggest pathological narcissism, a characteristic expected in psychopaths.

Psychodynamics

Impulses.   Libidinal and aggressive drive derivatives (Kernberg, 1984) are ubiquitous in Huntley's Rorschach. Sexual responses, rare in normals but expected in antisocial personality disordered males (Gacono & Meloy, 1992), are verbalized by Huntley in a devalued and sadistic manner (3, 13; Meloy & Gacono, 1992). Characterological sadism (Kernberg, 1982) has been associated with sexual homicide (Gacono, 1992; Meloy, 1988) and is consistent with his sexually sadistic fantasies. Sudden psychotic regression in the midst of sadistic sexual arousal is suggested by his loss of reality testing on Responses 3 and 13. Sadomasochistic responses (Gacono, 1990; Meloy, 1988; Meloy & Gacono, 1992) are prevalent (1, 3, 13, 18) and are linked with gender confusion (1), sex organs (3, 13), or predation (18).

Aggression is manifested in his aggressive potential responses (1, 7, 18, 19), aggressive content of an oral and phallic nature (1, 7, 19), and present aggression (19; Exner, 1986). What is notable about these responses is their pervasiveness, their link with sadism (1, 18), and their separation from Huntley's sexual responses (3, 13). The mediating factor that links his aggression and sexuality, however, is sadism (3, 13), which implies pleasure through the infliction of pain or suffering on another and, by necessity, requires a certain amount of aggression against the object. The complete absence of aggressive past responses in Huntley's protocol suggests a predominantly sadistic, rather than masochistic, orientation to the object (Meloy & Gacono, 1992). The presence of unmodulated sexual and aggressive drives in this protocol, mediated by sadism, provides some concurrent validity for his real-world sexual assault risk.

The softer libidinal aspects of Huntley's impulses are found in his desire for attachment. Unfortunately, objects of attachment are perceived as threatening, suffused with aggression (7), or unpleasant and negated (19). The reptilian nature of this "negated T" response (19) is particularly intriguing ("It's ugly, slimy, mean looking, I wouldn't touch them. I have had lizards before") and is clinically consistent with certain theoretical aspects of the reptilian cerebrotype (MacLean, 1976) in psychopathy (Meloy, 1988). In this case, however, Huntley experiences this part of himself in a projected form.

Defenses.   Kernberg (1984) noted that psychotic defenses are generally the same as borderline defenses, but serve a different purpose. Borderline defenses prevent conflict; psychotic defenses prevent disintegration. Prominent defenses (Cooper & Arnow, 1986; Gacono, 1990) in Huntley's protocol include devaluation (3, 13, 17, 18, 19), projective identification (1, 7, 9, 19), and dissociation (1, 5, 19). Idealization is predictably absent (Gacono, 1990). The fluidity of defensive operations and the failure of higher level defenses are vividly displayed in Response 19: "I see alien life (devaluation, distancing) invading a dance. I see all kinds of bugs and insects also invading the dance. Scorpions too (projective identification)." Inquiry: "The top looks like a space ship (intellectualization), the way it is shaped, the color, gray and white. Could write a story about this one (omnipotence). Serpents (projective identification). It's ugly, slimy (devaluation), mean looking (projection), I wouldn't touch them (attempted reaction formation). I have had lizards before (attempted repression). Alien bugs from another planet (devaluation, distancing). The blue, scorpions (projective identification), got a lot of legs, on the attack, ready to kill and devour anything (projection) that they can get their hands on, or pinchers, or whatever you want to call it (rationalization). The dance, pink things represent (dissociation) two people having a good time at a dance (prestage splitting). Just having fun at a dance (pollyannish denial)." The rapid and sequential shifting of defenses in this one Rorschach response captures a moment of time in Huntley's intrapsychic life.

Projective identification can function as either a borderline or psychotic defense (Goldstein, 1991; Meloy, 1991). Goldstein (1991) theorized that the projection of self-representations may necessitate the psychotic use of projective identification. Likewise, the projection of object representations may signal the borderline use of projective identification. Clinical distinction, however, remains elusive. The four projective identification responses in this protocol may suggest the difference. Responses 1 and 19 appear to involve the projective identification of a self representation. They contain aggression or aggressive potential (*Ag* or *AgPot*) and human movement (*M*): all characteristics that are ego syntonic for Huntley and convey a sense of himself from the case history. Other data suggest that projective identification and dissociation may indicate a psychotic process in sexual homicide (Gacono, 1992). Responses 7 and 9, on the other hand, appear to involve the projective identification of an object representation. None of the content and determinants in the "self" responses are present here, suggesting an ego dystonic quality. The sole content are animal figures, alien to the human form. If these inferences are accurate, Huntley defensively shifts between a psychotic and borderline use of projective identification in the service of intrapsychic self-cohesion and conflict reduction, respectively.

Object Relations.   Psychotic personality organization implicates a loss of reality testing, preoedipal defenses, and identity diffusion (Kernberg, 1984). A psychotic Rorschach should likewise manifest object relations that are rooted in the autistic or symbiotic developmental stages, rather than the more progressed stage of separation–individuation (Mahler, Pine, & Bergman, 1975). Although controversy abounds concerning the time frames of infant development, there is some consensus that a "symbiotic dual unity" (p. 46) exists between mother and infant prior to the autonomous strivings of the toddler:

> the infant begins dimly to perceive need satisfaction as coming from some need satisfying part-object—albeit still from within the orbit of the omnipotent symbiotic dual unity—and he turns libidinally toward that mothering source or agency. The need gradually becomes a wish and later the specific "object-bound" affect of longing. (Mahler et al., 1975, p. 46)

Huntley's object relations suggest fixation and conflict during the symbiotic stage of development. Primitive object relations (Kwawer, 1980) include engulfment (16); violent symbiosis, separation, and reunion (17); and womb imagery (4). Affectional striving (7) encounters a threatening and penetrating object or an object unpleasant to the touch and "cold blooded" (19). These are not conflicts around mirroring, resulting in the expected narcissistic pathology of borderline psychopaths, but are primitive fears of merging with a penetrating ("claws . . . they are sharp") and devouring ("ready to kill and devour") maternal object. This is the basic annihilatory fear of the psychotic (Frosch, 1983). How does Huntley defend against this atavistic emotion? He uses sadism to hurt and control the maternal object so that it will not be destroyed by his own hatred. In this case, sadism and psychosis walk hand in hand (Gabbard, 1989; MacCulloch, Snowden, Wood, & Mills, 1983; Shapiro, 1981).

CONCLUSION

We think there is a high probability that Huntley will commit a sexual homicide in the future if left to his own devices. It would be impulsive and marked by dyscontrol (Ressler, Burgess, & Douglas, 1988), but also a product of years of rehearsal fantasy (Prentky et al., 1989). The victim would most likely be a female acquaintance or girlfriend who unwittingly stimulated his annihilatory fear and defensive, sadistic rage.

Table 4.1 summarizes the clinical signs for an underlying compulsive syndrome for violence, the typical motivation for serial sexual murder (Litwack & Schlesinger, 1987; Revitch & Schlesinger, 1981). Huntley is positive for seven of these nine signs. Overprediction of violence is always expected, but in this case we think the intrapsychic characteristics of Huntley, inferred from his Rorschach, are deeply endogenous and will overshadow both psychiatric and psychological efforts to attenuate his future violence. Time and the nature of his clinical management will tell.

ADDENDUM

Six years after this patient was evaluated and readmitted to a forensic hospital, he was released, once again, to the community. The Superior Court concurred with the hospital staff and the independent evaluations that Huntley would not constitute a danger to others if supervised by an involuntary outpatient treatment program.

Within a month of release Huntley reported to his treating clinician that his frequency of sexually sadistic fantasies had increased, and he had "followed" a woman for several blocks, unknown to her. He was immediately recommitted to the same forensic hospital. Despite the eternal optimism of clinicians, there is no demonstrable treatment for sexual sadism (Meloy, 1992).

TABLE 4.1
Clinical Signs of an Underlying Compulsive Syndrome for Violence

1. A history of mistreatment of women or fantasies of assaulting women.
2. Breaking and entering committed alone and under bizarre circumstances.
3. Fetishism for female underclothing and destruction of female clothes.
4. Expression of hatred, contempt, or fear of women.
5. Dislike for cats or actual violence against cats or other animals.
6. Violent and primitive fantasy life.
7. Confusion of sexual identity on projective tests.
8. Sexual inhibitions and moral preoccupation with sexual conduct.
9. Feelings of isolation and poor reality testing.

Note. Cited in Litwack and Schlesinger (1987).

ACKNOWLEDGMENTS

We thank Linda Helinski, PhD, for her clinical contribution to this chapter, Phil Erdberg, PhD, for his scoring help, and Jeffrey Hammond, PhD, for his insightful comments.
This chapter was originally part of a symposium entitled, "Psychotic Personality Organization: Through the Looking Glass," presented at the Society for Personality Assessment, Midwinter Meeting, New Orleans, March 9, 1991.
The views expressed are ours and do not necessarily reflect those of the Department of Psychiatry, University of California, San Diego, School of Medicine or Atascadero State Hospital.

REFERENCES

American Psychiatric Association. (1987). *Diagnostic and statistical manual of mental disorders* (3rd ed., rev.). Washington, DC: Author.

Cooper, S., & Arnow, D. (1986). An object relations view of the borderline defenses: A Rorschach analysis. In M. Kissen (Ed.), *Assessing object relations phenomena* (pp. 143–174). New York: International Universities Press.

Exner, J. (1986). *The Rorschach: A comprehensive system. Vol. 1, Foundations* (2nd ed.). New York: Wiley.

Exner, J. (1990). *Rorschach interpretation assistance program: Version 2.* Asheville, NC: Rorschach Workshops.

Frosch, J. (1983). *The psychotic process.* New York: International Universities Press.

Gabbard, G. (1989). Patients who hate. *Psychiatry, 52,* 96–106.

Gacono, C. (1990). An empirical study of object relations and defensive operations in antisocial personality disorder. *Journal of Personality Assessment, 54,* 589–600.

Gacono, C. (1992). *A Rorschach case study of sexual homicide.* Manuscript submitted for publication.

Gacono, C., & Meloy, R. (1991). A Rorschach investigation of attachment and anxiety in antisocial personality disorder. *Journal of Nervous and Mental Disease, 179,* 546–552.

Gacono, C., & Meloy, R. (1992). The Rorschach and *DSM–III–R* antisocial personality: A tribute to Robert Lindner. *Journal of Clinical Psychology, 48,* 393–406.

Gacono, C., Meloy, R., & Berg, J. (1992). Object relations, defensive operations, and affective states in narcissistic, borderline, and antisocial personality disorder. *Journal of Personality Assessment, 59,* 32–49.

Gacono, C., Meloy, R., & Heaven, T. (1990). A Rorschach investigation of narcissism and hysteria in antisocial personality disorder. *Journal of Personality Assessment, 55,* 270–279.

Goldstein, W. (1991). Clarification of projective identification. *American Journal of Psychiatry, 148,* 153–161.

Kernberg, O. (1982). An ego psychology and object relations approach to the narcissistic personality. In The American Psychiatric Association (Ed.), *Psychiatry: Annual review* (pp. 510–523). Washington, DC: American Psychiatric Association.

Kernberg, O. (1984). *Severe personality disorders.* New Haven, CT: Yale University Press.

Kwawer, J. (1980). Primitive interpersonal modes, borderline phenomena and Rorschach content. In J. Kwawer, A. Sugarman, P. Lerner, & H. Lerner (Eds.), *Borderline phenomena and the Rorschach test* (pp. 89–105). New York: International Universities Press.

Litwack, T., & Schlesinger, L. (1987). Assessing and predicting violence: Research, law, and applications. In I. Weiner & A. Hess (Eds.), *Handbook of forensic psychology* (pp. 205–257). New York: Wiley.

MacCulloch, M., Snowden, P., Wood, P., & Mills, H. (1983). Sadistic fantasy, sadistic behaviour and offending. *British Journal of Psychiatry, 143,* 20–29.

MacLean, P. (1976). Sensory and perceptive factors in emotional functions of the triune brain. In R. Grenell & S. Gabay (Eds.), *Biological foundations of psychiatry* (pp. 177–98). New York: Raven.

Mahler, M., Pine, F., & Bergman, A. (1975). *The psychological birth of the human infant.* New York: Basic Books.

Meloy, J. R. (1988). *The psychopathic mind: Origins, dynamics, and treatment.* Northvale, NJ: Aronson.

Meloy, J. R. (1991). The "blurring" of ego boundary in projective identification [Letter to the editor]. *American Journal of Psychiatry, 148,* 1761–1762.

Meloy, J. R. (1992). *Violent attachments.* Northvale, NJ: Aronson.

Meloy, J. R., & Gacono, C. (1992). The aggression response and the Rorschach. *Journal of Clinical Psychology, 48,* 104–114.

Meloy, J. R., Haroun, A., & Schiller, E. (1990). *Clinical guidelines for involuntary outpatient treatment.* Sarasota, FL: Professional Assessment Resources.

Meloy, J. R., & Singer, J. (1991). A psychoanalytic view of the Comprehensive System "special scores." *Journal of Personality Assessment, 56,* 202–217.

Prentky, R., Burgess, A., Rokous, F., Lee, A., Hartman, C., Ressler, R., & Douglas, J. (1989). The presumptive role of fantasy in serial sexual homicide. *American Journal of Psychiatry, 146,* 887–891.

Ressler, R., Burgess, A., & Douglas, J. (1988). *Sexual homicide: Patterns and motives.* Lexington, MA: D.C. Heath.

Revitch, E., & Schlesinger, L. (1981). *Psychopathology of homicide.* Springfield, IL: Thomas.

Shapiro, D. (1981). *Autonomy and rigid character.* New York: Basic Books.

The Rorschach Protocol of a Psychotic (Sexual) Psychopath

I.

1. Looks like a Halloween mask.

The whole thing. They look like horns on top and on the side (?) Idk. Just does. Also it is black. (?) Eyes right where eyes should be on the face. (?) The nose, not exactly a nose, a place to breathe out. Just looks like a Halloween mask. A sinister smile. Divided by a line, still looks like a mouth. Sinister. Grey lines resemble teeth to me. It'll do a.t. it can to get to you. Not going to let it [smiles].

2. I see two people standing together, a man and a woman.

Got it backwards, a woman over here, man over here, sorry about that. Doing the best I can. Shape of the head. Looks like she got a good haircut, hairstyle, looks feminine. The shape of the head, outline of the body. Facing each other, looking at each other. Way the head's shaped and body is outlined. Looks ragged. Line here, right by shoulderblades might be a crease in a shirt or muscles, looks like the outdoors type. Idk. In my imagination. See him with a shirt or climbing up mountains.

II.

3. This one you're not going to like. Looks like a vagina after a period.

Using the whole thing. (Vagina?) Do I have to [laughs] outside of a vagina (?) first thing that came to my mind it is similar. Inside space, looks like a vagina (?) blood stains here and here. I've seen them before. That's what they look like. Big spots, real red.

4. Looks like a cave.

These are rocks, on both rocks. The color, the shape (?) Black. This hole right here. Kind of looks endless. Enter to nowhere yet somewhere. Who knows, maybe entering to a lost tunnel.

III.

5. Two people dancing at a party. A man and a woman. The red symbolizes the decorations of the party.

All of it. Way they are shaped. Color helps, too. Black. (?) Way they are formed. (Symbolized?) It looks like decorations hanging from a ceiling, and hanging off the wall.

6. Also looks like some dolphins swimming around some rocks.

All the black Dolphins. Each has got a fin showing, that goes upward like a dolphin swimming. I love dolphins playing around. They are sweet. Next to a dog, man's best friend. Don't hurt them. Rocks are the shape and black.

IV.

7. I see two things. A big monster approaching.

It looks black and gray. Looks hairy to me. Evil eyes. Big hands. (hairy?) Way black and gray are blended together. (?) The type of thing you'd want to get away from fast. Gives me the creeps. (Approaching?) The way the feet are pointed. Paws actually, no claws. Only two fingers on the whole hand and they are sharp, kind of like pincers on a crab. *(continued)*

8. Also, a giant tree. How am I doing?

Trunk of the tree (?) I've seen alot of trees and it looks like one. Like I said, leaves (?) shape and color. Looks like a tree in autumn. They are dark. Not bright green. Looks like it's ready to fall. Fall is my favorite time of year. (Giant?) I'm about 5'10". This tree looks like it towers over me at least six hundred times. I see myself at the base of the tree and it's towering up, up, up, forever up. I don't want to miss lunch.

V.

9. A bat or a butterfly.

Whole thing. (bat?) The wings, feet, ears here. Coming at me (?) Just, I don't know. (butterfly?) Way it is shaped, the antenna (?) Way shaped. Next to the smallest thing on the drawing (?) I can't explain it.

10. A moth.

Basically the same thing that made it look like a butterfly.

VI.

11. A sky vision to a highway road with mountains on both sides.

(?) Whole thing. Looking down on it. I've seen freeways before. (Highway?) White line going down the middle of it. The blackness of the road. (mountains?) I've gone to mountains before and seen a lot of hills, it reminds me of hills and mountains.

12. And two cars on a road going toward each other.

The shape, the color, makes it look like it's got headlights on.

13. Also looks like somebody's rectum [smiles].

The crack (?) The line that goes down to it, and the opening, the color (?) gray and black.

VII.

14. One is two girls with ponytails getting ready to kiss each other.

Facial features, shape. Looks like two girls. Ponytails standing straight up. First thing I thought of. Lips puckered up ready to kiss each other slowly but surely (?) going in slow motion to get to each other.

15. A bunch of rain clouds forming. I found a third one.

Clouds, the whole thing. Puffy and shape. (?) the color, it's gray. Rain clouds, dark clouds, the color. Coming together from top to bottom.

16. A cricket caught in the midst of a bunch of rain clouds.

It just does! Long, slender. Got its legs tucked in, just reminded me of a cricket. (caught?) Pressed in between the two clouds, coming closer and closer, pressing on the beetle, cricket, rather.

VIII.

17. Two aardvarks pulling on the sails of an old ship.

The whole thing. They are long and slender, the nose being the only difference between these and the real ones. These have a shorter snout, way the lines are. Long. (?) just pulling on the sails, just looks like old, beat up sails. Raggedy edges, torn all to hell. Ragged edges. Rest of the boat is right here. The only solid thing here.

IX.

18. Okay, I see two old men searching for something.

Here's the eyes, nose, and mouth, the way the lip hangs down. Searching (?) way the eyes look, wide open and concentrating on whatever they can see. Ready to zero in on any one thing at any minute. Maybe a couple of old ladies [laughs].

X.

19. I see alien life invading a dance. I see all kinds of bugs and insects also invading the dance. Scorpions too.

The top looks like a space ship, the way it is shaped, the color, gray and white. Could write a story about this one. Serpents (?) It's ugly, slimy, mean looking, I wouldn't touch them. I have had lizards before. Alien beings from another planet. The blue, scorpions, got a lot of legs, on the attack, ready to kill and devour a.t. that they get their hands on, or pinchers or whatever you want to call it. The dance, pink, things represent two people having a good time at a dance (?) just having fun at a dance.

APPENDIX B
Comprehensive System Sequence of Scores From the Rorschach of a Psychotic (Sexual) Psychopath

Card	No.	Loc.	#	Determinant(s)	(2)	Content(s)	Pop Z	Special Scores
I	1	WSo	1	FC'.Mpo		(Hd)	3.5	DR
	2	Dd+	99	Mpu		H, Cg	4.0	DR
II	3	WSo	1	CF–		An, Sx, Bl	4.5	PER
	4	DS/	6	C'F.FDu		Ls	4.5	DR2
III	5	W+	1	Ma.FC'.mp.CFo		H, Art	P 5.5	AB, COP
	6	D+	1	FMa.FC'u	2	A, Ls	3.0	DR2
IV	7	Do	7	FMa.FTo		(A)		DR
	8	Ddo	99	FY.FDo		Bt		PER, DR
V	9	Wo	1	FMao		A	P 1.0	DR
	10	Wo	1	Fo		A	1.0	
VI	11	W+	1	FC'.FDu		Ls	2.5	PER, DV
	12	D+	5	ma.FC'u	2	Sc, Ls	2.5	
	13	Do	5	FC'–		An, Sx		
VII	14	D+	2	Mp.mpo	2	Hd	P 3.0	COP
	15	W/	1	C'F.mao	2	Cl	2.5	
	16	W+	1	ma.FMp–		A, Cl	2.5	FAB2
VIII	17	W+	1	FMau	2	A, Sc	P 4.5	FAB2, MOR
IX	18	DS+	1	Mpu	2	Hd	2.5	DR
X	19	W+	1	Ma.FC'.CF–	2	Sc, (H), A	5.5	FAB2, AG, COP, PER

Summary of Approach

I:WS.Dd	VI:W.D.D
II:WS.DS	VII:D.W.W.
III:W.D.	VIII:W
IV:D.Dd	IX:DS
V:W.W	X:W

APPENDIX C
Rorschach Structural Summary

LOCATION FEATURES	DETERMINANTS		CONTENTS	S-CONSTELLATION
	BLENDS	SINGLE		YES..FV + VF + V + FD > 2
			H = 2,0	YES..Col-Shd Bl>0
Zf = 16	FC'.M	M = 2	(H) = 0,1	NO..Ego<.31,>.44
ZSum = 52.5	C'F.FD	FM = 2	Hd = 2,0	NO..MOR>3
ZEst = 52.5	M.FC'.m.CF	m = 0	(Hd) = 1,0	NO..Zd > ± 3.5
	FM.FC'	FC = 0	Hx = 0,0	YES..es>EA
W = 10	FM.FT	CF = 1	A = 5,1	YES..CF+C>FC
(Wv = 0)	FY.FD	C = 0	(A) = 1,0	YES..X+%<.70
D = 7	FC.'FD	Cn = 0	Ad = 0,0	YES..S>3
Dd = 2	m.FC'	FC' = 1	(Ad) = 0,0	NO..P<3 or >8
S = 4	M.m	C'F = 0	An = 2,0	NO..Pure H <2
	C'F.m	C' = 0	Art = 0,1	NO..R<17
DQ	m.FM	FT = 0	Ay = 0,0	6.....TOTAL
.........(FQ–)	M.FC'.CF	TF = 0	Bl = 0,1	
+ = 10(2)		T = 0	Bt = 1,0	SPECIAL SCORINGS
o = 7 (2)		FV = 0	Cg = 0,1	Lvl Lv2
v/+ = 2 (0)		VF = 0	Cl = 1,1	DV = 1x1 0x2
v = 0 (0)		V = 0	Ex = 0,0	INC = 0x2 0x4
		FY = 0	Fd = 0,0	DR = 6x3 2x6
		YF = 0	Fi = 0,0	FAB = 0x4 3x7
		Y = 0	Ge = 0,0	ALOG = 0x5
FORM QUALITY		Fr = 0	Hh = 0,0	CON = 0x7
		rF = 0	Ls = 2,2	SUM6 = 12
FQx FQf MQual SQx		FD = 0	Na = 0,0	WSUM6 = 52
+ = 0 0 0 0		F = 1	Sc = 2,1	
o = 8 1 3 1			Sx = 0,2	AB =1 CP = 0
u = 7 0 2 2			Xy = 0,0	AG =1 MOR = 1
– = 4 0 1 1			Id = 0,0	CFB =0 PER = 4
none = 0 – 0 0		(2) = 7		COP =3 PSV = 0

RATIOS, PERCENTAGES, AND DERIVATIONS

R = 19	L = 0.06		FC:CF+C =0:3	COP = 3	AG =1
			Pure C =0	Food	= 0
EB = 6: 3.0	EA = 9.0	EBPer = 2.0	Afr =0.19	Isolate/R	= 0.47
eb = 10:11	es = 21	D = –4	S =4	H:(H)Hd(Hd)	= 2:4
	Adj es = 17	Adj D = –3	Blends:R =12:19	(HHd):(AAd)	= 2:1
			CP =0	H+A:Hd + Ad	= 10:3
FM = 5	C' = 9	T = 1			
m = 5	V = 0	Y = 1			
			P = 4	Zf =16	3r+(2)/R = 0.37
a:p = 9:7	Sum6 =12		X+% = 0.42	Zd = +0.0	Fr+rF = 0
Ma:Mp = 2:4	Lv2 = 5		F+% = 1.00	W:D:Dd =10:7:2	FD = 3
2AB+Art+Ay = 3	WSum6 = 52		X–% = 0.21	W:M =10:6	An + Xy = 2
M– = 1	Mnone = 0		S–% = 0.25	DQ+ =10	MOR = 1
			Xu% = 0.37	DQv =0	

SCZI = 3	DEPI = 5*	CDI = 3	S-CON = 6	HVI = No	OBS = No

5

Toward a Synthetic Approach to the Rorschach: The Case of a Psychotic Child

James F. Murray
Knoxville. TN

Increasingly the teaching of the Rorschach and Rorschach research have come to be grouped into two camps: the psychoanalytic camp and the empirical camp. Each side tends to muster arguments and/or research to support its style of approach, measures, ratios, and scales. Frequently these presentations fail to acknowledge the existence of the other camp's attempts to address similar issues or diagnostic concerns. Often one is left with a growing sense of an isolation or fundamental dichotomization between these two camps.

This apparent incompatibility is unnecessary and generally avoided by sophisticated clinicians. In day-to-day clinical practice, astute clinicians tend to call upon a number of scoring systems, scales, and perspectives in attempting to deal with a particular assessment issue or refining a given diagnostic concern. Familiarity with a number of systems, scales, and perspectives provides a clinician with an awareness of the strengths and weaknesses of each approach in addressing a given clinical issue. Using this type of synthetic approach, one can develop a stable of systems, scales, and perspectives that can be "plugged in" as the clinical situation dictates. Employing a process of sophisticated analysis and integration of Rorschach tools and perspectives (regardless of the camp) allows the clinician to best understand and be of help to patients undergoing assessment. This sense of analysis and synthesis is lost in the more unidimensional approaches to the Rorschach.

The aim of this chapter is not to present a specific "how-to" approach to the diagnosis of psychosis per se, but to demonstrate a process of clinical inference building that employs and integrates a variety of approaches to the Rorschach. This approach requires the clinician to give a Rorschach; not a particular system or scale. Specific systems or scales may be useful in comprehending the Rorschach process and what it says about the person under study, but the measures must be guided by the clinician rather than the clinician being excessively guided by the measures.

With this in mind, the Rorschach of a psychotic child is presented to illustrate this synthetic clinical decision-making process. I do not show the utility of the Rorschach in arriving at this diagnosis—which is not a particularly difficult task given the clinical and Rorschach material in this selected case—but to demonstrate, to a limited extent, the process of integration of Rorschach knowledge in the service of clinical inference and decision making.

CLINICAL DATA

K was a 9-year, 8-month-old White female who was tested as an inpatient at a children's psychiatric facility. Hospitalization was ascribed to the patient's wild imagination and bizarre behavior which included: (a) K's attempt to burn her house down through the use of a heater; (b) K telling her parents "Jesus put his tongue in my mouth at school" after she french kissed a boy at school; (c) K killing a kitten by placing it in a plastic bag, tying the bag on the handlebars of a bike, and then allowing the cat to become caught up in the spokes and be crushed; (d) poor peer interaction and disruptive behavior in the classroom; (e) frequent instances of stealing and lying; (f) instances of K placing foreign objects in her mouth, ears, and vagina; (g) K purposely cutting her knee with a razor blade and repeatedly pulling at teeth that were not ready to be loosened so that she could enjoy seeing her own blood; (h) reported auditory hallucinations; and (i) K's repeated discussions of her fantasy of having a Black baby.

K's developmental history was notable for her removal from her birth parents' home when she was 22 months old due to severe neglect. Reportedly, K's mother could not read or write and had a long history of drug abuse, and her biological father reportedly spent a considerable period of time in jail. The adoptive family reported a strong suspicion that K was physically and sexually abused by her natural parents in addition to severe neglect. The patient had been diagnosed several years previously as having petit mal seizures of the absence nature and was treated with medication.

Intellectual assessment at the time that projectives were given revealed a Verbal Scale IQ score of 69, a Performance Scale IQ score of 81, and a Full Scale IQ score of 73. Although these scores were seen as reflecting current functional capacity, they were viewed as an underestimate of innate capability.

RORSCHACH ASSESSMENT

The Rorschach was administered to K as part of a battery of tests that included the Wechsler Intelligence Scale for Children–Revised (WISC–R), the Thematic Apperception Test (TAT), and projective drawings. The testing took place within the first 2 weeks of admission. Administration and scoring of the Rorschach was according to Exner's Comprehensive System (Exner, 1986; Exner & Weiner, 1982). (See Appendices A, B, and C for Rorschach protocol and related scoring materials.)

Exner and Weiner (1982) described a conceptual framework for the diagnosis of schizophrenia and outlined specific empirically derived or tested Rorschach indices to aid in diagnostic decision making. These indices led to the development of the Schizophrenia index (*SCZI;* Exner, 1986).

Table 5.1 shows the general conceptual categories and K's performance on a number of the indices. Specifically, K displays distorted thinking in the form of 16 Special Scores. Her protocol includes two instances of contaminated thinking (CONTAM) and one instance of autistic logic (ALOG); these two scores represent more severe types of disturbance in thinking.

K displays inaccurate perception in her very low good form level (*X*+%), an extremely high poor form level (*X*–%), and in her tendency for perceptual inaccuracy to occur pervasively. That is to say that her impairment in perception, or reality testing, does not appear to be in response to specific or circumscribed Rorschach card properties (e.g., color, cognitive complexity, shading, aggressive or interpersonal content). In simple language, this suggests that her reality testing is just plain bad; regardless of the external setting or stimulus.

K also exhibits significant disturbance in the interpersonal realm. To begin with, all of her human movement (*M*) responses are of poor form quality. Even more ominous, each *M* response is infused with a Special Score. Thus, K appears to not only inaccurately perceive others, but to interpret or elaborate upon these inaccurate perceptions in peculiar, bizarre, and highly illogical fashions. Furthermore, all *M* responses are (*H*) or animals engaged in human activity. This tends to reflect very primitive modes of conceptualizing people and interpersonal relations. Finally, K frequently "spoils" popular responses, indicating that she can take material that is simple and obvious to most

TABLE 5.1
Rorschach Indicators of Impairment—Protocol

Disordered thinking	1.	16 Special scores—including 2 CONTAMS and 1 ALOG.
Inaccurate perception	1.	*X*+% = 19%.
	2.	*X*–% = 55%.
	3.	Inaccuracies pervasive.
Interpersonal ineptness	1.	All *M* responses are u or –.
	2.	Each *M* response is infused with a special score.
	3.	All *M*s are (*H*) [vampire/skeletons, caveman/skeletons, or monster/vampires] or are *A*s engaged in *H* activities.
	4.	*P*s are frequently spoiled.
Inadequate controls	1.	Disturbed content with 5 *AG*s—and much more aggressive material in nonmovement responses.
	2.	Poor control over affect with 3 *C*s and *FC:CF* + *C* = 2:7.
	3.	General response to the material reflecting sense that the bizarre and out of control was "OK" and even enjoyable.

everyone and ruin or distort her perception. This bespeaks a severe impairment in her capacity to view even the most mundane material in a conventional fashion and tends to reflect severe disturbance.

K's Rorschach reflects serious problems with control over affects and impulses. She has five aggressive (AG) responses, and there are numerous responses reflecting aggression or violence that are not scored in the Exner system (Gacono & Meloy, 1994). These responses clearly reflect her preoccupation with the control of aggression (in herself and others) and raise questions about her capacity to contain aggressive impulses. Her ratio of form dominated to nonform dominated responses (FC:CF + C) is 2:7, indicating that when emotion is displayed it tends to be poorly integrated with or contained by cognition, and given an overall context of limited resources for containment and control, has the potential to fuel impulsive behavior. Her frequent peculiar or bizarre responses reflect a difficulty with control of thinking as well. Equally ominous was the sense she conveyed that the bizarre and out of control behavior was expected and even enjoyable. This occurred most vividly in her side comment to a particularly bizarre and aggressive response on Card X as she stated that it was a "good picture, though scary." This acceptance of severe pathology reflects a deeply ingrained and chronic disturbance.

SYNTHETIC APPROACH TO RORSCHACH DATA

With this information regarding K's Rorschach, it should come as little surprise to discover that she scored a perfect 5 for 5 on Exner and Weiner's (1982) old Schizophrenia index (SCZI). Using the new or revised SCZI (Exner, 1990) resulted in K scoring 5 out of 6 of the index markers. Estimates are that this revised index is more conservative with a false positive rate of 8%–10% when SCZI is 4–6, even in children (I. B. Weiner, personal communication, June 17, 1991). Although this "fine tuning" of the SCZI appears to increase the predictive power of the instrument, it does so at the cost of reducing the conceptual utility of the SCZI that served as the framework for Exner and Weiner's (1982) original presentation of the index. So using either the old or new SCZI exclusively would be a relatively easy case, and one could offer very strong support for a diagnosis of schizophrenia.

My clinical experience suggests that the simple application of the old SCZI can result in inaccurate diagnosis, and with these cases I have found it useful to go to other Rorschach measures to help in discriminations. The old SCZI tends to give frequent false positives in certain types of learning disability and attention deficit disorder populations. Although both Exner and Weiner (1982) and Acklin (1990) pointed out that learning disabled children exhibit inaccurate perception (poor $X+\%$), both suggested that disordered thinking (i.e., Special Scores) does not tend to be prevalent. I have found that to be true to the extent one is looking at older children (ages 9 and up) and to the extent that the disability is relatively circumscribed. Perhaps the absence of

Special Scores for this population reflects the fact that growing up has allowed children to develop compensatory mechanisms that overcome or limit the impact of the disability, or the circumscribed nature of the disability readily allows for these compensatory mechanisms. However, for younger children (ages 5–8) with more severe or pervasive disabilities, one tends to get inaccurate perception (low $X+\%$), interpersonal impairments ($M-$, (H)), and disturbances in reasoning (Special Scores). When using the old $SCZI$, it was not at all unusual to obtain $SCZI$ scores of 3, 4, or 5 in the absence of any clinical data or test behavior that "feels" schizophrenic.

Those scoring high on the $SCZI$ who do not "feel" schizophrenic are generally children with severe cognitive processing difficulties, and they often have so-called "hyperactivity," which tends to result in behavioral discontrol and significant conflict with both peers and adults. Thus, they have difficulty establishing articulated, consistent, and realistic cognitive–perceptual maps of the world around them, and they experience or induce highly conflictual and distorted interpersonal relationships. Often their major source of solace is being "plugged into" fantastic and violent cartoons or Nintendo games. In these types of cases it is useful to review the work of Blatt and his co-workers (Blatt, Brenneis, Schimek, & Glick, 1976; Blatt, Wild, & Ritzler, 1976) as well as the large body of research based on Holt's (1977) system for assessing primary and secondary process thinking on the Rorschach.

Blatt and his co-workers looked at special scorings and the overall articulation of the object representation in terms of psychoanalytic formulations on boundary formation and impairment. They viewed schizophrenia as an impairment in the capacity to experience, perceive, and represent boundaries and special scorings as an individual's manifestations of difficulties in this area of boundary functioning.

As we can see in K's protocol, instances of boundary impairment come fast and furious. The first response ends up as a bat-grabber-bee: a gross violation of boundaries in that two reality-based images (a bat and a bee) are fused together along with some very primitive image of a "grabber." Blatt's perspective gives a theoretical framework for why the CONTAM response is so rare and so pathognomonic. This very primitive boundary impairment continues in Response 2—butterfly-bat—and in Card II Response 6—an airplane hanging inside of a bat.

K also displays severe disturbance in maintaining appropriate boundaries between ideas or percepts. For example, in Card III there is not only the boundary violation of the cavemen-skeletons killing the elephant and eating his blood, but the severely distorted reasoning in judging the external red to be their hearts and having this signify they are "in love."

This theme of boundary violation and fusion of objects into one is pervasive in K's protocol and consistent with Blatt's theories regarding the basis for severe boundary impairment occurring in earliest mother–infant interaction. Note on Card IV the response of a "monster-vampire that eats, eats, eats people." As she continues, suddenly the "he" turns into a "mommy." Similarly on Card X, one set of figures moves inside of another to kill him (again, presumably this him is a mommy) because they want to devour "his" eggs.

One of the features that differentiates K's Rorschach from the Rorschachs of learning disabled/attention deficit disorder (LD/ADDH) children who may have SCZI scores of 4 or 5 is the driven and ego syntonic nature of the boundary violations. One gets a sense that the boundary impairment occurs not just on a cognitive-processing level, but that she has a driven wish to fuse, in very primitive libidinal and aggression filled ways, with maternal objects. Essentially, she has a wish to both be blissfully reunited with and to kill her mother as the result of very early and severe disturbance in the mother–infant relationship.

In contrast, learning disabled children's boundary violations tend to have a much more cognitive-processing impairment as opposed to a developmentally driven feel to them. Sometimes their Special Scores have good or only moderately poor form quality, but they impose unrealistic or fantastic relationships. More often their unrealistic and fantastic percepts reflect a defensive withdrawal from the tension-filled and failure-ridden involvement with the external world into the relatively safe quasi-fantasy world of cartoons and Nintendo (or, in later years, Stephen King novels or science fiction/fantasy books or games). In this world, animals talk and things can be magically transformed right before one's eyes. These children tend to deliver much of this fantastic world onto the Rorschach as they truly have never surrendered their cartoon logic for more realistic concerns.

A knowledge of different Rorschach scoring systems can be helpful in this instance. The Holt system examines manifestations of primary process thinking: either in terms of drive material (i.e., sexual or aggressive) or in terms of structural fluidity in thinking (i.e., loose logic or the kind of thinking that strains or breaks logical boundaries). There is a very extensive body of research indicating that the presence of primary process thinking on the Rorschach, under certain conditions, is correlated with a host of positive cognitive, emotional, and interpersonal capabilities in children and adults (Holt, 1977; Russ, 1988). What are the conditions in which primary process thinking may be adaptive in nature? They are: (a) when the material occurs in the context of good form level; and (b) when the primitiveness of the drive or structural material is in some way contained, mitigated, or made more acceptable by reference to an appropriate social context.

The Special Scores of LD/ADDH individuals are often of relatively poor form level, so that is not of much help in making the distinction from the Rorschachs of schizophrenic children. But many of the more fantastic or Special Score responses tend to be things these children have seen on television or in Nintendo. Thus, their distortions in thinking or reasoning have a "salvaging" cultural referent or context. This is in stark contrast to K's material; her Special Scores tend to reflect highly idiosyncratic ideation. Strange as it may seem, there is a cultural referent for a child seeing a mustachioed Italian gentleman hitting a gorilla over the head with a sledgehammer, thanks to Mario Brothers. To my knowledge, there is no television show or game that features cavemen-skeletons, in love, killing elephants and drinking their blood.

By working with the Rorschach in this manner, one can best understand patients, essentially by using the Exner system as an initial approach and then employing other systems or perspectives when one runs into specific issues or weaknesses within the Exner system. The Exner system offers a solid, empirically grounded analysis of cognitive–perceptual functioning, general affective state including affective control and capacity to integrate cognition and affect, as well as a basic, albeit limited, analysis of interpersonal perceptions and functions. The Exner system is weak in the areas of the analysis of drives and a more sophisticated analysis of the integration of drives and affective experience in the context of interpersonal interaction. The Exner System's reliance on empirically based data, ratios, and indexes can result in a blind or cookbook approach to the Rorschach, with the clinician failing to comprehend the nuances of a specific or atypical patient and the nature of meaning of specific elements within the Rorschach process. Although these are inherent (and perhaps unavoidable) weaknesses in an empirical approach, the failure to be sensitive to these possibilities and attempt to compensate for them is not the fault of the Exner System per se, but rather the result of a lack of training or sophistication on the part of the clinician.

A number of other psychoanalytically oriented approaches are far more attuned to these areas and can potentially compensate. However, these approaches generally lack a strong empirical base, and because of their tendency to focus on the interpersonal realms, often fail to provide a thorough analysis of basic personality features. Additionally, these more conceptually based approaches allow for significant shaping (and potentially distortion) of interpretation as a result of the clinician's particular theoretical bias or countertransference difficulties. In these instances, an empirically based system offers a potential check to these more idiosyncratic pulls. A flexible, synthetic integration of these two approaches allows one to compensate for the weaknesses of one with the strengths of the other. However, this synthetic approach requires a fairly thorough knowledge of the strengths and weaknesses of a variety of Rorschach approaches. Without this knowledge one is in danger of concocting a haphazard "grab bag" approach. It is important for the clinician to know the Rorschach, not a particular Rorschach system, and an integrated approach can be especially helpful when attempting to rule in, or more frequently, rule out difficult or atypical diagnoses.

ACKNOWLEDGMENT

A version of this chapter was initially presented at the Midwinter Meeting of the Society for Personality Assessment, March 9, 1991, New Orleans, as part of a symposium entitled, "Psychotic Organization: Through the Looking Glass."

REFERENCES

Acklin, M. (1990). Personality dimensions in two types of learning-disabled children: A Rorschach study. *Journal of Personality Assessment, 54,* 67–77.

Blatt, S., Brenneis, C., Schimek, J., & Glick, M. (1976). Normal development and psychopathological impairment of the concept of the object on the Rorschach. *Journal of Abnormal Psychology, 85,* 364–373.

Blatt, S., Wild, C., & Ritzler, B. (1976). Disturbances of object representation in schizophrenia. *Psychoanalysis and Contemporary Science, 4,* 235–288.

Exner, J. E., Jr. (1986). *The Rorschach: A comprehensive system* (Vol. 1, 2nd ed.). New York: Wiley.

Exner, J. E., Jr. (1990). *A Rorschach workbook for the comprehensive system.* Asheville, NC: Rorschach Workshops.

Exner, J. E., Jr., & Weiner, I. B. (1982). *The Rorschach: A comprehensive system. Vol. 3: Assessment of children and adolescents.* New York: Wiley.

Gacono, C., & Meloy, R. (1994). *Rorschach assessment of aggressive and psychopathic personalities.* Hillsdale, NJ: Lawrence Erlbaum Associates.

Holt, R. (1977). A method for assessing primary process manifestations and their controls in Rorschach responses. In M. Rickers-Ovsiankina (Ed.), *Rorschach psychology* (pp. 375–420). Huntington, NY: Krieger.

Russ, S. (1988). Primary process thinking on the Rorschach, divergent thinking, and coping in children. *Journal of Personality Assessment, 52,* 539–548.

I.

1. A bat . . . a bat w/hands and a grabber—a bee—a bat-grabber-bee

A messy bat
A messy bat . . .
He's got holes in his wings

2. A butterfly
A butterfly-bat

3. A pincher bug

II.

4. ST that kills . . . a bird—the white part—to me is a bird . . . and the dark part is the vampire and this is the snapper and this is the blood

5. A butterfly

6. A bat . . .
A butterfly and an airplane

III.

7. A skeleton

8. People picking up food and their hearts are just beating and they killed an elephant and they cut up and there's blood—yuck! Cavemen, skeletons—all I can tell—Heart's there—cave people This is hers, this is his (heart). They're in love anyway

IV.

9. A monster!

1. Right there—the beetle, there's the bee and there's the bat Q. (All together?) Q. (One A?) A bat-grabber bee-yea

2. [points]
Wings are the bat eyes are the bee's, and the body is the bat and wings is the bat, eyes for the bat, too . . . one eye is for the bat and one isn't

3. Yea, those hands . . . when he catches things pinches 'em and kills 'em, yuck!

4. Yes—This here is the vampire—all this Q. (Blood?)-the red

5. The wings—part butterfly and part vampire right there . . . a juicy beetle that the vampire ate

6. Yea—a bat—vampire and part everything. There's an airplane hanging right inside of him—hanging right inside of the bat.

7. One is a skeleton and one is a vampire—he (the vampire) sucked the most blood and spit it out at the skeleton and then they ate the meat they didn't like. . . just blood—then they got in a fight because one does (like meat) and one doesn't—skeleton does like meat—The vampire just likes blood.

8. All that
Q. (Show me) (points)
How come they're like they're crunched?
Q. Crunched?
That thing they killed stepped on 'em—Crunched them and then they stuck a knife in the heart—that's the easiest way to kill—kill him, cut him up and eat him—even eat blood. They're sick people, cave people.

9. He looks like one, doesn't it? With a dragon tail and big boots on him—also got wings—white wings—he's also a vampire . . . he eats people—that's why he's so big, he eats, eats, eats, eats, people. It's a mommy. It's a mommy and a mommy's crunched him.

(continued)

10. A dinosaur

10. There's the dinosaur—got a tranasix (sic) tail—I didn't eat my breakfast today—oh well—who cares!—(Talks about phone calls from mother and father)

11. Monster/vampire . . . Who made these? . . . you? They could have made blood all over—dinosaurs are dangerous-definitely a meat eater.

V.

11. (Same as first response.) with a beak—cut things up

12. Like a butterfly and a caterpillar

12. Yea—antenna, head and these two things here, and wings just like a bat

13. Like a bat—a vampire bat

13. Yea—it's wings

14. And a dinosaur—bat

14. Oh yea—wings and body—whole body—kinda like a tyranasaurus—not an airplane (Q. Made it look like a dinosaur bat.) It's wings, thin wings

VI.

15. Like a bird . . . what is a bird called in dinosaur ages? Does it look like a bird?

15. This is not a bird . . . Oh yea—kinda like a . . . See this part? See bird's eye's (points to Dd)

16. When you spin it looks like a point on a game

16. They're like playing a game (spins card)

VII.

17. This here looks like a butterfly

17. Right here—and there's the biggest wings in the world

18. 2 bats

18. Right here

19. 2 clouds

19. Right there
Q. (made look like?)
Shaped like clouds—with grey paint

VIII.

20. A rainbow—right here

20. (points)
Q. (Made look like?)
The colors and shapes

21. These look like dinosaurs

21. Yea—and they're like climbing up the rainbow and you can see the mouth

22. This looks like a butterfly—four butter-flies

22. That one
That one
That one
That one

IX.

23. Worms

23. The orange parts

24. Clouds

24. In the middle-shapes

25. Those could be apples

25. 4 apples
Q. (Made look like?)
The shapes and they're red

26. Trees

26. The cloud's parts are . . .
Q. (Made it look like?)
The color

27. And the blue right there could be the skyway

27. Yea, right in there
Q. (skyway?) the sky

X.

28. Spiders, these 2

29. These 2 spiders

30. Pinch bug, bug wings

31. Eggs, worm . . . These 2 look like eggs too These things here . . . These here caught a measle . . . There's a knife here going into him—They got him locked up, and if he moves . . . ehhh! he gets picked . . . and they want his eggs out of him—gerbils here and when the butterfly moves and gets killed, they're the ones gonna be guilty. That's a good picture, though, scary.

28. This is kinda scary—These 2 . . . and they caught something—what did I call those—it's a baby and callin' for help—scary—measles! that's what they are measles
Q. (Measles?)
Something that can't crawl—just stays there, have no blood. Green slimy stuff squished. It made me sick and throw up.

29. These 2

30. (points)

31. Right here's the knife
Right here's the eggs
They want to kill him and kill his eggs to—gonna eat his eggs

APPENDIX B
Exner System Sequence of Scores for K

Card	No.	Loc.	#	Determinant(s)	(2)	Content(s)	Pop Z	Special Scores
I	1	WSo	1	F–		(A)	P 1.0	CON, MOR
	2	Wo	1	F–		(A)	P 1.0	CON
	3	Do		Fo		A		
II	4	W+	1	CF–		A, Bl	4.5	MOR
	5	W+	1	FMa–		A	4.5	INC, AG
	6	DS+		mp–		A, Sc	4.5	FAB
III	7	W+	1	Ma.Cu	2	(H), Bl, Fd	P 5.5	DR, MOR, AG
	8	W+	1	Ma.C–	2	(H), Bl, An	P 5.5	DR, FAB, ALOG, MOR, AG
IV	9	WSo	1	FC'u		(H)	P 2.0	INC, DR
	10	Wo	1	F–		A	2.0	
	11	Wo	1	Fu		(H)	2.0	
V	12	Wo	1	Fo		A	P 1.0	
	13	Wo	1	Fo		A	P 1.0	PSV
	14	Wo	1	F–		(A)	1.0	INC
VI	15	Wo	1	F–		A	2.5	
	16	Wo	1	F–		Hh	2.5	
VII	17	Do		Fo		A		
	18	Do		F–	2	A		
	19	Dv		FYu	2	Cl		
VIII	20	Do		CF–		Na		
	21	W+	1	FMa.CF–	2	A, Na	P 4.5	FAB
	22	Do		F–	2	A		
IX	23	Do		F–	2	A		
	24	Dv		Fu	2	Cl		
	25	Do		FCo	2	Fd		
	26	Dv		CFo		Na		
	27	Dv		C		Na		DV
X	28	D+		Mpu	2	A	P 4.0	AG, MOR, DV
	29	Do		Fu	2	A		
	30	Do		F–		A		
	31	Dd+		Ma.FC–	2	(A), Fd, Id	4.5	AG, DR, INC

APPENDIX C
Rorschach Structural Summary

LOCATION FEATURES	DETERMINANTS BLENDS	SINGLE	CONTENTS	S-CONSTELLATION
			H = 0,0	..FV + VF + V + FD > 2
				..Col-Shd Bl>0
Zf = 18	M.C	M = 1	(H) = 4,0	..Ego<.31,>.44
ZSum = 53.5	M.C	FM = 1	Hd = 4,0	..MOR>3
ZEst = 59.5	FM.CF	m = 1	(Hd) = 0,0	..Zd > ± 3.5
	M.FC	FC = 1	Hx = 0,0	..es>EA
W = 15		CF = 3	A = 16,0	..CF+C>FC
(Wv = 0)		C = 1	(A) = 4,0	..X+%<.70
D = 15		Cn = 0	Ad = 0,0	..S>3
Dd = 1		FC' = 1	(Ad) = 0,0	..P<3 or >8
S = 3		C'F = 0	An = 0,1	..Pure H <2
		C' = 0	Art = 0,0	..R<17
DQ		FT = 0	Ay = 0,0	x.....TOTAL
.........(FQ–)		TF = 0	Bl = 0,3	
+ = 8 (6)		T = 0	Bt = 0,0	SPECIAL SCORINGS
o = 19(11)		FV = 0	Cg = 0,0	Lvl Lv2
v/+ = 0 (0)		VF = 0	Cl = 2,0	DV = 2x1 0x2
v = 4 (0)		V = 0	Ex = 0,0	INC = 4x2 0x4
		FY = 1	Fd = 1,2	DR = 4x3 0x6
		YF = 0	Fi = 0,0	FAB = 3x4 0x7
		Y = 0	Ge = 0,0	ALOG = 1x5
FORM QUALITY		Fr = 0	Hh = 1,0	CON = 2x7
		rF = 0	Ls = 0,0	SUM6 = 16
		FD = 0	Na = 3,1	WSUM6 = 53

	FQx	FQf	MQual	SQx						
+	= 0	0	0	0	F = 17	Sc = 0,1				
o	= 6	4	0	0		Sx = 0,0	AB =0	CP = 0		
u	= 7	3	2	1		Xy = 0,0	AG =5	MOR = 5		
–	= 17	10	2	2		Id = 0,1	CFB =0	PER = 0		
none	= 1	–	0	0	(2) = 12		COP =0	PSV = 1		

RATIOS, PERCENTAGES, AND DERIVATIONS

R = 31	L = 1.21			FC:CF+C =2:7	COP = 0	AG =5
				Pure C =3	Food	= 3
EB = 4: 9.5	EA = 13.5	EBPer = 2.4		Afr =0.63	Isolate/R	= 0.39
eb = 3:2	es = 5	D = +3		S =3	H:(H)Hd(Hd)	= 0:4
	Adj es = 5	Adj D = +3		Blends:R =4:31	(HHd):(AAd)	= 4:4
				CP =0	H+A:Hd + Ad	= 24:0
FM = 2	C' = 1	T = 0				
m = 1	V = 0	Y = 1				
			P = 9	Zf =18	3r+(2)/R = 0.39	
a:p = 5:2	Sum6 =16	X+% = 0.19	Zd =−6.0	Fr+rF = 0		
Ma:Mp = 3:1	Lv2 = 0	F+% = 0.24	W:D:Dd =15:15:1	FD = 0		
2AB+Art+Ay = 0	WSum6 = 53	X–% = 0.55	W:M =15:4	An + Xy = 1		
M– = 2	Mnone = 0	S–% = 0.12	DQ+ =8	MOR = 5		
		Xu% = 0.23	DQv =4			

SCZI = 5*	DEPI = 4	CDI = 2	S-CON = N/A	HVI = No	OBS = No

6

A Fall From Grace

Mark J. Hilsenroth
The Cambridge Hospital and Harvard Medical School

"All sinners will burn, cast down into the lake of fire to be tormented by the devil and his imps forever!" With this last statement Thomas sprang to his feet, a vitriolic liturgy spat from his mouth: "All who sin against the Lord my father will burn, burn, burn! All sinners will burn!" His finger jabbed accusingly at the group members, pointing at each in turn, shouting "You will burn, you will burn, you will burn. . . ." The very depressed woman sitting next to me let out an almost inaudible whimper as his finger fell upon her. I noticed out of the corner of my eye that Martin, a chronic inpatient with a history of violent episodes, had begun to slowly clench and unclench his fist. Sensing that I was about to speak Thomas suddenly lept in front of me, his face less than a foot from my own and bellowed "Demon, vile demon, you are the imp of Satan and soon you will be punished by the angels in the army of heaven!" I looked up into Thomas' ruddy face standing above me as he barked "Would you dare to harm the son of God? I am alpha and omega, the beginning and the end!" After looking into each other's eyes for what seemed an eternity, my first attempt to speak ended only in silence. The only sound that I could hear was the pounding of my fearful heart that seemed to reverberate throughout the room.

A comprehensive evaluation of the psychological functioning and inner world of a patient provides the therapist with useful information in understanding a patient's experience that, in turn, may help the therapist develop an empathic response. In addition, proper diagnosis of various psychotic syndromes, as well as their respective subcategories, has important ramifications concerning determination of acute versus chronic adjustments and treatment outcome (Bell, Lysaker, & Milstein, 1992; Blatt & Ford, 1994; Endicott, Nee, Cohen, Fliess, & Simon, 1986; Fenton & McGlashan, 1987; Goldberg, Schooler, & Mattsson, 1967; Gunderson, Frank, & Katz, 1984; Karon & Vandenbos, 1981; Kendler, Gruenberg, & Tsuang, 1984; Nicholson & Neufeld, 1993; Strauss & Carpenter, 1974; Strauss, Sirotkin, & Grisell, 1974; Vaillant, 1962). In many instances the use of routine clinical interviews to identify or describe psychiatric patients with the utilization of unspecified diagnostic criteria has been found to be grossly inadequate (Spitzer, Endicott, & Robbins, 1975, 1978; Spitzer & Fliess, 1974). Incorrect diagnosis may lead to the faulty application of psychopharmacological and/or psychological treatment interventions. Such mismatches of treatment with patients will likely lead to poor outcomes (Smith, Macewan, Ancill, & Honer, 1992).

My purpose is to examine the psychotic personality organization as manifested on the Rorschach. Thomas' Rorschach protocol (see Appendix A) is particularly germane to his treatment and illustrates salient features of a delusional system. I discuss the importance of integrating both structural and psychodynamic aspects of Rorschach interpretation to more fully understand the experience of this young man.

I attempt to distill a process of constructing a formulation through a sequence of steps. I describe the formal aspects of this synthesis by presenting a sequential analysis of each response, followed by an examination of different areas of personality functioning. An integration of the various inferences developed from both of these stages is constructed in a holistic manner. In addition, I weave together clinical interactions that illustrate how various aspects of Rorschach data can aid in the deciphering of behavior. This approach to interpretation is designed to facilitate the generation of hypotheses about a patient's character structure. These hypotheses may then be retained, modified, or discarded depending on whether or not they receive sufficient support from other assessment data. It is important to note that in a comprehensive assessment hypotheses should be generated across various tests and integrated with countertransference reactions and behavioral observations (Phillips, 1992; Sugarman, 1981). I have found that this synthesis of structural and psychoanalytic interpretation contributes to a richer formulation of an individual's personality structure and his or her phenomenological experience of the world.

CLINICAL MATERIAL

Thomas was the only child born into a lower income working-class family. His mother was described as an authoritarian who was intrusive and placed many demands on her son. His father was a remote individual who abandoned his wife and son when Thomas was 6. Thomas reports that in his last memory of his father they walked out to the driveway together, his father ran his fingers through Thomas' hair and said, "be a good boy for your mother."

Indeed, for the next 12 years it would appear that Thomas took his father's words quite literally, perhaps interpreting his father's last statement to him as a precondition for his return. Thomas approached the tasks of being "a good boy" with zeal. He would dote on his mother, completing the large number of chores she assigned him without opposing her in any significant way. His mother seemingly thought nothing of the amount of work she expected from him and encouraged his indulgence of her.

Church began to play an important role in Thomas' life as he matured. At first this consisted of simply attending church with his mother every Sunday, then he started attending biweekly Bible study classes, and eventually Thomas became a central member in the local Christian youth association chapter. Snake-handling, speaking in tongues, belief in possessions, and weekend revivals were commonplace in the church that Thomas attended. Thomas also began to form a deep attachment to the minister of the church who was known for his Cotton Mather-like disposition concerning sin, as well as being widely regaled for his vociferous "fire and brimstone" speeches. At the early age of 12 Thomas announced to his mother his plan to enter the ministry, "in order to become one with the Lord our Father." Having found the method for achieving a childhood dream, Thomas threw himself into the study of scripture.

As Thomas grew into adolescence he became increasingly ensconced in religious study, forsaking the normal pursuits of a teenage boy in the rural southeast. At about the age of 16 Thomas began to take the word of the Lord to the streets and began preaching the gospel to all who would listen. Unfortunately, Thomas did not stop at merely taking the word of the Lord to the streets, but also to the local grocery, diners, movie theaters, shopping malls, and school. It was at the last of these venues where Thomas' faith would be severely tested. Having been a devoted student, Thomas had learned the art of preaching all too well for the liking of the rest of the student body. The intensity of his need to ferret out sin and preach loud righteousness led to a number of severe beatings at the hands of other students, singled out by Thomas as leading "sinful lives." After the advent of a particularly harsh pummeling, Thomas' mother was successful in petitioning for a "home-bound" educational alternative. Thus, Thomas spent the last 2 years of high school at home with his mother; he was an already socially isolated youth who developed into an even more alienated young man.

Thomas became increasingly reclusive, but his life was outwardly uneventful until some time past his 19th birthday. Four weeks before his admission, Thomas' mother reports that his behavior around the house became increasingly bizarre. He spent much of his time locked in his room, not allowing his mother to enter or clean it, constantly mumbling to himself, eating alone, and having fits of laughter and sobbing. At a church fair one Sunday afternoon, Thomas began to preach uncontrollably about the of evils of sexuality and began to wildly assail the various booths and tables, knocking them to the ground before he could be subdued by a number of men in the parish. Given his involvement with the church, Thomas was merely transported home to the custody of his mother. However, when she attempted to console him he pushed her to the ground and called her a demon and a witch sent from Satan to ruin him. He then ran to the kitchen, grabbed a large knife, and threatened to kill her if she came near him. The police were contacted and arrived, disarming the young man and transporting him to the nearest state inpatient facility where we met the following day.

After a few quick swallows to clear my throat and again noticing Martin's now rapidly clenching fist, I was finally able to jar myself from the trance-like state I was in. "No, Thomas." I spoke rather tentatively, "I have no wish to harm the son of God, . . . but you know I'm confused about something . . . and I'm afraid you're the only person who can help me to understand it." "Yes, sinner!" Thomas snapped suspiciously. I continued, "How is it . . . that the son of God . . . has come to find himself here?" while I simultaneously gestured across the 1970s furnishings, cinder block walls, stopping at the steel double-locked door to the ward within the group therapy room of an inpatient hospital which had seen better days. The expression on Thomas' face changed from contempt to one of pain. He slouched into an adjacent empty chair, slowly placed his face in his hands and began to sob, "I have sinned . . . I have sinned against my father and now I must pay." Suddenly the tension which had previously filled the room was quickly replaced by a great sadness as Thomas cried softly, "I'm gonna burn, . . . burn, . . . burn, . . . burn."

RESPONSE ANALYSIS

Card I

In many respects Thomas' approach to Card I is very similar to the manner in which I first came to know him. Simply stated, he has lost his mind ("He has no head") and is relying on prayer and religion as protection (Cg), as a robe so to speak, to shield him from anxiety (m). His understanding of other people is seen from a perspective that is idiosyncratic (INC), fantasied (H), and highly personalized (PER). From this somewhat askew stance he combines interpersonal themes of damaged objects (MOR) and victimization (victim of aggression) with idealized figures. From a sequence analysis of these two responses one might infer that Thomas will defend against anxiety-provoking and threatening stimuli by a flight into idealized fantasy. At this point one may begin to wonder if he dichotomizes his interactions with the world into overarching dualities of devalued and idealized percepts, seeing others as all good or all bad. Such a stance, which splits the representation of others, will often be experienced by those people he interacts with as self-righteous and judgmental. It is also worth noting that two of the three movement responses developed on Card I are passive in nature and may denote a tendency to engage in fantasy or wishful thinking, expressing the hope that someone else will do something either for or to him. Thomas is enveloped in religiosity and, like the angels in Response 2, he often looks up to the heavens for answers or direction, which until recently has been eagerly awaited.

Card II

In Response 3 others are seen in cooperative activity (*Ma, COP*). However, as in Card I (Response 1 and 2), the perception of another is coupled with an unusual (*u*) and fantasied (*H*) understanding of this interaction. In conjunction with primitive ritualistic actions ("tribal dance") and a devaluation of a human percept ("troll people"), Thomas appears to be effectively distancing himself from mature relational interactions. Subsequently, the following response shows boundary disturbance (*DR*) in relation to primitive aggression that bubbles to the surface. His attempts at denial ("I don't like to think about that") are faltering. Also, one might hypothesize that Thomas will experience emotions as intense, labile, and overwhelming. Given his personalization of this response, one might hypothesize that the "someone who is hurt" is Thomas.

Card III

Thomas appears to have problems with identifying the gender of the two figures in Response 5. Although he originally labels them as *male* ("two guys"), he later perceives them to be wearing "high heel shoes," having "tits," and "peckers." This mixture of sexual attributes may reflect a sense of confusion concerning sexuality and gender identification. The spoiling (*FQ–*) of a relatively ordinary response of two humanlike figures to the D1 location (the inclusion of an illogical relation between those figures looking at their own hearts that are suspended outside of their bodies; *INC*) further supports the hypothesis that sexuality is particularly disorganizing for him. Furthermore, his development of exposed organs (*An*) and his personalization of this response indicate a focus on bodily concerns marked by distress.

Finally, two further psychodynamic hypotheses should be raised before moving from this response. The first is related to his perception of "pointed mouths" on the figures of this response. This may indicate oral aggression, expressed as verbal hostility, and/or a problem with his ability to accept nurturance from others. The second hypothesis concerns the manner in which the hearts of the figures are seen to reside outside of their bodies. Given that a person's heart has long been associated as the source of emotional expression, one might speculate that Thomas will place his emotions outside of his body and/or experience emotions in a split-off, poorly integrated manner.

Card IV

In Response 6 Thomas identifies a male humanlike figure that is seen as large, imposing, and aggressive (*AG*). However, it should be noted that this figure requires external support ("sittin' on a stump") and Thomas employs a fantasy-based, childlike perception [(*H*)] of the male figure. This is his third percept (also see Responses 2 and 3) involving a human figure that is fictional or mythological. In addition, Thomas' two other percepts involving a human figure (see Responses 1 and 5) were marked by an incongruous combination of an object. At this point one might begin to wonder if Thomas' interpersonal world is greatly influenced by fantasy and distortion.

Given that Thomas also employs some self-inspection while formulating this response (FD), one hypothesis might be that Thomas' subjective experience is to wish for support from others, while also being simultaneously defiant and uncompromising. This theme is also indicative of a passive–aggressive stance toward others, in which he finds strength in being stubborn. This interpretation is also congruent with the discussion of a conflict surrounding his ability to accept nurturance from others, which was raised in the discussion of his responses on Card III.

Card V

Perceptually, Thomas' responses to Card V were ordinary (FQo) and often developed by individuals taking the Rorschach (P). However, the elaboration of both percepts shows signs of reality perception that are more than slightly askew and hypervigilant in nature. Both responses include deviant verbalizations that are expressed in an odd use of a word (DV) or an inappropriate elaboration circumstantially related to the response (DR). His use of the phrase "sensitivity skills" in both responses is quite idiosyncratic; "sensitivity" seems to be a way in which to determine the distance and location of others from himself. This odd understanding of what it means to be sensitive to others suggests a guarded orientation toward the world.

His tangential (DR) and personalized (PER) elaboration in Response 8 may offer some understanding as to why he is highly attuned to the external world. Thomas is fearful of being harmed and placed in danger. Personalized idiosyncratic thoughts may motivate his fears of the external world. Reality for him is being afraid of becoming infected with a contagion. To avoid this he must maintain a watchful eye or he will perish. In regard to his prognosis for treatment it is also interesting to note that he does not have much faith in any help he may receive: "I'd have to go to the hospital and die." This statement conveys the expectation that once he is infected or damaged there is no hope for recovery. Finally, we again see orality coupled with aggressiveness (also see Response 5), which in this response is projected outward.

Card VI

A structural analysis of Response 9 would focus on how the percept is developed in a manner that is somewhat vague (DQv/+) and unusual (FQu). Incorporating a psychodynamic formulation to the aforementioned interpretation adds a great deal of understanding to what seems, now, to be a recurrent theme of religion in Thomas' protocol. Given the sexual underpinnings associated with this card one might hypothesize that he has escalating concerns about his sexuality and has used religion to make himself and his actions virtuous. He desires perfection (he notes the potential straightness of the cross and finds this aesthetically pleasing); thus religiosity is transposed on sexuality. He sublimates his sexual urges through religious preoccupations and settles all conflict over sexual issues by turning to the cross and religiosity.

Later that week Thomas and I would again find ourselves in a situation similar to the end of the group psychotherapy session. Thomas sat ensconced in shadow in the corner of my office, his face in his hands sobbing, "I'm gonna burn." "Why would the Lord want to damn his son?" I ventured softly. "Because I was impure, wretched and . . . dirty," Thomas spoke. "How is it that you have come to feel so impure and dirty?" I asked. "I've broken a law, I've sinned and now I will pay like Onan, I will be struck down by the Lord," winced Thomas. "Why was Onan struck down?" I queried. Thomas said nervously, "He spilled his semen upon the ground which angered the Lord who killed him dead." After a long silence I asked, "Thomas . . . are you trying to say that the sin you committed . . . was masturbation?" Thomas slowly raised his head a few inches out of his hands and with a sob whispered "Yes."

Card VII

Thomas has begun to show a consistent pattern in perceiving human or humanlike figures in a manner infused with ideational material and characterized by idiosyncratic perception of human interactions (also see Responses 1, 2, 3, 5, and 6). In Response 10 Thomas again shows this pattern where structurally his perception of the human figures is unusual and the individuals are connected in a fabulized manner. This distortion occurs even though he develops a popular (*P*) response to Card VII, a female head or face. Initially the figures are distanced from his experience by identifying them as foreign (Japanese or Chinese). However, as they become sexualized (i.e., being pregnant) this distancing fails, his reality testing becomes compromised, and the maternal object that was once foreign becomes the source of a boundary disturbance. One hypothesis derived from this response would be that Thomas can become particularly disorganized, or at least confused, when confronted with issues of interpersonal connectedness or sexuality. Further, his relationship with his mother is replete with merger/fusion concerns that are especially confounding for him.

I met Thomas' mother for the first time about two weeks into her son's hospitalization. She was a very attractive woman, in her late thirties, who arrived for a family therapy session with her son approximately 20 minutes late. While many of the things that were discussed during this meeting were important regarding his treatment, the interaction between the two of them at the beginning and the end of the session was especially salient. When Thomas' mother entered the room he rose to greet her. Walking over, he stopped about two to three feet from her, extended his upper torso and arms across this final distance, and hugged her, all the while keeping everything except his shoulders and arms well away from her. Thomas did all of this in a quiet, automatonlike manner. His mother's reaction, on the other hand, was fluid and emotional. Wiggling in his grasp she snapped, "Thomas stop that, you're suffocating me!" At this Thomas disentangled himself from her and meekly returned to his seat without a sound. However disconcerting this was to watch, it paled in comparison to the nature of the separation enactment that would follow at the end of the session. As she was leaving, Thomas' mother stopped at the door, turned, and said to Thomas in an accusing manner, "Aren't you going to hug me good-bye?" I immediately felt shock and confusion sweep over me. I looked at Thomas who likewise seemed paralyzed, but after a few moments scurried to obey his mother's wish. "There, there, that's a good boy," she cooed while running her fingers through his sandy brown hair.

Card VIII

As anticipated earlier in his protocol, Thomas continues to show signs that affect, in addition to interpersonal relatedness, is disorganizing for him. In Response 11 he contains the affect stimulated by the color of this card by viewing it as a painting. This transformation of the stimulus represents a defensive intellectualization of affect. However, it is sufficiently disconcerting enough that he becomes confused and tangential concerning the type of artwork the blot represents. An analysis of sequence may provide useful information in determining the way in which Thomas manages such disorganization. In the next response (12) Thomas focuses his attention on an unusual or infrequently identified area of the blot, but does so in a way that utilizes good form. Although the perception of this response is clear, the content of the response is that of bony anatomy and again may reflect anxiety regarding body integrity or self boundaries. Taken together one may hypothesize that when Thomas becomes anxious or feels threatened he will focus on minute details in a hypervigilant, rigid, and steadfast manner. Also, in regard to issues of body integrity, the lions in his response are missing their tails, raising the worry about castration of a successful and virulent creature. Being masculine or the "king" can place him in an especially perilous position.

Card IX

The unstructured color of this card is initially disorganizing for him. Again, as in Card I, Thomas perceives a man without a head. His "card extension" may belie a manic reaction (Wagner & Heise, 1981) to affective overstimulation, indicating that when he does become agitated or excited he is unable to calm himself and will need external constraints to do so. If he could be powerful, important, strong, courageous, and capable of managing his body with great precision then he would have the capacity to solve his conflicts around relatedness, affection, and sexuality. In many respects this idealized image of a strong dominant male would be one solution to many of his problems, but even this perception is spoiled because this figure lacks a head and is not a whole being.

Card X

The last card is particularly disorganizing for Thomas with special scores in each of the four responses to it. Two are related to circumstantial overelaborations and two indicate a merger of two disparate images within a single object. Also, these responses become increasingly disorganized as he continues to associate to Card X. In Response 14 he responds with an aggressive part-object (the face of a tiger). The use of achromatic color may reflect a state of anxious dysphoria that will be acted on under times of stress. He attempts to utilize religiosity in Response 15, possibly in an effort to organize or calm himself, but his attempt at idealization fails and leaves him confused about the perception of extreme good and bad images. Like the previous association, Response 16 also is developed initially in an idealized manner: a glorious, magical, fantasy creature that flies through the heavens. This percept employs representations of being phallic (unicorn horn) and masterful (flying). Thomas tries desperately to embody both of these attributes. However, this feeling of success is short lived and his attempts at mastery end in failure. This marvelous beast, like Thomas, has become damaged and now hurtles toward its impending doom. Sequentially, his reaction to this injury, depression and disorganization, has increased his level of paranoia dramatically. Thus, he signs off (last response, 17) with a highly disorganized hypervigilance intent on protecting himself from further diminution and insults.

CATEGORICAL ANALYSIS

Thomas' Rorschach suggests a psychotic personality organization replete with impaired reality testing, ego functions, defensive organization, and affect modulation. In addition, his internalized representations of self and others are fragmented, chaotic, or merged. Having generated a number of hypotheses for each of the individual responses, I now turn to an integration of these inferences organized in a number of different areas of personality functioning. An analysis of both the structural and psychodynamic aspects of the protocol will highlight ways in which the diagnosis of psychotic personality organization is assisted and facilitated by the use of the Rorschach.

However, some of the structural characteristics (scores, percentages, indices, and constellations) found in Thomas' protocol were not as highly elevated as one might expect, given the history and current symptom picture of this delusional young man. I believe that in these circumstances, where some of the structural scores are equivocal, the integration of psychodynamic-content features of the protocol with the structural scores becomes especially salient for an accurate understanding of the patient's phenomenological world and diagnostic formulation. What is most readily apparent in an examination of the structural summary data (see Appendix B) is the lack of a significant elevation on the *SCZI* index. Within the evaluation of this index (see Appendix C) we can see that the criteria that focus on a diminution of the $X+\%$ and the occurrence of special scores are found to be positive (*SCZI* criteria 1, 4, and 5). However, Thomas' protocol does not have an overabundance of responses with a minus form quality ($X-\%$; *SCZI* criteria 2 and 6). Instead, Thomas produced significantly more unconventional and idiosyncratic perceptions, as indicated by the elevated $Xu\%$ (.29), in contrast to frank reality distortions. Where Thomas' psychotic process is most evident is in two thirds of his responses where they warrant a special score, showing signs of seriously disturbed thinking. This indicates his ideational activity is characterized by fabulized conceptualizations, impaired judgment, diffuse boundaries, disorganized representations, and bizarre patterns of thinking that indicate a robust level of psychopathology from a number of different scoring approaches (Blatt, Brenneis, Schimek, & Glick, 1976; Blatt & Ritzler, 1974; Cooper & Arnow, 1986; Exner, 1993; Holt, 1977; Johnston & Holzman, 1979; Kwawer, 1980; Lerner & Lerner, 1980; Masling, 1986; Urist, 1977; Wagner, Wagner, Hilsenroth, & Fowler, 1995).

A second, somewhat surprising aspect on his structural summary are the *D* (0) and *Adj D* (+1) scores, which are suggestive of an acute increase in situationally related stressors. These stressors contribute to his cognitive disorganization and confusing emotional experiences, and also imply that Thomas possesses some internal resources that are readily accessible to him. However, within a patient population Exner (1993) suggested that 0 or positive scores are characteristic of poor prognostic cases in which long-standing symptomatic patterns are deeply entrenched and resistant to change. Although Exner cautioned clinicians to examine all Rorschach data when developing interpretive formulations, Kleiger (1992) pointed out that faulty inferences regarding the *D* and *Adj D* scores may result from an unsophisticated use of the component scores (*EA:es*) that make up theses indices, which can lead to confusing and at times contradictory inferences. Despite the unelevated *SCZI*, *D*, and *Adj D* scores, a psychotic level of personality organization is suggested by structural aspects that assess ideational, cognitive, affective, and interpersonal areas of functioning.

Ideation

Thomas appears to live much more in his head than in his body. He has an introversive character style, in which feelings are minimized and in which he relies heavily on private internal evaluations in forming judgments (*EB* = 6:2.5;

EBPer = 2.4). He will use this extensive inner fantasy life as a source of gratification and refuge; *a:p* = 5:5; *Ma:Mp* = 2:4; *(H)* = 4; *(A)* = 2. The situational stress he is currently experiencing *(D* = 0; *Adj D* = +1) has hindered his ability to stay focused and has increased his flight into fantasy. Most prominent in his style of thought is an overinvolvement in the use of fantasy (*Ma:Mp* = 2:4), which he uses defensively in response to anxiety. His flight from reality is particularly detrimental because his ideational (*M–* = 1, *S* = 1) and fantasy-prone thought processes are the substrate from which his burgeoning psychotic process is built (*Sum6* = 12; *Lv2* = 4; *WSum6* = 41). The presence of 1 *Mp–* and 1 *Mpu* suggest delusions and are linked to formal thought disorder, as do the numerous *INC* (4) and *FAB* (1) scores, which indicate a bizarre understanding of the relations between objects. Also, the presence of an *M–* raises concerns about the peculiarity of ideation that is associated with deficient social skills and poor interpersonal relations. Formal thought disorder is pervasive and severe (*WSum6* = 41, *Lv2* = 4). This high level of unusual ideation or cognitive slippage can be observed through the mismanagement of language (*DV* = 1), faulty reasoning (*X+%* = .47), affective instability (*C* = 1), and difficulty with boundaries (*DR* = 6), which involves an irrational synthesis of action and ideation. This impairment in thinking and reasoning is also accompanied with a high level of paranoid ideation (Paranoid Process = 4).

Perception

Thomas views the world as if he were looking through a cloudy lens and his perception of objects and understanding of others' actions are often distorted. It is often the case when visiting a house of mirrors that relatively neutral images may take on an immature or comical likeness, become larger than life, be drastically reduced in size, and at times become menacing and aggressive through these alterations. Thomas carries his house of mirrors with him and subsequently feels that his surroundings are unreal, tenuous, and threatening.

For Thomas, perceptions become infected with bizarre thoughts during the process of translating or understanding the information he scans (*Sum6* = 12; *Lv2* = 4; *WSum6* = 41). He shows difficulty in understanding complex perceptual inputs appropriately or accurately (*X+%* = .47; *DQv* = 4). These serious deficiencies in perceptual accuracy occur in conjunction with a substantial delusional system and hallucinations. Perceptual inaccuracies and distortions are accompanied by impoverished judgment and a poor understanding of social conventionality (special scores accompany all *H*; *M–* = 1; *Xu%* = .29; *X–%* = .18).

Thomas' use of the story of Onan as the basis of his fears provides one example of his perceptual inaccuracy and idiosyncratic understanding of information, which is evident in his misinterpretation of why the Lord slew Onan. This act of divine aggression occurs in the book of Genesis (38:9) and is part of the story of Judah and Tamar. Upon reading this passage closely it is quite clear that Onan, in fact, was not slain because he masturbated, but rather because he broke the levirate law. According to the ancient widespread custom of levirate marriage, the duty of a brother-in-law was to raise up a male descendant for his deceased brother and thus perpetuate his brother's name and inheritance. At the beginning of this chapter Tamar was originally married to Judah's first-born son Er who was killed by the Lord for being sinful. His death occurred before the couple was able to conceive a child. Judah then sent his second son, Onan, to perform the duty of his older brother. However, Onan, knowing that any children he would have with Tamar would be considered his brothers, and not his own, decided to renege on the levirate duty by spilling his semen on the ground rather than impregnating Tamar. This act angered the Lord who slew him also. Tamar is finally made pregnant, fulfilling the levirate obligation, by tricking her father-in-law, Judah, into having sex with her while disguised as a prostitute! This story may be especially disorganizing for Thomas due to its emphasis on punitive aggression, incestuous sexual boundaries, and a strict adherence to a rigid set of standards. Thus, he focuses on a concrete interpretation of consecutive actions (i.e., Onan spilling his semen on the ground and his subsequent destruction), missing a holistic understanding of the story.

It is also important to note that most of his perceptual inaccuracies are limited to the color cards (FQ–) indicating that he is especially disorganized around affective material. However, Thomas' idiosyncratic perceptions do not appear to impact his understanding of stimuli that are not overly complex (F+% = .80). It appears that the stimuli that he perceives most accurately are mundane, obvious, and simple. He is capable of responding appropriately to situations that are precisely defined and require minimal processing.

Affect

For Thomas, affect seems to be on or off, suggesting that he reacts to the world with either flatness of affect or extreme impulsivity and wild emotion. Although he struggles to control affect displays, when he does experience emotions it is likely to lead to discharges of affect that are poorly controlled, feel overwhelming, and contribute to the distortion of his perceptions (C = 1; special scores accompany all color responses and at least one occurs on each of the color cards; FQu and FQ– for many responses to color cards). Affective experience can also be characterized as confusing because both pleasure and pain are often mixed together and experienced simultaneously (color-shading blends > 0).

One interpretive heuristic I have found useful in understanding patients' affective experiences is to consider that the first color response (FC, CF, or C) to occur may indicate the most prominent affective tendency of that patient (Rorschach & Oberholzer, 1923). This would lead us to posit that

Thomas' primary affective experience (C, in conjunction with a DR special score), when it does occur, will be labile, irritable, impulsive, and egocentric. When he does experience affect he has much difficulty controlling, modulating, and integrating these emotions.

Perception of Self and Others

Thomas' perception of himself is based largely in fantasy rather than in reality, which in turn distorts notions of himself and others; $M- = 1$; $Mu = 2$; $Ma:Mp = 2:4$; $(H) = 4$; $(A) = 2$; $X+\% = .47$. Because he does not perceive the world in a conventional manner, it might be expected that Thomas will also exhibit a high frequency of behaviors that disregard social demands or expectations. His impairment in social appropriateness seems to be related to Thomas' perception and understanding of external stimuli in a very personalized and idiosyncratic manner ($Xu\% = .29$; $DQv = 4$; $DR = 6$; $PER = 3$). This lack of reality contact will influence his interpersonal style, because others will find him odd, hard to understand, and will subsequently avoid interacting with him. Thus, Thomas' interpersonal world is lonely, filled with isolation and lack of support. His distorted view of human interactions will lead him to wishful or magical thinking, expressing the hope that an external force will save or rescue him; $Ma:Mp = 2:4$; $(H) = 4$; $(A) = 2$.

Thomas avoids relating to others and he is highly threatened in close affectionate relationships. This does not mean that Thomas does not experience needs for emotional closeness, but rather, that these needs are denied, defended against, and split-off. He will maintain distance in relationships, and one might suspect that this is done for safety. The lack of Texture ($T = 0$) in his Rorschach may indicate that highly traumatic early experiences have extinguished the desire for closeness. Vigilant against future insults, he has his "antennae" out, feeling his way through the world that he views as hostile and dangerous. This hypervigilant stance is congruent with his cognitive style of searching for details, or "clues," but failing to adequately integrate and understand this material in a holistic or reality-based manner ($X+\% = .47$). It would appear that Thomas has very little understanding of how people participate in pleasurable relationships that involve mutual interchange of positive feelings and interactions.

Thomas' idiosyncratic understanding of the world also gives rise to a defensiveness that may be perceived by others as hostility. His rigid interpretation of the "right" way to understand a situation or information may impair relations with others, and probably signals an underlying sense of insecurity around challenges to his way of seeing things ($PER = 3$). His self-image includes a certain pessimistic orientation toward himself and others. This poor outlook may also be conceptualized as coming from a sense of feeling damaged ($MOR = 2$) or, more likely, feeling incomplete or fragmented. Parallel to these problems of self-image are anxious concerns regarding body integrity and vulnerable self–other boundaries ($An + Xy = 2$).

Character and Defensive Structure

A review of psychoanalytic content scores identifies sexuality, experience of affect, disorganized thought processes, religiosity, paranoid process, anxiety concerning a loss of self-cohesion, and the receiving or acceptance of nurturance as central issues concerning Thomas' psychological functioning. In particular, he seems especially uncomfortable with a dependency conflict in which he both longs for and shuns sources of nurturance. In Thomas' experience, needs for succorance are associated with the threat of annihilation. He is motivated to avoid this threat at all costs and has erected an omnipotent facade to protect himself from feeling needy.

Given his hyper-religiosity, Thomas tends to polarize, or split the world into objects that are seen to be all good or all bad. There is little sense of a middle ground and he is unable to tolerate opposite feelings toward the same individual. His feelings about himself have this same polarized good and bad quality. Bolstering his tendency toward splitting is his proclivity to either devalue or idealize both himself and others. This leads to an increase of fragmentation of the Ego contributing to a limited sense of cohesion and precarious sense of self. In a classical drive-theory formulation, one can envision the intrapsychic structure of Thomas' mind to include prominent Id and archaic Superego structures.

Thomas' defensive style can be characterized by denial and a related group of primitive defenses (such as devaluation, splitting, and projective identification) that are being used in an inflexible manner. Along with this, Thomas has a distinct hypomanic style in his behavioral presentation as well as activity-laden fantasy ideation. When his anxiety reaches intolerable levels he discharges it by acting out in a paranoid manner. Primary in Thomas' defensive schema is a primitive regression to his feelings of depression and anxiety. Again, like feelings of neediness, depressed and anxious feelings are highly threatening and overwhelming. When he begins to experience these feelings Thomas will respond with heightened levels of grandiosity.

Six months after I had first met him Thomas was preparing to leave the hospital in the coming week. In what would be one of our final sessions together Thomas would again return to the topic of masturbation. "When I'd do that . . . my thoughts are impure too," said Thomas. "Can you tell me some about your thoughts," I asked. "I'd remember the day that I saw her . . . I didn't mean to but I did and then I just couldn't help thinking about her," Thomas said in a pressured tone. "You saw something that was exciting?" I clarified. After a long silence and a period of nervously looking around the room Thomas quietly spoke: "One day I had just come back from church and the phone rang; it was for her. We have a cordless phone so I just took it upstairs. She was in the bathroom and she told me

to come in . . . she told me to. I went in to give her the phone and she was standing
there . . . she had just taken a shower and she was all . . . wet. I tried not to look,
but I couldn't help it she was just standing there, she looked perfect . . . like an
angel . . . a beautiful angel. I tried not to look, so I ran away . . . but I couldn't
get away from the burning. I started burning the moment I saw her."

SUMMARY

Thomas' functioning is characterized by marked ego fragmentation that leaves
him vulnerable to impulsivity, poor judgment, and poor reality testing. He
displays distinct paranoid ideation as well as disorganization both in perception
and boundary issues. Thomas' ideational style, coupled with a marked hy-
pervigilence, would warrant consideration of a diagnosis of paranoid schizophrenia, schizophreniform, or delusional disorder given the clinical presence
of prominent delusional material, confusion, ideas of reference, social dysfunction, and grossly disorganized behavior. Intense emotional disruptions interfere
with his abilities to process information in a planful manner, affect his
inhibitions against acting impulsively, and increase hypervigilant thought processes.

Thomas presented with significant unresolved issues around dependency,
orality, and the acceptance of nurturant supplies. He is confused and conflicted
about being a man, predominantly due to his incestuous desires toward his
mother and his (Oedipal) fear that he has destroyed his father. His sexual
desire is therefore increasingly infused with aggression and he defends against
enormous guilt by relying on religious convictions to purify himself into a
virtuous person. He has developed both religious delusions and paranoia as a
means of managing hateful and rageful outbursts that are oral, primitive, and
frightening to him. Any sexual thoughts or stimuli lead to disorganization. He
is afraid of his own needs for closeness and nurturance because he might
become primitively fused to the "other" and lose a coherent sense of himself.

Affective and interpersonal interactions are also disorganizing for him.
There is a marked deficit in his capacity to mediate affect, which is experienced in relationships with others (i.e., a diminished Ego and its attendant
functions). In relationships with others he will make active use of an extensive
fantasy life that provides illusory interpersonal sustenance. Images of people
are often distorted, devalued, idealized, and are immature caricatures. This
may not only reflect what he feels towards others, but also suggests a poor
sense of self-esteem. At times he feels depressed, empty, alone, and helpless;
believing that he is bad, or worse, worthless, and less than human. At other
times he defends against these feelings by developing fantasies of being
all-powerful and omnipotent as an attempt at compensation. His choice of
delusion is defensive in that it allows him to remain connected to an ever-present, all-knowing, all-powerful, ever-watchful father in a pristine idealized
state. Perhaps this father, unlike his own, is strong enough to prevent the

incestuous fantasies that both excite and repel him. This delusional system helps to organize a defense against maternal merger/fusion longings that have become hypersexualized (in the absence of his father and given his mother's perceived seductiveness) and threaten him with annihilation.

There is, on one hand, the desire for fusion, which has become sexualized, coupled with self-loathing and disgust with himself for having such "filthy thoughts." Thomas' rigid use of religion helps him to maintain moral boundaries, which gives him a structure to avoid his "impure" thoughts. However, masturbation, coupled with incest fantasies, pushes him toward psychosis because his defenses are brittle and unable to contain these powerful impulses. In this sense the Oedipal-like fears of retribution are even more primitive and devastating, especially in the absence of a paternal figure as a source of benevolent prohibition and phallic identification. Instead, Thomas can only employ a punitive set of rules for himself to live by, with which it is impossible for him to comply.

In conclusion, one metaphor that might best communicate Thomas' experience is that of the tightrope performer perched on the highwire. In this role he is elevated above the throng of spectators whose attention is riveted on his every step. He must have complete balance as he walks across the cable, as there is no margin for error. An immense amount of energy is being expended to stay focused on his goal, which is all he can let himself be aware of. If he can only make it to the landing across from him he will be safe. If he can be perfect, he will attain his most coveted wish: a reunion with an all-loving, protecting father who will provide him with rules and boundaries so that he can worry less about his "burning fantasies." In his hands religion is the pole, a powerful defense he has chosen, which helps him to maintain his balance. As he walks he must believe that he is perfect, there can be no room for doubt. Thomas' very existence is tied to the success of his religious effort to maintain boundaries. However, there are ever-present enemies he must battle with each step. These foes are sexual and affective yearnings that like gravity seek constantly to pull him from his precipice. The struggle is ongoing, to be virtuous means to forsake the authority of affects. Nothing must divert him from his appointed route or he risks losing his sense of uniqueness, and without this, he is nothing at all. Anxiety is expressed like the sweat on his brow. Sexuality and aggressive impulses have condemned him to be human. His hands become slippery on the pole. He may not deny his humanness for long. A realization sweeps over him that he is not perfect and to be imperfect therefore means that he is bad and undeserving. He slips into the abyss, and in the end Thomas' fall from grace can be understood as a fall toward the recognition of basic human desires, needs, and feelings.

ACKNOWLEDGMENTS

I would like to extend my gratitude to Andrea Celenza, Marla Ebby, Christopher Fowler, and Leonard Handler for their insightful comments and suggestions on earlier versions of this chapter. I would like to recognize the assistance of Linda Arsenault, Jessica Hilsenroth, and Randy Padawer in the preparation of this chapter. Finally, I am indebted to Father Thomas Tavella, Trenice Harris, and her husband Reverend Orlando Harris for the spritual consultation they provided regarding this case material.

REFERENCES

Bell, M., Lysaker, P., & Milstein, R. (1992). Object relations deficits for the diagnosis of schizophrenia. *Journal of Clinical Psychology, 48*, 433–444.

Blatt, S., Brenneis, B., Schimek, J., & Glick, M. (1976). *A developmental analysis of the concept of the object on the Rorschach.* Unpublished manuscript, Yale University, New Haven, CT.

Blatt, S., & Ford, R. (1994). *Therapeutic change: An object relations perspective.* New York: Plenum.

Blatt, S., & Ritzler, B. (1974). Thought disorder and boundary disturbances in psychosis. *Journal of Consulting and Clinical Psychology, 42*, 370–381.

Cooper, S., & Arnow, D. (1986). An object relations view of the borderline defenses: A review. In M. Kissen (Ed.), *Assessing object relations phenomena* (pp. 143–171). New York: International Universities Press.

Endicott, J., Nee, J., Cohen, J., Fliess, J., & Simon, R. (1986). Diagnosis of schizophrenia: Prediction of short-term outcome. *Archives of General Psychiatry, 43*, 13–19.

Exner, J. E., Jr. (1993). *The Rorschach: A comprehensive system: Vol. 1. Basic foundations* (3rd ed.). New York: Wiley.

Fenton, W., & McGlashan, T. (1987). Prognosis scale for chronic schizophrenia. *Schizophrenic Bulletin, 13*, 277–286.

Goldberg, S., Schooler, N., & Mattsson, N. (1967). Paranoid and withdrawal symptoms in schizophrenia: Differential symptom reduction over time. *Journal of Nervous and Mental Disease, 145*, 158–162.

Gunderson, J., Frank, A., & Katz, H. (1984). Effects of psychotherapy in schizophrenia II: Comparative outcomes of two forms of treatment. *Schizophrenia Bulletin, 10*, 564–598.

Holt, R. (1977). A method for assessing primary process manifestations and their controls in Rorschach responses. In M. Rickers-Ovsiankina (Ed.), *Rorschach psychology* (2nd ed., pp. 375–420). Huntington, NY: Krieger.

Johnston, M., & Holzman, P. (1979). *Assessing schizophrenic thought.* San Francisco: Jossey-Bass.

Karon, B., & Vandenbos, G. (1981). *Psychotherapy of schizophrenia: The treatment of choice.* Northvale, NJ: Aronson.

Kendler, K., Gruenberg, A., & Tsuang, M. (1984). Outcome of schizophrenic subtypes defined by four diagnostic systems. *Archives of General Psychiatry, 41*, 149–154.

Kleiger, J. (1992). A conceptual critique of the EA:es comparison in the Comprehensive Rorschach System. *Psychological Assessment, 4*, 288–296.

Kwawer, J. (1980). Primitive interpersonal modes, borderline phenomena and Rorschach content. In J. Kwawer, H. Lerner, P. Lerner, & A. Sugarman (Eds.), *Borderline phenomena and the Rorschach test* (pp. 89–107). New York: International Universities Press.

Lerner, P., & Lerner, H. (1980). Rorschach assessment of primitive defenses in borderline personality structure. In J. Kwawer, H. Lerner, P. Lerner, & A. Sugarman (Eds.), *Borderline phenomena and the Rorschach test* (pp. 257–274). New York: International Universities Press.

Masling, J. (1986). Orality, pathology, and interpersonal behavior. In J. Masling (Ed.), *Empirical studies of psychoanalytic theories* (Vol. 2, pp. 73–106). Hillsdale, NJ: Lawrence Erlbaum Associates.

Nicholson, I., & Neufeld, R. (1993). Classification of schizophrenias according to symptomatology: A two factor model. *Journal of Abnormal Psychology, 102,* 259–270.

Phillips, L. (1992). A commentary on the relationship between assessment and the conduct of psychotherapy. *Journal of Training and Practice in Professional Psychology, 6,* 46–52.

Rorschach, H., & Oberholzer, E. (1923). The application of the interpretation of form to psychoanalysis. *Zeitschrift fur gesamte Neurlogie und Psychiatrie, 82,* 240–274.

Smith, G., Macewan, G., Ancill, R., & Honer, W. (1992). Diagnostic confusion in treatment-refractory psychotic patients. *Journal of Clinical Psychiatry, 53,* 197–200.

Spitzer, R., Endicott, J., & Robbins, E. (1975). Clinical criteria for psychiatric diagnosis and *DSM–III. American Journal of Psychiatry, 132,* 1187–1192.

Spitzer, R., Endicott, J., & Robbins, E. (1978). Diagnostic criteria: Rationale and reliability. *Archives of General Psychiatry, 35,* 773–782.

Spitzer, R., & Fliess, J. (1974). A re-analysis of the reliability of psychiatric diagnosis. *British Journal of Psychiatry, 125,* 341–374.

Strauss, J., & Carpenter, W. (1974). The prediction of outcome in schizophrenia II: Relationships between predictor and outcome variables. *Archives of General Psychiatry, 31,* 37–42.

Strauss, M., Sirotkin, R., & Grisell, J. (1974). Length of hospitalization and rate of re-admission of paranoid and nonparanoid schizophrenics. *Journal of Consulting and Clinical Psychology, 42,* 105–110.

Sugarman, A. (1981). The diagnostic use of countertransference reactions in psychological testing. *Bulletin of the Menninger Clinic, 45,* 473–490.

Urist, J. (1977). The Rorschach test and the assessment of object relations. *Journal of Personality Assessment, 41,* 3–9.

Vaillant, G. (1962). The prediction of recovery in schizophrenia. *Journal of Nervous and Mental Disease, 135,* 534–543.

Wagner, E., & Heise, M. (1981). Rorschach and Hand Test data comparing bipolar patients in manic and depressive phases. *Journal of Personality Assessment, 36,* 62–64.

Wagner, E., Wagner, C., Hilsenroth, M., & Fowler, C. (1995). A taxonomy of Rorschach autisms with implications for differential diagnosis among thinking disordered patients. *Journal of Clinical Psychology, 51,* 290–293.

Free Association	Inquiry

I 12"

1) A person in the middle

(Rpt response) A person . . . with a robe on. He has no head. His hands and shoulders are lifted up in prayer. (robe?) The shape, the way it's hangin' down. This sort of l.l. the art work I've seen somewhere, I know I've seen stuff like this before.

Structural Scoring: Do 4 Ma.mpo H,Cg INC 1, PER, MOR
Psychoanalytic Content: Religiosity, Devaluation, Victim of Aggression

2) Two angels

(Rpt response) The wings, the body here. They're both lookin' up. They look pretty.

Structural Scoring: Do 2 Mpo 2 (H)
Psychoanalytic Content: Religiosity, Idealization, Orality

II 3"

3) l.l. sm. kinda tribal dance, these two things are smakin' they're hands together

(Rpt response) Their hands and knees are together, dancin' in a religious ritual. (two things?) They l.l. troll people. (troll ppl?) The shape.

Structural Scoring: D+ 6 Mau 2 (H) 3.0 COP
Psychoanalytic Content: Religiosity, Devaluation

4) IDK what the red is ... c.b. blood, but I don't like to think about that!

(Wht abt it mks it l.l. Bl?) b.c. it's red. I don't like to think about Bl b.c. that means smone is hurt.

Structural Scoring: Dv 3 C Bl DR, PER
Psychoanalytic Content: Denial, Result of Aggression, Confabulation Tendency

III 4"

5) l.l. two things ... two guys

(Rpt response) They got tits, high heel shoes on, pointed mouths and peckers on'em. This thing in the middle that's b.f. shaped is their hearts. They're lookin' at their hearts (Wht abt it mks it l.l. a heart?) the shape. You know I've seen pictures like this before!

Structural Scoring: Dd+ Mp- 2 H, An, Sx P 3.0 INC2, PER
Psychoanalytic Content: Libidinal Content-Sexual, Devaluation, Libidinal Content-Oral, Orality, Contamination Tendency

IV 6"

6) A great big thing sitin' on a podium with his arms crossed and his feet kicked out lookin' like he's not movin' for nothing. Like he's darin' you "Try and move me."

(Rpt response) Here's his feet, he's sitin' on a stump, leaning back with his body extended. Arm like things here, comin' off his shoulders. (leaning back?) his feet are bigger in proportion to the rest of his body.

Structural Scoring: Wv Mp.FDo (H) P 4.0 AG
Psychoanalytic Content: Passive-Aggressiveness, Devaluation

V 2"

7) l.l. sm kinda b.f.

(Wht abt it mks it l.l.b.f?) The shape, tail, the antenna for their sensitivity skills.

Structural Scoring: Wo Fo A P 1.0 DV
Psychoanalytic Content: Paranoid Process

(continued)

8) A bat

(Wht abt it mks it l.l. bat?) Same shape as the b.f., except they use an echo for their sensitivity skills. They bounce waves off of things to tell how close they are. Bats are fast and sneaky and they bite you. I don't want to get bit by a bat, then I'd have to go to the hospital and die of rabies.

Structural Scoring: *Wo Fo A P* 1.0 *DR*
Psychoanalytic Content: Projective Identification, Aggression, Libidinal Content-Oral, Orality, Paranoid Process, Confabulation
VI 4"

9) Sm kinda structure. It comes up into a great big cross.

(Rpt response) If this were drawn perfect it would look real pretty. It has a straightness in its shape. The rest is shaped like a rock or a mountain.

Structural Scoring: *Wv/+ Fu Ls* 2.5
Psychoanalytic Content: Religiosity
VII 12"

10) Two sorda . . . sm kinda people look'in at e.o.

(Rpt response) The shape of their faces look Japanese or Chinese. Their hair is up in that style to. They look pregnant, their stomachs are connected together.

Structural Scoring: *W+ Mpu* 2 *H P* 2.5 *FAB2*
Psychoanalytic Content: Fusion, Libidinal Content-Sexual, Orality, Devaluation, Contamination
VIII 4"

11) Sm. kinda art, IDK. I *should* know what kind but I forgot!

(Rpt response) A lion or a panther coming up the side of a hill or mtn. (Wht abt it mks it l.l. a LN or PN?) The shape of the body, but they're missing their tails. (Wht abt it mks it l.l. a HL or MTN) The shpe. (originally you said that this was sm. kinda art?) It's an art painting of a lion climbing a mountain.

Structural Scoring: *Wv/+ FMao* 2 *Art,(A),Ls P* 4.5 *MOR, DR*
Psychoanalytic Content: Castration, Victim of Aggression, Confabulation Tendency

12) A backbone.

(Wht abt it mks it l.l. bkbone?) The shape.

Structural Scoring: *Ddo* 30 *Fo An*
Psychoanalytic Content: Paranoid Process
IX 1"

V 13) Wow, this picture is great! It kinda l.l. a person.

(Wht abt it mks it l.l. a person?) The feet, they're pointed inward. The stomach, chest, arms, baggy pants. But it doesn't show his shoulders or head, it would be up here (he identifies an area which is extended beyond the inkblot on the card). It's a picture of one of those samuri guys. (Samuri guys?) Yeah, the pants are real baggy for flexibility and hanging loose on him. Also, he's got a strong build and the colors. They're nice on this one they don't sting my eyes, they're not harsh.

Structural Scoring: *Wv ma.FCu H,Cg DR*
Psychoanalytic Content: Idealization, Libidinal Content-Oral, Orality, Aggression, Confabulation

X 1"

14) My gosh, this is an excellent artist who made these! An animal's face.

(Rpt response) A nose here, a tiger stripe. The white lines make it l.l. a tiger's face.

Structural Scoring: DSo 11 FC'– Ad DR
Psychoanalytic Content: Aggression

15) Two angels.

(Rpt response) The mouth, nose, eyes. An angel, not a demon! Demons are real and they look more scary than that.

Structural Scoring: Do 9 Fo 2 (H) DR2
Psychoanalytic Content: Religiosity, Idealization, Denial, Libidinal Content-Oral, Orality, Confabulation Tendency

16) A unicorn dragon.

(Rpt response) The eyes, nose, horn, wings. But it's messed up it's been in a fight and falling to the ground, it's gonna crash.

Structural Scoring: Dv 1 FMau (A) MOR, INC
Psychoanalytic Content: Victim of Aggression, Phallic Symbol, Fabulized Combination-Serious

17) Eyeballs with antennae coming out of'em.

(Rpt response) The shape, the white and the green. The different shades of the green. (different shades?) It's light and dark in different places.

Structural Scoring: Dv 5 FC.FY– Hd, Ad INC2
Psychoanalytic Content: Paranoid Process, Fabulized Combination-Serious

APPENDIX B
Rorschach Structural Summary

LOCATION FEATURES	DETERMINANTS BLENDS	SINGLE	CONTENTS	S-CONSTELLATION
				NO..FV + VF + V + FD > 2
			H = 4,0	YES..Col-Shd Bl>0
Zf = 8	M.m	M = 4	(H) = 4,0	NO..Ego<.31,>.44
ZSum = 21.5	M.FD	FM = 2	Hd = 1,0	NO..MOR>3
ZEst = 23.0	m.FC	m = 0	(Hd) = 0,0	NO..Zd > ± 3.5
	FC.FY	FC = 0	Hx = 0,0	NO..es>EA
W = 7		CF = 0	A = 2,0	NO..CF+C>FC
(Wv = 1)		C = 1	(A) = 1,1	YES..X+%<.70
D = 8		Cn = 0	Ad = 1,1	NO..S>3
Dd = 2		FC' = 1	(Ad) = 0,0	NO..P<3 or >8
S = 1		C'F = 0	An = 1,1	NO..Pure H <2
		C' = 0	Art = 1,0	NO..R<17
DQ		FT = 0	Ay = 0,0	2.....TOTAL
.........(FQ–)		TF = 0	Bl = 1,0	
+ = 3 (1)		T = 0	Bt = 0,0	SPECIAL SCORINGS
o = 7 (1)		FV = 0	Cg = 0,2	Lvl Lv2
v/+ = 3 (0)		VF = 0	Cl = 0,0	DV = 1x1 0x2
v = 4 (1)		V = 0	Ex = 0,0	INC = 2x2 2x4
		FY = 0	Fd = 0,0	DR = 5x3 1x6
		YF = 0	Fi = 0,0	FAB = 0x4 1x7
		Y = 0	Ge = 0,0	ALOG = 0x5
FORM QUALITY		Fr = 0	Hh = 0,0	CON = 0x7
		rF = 0	Ls = 1,1	SUM6 = 12
FQx FQf MQual SQx		FD = 0	Na = 0,0	WSUM6 = 41
+ = 0 0 0 0		F = 5	Sc = 0,0	
o = 8 4 3 0			Sx = 0,1	AB =0 CP = 0
u = 5 1 2 0			Xy = 0,0	AG =1 MOR = 2
– = 3 0 1 1			Id = 0,0	CFB =0 PER = 3
none = 1 – 0 0		(2) = 6		COP =1 PSV = 0

RATIOS, PERCENTAGES, AND DERIVATIONS

R = 17	L = 0.42		FC:CF+C =2:1	COP = 1	AG = 1	
			Pure C =1	Food	= 0	
EB = 6: 2.5	EA = 8.5	EBPer = 2.4	Afr =0.70	Isolate/R	= 0.12	
eb = 4:2	es = 6	D = 0	S =1	H:(H)Hd(Hd)	= 4:5	
	Adj es = 5	Adj D =+1	Blends:R =4:17	(HHd):(AAd)	= 4:2	
			CP =0	H+A:Hd + Ad	= 12:3	
FM = 2	C' = 1	T = 0				
m = 2	V = 0	Y = 1				
			P = 6	Zf =8	3r+(2)/R = 0.35	
a:p	= 5:5	Sum6 =12	X+% = 0.47	Zd =–2.5	Fr+rF = 0	
Ma:Mp	= 2:4	Lv2 = 4	F+% = 0.80	W:D:Dd =7:8:2	FD = 1	
2AB+Art+Ay = 1		WSum6 = 41	X–% = 0.18	W:M =7:6	An + Xy = 2	
M–	= 1	Mnone = 0	S–% = 0.33	DQ+ =3	MOR = 2	
			Xu% = 0.29	DQv =4		

SCZI = 3	DEPI = 2	CDI = 1	S-CON = 2	HVI = No	OBS = No

SCZI (SCHIZOPHRENIA INDEX):
Positive if 4 or more conditions are true:
YES...EITHER: (X+% < .61) AND (S-% < .41)
  OR...: (X+% < .50)
No...(X-% > .29)
No...EITHER: (FQ- > = FQu)
  OR...: (FQ- > FQo + FQ+)
YES...(Sum Level 2 Sp. Sc. > 1) AND (FAB2 > 0)
YES...EITHER: (Raw Sum of 6 Spec. Scores > 6)
  OR...: (Weighted Sum of 6 Sp. Sc. > 17)
No...EITHER: (M- > 1)
  OR...: (X-% > .40)

DEPI (DEPRESSION INDEX):
Positive if 5 or more conditions are true:
No...(FV+VF+V> 0) OR (FD> 2)
YES...(Col-Shd Blends > 0) OR
  (S > 2)
No...(3r+(2)/R > .44 and Fr+rF = 0)
  OR (3r+(2)/R < .33)
No...(Afr < .46) OR (Blends <4)
No...(SumShading > FM+m) OR
  (SumC' > 2)
No...(MOR > 2) OR
  (2AB+ (Art+Ay) > 3)
YES...(COP < 2) OR
  (Isolate/R > .24)

CDI (COPING DEFICIT INDEX):
Positive if 4 or 5 conditions are true:
No...(EA < 6) OR (Adj D< 0)
YES...(COP < 2) AND (AG < 2)
No...(Weighted Sum C < 2.5)
  OR (Afr < .46)
No...(Passive > Active+1) OR
  (Pure H < 2)
No...(SumT > 1) OR
  (Isolate/R > .24) OR
  (Food > 0)

HV (HYPERVIGILANCE INDEX):
Positive if Condition 1 is true and at least
4 of the others are true.

YES...(1) FT+TF+T = 0

No...(2) Zf >12
No...(3) Zd > +3.5
No...(4) S > 3
YES...(5) H+(H)+Hd+(Hd) > 6
YES...(6) (H)+(A)+(Hd)+(Ad) > 3
No...(7) H+A:Hd+Ad < 4:1
No...(8) Cg > 3

OBS (OBSESSIVE STYLE INDEX):

No...(1) Dd > 3
No...(2) Zf > 12
No...(3) Zd > +3.0
No...(4) Populars > 7
No...(5) FQ+ > 1

Positive if one or more is true:
No...Conditions 1 to 5
  Are All True
No...2 or more of 1 to 4
  are true AND FQ+ > 3
No...3 or more of 1 to 5
  are true AND X+% > .89
No...FQ+ > 3 AND X+% >.89

7

A Psychotic and Bulimic Female Adolescent

Rebecca E. Rieger
Chestnut Lodge Hospital

This chapter presents the case of "Mary," a psychotic and personality-disordered inpatient female adolescent with admitting diagnoses of schizoaffective disorder and bulimia (Axis I, Diagnostic and Statistical Manual of Mental Disorders [4th ed.; American Psychiatric Association, 1994]) and a comorbid low level borderline and psychotic personality organization. Although bulimia is included among the Axis I disorders (APA, 1994), in psychoanalytic studies eating disorders are widely subsumed under and presumed to share many aspects of borderline personality disorder. Rorschach interpretation will be discussed from an integrated perspective utilizing Comprehensive System analysis (Exner, 1991; Exner & Weiner, 1995), psychodynamic content (Cooper & Arnow, 1985; Kwawer, Lerner, Lerner, & Sugarman, 1980), and sequential analysis. The relation between Mary's psychotic Axis I disorder and Axis II personality disorder is discussed with particular attention to symptomatology, interactional effects, and probable early developmental factors.

Mary was the second of three children from an intact, middle-class family from the Midwest. Mary's parents reported that she had been "the perfect child"; she was beautiful, intelligent, and well behaved. The clinical interview suggested, however, an attentional/hyperactivity problem during her early school years. Mary's mother reported that as a young child she "bounced off the walls." When questioned concerning a depressive history, the mother recalled that at age 5, Mary's maternal grandmother had described her as "a very unhappy little girl."[1]

Mary was admitted to the hospital at age 16 after a 1- to 2-year period of deteriorating school performance, rebellious behavior with counterculture friends, substantial substance abuse (primarily alcohol and marijuana), severe bulimia, temper tantrums, and depression. In the admission interview Mary

---

[1]Mary's history as solicited from her parents proved to be elusive. The history has been altered to protect confidentiality.

reported anxiety, panic feelings, and a vague sense of identity. She had also evidenced mood swings and self-mutilation (cutting). Previous attempts at outpatient and day treatment found her resistant and "amotivational." Psychopharmacological intervention had included a combination of lithium, antidepressant, and antianxiety drugs. Medication had proven partially effective, but the added structure and containment of the hospital enhanced psychotropic intervention effectiveness. Mary had a 4-year course of improvements and regressions, with moves between inpatient and less restrictive levels of care. Psychotherapeutic intervention consisted of individual, intensive, analytically-oriented therapy with the same female therapist throughout, and group therapy, including a substance abuse group. Additionally, Mary attended the hospital-based "therapeutic school," from which she graduated with a high school diploma. In individual therapy she gradually became attached to her therapist, but was "passive" in treatment and found it difficult to express her feelings or dwell on painful events in her life.

The high level of parental denial of her escalating difficulties was somewhat modified in the course of parent and family work, but continued to manifest, for example, in the parents' insistence on having Mary accompany them on an extended family vacation despite clear evidence of her fragile gains.

PSYCHOLOGICAL TESTING

Mary was tested within 2 weeks of her admission to the hospital adolescent unit. She presented as a very attractive midadolescent in all-black apparel. She was given the Wechsler Adult Intelligence Scale–Revised (WAIS-R), Bender Visual Motor Gestalt Test, Human Figure Drawings, Most Unpleasant Concept Test (Harrower, 1950), Rorschach, and Thematic Apperception Test (TAT), and was able to cooperate and tolerate the initial testing session (1.5 hr); she did ask to postpone the last task (TAT) until the following day. She was markedly self-deprecating, dwelling on her inability to meet her own high standards and distorting her perception of the level of her performance. She was also subtly passive-aggressive. Cognitive testing revealed a level of functioning in the superior range (WAIS–R Verbal Scale IQ = 128, Performance Scale IQ = 128, Full Scale IQ = 131), and other graphomotor tasks (Bender and drawings) showed no evidence of structural (neurological) deficits. At the time of testing Mary was prescribed Trilafon and Lithium.

RORSCHACH AND PSYCHOTIC STRUCTURE

Acklin (1992) discussed psychotic personality organization, "translated into a contemporary Rorschach psychology, which integrates nomothetic and idiographic approaches" (p. 460). Among the "structural" indications, he identified the following Comprehensive System indices (Exner, 1991): Elevation in the frequency of Special Scores, especially Level 2; heavily weighted *Sum* 6; deterioration of Form Level (*X–%*); and the Schizophrenia Index ≥ 4. Acklin further noted disturbances and oddities of syntax and representation indicative of thought disorder (Berg, Packer, & Nunno, 1993), and disturbances in the structural features of percepts, especially human percepts (Acklin, 1992). The analysis of sequence and content permits observations relating to the failure of defenses, utilization of primitive defenses (Cooper & Arnow, 1986; Cooper, Perry, & Arnow, 1988; Cooper, Perry, & O'Connell, 1991; Kwawer et al., 1980), expression of raw, drive-laden, primary process material; themes of barrenness, emptiness, and malevolent interaction; and fragmented, chaotic, or merged internalized representations of self and others (Blatt et al., 1990).

Murray (1992), in his discussion of a psychotic child, listed Rorschach characteristics under four headings: (a) disordered thinking (*WSum6* Special Scores); (b) inaccurate perception (low *X+*, high *X–*, and the pervasiveness of inaccuracies); (c) interpersonal ineptness (all *M* responses are unusual or minus, each *M* is infused with a Special Score, *M*s are [*H*] or animals in human activities, and frequently spoiled populars); and (d) inadequate controls (disturbed content with high *AG*; *CF* + *C* > *FC*; and a sense that the bizarre and out of control material is acceptable or even enjoyable). Mary's Rorschach will be analyzed following the Acklin and Murray criteria as templates (Acklin, 1992; Murray, 1992).

MARY'S RORSCHACH

Mary produced a valid Rorschach protocol of 19 responses (Lambda = .36, see Appendix A). Attention is immediately drawn to the Schizophrenia Index (*SCZI* = 6), which strongly suggests a psychotic process (Exner, 1986). The *SCZI* is made up of 10 variables across six tests, reflecting problems in both inaccurate perception and thought disorder (Exner, 1991). Mary is positive on all six, indicating a high probability of schizophrenia.

SCZI

1. *X+%* < .61 and *S–%* < .41 *or X+%* < .50. [Mary's *X+* of .32 and *S–%* of .33, as well as her *X+%* of 32, are both positive.]
2. *X–%* > .29. [Mary's *X–%* is .47.]
3. *FQ–* > Sum FQu *or FQ–* > Sum (*FQo* + *FQ+*). [Both are true for Mary.]
4. Sum Level 2 Special Scores > 1 *and* Fabcom 2 > 0. [Mary has four Level 2 Special Scores and four Level 2 Fabcoms.]
5. Raw Sum 6 Special Scores > 6 *or* Weighted *Sum6* Special Scores > 17. [Mary's raw *Sum6* is 16, and her Weighted *Sum6* Special Scores is 60!]

6. $M-$ > 1 or $X-\%$ > .40. [Mary has 2 $M-$ and $X-$ = .47.]

In Exner and Weiner's (1995) first admission schizophrenic adolescents sample (N = 100), 19% were extratensive and only 8% were pervasively extratensive. The $CF + C$ > $FC + 2$ in the sample was 3%, and only 1% had an AFR < .40. Thirteen percent had MOR > 2. Mary differs from the schizophrenic adolescent sample (see Appendix A). Mary's 4 INCs, 5 DRs, 2 FAB 1s and 4 FAB 2s warrant consideration of affective features, particularly of a manic nature (Singer & Brabender, 1993).

Affective stimulation and reactivity significantly impact Mary's perceptual accuracy and thinking (see Appendix A): 67% of her nine minus form responses are on color cards; 63% of her eight color responses have minus form and/or special scores (FAB 1 and 2, DR). The marked elevation in space responses (S = 5), another affective indicator relating to a chronic, angry, negative attitude to the world, suggests that her anger is likely to manifest itself in more intense, affective displays and to have considerable impact on her decision making (Exner, 1991). Together with her pervasive Extratensive style (EB = 3:7.5) and predominance of poorly modulated affect, it indicates the vulnerability of her thinking and reality testing in the presence of affective stimulation and reactivity, and offers some support for a diagnostic formulation that includes an affective component. In Mary's case, this pattern points to the probability of a schizoaffective disorder, her admitting diagnosis. Subsequent consultation with a psychopharmacologist led to his formulation of a rapidly cycling bipolar disorder.

Consistent with Acklin's (1992) and Murray's (1992) criteria, Mary's human contents are heavily weighted on the side of parenthesized and part objects (H:[H]Hd[Hd]) = 1:4, and two of her three M responses are minus, suggesting a grossly impaired and distorted understanding of people and interpersonal interactions. Her positive CDI strengthens the impression of interpersonal ineptness, with elements of social immaturity and feelings of isolation from active interchange with others. It is interesting that her one pure H and COP response on Card II.3 is presented as a failed or inept interaction ("Two little kids playing patty-cake, but keep missing and slapping their faces").

Acklin (1992) referred to raw, drive-laden, primary process material. Mary's responses to Card III 5 and 6 ("bird *shit*"), and Card V 11 ("slug . . . wings look like *smushed banana*") and IX 16 ("Forest fire . . . fire is coming out in *tongues*") reveal an open channel to primitive anal and oral ideation. Her initial responses to Card I, a theme of engulfment, loss of boundaries, and malevolent interaction, illustrates her fragmented, chaotic, or merged internal representations. With Card IV 10 ("bleached cow's skull . . . something dead") and Card VII 13 ("statues on Easter Island . . . black statues facing each other . . . the ones on Easter aren't talking"), her theme of barrenness and emptiness in object relations is expressed, the latter possibly reflecting a maternal object representation.

The following sequences illustrate Mary's use of splitting and the failure of narcissistic self-focus to protect the object world from malevolent introjects: After the object unavailability on VII 13, she follows on VIII 15 with a pleasurable narcissistic gratification—"I love that one . . . (wolf) can look down at his reflection, beautiful"—but her next response to IX is a raging, destructive force ("forest fire") that she defends against with a magical image of resurrection, that is, denial. She then returns to the theme of danger in her playful hypomanic image of a "pink elephant with a green cape and his legs are on fire" (IX 17). On Card X 18 the bucolic nonhuman landscape scene ("This is beautiful"), with its pleasant affective tone is followed by her final sign-off: "A goat with fiery eyes, and they put like a muzzle on him, but I think he'll get out pretty soon," her fear (and wish) that her rage cannot be contained. There is also evidence of other primitive defenses (Cooper & Arnow, 1986) like devaluation (2), idealization (15), denial (16), and projective identification (19) (see Appendix B).

Murray (1992) observed that in the psychotic protocol one finds inadequate controls and a sense that the bizarre and out-of-control material is acceptable or even enjoyable. The Comprehensive System computer-generated analysis (RIAP 3), noting the *SCZI* = 6, raised the possibility of some form of exaggeration or malingering. Mary's dramatic Rorschach presentation may be understood in light of the significant affective component, but also in her seeming pleasure in, but fear of, her sadistic impulses.

BORDERLINE CHARACTERISTICS

Acklin (1993) identified some borderline characteristics found in Mary's Rorschach protocol (see Appendix B): raw content; a mixture of human percepts with both cooperative and malevolent interaction; an unstable range of functioning, including rapid deterioration and recovery; a loss of distance from the blots; primitive relational modes; labile emotionality; boundary disturbances mainly in the form of fabulized combinations rather than contaminations; and primitive defenses focused on splitting, including devaluation and projective identification. However, she does not show a well-developed representation of humans, nor does she have a high percentage of unusual over minus form qualities.

Two thirds of all her minus responses (six of nine) were accompanied by object relational scores pertaining to primitive interpersonal modes or primitive defenses. Furthermore, all of her six severe *MOA* scores (Level 5 and 6, see Appendix B) were associated with special scores (3 *FAB2*, 2 *FAB1*, 1 *DR*); all had aggression-associated content (3 *AG* Past, 3 *AG* Potential; Gacono, 1990; Gacono & Meloy, 1992, 1994; Meloy & Gacono, 1992); and all but one were minus form quality. Here we see the coexistence of thought disorder indicators, disturbed object representations, and a negative affective tone reflecting concerns about aggression and pessimism about the self (reflected in the $MOR = 7$). It should be noted in the case of the higher MOA scores that Blatt, Tuber, and Auerbach (1990) concluded they primarily assess aspects of psychopathology, such as the severity of clinical symptoms and the extent of thought disorder, and only secondarily, the quality of interpersonal relationships.

INDIVIDUAL DIFFERENCES

Although it is useful, and even necessary, to clarify diagnostic formulations with implications for treatment and prognosis, it is possible to lose the person in the process. Mary's structural summary (Appendix A) and content provide an individualized picture of her psychopathology.

SELF PERCEPTION

$3r + (2)/R = 0.37$	$FD = 0$	$MOR = 7$	$Hx = 0$	$An + Xy = 0$
$Fr + rF = 1$	$Sum\ V = 0$	$H:(H)+Hd+(Hd) = 1: 4$		$Sx = 0$

MOR Responses	FQ– Responses	M Responses	FM Responses	m Responses
2, 3, 6, 10, 11, 12, 17	1, 2, 5, 6, 8, 9, 16, 17, 19	1, 2, 3	1, 11, 15	2, 16

The egocentricity index (Ego $= .37$) is inflated by one reflection response, but remains low (expected range for age is .33 to .48). If the Fr is experimentally scored as a pair, the egocentricity falls to .26, well below expectations for age. This suggests that the underlying poor self-estimate is weakly denied with narcissistic defenses. There is also the indication of pervasive negative features in her self-image and the likelihood of very pessimistic thinking ($MOR = 7$). Most of the MOR responses represent damage resulting from externalized past aggression (AG Past; Gacono & Meloy, 1994), giving the sense of her self-concept as victim. She sees herself as defective and different, a "mutant" butterfly, and vulnerable to disintegration (III.6). Difficulties with intentional behavior (II.3) are indicated in her image of children playing, but "keep missing and slapping their faces," resulting in injury. This response suggests a history of a hyperactive, poorly controlled child, later confirmed. Of the three M responses, two are minus (both on Card I), and convey a sense of impotent struggle against a fear of engulfment, a loss of integrity in the self-representation; II.3 is a spoiled COP with concern over out-of-control impulses (as noted in Appendix B).

There is no one content category in her nine minus responses, but two thirds appear on cards containing color (III 5, 6, 8; IX 16, 17; X 19), and seven of the nine have Special Scores indicating the presence of disordered thinking, while boundary disturbances also appear on II.2. Once again, her thinking deteriorates under the impact of affect, which is particularly problematic with a pervasive extratensive ($EB\ Per = 2.5$).

INTERPERSONAL PERCEPTION AND RELATIONS

$CDI = 4^*$	$a{:}p = 6{:}3$	$T = 0$	$Human\ Cont = 5$	$Pure\ H = 1$
$HVI = Pos$	$Food = 0$	$PER = 0$	$COP = 1$	$AG = 0$
		$Isolate/R = 0.42$		

Human Movement with Pair	Human Contents
3	1, 2, 3, 4, 8

The interpersonal perception and relations cluster adds to the picture of likely difficulties, discomfort, ineptness, and failure in object relationships ($CDI = 4$; Isolation Index = .42). There is, however, the additional positive Hypervigilance Index (HVI), which represents an anticipatory, hyperalert state that has its origins in a negative or distrustful expectation from the environment with marked guardedness in interpersonal relations (Exner, 1991). It rests fundamentally on the lack of any texture responses ($T = 0$), which suggests unease with close relationships, and the probability of past disappointment or early experiences that Mary perceived as rejecting or anxiety provoking. Taken together with her significant problems in accurate perception and ideation, the HVI may represent a more paranoid, interpersonally distorted outlook. Despite the angry affect represented by the elevation in S, she has no scores for aggression. In the Exner system, AG can only be scored with movement responses when the action is taking place in the present. The presence of some AG (e.g., $AG = 2$) is within normative expectations, and seems to signal an active, not necessarily hostile, interaction with the environment. In the presence of elevated S, the absence of AG in her case demands a further examination of a spectrum of experimental AG scores (Gacono & Meloy, 1994): AG Past (often scored with Exner's MOR); AG Content (which includes weapons); AG Potential, in which the action is foreshadowed; and SM, Sadomasochism, in which destructive content is associated with evidence of pleasurable affect, such as smiling. Although Mary's Exner $AG = 0$, she does have 3 $MORs$ that are AG Past (I.2, VI.12, IX.17), one AG Potential (X.19), one SM (VI.12) and one AG denied or unintended (II.3). On some level she is preoccupied with and concerned about aggressive impulses. She sees herself as not only damaged or vulnerable ($MOR = 7$) but aggressed against (AG Past = 3). There is the further element of her own unacknowledged aggressive thinking, and the probability of the use of the pathological defense of projection, perhaps reflected in her positive HVI.

In view of her intense affect, including anger, it is important to examine her capacity for control and stress tolerance.

CAPACITY FOR CONTROL AND TOLERANCE FOR STRESS

$EB = 3: 7.5$ $EA = 10.5$ $D = 0$
$eb = 5: 3$ $es = 8$ $Adj\ es = 7$ $Adj\ D = +1$

$FM = 3$ $C' = 2$ $T = 0$ $CDI = 4^*$
   $m = 2$ $V = 0$ $Y = 1$

From $D = 0$, based on an $EA = 10.5$ and $es = 8$, it would appear Mary's controls and stress tolerance are currently adequate, that is, she is unlikely to be impulsive because of overwhelmed resources. She also appears to have a sturdier tolerance for stress than most people ($AdjD = +1$). These assumptions, however, need to be challenged; where her 3 Ms include $2M-$, and where her sum color points to poorly modulated affect, her resources for deliberate decision making are fragile. The minimal elevation in the situational variable ($m = 2$), which changes the $es = 8$ to the Adjusted $es = 7$, questions the assumption of her habitual stress tolerance as "sturdier" than most. The positive CDI likely reflects social ineptness that manifests as inappropriate behavior rather than loss of control.

A significant symptom of Mary's psychopathology is her bulimia, which involves both binging and purging, and has waxed and waned, but remains an available channel for the expression of her internalized object representations. A series of studies using the Rorschach, summarized by Lerner (1991), reported differences between female restricting anorexic and bulimic patients in thought disorder, boundary disturbance, primitive defenses, object relations, and developmental object representations. When compared to restricting anorexics, bulimics manifest a lower level of reality testing and a pathological range of thought disorder; more severe boundary disturbances, producing many fabulized combinations; primitive defenses emphasizing projective identification and low-level devaluation; object relations that are more malevolent; sadistic responses that are unique to the bulimic patients; and primitive interpersonal themes, with more engulfment. A key difference lies in the bulimic patient's active involvement in a struggle with an internal "bad object," which has to be incorporated but then expelled.

Mary's Rorschach shows significant similarities to these features of bulimic patients. In addition, there is the prominent theme of orality, mainly in its aggressive/destructive aspects. For example, on Card V she introduces a devalued food response in describing the "Flying slug with legs. Wings sorta look like smushed banana," which is suggestive of primary process intrusion; to Card IX, she introduces food content (albeit magically transformed) and oral imagery related to destructive forces: "Forest fire. Like an egg (a phoenix's egg) emerging from the fire . . . Fire is coming out in tongues"; and to Card X, in her last response, she associates rageful feeling with the need for external control, expressed as "A goat with fiery eyes and they put like a muzzle on him, but I think he'll get out pretty soon." This is her dangerous and aggressive oral incorporation.

OTHER TESTING

Although the Rorschach "speaks more to the structural aspects of personality . . . other, more explicitly object relational instruments like the TAT speak more to the characterological stylistic aspects of personality" (Athey, Fleischer, & Coyne, 1980, p. 297).

To offer corroboration and strengthen the evidence of Mary's bulimic dynamics, we can turn to other test data and briefly note the following: She described her figure drawings, first of a somewhat bizarre counterculture adolescent male, as "the man with bear slippers . . . or cow's udders," and the second very demure female figure as "She lives with the man with bear slippers. She has no name." The intrusion of primary process orality ("cow's udders"), and the female's lack of identity are suggestive of borderline issues of symbiotic attachment, fear of separation, and identity diffusion.

When asked to draw "the most unpleasant thing you can think of" (Harrower, 1950), her first response was to draw a platter with a lump of "Spam," which she then elaborated (see Fig. 7.1) to a picture of a horrendous octopuslike creature with a huge open mouth showing sharp teeth, topped by the platter of "Spam" and then extended to a little stick figure that she labeled her sibling. The initial theme of unacceptable "ersatz" food gave way to the voracious destructive mouth, which was then related to an object representation. It illustrates her rage at the frustration of her early dependent needs and her consuming, but unfulfilling orality.

Mary's TAT stories fill out the picture of desperate, sadistic ideation, the sense that she is herself a dangerous "bad object," and her fear that her defenses are failing to protect her from increasing depression and pessimism about her future. However, it is her story to the first card of the Michigan Picture Test (a TAT-like story telling task; see Hutt, 1980) that reveals the depth of her underlying distrust of the maternal object. The scene is a family at breakfast, including an adolescent girl, the father, and a mother spoon-feeding a little boy. The most "popular" story relates to sibling rivalry and resentment of the mother's attention to the boy. Mary's story is as follows: "This *happy* little family is sitting around eating breakfast when the kid looks down at his spoon, which is full of worms. The mother shoves it in his mouth, and the worms eat his esophagus and innards and he dies."

She identifies with the boy and describes the mother's "nurturance" as malevolent and totally destructive. With such an early internalized sadistic image of the maternal relationship, it is not surprising that the Rorschach yields a $T = 0$ and a positive HVI, at the least a pathological generalization about object relations. But there is also evidence that some of the malevolence, her

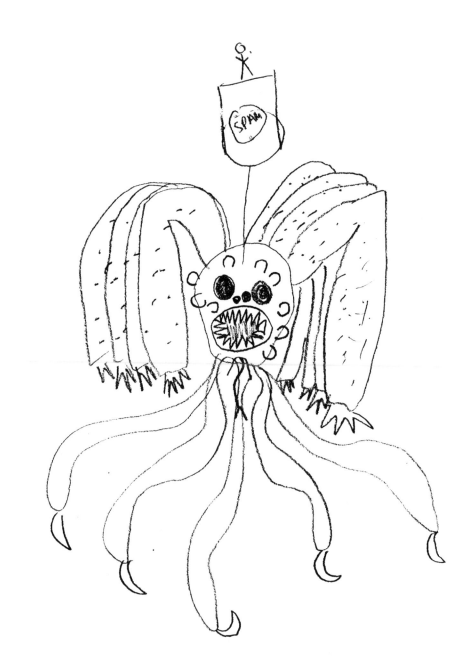

FIG. 7.1. Drawing of the "most unpleasant thing you can think of" (Harrower, 1950).

own rage, is unconsciously managed by projection and projective identification. The available developmental history is too sketchy to permit more than probablistic statements about etiology. The confirmed early hyperactivity likely resulted in a stressful mother–child relationship. There is evidence in the history of a lack of maternal empathy (or awareness) of Mary's needs, and an unrealistic denial of her growing difficulties. The maternal deficit or unavailability in the presence of an infant's vulnerability and needs can compound the constitutional predisposition and lead to the child's rageful frustration and internalized representation of a bad object. In a long-term prospective study of hyperactive children, Weiss and Hechtman (1993) noted developmental risk factors in cognitive learning, troubled object relations, and impaired social skills.

SUMMARY

The Rorschach reveals the complex nature of Mary's psychopathology. Her therapist reported that despite medication efforts, her "rapidly cycling bipolar disorder has been quite resistant to adequate regulation" and referred to this affective disorder as a severe, persistent disability. Her compromised reality testing and unreliable judgment and her very unstable mood disorder made living in the community quite problematic, as evidenced by inappropriate behavior on passes from the hospital. But her problems in living have been greatly compounded by the nature and extent of her internalized object representations and relations, mainly in her great unease and distrust of intimacy and the ongoing, current strength of her preoccupation with preoedipal issues around trust, separation, individuation, and mastery. The comorbidity of the Axis I probable biological mood disorder,[2] the ego weaknesses permitting psychotic regression in the presence of intense affect, and the Axis II personality disorder with its object-directed rage, distrust, and pathological, brittle defensive structure, have been delineated by the combined structural and dynamic approach to Rorschach interpretation.

REFERENCES

Acklin, M. W. (1992). Psychodiagnosis of personality structure: Psychotic personality organization I. *Journal of Personality Assessment, 58,* 454–463.
Acklin, M. W. (1993). Psychodiagnosis of personality structure II. Borderline personality organization. *Journal of Personality Assessment, 61,* 329–341.

---

[2]The observed and documented attention deficit hyperactivity disorder may have been prodromal to the developing affective disorder.

American Psychiatric Association. (1994). *Diagnostic and statistical manual of mental disorders* (4th ed.). Washington, DC: Author.

Athey, G. I., Fleischer, J., & Coyne, L. (1980). Rorschach object representation as influenced by thought and affect organization. In J. S. Kwawer, H. Lerner, P. Lerner, & A. Sugarman (Eds.), *Borderline phenomena and the Rorschach test* (pp. 275–298). New York: International Universities Press.

Berg, J. L., Packer, A., & Nunno, V. J. (1993). A Rorschach analysis: Parallel disturbance in thought and in self/object representation. *Journal of Personality Assessment, 61,* 311–323.

Blatt, S. J., Tuber, S. B., & Auerbach, J. S. (1990). Representation of interpersonal interactions on the Rorschach and level of psychopathology. *Journal of Personality Assessment, 54,* 711–728.

Cooper, S., & Arnow, D. (1986). An object relations view of the borderline defenses: A Rorschach analysis. In M. Kissen (Ed.), *Assessing object relations phenomena* (pp. 143–171). New York: International Universities Press.

Cooper, S. H., Perry, J. C., & Arnow, D. (1988). An empirical approach to the study of defense mechanisms: I. Reliability and preliminary validity of the Rorschach Defense Scales. *Journal of Personality Assessment, 52,* 187–203.

Cooper, S. H., Perry, J. C., & O'Connell, M. (1991). The Rorschach Defense Scales: II. Longitudinal perspectives. *Journal of Personality Assessment, 56,* 191–201.

Exner, J. E., Jr. (1986). Some Rorschach data comparing schizophrenics with borderline and schizotypal character disorders. *Journal of Personality Assessment, 50,* 455–471.

Exner, J. E., Jr. (1991). *The Rorschach: A comprehensive system: Vol. 2. Interpretation* (2nd ed.) New York: Wiley.

Exner, J. E., Jr., & Weiner, I. B. (1995). *The Rorschach: A comprehensive system: Vol. 3. Assessment of children and adolescents* (2nd ed.). New York: Wiley.

Gacono, C. B. (1990). An empirical study of object relations and defensive operations in antisocial personality disorder. *Journal of Personality Assessment, 54,* 589–600.

Gacono, C. B., & Meloy, J. R. (1992). The Rorschach and the *DSM–III–R* antisocial personality: A tribute to Robert Lindner. *Journal of Clinical Psychology 48,* 393–406.

Gacono, C. B., & Meloy, J. R. (1994). *The Rorschach assessment of aggressive and psychopathic personalities.* Hillsdale, NJ: Lawrence Erlbaum Associates.

Harrower, M. R. (1950). The Most Unpleasant Concept test. *Journal of Clinical Psychology, 6,* 213–233.

Hutt, M. L. (1980). *The Michigan Picture Test–Revised.* New York: Grune & Stratton.

Kwawer, J. S., Lerner, H. D., Lerner, P. M., & Sugarman, A. (Eds.) 1980. *Borderline phenomena and the Rorschach test.* New York: International Universities Press.

Lerner, P. M. (1991). *Psychoanalytic theory and the Rorschach.* Hillsdale, NJ: The Analytic Press.

Meloy, J. R., & Gacono, C. B. (1992). The aggression response and the Rorschach. *Journal of Clinical Psychology, 48,* 104–114.

Murray, J. F. (1992). Toward a synthetic approach to the Rorschach: The case of a psychotic child. *Journal of Personality Assessment, 58,* 494–505.

Singer, H. K., & Brabender, V. (1993). The use of the Rorschach to differentiate unipolar and bipolar disorders. *Journal of Personality Assessment, 60,* 333–345.

Weiss, G., & Hechtman, L. T. (1993). *Hyperactive children grown up* (2nd ed.). New York: Guilford.

APPENDIX A
Rorschach Structural Summary

LOCATION FEATURES

Zf	= 15
ZSum	= 61.5
ZEst	= 49.0
W	= 13
(Wv	= 0)
D	= 4
Dd	= 2
S	= 5

DQ

	..........(FQ–)
+	= 9 (5)
o	= 8 (3)
v/+	= 1 (0)
v	= 1 (1)

DETERMINANTS

BLENDS	SINGLE	
M.FM	M	= 0
M.m	FM	= 1
M.CF	m	= 0
Fr.FM.CF	FC	= 1
CF.m	CF	= 4
	C	= 0
	Cn	= 0
	FC'	= 2
	C'F	= 0
	C'	= 0
	FT	= 0
	TF	= 0
	T	= 0
	FV	= 0
	VF	= 0
	V	= 0
	FY	= 0
	YF	= 1
	Y	= 0
	Fr	= 0
	rF	= 0
	FD	= 0
	F	= 5
	(2)	= 4

CONTENTS

H	= 1,0
(H)	= 1,1
Hd	= 1,1
(Hd)	= 0,0
Hx	= 0,0
A	= 5,1
(A)	= 2,1
Ad	= 2,0
(Ad)	= 2,0
An	= 0,2
Art	= 0,0
Ay	= 1,1
Bl	= 0,2
Bt	= 2,0
Cg	= 0,2
Cl	= 0,1
Ex	= 0,0
Fd	= 0,0
Fi	= 0,2
Ge	= 0,0
Hh	= 0,0
Ls	= 0,0
Na	= 1,1
Sc	= 0,0
Sx	= 0,1
Xy	= 0,0
Id	= 1,2

S-CONSTELLATION

- NO..FV + VF + V + FD > 2
- NO..Col-Shd Bl>0
- NO..Ego<.31,>.44
- YES..MOR>3
- YES..Zd > ± 3.5
- NO..es>EA
- YES..CF+C>FC
- YES..X+%<.70
- YES..S>3
- YES..P<3 or >8
- YES..Pure H <2
- NO..R<17
- 7.....TOTAL

SPECIAL SCORINGS

	Lvl	Lv2
DV	= 1x1	0x2
INC	= 4x2	0x4
DR	= 5x3	0x6
FAB	= 2x4	4x7
ALOG	= 0x5	
CON	= 0x7	
SUM6	= 16	
WSUM6	= 60	

AB	=0	CP	= 0
AG	=0	MOR	= 7
CFB	=0	PER	= 0
COP	=1	PSV	= 0

FORM QUALITY

	FQx	FQf	MQual	SQx
+	= 0	0	0	0
o	= 6	3	1	0
u	= 4	0	0	2
–	= 9	2	2	3
none	= 0	0	0	0

RATIOS, PERCENTAGES, AND DERIVATIONS

R	= 19	L	= 0.36		
EB	= 3:7.5	EA = 10.5		EBPer = 2.5	
eb	= 5:3	es = 8		D = 0	
		Adj es = 7		Adj D = +1	

FC:CF+C	=1:7	COP = 1		AG = 0	
Pure C	=0	Food			= 0
Afr	=0.36	Isolate/R			= 0.42
S	=5	H:(H)Hd(Hd)			= 1:4
Blends:R	=5:19	(HHd):(AAd)			= 2:5
CP	=0	H+A:Hd + Ad			= 12:6

FM	= 3	C' = 2		T = 0	
m	= 2	V = 0		Y = 1	

				P = 1	Zf	=15	3r+(2)/R	= 0.37
a:p	= 6:2	Sum6	=16	X+% = 0.32	Zd	=+12.5	Fr+rF	= 1
Ma:Mp	= 3:0	Lv2	= 4	F+% = 0.60	W:D:Dd	=13:4:2	FD	= 0
2AB+Art+Ay	= 2	WSum6	= 60	X–% = 0.47	W:M	=13:3	An + Xy	= 2
M–	= 2	Mnone	= 0	S–% = 0.33	DQ+	=9	MOR	= 7
				Xu% = 0.21	DQv	=1		

SCZI = 6*	DEPI = 4	CDI = 4*	S-CON = 7	HVI = Yes	OBS = No

I.

1. Looks like—still looks like the dog on Ghostbusters, but also has hands reaching out of its head, people in its brain . . . duck hanging out of mouth.

Head. Little hands, somebody's feet, trying to break out of there.

(Lower d) Like a beak.

Structural Scoring: *W*+ *Ma.FMp–*   *(Ad),Hd,(A),An* 4.0   *FAB2*
Primitive Modes of Relating: Engulfment, Boundary Disturbance
Primitive Defenses: Massive Denial
Aggression Scores: *AG* Past
MOAS: 6

2. Or a mutant butterfly—people trying to get out of its head.

Looks like a strange butterfly, wings all carved up; sort of bleeding, cut into. (People?) Same thing as dog.

Structural Scoring: *W*+ *Ma.mp–*   *(A),(H),Bl* 4.0   *MOR,FAB2*
Primitive Modes of Relating: Engulfment, Boundary Disturbance, Birth Re-birth
Primitive Defenses: Devaluation, Massive Denial
Aggression Scores: *AG* Past
MOAS: 6

II.

3. Looks like two little kids playing patty-cake, but keep missing and slapping their faces (I love kids).

Faces all bloody.

Structural Scoring: *W*+*Ma.CFo*   2   *H,Bl*   4.5   *MOR,COP*
Primitive Modes of Relating: None
Primitive Defenses: Splitting, Disavowal
Aggression Scores: *AG* Past
MOAS: 2

4. Or two little gnomes.

(W) Little hats, long noses and long pointy chins.

Structural Scoring: *Wo*   *Fo*   2   *(H),Cg*   4.5
Primitive Modes of Relating: None
Primitive Defenses: Devaluation
Aggression Scores: None
MOAS: None

III.

5. Bird shit.

(Top red) Didn't want to say splattered blood because it would have kept me in hospital. Red bird shit.

Structural Scoring: *Dv*   2   *CF–*   *Id*   *INC,DR*
Primitive Modes of Relating: None
Primitive Defenses: None
Aggression Scores: None
MOAS: None

6. Baboons and bird shit.

You know how baboons have crimson buttocks. Buttocks fell off and flew up.

Structural Scoring: *Dd*+   99   *FC–*   2   *A,Id,Sx*   4.0   *MOR,FAB2*
Primitive Modes of Relating: Violent separation
Primitive Defenses: None
Aggression Scores: None
MOAS: None

7. Butterflies.

(Center) Body and two wings.

Structural Scoring: *Do*   3   *Fo*   *A*
Primitive Modes of Relating: None
Primitive Defenses: None
Aggression Scores: None
MOAS: None

8. Eskimos.

(lower D) Face reminds me of an Eskimo. ? Just looks like an Eskimo.

Structural Scoring: *Do*   7   *F–*   *Hd*
Primitive Modes of Relating: None
Primitive Defenses: None
Aggression Scores: None
MOAS: None

IV.

9. This looks like the face of a butterfly, face of an insect.

(W) Eyes (top S). Scary.

Structural Scoring: *WSo*   *F–*   *Ad*   5.0   *INC*
Primitive Modes of Relating: None
Primitive Defenses: Projection
Aggression Scores: None
MOAS: None

10. Bleached cow's skull—something dead.

Same way as insect's face. (Bleached?) Because it's so black, it's white—like a negative was taken of cow in desert—bleached by sun.

Structural Scoring: *WSo*   *FC'u*   *(Ad)An*   5.0   *MOR*
Primitive Modes of Relating: None
Primitive Defenses: None
Aggression Scores: None
MOAS: None

V.

11. Flying slug with legs. Wings sorta look like smushed banana.

Slug's antennae, legs. Got these mushy wings. (Mushy?) I don't know—just does.

Structural Scoring: *Wo*   *FMau*   *A*   1.0   *INC,MOR,DV*
Primitive Modes of Relating: None
Primitive Defenses: Devaluation, Massive Denial
Aggression Scores: None
MOAS: None

VI.

12. (Laughed) Looks like Ed The Cat—really looks like him—got hit by a steam roller.

Totally flat. Inside of face, whiskers. They did this one on purpose.

Structural Scoring: *Wo*   *Fo*   *(A)*   2.5   *MOR,DR*
Primitive Modes of Relating: None
Primitive Defenses: Projection
Aggression Scores: *AG* Past, *SM*
MOAS: 5

VII.

13. Reminds me of statues on Easter Island.

Just these black statues facing each other. The ones on Easter Island aren't talking. ? Dark.

Structural Scoring: *W+*   *FC'u*   2   *Ay*   2.5   *DR*
Primitive Modes of Relating: None
Primitive Defenses: None

(continued)

Aggression Scores: None
MOAS: None

14. Looks like clouds in the sky.　　　　　(*W*, plus *S*) Moon should be here. The
　　　　　　　　　　　　　　　　　　　　clouds just broke up and moon here.

Structural Scoring: *WSv/+*　　*YFu*　　*Na,Cl*　　4.0　　*DR*
Primitive Modes of Relating: Separation, Division
Primitive Defenses: None
Aggression Scores: None
MOAS: None

VIII.

> 15. I love that one. Wolf walking by a　　　Sunset, bathes everything in colors. Can
lake at sunset and looks down on reflec-　look down at his reflection—beautiful.
tion—over a root, rocks, trees next to it.

Structural Scoring: *W+*　　*Fr.FMa.CFo*　　*A,Na*　　*P*　　4.5
Primitive Modes of Relating: Narcissistic Mirroring
Primitive Defenses: Idealization
Aggression Scores: None
MOAS: 4

IX.

> 16. Forest Fire. Like an egg emerging　　Here's the green of the trees and there's the
from the fire—big egg.　　　　　　　　　fire (orange and splattery areas). Fire is coming
　　　　　　　　　　　　　　　　　　　　out in tongues. Egg—a phoenix's egg.

Structural Scoring: *DS+*　　2　　*CF.ma–*　　*Bt,Fi,Ay*　　5.0　　*FAB2*
Primitive Modes of Relating: Metamorphosis-Transformation, Birth Re-birth
Primitive Defenses: Denial
Aggression Scores: *A*G Content
MOAS: 6

V 17. And I also see an elephant with a　　Head, trunk, ears, cape, legs. [Added: Ba-
green cape and his legs are on fire.　　　boon (in middle).]

Structural Scoring: *W+*　　*CF–*　　*A,Fi,Cg*　　5.5　　*FAB,MOR*
Primitive modes of Relating: None
Primitive Defenses: Splitting (pre-stage)
Aggression Scores: *A*G Content
MOAS: 5

X.

V 18. This is beautiful. Looks like underwa-　　(Beautiful?) Colors and shapes.
ter coral reef, little plants and animals. Beauti-
ful.

Structural Scoring: *W+*　　*CFo*　　*Bt,A*　　5.5
Primitive modes of Relating: None
Primitive Defenses: Idealization
Aggression Scores: None
MOAS: None

V 19. Also a goat in here - a goat with fiery　　(Yellow-orange) Eyes.
eyes and they put like a muzzle on him, but I
think he'll get out pretty soon.

Structural Scoring: *DdSo* 99　　*CF–*　　*Ad, Id*　　*FAB, DR, INC*
Primitive modes of Relating: None
Primitive Defenses: Projective Identification (fearful empathy)
Aggression Scores: *A*G Potential
MOAS: 5

Card	No.	Loc.	#	Determinant(s)	(2)	Content(s)	Pop Z	Special Scores
I	1	W+	1	Ma.FMp–		(Ad), Hd,	4.0	FAB2
						(A), An		
	2	W+	1	Ma.mp–		(A), (H),	4.0	MOR, FAB2
						Bl		
II	3	W+	1	Ma.CFo	2	H, Bl	4.5	MOR, COP
	4	Wo	1	Fo	2	(H), Cg	4.5	
III	5	Dv	2	CF–		Id		INC, DR
	6	D+	99	FC–	2	A, Id, Sx	4.0	MOR, FAB2
	7	Do	3	Fo		A		
	8	Do	7	F–		Hd		
IV	9	WSo	1	F–		Ad	5.0	INC
	10	WSo	1	FC'u		(Ad), An	5.0	MOR
V	11	Wo	1	FMau		A	1.0	INC, MOR, DV
VI	12	Wo	1	Fo		(A)	2.5	MOR, DR
VII	13	W+	1	FC'u	2	Ay	2.5	DR
	14	WS/	1	YFu		Na, Cl	4.0	DR
VIII	15	W+	1	Fr.FMa.CFo		A, Na	P 4.0	
IX	16	DS+	2	CF.ma–		Bt, Fi, Ay	5.0	FAB2
	17	W+	1	CF–		A, Fi, Cg	5.5	FAB, MOR
X	18	W+	1	CFo		Bt, A	5.5	
	19	DdSo	99	CF–		Ad, Id		FAB, DR, INC

Summary of Approach

I:W.W	VI:W
II:W.W	VII:W.WS
III:D.Dd.D.D.	VIII:W
IV:WS.WS	IX:DS.W
V:W	X:W.DdS

II

BORDERLINE PERSONALITY ORGANIZATION

8

Psychodiagnosis of Personality Structure: Borderline Personality Organization

Marvin W. Acklin
Honolulu, HI

Perhaps no single diagnostic category or type of patient has consumed more attention from theoreticians, diagnosticians, and therapists than the so-called "borderline" cases. Although borderline cases have been variously described in the clinical literature for over four decades (Stone, 1980), the attention focused on these demanding and perplexing cases has been intense since the early 1970s. Questions about the nature of borderline conditions—whether they represent a personality disorder (Spitzer, Endicott, & Gibbon, 1979), a stable personality configuration or syndrome (Grinker, Werble, & Drye, 1968; Gunderson & Singer, 1975), a mild form of schizophrenia (Kety, D. Rosenthal, Wender, & Schulsinger, 1968; Kety, 1985), a variant of affective disorder (Akiskal, Djenderedjian, T. Rosenthal, & Khani, 1977; Akiskal et al., 1984; Jacobson, 1953; Klein, 1977), a range of severity of functioning (Kernberg, 1975; Millon, 1981), or an unvalidated wastebasket diagnosis (Widiger, 1982)—have been and continue to be vigorously debated. Even the choice of the designation borderline has been subject to disagreement (Millon, 1981).

The history of the borderline concept is too familiar to be outlined in detail here, so a brief exposition will suffice. Descriptions of borderline cases, at least where the term *borderline* is formally used, date from the 1930s (Stern, 1938) and earlier (e.g., Kraepelin's "excitable personality," 1980; Schneider's "labile personality," 1980). Various theoreticians and clinicians delineated the borderland between psychosis and neurosis: Zilboorg's (1941) "ambulatory schizophrenia" (1941), Rapaport, Gill, and Schafer's "preschizophrenic character" (1945/1946), Schmideberg's "stably unstable" patients (1947), Hoch and Polatin's "pseudoneurotic schizophrenia" (1949), Bychowski's "latent psychosis" (1953), and Knight's (1953) further popularization of the borderline term. From early on, two trends were noted in the definitions of the borderline conditions: those describing clinical pictures on the border of schizophrenia

109

and those on the border of the psychoneuroses (Stone, 1980). For the most part, these early descriptions were anecdotal. Lack of agreement of definitions, mixed picture of clinical symptomatology, character pathology, and poor response to traditional—psychoanalytic—treatment confused attempts to delineate the disorder.

Three early contributions to the borderline literature deserve a brief consideration. Stern's (1938) description of the borderline is clinically astute, instructive from a definitional point of view, and remarkably prescient with respect to later formulations. He listed 11 characteristics of the borderline disorder: narcissism, psychic bleeding, inordinate hypersensitivity, psychic rigidity, negative therapeutic reactions, feelings of inferiority, masochism, wound-licking, somatic anxiety, projection mechanisms, and difficulties in reality testing.

Schmideberg (1947, 1959) employed the term borderline during the late 1940s, a term she used to describe individuals who could not tolerate routine, were incapable of insight, were inclined to lead chaotic lives, and were deficient in empathic capacity. Her description is quoted at length:

> It is not just quantitatively halfway between the neuroses and psychoses; the blending and combination of these modes of reaction produce something qualitatively different ... One reason why the borderline should be regarded as a clinical entity is that the patient, as a rule, remains substantially the same throughout his life. He is stable in his instability, whatever ups and downs he has, and often keeps constant his pattern of peculiarity. Borderlines should be broken down into major subgroups, such as depressives, schizoids, paranoids. . . . Borderlines suffer from disturbances affecting almost every area of their personality and life, in particular, personal relations and depth of feeling. (1959, p. 399, quoted in Millon, 1981)

Finally, Knight's (1953) description of borderline patients anticipated the current work of Kernberg, which emphasizes "ego weakness" as a crucial element of borderline personality structure. Knight wrote,

> We conceptualize the borderline case as one in which normal ego functions of secondary process thinking, integration, realistic planning, adaptation to the environment, maintenance of object relationships and defenses against primitive unconscious impulses are severely weakened. (1953, p. 5)

Like many theorists, Knight emphasized the value of psychological testing in illuminating borderline dynamics, specifically macroscopic and microscopic evidence of borderline ego functioning (Knight, 1953; Perry & Klerman, 1978).

More recently, sophisticated and methodical efforts at description and delineation of the borderline conditions have been undertaken. The work of Grinker and his colleagues (Grinker, Werble, & Drye, 1968) is particularly useful to the diagnostician. Using an empirical, ego psychological approach, they described a borderline spectrum with four clusters of patients falling along a continuum from psychosis to neurosis: on the psychotic border, the core borderline and "as if" characters falling in the middle, and a lesser disturbed group falling on the border with neuroses. Spitzer and his colleagues (1979) refined and described two diagnostic criterion sets for borderline personality: the "schizotypal personality," demonstrating similarity to "borderline schizophrenia" (odd use of language, ideas of reference, magical thinking, and social detachment; cf. Kety, 1985), and the "unstable borderline," with a much stronger affective component to their illness (Stone, 1980). D. Klein (1977) emphasized the dimensions of affective disorder in his "hysteroid dysphoria." He described overly sensitive individuals who demonstrate "crash-like," depressive symptoms following personal rejection, self-abusing and self-defeating behaviors, including substance abuse, self-mutilation, overidealization of love objects, and a personal style that is histrionic in nature. Gunderson's borderline personality disorder (Gunderson, 1978; Gunderson & Singer, 1975), which closely resembles the diagnosis in *DSM–III* (American Psychiatric Association, 1987), highlights the poor work capacity, impulsivity, manipulative suicide gestures, intolerance of being alone, and predominantly angry affects. Gunderson stressed (discussed later) the notion that these individuals will show good performance on structured psychological testing but will demonstrate the emergence of primitive ideation on unstructured psychological testing.

The latest version of the *Diagnostic and Statistical Manual* (3rd ed., rev. *[DSM–III–R];* American Psychiatric Association, 1987) has not improved the situation, because over 90 different variants of the disorder can be derived from the 8 diagnostic criteria. To the *DSM–III–R*'s credit, however, the borderline disorders were split into two separate personality disorder categories: schizotypal personality disorder, based on the borderline schizophrenics of D. Rosenthal, Kety, and Wender, and borderline personality disorder, an integration of the formulations by Gunderson, Kernberg, Stone, and Rinsley (Widiger & Francis, 1985). A recent study by Gacono, Meloy, and J. L. Berg (1992) suggests that the *DSM–III–R* Cluster B disorders (the dramatic, impulsive, emotional, erratic, and egocentric behavioral styles) are consistent with Kernberg's lower range of character pathology or borderline personality organization (Kernberg, 1984). In summary, despite numerous attempts to define and delineate what constitutes borderline psychopathology, the diagnosis continues to elude the sort of definitional clarity, reliability, and validity that is ideally demanded from a diagnostic category.

Eschewing descriptive approaches based on symptomatic presentation and history, Kernberg (1975, 1976, 1980, 1984) approached the borderline conditions utilizing a combination of ego psychological and object-relations concepts that view the borderline conditions as a range of psychological functioning, which reveals itself in underlying structural characteristics of personality organization. Kernberg's view is clearly described in his 1984 formulation:

> Neurotic, borderline, and psychotic types of organization are reflected in the patient's overriding characteristics, particularly with regard to (1) his degree of identity integration, (2) the types of defenses he habitually uses, and (3) his capacity for reality testing. I propose that neurotic personality structure, in contrast to borderline and psychotic personality structures, implies an integrated identity. Neurotic personality structure presents a defensive organization centering on repression and other advanced or high level defensive operations. In contrast, borderline and psychotic structure are found in patients showing a predominance of primitive defensive operations centering on the mechanism of splitting. Reality testing is maintained in neurotic and borderline organization but is severely impaired in psychotic organization. These structural criteria can supplement the ordinary behavioral or phenomemological descriptions of patients and sharpen the accuracy of the differential diagnosis of mental illness, especially in cases that are difficult to classify. (pp. 5–6)

In this framework, a number of psychological functions are arrayed across a tripartite continuum of functioning, from psychotic on the low functioning end, through the intermediate borderline conditions, to neurotic functioning on the high functioning end (see Table 8.1).

In differentiating level of personality organization, the psychodiagnostician has a large number of theoretically derived indices reflecting developmental lines (Freud, 1965), including ego functions, stages of defensive organization, affect development, and self and object concepts (Acklin, 1992). Kernberg pays particular attention to three of these: identity integration, defensive operations, and reality testing (see Fig. 8.1).

Kernberg proposes, further, that borderline structure is characterized by nonspecific manifestations of ego weakness (Kernberg, 1975), reflecting poor anxiety tolerance, poor impulse control, absence of sublimatory channels, and a shift toward primary process mentation, especially in situations of low structure, like psychoanalysis or projective psychological testing (Kernberg, 1967, 1975; Knight, 1953).

While Kernberg does not postulate a superordinate construct for understanding borderline structure, in psychoanalytic terms an underdeveloped, regressive, or chronically regressed ego accounts well for the borderline clinical picture (cf. Schmideberg's 1959 description of the borderline personality as "stably unstable"). The borderline's weak ego and tenuous ego balance reflect tendencies for regression in the face of stress, that is, a propensity to shift to developmentally earlier modes of adaptation and relatedness. In fact, the borderline individual's clinical history is typically characterized by erratic functioning and episodic, chaotic regressions, a tendency that is replicated in their projective test protocols.

TABLE 8.1
Kernberg's Differential Diagnosis of Personality Organization

Area	Neurotic	Borderline	Psychotic	Diff
Ego development	High	Moderate	Low	N/B/P
Reality testing	Generally intact	Good in distant relations, poor in intimate relations	Generally poor	N/B/P
Defenses	Predominantly high level	Predominantly low level	Predominantly low level	N/B
Affect	Modulated, stable, appropriate	Unmodulated, intense, unstable, inappropriate	Unmodulated, intense, unstable, inappropriate	N/B
Impulsivity	Highly selective, infrequent	Moderately selective, frequent	Unselective, frequent	N/B/P
Anxiety tolerance	High	Low	Low	N/B
Sublimatory channels	Yes	No	No	N/B
Superego integration	Contemporary, integrated, depersonified	Archaic, personified, unintegrated	Archaic, personified, unintegrated	N/B
Dynamics	Oral, anal, phallic, genital	Oral aggressive	Oral aggressive	N/B
Object relations	Contemporary, depersonified, abstract	Archaic, personified, concrete	Archaic, personified, concrete	N/B
Object constancy	Constant	Inconstant	Inconstant	N/B
Self–other differentiation	Good in most relations	Good in superficial relations	Poor in most relations	N/B/P
Identity	Intact	Diffusion likely	Diffusion	N/B/P
Interpersonal relationships	Stable with symptoms, anxiety inhibitions	Superficially stable, intimate relations chaotic	Unstable in all relations	N/B/P

Note. Adapted from Kernberg (1975, 1976, 1980). Diff = relevant differential diagnosis. N/B/P = neurotic, borderline, and psychotic personality organization, respectively.

A borderline designation as a broad measure of severity is not a sufficient diagnostic classification. Psychodiagnosis from Kernberg's structural point of view distinguishes between personality *organization*, a broad range of functioning sharing common structural characteristics, and personality *style*: histrionic, paranoid, narcissistic, obsessive–compulsive, hypomanic, and so forth. Consequently, diagnostic formulation is two-tiered; for example, a patient may be diagnosed as demonstrating a histrionic personality disorder organized at the borderline level of personality functioning.

Similar attempts to provide a definitive conceptualization of the borderline conditions have emerged from the psychological assessment literature. These attempts at discovering the borderline Holy Grail (Murray, 1992) have, similar

	Neurotic	Borderline	Psychotic
Identity integration	Self-representations and object representations are sharply delimited. Integrated identity: contradictory images of self and others are integrated into comprehensive conceptions.	Self-representations and object representations are poorly delimited, or else there is delusional identity. Identity diffusion: contradictory aspects of self and others are poorly integrated and kept apart.	
Defensive operations	Repression and high-level defenses: reaction formation, isolation, undoing, rationalization, intellectualization. Defenses protect patient from intrapsychic conflict. Interpretation improves functioning.	Mainly splitting and low-level defenses: primitive idealization, projective identification, denial, omnipotence, and devaluation. Defenses protect patients from disintegration and self-object merging. Interpretation leads to regression.	
Reality testing	Capacity to test reality is preserved—differentiation of self from nonself, intrapsychic from external origins of perceptions and stimuli. Capacity to evaluate self and others realistically and in depth.	Alterations in relationship with reality and in their feelings of reality.	Capacity to test reality is lost.

FIG. 8.1.   Kernberg's differentiation of personality structures.

to other conceptual approaches, foundered on definitional issues (Widiger, 1982). The role of psychological testing has been affirmed from early on. In 1953, Bychowski emphasized the importance of the Rorschach in detecting "schizophrenic disposition." In 1954, Knight noted the value of including both structured and unstructured stimuli in the psychological assessment of borderline patients. Kernberg (1975) similarly noted that the detection of primary process thinking "through the use of projective tests makes sophisticated psychological testing an indispensable instrument for the diagnosis" (p. 25).

Psychological evaluation studies have outlined a number of the presumably cardinal, but controversial, psychological assessment features of the borderline conditions (Gartner, Hurt, & Gartner, 1989). These include adequate functioning on high structure tests (e.g., the Wechsler Adult Intelligence Scale [WAIS] or WAIS–R) and deteriorated performance on projectives, especially the Rorschach (Kernberg, 1967; Knight, 1953; Rapaport, Gill, & Schafer, 1945/1946; Singer, 1977), evidence of loosened thinking, boundary disturbance and thought disorder (Singer & Larson, 1981), malevolent object relations (H. Lerner & St. Peter, 1984; Stuart et al., 1990), dysphoria, poor stress tolerance, and labile emotionality (Exner, 1986). Although these studies have done much to describe the range and quality of functioning of borderline patients, the "shifting aliases and category boundaries" (Widiger, 1982, p. 227) have weakened empirical support for definitive understanding of psychological test performance by borderline patients.

A number of studies have examined borderline personality functioning on psychological tests. In their definitive study, Gartner, Hurt, and Gartner (1989) noted that approximately 40 articles had been published since 1977 aimed at identifying test characteristics found in borderline test records. Although some of the findings have become points of controversy and share the same flaws as attempts to clarify what defines borderline (Widiger, 1982), they have become part of the clinical lore relating to borderline patients and are useful to the diagnostician. A selective review follows.

Exner's (1986) Rorschach study differentiating the two types of borderline disorder described by Spitzer et al. (1979; the schizotypal and emotionally unstable personality) tended to validate Spitzer's observations. Schizotypal personalities bore a strong resemblance on the Rorschach to schizophrenics with tendencies toward introversion, problems with odd or divergent thinking, and passive, social detachment. The borderline group was described as "very different from the other two [schizophrenics and schizotypal personalities] in both organization and functioning" (p. 468). They were described as more likely to be extratensive *(EB)*, affect-oriented *(Afr* and *FC: CF + C)*, self-centered *(3r + (2)/R)*, and immature individuals who are easily overwhelmed by stress *(es* and *D)*, with problems with dysphoria and affect modulation (shading and *FC:CF + C*). Exner noted that "the differences [between the two groups] are so extensive that it seems reasonable to question the *DSM–III* notion that the diagnoses of both borderline and schizotypal personality disorders could be used to identify the same patient" (p. 468). He concluded that "the current label borderline seems overly general and potentially misleading. Quite possibly, by reverting to an older category of inadequate personality, the label would be more appropriately descriptive" (p. 470).

With respect to reality testing and perceptual accuracy, borderline records have been shown to be distinguishable from both neurotics (Singer & Larson, 1981) and schizophrenics (Exner, 1986). Overall, a borderline patient's good form responses generally make up 65% to 70% of the record (Gartner, Hurt, & Gartner, 1989), with a higher level of weak or unusual form quality, indicating idiosyncratic rather than distorted reality perception.

Rorschach (1921/1942) and, later, Rapaport and his colleagues (1945/1946) described the oddities of thought in the Rorschach records of latent or ambulatory schizophrenics. Rapaport, Gill, and Schafer also were the first to note the borderline's intact performance on the WAIS and deterioration on the Rorschach. The work of Margaret Singer (Gunderson & Singer, 1975; Singer, 1977; Singer & Larson, 1981) on the psychological testing of borderlines has attracted significant attention in this regard. Singer asserted that the test records of borderlines demonstrate significant deterioration of thinking (revealed through a predominance of fabulized combination special scores). She asserted further that good performance on the "structured" WAIS and poor performance on the "less structured" Rorschach is "almost axiomatic" in the diagnosis of borderline psychopathology (1977, p. 194). Singer asserted, further, that Rorschach protocols of borderline individuals are "more openly filled with primary process associations" and "schizophrenic thinking" than are the Rorschach records of most schizophrenics (pp. 193–194). The seasoned Rorschach examiner, especially in the inpatient psychiatric setting, cannot help but validate the observation that borderline individuals demonstrate highly disturbed or florid records.

Observations about the role of structure in testing borderline patients have been subject to considerable debate and attempts at replication (Carr, Goldstein, Hunt, & Kernberg, 1979; Forer, 1950; Weiner, 1966; Zucker, 1952), including a well-reasoned review by Widiger (1982) that criticizes these assertions as being without empirical support. M. Berg's excellent review of borderline psychopathology on psychological tests (1983) notes that the absence of disturbed thinking on the WAIS or WAIS–R may be an artifact "of the typical practice of summarizing intelligence test responses to comply with the narrow space on the test forms, in contrast to the verbatim records made during projective testing," (p. 121) a point that bears consideration.

As an aid to diagnosis and means to test Kernberg's hypothesis that "low level" defenses characterize the functioning of borderline individuals in comparison to neurotics, P. Lerner and H. Lerner (1980) developed a scoring manual for borderline defenses. Human content (*H*) responses are scored for splitting, devaluation, idealization, projective identification, and denial. Preliminary findings for reliability and discriminability have been good.

Cooper, Perry, and Arnow (1988) developed a scoring manual for Rorschach defense scales across three broad categories: Neurotic (denial, intellectualization, isolation, reaction formation, repression, rationalization, and pollyannish denial), Borderline (splitting, primitive idealization, devaluation, omnipotence, projective identification, and projection), and Psychotic (massive denial and hypomanic denial). Suitable levels of interrater reliability have been obtained for the borderline defenses, and the scales have demonstrated preliminary validity.

Building on Mahler's (1971) theoretical notions of separation–individuation as important etiological factors in borderline psychopathology, Kwawer (1980) proposed a scoring system for Rorschach content that focuses on boundary disturbance and symbiotic modes of relatedness. In this framework, Rorschach percepts are scored for engulfment, symbiotic merging, violent symbiosis, separation and union, malignant internal processes, birth and rebirth, metamorphosis and transformation, narcissistic mirroring, separation–division, boundary disturbance, and womb imagery.

A series of studies by Gacono, Meloy, and their colleagues have demonstrated the robustness of the P. Lerner and H. Lerner, Kwawer, and Cooper, Perry, and Arnow scales in discriminating levels of character pathology (Gacono, 1990; Gacono & Meloy, 1991; Gacono, Meloy, & J. L. Berg, 1992; Gacono, Meloy, & Heaven, 1990).

Consideration of the borderline diagnosis cannot be complete without reference to emerging data that link borderline conditions to sex abuse trauma. Recent studies have demonstrated a high incidence of sex abuse histories in individuals carrying the borderline diagnosis (Brown & Anderson, 1991; Bryer, Nelson, Miller, & Krol, 1987; Herman, Perry, & van der Kolk, 1989; Ludolph et al., 1990; Ogata, Silk, Goodrich, Lohr, Westen, & Hill, 1990). Individuals with histories of sexual abuse present with posttraumatic symptoms (intrusive phenomena, nightmares, sensory numbing), disturbances in affect regulation and expression, dissociative control of awareness, identity disturbance (impaired self-concept and self-reference), and problems in tension reduction, often associated with substance abuse, sexual acting-out, and self-mutilation (J. Briere, notes from Sexual Abuse Trauma Workshop, Honolulu, HI, May 7, 1992; Cole & Putnam, 1992). The overlap between these clinical features and the clinical history and presentation of borderline personalities is now well recognized (Landecker, 1992), and as further studies of the overlap emerge, questions of etiology are likely to undergo rapid and perhaps dramatic change.

Given these considerations, what then can the diagnostician expect in viewing the Rorschach of a borderline individual? The first question is what kind of "borderline" are we talking about? Broadly speaking, one would anticipate a protocol that reflects ego weakness, general instability of psychic functioning, and easily provoked regression. The borderline Rorschach is typically, but not always, raw in content, in both affective and content spheres; it also offers a mixture of human percepts ranging from cooperative to malevolent. It demonstrates the following: a wide and unstable range of functioning, including rapid deterioration and recovery; loss of distance from the blots; and well-developed but malevolent representations of humans, including primitive relational modes. It yields structural data that reveal labile emotionality (in the case of the emotionally unstable borderline); poor stress tolerance; high percentage of unusual over minus form quality; boundary disturbance without the sort of arbitrary distortion observed in overtly psychotic records (e.g., fabulized combinations over contaminations); and primitive defensive operations focused on splitting, including devaluation and projective identification. Test-taking behaviors may, but do not always, demonstrate the borderline patient's problems in dealing with unstructured situations, where their own lack of internalized structure infiltrates the ambiguity of the test situation (Arnow & Cooper, 1984). Characteristic storminess and regression and problems with the inquiry may be noted.

The Rorschach is unable to clarify the definitional issues related to the borderline diagnosis, likely an impossible task given the heterogeneity of the patient population and theoretical points of departure. Nevertheless, when used in a manner that integrates empirically based nomothetic and theory-saturated idiographic analysis (Acklin, 1992), the test is unparalleled in graphically assessing and displaying the underlying structural, affective, and representational features of the borderline's inner world. Despite the controversies and unanswered questions surrounding the borderline diagnosis, the Rorschach's unique role and value in elucidating borderline dynamics assures its pre-eminent place in the diagnostician's tool box.

ACKNOWLEDGMENTS

This chapter was the introduction to the symposium entitled "Borderline Personality Organization: Through the Looking Glass II," presented at the Midwinter Meeting of the Society for Personality Assessment in Washington, DC, on March 14, 1992.

Special thanks to Dr. Charles A. Peterson for his continuing support and inspiration.

REFERENCES

Acklin, M. W. (1992). Psychodiagnosis of personality structure: Psychotic personality organization. *Journal of Personality Assessment, 58*, 454–463.

Akiskal, H. G., Chen, S., Davis, G. C., Puzantian, V. R., Kashgarian, M., & Bolinger, J. (1984). Borderline: An adjective in search of a noun. *Journal of Clinical Psychiatry*, 1138–1142.

Akiskal, H. G., Djenderedjian, A. H., Rosenthal, T., & Khani, M. K. (1977). Cyclothymic disorder: Validating criteria for inclusion in the bipolar affective group. *American Journal of Psychiatry, 134*, 1227–1233.

American Psychiatric Association. (1987). *Diagnostic and statistical manual* (3rd ed., rev.). Washington, DC: Author.

Arnow, D., & Cooper, S. H. (1984). The borderline patient's regression on the Rorschach test. *Bulletin of the Menninger Clinic, 48,* 25–36.

Berg, M. (1983). Borderline psychopathology as displayed on psychological tests. *Journal of Personality Assessment, 47,* 120–133.

Brown, G. R., & Anderson, B. (1991). Psychiatric morbidity in adult inpatients with childhood histories of sexual and physical abuse. *American Journal of Psychiatry, 148,* 55–61.

Bryer, J. B., Nelson, B. A., Miller, J. B., & Krol, P. A. (1987). Childhood sexual abuse and physical abuse as factors in adult psychiatric illness. *American Journal of Psychiatry, 144,* 1426–1430.

Bychowski, G. (1953). The problem of latent psychosis. *Journal of the American Psychoanalytic Association, 4,* 484–503.

Carr, A. C., Goldstein, E. G., Hunt, H., & Kernberg, O. (1979). Psychological tests and borderline patients. *Journal of Personality Assessment, 43,* 582–590.

Cole, P. M., & Putnam, F. W. (1992). Effects of incest on self and social functioning: A developmental psychopathology perspective. *Journal of Consulting and Clinical Psychology, 60,* 174–184.

Cooper, S. H., Perry, J. C., & Arnow, D. (1988). An empirical approach to the study of defense mechanisms: I. Reliability and preliminary validity of the Rorschach defense scales. *Journal of Personality Assessment, 52,* 187–203.

Exner, J. E. (1986). Some Rorschach data comparing schizophrenics with borderline and schizotypal personality disorders. *Journal of Personality Assessment, 50,* 455–471.

Forer, B. R. (1950). The latency of latent schizophrenia. *Journal of Projective Techniques, 14,* 297–320.

Freud, A. (1965). *Normality and pathology in childhood.* New York: International Universities Press.

Gacono, C. (1990). An empirical study of object relations and defensive operations in antisocial personality disorder. *Journal of Personality Assessment, 54,* 589–600.

Gacono, C., & Meloy, J. (1991). A Rorschach investigation of attachment and anxiety in antisocial personality disorder. *Journal of Nervous and Mental Disease, 179,* 546–552.

Gacono, C. B., Meloy, J., & Berg, J. L. (1992). Object relations, defensive operations, and affective states in narcissistic, borderline, and antisocial personality disorder. *Journal of Personality Assessment, 59,* 32–49.

Gacono, C., Meloy, J., & Heaven, T. (1990). A Rorschach investigation of narcissism and hysteria in antisocial personality disorder. *Journal of Personality Assessment, 55,* 270–279.

Gartner, J., Hurt, S., & Gartner, A. (1989). Psychological test signs of borderline personality disorder: A review of the empirical literature. *Journal of Personality Assessment, 53,* 423–441.

Grinker, R. R., Werble, B., & Drye, R. C. (1968). *The borderline syndrome.* New York: Basic Books.

Gunderson, J. G. (1978). Discriminating features of borderline patients. *American Journal of Psychiatry, 135,* 792–796.

Gunderson, J. G., & Singer, M. T. (1975). Defining borderline patients: An overview. *American Journal of Psychiatry, 132,* 1–10.

Herman, J. L., Perry, J. C., & van der Kolk, B.A. (1989). Childhood trauma in borderline personality disorder. *American Journal of Psychiatry, 146,* 490–495.

Hoch, P. H., & Polatin, P. (1949). Pseudoneurotic forms of schizophrenia. *Psychiatric Quarterly, 23,* 248–276.

Jacobson, E. (1953). Contribution to the metapsychology of cyclothymic depression. In P. Greenacre (Ed.), *Affective disorders* (pp. 49–83). New York: International Universities Press.

Kernberg, O. (1967). Borderline personality organization. *Journal of the American Psychoanalytic Association, 15,* 641–685.

Kernberg, O. (1975). *Borderline conditions and pathological narcissism.* New York: Aronson.

Kernberg, O. (1976). *Object relations and clinical psychoanalysis.* New York: Aronson.

Kernberg, O. (1980). Neurosis, psychosis, and the borderline states. In A. M. Freedman, H. I. Kaplan, & B. J. Sadock (Eds.), *Comprehensive textbook of psychiatry* (Vol. III). Baltimore: Williams & Wilkins.

Kernberg, O. (1984). *Severe personality disorders: Psychotherapeutic strategies.* New Haven: Yale University Press.

Kety, S. S. (1985). Schizotypal personality disorder: An operationalization of Bleuler's latent schizophrenia? *Schizophrenia Bulletin, 11,* 590–594.

Kety, S. S., Rosenthal, D., Wender, P. H., & Schulsinger, F. (1968). Mental illness in the biological and adoptive families of adopted schizophrenics. In D. Rosenthal & S. Kety (Eds.), *Transmission of schizophrenia* (pp. 345–362). Oxford: Pergamon.

Klein, D. F. (1977). Psychopharmacological treatment and delineation of borderline disorders. In P. Hartocollis (Ed.), *Borderline personality disorders* (pp. 365–383). New York: International Universities Press.

Knight, R. P. (1953). Borderline states. *Bulletin of the Menninger Clinic, 17,* 1–12.

Knight, R. (1954). Management and psychotherapy of the borderline schizophrenic patient. In R. P. Knight & C. R. Friedman (Eds.), *Psychoanalytic psychiatry and psychology* (pp. 110–122). New York: International Universities Press.

Kraepelin, E. (1980). Psychiatria: Ein Lehrbuch fur Studierende und Aertze. In M. Stone (Ed.), *The borderline syndromes: Constitution, personality, and adaptation.* New York: McGraw-Hill.

Kwawer, J. S. (1980). Primitive interpersonal modes, borderline phenomena, and Rorschach content. In J. Kwawer, H. Lerner, P. Lerner, & A. Sugarman (Eds.), *Borderline phenomena and the Rorschach test* (pp. 89–105). New York: International Universities Press.

Landecker, H. (1992). The role of childhood sexual trauma in the etiology of borderline personality disorder: Considerations for diagnosis and treatment. *Psychotherapy: Theory, Research, Practice, and Training, 29,* 234–242.

Lerner, P., & Lerner, H. (1980). Rorschach assessment of primitive defenses in borderline personality structure. In J. Kwawer, H. Lerner, P. Lerner, & A. Sugarman (Eds.), *Borderline phenomena and the Rorschach test* (pp. 257–274). New York: International Universities Press.

Lerner, H., & St. Peter, S. (1984). Patterns of object relations in neurotic, borderline, and schizophrenic patients. *Psychiatry, 47,* 77–92.

Ludolph, P., Westen, D., Misle, B., Jackson, A., Wixom, J., & Wiss, C. (1990). The borderline diagnosis in adolescents: Symptoms and developmental history. *American Journal of Psychiatry, 147,* 470–476.

Mahler, M. (1971). A study of the separation–individuation process. *The psychoanalytic study of the child,* 403–424.

Millon, T. (1981). *Disorders of personality DSM III: Axis II.* New York: Wiley.

Murray, J. F. (1993). The Rorschach search for the borderline Holy Grail: An examination of personality structure, personality style, and situation. *Journal of Personality Assessment, 61,* 342–357.

Ogata, S. N., Silk, K. R., Goodrich, S., Lohr, N., Westen, D., & Hill, E. M. (1990). Childhood sexual and physical abuse in adult patients with borderline personality. *American Journal of Psychiatry, 147,* 1008–1013.

Perry, C., & Klerman, G. (1978). The borderline patient: A comparative analysis of four sets of diagnostic criteria. *Archives of General Psychiatry, 35,* 141–149.

Rapaport, D., Gill, M., & Schafer, R. (1945/1946). *Diagnostic psychological testing* (Vols. 1–2). Chicago: Year Book Publishers.

Rorschach, H. (1942). *Psychodiagnostics* (5th ed.). Bern: Huber. (Original work published 1921)

Schmideberg, M. (1947). The treatment of psychopaths and borderline patients. *American Journal of Psychotherapy, 1,* 145–155.

Schmideberg, M. (1959). The borderline patient. In S. Arieti (Ed.), *American handbook of psychiatry* (Vol. 1, pp. 398–416). New York: Basic Books.

Schneider, K. (1980). Clinical psychopathology. In M. W. Stone (Ed. & Trans.), *The borderline syndromes: Constitution, personality, and adaptation.* New York: McGraw-Hill.

Singer, M. (1977). The borderline diagnosis and psychological tests: Review and research. In P. Hartocollis (Ed.), *Borderline personality disorders* (pp. 193–212). New York: International Universities Press.

Singer, M. T., & Larson, D. (1981). Borderline personality and the Rorschach test. *Archives of General Psychiatry, 38,* 693–698.

Spitzer, R., Endicott, J., & Gibbon, M. (1979). Crossing the border into borderline personality and borderline schizophrenia. *Archives of General Psychiatry, 36,* 17–24.

Stern, A. (1938). Psychoanalytic investigation of and therapy in the borderline group of neuroses. *Psychoanalytic Quarterly, 7,* 467–489.

Stone, M. (1980). *The borderline syndromes: Constitution, personality, and adaptation.* New York: McGraw-Hill.

Stuart, J., Westen, D., Lohr, D., Silk, K. R., Becker, S., Vorus, N., & Benjamin, J. (1990). Object relations in borderlines, major depressives, and normals: Analysis of Rorschach human responses. *Journal of Personality Assessment, 55,* 661–693.

Sugarman, A. (1980). The borderline personality organization as manifested on psychological tests. In J. Kwawer, H. Lerner, P. Lerner, & A. Sugarman (Eds.), *Borderline phenomena and the Rorschach test* (pp. 39–57). New York: International Universities Press.

Weiner, I. (1966). *Psychodiagnosis in schizophrenia.* New York: Wiley.

Westen, D., Ludolph, P., Misle, B., Ruffins, S., & Block, J. (1990). Physical and sexual abuse in adolescent girls with borderline personality disorder. *American Journal of Orthopsychiatry, 60,* 55–66.

Widiger, T. A. (1982). Psychological tests and the borderline diagnosis. *Journal of Personality Assessment, 46,* 227–238.

Widiger, T., & Francis, A. (1985). Axis II personality disorders: Diagnostic and treatment issues. *Hospital and Community Psychiatry, 36,* 619–627.

Zilboorg, G. (1941). Ambulatory schizophrenia. *Psychiatry, 4,* 149–155.

Zucker, L. J. (1952). The psychology of latent schizophrenia: Based on Rorschach studies. *American Journal of Psychotherapy, 6,* 44–62.

9

The Rorschach Search for the Borderline Holy Grail: An Examination of Personality Structure, Personality Style, and Situation

James F. Murray
Knoxville, TN

The renaissance of the Rorschach starting in the 1970s and continuing through the present has been widely noted, enjoyed, and applauded (Blatt, 1986; Sugarman, 1991; Weiner, 1983). The major factor in the rebirth of the Rorschach has rightly been attributed to Exner's (1974, 1986) work in the development of the Comprehensive System. Yet another spur to the re-emergence of the Rorschach in the 1970s and 1980s was the intense interest in the diagnosis, understanding, and treatment of borderline psychopathology.

Even with some of the earliest diagnostic prescriptions, for example, Singer's (1977) simplistic "good WAIS/bad Rorschach" formulation, the Rorschach was seen as being uniquely capable of reaching the inner world and primitive pathology of the borderline. And thus began the search for the Rorschach borderline holy grail: the set of variables, defense configurations, object representations, or object relational patterns that would definitively identify the borderline once and for all. The search has been fascinating, and in terms of helping us to understand aspects of both the Rorschach and borderline psychopathology, quite productive. But no holy grail has been found; no definitive borderline Rorschach profile has emerged. Now we could probably take refuge in discussions of sample criteria and the problems of reliable diagnosis of borderline states independent of the Rorschach (both realistic and valid points). However, it may also be that we have viewed the diagnosis of borderline pathology in too simplistic a fashion. The nature of borderline psychopathology may be far more complex and interactive than we have allowed for in our present conceptualizations. The Rorschachs of borderlines may confusingly, but potentially fortuitously, reflect that complexity.

As Acklin (1992) pointed out, psychodiagnosis has come to focus on two basic levels of analysis: a structural diagnosis involving identification of a level of personality organization, and a stylistic dimension, identifying preferred patterns of cognition, affect experience and expression, and defense processes. The manner in which these two factors are organized and viewed as interacting ranges from the chaos of the *Diagnostic and Statistical Manual of Mental Disorders'* (3rd ed., rev. [*DSM–III–R*]; American Psychiatric Association, 1987) Chinese menu approach (in which you get one from Axis I and one from Axis II) to the rather elegant work of Stone (1980), who created a diagnostic matrix in which a large number of character styles cut across the neurotic, borderline, and psychotic levels of personality organization. What is apparent from these approaches, and from the work of Kernberg (1975, 1976), is that the borderline diagnostic category has utility only to the extent that one recognizes that it represents a level of personality organization or a broad type of personality structure within which fit a variety of symptom pictures, personality styles, and characteristic patterns of defense. When the borderline diagnostic category is viewed in this fashion, one can begin to see that it is unrealistic to believe that such a diverse group of patients would present with any specific or particular type of Rorschach pattern—despite their having a common level of personality organization. If the Rorschach can assess with any depth or sophistication, it must surely measure or reflect aspects of personality structure or organization, personality style, and situational variables. Those searching for the Rorschach borderline holy grail have failed to consider the potential complexities when diversities within these three factors interact and influence each other.

This chapter attempts to examine how these three factors—personality structure, personality style, and situational variables—appear on the Rorschach. It attempts to explore (admittedly tentatively) how these factors interact and influence each other. To this end, two Rorschachs from a borderline patient will be compared. The first was administered at the beginning of treatment, and the second was administered approximately 4 years into treatment. It is hypothesized that structural elements change slowly and that, for a borderline, even 4 years of treatment can be a relatively brief period of time. Thus, structural elements would not be expected to change extensively over the two testings.

In successful psychotherapy of the borderline, the elements most likely to reflect change, at least initially, are those associated with personality style (cognitive style, affective control and experience, defensive orientation and flexibility) and aspects of the manner in which personality style interacts with structural factors. Thus stylistic factors would be expected to manifest the most change in the initial stages of treatment.

Situational factors are traditionally viewed as the Rorschach variables most likely to vary over time, and this view has been well supported by Exner and Weiner's (1982) work on retest correlations over brief and long-term intervals.

This research has identified inanimate movement (*m*) and diffuse shading (*Y*) as reflecting situational stressors and, therefore, prone to being highly unstable (in terms of reliability) because of the extent to which environmental stressors are relatively transient. However, this view may get somewhat more complicated for a borderline patient because borderlines are frequently described as being intolerant, reactive, or unusually vulnerable to even relatively minor stressors (Kernberg, 1975). Consistent "transient" or "situational" stress may be present in a borderline Rorschach and reflect not so much the presence of transient external stressors per se, but rather a long-term structural defect in anxiety tolerance or defensive functioning.

PATIENT HISTORY

The patient was 37 years of age at the time of the first testing and 41 at the second testing. She is a mental health professional who has an undergraduate degree and some graduate training. She was married for approximately 16 years at the time of the first testing and was divorced approximately 2 years at the time of the second. She is the mother of three children who were of junior high and high school age at the time of the second testing.

She described herself as having been disabled by anxiety attacks since she was a young child. At the time of her first testing she described multiple phobic symptoms, many of which involved medication and food. She became particularly panicked at the time of the Tylenol poisoning scare and was often fearful that her food was contaminated. To protect against poisoning she would have family members eat first in a manner that reminded the initial examiner of Oriental food tasters. She was hospitalized for 2 weeks some 3 years prior to the initial testing, ostensibly for diagnostic purposes. She has received various medications for anxiety and depression, reportedly with little or no success. Intellectual assessment with the Wechsler Adult Intelligence Scale–Revised revealed a Verbal Scale IQ Score of 117, a Performance Scale IQ Score of 98, and a Full Scale IQ Score of 108.

At the second testing the patient reported, and her therapist confirmed, a substantial diminution in overt anxiety symptomatology. She attributed this to her divorce and her work with her female therapist. She remained unemployed but was taking graduate coursework in a fairly sporadic fashion. Both therapist and patient were pleased with the course and progress made in treatment, and requested testing to assess progress and to offer recommendations regarding the necessity for and/or course of future treatment efforts. Therapy was generally supportive in nature, and the patient seemed to be wondering whether the decline in anxiety indicated that treatment had been completed.

RORSCHACH ANALYSIS

Weiner and Exner (1991) developed a series of Rorschach measures reflecting clusters of psychopathology and then explored changes in these measures over the course of long- and short-term psychotherapies. They found that both long- and short-term treatments could produce positive changes as assessed by Rorschach measures, but that long-term treatment resulted in changes in a larger number of variables, these changes tended to hold over time more than those of short-term treatment patients, and the type of variables changing seemed to reflect greater depth of change. This article employs the Weiner and Exner Rorschach variable clusters to assess changes in the Rorschach of the borderline individual just described over the course of treatment (see Appendices A, B, C, & D).

It is important to note that the application of the Weiner and Exner variables to a single case restricts this Rorschach analysis to structural data and does not allow for the careful examination of Rorschach content that can help "flesh out" the analysis of a clinical case. However, this approach does allow for an exploration of structural dynamics and changes, and a comparison of the changes made by this patient and by the Weiner and Exner patients.

Stress

The first item in the Stress cluster is the $D < 0$ item. As can be seen from Table 9.1, the change from the first to the second testing is in the direction of an apparent increase in pathology with the marker being absent in the first testing ($D = 0$) and present in the second ($D = -3$). This change stems from a moderate decrease in EA (from 6 to 4) and, to a much greater extent, from a major increase in es (from 5 to 13). To understand this change, one must examine the components of es to assess the source or nature of the increase in "stress". FM has gone from 2 to 5, V has gone from 1 to 3, and T has gone from 2 to 4. Also important to note is that m and Y (reflecting situational stress) are relatively unchanged from the first to the second testing. This factor is reflected in the second Stress variable ($Adj\ D < 0$) as $Adj\ D$ is D with situational stressor variables (m and Y) removed. Taken together, the $Adj\ D$ and D scores indicate that at the time of the second testing the patient is experiencing significant—perhaps even intense or overwhelming—overt distress, but that this increase in stress is not the result of situational or externally based stress.

Looking at the third variable in the cluster ($EA < 7$), one can get some sense of why she is in distress or prone to being distressed. Her EA score is in the pathological range in both testings, reflecting a fairly chronic deficit in organized or mature personality resources. However, as was mentioned previously, the relatively minor decline in EA from the first to the second testing is insufficient to account for the difficulties in stress reflected in the $Adj\ D$ score of -3. What the Stress cluster variables strongly suggest is that at the time of the second testing the patient is experiencing an increase in stress due to internal stressors rather than external or situational factors.

One possible speculation is that the patient previously discharged internal stressors through primitive defensive processes associated with her phobic symptomatology (her concerns about poisoning) and through somatization (she had a history of vague or peculiar physical complaints and saw a series of physicians with no real diagnostic conclusions). It is possible that this patient's distress (principally pan anxiety, depression, and an intense sense of object loss or object hunger) has gone from being discharged through more primitive realms (phobic and somatic) to more psychological realms (a more subjectively experienced depression, and a greater involvement with people—albeit a distant, peculiar, and conflictual involvement).

The final Stress cluster variable—CDI—is not present as a pathological marker for either testing. The absence of a positive CDI along with a positive *Adj D* suggests that this patient's vulnerability to loss of control tends to be restricted to situations that are unstructured and ambiguous. She is likely to function fairly effectively in situations that are familiar, routine, or well defined.

Thus, with regard to issues of stress and control, the following conclusions are warranted:

1. The patient has become more overtly and subjectively distressed as the result of treatment and more vulnerable to loss of control or impulsive action, but in examining her history, this increase in stress and vulnerability to control problems may be a trade-off for a reduction in primitive phobic and somaticizing symptomatology.

2. Although stress tolerance and control are limited, she is probably able to function reasonably effectively in structured or familiar settings.

In terms of character structure versus character style issues, these results suggest the following:

1. The patient has a structurally based deficit in handling anxiety. Previously, anxiety resulted in phobic, perhaps quasi-delusional behavior. Currently, anxiety results in vulnerability to loss of control.

2. Rorschach results reveal prominent hysteroid stylistic defenses and suggest that over the course of treatment there have been character style shifts along the hysteroid dimension from a very primitive quasi-phobic/paranoid somatization to a somewhat more advanced affectively/impulsively labile acting out.

3. There is some evidence of character style changes, but when the data are interpreted in this fashion, one has to jump through some hoops to explain why what looks on the surface like a worse Rorschach some 4 years into treatment might actually signify progress.

Difficulty Dealing With Experience

The first variable in this cluster is the Ambitent measure. This factor is positive when the two sides of the $M : Sum\ C$ ratio are roughly equivalent, and its

TABLE 9.1
Rorschach Measures in First and Second Testing: Rorschach Measures of Personality
Characteristics Related to Changes in Psychotherapy

Characteristic		First Test	Second Test
Stress			
1. $D < 0$	Subjectively felt stress resulting from inadequate resources to meet experienced demands	$D = 0$ –	$D = -3$ +
2. Adj $D = -3$	Persistently felt distress extending beyond transient or situational difficulties in meeting demands	$Adj\ D = 0$ –	$Adj\ D = -3$ +
3. $EA < 7$	Limited resources for implementing deliberate problem-solving strategies	$EA = 6$ +	$EA = 4$ +
4. $CDI > 3$	General deficit in capacities for coping with demands of daily living	$CDI = 3$ –	$CDI = 3$ –
Difficulty dealing effectively with lack of experience			
1. Ambitent	Lack of commitment to a cohesive coping style resulting in a sense of uncertainty	$EB = 3{:}3$ +	$EB = 2{:}2$ +
2. $Zd < -3.0$	Inattention to nuances of one's experience, superficial scanning, hastily drawn conclusions	$Zd = -10.5$ +	$Zd = +2.0$ –
3. Lambda $> .99$	Narrow, limited frames of reference, overly simplistic response	$L = 1.13$ +	$L = .73$ –
4. $X+\% < 70$	Inability/disinclination to perceive objects and events as most people would	$X+\% = .53$ +	$X+\% = .47$ +
5. $X-\% > 20$	Inaccurate perception and faulty anticipation of consequences	$X-\% = .29$ +	$X-\% = .32$ +
Problems with experience of self			
1. $Fr + Rf > 0$	Narcissistic glorification and externalization of blame	$r = 0$ –	$r = 0$ –
2. $3r + (2)/R < .33$	Low regard for self in comparison with others	.35	.47
3. $3r + (2)/R > .43$	Excessive self-focusing and self-preoccupation	–	+
4. $FD > 2$	Unusual extent of introspection	$FD = 0$ –	$FD = 1$
Comfort in interpersonal relations			
1. $p > a + 1$	Passivity and avoidance of initiative and responsibility	$a{:}p$ 4:2 –	$a{:}p$ 5:3 –
2. $T = 0$	Lack of expectation or seeking of close, intimate, nurturant, mutually supportive relationships	$T = 2$ –	$T = 4$ –
3. $T > 1$	Unmet needs for closeness and comfort leading to feelings of loneliness and deprivation	+	+
4. Pure $H < 2$	Disinterest in and/or difficulty identifying with others	$H = 1$ +	$H = 2$ –
5. $H < [(H) + Hd + (Hd)]$	Uneasiness in relatedness with real, live, fully functional people	1:3 +	2:5 +

(continued)

TABLE 9.1 (Continued)

Problems in modulating affect pleasurably and sufficiently

1. SumSh > FM + m	Negative emotional experience; dysphoria, loneliness	3:2 +	7:6 +
2. DEPI = 5	Depressive concerns	DEPI = 6 +	DEPI = 6 +
3. DEPI > 5	Likelihood of diagnosable depressive disorder	+	+
4. Afr < .50	Avoidance of emotional interchange and lack of involvement in affect-laden situations	Afr = .70 –	Afr = .58 –
5. CF + C > FC + 1	Overly intense feelings and unreserved expression of affect	1:5 –	2:1 +

Ideational difficulties

1. Sum6 Sp Sc > 6	Loose and arbitrary thinking	Sum6 = 9 +	Sum6 = 8 +
2. M– > 0	Strange conceptions regarding human experience	M– = 2 +	M– = 1 +
3. Mp > Ma	Excessive escapist fantasy substituted for constructive planning	1:3 –	0:2 –
4. Intellect > 5	Excessive reliance on intellectualization	Intel = 11 +	Intel = 11 +

Note. + signifies presence of variable at pathological level. – signifies absence of variable at

presence reflects difficulty establishing a preferred and elaborated style of coping. The patient is positive as an ambitent on both testings.

Exner's (1978) research indicates that compared to individuals weighted to one side or the other on the ratio, ambitents show less progress in treatment and display the highest frequency of return to therapy. As one continues through this patient's Rorschach, it becomes apparent that she employs a mixture of defensive styles. Hysteroid affective lability and a tendency to externalize/somaticize are combined with introtensive/pseudo-obsessive defenses (as seen in the Vista responses and the elevated Intellectualization Index). One could hypothesize that this represents a pan-defensive orientation that prevents the patient from developing a consistent, mature, and elaborated defensive orientation that would allow for more successful functioning. This pan-defensive orientation (as manifested in the variety of primitive defenses employed and in her ambitent status) is reminiscent of the early descriptions of borderlines as pseudoneurotic or pan-neurotic in their defensive make-up (Hoch & Polatin, 1949).

Continuing in this cluster, one arrives at the *Zd* and *Lambda (L)* variables. Probably the most substantive changes in this patient's Rorschach occur in these two measures. The positive marking for *Zd* at the first testing indicates quite clearly that at the initial testing she was an "underincorporator" and tended to neglect critical bits of information when arriving at judgments. In this case this probably reflects a reliance on defenses involving more simplistic or blatant forms of denial. Similarly, *Lambda* is positive in the first testing and not present at a pathological level in the second. A high *Lambda* reflects a tendency to ignore or neglect the complexities of experience, again revealing a reliance on denial or avoidance and a tendency toward impulsive, simplistic solutions.

These positive changes in *Zd* and *Lambda* appear to be the most significant effects of treatment. Although *Zd* and *Lambda* do not signify this in all cases, in this case these two factors signal a reliance on primitive modes of defense involving the use of denial and splitting. These defenses are fundamental to the more severe forms of character pathology present at the borderline level of personality organization (Kernberg, 1975). These more primitive defenses probably supported her somatization and phobic defenses because these latter defenses would require blatant denial and splitting off of impulses, affects, and aspects of cognition. The primitive role of these defenses is reflected in their power to severely bend or distort reality testing. It is apparent from the other two measures in this cluster ($X+\%$ and $X-\%$) that impairments in reality testing were present in the first testing and persist to the second. Although these ongoing impairments in reality testing make it difficult to argue that improvements in *Zd* and *Lambda* indicate that she no longer employs primitive defenses involving splitting and denial, these improvements do suggest that she has plugged in somewhat more flexible and adaptive defenses (probably involving rationalization and intellectualization). However, the more blatant and primitive cognitive denial and splitting necessary to allow for her previous somatic and phobic symptomatology may well have been relinquished.

Problems With Experience of Self

The patient displays relatively little pathology in this cluster category. She has no reflection responses (*r*), suggesting that she manifests no severe or overt narcissistic difficulties at either of the two testings. The Egocentricity Index is negative in the first testing and positive in the second. This elevation reflects an increased attention to the self, and, given her capacity for denial, externalization, and somatization, this is probably not a bad thing. There is further support for this from the fourth measure in this cluster: the form dimension (*FD*) response. The presence of one *FD* response in the second testing (after having none in the first) supports the hypothesis that she is more capable of focusing on herself in a potentially productive fashion.

Interpersonal Relations

The first two markers in this cluster are not noteworthy because they are not in the pathological range for either of the two testings. The third variable reflecting Texture responses greater than one ($T > 1$) is of note. This variable is positive on both testings and furthermore, there is a significant increase in T from the first testing to the second (from 2 to 4). Clearly this is a person chronically object-hungry and highly sensitive to loss, despite her conflicts and ambivalances in relationships. A reasonable speculation would be that this increase in T in the second testing represents a shift from her somatic/phobic position to a more overt and subjectively experienced depression: at least in the form of increased loneliness, neediness, as well as an increased awareness of or sensitivity to loss. This hypothesis is supported by the fourth variable in this cluster. She goes from having a single pure Human response (H) in the first testing (in the pathological range) to having two Hs in the second testing (outside the pathological range). This shift suggests that she is more interpersonally involved, with increased interest in and identification with people. However, the fifth item in this cluster ($H < [(H) + Hd + (Hd)]$) indicates that she continues to have difficulty seeing whole, real people on the Rorschach, and consequently, she still tends to view others in very primitive terms that result in distorted perceptions and unrealistic expectations.

Problems Modulating Affect

Over both testings there is a significant level of dysphoria and anxiety. As seen in the first measure in this category (*Sum Shading* $> FM + m$), there is a significant increase in both sides of *eb* in the second testing—a not unexpected and almost certainly positive sign as she explores her inner world and past and confronts painful aspects of both.

In looking at components of this increase in *eb*, one finds the following:

1. a significant increase in FM
2. a slight increase in m
3. a significant increase in V
4. a significant increase in T

These results suggest increased ideational press or distress over issues of object loss or a very painful introspection, and probably reflect aspects of both an anaclitic and introjective depression.

The next two measures deal with the Depression Index (*DEPI*), and the results reflect an ongoing depression. In the first testing, the only *DEPI* item that was not positive was the Egocentricity Index/Reflection Response item. In the second testing, that item was positive, and only the item dealing with *Afr* or *Blends* was not positive. Clearly this is an individual with significant, long-standing depression.

The negative findings for Item 4 (*Afr* $< .50$) indicate that this is not a person who avoids emotionally charged situations. In fact the next variable ($CF + C > FC + 1$) suggests a change from a hypercontrol of affect to possible difficulty with containment of affect. Although this may, at present, be somewhat problematic for her in day-to-day functioning (and more likely problematic for those around her), this may well represent growth in that affect was previously bound up in somatic and phobic symptomatology. It is important to note that this measure reflects only two C*F*s.

Ideational Difficulties

Probably the most striking factor here is the lack of change: All variables in the category are virtually identical from the first testing to the second. As is seen in the first variable (*Sum 6 Sp Sc* > 6) she continues to display distorted, disorganized, or disturbed thinking and reasoning. One can analyze various scores to see if severity of disturbance has changed, but *WSum 6* = 21 in both cases, and she essentially trades a Level 2 *FAB* in the first testing for an *ALOG* in the second. There is nothing here to argue for a decrease in distorted thinking or reasoning.

The second item (*M*– > 0) is also positive over both testings. This indicates that she can still significantly distort or misinterpret the motives and actions of others. This has diminished somewhat with treatment, but it is still a concern.

One sees in the next measure (*Mp* > *Ma*) that she does not withdraw into fantasy, and it is apparent from the next measure (Intellectualization Index > 5) where she goes with her ideational defenses. With the Intellect Index this high and this consistent over time, it reflects a massive and pervasive reliance on intellectualization to deny or fend off distressing and conflictual experience. At this level the use of these defenses is almost certainly not an adaptive, sophisticated defensive effort, but rather a pseudointellectualization/rationalization that rigidly and blatantly denies affective experience (internal reality) as well as denying aspects of the external world (external reality). It is highly likely that this denial-based defense contributes to impaired reality testing and instances of peculiar or illogical reasoning. However, this reliance on an ideationally based defensive containment of disorganizing affective and impulsive experience may be the only containment or modulating defense to which she has ready access at the present time. These defenses are probably more adaptive than the denial-based defenses she used in the past that centered on phobic externalization and somatization. These findings suggest that a therapist would need to be somewhat circumspect in aggressively attacking or stripping away these defenses.

CONCLUSIONS

The preceding case analysis offers clinical support for the theoretical position that personality functioning (and the Rorschach as a measure of personality) can best be understood with an examination of personality structure, personality style, and situational influences. Situational variables are best identified through reliability studies involving test–retest correlations with nonclinical populations (Weiner & Exner, 1982). These variables reflect anxiety and relatively mild dysphoria. However, the situational nature of these factors can be somewhat obscured for the borderline patient, because borderlines tend to have fairly chronic levels of anxiety and dysphoric affective experience. Thus, these "situational" variables, when seen chronically in a patient, probably reflect underlying long-term or structural pathology involving difficulty in modulating or containing anxiety or affective experience, as well as a proclivity for conflictual interpersonal relations (cf. Kernberg, 1975, 1976). These variables may be truly situational only for those individuals that have the personality resources (i.e., the personality structure) to modulate or contain anxiety and affect consistently over time.

What about the identification of Rorschach variables reflecting personality structure and personality style? The results of this case analysis suggest that these variables may be identified through approaches similar to that of Weiner and Exner (1991). They found that, unlike long-term patients, short-term patients did not display changes in:

1. *Sum 6 Sp Sc* > 6
2. Intellectualization Index > 5
3. Egocentricity Index > .43
4. $T = 0$

In addition, they found that 4 years later the short-term group was substantially more likely to display:

1. $D < 0$
2. Ambitence (in *EB*)
3. $CF + C > FC + 1$
4. $M- > 0$
5. $X+\% < 70$
6. $T = 0$

With the exception of the $T = 0$ items, the borderline patient I have presented is positive on each of the variables listed after some 4 years of psychotherapy. So the question arises, what would a borderline patient some 4 years into a fairly supportive psychotherapy have in common with a variety of patients who have undergone a short-term psychotherapy? It strikes me that with both a 4-year supportive treatment of a borderline and short-term treatment of a variety of patients, one would not anticipate major change in aspects of personality structure or level of personality organization. Thus, one way of looking at the variables that did change for both Weiner and Exner's short-term group and this borderline patient is that these variables reflect nonstructural factors that are probably related to situational factors or aspects of character style. Similarly, one might tentatively identify the variables that were resistant to change in both the short-term treatment group and this borderline patient as reflecting structural factors, or at least stylistic factors closely related to character structure and thus resistant to change. When viewed in this vein, one can see why efforts to identify basic borderline signs or concrete patterns in the Rorschach have generally proved to be only marginally successful. The Rorschach is a complex instrument that reflects a complex interaction between level of personality structure (or level of personality organization), personality style, and situational factors. Efforts at oversimplification fail to do justice to the intricacies of the Rorschach and to the complexities of personality functioning. An approach is needed that allows for an understanding of the complex interaction of these factors as they are reflected in the Rorschach and, more importantly, as they are reflected in the patient.

REFERENCES

Acklin, M. (1992). Psychodiagnosis of personality structure: Psychotic personality organization. *Journal of Personality Assessment, 58*, 454–463.

American Psychiatric Association. (1987). *Diagnostic and statistical manual of mental disorders* (3rd ed., rev.). Washington, DC: Author.

Blatt, S. J. (1986). Where have we been and where are we going? Reflections on 50 years of personality assessment. *Journal of Personality Assessment, 50*, 343–346.

Exner, J. E. (1974). *The Rorschach: A comprehensive system. Vol. 1.* New York: Wiley.

Exner, J. E. (1978). *The Rorschach: A comprehensive system: Vol. 2. Recent research and advanced interpretation.* New York: Wiley.

Exner, J. E. (1986). *The Rorschach: A comprehensive system: Vol. 1. Basic foundations* (2nd ed.). New York: Wiley.

Exner, J. E., & Weiner, I. B. (1982). *The Rorschach: A comprehensive system: Vol. 3. Assessment of children and adolescents.* New York: Wiley.

Hoch, P. H., & Polatin, P. (1949). Pseudoneurotic forms of schizophrenia. *Psychiatric Quarterly, 23*, 248–276.

Kernberg, O. (1975). *Borderline conditions and pathological narcissism.* New York: Aronson.

Kernberg, O. (1976). *Object relations theory and clinical psychoanalysis.* New York: Aronson.

Singer, M. T. (1977). The borderline diagnosis and psychological tests: Review and research. In P. Hartocollis (Ed.), *Borderline personality disorders* (pp. 193–212). New York: International Universities Press.

Stone, M. (1980). *The borderline syndromes: Constitution, personality, and adaptation.* New York: McGraw-Hill.

Sugarman, A. (1991). Where's the beef? Putting personality back into personality assessment. *Journal of Personality Assessment, 56*, 130–144.

Weiner, I. B. (1983). The future of psychodiagnosis revisited. *Journal of Personality Assessment, 47*, 451–459.

Weiner, I. B., & Exner, J. E. (1991). Rorschach changes in long-term and short-term psychotherapy. *Journal of Personality Assessment, 56*, 453–465.

APPENDIX A
Sequence of Scores—First Testing

Card	No.	Loc.	#	Determinant(s)	(2)	Content(s)	Pop Z	Special Scores
I	1	Wo	1	Fo		An	1.0	
	2	Wo	1	Fo		A	1.0	MOR
II	3	Wo	1	FT.FC.Ma–		(Ad), Hx	4.5	AB, PER, INC, MOR
III	4	D+		Mao	2	H, Hh	P 3.0	AB, DV
IV	5	Wo	1	Fu–		(A), Hx	2.0	AB, DR, MOR
V	6	Wo	1	Fo		A	P 1.0	
	7	Wo	1	Fo		A	P 1.0	PSV
VI	8	Wo	1	Fu		A	2.5	
	9	Wo	1	FMp.FTo		(A)	2.5	DV, AB, MOR
VII	10	W+	1	Fo	2	(Hd), Art	P 2.5	
VIII	11	Do		Fo	2	A	P	PER
	12	Do		F–	2	An, Xy		PER
IX	13	Dd+		Ma–p.CF.VF–		Hx, Sx	2.5	AB, DV
X	14	Do		FCo	2	A	P	INC
	15	D+		FMau	2	(A), Sc	4.0	FAB2
	16	Do		FC–		Hd		INC
	17	Do		FC–		Hd		INC

135

APPENDIX B
Rorschach Structural Summary—First Testing

LOCATION FEATURES	DETERMINANTS BLENDS	SINGLE	CONTENTS	S-CONSTELLATION
			H = 1,0	NO..FV + VF + V + FD > 2
				YES..Col-Shd Bl>0
Zf = 12	FT.FC.M	M = 1	(H) = 0,0	NO..Ego<.31,>.44
ZSum = 27.5	FM.FT	FM = 1	Hd = 2,0	YES..MOR>3
ZEst = 38.0	M.CF.VF	m = 0	(Hd) = 1,0	YES..Zd > ± 3.5
		FC = 3	Hx = 1,2	NO..es>EA
W = 9		CF = 0	A = 6,0	NO..CF+C>FC
(Wv = 0)		C = 0	(A) = 3,0	YES..X+%<.70
D = 7		Cn = 0	Ad = 0,0	NO..S>3
Dd = 1		FC' = 0	(Ad) = 1,0	NO..P<3 or >8
S = 0		C'F = 0	An = 2,0	YES..Pure H <2
		C' = 0	Art = 0,1	NO..R<17

	DQ		
..........(FQ–)		
+ = 4 (1)		
o = 13(4)		
v/+ = 0 (0)		
v = 0 (0)		

FORM QUALITY				
	FQx	FQf	MQual	SQx
+	= 0	0	0	0
o	= 9	6	1	0
u	= 3	2	0	0
–	= 5	1	2	0
none	= 0	–	0	0

Single contents (continued):
FT = 0, TF = 0, T = 0, FV = 0, VF = 0, V = 0, FY = 0, YF = 0, Y = 0, Fr = 0, rF = 0, FD = 0, F = 9

Contents (continued):
Ay = 0,0, Bl = 0,0, Bt = 0,0, Cg = 0,0, Cl = 0,0, Ex = 0,0, Fd = 0,0, Fi = 0,0, Ge = 0,0, Hh = 0,1, Ls = 0,0, Na = 0,0, Sc = 0,1, Sx = 0,1, Xy = 0,1, Id = 0,0, (2) = 6

	5.....TOTAL		

SPECIAL SCORINGS			
	Lv1		Lv2
DV	= 3x1		0x2
INC	= 4x2		0x4
DR	= 1x3		0x6
FAB	= 0x4		1x7
ALOG	= 0x5		
CON	= 0x7		
SUM6	= 9		
WSUM6	= 21		
AB	=5	CP	= 0
AG	=0	MOR	= 4
CFB	=0	PER	= 3
COP	=0	PSV	= 1

RATIOS, PERCENTAGES, AND DERIVATIONS

R = 17	L = 1.13			FC:CF+C =4:1	COP = 0	AG =0
				Pure C =0	Food	= 0

EB = 3: 3.0	EA = 6.0	EBPer = N/A		Afr =0.70	Isolate/R	= 0.00
eb = 2:3	es = 5	D = 0		S =0	H:(H)Hd(Hd)	= 1:3
	Adj es = 5	Adj D = 0		Blends:R =3:17	(HHd):(AAd)	= 1:4
				CP =0	H+A:Hd + Ad	= 10:4

FM = 2	C' = 0	T = 2				
m = 0	V = 1	Y = 0				
			P = 6	Zf =12		3r+(2)/R = 0.35
a:p = 4:2	Sum6 =9		X+% = 0.53	Zd =–10.5		Fr+rF = 0
Ma:Mp = 3:1	Lv2 = 1		F+% = 0.67	W:D:Dd =9:7:1		FD = 0
2AB+Art+Ay = 11	WSum6 = 21		X–% = 0.29	W:M =9:3		An + Xy = 3
M– = 2	Mnone = 0		S–% = 0.00	DQ+ =4		MOR = 4
			Xu% = 0.18	DQv =0		

SCZI = 4*	DEPI = 6*	CDI = 3	S-CON = 5	HVI = No	OBS = No

Sequence of Scores—Second Testing

Card	No.	Loc.	#	Determinant(s)	(2)	Content(s)	Pop Z	Special Scores
I	1	Wo	1	Fo		A	P 1.0	DR
	2	W+	1	FMau	2	(A)	4.0	AG
II	3	WSo	1	FT.FMa.CF–		Ad	4.5	AB, AG, ALOG
	4	Do		FV.FMpu		A		PER
III	5	Do		Fo		H, Ay, Sx	P	
	6	Ddo		Fu	2	H, Ay		DR
	7	Do		FV–		A, (Hd), Ay		
IV	8	Wo	1	Fo		A	2.0	DV, INC, MOR
V	9	Wo	1	FMa.FDo		A	P 1.0	
VI	10	Wo	1	FMp.FT.FVo		(A)	P 2.5	MOR
VII	11	Do		Fo	2	Hd	P	
	12	W+	1	mpo	2	Art, Hd	P 2.5	
VIII	13	Do		Fo	2	A	P	
	14	DSo		CF–		An		INC
IX	15	Do		F–		(H), Hx		AB, DR
	16	DSo		TF.Ma–		A, Hx	5.0	INC
X	17	Do		FTo	2	A	P	
	18	D+		Mau	2	(A)	4.5	AB
	19	DdSo		F–		(Hd), Art	6.0	

APPENDIX D
Rorschach Structural Summary—Second Testing

LOCATION FEATURES	DETERMINANTS		CONTENTS	S-CONSTELLATION
	BLENDS	SINGLE		YES..FV + VF + V + FD > 2
			H = 2,0	YES..Col-Shd Bl>0
Zf = 10	FT.FM.CF	M = 1	(H) = 1,0	YES..Ego<.31,>.44
ZSum = 33.0	FV.FM	FM = 1	Hd = 1,1	NO..MOR>3
ZEst = 31.0	FM.FD	m = 1	(Hd) = 1,1	NO..Zd > ± 3.5
	FM.FT.FV	FC = 0	Hx = 0,2	YES..es>EA
W = 7	TF.M	CF = 1	A = 8,0	YES..CF+C>FC
(Wv = 0)		C = 0	(A) = 3,0	YES..X+%<.70
D = 10		Cn = 0	Ad = 1,0	YES..S>3
Dd = 2		FC' = 0	(Ad) = 0,0	NO..P<3 or >8
S = 4		C'F = 0	An = 1,0	NO..Pure H <2
		C' = 0	Art = 1,1	NO..R<17
DQ		FT = 1	Ay = 0,3	7.....TOTAL
.........(FQ–)		TF = 0	Bl = 0,0	
+ = 3 (0)		T = 0	Bt = 0,0	SPECIAL SCORINGS
o = 16(6)		FV = 1	Cg = 0,0	Lvl Lv2
v/+ = 0 (0)		VF = 0	Cl = 0,0	DV = 1x1 0x2
v = 0 (0)		V = 0	Ex = 0,0	INC = 3x2 0x4
		FY = 0	Fd = 0,0	DR = 3x3 0x6
		YF = 0	Fi = 0,0	FAB = 0x4 0x7
		Y = 0	Ge = 0,0	ALOG = 1x5
FORM QUALITY		Fr = 0	Hh = 0,0	CON = 0x7
		rF = 0	Ls = 0,0	SUM6 = 8
FQx FQf MQual SQx		FD = 0	Na = 0,0	WSUM6 = 21
+ = 0 0 0 0		F = 8	Sc = 0,0	
o = 9 5 0 0			Sx = 0,1	AB =3 CP = 0
u = 4 1 1 0			Xy = 0,0	AG =2 MOR = 2
– = 6 2 1 4			Id = 0,0	CFB =0 PER = 1
none = 0 – 0 0		(2) = 9		COP =0 PSV = 0

RATIOS, PERCENTAGES, AND DERIVATIONS			
R = 19 L = 0.73	FC:CF+C =0:2	COP = 0	AG = 2
	Pure C =0	Food	= 0
EB = 2:2.0 EA = 4.0 EBPer = N/A	Afr =0.58	Isolate/R	= 0.00
eb = 6:7 es = 13 D = –3	S =4	H:(H)Hd(Hd)	= 2:5
Adj es = 13 Adj D =–3	Blends:R =5:19	(HHd):(AAd)	= 3:3
	CP =0	H+A:Hd + Ad	= 14:5
FM = 5 C' = 0 T = 4			
m = 1 V = 3 Y = 0			
	P = 8 Zf =10		3r+(2)/R = 0.47
a:p = 5:3 Sum6 = 8	X+% = 0.47 Zd = +2.0		Fr+rF = 0
Ma:Mp = 2:0 Lv2 = 0	F+% = 0.63 W:D:Dd =7:10:2		FD = 1
2AB+Art+Ay = 11 WSum6 = 21	X-% = 0.32 W:M =7:2		An + Xy = 1
M– = 1 Mnone = 0	S-% = 0.67 DQ+ =3		MOR = 2
	Xu% = 0.21 DQv =0		

| SCZI = 4* | DEPI = 6* | CDI = 3 | S-CON = 7 | HVI = No | OBS = No |

10

A Borderline Psychopath: "I was basically maladjusted . . ."

J. Reid Meloy
University of California, San Diego

Carl B. Gacono
U.S. Department of Justice

Despite Knight's (1953) seminal paper in which he paradoxically recommended that *borderline* not be used as a diagnostic term, an enormous amount of research literature concerning borderline psychopathology has emerged in the past 40 years (Grotstein, Solomon, & Lang, 1987). Kernberg's early work (1966, 1967, 1968) advanced the concept of neurotic, borderline, and psychotic personality organization, culminating in his more recent explication (Kernberg, 1984) of the reality testing, identity, and defensive aspects that demarcate these "levels" of personality. Various character formations are theorized to cut vertically across these horizontal latitudes of development (Kernberg, 1975).

In this study, the fourth in a series of idiographic explorations of personality organization and character formation (Gacono, 1992; Meloy, 1992a; Meloy & Gacono, 1992b), we present the case of a young man who is organized at a borderline level of personality and is a psychopathic character. Rorschach findings are used to empirically understand these two dimensions of personality. Our approach to the Rorschach data is both psychostructural and psychodynamic.

CASE STUDY

Chet is a 21-year-old White man, the second child born to an intact family. His mother was raised in Jamaica and is employed as a medical technician. His father was born in Iowa and was following a Naval career; he now owns a bar. Father is described by both mother and son as a paranoid alcoholic who has attempted suicide on three different occasions. There is also a paternal familial history of alcoholism, depression, and schizophrenia.

Although the pregnancy and delivery of Chet are reported to have been normal, within several months his mother moved away from her support system, became increasingly anxious, and had difficulty feeding Chet. In spite of these problems, which required medical attention, Chet gained weight and appeared to be developing normally.

Chet was enuretic until age 4, and by age 6 was exhibiting defiance toward his parents and teachers and aggression toward toys. His anger and aggression were reciprocated by his father, who was physically, although not sexually, cruel and abusive to both him and his mother. He later reported that he had been raped and molested when he was 6 years old but subsequently said that he had lied, adding, "when you're going to be an actor, you need to set the stage right." The frequent changes of living due to his father's career, and Chet's large physical size, resulted in continuous teasing and challenging from older children and left few opportunities for enduring peer relationships.

At age 8, Chet's psychiatric history began. His parents were told that he would function better if they separated. His mother disagreed. Chet was tried on methylphenidate for 1½ years to address his hyperactivity. His mother became isolative and depressed when his father would return home from a Navy deployment and abuse Chet. Mother turned to astrology and religious groups to cope.

Chet started to hang around with other children who were delinquent. Consistent with a diagnosis of conduct disorder, his behavioral problems manifested in petty crimes, drug use, poor school performance, truancy, and chronic arguments within the family. By midadolescence he was diagnosed with a reactive depression to the violence he experienced with his father. As the doctor got to know him, he wrote, "despite paranoid trends and a symbiotic attachment to his mother, Chet in relationship is very shallow and talks about grandiose schemes to be someone, usually involving sociopathic ideas such as selling drugs and becoming rich." His drug history during adolescence involved marijuana, phencyclidine, LSD, methamphetamine, and alcohol.

Three years before the instant offense, when Chet was 17, his mother divorced his father. Chet threatened to kill his father and self-reported two suicide attempts. During that same year, Chet became more secretive and withdrawn from his mother. Following her mild rebuke, he set a fire at his high school, and was arrested while watching the firemen work. He was detained at Juvenile Hall and subsequently admitted to a psychiatric hospital for 2 months.

His physical exam was normal. Psychological testing, now 2 years before the instant offense, indicated an average range of intellectual ability. There was no evidence of organic impairment. Projective testing revealed,

significant disturbance in the area of interpersonal relations and extremely low self esteem. Frustration tolerance and ability to handle stress are quite tenuous, and depression as well as aggressive feelings are prominent. Typical defense mechanisms are projection and denial, and a latent thought disorder is present.

The discharge summary stated, in part,

> there are significant pseudo-sociopathic tendencies as well as deep seated latent, and sometimes not latent, aggressive feelings. Underlying narcissistic disturbance is quite severe and, though not formally psychotic, he at times does manifest rather extreme disturbances of thought and cognition indicative of a severe emotional disturbance.

The discharge diagnosis was conduct disorder and a borderline personality disorder with narcissistic features.

Instant Offense

The victim was a 56-year-old church organist and retired Baptist minister who had been dead in his apartment for at least 5 days before the police discovered the body. The autopsy revealed bruises to the trunk and face, as well as fractures to the nasal bones. There were additional fractures of the supraorbital portion of the bones around his eyes, and a linear fracture at the base of his skull. The cause of death was head injury. The victim was found fully clothed, and his hands and feet were bound with telephone cord. His face was covered with a towel (Geberth, 1990).

Police investigation led to a 14-year-old boy who had been present during the killing. He had been taken to dinner by the victim, a known pedophile, and had subsequently granted him two sexual favors before Chet and another young man arrived at the victim's apartment. The four sat in the living room talking, and then Chet returned from the kitchen and placed a fork at the victim's throat, threatening him with harm. The boy was handcuffed and taken by the other man into the victim's bedroom, where he was later tied up. He did not see the killing, but heard noises consistent with blows to the victim's head, throat, stomach, and chest, and pleas for medical help. After the killing, Chet and his companion stole the victim's stereo, credit cards, and other property. They decided to let the juvenile live. Chet was heard to say to the victim, "I'm going to kill you. I am a crazy motherfucker. If I get caught they will put me in a mental hospital."

When Chet was arrested, he confessed to the crime.

> I beat up the guy, kicked him, twisted his head around, then killed him because the guy had raped one of my little friends and the little boy's mother was not able to go to the police and tell them.

He reported that he was a "drug addict" and a "well-minded loner" whose relationships centered around criminal activity, such as vandalism, burglary, and car theft. He maintained that he and his friend planned to rob and kill the victim before they got to his apartment. He reported feeling "upset" about the crime, but acknowledged that he might have killed again, because he had heard that it gets easier. He said, "my crime merits imprisonment."

During his incarceration and trial he was briefly treated in a forensic inpatient unit for suicidality, depression, crying, anxiety, and self-reported auditory and visual hallucinations. He did not respond, however, to antipsychotic medications but did respond to hydroxyzine pamoate (an antihistamine) and doxepin hydrochloride (an antidepressant). At the time of testing he was taking doxepin 50 mg bid and 100 mg hs. Chet was also administered the MMPI, the Wechsler Adult Intelligence Scale–Revised (WAIS–R; Wechsler, 1981) and the Thematic Apperception Test (TAT; Murray, 1943). His MMPI was an invalid, "fake bad" profile. On the WAIS–R he scored a VIQ of 96, a PIQ of 90, and a FSIQ of 94, consistent with prior testing. He defined the word *tirade* on the vocabulary subtest as "sadistic talk". In response to the comprehension subtest concerning finding an envelope in the street, he stated, "I'm supposed to mail it, but I would open it." His TAT response to Card 18GF is noteworthy: "This girl is a psychopathic killer, and she has her mom pinned up against the staircase and she is choking her to death. And then the old lady's body is limp because she's made her life miserable and she just got tired of it and she evened up the score and she is enjoying what she's doing to her mom cause she made her crazy." The Rorschach was administered 2 weeks after the homicide.

RESULTS

Appendix A shows the Rorschach protocol. Appendix B shows the sequence of scores, and Appendix C shows the structural summary, both generated by Rorschach Scoring Program, Version 2 (Exner, Cohen, & McGuire, 1990). Table 10.1 contains categories that define primitive interpersonal modes of relating (Kwawer, 1980), Table 10.2 shows the Rorschach defenses (Cooper, Perry, & Arnow, 1988), and Table 10.3 shows the aggression scores (Exner, 1986a; Meloy & Gacono, 1992a) for this protocol.

DISCUSSION

Chet's Rorschach indicates both borderline personality organization and psychopathic character formation. Our approach to these idiographic data, which are both psychostructural and psychodynamic, is in the context of concurrent validity. What expectable clinical hypotheses could we generate, based on Chet's background and behavior, and does the Rorschach support these hypotheses? We address each one in turn.

TABLE 10.1
Primitive Interpersonal Modes (Kwawer, 1980)

Criteria	Frequency
1. Engulfment	0
2. Symbiotic merging	0
3. Violent symbiosis, separation, and reunion	6
4. Malignant internal processes	1
5. Birth and rebirth	1
6. Metamorphosis and transformation	0
7. Narcissistic mirroring	1
8. Separation–division	0
9. Boundary disturbance	3
10. Womb imagery	0

Total	12
	% of R = 30

TABLE 10.2
Rorschach Defense Scales (Cooper, Perry, & Arnow, 1988)

Level of Personality Organization	Defense	Frequency	%
Neurotic	Higher level denial	2	
	Intellectualization	0	
	Isolation	2	
	Reaction formation	0	
	Repression	0	
	Rationalization	0	
	Pollyannish denial	0	

	Total	4	15%
Borderline	Devaluation	5	
	Omnipotence	0	
	Primitive idealization	0	
	Projection	5	
	Projective identification	2	
	Splitting	3	

	Total	15	58%
Psychotic	Hypomanic denial	0	
	Massive denial	7	

	Total	7	27%
	Total scored	26	100%

TABLE 10.3
Aggression Scores (Meloy & Gacono, 1992a)

Aggression (Exner, 1986a)	3
Aggressive content	7
Aggressive past	3
Aggressive potential	0
Sadomasochism	1

Total aggression	14

Hypothesis 1: There Is a Strong Identification With the Aggressor, in This Case, the Father.   Meloy (1988) theorized that the primary identification of the psychopath is with the "stranger selfobject" (Grotstein, 1982) or, in Freudian terms, with the aggressor (A. Freud, 1966). It would be expected that Chet's internal representations would be suffused with aggression, with indications that he also identified with the aggressor. Such is the case. Perusal of his protocol (Appendix A) indicates many aggression responses: Comprehensive System (Exner, 1986a) aggression occurring only in the present (8, 11, 26) and other, more refined aggressive indices—aggressive content (1, 7, 10, 14, 22, 26, 27), aggressive past (16, 17, 26), and sadomasochism (16). Table 10.3 indicates a total of 14 aggression responses.

Although the relation of aggressive responses on the Rorschach to real-world aggression is problematic in forensic populations (Gacono, Meloy, & Berg, 1992; Meloy & Gacono, 1992a), idiographic support abounds in this case for such a correlation. The aggression is particularly atavistic and cruel, apparent in the reader's probable visceral reactions to looking at the responses (see, e.g., Responses 21 and 26). Aggressive drive derivatives predominate among his internal objects.

Weapons ("Gun," "shotgun") also emerge as aggressive content (14, 27) and can be theoretically understood as a hard object identification or attachment in psychopathy (Meloy, 1992b). Percepts of weapons are often imbued with characteristics of omnipotent control, grandiosity, and narcissistic invulnerability.

The absence of anxiety or felt helplessness ($Y = 0$), coupled with an abundance of aggressive indices, suggests the egosyntonic nature of Chet's aggression. In this case, $Y = 0$ is accompanied by emotional detachment ($T = 0$), which both enhance the capacity for predatory violence toward the victim (Gacono & Meloy, 1994), verified by Chet's preparation and planning for the robbery and killing. Both chronic detachment and predatory violence (Meloy, 1988) have been found to differentiate between psychopathic and nonpsychopathic criminals (Gacono & Meloy, 1991; Williamson, Hare, & Wong, 1987). Psychopaths usually seek male strangers as victims, somewhat consistent with this case.

The final index of support for this hypothesis are the four space responses. Unexpected in adult normals (Exner, 1986a) but characteristic of antisocial personality disorder (Gacono & Meloy, 1992), these suggest a characterologically angry individual who will be sullen and oppositional. Inconsistent with this hypothesis is the mild expectation of cooperativeness from others ($COP = 2$). The first cooperative response, however, is somewhat ambiguous (24), and the second one is spoiled by an aggressive content during the inquiry (27) and cognitive slippage (FAB). Both responses are perceptually idiosyncratic (Fu).

Hypothesis 2: There Is a Secondary Identification With the Victim.
Chet produced three aggressive past responses (16, 17, 26), which we and others (Meloy & Gacono, 1992a) have theoretically linked to a masochistic

orientation. There are also five Morbid responses (8, 16, 17, 21, 26) that strongly suggest a sense of self as injured and damaged, data consistent with samples of individuals with posttraumatic stress disorder (Hartman et al., 1990) who often perceive themselves as victims. Elevated Morbid responses ($M = 1.73$) were also found in a sample of Antisocial Personality Disordered (ASPD) incarcerated men (Gacono & Meloy, 1992), which provides some empirical support for the theoretical notion of grandiosity as a defense against a damaged self in some ASPD men.

There is also a serious preoccupation with physical vulnerability found in the three anatomy responses (3, 21, 22). This is most graphic in Response 21, "the head and body of a baby—they didn't tie the umbilical cord and the guts are shooting out . . ." This regressive response occurs with a loss of reality testing and is determined by both partially modulated affect (CF) and an ideational sense of helplessness (m). It also involves three special scores, including two indices of formal thought disorder (DR, INC). It is solely redeemed by a whole human representation (H), but in the milieu of a perinatal experience that is a wrenching, violent separation from the mother.

Hypothesis 3: There Is a Primary Object Relation Marked by Violent Attachment.   Kwawer's (1980) categories for primitive modes of interpersonal relatedness are listed in Table 10.1. Twelve of these responses are present and occur in 30% of R. Unlike the psychopathic character organized at a psychotic level of personality (Meloy & Gacono, 1992b), in which engulfment and womb imagery would be expected, organization at a borderline level would predict a plethora of symbiotic responses (Gacono, 1992). There are six in this protocol (8, 11, 16, 17, 21, 26), and they would all be categorized as violent symbiosis, separation, and reunion responses. Eighty-three percent of these responses are linked with Morbid special scores, and two thirds contain minus form quality or massive denial as a psychotic defense (Cooper et al., 1988); for example, (11), "A horse being eaten by a bear. (?) The horse head and hoof trying to get away."

Chet also produced one food ambivalence response (8), "broken mayonnaise jars—but mayo isn't red, strawberry jelly." Such responses may be a metaphor for early ambivalent experiences wherein nurturing was suffused, at times, with aggression from the primary object (Gacono, 1992; Gacono & Meloy, 1991).

The adaptation by Chet to this internal world of violent symbiotic objects is sequentially evident in Responses 17 through 19. In Response 17, the violent symbiosis is startlingly evident, "bits and pieces of a pig, his head, they tore his stomach off," and is accompanied by a loss of reality testing (F–). Reality testing is recovered on the next response (18) through the use of the borderline defense of devaluation: "Two Mexicans, you know with that on their head? They're snobby and looking over their shoulder," a ubiquitous defense in psychopathy (Gacono, 1990). But then reality testing is lost once again (F–)

when the neurotic defense of isolation is attempted on Response 19, "A nut and bolt here."

In contrast to this failure of neurotic adaptation, pathological narcissistic adaptation is successful in the sequence of Responses 11 through 13. Response 11, noted previously as a violent symbiotic response accompanied by a loss of reality testing, is followed by a narcissistic mirroring response with unusual form level (12), "a bird . . . skimming across the water, and the reflection," and then a popular response (13), "a butterfly." Reality convergence is attained and recovered from a violent symbiotic object relation through the use of a narcissistic defense (Rf).

Hypothesis 4: There Is Poor Modulation of Affect and an Absence of Unpleasant Emotion.   One of the paradoxes of psychopathy is the presence of a primitive and violent object relational world and the absence of dysphoric or anxious affect. We would expect stimulus overload, dysphoria, and anxiety in other subjects with similar object relational worlds (Gacono et al., 1992) and find it in Borderline Personality Disorder (Exner, 1986b).

Chet's affective experience, despite his identifications and object relations, is like the quiet and calm reflecting pool, a marker of his fundamentally alloplastic character. He is avoidant of external stimuli that is emotionally provoking (Afr = .42, 2 standard deviations below the mean for nonpatient men), and is highly defended against his own affect ($Lambda$ = .93). His nonvolitional affective experience is detached and empty (C' = 0, V = 0, T = 0, Y = 0), suggestive of the conceptual meaninglessness of his experience in which two-dimensional perception ($Pure\ F$) is rarely imbued with the third dimension of affective depth, whether joyful or dysphoric. These data are also consistent with the inability of psychopaths to discriminate between words with and without affective meaning (Hare, 1991), which may have a biological substrate in the limbic system (Meloy, 1988).

Although Chet does not have an expected $Pure\ C$ response, given his explosive violence, his modulation of affect (FC:CF + C = 1:3) is consistent with ASPD men (1:3; Gacono & Meloy, 1994) and like that of a 7-year-old boy (Exner, 1986a). His stress tolerance and controls, however, are average, and even better than average when adjusted for situational factors ($Adj\ D$ = +1). We would expect Chet to use his unmodulated affect, usually anger, in a deliberate and predictable manner to control objects in his environment, a proposition dramatized in the instant offense, and reinforcing the psychopathic fantasy of omnipotent control.

Hypothesis 5: There Is a Fusion of Aggressive and Sexual Drives, Linked to Sadomasochism, in the Context of the Self as an Injured Object. The psychopathic character restores meaning through cruelty to others. Chet produced one SM response (Gacono, 1990; Meloy, 1988; Meloy & Gacono, 1992a), scored when pleasurable affect accompanies a Morbid, aggressive, or devalued response (16): "a lady dancing and her hair's on fire. Buttocks, pointy shoes, one hand and one arm up through here—she got her head blown off (laughs)." Chet's sadomasochism, moreover, is closely linked to both anality and homophobia. He remembers as a child watching his father masturbate in front of the television. He reported positive feelings while killing the victim because he was a "faggot" just like his father. He also remembered tying up an adolescent and "torturing" him 2 years before the homicide, and also cruelty to animals as an adolescent. He described his internal state at the time of the homicide as feeling "dismembered" because he had been reduced to "just two big eyes." This may be suggestive of dissociation at the time of the killing, and is a memory pervaded with an unconscious, paranoid fear of castration.

After Chet was in custody he assaulted another inmate whom he found shackled in a "holding tank." He laughed when he described this assault to clinical staff. Like the homicide, the victim was being held and controlled, an anal metaphor, just before Chet became violent, literally acting out the "beating fantasy" (Freud, 1919/1958).

The sadistic pleasure that Chet derives from these actions is a consequence of the complete control and domination of the victim and the projective identification of his passive feminine internal objects into the victim. It is also a retaliatory product of his feelings of helplessness as the victim of his father and is driven by the wish to convert passive into active (Freud, 1919/1958). The homophobic context of the killing probably contains both a wish and a fear of homosexual assault as "buttocks" are juxtaposed with "pointy shoes" (16), and "ladies" deteriorate into "chickenpeople" (8). This latter response, similar to the term "chickenhawks" used to describe young men in custody that may be prey to homosexual assault, also links sexual and aggressive content; both sex responses (8, 16) contain a Morbid, suggesting a dynamic association between erotic arousal and the self as an injured object, a sexually masochistic orientation. Although sadomasochism is endemic in Chet's intrapsychic economy and real-world behavior, there is no irrefutable evidence for sexual sadism, unlike several of our previous case studies (Gacono, 1992; Meloy & Gacono, 1992b). Nevertheless, Chet has failed to integrate the "mother of pleasure and the mother of pain" (Bach, 1991, p. 85) during his development and sexual maturation.

Hypothesis 6: There Is a Borderline Personality Organization. We think the *SCZI* score of 4 on this protocol is a false positive for schizophrenia. There is a 13% false positive rate for BPD on the *SCZI* (Exner, 1986a). We would argue that Chet's protocol evidences a "lower level" character disorder (Kernberg, 1975) and a quite primitive borderline personality organization, perhaps developmentally near the psychotic border. An analysis of the Rorschach data concerning reality testing, unintegrated identity, and defensive operations is instructive.

First, Chet's cognitive mediation is unconventional and idiosyncratic ($X+\%$ = 30, $F+\%$ = 38), and his gross distortion of perceptual reality is significant ($X-\%$ = 30). Although this last index suggests severely impaired reality testing, it is still within 1 standard deviation of a sample of antisocial personality disordered men without a diagnosable psychosis (M = 23, SD = 11; Gacono & Meloy, 1992). Formal thought disorder is also pervasive in this record ($WSum6$ = 45), but all the Level 2 scores occur within a violent symbiosis response (8, 16, 26), suggesting a psychodynamic, rather than structural, basis for thought disorder (Meloy & Singer, 1991). Thought disorganizes in this young man when early emotional trauma surrounding the differentiation subphase of separation–individuation is recathected (Mahler, Pine, & Bergman, 1975).

Second, Chet's lack of an integrated identity is manifest in his use of splitting to alternate between his primary identification as an aggressor and his secondary identification as a victim. Splitting between good and bad objects is evident in the sequencing of Responses 1 and 2: "looks like the Devil (1) . . . two hummingbirds (2)." Confusion between internal and external reality, pathognomonic of borderline rather than psychotic organization, is evident in the Kwawer (1980) category of boundary disturbance (8, 21, 22). Response 22, for example, "A bug, eyeballs, skeleton, armor, feet, claws, his tail", suggests the rapidly oscillating shift between internal (skeleton) and external (armor), implicates the defensive use of both projection and introjection, and points to the borderline person's confusion with the origin of stimuli: Is it within me or out there? In psychotic states, we see no confusion because the boundary is lost (Meloy, 1991). Likewise, Special Scores that mark psychotic perception ($CONTAM$) and psychotic association ($ALOG$) are absent in Chet's Rorschach protocol (Meloy & Singer, 1991).

And third, the defensive operations also implicate a borderline personality organization. Of the identifiable defenses in this protocol, 58% are borderline, 27% are psychotic, and 15% are neurotic (see Table 10.2; Cooper et al., 1988). Prominent borderline defenses include devaluation and projection, findings consistent with psychopaths in general (Gacono, 1990). Devaluation as a defense is used with instinctual aggression in Response 26: "Looks like a bug here—someone used a drill press on him, blood here, drilling through one leg, the handle and power unit here." This response would also be scored for projective identification and is another example of the psychopathic character relating to objects on the basis of power rather than affection. This method of quantifying the proportion of defenses at each level of personality is useful because it emphasizes the dynamic and changeable nature of intrapsychic life and also allows for statements concerning the most prominent level of defensive organization.

Hypothesis 7: Psychopathic Character Formation Is Present.   Chet is positive for four of the five select Comprehensive System variables that discriminated between psychopathic and nonpsychopathic criminals (Gacono & Meloy, 1991; Gacono, Meloy, & Heaven, 1990). Indices suggest pathological narcissism (Rf = 1), chronic emotional detachment (T = 0), increased self-absorption ($EgoC$ = .41), and an absence of anxiety or felt helplessness (Y = 0). This latter measure is consistent with the psychophysiological research on psychopathy (Hare, 1991). The one aspect of psychopathy that is missing in this protocol is grandiosity, measured by Personals (Exner, 1986a) and omnipotent defenses (Cooper et al., 1988). Although grandiosity is expected in most psychopaths (Gacono et al., 1990), it appears to fail continuously in this particular case, perhaps due to inherited cognitive and affective vulnerabilities.

Not that Chet does not try. The absence of idealization as a defense is expected in psychopathy, overshadowed by a plethora of devaluation responses (Gacono, 1990). Both findings are consistent with this protocol (see Table 10.2) and suggest repetitive attempts to shore up the grandiose self-structure (Kernberg, 1975) through the devaluation of others. And the one sadomasochism response (16) in this protocol, a specific although not necessarily sensitive indicator (Meloy & Gacono, 1992a) of sadism, has been found to distinguish between psychopathic and nonpsychopathic criminals.

CONCLUSION

We have explored the case of a psychopathic character organized at a borderline level of personality. In the absence of a stable grandiose self-structure (Kernberg, 1975), intense aggression, often linked with homosexual impulse, is managed through an intricate defensive operation: Devaluation, projection, and projective identification keep the perceived (homo)sexual aggressor at bay, whereas splitting and massive denial facilitate the use of sadism toward real objects. This attempt to induce a "mutual sexualized misery" (Bach, 1991, p. 83) facilitates the conversion of passive into active, the projection of the injured self, the omnipotent control of the (father) aggressor, and momentary pleasure through the infliction of pain, the *lex talionis*, or law of revenge. To risk a condensation of the wisdom of Drs. Melitta Schmideberg and Hervey Cleckley, this young man wears a "stably unstable mask of sanity."

ACKNOWLEDGMENTS

This chapter was initially part of a symposium entitled, "Borderline Personality Organization: Through the Looking Glass II," organized by Marvin Acklin, PhD, and presented at the Society for Personality Assessment Midwinter Meeting, Washington, March 14, 1992.

We thank Marilyn Clarke for the preparation of the manuscript. The views expressed in this article are those of the authors and do not necessarily reflect those of the Departments of Psychiatry, University of California, San Diego, or San Francisco.

REFERENCES

Bach, S. (1991). On sadomasochistic object relations. In G. Fogel & W. Meyers (Eds.) *Perversions and near-perversions in clinical practice* (pp. 75–92). New Haven, CT: Yale University Press.

Cooper, S., Perry, J., & Arnow, D. (1988). An empirical approach to the study of defense mechanisms: I. Reliability and preliminary validity of the Rorschach defense scales. *Journal of Personality Assessment, 52,* 187–203.

Exner, J. (1986a). *The Rorschach: A comprehensive system: Vol. 1. Foundations* (2nd ed.). New York: Wiley.

Exner, J. (1986b). Some Rorschach data comparing schizophrenics with borderline and schizotypal personality disorders. *Journal of Personality Assessment, 50,* 455–471.

Exner, J., Cohen, J., & McGuire, H. (1990). *Rorschach scoring program, version 2.* Asheville, NC: Rorschach Workshops.

Freud, A. (1966). *The ego and the mechanisms of defense* (rev. ed.). New York: International Universities Press. (Original work published 1936)

Freud, S. (1958). A child is being beaten. In J. Strachey (Ed. & Trans.), *The standard edition of the complete psychological works of Sigmund Freud* (Vol. 17, pp. 179–204). London: Hogarth. (Original work published 1919)

Gacono, C. (1990). An empirical study of object relations and defensive operations in antisocial personality disorder. *Journal of Personality Assessment, 54,* 589–600.

Gacono, C. (1992). A Rorschach case study of sexual homicide. *British Journal of Projective Psychology, 37,* 1–21.

Gacono, C., & Meloy, J. R. (1991). A Rorschach investigation of attachment and anxiety in antisocial personality disorder. *Journal of Nervous and Mental Disease, 179,* 546–552.

Gacono, C., & Meloy, J. R. (1992). The Rorschach and DSM–III–R antisocial personality: A tribute to Robert Lindner. *Journal of Clinical Psychology, 48,* 393–406.

Gacono, C., & Meloy, J. R. (1994). *Rorschach assessment of aggressive and psychopathic personalities.* Hillsdale, NJ: Lawrence Erlbaum Associates, Inc.

Gacono, C., Meloy, J. R., & Berg, J. (1992). Affect states, defenses, and object relations in borderline, narcissistic, and antisocial personality disorder. *Journal of Personality Assessment, 59,* 32–49.

Gacono, C., Meloy, J. R., & Heaven, T. (1990). A Rorschach investigation of narcissism and hysteria in antisocial personality disorder. *Journal of Personality Assessment, 55,* 270–279.

Geberth, V. (1990). *Practical homicide investigation* (2nd ed.). New York: Elsevier.

Grotstein, J. (1982). Newer perspectives in object relations theory. *Contemporary Psychoanalysis, 18,* 43–91.

Grotstein, J., Solomon, M., & Lang, J. (1987). *The borderline patient: Emerging concepts in diagnosis, psychodynamics, and treatment* (Vols. 1–2). Hillsdale, NJ: The Analytic Press.

Hare, R. (1991). *The Hare Psychopathy Checklist–revised manual.* Toronto: Multi-Health Systems, Inc.

Hartman, W., Clark, M., Morgan, M., Dunn, V., Fine, A., Perry, G., Jr., & Winsch, D. (1990). Rorschach structure of a hospitalized sample of Vietnam veterans with PTSD. *Journal of Personality Assessment, 54,* 149–159.

Kernberg, O. (1966). Structural derivatives of object relationships. *International Journal of Psychoanalysis, 47,* 236–253.

Kernberg, O. (1967). Borderline personality organization. *Journal of the American Psychoanalytic Association, 15,* 641–685.

Kernberg, O. (1968). The treatment of patients with borderline personality organization. *International Journal of Psychoanalysis, 49,* 600–619.

Kernberg, O. (1975). *Borderline conditions and pathological narcissism.* New York: Aronson.

Kernberg, O. (1984). *Severe personality disorders.* New Haven, CT: Yale University Press.

Knight, R. (1953). Borderline states. *Bulletin of the Menninger Clinic, 17,* 1–12.

Kwawer, J. (1980). Primitive interpersonal modes, borderline phenonema, and Rorschach content. In J. Kwawer, A. Sugarman, P. Lerner, & H. Lerner (Eds.), *Borderline phenonema and the Rorschach test* (pp. 89–105). New York: International Universities Press.

Mahler, M., Pine, F., & Bergman, A. (1975). *The psychological birth of the human infant.* New York: Basic Books.

Meloy, J. R. (1988). *The psychopathic mind: Origins, dynamics and treatment.* Northvale, NJ: Aronson.

Meloy, J. R. (1991). The "blurring" of ego boundary in projective identification. [Letter to the editor]. *American Journal of Psychiatry, 148,* 1761–1762.

Meloy, J. R. (1992a). Revisiting the Rorschach of Sirhan Sirhan. *Journal of Personality Assessment, 58,* 548–570.

Meloy, J. R. (1992b). *Violent attachments.* Northvale, NJ: Aronson.

Meloy, J. R., & Gacono, C. (1992a). The aggression response and the Rorschach. *Journal of Clinical Psychology, 48,* 104–114.

Meloy, J. R., & Gacono, C. (1992b). A psychotic (sexual) psychopath: "I just had a violent thought . . .". *Journal of Personality Assessment, 58,* 480–493.

Meloy, J. R., & Singer, J. (1991). A psychoanalytic view of the Comprehensive System "Special Scores." *Journal of Personality Assessment, 56,* 202–217.

Murray, H. (1943). *Thematic Apperception Test manual.* Cambridge, MA: Harvard University Press.

Wechsler, D. (1981). *Wechsler Adult Intelligence Scale–Revised.* New York: The Psychological Corporation.

Williamson, S., Hare, R., & Wong, S. (1987). Violence: Criminal psychopaths and their victims. *Canadian Journal of Behavioral Science, 19,* 454–462.

APPENDIX A
Rorschach Protocol

I.

1. ll the devil—see the ears, eyes, and horns on the head—that's what it's supposed to be isn't it?

ears, horn, mouth, teeth, chin here.

2. Two hummingbirds trying to suck the nectar out of a flower—wings, beak, flower here.

the beak, wings, flower here.

3. ll a skull cuz it's hollowed out.

a cattle skull, bull, like on the ground in the desert (?) Bone, horns, eyes, nostrils.

II.

It doesn't ll anything—blobs on a piece of paper.

4. An upside down monarch butterfly.

the red ll two wings.

5. Two cartoon characters, clowns slapping their wrists together like this (gestures).

the hands and faces are red on each side, you could make the body ll that.

6. A technical instrument.

the shape, Idk, it looks manmade.

III.

7. A big fat creature—look at it this way, maybe a black widow cuz the thing in the middle—ever seen one? It ll a spider, claws, teeth, eyes here.

the arms, crab joints, shape.

8. Two ladies, fighting over some grocery bags, the red stuff is the mess they're making, trying to rip the shopping cart bag in half, here's the stuff coming out of it.

legs, hip, boobs, neck—they're chickenpeople (?) Yea, no mouths, just beaks. Marks here are rips. Stuff (stuff?) like Idk broken mayonnaise jars—bat mayo isn't red, strawberry jelly.

IV.

9. It ll some kind of creature.

goat's head with wings folded, feet here, the tail.

10. A creature with floppy feet, head, two eyes, hands like claws on each side.

like a dinosaur, the tail here, on each side eyes, hands like claws, tail is here, and floppy feet.

V.

11. A horse being eaten by a bear.

here, the horse head and hoof trying to get away.

12. Also ll a bird.

here, skimming across the water, and the reflection.

13. A butterfly.

this way, the whole thing.

VI.

14. A gun being fired, that's all it ll.

watch this (covers up half the card) it muffles the sound, handle trigger, shell.

VII.

15. ll a pig, doesn't it? Just like it here, the eyes, nose, teeth right here.

the nose, teeth here.

16. A lady dancing and her hair's on fire. Buttocks, pointy shoes, one hand and one arm up through here—she got her head blown off (laughs)—she's dancing.

the hair, arm here, head blown up.

(continued)

152

17. Bits and pieces of a pig, his head, they tore his stomach off, leg, head here. He's been chopped into little pieces, ya know?

right here.

18. Two Mexicans, you know with that on their head? They're snobby and looking over their shoulder.

like when you stick your tongue out, stuck up.

19. A nut and bolt here.

the space here.

VIII.

20. The rock he's on, a stump, branches, he's trying to fix it, the beaver, walk on it, fix it—one foot here, one in the air, on logs or branches.

like right here, log, branch, rock, a rodent.

IX.

21. The head and body of a baby—they didn't tie the umbilical cord and the guts are shooting out—can that really happen? Can it bleed to death?

nose, the color, more of a flesh tone—he's red when he comes out—this is green and orange guts coming out.

22. A bug, eyeballs, skeleton, armor, feet, claws, his tail.

here, the eyes, claws, skeleton, armor and tail receding.

X.

23. It reminds me of sea crustaceans. That large red area on both sides, crustaceans.

red coral like that.

24. Some guy's handing another guy something.

blue here, on a cliff.

25. These are like lobsters.

all the feet.

26. ll a bug here—someone used a drill press on him—blood here—drilling through one leg—the handle and the power unit here.

cockroaches, two antenna and feet, and a wishbone here, the yellow handle.

27. A man here, pulled along by two seahorses—like with Shamu—guy gets on his back, you ever been there?

the hair, feet, and seahorses, a shotgun here.

153

Sequence of Scores

Card	No.	Loc.	#	Determinant(s)	(2)	Content(s)	Pop Z	Special Scores
I	1	WSo	1	Fu		(Hd)	3.5	DR
	2	W+	1	FMau	2	A, Bt, Fd	4.0	
	3	WSo	1	Fo		An	3.5	
II	4	Do	3	Fo		A		
	5	W+	1	Ma.FCo	2	(H)	4.5	DR
	6	DSv	5	Fu		Sc		
III	7	Wo	1	F–		(A)	5.5	INC
	8	W+	1	Ma.CF.mau	2	(H), Hh, Sx, Fd	5.5	AG, INC2, MOR
IV	9	Wo	1	F–		(A)	2.0	INC
	10	Wo	1	Fo		(A)	2.0	
V	11	D+	4	FMa–		A, Ad	2.5	AG, FAB
	12	W+	1	FMa.Fru		A, Na	2.5	
	13	Wo	1	Fo		A	P 1.0	
VI	14	Ddo	99	mau		Sc, Ex		
VII	15	Do	3	Fo		Ad		
	16	Dd+	22	Mau		H, Fi, Sx, Cg	1.0	FAB2, MOR
	17	Ddo	23	F–		Ad		MOR
	18	Wo	1	Mpu	2	Hd	2.5	
	19	DSv	7	F–		Sc		
VIII	20	D+	1	FMao		A, Na	P 3.0	
IX	21	Dd+	99	ma.CF–		H, Bl, An	2.5	MOR, DR, INC
	22	Wo	1	F–		A, An	5.5	INC
X	23	Do	9	CFo		Ls		
	24	D+	6	Mau	2	H, Ls	4.0	COP
	25	Do	1	Fu	2	A		INC
	26	D+	7	Ma–	2	A, Hh, Bl	4.0	MOR, FAB2. AG
	27	D+	10	FMau	2	H, A	4.0	FAB, COP

Summary of Approach

I:WS.W. WS	VI:Dd
II:D.W. DS	VII:D.Dd.Dd.W.DS
III:W.W	VIII:D
IV:W.W	IX:Dd.W
V:D.W.W.	X:D.D.D.D.D

Rorschach Structural Summary

LOCATION FEATURES	DETERMINANTS BLENDS	SINGLE	CONTENTS	S-CONSTELLATION

LOCATION FEATURES	DETERMINANTS BLENDS	SINGLE		CONTENTS		S-CONSTELLATION
			H	= 4,0		NO..FV + VF + V + FD > 2
Zf = 19	M.FC	M	= 4	(H)	= 2,0	NO..Col-Shd Bl>0
ZSum = 63.0	M.CF.m	FM	= 4	Hd	= 1,0	NO..Ego<.31,>.44
ZEst = 63.0	FM.Fr	m	= 1	(Hd)	= 1,0	YES..MOR>3
	m.CF	FC	= 0	Hx	= 0,0	NO..Zd > ± 3.5
W = 12		CF	= 1	A	= 9,1	NO..es>EA
(Wv = 0)		C	= 0	(A)	= 3,0	YES..CF+C>FC
D = 11		Cn	= 0	Ad	= 2,1	YES..X+%<.70
Dd = 4		FC'	= 0	(Ad)	= 0,0	YES..S>3
S = 4		C'F	= 0	An	= 1,2	YES..P<3 or >8
		C'	= 0	Art	= 0,0	NO..Pure H <2
DQ		FT	= 0	Ay	= 0,0	NO..R<17
..........(FQ–)		TF	= 0	Bl	= 0,2	5.....TOTAL
+ = 11(3)		T	= 0	Bt	= 0,1	SPECIAL SCORINGS
o = 14(4)		FV	= 0	Cg	= 0,1	

DQ

..........(FQ–)			FT	= 0	Ay	= 0,0
+	= 11(3)		TF	= 0	Bl	= 0,2
o	= 14(4)		T	= 0	Bt	= 0,1
v/+	= 0 (0)		FV	= 0	Cg	= 0,1
v	= 2 (1)		VF	= 0	Cl	= 0,0

	Lvl	Lv2
DV	= 0x1	0x2
INC	= 5x2	1x4
DR	= 3x3	0x6
FAB	= 2x4	2x7
ALOG	= 0x5	
CON	= 0x7	
SUM6	= 13	
WSUM6	= 45	

FORM QUALITY

	FQx	FQf	MQual	SQx			
+	= 0	0	0	0	V	= 0	Ex = 0,1
o	= 8	5	1	1	FY	= 0	Fd = 0,2
u	= 11	3	4	2	YF	= 0	Fi = 0,1
–	= 8	5	1	1	Y	= 0	Ge = 0,0
none	= 0	–	0	0	Fr	= 0	Hh = 0,2

rF	= 0	Ls	= 1,1					
FD	= 0	Na	= 0,2					
F	= 13	Sc	= 3,0					
		Sx	= 0,2	AB	=0	CP	= 0	
		Xy	= 0,0	AG	=3	MOR	= 5	
		Id	= 0,0	CFB	=0	PER	= 0	
(2)	= 8			COP	=2	PSV	= 0	

RATIOS, PERCENTAGES, AND DERIVATIONS

R = 27	L = 0.93		FC:CF+C =1:3	COP = 2	AG = 3
			Pure C =0	Food	= 2

EB = 6:3.5	EA = 9.5	EBPer = 1.7	Afr =0.42	Isolate/R = 0.26
eb = 8:0	es = 8	D = 0	S =4	H:(H)Hd(Hd) = 4:4
	Adj es = 6	Adj D = +1	Blends:R =4:27	(HHd):(AAd) = 3:3
			CP =0	H+A:Hd + Ad = 19:5

FM = 5	C' = 0	T = 0
m = 3	V = 0	Y = 0

				P = 2	Zf =19	3r+(2)/R = 0.41
a:p	= 13:1	Sum6	=13	X+% = 0.30	Zd = +0.0	Fr+rF = 1
Ma:Mp	= 5:1	Lv2	= 3	F+% = 0.38	W:D:Dd =12:11:4	FD = 0
2AB+Art+Ay	= 0	WSum6	= 45	X–% = 0.30	W:M =12:6	An + Xy = 3
M–	= 1	Mnone	= 0	S–% = 0.13	DQ+ =11	MOR = 5
				Xu% = 0.41	DQv =2	

SCZI = 4*	DEPI = 4	CDI = 2	S-CON = 5	HVI = Yes	OBS = No

A Borderline Policeman: AKA, A Cop With No COP

Charles A. Peterson
Department of Veterans Affairs, Minneapolis Medical Center,
and University of Minnesota

Among the many objections analysands offer to the fundamental rule in psychoanalysis, Ferenczi (1919/1976) reported on patients who have difficulty distinguishing between thinking and doing: To think or say it is to risk doing it. For example, a patient might be hesitant to report being angry at someone, fearing that discussion presages loss of control. With developmental immaturity (whether arrest or regression), thought or impulse soon becomes action. Such patients had not reached the level of mature thought, which Freud (1911/1958) described as trial work or experimental action. To look at something intrapsychically does not mean that we have to leap interpersonally. Displaying the same diagnostic naivete that led Freud to regard the Wolf-Man as neurotic, and having no access to an "expert diagnostic consultant" (Weiner, 1972), Ferenczi dismissed the matter cavalierly: "We can reassure these overanxious folk that this fear is only a reminiscence of childhood when they actually were not capable of such a differentiation" (1976, p. 93).

A BORDERLINE POLICEMAN

Many borderline level patients are not so readily reassured by their psychotherapists, as verbal opportunity is transformed into preemptive strike. Mr. C., a combat medic in Vietnam and a street policeman in a large midwestern city, was such a patient. Burdened with fears of his own indiscriminate violence, he presented to an outpatient facility for Vietnam veterans. After an initial history and a screening MMPI (2–4–8), he was placed in a therapy group with other combat-exposed veterans. Not only was he unresponsive to the usual crisis center formula of reassurance, catharsis, and limit-setting, it became apparent that the emotional contagion overstimulated and exacerbated his fears of losing control. With an eye on understanding and soothing, he was subsequently referred for individual therapy, and prudently, a diagnostic consultation based on the Rorschach about to be presented.

Mr. C. is an English-speaking, college-educated, full-time employed, married 46-year-old White man. He grew up in a large midwestern city, the oldest of seven children raised in a violence-ridden family. His father, a strongly patriotic tradesman, was a hot-tempered alcoholic who often exploded in rage against his wife and children and, eventually, fittingly, was killed in a furnace explosion. His memories of his father are generally negative, a man who paid the bills and paid none but violent attention to the family. His most painful childhood recollection witnessed him protecting his younger brother from one of his father's rages. His mother, in a contrast that may favor the use of splitting as a defense, is recalled as a warm, loving, submissive, invariably nurturant woman, the affective glue that held the family together. After an adolescence filled with counterphobic thrills and minor-league criminality, he joined the armed service. Attending jump school and combat medic school provided some of the same excitement that would later influence his decision to become a policeman, about which he stated: "I hate it when things are boring."

Despite having held a job for 15 years and remaining married to the same woman for 20 years, the years since discharge from the Armed Forces have been difficult and tumultuous. His fears of violence have been precariously contained in a personality structure marginally equipped to deal with the demands of loving and working. His relationships have been distant, and when impingement is unavoidable, very turbulent. His impulsiveness has propelled him into a variety of self-damaging behaviors, among them reckless driving, job syntonic provocation of aggression, and alcoholism. Moodiness, irritability, and chronic, intense (if denied) anger, are perennial challenges, as are his efforts to escape boredom. Further destabilizing this unstable personality are the residuals of his war experience, among them intrusive recollections (although they may be memories screening childhood trauma), startle, and re-enactment. Put bluntly, he suffers from reminiscences that threaten to spill into action. Beyond this descriptive diagnosis, what might a psychoanalytically inspired Rorschach psychodiagnosis contribute to our understanding of Mr. C? Might the Rorschach document and provide some understanding of his fears of loss of control? The diagnostician was asked, in effect: Is this a good cop or a bad cop?

RORSCHACH PSYCHODIAGNOSIS OF BORDERLINE PERSONALITY STRUCTURE

Our ability to describe the borderline, whether with the language of experience-distant psychoanalysis or experience-near descriptive psychiatry, has not eliminated the numerous conceptual and methodological controversies surrounding the psychodiagnosis of the borderline. First, there is tremendous conceptual and nosological confusion surrounding the borderline diagnosis. Is it a state, a character disorder, an affective disorder, or a larval psychosis

(Sugarman & Lerner, 1980)? Even the pseudoprecision of the *Diagnostic and Statistical Manual of Mental Disorders* (3rd ed., rev.; American Psychiatric Association, 1987) tolerates, amazingly enough, some 90 different symptom configurations that would warrant the borderline diagnosis (Widiger, Sanderson, & Warner, 1986).

Second, just as there is no such thing as "THE Rorschach," there is no such thing as "THE borderline Rorschach." Even the vaunted pattern of a tidy Wechsler Adult Intelligence Scale—the response to a structured test demonstrating the borderline's good response to structure—and a messy Rorschach—the bad response to an unstructured test demonstrating their inner chaos and regressive potential—has been shown to be an unreliable Wasserman, likely a true positive when it occurs for a small fraction of cases, but a false negative when absent for the vast majority of borderlines (Widiger, 1982). The organizing stamp of different symptoms and character styles will defeat any atheoretical sign approach to the psychodiagnosis of borderline conditions. There is, in short, no "borderline sign" (Sugarman, 1980; Widiger, 1982).

Third, despite the inherent deficits and the lack of conceptual fulfillment in an atheoretical approach, an empirical and normative perspective (e.g., Exner, 1986a) does anchor the Rorschach clinician's speculation. Norms without theory are numbers; theory without norms is fantasy. In light of the general agreement that a theoretical/conceptual approach can best guide test research (Jackson, 1971; Weiner, 1977), a theoretical/conceptual (developmental psychoanalysis) viewpoint will guide this analysis.

The psychodiagnosis of the borderline is best approached in structural terms as a level of (immature) personality organization (Kernberg, 1975, 1980, 1981). That is, all clinicians know there is a vast middle ground between the obviously psychotic patient and the neurotic patient, the former denying the outer world, the latter denying the inner world, and the patients in between suffering more from cumulative trauma than conflict. That diagnostic borderland is the home of the borderline, a "star" (Pruyser, 1975) word in today's nosology, used to describe troubled and troublesome patients. The metapsychology has necessarily evolved, ego and id giving way to Self and Other, oedipal conflicts deferring to arrests in separation–individuation. Self is inadequately differentiated from Other, stuck in or around the rapprochement subphase. Object constancy has not been achieved. Identity is poorly integrated, vulnerable to dissociation. Affects remain preambivalent, labile, preemptory, and tyrannical; good is sharply, artificially, and often explosively separated from bad. Controls are both rigid and riddled with lacunae. Relations with the Other are typically—but can oscillate between—detached or merged, inevitably causing turbulence in the interpersonal field.

RESULTS

The results of the Rorschach testing are reported in the free association/inquiry (Appendix A), sequence of scores (Appendix B), and the structural summary

(Appendix C). They serve as the basis for a determination of the test's reliability and validity and an exploration of the patient's thought organization, affect organization, security operations, and interpersonal modes.

DISCUSSION

Reliability and Validity

This is a reliable, valid, and interpretively useful protocol. R (total responses) and *lambda* (ratio of pure form responses to responses with all other determinants) demonstrate good involvement with the stimuli. Dissatisfied with and hoping to complement a purely quantitative approach, the psychoanalytic psychodiagnostician also looks to the nature of the interaction to determine the meaningfulness of the patient's involvement with the test situation. Mr. C. participated in a pressured, labored interaction, producing long-winded and self-protective responses. Lest the reader be critical of the examiner's occasionally too-persistent inquiry, it is worth remembering that participant observation is required in psychodiagnosis as well as psychotherapy, the occasionally overactive inquiry probably suggesting that the examiner unconsciously knew that Mr. C. required some external prosthesis to structure his inefficient thinking and cascading affects. That the examiner is unwittingly drawn into an interaction that is laced with defensive filibuster, gratuitous evidence, and excessive query will certainly have relevance (later) when the sense of Self and Other is explored.

Thought Organization

Following Rapaport, Gill, and Schafer (1945–1946) and Blatt and Ritzler (1974), the nature of the thought process is the key to the level of structural diagnosis. The structural summary quickly suggests that this is neither a neurotic nor a psychotic protocol. Although the *WSum6* (the weighted sum of Special Scores) is relatively high, the Special Scores are all level 1, relatively free of the implications of a more malignant psychosis (Exner, 1986b). There are no instances of the gross, pervasive disturbances of thought process or specific ego weakness and boundary disturbance that accompany the CON-TAM (contamination) response. Thus, the SCZI (schizophrenia) index is likely a true-negative two. Even though Mr. C. can respond to banal consensual reality as represented in the P (popular) response, Mr. C.'s reality testing is poor, with distortion in both conflict and conflict-free spheres. Closer examination, response by response, reveals that many of the percepts were intially adequate but eventually degraded, much like the borderline who may look better on the surface, only to regress as the initial regulatory impact of the stimulus is overrun by internal factors. A failure of affective modulation rather than a gross failure of reality testing is implicated here. Further, his $X-\%$ (ratio of bad form responses to all responses) of 17% is more consistent with a primitive character than with schizophrenia. His cognitive style is ambitious, overincorporative, scanning the environment, alert for cues/clues. The two $DQv/+$ (developmental quality that involves the combination of 2 > vaguely perceived areas) and the W/M (whole responses compared with human movement responses) expose his unsuccessful attempt to present his cognitive style as more sophisticated than it is. Often overwhelmed, he prefers and perceives a simple, less complex, easily managed stimulus field, in which decisions become easy and/or superficially dichotomous: Reality is sorted into boxes of black and white. Despite an effort to promote a cognitive good front, vagueness persists, often followed by impulsive action, although the latter may prompt another round of rambling justification. There are several instances (e.g., Response 13) where a strained percept is followed with efforts to appear "logical." He disregards and distorts social demands and convention, thinking and behaving illogically, erratically, obviously under the influence of central mediational pressure and light slippage. This style of information processing is more common to children and betrays developmental immaturity. The nonspecific ego weakness that accompanies immaturity is further indicated in his poor affect neutralization and containment: Mr. C. almost invariably merges feeling with thinking during problem solving, vitiating his response to adaptive demand. Conflict-free ideational resources are almost nonexistent. Optimally autonomous ego functions are infiltrated by affects, sabotaging judgment, synthetic function, and safe regression. Psychoanalytic concepts such as the relative loss of autonomy from both id and environment (Rapaport, 1958), as opposed to the generic descriptor "poor information processing," facilitate an assignment to the borderline level of personality organization.

Affective Organization

Discrete and cumulative trauma, excess constitutional aggression, and poor match between infant and caregiver(s) predispose borderline patients to have difficulty modulating/containing and integrating thought with affect. Mr. C. is no exception to this theory-driven and experience-based guidance. An EB (experience balance) of 1:9 is heavily weighted in the direction of difficulty with affect regulation. He is driven by emotion, goaded rather than guided by his affects. An $FC/CF + C$ (the ratio of reality regulated to deregulated affect) clearly shows that affect often overwhelms reality regulation, the former swamping the latter. This reflects a passivity to emotions that is expressed in poorly modulated, often arbitrary expression of affect and impressionistic percepts and verbalizations (e.g., the vagueness on Response 1). This pressure and excitability results in a trial-and-error, nearly chaotic shot-in-the-dark approach to problem solving. Nearly every decision will be markedly influenced by his emotions, which, in light of his father's volatility, may be the inadvertent identification with the aggressor in the children of frightening, alcoholic parents. The *Afr* (affective ratio) provides further documentation that he will be caught up in and become overreactive to environmental stimulation. Overreactive? That has a pejorative ring to it. As nomothetic scientists, we are instructed to describe, not judge, someone's basic style. However, as idiographic ethnographers, we evoke, explore, and evaluate the adequacy of the sufferer's response to adaptive demand. Mr. C., as befits a street policeman, is a man of action, ready to leap into the fray. On the other hand, many hair-trigger situations require affect/frustration tolerance and well-developed sublimatory channels inconsistent with his apparent drive strength and nonspecific ego weakness.

What affects are pressing on and leaking through his controls? The protocol holds two *AG* (aggressive) responses, a figure higher than Exner's (1986a) sample of outpatient character disorders. Both *AG* responses involve fire, explosions, and military armament: The aggression involves things, suggesting that he may depersonalize and dissociate his aggression onto things (or people who become things!). Meloy and Gacono's (1992) expansion of the Comprehensive System's strategy for scoring aggression responses reveals additional aggressive content. There is an *AgContent* (Aggressive Content) response for the "sinister stingray" on Response 7 (Card IV) and a somewhat sublimated *AgPast* (Aggressive Past) for the cut up filet of meat on Response 11 (Card VI). His extratensive proclivity toward angry discharge conflicts sharply with his tendency to internalize his feelings, a trait represented in the five achromatic responses. He is a burnt child who attempts to hold and bury the pain he experiences. This, in turn, leads to the experience of pressure, friability, oversensitivity, and a readiness to explode. The brittle containment of his anger is consciously experienced as irritability, disgruntlement, and grudge, displayed as a nagging negativity in interpersonal situations. These contradictory trends indicate how poorly integrated are his aggressive affects.

As regards the assessment of depression, the *DEPI* (Depression Index) matches the interview assessment that did not diagnose a depressive disorder. Nevertheless, the contents of the true negative *DEPI* reveal retroflected anger, anxious helplessness, low self-esteem, and withdrawal, collectively indicative of unhappiness if not full-blown clinical depression. Coupled with the more vigilant, projective, paranoid-like anger, the absence of *Vista* determinants and relatively low incidence of *MOR* (Morbid) content suggest that he may have an intrapsychic intolerance for or an incapacity to bear depression (Zetzel, 1965). Anxiety is captured in the *Y* (general diffuse shading) determinants. But what is the source of the anxiety? Two of the responses are *FY* (form dominant general shading) with good form and benign popular content but suggest anxiety about the security of masculinity. With potential intimacy this anxiety becomes nearly catastrophic and disorganizing; witness the determinants within the blend on Card III: *YF.C'F.CF–*. The Sex, Blood and X-ray content further attest to the anxiety that presages his loss of control, although the *PER* (personalized content) indicates that he may defensively rationalize motives and repair his injuries with aggrandizement.

Additional misery (a purposely imprecise term, because his distress may not be clearly differentiated) is reflected in the Anatomy and X-ray content, both of which indicate a somatically deployed distress. Exner (1986a) said little on the differential significance of the two types of content and says even less on the meaning of different types of anatomy. Although psychologists have been cautioned (Schafer, 1954) about the practice of "wild analysis" in the interpretation of content, Phillips and Smith (1953) provided hypotheses that can be tested for coherence with the entire protocol and clinical history. Bony anatomy, Mr. C.'s spinal/vertebral imagery, reflects a barely repressed hostility, a hypothesis consistent with other structural variables. The soft anatomy, that is, the gynecological imagery offered by Mr. C., expresses vulnerability, which is disowned and warded off by violent PTSD (post-traumatic stress disorder) imagery and the masculine prosthesis anchored in choice of occupation (policeman). Card IV, Response 7, the denial of a childhood fear, nicely illustrates the counterphobic dimension. His *D* score of –2 reveals inefficient coping due to situational stress. This so-called situational stress may be a constant for a policeman, but it may also represent the chronic instability pathognomonic of the borderline diagnosis. There is no doubt that environmental press/stress will strain his pressured, impulsive, overcontrolled, affective style, continuously threatening a fulminating loss of control. Hypothetically, his coping will improve with a cessation of stress (*Adjusted D* = 0), but he may paradoxically crave too much stimulation to be able to calm down.

Defenses/Security Operations

It has become a clinical cliché that borderlines overemploy splitting as a means of protecting themselves from the unintegratable collisions of antipodal affects. Splitting versus repression has been the litmus in the diagnosis of structural level of personality. Symptomatic and characterological diversity render this rule too simple. The Rorschach diagnostician must be alert for defenses ranging from the primitive to the developmentally more advanced, all influenced by character, and all of which might be represented and displayed structurally, content-thematically, or interactionally during the testing. There are no simple signs, rules, or tips for the diagnostician adrift without theory's guidance.

One of the most frequently used systems available for the analysis of defenses in borderline disorders (Lerner & Lerner, 1980) depends on the presence of *H* (human) content in Rorschach responses. This methodology, in turn, assumes one variant or subtype of the borderline, namely, the overinvolved borderline, careening amidst turbulent, often chaotic object relations. The more detached, schizoid underinvolved borderline is less likely to have a densely populated inner world and correspondingly less H content available to the Rorschacher (cf., Rapaport et al., 1945–1946). Parenthetically, this clinical reality and methodological problem may caution the psychodiagnostician against an overreliance on Kernberg's (e.g., 1975) view of the borderline, namely, the one teeming with malevolent introjects. Further, a low H may signal a characterological defense against painful impingement and involvement. Many a vulnerable individual has mused the words of the old blues song, "If I don't get involved, I can't be hurt." Minimal attachment may bring less pain. However, the minimal attachment documented in the low H and T content further favors aggressive acting out. Attachment to and concern for others generally inhibits acting out (Weber, Meloy, & Gacono, 1992). Given Mr. C.'s low H production, further analysis will draw on Cooper and Arnow's (1986) system for the analysis of borderline defenses, because it is not dependent on the presence of human content. It may also be that another instrument, such as the TAT, might be better suited to evoke object relational themes with some low H character styles.

Mr. C.'s extra-extratensive EB and the massing of CF (color–form) responses favor discharge and acting out as the primary defensive strategy. Affects gush out, goading rather than guiding his behavior, overwhelming the adaptive demands of reality. With this much internal pressure, it is highly likely that his affects will not serve a signal function (Freud, 1926/1959), as they cascade to fulminating levels. The ratio of animal and inanimate to human movement $(FM + m > M)$ emphasizes the propensity to instinctual discharge and suggests that aggression might overwhelm ideational resources/controls. Fortunately (for Self and Other), the aggressive acting out is not conflict-free. The numerous C' responses indicate considerable affective inhibition. He is thus internally at war, tense and pressured, an affective instability reflected in the splitting on Card IX: A pretty, favorite, blossoming flower is followed by a bubbling, malevolent explosion. Following Schachtel's (1966) comments on (self-) percepts issuing from the center of the blot, the diagnostician recalls and understands Mr. C.'s concern that if he were to open up he might explode.

Other borderline level defensive operations are present. Projective identification is implicated in Response 3, where something hurtful (shells) are projected ("anti-aircraft fire") and put into something else ("airplane"). Another instance occurs in Response 6, where Mr. C. signals his alertness to external threat, in this instance a "sinister . . . stingray," a creature capable of putting its toxin in another creature. Omnipotence (more below on the PER responses) is evidenced in Responses 6 and 19, where he makes reference to his service in "the medical corps," his "medical training," and the "caduceus" or "insignia" that he had worn. Devaluation is present in many of his self-deprecatory remarks (e.g., Response 8) and may also be implied in Response 3 where there are attempts to "shoot down" an airplane.

A deficient "background of safety" (Sandler, 1960) is signaled by the low *Egocentricity Index* $(3r + (2)/R)$ and suggests that his defensive repertoire has failed to help him feel good about himself, even if it has precariously contained his acting out. This vulnerability is repaired primarily through a rigid compensatory reactivation of omnipotence and the Grandiose Self (Kohut, 1971), here represented in the numerous PER responses. The 10 PER responses are at a minimum, extraordinary, betraying an extreme narcissistic deficit, covered with a thin veneer of brittle defensiveness and grating grandiosity. The protocol—as record of examiner–patient interaction—is witness to this vigorous shoring up of a sense of Self that is friable. Mr. C. fends off challenges from the examiner and potential critics lurking everywhere, appealing to personal experience to buttress his perspective. This vigorous defense of the Self in an interactional setting may be regarded by the psychoanalytic diagnostician as a guide to the location of the bad object, here perceived as an unbelieving, critical examiner, helping place the testee along the depressive–paranoid continuum. Coupled with the low DEPI, Mr. C.'s vigorous defense suggests a brittle paranoid facade: Better to be pugnacious and lofty than vulnerable and depressed. This paranoid and narcissistic defense against vulnerability and depression was likely reinforced by, and defends against, his memories of vulnerability during his Vietnam experience (Hendin, 1984; it is interesting that Hendin's case was also a policeman, where vigilance is an occupational requirement and aggression is an occupational entitlement). Toughness defending against vulnerability is apparent in the content on Response 5, where he describes "a heavy bone structure protect[ing] the delicate spinal column," or on Response 6 where a "pelvic bone [is] protecting . . . a woman's reproductive organs." Denial and angry negativism are further underlined in his numerous S (White Space) responses and the psychological tongue-biting represented in the already-mentioned achromatic responses.

Self/Other and Interpersonal Modes

Theorists differ on the nature of the borderline's inner world, Kernberg (1975, 1980, 1981) favoring an excess of malevolent introjects, Adler (1985; Adler & Buie, 1979) favoring a paucity of introjects, particularly the holding–soothing variety, which should have been solidified with the attainment of object constancy. Not only is there an outright absence of malevolence, Mr. C. is clearly H deficient, producing only one H response. His one texture response, an FT (form–texture) involved an animal detail, and was not attached (!) to human content. In general, it appears that Mr. C. shows indifference to others as whole, unique, meaningful objects. A scarcely populated inner world can result in different behavioral patterns, among the many possibilities, object-indifference or object-hunger. The Isolate/R Index (the ratio of Botany, Cloud, Geography, Nature, and Landscape content to total responses) further indicates that Mr. C. prefers social isolation.

His only H response occurred on Response 12 on Card VII where the compelling popular response regulates his associative train. He begins with a relatively benign response, "Two Indian girls looking at each other." However, it is apparent that he has not recovered from the aggression released on the prior response/card. Commenting on the bottom center of the card, he spoils the popular by adding "the straight line reminds me of an incision or a cut, like they have been cut and laid open," like the meat reported on the prior response (11). This is a telling example of how aggression intrudes upon his object relations, no matter how vigorously it might be avoided. The aggressive incision and division between two humans, occurring on a card with a regressive lure, represents a defense against reincorporation and symbiosis. Better to be angry, edgy, wary, and separate than to risk intimacy and potential loss of Self. This defense transference is again witnessed in the absence of any cooperative (COP) human interaction.

Kwawer's (1980) classification of primitive modes of relatedness parallel these findings: Responses 3, 6, 18, and 20 collectively show themes of violent symbiosis and expulsive birth and loss/fragmentation of identity. Relations with the Other are avoided even in response to the powerful stimulus demand or pull on Card III, where inner emptiness triumphs over opportunities for relatedness. He offers the ultimate in nonhuman content, "two things," which he eventually refined/covered with a slightly more socially acceptable response, "chickens or birds." This is hardly an indicator of developmental maturation: Self and Other remain poorly, precariously differentiated, warily related, gender and sexual identity vigorously protected with barriers to involvement and intimacy.

The detachment from others is paralleled in his poor hold on the Self. The final response (24) to the Rorschach—often considered a sort of summary self-statement—hints at a rather fluid Self, an "amoeba . . . float[ing] through the sea [of life] . . . protoplasm around a nucleus." What might that nucleus of the Self be (Glover, 1939)? Although the absence of *Vista* responses indicates that Mr. C. may be free from morbid self-reflection, the absence of *FD* (form dimension) responses indicates that he has little productive introspection either, no doubt boding poorly for psychotherapy. His inner world may be too painful and too poorly differentiated to allow much introspection: Self-esteem, measured by the *Egocentricity Index*, is abysmally low. The average number of *FM* (Animal Movement) responses, combined with the large number of *m* (Inanimate Movement) responses suggest that Mr. C. has a great many unmet needs, causing a great deal of frustration and disgruntlement—distress that he cannot consciously pinpoint. It may be that the nucleus of the Self is built around an affective pressure, a generic pleasure–unpleasure. He may not know who he is, only that he is because he feels.

The high incidence of Anatomy and X-ray content not only signals distress, but a hypercathexis of the body, a preoccupation with his innerds, both expressing vulnerability and staving off fragmentation. In the absence of definite physical findings/pathology, something is definitely wrong with the historical and palpable core sense of Self, the bodily ego. Many of Mr. C.'s Anatomy responses involved gynecological imagery, suggesting uncertainty about sexual identity, with resultant attempts to disown and eject female parts of the Self. His emptiness and disowned femininity are covered with a grandiose, rigid, edgy, pompous false Self. The *PER* responses, when combined with a low T (Texture) and low H, will result in an authoritarian stance in his interpersonal relations. He will dominate and use the Other (as extratensives tend to do) while rigidly insisting that the Other follow a narrow code of conduct. The *PER* responses indicate that he will aggressively defend his views, as he believes that the Other will doubt, criticize, and potentially attack him. With his feelers out, he experiences the world as hostile, a place where he is under siege. The creation of a paranoid pseudocommunity creates and renews his great inner pressure, reflected in the four m responses, which, when coupled with some CF in the blend, could lead to some impulsive acting out against the Other whom he has defined (projectively) as aggressive.

The free association and inquiry (Appendix A)—as witness to the interaction between Self and Other—provide evidence of this paranoid trend. Schachtel (1966) has reasoned that the inquiry may evoke some defensiveness, as some testees experience the second phase of the Rorschach as a demand to account for or justify their percept. However, Mr. C. offered *PER* content in both free association and inquiry. His amazingly vigorous efforts to provide real-world historical evidence help justify any potential irregularities in his percepts, buttressing vulnerabilities in the sense of Self. In general, it is safer for him to stick to "Just the facts, Ma'am," and eschew the regressive lure of fantasy and potential space (Smith, 1990). However, even the facts of reality are misused: The combination of poor reality-testing/judgment (low $X+\%$), paranoid "set" (10 *PER* responses), scanty knowledge about and genuine involvement with people (low M and H, an Mp [passive human movement response]) will result in transient ideas of reference (Rapaport et al., 1945–1946). That is, he will alter his set to reality, responding to neutral reality as if it had compelling personal relevance. With access to the tester's countertransference (imagine what it feels like sitting with someone offering 10 *PER* responses), it is easy to envision him scanning his environment, brimming with unexpressed bitterness, distorting the interpersonal world, responding like the alienated paranoid character (Travis) in Martin Scorsese's *Taxi Driver*. Standing before a mirror, in the absence of actual human interaction, Travis says, "You talkin' to me? I don't see no-one else? You talkin' to me?" Hostility, pugnacity, rigidity, and pomposity are the order of the day on this policeman's watch. Living in a borderline world of good and evil, he is, in short, a cop with no COP. Just as a good therapist will help Mr. C. integrate the good and the bad, sophisticated Rorschachers will strive to integrate atheoretical, nomothetic, and developmental, theory-driven, idiographic approaches.

ACKNOWLEDGMENTS

This chapter was initially part of a symposium entitled "Borderline Personality Organization: Through the Looking Glass, Part II" presented at the midwinter meeting of the Society for Personality Assessment in Washington, DC, on March 14, 1992.

I thank Drs. Ernie Boswell and Michael Craine for access to case material, the other members of this symposium for their mutual stimulation, and the Department of Veterans Affairs for supporting this research.

REFERENCES

Adler, G. (1985). *Borderline psychopathology and its treatment.* New York: Aronson.

Adler, G., & Buie, D. H. (1979). Aloneness and borderline psychopathology: The possible relevance of child development issues. *International Journal of Psycho-Analysis, 60,* 83–96.

American Psychiatric Association. (1987). *Diagnostic and statistical manual of mental disorders* (3rd ed., rev.). Washington, DC: Author.

Blatt, S. J., & Ritzler, B. A. (1974). Thought disorder and boundary disturbance in psychosis. *Journal of Consulting and Clinical Psychology, 42,* 370–381.

Cooper, S., & Arnow, D. (1986). An object relations view of the borderline defenses: A review. In M. Kissen (Ed.), *Assessing object relations phenomena* (pp. 143–171). New York: International Universities Press.

Exner, J. E. (1986a). *The Rorschach: A comprehensive system: Vol. 1. Basic foundations* (2nd ed.). New York: Wiley.

Exner, J. E. (1986b). Some Rorschach data comparing schizophrenics with borderline and schizotypal personality disorders. *Journal of Personality Assessment, 50,* 455–471.

Ferenczi, S. (1976). On the technique of psycho-analysis. In M. S. Bergmann & F. R. Hartman (Eds.), *The evolution of psychoanalytic technique* (pp. 89–98). New York: Basic Books. (Original work published 1919)

Freud, S. (1958). Formulations on the two principles of mental functioning. In J. Strachey (Ed.), *The standard edition of the complete psychological works of Sigmund Freud* (Vol. 12, pp. 213–226). London: Hogarth. (Original work published 1911)

Freud, S. (1959). Inhibitions, symptoms and anxiety. In J. Strachey (Ed.), *The standard edition of the complete psychological works of Sigmund Freud* (Vol. 20, pp. 77–174). London: Hogarth. (Original work published 1926)

Glover, E. (1939). The psycho-analysis of affects. *International Journal of Psycho-Analysis, 20,* 299–307.

Hendin, H. (1984). Combat never ends: The paranoid adaptation to posttaumatic stress. *American Journal of Psychotherapy, 38,* 121–131.

Jackson, D. N. (1971). The dynamics of structured personality tests. *Psychological Review, 78,* 229–248.

Kernberg, O. (1975). *Borderline conditions and pathological narcissism.* New York: Aronson.

Kernberg, O. (1980). Neurosis, psychosis, and the borderline states. In A. M. Freedman, H. I. Kaplan, & B. J. Saddock (Eds.), *Comprehensive textbook of psychiatry* (Vol. 3, 3rd ed., pp. 1079–1092). Baltimore: Williams & Wilkins.

Kernberg, O. (1981). Structural interviewing. *Psychiatric Clinics of North America, 4,* 169–195.

Kohut, H. (1971). *The analysis of the self.* New York: International Universities Press.

Kwawer, J. S. (1980). Primitive interpersonal modes, borderline phenomena and Rorschach content. In J. Kwawer, H. Lerner, P. Lerner, & A. Sugarman (Eds.), *Borderline phenomena and the Rorschach test* (pp. 89–105). New York: International Universities Press.

Lerner, P., & Lerner, H. (1980). Rorschach assessment of primitive defenses in borderline personality structure. In J. Kwawer, H. Lerner, P. Lerner, & A. Sugarman (Eds.), *Borderline phenomena and the Rorschach test* (pp. 257–274). New York: International Universities Press.

Meloy, J. R., & Gacono, C. (1992). The aggression response and the Rorschach. *Journal of Clinical Psychology, 48*, 104–114.

Phillips, L., & Smith, J. G. (1953). *Rorschach interpretation: Advanced technique.* New York: Grune & Stratton.

Pruyser, P. W. (1975). What splits in "splitting"? *Bulletin of the Menninger Clinic, 39*, 1–46.

Rapaport, D. (1958). The theory of ego autonomy. *Bulletin of the Menninger Clinic, 22*, 13–35.

Rapaport, D., Gill, M., & Schafer, R. (1945–1946). *Diagnostic psychological testing.* Chicago: Year Book Publishers.

Sandler, J. (1960). The background of safety. *International Journal of Psycho-Analysis, 41*, 352–356.

Schachtel, E. G. (1966). *Experiential foundations of Rorschach's test.* New York: Basic Books.

Schafer, R. (1954). *Psychoanalytic interpretation of Rorschach testing.* New York: Grune & Stratton.

Smith, B. (1990). Potential space and the Rorschach: An application of object relations theory. *Journal of Personality Assessment, 55*, 756–767.

Sugarman, A. (1980). The borderline personality organization as manifested on psychological tests. In J. S. Kwawer, H. D. Lerner, P. M. Lerner, & A. Sugarman (Eds.), *Borderline phenomena and the Rorschach test* (pp. 39–57). New York: International Universities Press.

Sugarman, A. S., & Lerner, H. D. (1980). Reflections on the current state of the borderline concept. In J. S. Kwawer, H. D. Lerner, P. M. Lerner, & A. Sugarman (Eds.), *Borderline phenomena and the Rorschach test* (pp. 11–37). New York: International Universities Press.

Weber, C. A., Meloy, J. R., & Gacono, C. B. (1992). A Rorschach study of attachment and anxiety in inpatient conduct-disordered and dysthymic adolescents. *Journal of Personality Assessment, 58*, 16–26.

Weiner, I. B. (1972). Does psychodiagnosis have a future? *Journal of Personality Assessment, 36*, 534–546.

Weiner, I. B. (1977). Approaches to Rorschach validation. In M. A. Rickers-Ovsiankina (Ed.), *Rorschach psychology* (2nd ed., pp. 575–608). Huntington, NY: Krieger.

Widiger, T. A. (1982). Psychological tests and the borderline diagnosis. *Journal of Personality Assessment, 46*, 227–238.

Widiger, T. A., Sanderson, C., & Warner, L. (1986). The MMPI, prototypal typology, and borderline personality disorder. *Journal of Personality Assessment, 50*, 540–553.

Zetzel, E. R. (1965). Depression and the incapacity to bear it. In M. Schur (Ed.), *Drives, affects, behavior* (Vol. 2, pp. 243–274). New York: International Universities Press.

I.

1. A bat. I don't know exactly why. There's kind of a nose there, wings. I can't see much else in there. The darker part is kind of a body that a bat would have. I don't have a very creative imagination. I kind of deal with what's in front of me. Many time I'll go with my first impression. For the most part, the first impression is the right one. (a.t.e.?) Once I see something, I have a difficult time seeing anything else. No that's about all I can see in this one. I can't come up with anything else.

(?) These are kind of the feet folded up underneath the head here. These would be wings, raggedy kind of wings. (?) The outline. It looks like it's a pretty tough life. It's also nature's design, but it's not a nice flowing line along the outline of the wings. (?) These could be like a thumb and fingers. As I recall, bats have gripping feet. (?) It kind of goes in. It would be something that would bite on. I'm ignoring the projection on the side. The dark color has something to do with that, too. I consider bats sinister and this color is sinister, too. It's about the color I would expect a bat to be. I see the bat as going this way because the wings are swept back and that's how I would picture the wings to be.

II.

2. This is a cat's face. The white spot I would picture as a nose. It sweeps back kind of like whiskers.

(?) The white part reminds of a nose, although a cat's nose would actually be black. This is the mouth and the whiskers on it. There seems to be a pattern. I don't know if it's brush strokes or what but it reminds me of a cat's fur around the nose. Eyes are reddish color with stripes in, kind of like tiger stripes.

3. I can also imagine this to be an airplane. It'd be going in that direction. This could be tail-flames shooting out the back of the plane. This I could picture as anti-aircraft fire. Don't know if I see anything else in there. I don't see anything else.

(?) This would be the nose of the plane, kind of a pointed nose. The blast, red hot blast coming out the back of the plane. (?) The redness and lines coming out, to me, is a force coming out, away from the silhouette. This red up here I could picture as anti-aircraft fire, the red being hot. It's in front of the plane trying to shoot it down. The dark color gives me the impression it's flying in overcast conditions.

III.

4. Two things facing each other. I guess I'd say there were chickens or birds. Points remind me of beaks and the tail.

(?) Those look like beaks to me. (?) They're pointed with kind of a round head right about where a beak would be. Near the end where the tail of a bird would be I remember bird tails project. Front part could be a wing. The length makes it look like a folded wing. It projects out too much. This would be a very abstract bird.

5. The other thing I can think of is a vertebrae column.

(?) The outline reminds me of a vertebrae down here and the vertebrae are stacked on each other. (?) A heavy bone structure protects the delicate spinal column in between. (?) Thicker, it looks thicker, thinner in the middle, more delicate.

6. This is kind of long shot, but it might also be a diagram of a woman's reproductive organs, too. This could be the vagina, the uterus and the fallopian tubes up here. That's about all I can see on that one.

(?) I was in the medical corps and had a lot of medical training and I've seen a lot of these diagrams. Dark parts remind me of an x-ray. White areas in here remind me of a pelvic bone protecting that area. This is the vagina entry into the uterus, the birth canal leading into the uterus. (?) It's light colored dark around the middle. Fallopian tubes curl up and around this way. Red reminds me of the blood inside the human body.

IV.

7. This is kind of a sinister one to me. Some kind of sea creature like a sting ray or something like that. This, the head with tentacles sticking out. Two eyes there. Wings or fins; I guess you call them fins on a sea creature. These I see as tentacles or stingers. I'm always thinking there's a hidden picture there I should see, but I don't see it.

(?) It's dark. It doesn't have nice flowing lines; it has a jagged outline. It just looks threatening. If I saw this in the water, I would want to get out. Like when I was a boy, they told me not to touch the stingers of bullheads. Ironically now I'm not afraid of bullheads. I just grab them. When I was a young boy, I'd cut the line before I'd touch it. (?) The length suggests tentacles or stingers. They could be feelers for feeling around or they could be used for stinging. The dark spots suggest two eyes. That's what strikes me right away. Two eyes remind me of a creature. I've never seen anything like this in the water, but I wouldn't be surprised to see this swimming by. I say sea creature because it looks too bulky to be on land. It's not streamlined. (?) This looks like a big neck. It just looks too heavy to be a flying creature. I'm not saying it's huge. It might be small, but I would still stay away from it. Its proportion is such that I don't see it a flying thing. (?) They're spread out, loose. They would flap on the upward stroke.

V.

8. A moth, here again, the wings, the jagged edge around the wings. These would be the tentacles. These would be, I don't know what they call them, but on moths and butterflies they have these things trailing off the back. I think they have something to do with stabilizing in flight. I look at this as a moth instead of a butterfly. Butterfly has straight-edged wings and pretty colors. That's about it. I'm just not a creative person. I know an artist could see dozens of things in here, but I'm, I just see what I see and tell it like it is.

(?) Here again the pattern extends out, reminds me of wings, aerodynamic like a flying creature. These would remind me of feelers. (?) The way they project out. I see this as a head and this is the way they project out. I, most of these I see, this as a natural formation because nature has a way of duplicating on each side. There is a jagged edge because nature has duplicated it. I don't know the reason but I figure there must be a reason. (?) The irregularities just don't follow my sense of order. I like things round or straight. Anything else is an imperfection. Like I say there might be a perfectly logical explanation but I don't know what it is. A butterfly's wings would come out straight and curve nice and flowing without any irregularities. If there were different colors in here I might see this as a very beautiful . . . but right now it's not something I see as beautiful.

(continued)

171

VI.

9. This is a tough one. It reminds me of a hide or a skin staked out on a wall to dry. It reminds me of a Western scene. You might see this in an Indian village or on the side of an old Western trading post or something.

10. The top part reminds me of an Indian symbol. I believe they call it a thunderbird from Indian lore or religion or mythology.

11. It reminds me of a piece of meat cut open, a filet of some type. I used to work in a grocery store behind a meat counter, and I would cut open a filet like this. See the knife line right down the middle. Then I would cut, make it nice and neat for the customer and throw away the excess in the hamburger grinding bin. That's about all I can see on that one.

VII.

12. Two Indian girls looking at each other. This would be the feather. Their faces here. Probably sitting on rocks, identical rocks. All these patterns have that straight line down the middle that reminds me of an incision or a cut, like they've been cut and laid open.

(?) Pattern looks like it might be a hide, back legs here, front legs here. (?) The shape of it, like somebody cut it right down the middle and laid it open. It's something I might have seen in my youth in a cowboy and Indian movie, a hide staked to the side of a wall.

(?) These look like wings sticking straight out. Here again both sides are duplicates of each other. It looks like something that might be on a totem pole or stand. That could be the head. It's very abstract, but from memory, that could be the head. The color indicates, as I recall, Indian artifacts have different colors in them. (?) Different shades, lighter here, wings are a darker shade.

(?) Here again, it's an irregular pattern, but the same on both sides. Cut open a piece of meat and it looks like that, irregular but similar. Again, you cut off the protruding pieces. People not only want a good tasting piece of meat but they want one that looks good, too.

(?) This looks like a face here, hair curled out to front, eyes, nose, face, chin, neck. I can't explain this projection, maybe a pack. This looks like a feather straight up in the air. (?) The swirl. It sticks out past the forehead. That's why I say girl, because more hair. Indian boys wore their hair much shorter traditionally, so I wouldn't see the hair out front. Bunch back here reminds me of hair because of the bunching. (?) This is pretty abstract again. It's a pretty thick feather, but it comes up to a point. I thought it might be a ponytail but a ponytail would hang down. The only other explanation would be a feather. (?) I think of a feather as delicate, thinner. It's wide at the base and the darkness of the inside kind of gives me the impression of a feather, too. (?) The only explanation I could give for this is bulk. I think of Indians as outdoor people. Also, irregular shape again.

13. I'm not supposed to turn these, am I. (whatever you'd like). Being as how there are identical patterns on both sides, I feel the only proper way to observe this would be this way (∧) or this way (∨). If I hold it this way, this appears to be a foundation the figure is standing on. If I hold it this way, it could stand on these two points. As I hold it on the side, it doesn't appear to be the logical way to hold it because if I set it down it would tip or this point would break off. That's about all I can see in that one. I get hung up on that first impression and then it's hard for me to see anything else.

VIII.

14. I remember some of these from the --- Center. No, was you show them to me. The minute you showed me this, it reminded me of two rodents climbing up a rock formation, maybe a coral formation.

15. This middle part again could be a vertebrae column or spinal column. It looks kind of like that.

16. This lower part kind of reminds me of a flower. I can't think of the name of it right now. These definitely I can't get away from thinking they're some kind of rodents probably. I'm really hung up on those rodents. That's about all I can see.

IX.

17. They don't get any easier, do they. This way it reminds me of a flower blossoming out.

(?) It's bulkier down here, heavy and strong. (?) Just the size. It looks like something strong to me. If you put it like this, it could balance on the columns like engineers build with two columns, so all things being equal it could balance. Here it would be supported by this point and it would fall to the bulkier side. (?) The size. Points give me the center line. There's more mass on this than the other side.

(?) A coral formation would probably more correct. A rock formation would be more massive, a coral formation more delicate with color. A rock is grey. (?) These lines structures, they don't look like strong structures. They might be very pretty structures, but . . . I see the legs, stepping up to another formation, kind of a pointed nose, dark spots are eyes. A little rise here, like it's an ear.

(?) I see a mass of bone. I can't explain the color, but I see the mass protecting the precious spinal column. (?) The shape, it's kind of all in a line on the side, to the pointed coccyx. I think that's what they call it. Bones, especially vertebrae are irregularly patterned.

(?) It has an irregular but similar pattern like nature does. It's kind of like an opening flower, spread out. The color pink gives me the idea of a delicate flower.

(?) Actually, this turned out to be my favorite one after I looked at it for a while. After a while it looked pretty to me, like an open flower with pretty colors. There's a projection in the middle to the pollen. Again, irregular but similar on both sides like nature does things. I see petals on a flower being irregular but similar. The color in the middle indicates space in between.

(continued)

18. This way it reminds me of an explosion.

(?) Pattern is kind of a multiple explosion, explode, implode, explode, kind of like a mushroom cloud, not a perfect mushroom cloud, a bubbling mushroom cloud. It's still taking shape. The lighter orange reminds me of flame heat in the middle. Green in the middle is a mixture of things being blown up. It's a darker color. I can't explain the pink on top. Maybe it's an explosion in red clay with pink dust. That could be vegetation in the middle with the flame below it.

19. For some reason. I don't know why, it reminds me of the medical caduceus we used to wear. I don't know why, it kind of does. That had a staff right in the middle. The insignia had wings on the side.

(?) I think of the lighter colors. If I eliminate them, I see the staff and the wings. The darker colors dominate the lighter ones and that's where I see the caduceus or insignia.

X.

20. I hate to say this because I don't want anyone to think I have a hang-up about this, but to me again it kind of reminds me of a diagram of a woman's reproductive organ.

(?) Diagrams I've seen are similar on the same side. I'm trying to look at that and say what did I see here.

21. Pelvic bone again, it's out of proportion. It kind of reminds me of the pelvic bone area.

(?) Shape again. The pelvic bone flares out. This bridge reminds me of a structure holding it together. I have to eliminate all this other stuff. That seems to be stretching it. I look at it now and think the seascape is more appropriate.

22. I also see a coral scene here in the clear tropic waters of the Carribean, maybe, the Bahamas or something like that. These are the coral patterns.

(?) The color. I haven't had much experience with the sea or coral but I understand coral is colored and there is red coral. I've eliminated that grey structure, though I suppose that could be a sea structure, too. It just looks like it would not be very stable. It would fall over. Of course, coral would be delicate, too. (?) The small structure, thin pieces holding together, even vegetation. This could be underwater plants or flowers. (?) The colors. This is green. This is yellow. If I were a scuba diver and had plenty of experience with coral, this probably wouldn't look anything like it. But I don't have that.

23. There are a couple of sea horses in the middle of the pattern.

(?) This pattern is probably what led me into the seascape thing. I've seen sea horses, too. This is definitely the pattern of a sea horse. (?) The shape, long body flows over the top to a pointed nose. As I recall they actually do have a structure on their back and head that looks like the mane of a horse.

24. Various sea amoeba and things that float in the area. That's all about I can see in there, right now.

(?) This might be a little piece of plant life that floats through the sea. This looks like protoplasm surrounding a nucleus, if I can remember from my science classes. (?) Kind of the color again, suggests seed pods, stalks. This green color could be vegetation.

APPENDIX B
Sequence of Scores

Card	No.	Loc.	Determinant(s)	(2)	Content(s)	Pop Z	Special Scores
I	1	Ddo	FC'.FMpo		A		PER, MOR
II	2	WSo	FT.FCu		Ad	5.5	
	3	WS+	ma.CF.C'Fu		Sc, Fi, Ex	5.5	AG, DV
III	4	Do	FMpu	2	A		
	5	DSo	Fu		An		
	6	DdSo	YF.C'F.CF–		Xy, Sx, Bl		PER
IV	7	Wv	C'Fu		A		PER, ALOG
V	8	Wo	Fo		A	1.0	INC, ALOG
VI	9	Dv	Fo		Ad	P	PER
	10	Do	FYo		Ay		PER
	11	Dv	F–		Fd		PER
VII	12	W+	Mp.FYo	2	H, Ls	P 2.5	
	13	Wv	F–		Id		DR
VIII	14	W+	FMa.CFo	2	A, Ls	P 4.5	FAB
	15	Ddo	Fu		An		
	16	Dv	CF.mpo		Bt		
IX	17	DdS/	CF.mp.C'Fo		Bt	5.0	
	18	W/	ma.CFo		Ex, Fi	5.5	AG
	19	Wo	FCu		Cg	5.5	PER, DV
X	20	Wv	F–		An, Art		PER, DV
	21	DdSo	Fu		An		
	22	Wv	CFo		Na		
	23	Do	Fo	2	A		PER
	24	Wv	CFu		A, Bt		PER

Summary of Approach

I:Dd	VI:D.D.D.
II:WS.WS	VII:W.W
III:D.DS.DdS	VIII:W.Dd.D
IV:W	IX:DdS.W.W
V:W	X:W.DdS.W.D.W

APPENDIX C
Rorschach Structural Summary

LOCATION	DETERMINANTS	CONTENTS	S-CONSTELLATION
FEATURES	BLENDS SINGLE		NO..FV + VF + V + FD > 2

LOCATION FEATURES

Zf = 8	
ZSum = 35.0	
ZEst = 24.0	
W = 12	
(Wv = 5)	
D = 7	
Dd = 5	
S = 6	

DETERMINANTS — BLENDS

FC.'FM
FT.FC
m.CF.C'F
YF.C'F.CF
M.FY
FM.CF
CF.m
CF.m.C'F
m.CF

DETERMINANTS — SINGLE

M = 0	FM = 1	m = 0	FC = 1
CF = 2	C = 0	Cn = 0	FC' = 0
C'F = 1	C' = 0	FT = 0	TF = 0
T = 0	FV = 0	VF = 0	V = 0
FY = 1	YF = 0	Y = 0	Fr = 0
rF = 0	FD = 0	F = 9	

CONTENTS

H = 1,0	(H) = 0,0
Hd = 0,0	(Hd) = 0,0
Hx = 0,0	A = 7,0
(A) = 0,0	Ad = 2,0
(Ad)= 0,0	An = 4,0
Art = 0,1	Ay = 1,0
Bl = 0,1	Bt = 2,1
Cg = 1,0	Cl = 0,0
Ex = 1,1	Fd = 1,0
Fi = 0,2	Ge = 0,0
Hh = 0,0	Ls = 0,2
Na = 1,0	Sc = 1,0
Sx = 0,1	Xy = 1,0
Id = 1,0	

S-CONSTELLATION

- YES..Col-Shd Bl>0
- YES..Ego<.31,>.44
- NO..MOR>3
- YES..Zd > ± 3.5
- YES..es>EA
- YES..CF+C>FC
- YES..X+%<.70
- YES..S>3
- NO..P<3 or >8
- YES..Pure H <2
- NO..R<17
- 8.....TOTAL

DQ

..........(FQ–)

+ = 3 (0)	
o = 11(1)	
v/+ = 2 (0)	
v = 8 (3)	

FORM QUALITY

	FQx	FQf	MQual	SQx
+	= 0	0	0	0
o	= 11	3	1	1
u	= 9	3	0	4
–	= 4	3	0	1
none	= 0	–	0	0

(2) = 4

SPECIAL SCORINGS

	Lvl	Lv2
DV	= 3x1	0x2
INC	= 1x2	0x4
DR	= 1x3	0x6
FAB	= 1x4	0x7
ALOG	= 2x5	
CON	= 0x7	
SUM6	= 8	
WSUM6	= 22	

AB =0		CP = 0
AG =2		MOR = 1
CFB =0		PER = 10
COP =0		PSV = 0

RATIOS, PERCENTAGES, AND DERIVATIONS

R = 24	L = 0.60	

FC:CF+C =2:8	COP = 0	AG = 2
Pure C =0	Food	= 1

EB = 1:9.0	EA = 10.0	EBPer = 9.0	Afr =0.85	Isolate/R	= 0.29
eb = 7:9	es = 16	D = –2	S =6	H:(H)Hd(Hd)	= 1:0
	Adj es = 11	Adj D =0	Blends:R =9:24	(HHd):(AAd)	= 0:0
			CP =0	H+A:Hd + Ad	= 8:2

FM = 3	C' = 5	T = 1
m = 4	V = 0	Y = 3

			P = 3	Zf =8	3r+(2)/R = 0.17
a:p = 3:5	Sum6 =8	X+% = 0.46	Zd = +11.0	Fr+rF = 0
Ma:Mp = 0:1	Lv2 = 0	F+% = 0.33	W:D:Dd =12:7:5	FD = 0
2AB+Art+Ay = 2	WSum6 = 22	X–% = 0.17	W:M =12:1	An + Xy = 5
M– = 0	Mnone = 0	S–% = 0.25	DQ+ =3	MOR = 1
		Xu% = 0.38	DQv =8	

SCZI = 2	DEPI = 4	CDI = 2	S-CON = 8*	HVI = No	OBS = No

12

A Rorschach Case Study of Stalking: "All I wanted was to love you . . ."

J. Reid Meloy
University of California, San Diego

The crime of stalking is usually defined as the willful, repeated, and malicious following or harassing of another person that threatens his or her safety. There are now explicit laws that prohibit this conduct throughout the United States and Canada, progenies of the first law born in California in 1990.

Although prosecuting people for stalking is quite new, the behavior itself is quite old. Louisa May Alcott was probably the first to write about it in her recently discovered and published novel, *A Long Fatal Love Chase* (Alcott, 1866/1995). The French psychiatrist de Clérambault (1942) vividly described it in the context of erotomanic delusional disorder. And two prominent forensic cases in the United States, *U.S. v. John Hinckley, Jr.* (No. 81-306) and *Tarasoff v. Regents of the University of California* (17 Cal. 3d 425, 1976), captured its essentials in the latter half of the 20th century.

Stalking, clinically labeled "obsessional following" (Meloy & Gothard, 1995), has received an enormous amount of legal attention (Guy, 1993). Clinical research, however, has been meager. I reviewed the extant studies published during the past 25 years—10 scientific papers involving 180 subjects—and offered, in part, the following preliminary findings: Individuals who engaged in stalking were usually above average IQ, single or divorced males in their 30s, with prior criminal, psychiatric, and drug abuse histories. They pursued women about their age, the majority of whom were prior acquaintances (neither former sexual intimates nor complete strangers).[1] Pursuits

---

[1] This empirical finding contradicts the passionate assertions of professionals who work with victims of domestic violence that all stalking arises from violent marriages that were torn asunder. Stalking is not a synonym for domestic violence, but may be a variant of it in some cases (Kurt, 1995). Zona recently reported that less than half of their sample of 200 obsessional followers (of whom 74 were included in my review) were preceded by domestic violence (M. Zona, personal communication, August 1995).

usually were accompanied by threats and lasted for months or years, likely inducing psychiatric symptoms, such as anxiety and depression, in many victims. Face-to-face contact, phone calls, and letters were the most frequent means of approach, but most stalking cases did not result in personal violence. If it did, the victim was pushed, grabbed, hit, punched, or fondled. Homicide was rare (< 2%;[2] Meloy, 1996).

The most parsimonious and useful psychodynamic formulation posits that pathological narcissism, and a linking fantasy (Bion, 1959/1984), are central to stalking, and rejection by the object of desire stimulates a deep humiliation that is defended against with rage; the obsession is fueled, devaluation ensues, and acts begin to hurt or injure the object to restore the linking narcissistic fantasy. Stalkers do not mourn the loss of their objects and form new attachments, a common denouement of unrequited love among normals (Meloy, 1989, 1996). This inability to grieve the loss of a whole object, and instead, rage against the victim as a part object or selfobject (Kohut, 1972), is consistent with borderline personality organization (Kernberg, 1984) and the lack of attainment of the depressive position (Klein, 1957/1975). Empirical testing of these hypotheses, however, has not been done.

Published psychological test data on samples of stalkers are virtually nonexistent. Some data on a small sample ($N = 6$) of erotomanic and borderline erotomanic individuals who were violent have been published (Meloy, 1992), and do not contradict theoretical formulations. Such nomothetic data collection, however, has little discriminant validity because psychological heterogeneity (variance) is likely when subject sampling is defined by one pattern of behavior—the intentional and repeated following of another. Psychiatric heterogeneity among stalkers has already been empirically found (Harmon, Rosner, & Owens, 1995; Meloy & Gothard, 1995; Mullen & Pathé, 1994; Zona, Sharma, & Lane, 1993). I take an idiographic approach in the following case to scrutinize the behavior, history, psychodynamics, motivation, and psychiatric diagnoses of one man who was charged with and convicted of stalking.

CASE STUDY

In the early morning hours of October 17, 1994, a police officer investigated a Saab 900 Turbo convertible parked along the street with a man slouched down in the driver's seat, pretending to be asleep. He had a pair of binoculars in his lap, told the officer his name was Victor, and he was, "just hanging out

---

[2]Zona reported no homicides caused by his sample of 200 subjects from the Threat Management Unit of the Los Angeles Police Department. About half of his subjects threatened as expected, and the highest frequency of personal violence was 17% among the erotomanic subgroup (M. Zona, personal communication, August 21, 1995). Note, however, that the probability of being intentionally killed (1:50) if one is being stalked is 200 times greater than the risk of being intentionally killed just by virtue of living in the United States (1:10,000).

enjoying the scenery." When prompted by the officer, he admitted to parking there to see if his girlfriend would drive by. He was one half mile from her residence. When the officer verbally confronted Victor about the restraining order that was in effect, he replied, "I can't help it. I'm in love with her."

Victor had a folding buck knife in his waistband and a Swiss army knife in his pocket. On the right front passenger floorboard was an unsheathed sword and a machete. In his briefcase was another 6-in. knife. Another briefcase in the trunk produced a Charter Arms Model AR–7 .22 caliber rifle and 86 rounds of ammunition. In the back seat, wrapped in a blanket, was a 16 gauge Remington shotgun loaded with five rounds, one in the chamber. Victor was 146 ft outside the perimeter established by a restraining order that had been issued 4 days earlier. He was subsequently booked into custody and charged with several crimes, including stalking with a temporary restraining order in effect, a felony.[3]

Criminal investigators found that Victor had lived with the victim, Uma, for 6 years, and they had produced a son, Victor's third child. The 2 months preceding his arrest and following their separation were filled with tempestuous behavior and amphetamine-laced angst. Uma left Victor because of his violence toward her. He then threatened to kill her and her friends, followed her in his car, telephoned her multiple times, and on one occasion 10 days before his arrest went to her residence and tried, with a certain neanderthal bravado, to drag her away with him. Two male friends confronted him with a pipe and bat, Victor drew a knife, but he then let Uma go.

A week before the arrest, however, it appears that Victor was the intended victim of a "drive-by" shooting at the home in which he was staying. Uma also continued to telephone him and have sexual intercourse with him, subsequent to their separation. The defendant, the victim, and her friends were using amphetamine continuously through the summer.

Victor's letters to Uma were filled with rage: "You are the worst person on the planet and the sooner you die the better, the despicable bitch that you are . . . I hate you with all my heart, you cum catcher." On the other hand, his loss and grief were painfully apparent: "I'm the one who wants to die . . . all I wanted was to love you. I never meant to hurt you physically, I didn't want that. I felt you slipping away." Uma characterized Victor as possessive, jealous, and paranoid. He would accuse her of being with many men. When he would blow up, he would yell obscenities, throw things, and leave.

I examined Victor at the request of his defense counsel. He was a 42-year-old White male of Irish and Eastern European heritage, 6'4" tall and weighed 220 pounds. He was partially balding, had a bushy, handlebar moustache, and reminded me of Paul Bunyan. Despite his intimidating size and appearance, he remained friendly and cooperative throughout our day together.

---

[3]California Penal Code Section 646.9. Subsequent to this case the California law was changed so that the first offense of stalking could be charged as a felony without a restraining order in effect.

Although Victor was not grossly psychotic, his mental status exam showed some abnormalities. He was mildly circumstantial and tangential, his mood was dysthymic, and he was obviously grieving a number of losses, crying openly in front of me. As the interview progressed, he reported many suspicious, jealous, and persecutory beliefs concerning his love object and her friends. He showed no anger or suspicion toward me.

Victor was the second-youngest child in a family of five children from an intact, middle-class family. He described his developmental years as "intense." His earliest memory (Bruhn, 1990) was, "Tossing my bottle out of the crib, breaking the crib with my feet. I was thrilled." He was very athletic without a corollary history of conduct disorder. His parents divorced when he was 7, and he endured his first major emotional loss when father left after asking him, "'Don't you want to go with me?' I turned him down cause I didn't want to leave my mother." Victor began to sob.

His chronic, but nonviolent criminal history began when he was 18 and arrested for possession of seconal, and remained embedded in his extensive polydrug use history that continued until this arrest almost 25 years later. Cannabis was his favorite drug, amphetamine was his most recent drug, and heroin was his most problematic drug. His work history was intermittent, usually employed by a family member in the construction business. His psychiatric history was negative except for counseling related to drug use, but two of his siblings also had heroin and amphetamine dependence problems. His violence history included mostly fist-fights, but Victor reported a fascination with knives since age 15: "the perfection, the skill, they are a work of art." Anger management was learned through drug counseling. "I blow off stress by cussing, a catharsis. Did you read about the 'screaming tree' in James Clavell's *The Noble House?*" I had not.

Victor reported a history of serial polygyny. He married Barbara for 2 years and produced two children. They separated, he took the children, and began living with Stella. This relationship lasted for 2 years, they separated, and 2 years later he met Uma. She became pregnant, disliked his children, and he relinquished them to his first wife and sister. Uma and he remained together for 6 years. "I told Barbara I'm never going to leave these kids. There was alot of lust with Uma, a pretty girl. But she was cold hearted. I lost my kids because of her. On a daily basis I have to stop myself from crying. Am I going to leave him (his youngest son) without a father too?" Victor began to sob again. His youngest son, Frank, is now the same age as he was when his father abandoned him.

Victor was "mad and hurt" the night of the offense. He thought about suicide, but was also determined to assault Uma's perceived boyfriend. "Uma had called me six times that day, but no return number. I was still thinking there was a chance. If she came back now I'd take her back. I'm still stewing in it. It's so stupid . . . I honestly feel I showed a lot of restraint in this deal. They were actively trying to make me believe I was crazy. She should be on trial. Playing a vicious game. I caught her in lies."

PSYCHOLOGICAL TESTING RESULTS

Victor was on no psychotropic medication at the time of testing. He completed the Quick Test, the Rorschach, the Minnesota Multiphasic Personality Inventory–2 (MMPI–2), and the Millon Clinical Multiaxial Inventory–II (MCMI–II). I also scored him on the Psychopathy Checklist–Revised (Hare, 1991). On the Quick Test (Ammons & Ammons, 1962), a measure of estimated verbal intelligence, he scored 110, placing him at the 75th percentile. The MMPI–2 (Hathaway & McKinley, 1989) evidenced a spike 4 profile (Pd = 72), with a valid, but self-favorable LFK configuration. He produced a raw MacAndrew score of 27 (T = 62) and a T = 69 on the Overcontrolled Hostility scale. Harris and Lingoes subscales were unremarkable except for Ma3 (T = 65), imperturbability. The MCMI–II (Millon, 1976) showed mild elevations on the Schizoid (BR = 69) and Dependent (BR = 65) scales, a curious clinical conundrum. The Rorschach protocol is reproduced in Appendix A. The Sequence of Scores is in Appendix B. The Structural Summary is in Appendix C.

DISCUSSION

Rorschach Comprehensive System Findings

Victor produced a constricted (R = 16) but valid protocol ($Lambda$ = 0.60). His core characteristics indicate a man with significantly less volitional resources (EA = 3) than normal adults (EA = 8.28; Exner, 1986). Given his current stressors and chronic patterns ($AdjD$ = –1), he is likely to show lapses in his ability to organize his behaviors in a predictable manner. In other words, intermittent losses of impulse control, probably stimulated by interpersonal difficulties ($H:[H]$ + Hd + $[Hd]$ = 0:6, M = 1), are expected.

Victor is chronically characterologically angry (S = 3), likely caused by his grandiose notions of accomplishment ($W:M$ = 10:2) and shortcomings in his abilities to love and work (CDI = 4), despite his bright normal IQ. He constrains his emotions (C' = 4, $FC:CF$ + C = 2:0, $WgtSumC$ = 1) and tries to avoid emotional stimuli in others (Afr = 0.45). At present he has an elevated sense of "being shot at" (m = 2), but has no difficulty discharging states of tension (FM = 1), perhaps at the expense of others' feelings of safety. He does not have a clear problem-solving style (EB = 2:1), unexpected in psychiatric samples (Exner, 1993). He likely experiences no remorse (V = 0), has a normative amount of anxiety (Y = 1), and is chronically emotionally detached from others (T = 0). He is confused by his emotions (Response 3, $FC'.FC–$). He does produce, however, a "negated T" on Response 10, perhaps a marker for the use of denial as a defense against affectional neediness (Meloy & Gacono, 1992).

Rorschach data concerning Victor's interpersonal relations suggest a man who is schizoid ($COP = 0, Ag = 0, Food = 0$), expecting neither cooperation nor aggression from others. He does not represent himself or others in his mind as whole, real, and meaningful individuals (*Pure H* = 0), and may have a paranoid disorder ($H + A:Hd + Ad < 4:1, Zf = 13, R = 16$; Meissner, 1978). Consistent with the behavior of stalking, his relations with others appear to depend more on wish fulfillment and fantasy than actual reality ($[H] = 2$, $[Hd] = 2, Mp > Ma$). His perceptions are chiefly characterized by self-criticism in relation to others (*EgoC* = 0.25), consistent with a deep sense of injury, perhaps a narcissistic wound (*MOR* = 3) that is continuously reinfected by a repetition compulsion to master abandonment and his subsequent hurt as a child through poor object choices as an adult. He is not somatically preoccupied ($An + Xy = 1$). He has a normative capacity for insight (*FD* = 1), a positive treatment indicator.

Victor's cognitive processing is quite efficient ($Zf = 13$), but not very effective ($Zd = -2.0$). He has a tendency to miss important details in his environment. He will likely not see the big picture, although he tries to and fails ($W:D = 10:4$). His cognitive mediation is also quite faulty. Victor perceives the world in an unconventional and idiosyncratic manner, but better when affect is involved ($X+\% = 50, F+\% = 33$). His reality testing is impaired, and in the borderline range ($X-\% = 19$), like most antisocial males in custody (Gacono & Meloy, 1994). This variable also suggests a borderline level of personality organization and the utilization of defenses, such as projection, which contribute to the confusion of internal fantasy and external stimuli. For instance, Victor may perceive aggressive threats in others when they actually originate in himself. He may be prone to become psychotic when in a rage ($S-\% = 100$), but this Rorschach correlate needs more validation (Exner, 1993). In this case, $S-\%$ may be related to a more hysterical and dissociative explosiveness (Response 3, "Whoa!"; Response 14, "Wow!") that accompanies his aggression.

Victor shows mild formal thought disorder ($WSum6SpecScores = 12, Level 2 = 0$), and is prone to withdraw into fantasy and depend on others, rather than actively problem solve ($Ma:Mp = 0:2$). This is especially conflictual given his schizoid and paranoid proclivities (Klein, 1946/1975). A major mood disorder is likely ($DEPI = 6$).

Rorschach Psychoanalytic Findings

A psychoanalytic approach to the Rorschach further details his intrapsychic life. Victor utilizes several borderline defenses (Cooper, Perry & Arnow, 1988): devaluation (Responses 1, 7, 13, 15), primitive idealization (Responses 5, 6, 14), and splitting ($2 \rightarrow 3, 6 \rightarrow 7$). These defenses, and their dynamic relationship across the Rorschach protocol, point toward an oscillating pattern to fend off his own wishes for need fulfillment (devaluation) and to ensure his protection against bad objects (primitive idealization). Such intrapsychic vicissitudes would predict havoc in his interpersonal field.

Affectional neediness is denied (Response 10) and defended against with narcissistic pseudo-autonomy (Response 11), accompanied by a strong, voyeuristic, and interpersonal pull: "two looking in a mirror at each other, little statuettes or something." His gazing on others is likely imbued with both erotic and affectional desires (Response 12), perceptions distorted by confusion around boundaries (Response 11). Narcissistic enhancement is never quite successful, and quickly leads to a need to protect the inflated, yet vulnerable self (Response 14; "crown, helmet").

Most interesting is the finding that all of Victor's space responses are a minus form quality stimulated by part-object human content and accompanied by clothing (Responses 3, 5, 14). This repetitive pattern of Rorschach responding defines an intrapsychic vulnerability to loss of reality testing when unpleasant, angry affect (Kohut, 1972) surrounding part-object representations (Kernberg, 1975) is stimulated. Attention to surface and appearance (Cg = 2) may help manage such disturbing feelings, images, and perceptions. On occasion intellectualization is utilized (Responses 6, 7), but often affective constraint leads to ideational helplessness (Response 9 to Response 10). Anxiety is associated in Victor's mind with his damaged and devalued self (Response 13, $FY + MOR$).

There is no present aggression (Ag) in the entire protocol, similar to many antisocial personality disordered individuals (Gacono & Meloy, 1994). This is contrary to normal populations, wherein tensions of ego-dystonic aggression are often apparent in their Rorschachs. We theorized that aggressive impulses in antisocial individuals are ego-syntonic and rapidly discharged; therefore, such impulses do not create internal states of tension, and consequent symbolization, when evoked during Rorschach administration (Gacono & Meloy, 1994).

Victor does produce three aggressive content (AgC) responses (1, 2, 15), the most common experimental aggression score analyzed to date in clinical and normal samples (Gacono & Meloy, 1994). In this protocol, the aggressive content is a marker for oral ("sharp teeth") and phallic ("stinger") impulses. The identification of certain impulses that infer "stages" of instinctual development in a Rorschach protocol (Schafer, 1954) is not diagnostic per se, but the transparency and coarseness of their expression during testing may correlate with the degree to which these impulses are, or are not, inhibited or sublimated in real world behavior. In Victor's case, maturation of defenses (Vaillant, 1993) around primitive instincts could have been better. As he described his heavy construction work, "when I'm on a dozer I'm happier than a dog with two dicks."

Integration With Other Testing

The MMPI-2 results were quite consistent with the Rorschach data. Despite his spike 4 profile (T = 72), Victor is not a primary psychopath ($PCL-R$ =

20; Hare, 1991). He has a pattern of chronic antisocial behavior, but it was usually nonviolent and associated with his drug dependencies. His MMPI–2 *ASP* score (*T* = 53) further validates an antisocial picture that loads on Factor 2 of the *PCL–R* (chronic antisocial behavior) rather than Factor 1 (aggressive narcissism).

His *OH* scale (*T* = 69), coupled with *Pa1* (*T* = 58), prompted the Caldwell Report to print, "this pattern has been associated with hysteroid and emotionally explosive trends and in a few cases with paranoid disorders. He tests as rigidly repressed and overcontrolled." The MCMI–II found predominately schizoid and dependent traits.

The most striking test discrepancy was the positive *DEPI* on the Rorschach and the complete absence of any depression elevations on the MMPI–2 (*D* = 53, *D1* = 48, *D2* = 54, *D3* = 51, *D4* = 43, *D5* = 45, *DEP* = 51, *FRS* = 41, *CYN* = 49). Some of this is likely due to his *K* (*T* = 62), but his clinical presentation of lability and sadness was much more consistent with the Rorschach findings. He may have successfully masked through self-report a major depression or dysthymia on both the MMPI–2 and the MCMI–II (Dysthymic *BR* = 18, Major Depression *BR* = 38).

Although psychosis was not indicated on any of the personality testing, there were enough indices of a possible paranoid condition on both the Rorschach and MMPI–2 to warrant a careful clinical exploration for an encapsulated delusional disorder. Evidence confirmed a diagnosis of either amphetamine delusional disorder (*Diagnostic and Statistical Manual of Mental Disorders*; 4th ed. [*DSM–IV*]; American Psychiatric Association, 1994) or delusional disorder, jealous subtype (*DSM–IV*). The differential diagnosis would need to be made on subsequent retesting due to his chronic amphetamine use prior to incarceration. Victor had a preliminary Axis II diagnosis of Personality Disorder NOS with dependent, isolative, emotionally explosive, and antisocial features.

FINAL THOUGHTS

Victor was a prototypical "stalker." He was older and smarter than most criminal offenders. He was not in a stable, bonded relationship at the time, and had a prior criminal and drug abuse history. He threatened his victim, pursued multiple and various contacts with her, and evidenced both an Axis I and Axis II disorder. Most poignantly, Victor could not separate from Uma, despite her rejection of him. His feelings of humiliation and loss were defended against with rage, he devalued her, and posed an imminent threat to her when he was arrested. Victor's behavior is inexplicable without understanding through clinical interview and testing his early paternal attachment disruption, his borderline personality organization and antisocial-dependent character style, his paranoid delusional disorder, the fueling of his aggression with stimulants, and his obsession (preoccupation) with a woman whom he had once idealized. As Victor had written to Uma, "all I wanted was to love you."

REFERENCES

Alcott, L. M. (1866/1995). *A long fatal love chase.* New York: Random House.

American Psychiatric Association. (1994). *Diagnostic and statistical manual of mental disorders* (4th ed.). Washigton, DC: Author.

Ammons, R., & Ammons, C. (1962). *Psychological Reports Monograph Supplement, 1–V11,* 111–161.

Bion, W. (1984). Attacks on linking. In *Second thoughts: Selected papers on psycho-analysis* (pp. 93–109). New York: Aronson. (Original work published 1959)

Bruhn, A. (1990). *Earliest childhood memories: Theory and application to clinical practice, Vol. 1.* New York: Praeger.

Cooper, S., Perry, J., & Arnow, D. (1988). An empirical approach to the study of defense mechanisms: I. Reliability and preliminary validity of the Rorschach defense scale. *Journal of Personality Assessment, 52,* 187–203.

de Clérambault, G. (1942). Les psychoses passionelles [The passionate psychoses]. In *Oeuvres Psychiatriques* (pp. 315–322). Paris: Presses Universitaires de France.

Exner, J. E. (1986). *The Rorschach: A comprehensive system: Vol. 1. Basic foundations* (2nd ed.). New York: Wiley.

Exner, J. E. (1993). *The Rorschach: A comprehensive system: Vol. 1. Basic foundations* (3rd ed.). New York: Wiley.

Gacono, C. B., & Meloy, J. R. (1994). *The Rorschach assessment of aggressive and psychopathic personalities.* Hillsdale, NJ: Lawrence Erlbaum Associates.

Guy, R. (1993). The nature and constitutionality of stalking laws. *Vanderbilt Law Review, 46,* 991–1029.

Hare, R. (1991). *Scoring manual for the Psychopathy Checklist–Revised.* Toronto, Canada: Multihealth Systems.

Harmon, R., Rosner, R., & Owens, H. (1995). Obsessional harassment and erotomania in a criminal court population. *Journal of Forensic Sciences, 40,* 188–196.

Hathaway, S., & McKinley, J. (1989). *MMPI-2 Manual for administration and scoring.* Minneapolis: University of Minnesota Press.

Kernberg, O. (1975). *Borderline conditions and pathological narcissism.* New York: Aronson.

Kernberg, O. (1984). *Severe personality disorders: Psychotherapeutic strategies.* New Haven, CT: Yale University Press.

Klein, M. (1975). Notes on some schizoid mechanisms. In *The writings of Melanie Klein. Vol. III. Envy and gratitude and other works 1946–1963* (pp. 1–24). New York: The Free Press. (Original work published 1946)

Klein, M. (1975). Envy and gratitude. In *The writings of Melanie Klein. Vol. III. Envy and gratitude and other works 1946–1963* (pp. 176–235). New York: The Free Press. (Original work published 1957)

Kohut, H. (1972). Thoughts on narcissism and narcissistic rage. *Psychoanalytic Study of the Child, 27,* 360–400.

Kurt, L. (1995). Stalking as a variant of domestic violence. *Bulletin of the American Academy of Psychiatry and the Law, 23,* 219–230.

Meissner, W. (1978). *The paranoid process.* New York: Aronson.

Meloy, J. R. (1989). Unrequited love and the wish to kill: Diagnosis and treatment of borderline erotomania. *Bulletin of the Menninger Clinic, 53*, 477–492.

Meloy, J. R. (1992). *Violent attachments.* Northvale, NJ: Aronson.

Meloy, J. R. (1996). Stalking (obsessional following): A review of some preliminary studies. *Aggression and Violent Behavior, 1*, 147–162.

Meloy, J. R., & Gacono, C. B. (1992). A psychotic (sexual) psychopath: "I just had a violent thought . . ." *Journal of Personality Assessment, 58*, 480–493.

Meloy, J. R., & Gothard, S. (1995). Demographic and clinical comparison of obsessional followers and offenders with mental disorders. *American Journal of Psychiatry, 152*, 258–63.

Millon, T. (1976). *Millon Clinical Multiaxial Inventory–II.* Minneapolis, MN: National Computer Systems.

Mullen, P., & Pathé, M. (1994). Stalking and the pathologies of love. *Australian and New Zealand Journal of Psychiatry, 28*, 469–477.

Schafer, R. (1954). *Psychoanalytic interpretation in Rorschach testing.* New York: Grune & Stratton.

Vaillant, G. (1993). *The wisdom of the ego.* Cambridge, MA: Harvard University Press.

Zona, M., Sharma, K., & Lane, J. (1993). A comparative study of erotomanic and obsessional subjects in a forensic sample. *Journal of Forensic Sciences, 38*, 894–903.

I.

1. A bat.

Black wings, horned and sharp edges, sharp teeth.

2. A bug through here. A demented bee or hornet.

Stinger, wings pushed forward, rough edges.

II.

3. Whoa! A clown, eyes closed, black makeup, red moustache, a stretch.

Eyes, lids, nose, shape of nose.

III.

4. Small butterfly.

Shape.

5. Neck, bowtie, outer part hair, shirt, shoulder, like a President, if any have bowties.

Whole card, shoulders up.

IV.

6. Georgia O'Keeffe. Negative of her skull of cattle. Yea.

Eyes, nose part, black instead of white, bone.

7. Head, small, perspective, feet, laying prone like a monster, this is something bad (points).

Head is smaller than feet, arms smaller too, demented.

V.

8. A bat definitely.

Rough edges, pointy things, feet.

9. Or a black butterfly.

Horns, things here.

VI.

10. Looks like stretched skin, deerskin on a tanning deal.

Legs, neck area here, butt area (?) doesn't have shape of it (?) no furry qualities to it (?) shape.

VII.

11. Cartoon from Peanuts. Face and feathers. Two looking in a mirror at each other, little statuettes or something.

Two looking at each other, the shape, vague.

VIII.

12. Bear walking up a cliff, two bears, trying to get some honey or something.

Shape, here, stepping up, about it.

IX.

13. A clown who didn't do his makeup right. I'm reaching with a clown.

Blotted it out. Shape is round. Shoulders here. Neck here. Smooched it wrong. Line marks here, smudged.

X.

14. Wow! Weird moustache, nose, eyes, crown, helmet, on top.

Green moustache, helment popped off, motion jobs.

15. Two spiders, crabs.

Too many feet, claw.

16. Two psychedelic birds on branch and leaf.

Imagination, no shape, what would be on a branch.

APPENDIX B
Sequence of Scores

Card	No.	Loc.	#	Determinant(s)	(2)	Content(s)	Pop Z	Special Scores
I	1	Wo	1	FC'o		A	P 1.0	DV
	2	Wo	1	Fu		A	1.0	MOR
II	3	WS+	1	FC'.FC–		(Hd)	4.5	
III	4	Do	3	Fo		A		
	5	WS+	1	F–		Hd, Cg	5.5	DR
IV	6	Wo	1	FC'u		(Ad), An, Art	2.0	
	7	Wo	1	Mp.FDo		(H)	2.0	MOR
V	8	Wo	1	Fo		A	P 1.0	DV
	9	Wo	1	FC'o		A	P 1.0	INC
VI	10	Do	1	mpo		Ad	P	
VII	11	D+	2	Mpo	2	(Hd), Art	P 3.0	
VIII	12	W+	1	FMao	2	A, Ls	P 4.5	
IX	13	Wo	1	FYu		(H)	5.5	MOR, DV
X	14	DdS+	99	FC.ma–		Hd, Cg	4.5	INC
	15	Ddo	99	Fu	2	A		
	16	Dv/+	15	Fu	2	(A),Bt	4.0	INC

Summary of Approach

I:W.W	VI:D
II:WS	VII:D
III:D.WS	VIII:W
IV:W.W	IX:W
V:W.W.	X:DdS.Dd.D

188

APPENDIX C
Rorschach Structural Summary

LOCATION FEATURES	DETERMINANTS BLENDS	SINGLE	CONTENTS	S-CONSTELLATION
			H = 0,0	NO..FV + VF + V + FD > 2
				YES..Col-Shd Bl>0
Zf = 13	FC'.FC	M = 1	(H) = 2,0	YES..Ego<.31,>.44
ZSum = 39.5	M.FD	FM = 1	Hd = 2,0	NO..MOR>3
ZEst = 41.5	FC.m	m = 1	(Hd) = 2,0	NO..Zd > ± 3.5
		FC = 0	Hx = 0,0	YES..es>EA
W = 10		CF = 0	A = 7,0	NO..CF+C>FC
(Wv = 0)		C = 0	(A) = 1,0	YES..X+%<.70
D = 4		Cn = 0	Ad = 1,0	NO..S>3
Dd = 2		FC' = 3	(Ad) = 1,0	NO..P<3 or >8
S = 3		C'F = 0	An = 0,1	YES..Pure H <2
		C' = 0	Art = 0,2	YES..R<17
DQ		FT = 0	Ay = 0,0	6.....TOTAL
.........(FQ–)		TF = 0	Bl = 0,0	
+ = 5 (3)		T = 0	Bt = 0,1	SPECIAL SCORINGS

o = 10(0)	FV = 0	Cg = 0,2	Lvl Lv2
v/+ = 1 (0)	VF = 0	Cl = 0,0	DV = 3x1 0x2
v = 0 (0)	V = 0	Ex = 0,0	INC = 3x2 0x4
	FY = 1	Fd = 0,0	DR = 1x3 0x6
	YF = 0	Fi = 0,0	FAB = 0x4 0x7
	Y = 0	Ge = 0,0	ALOG = 0x5
FORM QUALITY	Fr = 0	Hh = 0,0	CON = 0x7
	rF = 0	Ls = 0,1	SUM6 = 7

	FQx	FQf	MQual	SQx	FD = 0	Na = 0,0	WSUM6 = 12
+	= 0	0	0	0	F = 6	Sc = 0,0	
o	= 8	2	2	0		Sx = 0,0	AB =0 CP = 0
u	= 5	3	0	0		Xy = 0,0	AG =0 MOR = 3
–	= 3	1	0	3		Id = 0,0	CFB =0 PER = 0
none	= 0	–	0	0	(2) = 4		COP =0 PSV = 0

RATIOS, PERCENTAGES, AND DERIVATIONS

R = 16	L = 0.60		FC:CF+C =2:0	COP = 0	AG = 0
			Pure C =0	Food	= 0
EB = 2:1.0	EA = 3.0	EBPer = N/A	SumC':WSumC =4:1.0	Isolate/R	= 0.13
eb = 3:5	es = 8	D = –1	Afr =0.45	H:(H)Hd(Hd)	= 0:6
	Adj es = 7	Adj D = –1	S =3	(HHd):(AAd)	= 4:2
			Blends:R =3:16	H+A:Hd + Ad	= 10:6
FM = 1	C' = 4	T = 0	CP =0		
m = 2	V = 0	Y = 1			
		P = 6	Zf =13	3r+(2)/R = 0.25	
a:p = 2:3	Sum6 =7	X+% = 0.50	Zd =–2.0	Fr+rF = 0	
Ma:Mp = 0:2	Lv2 =0	F+% = 0.33	W:D:Dd =10:4:2	FD = 1	
2AB+Art+Ay = 2	WSum6 = 12	X–% = 0.19	W:M =10:2	An + Xy = 1	
M– = 0	Mnone = 0	S–% = 1.00	DQ+ =5	MOR = 3	
		Xu% = 0.31	DQv =0		

SCZI = 1	DEPI = 6*	CDI = 4*	S-CON = 6	HVI = No	OBS = No

13

White Bird: Flight From the Terror of Empty Space

Bruce L. Smith
University of California, Berkeley and San Francisco

Man does not live by scores alone.

The amount of data available in a Rorschach protocol is unfathomable. Even if one were to limit consideration to the Structural Summary, there are quite literally hundreds, if not thousands, of scores, ratios, and relationships among scores that are potentially interpretable. How, then, to integrate this mass of data in a way that results in a meaningful, coherent picture and does not do violence to the complexity of the individual assessed. As I have suggested elsewhere (Smith, 1991), it is necessary to have a theoretical framework within which to fit the observations and interpretations of a test battery if assessment is to be meaningful. Sugarman (1991) suggested that a comprehensive personality theory serves four functions in assessment: providing an organizing framework, helping to integrate data (especially seemingly contradictory data), filling in gaps in the data, and allowing for clinical prediction.

In terms of Rorschach assessment, a coherent theory operates in at least three distinct aspects of the interpretative process. First, the interpretation of idiographic data is impossible without a consistent personality theory. For example, if a patient reports that Card I reminds him of a "dried, moth-eaten oak leaf," we may hypothesize that this response reflects despair and hopelessness associated with narcissistic injury. Why? Because we know that responses to the first card often reflect key aspects of a patient's self-concept; that "dried" and "moth-eaten" are images that suggest a loss of vitality, whereas "oak leaf," in addition to being a botanical response is also a decoration suggestive of exalted rank, and we know from a psychoanalytic perspective that injuries to a patient's narcissism usually lead to despair and depression. We may tentatively speculate that this patient currently experiences himself as having lost a previously held honorable status. That the leaf is dried suggests his belief that this reversal of fortune is permanent. Schwartz and Lazar (1979) suggested that the interpretation of a Rorschach is a semantic exercise, a creation of meaning. To interpret the meaning of a response or set of responses, a system of meaning (i.e., a theory) is necessary.

Second, theory operates in the selection, interpretation, and organization of hypotheses derived from nomothetic data. The Comprehensive System yields a variety of predictive statements based on scores, ratios, and indices. Unintegrated, these say precious little about the person in question. How does one determine what statements reflect core psychological processes and what are epiphenomena? How does the clinician reconcile contradictory findings? Only a comprehensive theory of personality that posits which processes are a consequence of which can order these data.

Third, theory operates in the derivation of prognostic and therapeutic statements from the Rorschach data. The Rorschach itself tells us nothing about which psychological processes are amenable to treatment, or which interventions are likely to be most efficacious. Nor does it say anything about the prognostic implications of various findings. Again, a personality theory gives the clinician the tools with which to derive such important conclusions from the assessment data.

Atheoretical nomothetic interpretation is only as good as the specific predictive statements that are generated. As is well known, even the best predictors from a Structural Summary are often inaccurate in specific cases. Without a theoretical understanding of how personality variables interact with each other, it becomes impossible to know what to do with "false" predictions. For example, a 40-year-old woman, employed as a legal secretary, is tested to better understand a therapeutic impasse. She attains a positive Schizophrenic Index (*SCZI*), with a *WSum6* of 30. This woman has never experienced a formal decompensation, been hospitalized, or complained of psychotic symptoms. Clearly, interpreting these data as indicative of schizophrenia would be in error. Yet, they cannot be dismissed either. When coupled with her "clean" Wechsler Adult Intelligence Scale–Revised (WAIS–R; Wechsler, 1981) profile, her complaint that her life becomes difficult "when there is a man in the picture," and the fact that all of the responses meriting special scores contain overtly sexual content usually accompanied by violent images, we begin to formulate the hypothesis that this patient has a low-level borderline personality organization, that she generally has an intact conflict-free ego sphere (as evidenced by the intact WAIS–R and her capacity to function in a high-stress occupation), but that she is preoccupied with sexual concerns, easily becomes compromised when stimulated by sexual thoughts, and is prone to masochistic behavior vis à vis men. If this hypothesis is supported by other data from the testing, we can then begin to develop a dynamic formulation that includes genetic considerations and has implications for treatment (in this case, e.g., her proneness for developing transient sadomasochistic psychotic transferences to her male therapist).

Of course, all personality theories are not created equal. Only a dynamic model, such as psychoanalytic theory, that contains propositions capable of linking test results with underlying psychological processes, genetic or developmental considerations, and observable behavior can provide the framework for a comprehensive psychological evaluation. In particular, modern object relations theory permits the interpretation of test data from a perspective that is both experience-near and of sufficient complexity to comprehend the mass of data produced by a Rorschach protocol (Lerner, 1991; Smith, 1994). By framing propositions about the patient in terms of his or her object relations and object representations, it is possible to derive interpretive statements that are immediately relevant to the treating clinician. Although observations about the relative distribution of attentional cathexes may be impressive-sounding, they rarely lead to useful interventions. By contrast, a statement that the patient tends to experience male objects as primarily malevolent and that his inner world is populated by frightening representations that are relatively unaffected by external reality has immediate implications for the transference and how it may be handled.

One particular object relational construct that I have found especially relevant for Rorschach interpretation is Winnicott's idea of "potential space" (Winnicott, 1971). He postulated that there was a potential space between the self and object that both facilitated and was a consequence of the process of separation: "I refer to the hypothetical area that exists (but cannot exist) between the baby and the object (mother or part of mother) during the phase of the repudiation of the object as not-me, that is, at the end of being merged in with the object" (p. 107).

Potential space lies, in a sense, between reality and fantasy and becomes the area in which experience is given meaning, that is, reality and fantasy are reconciled. Winnicott (1971) described it as the "place where we live" (p. 104). Potential space develops out of a more or less successful process of separation in which the mother gradually disillusions the fantasy of an undifferentiated dyad by titrated absences and failures. Where the process has been too abrupt or traumatic or care has been too inconstant, the space between self and other is experienced as a frightening void that cannot be filled or symbolized.

Ogden (1989) elaborated on Winnicott's ideas by suggesting that there was a dialectical process between reality and fantasy in which each create and negate the other. In this model, defenses can be thought of as disruptions in the dialectical process in which fantasy and reality become dissociated from each other resulting in a loss of meaning. He referred to this process as a collapse of potential space and suggested that many forms of psychopathology could be conceptualized as particular manifestations of collapse.

In a previous article (Smith, 1990), I suggested that Rorschach percepts can be conceptualized as transitional phenomena and, therefore, located in potential space. This reflects the fact that percepts are both created—in the sense that the blot is amorphous and only given meaning by the subject's own creative process—and found—in the sense that the resulting image must be reconciled with the properties of the blot. Where there is a collapse of potential space, this can be detected in the resulting Rorschach percept. These observations have important implications for understanding the patient's deepest concerns and his or her object relations, including transference relationships.

EVA

An attractive, if somewhat naive-looking, 27-year-old, Eva was referred for assessment because her psychiatrist was befuddled. She had begun treatment initially for depression following the end of a clandestine affair with a prominent married man about 25 years her senior. She reported that this was not the first such episode in her life (although it was the first time she had sought help) and that at other times she experienced periods in which she was active, energetic, and often went without sleep. Despite this history, she gave no clinical evidence of a bipolar illness in over 3 months of therapy.

Eva was the middle of three children, with a brother 1 year older and a half-brother 12 years younger. Her parents divorced when she was only 1 year old, and she had no subsequent contact with her father, who had moved to another country. She was born in eastern Europe, spent much of her early childhood in France, and came with her family to the United States at the age of 12, initially settling in the South. She is a highly intelligent young woman who is fluent in three languages in addition to her unaccented English. She moved to California following her graduation from university. She claimed to have a "firm commitment" to attend medical school, but had been working as a part-time waitress for 5 years.

She presented herself in a friendly, casual¹ manner but appeared rather scatter-brained, especially given her intelligence and aspirations. She tended to be rather histrionic, frequently peppering her testing responses with interjections such as "Oh my God!" or inappropriate laughter. She was especially preoccupied with avoiding boredom, rejecting Rorschach or other test responses as "boring," filling the space at other times with a flurry of verbal activity. It seemed as if she equated boredom with a kind of psychic emptiness and rapidly moved to fill the space.

On the WAIS, she gave a performance that was extremely variable. Although her Full Scale IQ was in the above-average range, as a summation it was almost meaningless, given the variability of her performance. She would answer correctly many difficult items, giving responses that were remarkably sophisticated. On the same subtests, however, she would make striking errors on far simpler ones. Her long-term memory and general fund of information was quite spotty (e.g., she had no idea how far New York was from Paris despite her obvious personal experience). This is, of course, in keeping with her histrionic cognitive style, one in which she focuses on global impressions rather than on specific details. In particular, she showed lapses in tasks that required abstract reasoning and judgment. When asked, for example, what to do if in the movies she were the first person to see smoke and fire, she responded, "Get up and say, 'Smoke over there!'" After a pause, she added, "I'd yell it REAL loud!" It was also clear that she seemed to lack the capacity for self-reflection; even if a response were given tentatively, once she verbalized, she remained committed to it, never revising her answer. It seemed as if she treated associations as equivalent to reasoned thoughts. When asked to interpret the proverb, shallow brooks are noisy, she first acknowledged that she had never heard the proverb, then attempted to make sense of it, finally coming up with "Little kids are allowed in shallow water only, and they are noisy." This answer, unlikely as it may be, satisfied her.

THE RORSCHACH

The mass of data available in a typical Rorschach protocol is magnified in Eva's case both by her productivity and her many comments about her responses. When faced with this mass of data, how does one reduce it to manageable proportions while still ensuring that significant interpretations are not lost? Weiner (1994) suggested that a profitable way of conceptualizing Rorschach data is into two classes—structure (i.e., the formal properties reflected in the Structural Summary), and content—which parallel two aspects of personality, structure and dynamics. Although there is much utility in such a conceptualization, there are also problems with so clear a distinction between these two classes. In the first place, the distinction between structure and dynamics of personality is to some degree a spurious one. As Rapaport (1959/1967) noted, structure is actually nothing more than dynamics with a slow rate of change. Secondly, it is not necessarily true that structural aspects of a subject's personality are only evident through summary variables such as those in the Structural Summary, or that psychodynamics cannot be inferred from formal properties of a protocol. Thus, I recommend a more fluid interpretive process in which the interpreter moves back and forth between structural variables and more narrative data. I do, of course, begin with the structural variables, as these are most descriptive of the protocol as a whole and therefore most likely to produce descriptions of the subject's characteristic modes of functioning. Although Exner (1993) recommended an interpretive strategy based on key variables, I prefer to begin my interpretation by examining the protocol for the most striking findings, especially those that were noteworthy during the administration. Following this, I tend to focus next on cognitive variables, then affects, defenses, self- and object-representations, and dynamics. I do this because this is the format in which I generally write my reports.

The Rorschach protocol is given at the end of this chapter in Appendix A, the Sequence of Scores in Appendix B, and the Structural Summary in Appendix C.

In the case of Eva's Rorschach, we are struck initially by her 41 responses. Usually, an R of this magnitude is suggestive of either an obsessive need to account for every detail (as evidenced by many small Dd responses) or a hypomanic or manic flight of ideas. A careful examination of Eva's protocol, however, reveals that rather than giving many responses to each card, she gave only three or fewer for five of the cards (I, IV, V, VI, and IX) and five or more to the others (II, III, VII, VIII, and X). It would appear that this process is stimulated by certain cards only. This further suggests that whatever this process represents, it is highly stimulus-dependent.

The other variable that is most striking is the total of 10 space responses. Because this is going to be a central focus of the analysis of this Rorschach, I defer discussion of the meaning of space responses for Eva until later.

Thought Organization

The Structural Summary reveals several indicators of thought disturbance, most notably a Raw *Sum6* of 7 (sum of six key Special Scores) and a *WSum6* of 18 (weighted sum of these variables). Five of these responses involve evidence for boundary disturbance: four Incongruous Combinations and one Fabulized Combination. None, however, were serious enough to be scored at Level 2. This is strongly suggestive of a tendency to blur boundaries under the pressure of primitive impulses. Indeed, all but one of these responses involve percepts of an aggressive nature. The boundary disturbance in these instances can be seen either as the aggression bleeding through initial defenses as in Response 23 (pigs with a shark's mouth), or an attempt to bind the initial aggressive impulse as in Response 15 (a giant monster with the "tiny, tiny" face of an anteater). What is important to note at this point is that these attempts to deal with aggressive associations lead to failures of logical thinking. We may conclude that her thinking, although generally intact, is quite vulnerable to disruption.

Eva's reality testing, as reflected in her Form Quality scores, is likewise quite variable. Although her *X+%* and *X–%* suggest some difficulties with perceptual accuracy, an examination of the responses themselves reveals that she can be highly accurate at times, while her reality testing suffers at others. The nature of the specific contents that cause a disruption in reality testing will be explicated later.

Affects and Defenses

The positive Depression Index (*DEPI*; a summation of variables thought to be predictive of clinical depression), and the extratensive Experience Balance (a predominance of color over movement responses) are strongly suggestive of a person who is highly responsive to affective stimuli and affectively labile. Although Comprehensive System interpretations of extratensive protocols tend to stress the role of affect in the individual's problem solving, in this case we may say that affect and its control are the problems to be solved. Although she is usually able to integrate her affective experience into her ideational life as evidenced by the preponderance of *FC* over *CF* or *C* responses, there are clearly instances in which she is flooded by affect and consequently unable to make sense of these experiences as evidenced by the *CF–* responses to Card VIII. Despite her histrionic self-presentation, there is little evidence in the record for repression as would be expected were her character structure primarily hysterical.[1] Although there is evidence for intellectualization and reaction formation, it is clear that she relies most heavily on the mechanisms of denial—especially denial in fantasy—and projection, especially projective identification. Lacking the capacity to keep out of awareness threatening affects or impulses, Eva blandly denies their existence (The "giant monster" on Card IV, she asserts, is "gentle, not threatening at all") or develops an elaborate compensatory fantasy to replace them. Often her more morbid responses would be followed by manic attempts to deny the image or to assert that it had no meaning: "if I stretch my imagination I can make up stories, but I don't think I will." Nowhere is this process clearer than on Card IX, where she initially perceives deformed witches, but subsequently reduces them to a figment of the imagination of "kids . . . infants . . . fetuses."

Projection as a defense reveals itself in the Rorschach in a variety of subtle ways. Of course, the most obvious responses are those in which the subject interjects him or herself directly into the percept, losing distance from the card in the process (e.g., the percept is experienced as looking at, threatening, about to attack, etc., the subject). More common, however, are responses in which affective dispositions are attributed to the percept, frequently without perceptual justification. Eva's emphasis on animate objects looking "omnipotent," "barbaric," or "bewitched" suggests a need to project her own aggressive impulses into objects in her world. Unfortunately, this leads her to feel vulnerable and at the mercy of the other, thus the need to deny that which she has just projected.

Projective identification differs from simple projection in that it involves the projection of a part of the self-representation rather than simply an impulse. Typically, in projective identification, the object is treated in such a way that he or she behaves in a manner consistent with the projection. The subject may then "empathize" with the object and reintroject the self representation, identifying with it as if it came from the other (Kernberg, 1975). Lerner and Lerner (1980) suggested two indices of projective identification on the Rorschach: (a) responses involving human content in which the form quality is poor and the response is overly embellished, usually with overtly sexual or aggressive material; or (b) human or human detail responses that are given to unusual details, use diffuse shading as a determinant, or use differ-

---

[1]I prefer to reserve the term *hysterical* to refer to a neurotic level character structure in which repression dominates the defensive structure, and the dynamic conflicts are primarily Oedipal. I am aware, of course, that histrionic traits may be found in more primitive personality structures such as the "oral" character (Sugarman, 1979) in which denial is the primary defense, but I believe that referring to these latter as hysterical leads to conceptual confusion.

ences in shading to "carve out" the response, and in which the figure is described either as aggressive or having been aggressed against. Eva's protocol is replete with responses that involve projective identification. Indeed, most of her animate percepts involve some kind of projected representation, usually of an aggressive, aggressed against, or negative nature. To cite just one example, Response 18 to Card V, "2 faces . . . actually silhouette. Kind of bewitched-looking; a big crooked nose, scraggly beard, ugly face. Kind of like a dunce's face . . . a stupid, ugly face. (Inquiry) . . . (they) look pathetic; the kind you'd feel sorry for."

One other defensive operation deserves mention. Despite her intelligence and willingness to engage with the blots, she tended to respond to single aspects in her percepts. Thus, she gave relatively few Whole (*W*) responses, and even fewer *Blends* (responses in which more than one determinant was used). Although the usual interpretation of such findings is that she has a "conservative" motivation in processing data and she tends to be somewhat constricted in her responsiveness, these statements are not particularly reve-latory of Eva's psychological makeup. A conservative motivation suggests a reluctance to take risks, an unlikely finding given her recent behavioral history and tendency to produce multiple responses with affect-laden content, and constriction suggests a lack of affectivity, again an interpretation contradicted by other data. Instead, these scores seem to reflect an attempt to keep representations separate from each other. This includes the wish to keep affect separate from other aspects of experience. Dynamically, this process can be understood as a defense against the tendency to blur boundaries and merge objects observed earlier. This process is known as *fragmentation*, and is a primitive defense mechanism akin to splitting (Kernberg, 1975).

Self and Object Representations

From an object relations theoretical point of view, self and object repre-sentations are the building blocks of personality. Affects, self images, interper-sonal relations, and even thinking all derive from the child's earliest relationships with significant objects. Winnicott (1971), for example, sug-gested that thinking develops out of the mother's early efforts to make sense out of the child's initially unsymbolized sense experiences.

Eva's affective lability, her primitive defenses, and her vulnerability to flooding all appear to be related to the primitive nature of her inner object world. The protocol reveals a predominance of part-object representations (as indicated by Human Detail or Quasi-Human Detail responses) over whole objects. Perceiving objects as parts reflects a tendency to see people as unidimensional and derives from the earliest stages of development when the child views the mother not as a fully differentiated other, but rather as a nurturing and frustrating breast. The capacity to perceive others as con-stant—not changing despite changes in one's affective disposition toward them—and as multidimensional is a developmental achievement that involves tolerating ambivalence, that one might feel differently toward the same object. Individuals whose inner world is populated by fragmented part-objects tend to have an equally fragmented and discontinuous set of self-representations. In other words, their sense of self is equally split, and they feel as if they were a different person at different times.

Eva's self- and object-representations are suffused with primitive affects. Although there are no responses scored for Aggressive Movement (*AG*), this is in large part an artifact of the scoring system, which limits scoring of aggression to movement responses and to aggression presently occurring. According to the system for scoring aggression proposed by Gacono and Meloy (1994), four responses would be scored for Aggressive Content (*AgC*) and three for Aggressive Past (*AgPast*). Thus, many of her representations involve the perception of objects that have been aggressed against (i.e., victims) or have the potential to be harmful. The fact that both are present suggests an oscillation in her sense of self between that of a victim and that of a potential aggressor. Similarly, sexual themes are also prevalent throughout the protocol. There is a preoccupation with female genitalia and whether or not they all look the "same." We may speculate that this concern reflects her uncertainties about her own sexuality—whether or not she is a "normal" woman. Male sexuality appears to be associated with aggression (e.g., the "mammoth" monster with a giant penis), whereas female sexuality is frequently represented as deformed or diseased.

Perhaps the most salient image for her is that which is represented by the bird. Not only does she perceive 4½ different sets of birds (the women on Card III have bird's heads), but they are frequently extremely well-articulated, with species noted, and so forth. Coupled with her percepts of other flying animals (butterflies, bats, even falling rats), this suggests that flight or the capacity to flee is a particularly salient aspect of her sense of self. This is, of course, in keeping with her preferred mode of defense that involves flights of fantasy as a means of denying painful experience. Fried (1980) suggested that images such as birds and other winged objects, especially when coupled with their thematic opposites (e.g., falling, dismemberment, being held down, etc.), reflect an Icarus Complex (Murray, 1955) in which flights of fantasy alternate with fears of abandonment, degradation, and disintegration. Dynamically, the former can be seen as a defense against the latter and indicates core narcissistic pathology.

Sequence Analysis

Analysis of the Structural Summary, even with a consideration of the specific responses that constitute the scores, yields a very incomplete picture of a subject's personality. To understand how someone functions, it is necessary to evaluate the process, that is, the interplay between impulses, affects, defenses, thoughts, and behaviors over time. This can be done by analyzing the sequence of responses, including the specific verbalizations used by the subject to articulate his or her perceptions. It is important to note that this differs from analyzing the content alone. In a comprehensive sequence analysis, formal properties of the responses are considered along with the contents.

Eva begins her encounter with the Rorschach with a nervous laugh, no doubt expressing some anxiety about an unknown task. Her first response, given after only 10 sec of consideration, is "this female figure. Do you want to know why? She sort of has her arms up, and she has sort of an omnipotent air—like this (she gestures, raising her arms)." Following this response, she sees "four ghost-like figures" and "two hawk-like birds perched on the shoulders." In analyzing the sequence of responses to this card, it is important to remember that they occur in the context of an interpersonal relationship; that is, she must not only organize and articulate her perceptions, she must communicate them to the examiner. In this instance, she begins by seeing a female figure, focusing on the center of the blot. This image may reflect an attempt to locate herself vis à vis the examiner; she is at the center of attention with "an omnipotent air." That this sense of omnipotence is fragile is suggested by her comment in the inquiry that the woman is essentially defined by her clothing. Her second response, four ghosts, continues the theme of insubstantiality. The clothing that defined the woman in this case obscures the ghosts, rendering their features indistinct. Finally, she introduces a theme that will be a preoccupation throughout this protocol—birds—with her final response. One of the interesting features to note is the fact that the birds are seen in conjunction with the image of a woman, a juxtaposition that will be repeated on Card III. Finally, it is important to note that despite the fact that the responses are distinct percepts, they are all nevertheless located in terms of the woman (under her arms, perched on her shoulders). This suggests a certain stickiness or fluidity to her self–other boundaries, a tendency that becomes more overt under stress.

Eva's asides during the administration of Card I are also noteworthy. She initially suggests that she could "go on and on" but later cuts herself off abruptly by saying, "There's more, but it is boring." It would appear that she is at least nascently aware of her tendency to lose control of her associative processes.

By contrast with the first card, Eva does "go on and on" on Card II. Although it may be the color that stimulates her associations, it is clear that it is specifically the lower central aspect of the blot (D3) that she is trying to cope with. Her initial response is a popular one, but is described in such a way that suggests that it stimulates primitive anxieties. The response is scored for both achromatic color and texture, suggesting dysphoria and nurturant needs at the same time. In addition, she stresses the size of the animals, "huge . . . mammoth-size, huge." The emphasis on size may suggest that she perceives the figures as masculine and herself as small or childlike in conjunction. If this is so, then there is the possibility that this image reflects sadness over the lack of nurturance from a paternal figure (recalling that Eva's father left when she was an infant). Her next response is obviously female, namely a vagina. But the vagina turns out to be "bloody." She then sees the identical area as a butterfly, specifically a "monarch." This may be seen as an attempt to restore the narcissistic equilibrium of the "omnipotent" woman from Card I that was destroyed in the previous image. The remaining responses appear to serve to pull her away from the "stuff on the bottom." The percept of a mask is especially noteworthy for the unusual negative color projection, perceiving a chromatic area as specifically black. This suggests an attempt to deny the affective pull of the card, just as perceiving the area as a mask, rather than a face, dilutes the impact of the barbarousness. Finally, she gives her first whole response on this card, but it is a poorly organized, perceptually inaccurate one. At least on this card with its strong affective pull, her attempt at integration fails. Her final comment, that the birds on Card I look more like cardinals than hawks is an interesting one. In the first place, it serves to underscore the salience of the image for her, the fact that she is still pondering it even after the multiple associations to the next card. Second, it denies the aggression that was implied in the initial response. The woman is in far less danger with cardinals perched on her shoulder than hawks. Finally, it may have been stimulated in part by the color red that she has been responding to on Card II. If this is so, we can understand it also as another attempt to restore the grandiosity that was undermined by the perception of a bloody vagina.

Card III reiterates the themes elucidated in the first two cards. Once again there are images of females connected to images of birds. Again, we see a highly articulated response to the white space. The bulldog response is interesting because of the ambiguous gender identity; bulldogs are usually associated with masculinity, but this one has a bow on its head. Finally, there is the most disturbing response so far, the mangled, bloody rats falling from the sky. As discussed earlier, this kind of image most likely reflects the operation of projective identification, in this case representation of the self as severely damaged. Because it is the color red that stimulates this association, because it occurs in the context of another perception of women, and because the previous perception of blood was associated with menses, there is at least the suggestion that there may be the unconscious equation of female = damage.

In contrast to previous cards, Card IV produces only one percept, albeit an interesting one. Once again, she denies the aggression manifest in the original association. Once again, the object comprises characteristics of two species. Her casual identification of an outsized penis in this context suggests that she associates aggression specifically with male sexuality.

On Card V, she makes a comment that is interesting in terms of her approach to the Rorschach when she states that it is a bat, "if you look at the whole thing." This remark underscores the fact that she is not in the habit of looking at the whole picture, preferring to focus on more manageable details. Once again, she produces a highly articulated response to the white space. What is especially interesting here is the juxtaposition of the figures in

Response 17, who are "very wise," with those in Response 18, who are "dunces
. . . stupid, ugly . . . (with) a scraggly beard . . . pathetic . . . the kind you'd feel
sorry for." This kind of overidealization/devaluation is a primitive defensive
operation typical of a borderline level of object relations in which objects are
split into all-good and all-bad part-objects. (Interestingly, in this instance, the
all-good is in the white space, and the all-bad is in the blot itself.) It should
also be noted that the examiner has a beard, thus the "scraggly beard" may
reflect a transference comment about the status of the relationship with the
examiner at this moment.

"Actually the skin of a dead cat as if somebody had emptied out the insides."
This disturbing response, reminiscent of the mangled rats, is suggestive of her
sense of herself as victimized, perhaps by the "pathetic" examiner. Note the
observation that the cat is "opened flat as if to study it or hang it on a wall."
The next response confirms once again the connection between aggression,
deformity, and female sexuality. She concludes her response to this card by
asserting that she "could make up stories" but chooses not to, as if to reclaim
control over her own thought processes.

Her responses to Card VII parallel those to Card VI in that there is once
again a representation of devalued femininity (the ballerina "past her time"),
an aggressive image (face with a shark's mouth), and an assertion of her own
control over her associations in the image of the impressionist painter who
smeared over his own painting. That this process is not successful ("you can
still detect eyes and the form of the head") is a poignant statement of the
ineffectiveness of denial as a defense. The combination of "pig" and "shark"
would seem to make clear that the aggression is primarily oral in nature. Once
again, we observe the relatively greater articulation of the response to the white
space. Finally, her comment about the female genitalia deserves comment. She
seems initially troubled that the genitals do not "look the same" as previous
ones, but then reassures herself that women's genitals are not necessarily
identical. We may wonder if this comment betrays concern about her own
femininity, perhaps a fear that she is not the same as other women, perhaps
not "normal" in some way. This is, of course, consistent with her tendency to
perceive women as deformed throughout this Rorschach.

Cards VIII, IX, and X are fully chromatic, and she produces a total of 16
responses to them. Once again, the affective stimulation causes stress on her
capacity to maintain control over her thought processes, and she produces
responses that are formally disturbed to each of the cards. In each instance,
the most disturbed response is the final one to the card (the X-ray on Card
VIII, the fetuses imagining witches on Card IX, and the face on Card X),
suggesting a progressive breakdown of defenses under the pressure of affective
stimulation. That she gives accurate percepts as her first responses to IX and
X suggests that she is able to reconstitute her defenses quickly once the
anxiety-provoking stimulus is removed. This observation has important implications for her capacity to recover from transient disruptions in her psycho-

logical functioning and has obvious ramifications for how crises should be handled in psychotherapy.

Her comment about the popular animals on Card VIII ("ground animals. . . . Don't look like they have wings") is striking. A bird is such a salient icon for her, that all other animals appear to be defined in terms of them. It is as if she looks first for wings. It is in the white space that she finally finds the bird she is looking for, but it is flying away from her.

Her most disturbed response from a standpoint of blurred boundaries is the final one to Card IX. Interestingly enough, this response shows accurate form quality (in fact, all of the responses scored for *INC* or *FAB* show adequate form quality). One may speculate that it is the effort to keep things separate that causes perceptual distortions. This response also demonstrates her tendency to regress in an attempt to gain control over her fantasies, as the faces go from being kids to infants to fetuses.

Throughout this sequence analysis, the variability of Eva's functioning is most striking. Under the pressure of anxiety-provoking stimuli, her thinking can become arbitrary, and her defenses extremely primitive. When the stimuli are removed, however, she can revert to much more intact functioning. Although the vulnerability to depression, especially when dependency needs are stimulated, can be seen, she does not appear to be primarily depressed. Rather, she seems easily flooded with affects that are relatively undifferentiated. Her reliance on primitive, fragmenting defenses gives her subjective experience an extremely discontinuous, and at times chaotic, quality. Her preoccupation with birds and flight suggests that getting away, perhaps avoiding attachment, is a crucial mode for her. One is reminded of the description of "Ruby Tuesday" in the Rolling Stones' song (Jagger & Richards, 1967) of the same name, "Good bye, Ruby Tuesday/Who could hang a name on you/When you change with every new day . . . "

Space: The Final Frontier

The space response is one of the least understood in Rorschach psychology. From the time of Rorschach's (1942) original research, space responses have been thought of as primarily reflecting an oppositional tendency. This interpretation would appear to stem from the fact that in responding to the white space, and reversing figure and ground, the subject is ignoring Rorschach's carefully wrought blots in favor of the surrounding space. Exner, for example, although urging caution in the interpretation of *S*, nevertheless suggested that the presence of four or more *S* responses, especially if one or more occurs after Card III, "indicates the presence of a very negative, angry attitude toward the environment" (Exner, 1993, p. 499).

Although research suggests that anger or negativism may be reflected in a tendency to respond to the white space, I believe that this is frequently epiphenomenal and that the *S* response represents far more complex processes. In the first place, most space responses require considerable cognitive-perceptual effort, as the subject must suppress the images that might be called forth by the blot itself in order to focus on the white space (of course, this is less true of the large central spaces on Cards II and VII). Thus, we may hypothesize that a high frequency of S responses implies, among other things, cognitive complexity. Second, we must ask what would motivate an individual to invest the energy required to find and maintain images in the white space. For example, Pechoux and Harmand (1967) examined 200 Rorschach protocols and found no differences between subjects who gave S responses, and those who did not, in social oppositionalism. They proposed that "oppositionalism" as manifested in the Rorschach may reflect a variety of motivations, including an affirmation of the self. This is consistent with the research of Spitz (1957), who argued that the genesis of human communication as well as the earliest sense of the self lay in the opposition to the "yes" of the caregiver.

Although a negativistic attitude in the form of a refusal to do what is expected is certainly one possibility, so, too, is defensive flight. In this case, the subject avoids something threatening in the blot by fleeing to the white space. Finally, we must consider the possibility that something about space itself generates an anxiety that must be bound by creating a percept. Merceron, Husain, and Rossel (1988) noted that for some borderline patients space responses reflect a need to deny deficiency, the prototype of which is the need to deny the differences between genders. In a similar vein, Beizman (1967) noted the relationship between space responses and separation anxiety. Space, without content, represents absence. At its best, this can reflect a respite from conflict, stimulation, or pain; at its worst, it triggers experiences of nothingness. This is especially salient for white spaces located in the center of the cards (Cards II, III, VII, and IX). This void represents for some subjects a gulf between two figures and triggers the experience of the pain of separation. Phillips and Smith (1953) noted, for example, that children of divorce tended to show an increase in S responses. For others, it represents the most primitive anxiety of all, that the core of the self is empty. These subjects need to bridge the gap or fill the emptiness with something solid.

What is most striking about Eva's space responses is that they are so exquisitely formed and well-articulated, far more so than her responses to the blots themselves. The form quality of her space responses is excellent. The only two minuses occur when she attempts to integrate space with the blots themselves. Not only are all of her "pure" space responses scored "o" or "u," they are frequently quite compelling. It is as if Eva comes alive in the interstices of her experience.

Given what is already surmised about Eva's psychology, it would appear that filling in the white space serves the function of keeping her objects separate, protecting her fragile boundaries. Thus, for example, she fills the space between the bears on Card II with a "pool hall light," perhaps preventing the bears, who are already touching, from merging altogether.

At the same time, we may observe that Eva also fills in spaces that are not between objects. Indeed, she manages to fill in virtually every white space on the entire Rorschach. This obsessive need suggests that there is something anxiety-arousing about space—or emptiness, itself—for her. Two of her most evocative space responses are of birds, one flying away from her, and the other (the dove from Noah's ark) presumably coming back. She also perceives two wise men who are out of touch with each other, not even quite in contact with the post that they share. Finally, there is the percept of the ballerina "past her time," described as old and misshapen, yet still ridiculously dressed in a tutu. Taken together, these responses suggest conflicts over separation/merger as well as a need to defend against despair that is provoked by the perception of nothingness. Indeed, we might speculate that this is precisely the experience that she attempts to avoid with her frantic mental activity.

FORMULATION

The observations, interpretations, and speculations that have been generated need to be put into a dynamic formulation in which the causal links among them are spelled out. In particular, it is important to stress those observations and interpretations that are likely to be clinically useful. Many of the interpretations of Structural Summary variables here differ from those commonly associated with them. It is not so much that I view the typical Comprehensive System interpretations as wrong; they are, after all, backed by some empirical research. Rather, I have attempted to interpret the data in terms that fit into a particular theoretical framework that in turn will generate statements that can be of the most utility to the referring clinician. Many statements such as "the level of ideational activity that is outside the focus of attention is about average" may be accurate, but of limited relevance to a psychotherapist. Other statements imply a trait-psychology (e.g., "she is an angry person") that says nothing about the underlying dynamics that produce the traitlike behavior. Indeed, statements such as this, although often accurate, tend to be superficial, reminding one of the cartoon character, Popeye: "I yam what I yam, and dat's all what I yam."

Diagnostically, Eva can best be described as a cyclothymic personality functioning at a borderline level of organization. In formulating a test diagnosis, I see little value in limiting myself to *Diagnostic and Statistical Manual of Mental Disorders* (4th ed. [*DSM–IV*]; American Psychological Association, 1994) terminology. The *DSM–IV* was developed to characterize patients' history and clinicians' behavioral observations, whereas testing is designed to get at underlying psychological structure. Although Eva does exhibit hypomanic trends as well as a vulnerability to depression, the tests do not suggest that she has a full-blown bipolar disorder. Rather, her flights of fantasy and affective storms appear to be related to specific dynamic concerns and tend to wax and wane depending on the stimulus configuration. Her primitive defenses, proneness to transient regressions, and primitive object relations are paradigmatic for a borderline personality.

At the core of her personality and psychopathology is the aforementioned conflict over separation. Close contact with others leads to a blurring of boundaries and the threat of a loss of individual identity. Separation, on the other hand, means abandonment and the terror of confrontation with her own inner emptiness. Her solution is to attempt to flee from closeness and fill the empty space that is left behind with manic activity. This process can affect her thinking quite substantially, at times, although her capacity to recover from temporary regressions is impressive. At the same time, there is evidence for considerable unconscious rage that was evinced by the images of squashed, eviscerated, or otherwise damaged creatures. These latter images would seem to reflect both her unconscious aggression and her own sense of herself as a victim, perhaps symbolizing a masochistic orientation in relationships.

Another important theme is her significant confusion around her sexual identity. At times it appears that Eva almost has a cross-gender identification. She appears fascinated with the sexuality of other women in a way that may reflect unconscious homosexual impulses. The identification with males seems to be primarily in the form of an identification with the aggressor; men are seen as gigantic, powerful, physically dominant figures with "tiny, tiny heads." Women, by contrast are perceived primarily as part-objects—breasts, faces, vaginas. Her preoccupation with female genitalia seems at once to be an expression of unconscious homosexual desires and a concern that she, herself, is not quite normal. One may also speculate that the identification with men is with the phallus, not only as a symbol of male aggressivity, but as a space-occupying organ, one that fills the empty inner space that she experiences as her femininity.

We may speculate that the loss of her father when she was an infant is a loss that she has been unable to overcome, and her rage over this abandonment has led to a partial identification with the aggressor (i.e., men) and a confusion over her own identity as a woman. It is also clear from the projective material that she sees little succor forthcoming from maternal figures. Thus, she has failed to internalize a stable good object and must resort to primitive defensive maneuvers to stave off awareness of disorganizing rage and a powerful sense of loss and abandonment.

Most impressive is the wide range of functioning that she demonstrates. Although her fundamental issues appear to be pre-Oedipal and her defenses are, at times, quite primitive, she is capable of a great deal of creativity. Unfortunately, her inability to control her powerful primitive affects has rendered her incapable of using her considerable talents in a steady goal-directed manner.

RECOMMENDATIONS

In making recommendations based on the Rorschach, it is important to go beyond "good/poor candidate for psychotherapy," and offer prognostic statements and recommendations that are likely to be useful to the treating clinician. In this case, given Eva's intelligence and her ability to symbolize her distress (as evidenced by the richness of her Rorschach protocol), psychodynamic psychotherapy would appear to be the treatment of choice. This observation about sympolization is an extremely important one. I have found that patients who are able to symbolize their pathology in a way that is understandable to another, even if unconsciously, are generally able to make use of analytic psychotherapy. This observation has been at least partially confirmed in the Austen Riggs study of long-term psychotherapy (Blatt & Ford, 1994). In addition, even though she does not have a full-fledged manic-depressive disorder, pharmacotherapy with a mood-stabilizing agent such as lithium might be considered as an adjunct to help her control the mood swings that seem to be such a problem for her.

Eva is likely to make an easier attachment to a male therapist (which, interestingly, was her choice). The initial transference is likely to revolve around the expression of rage and her testing of the therapist's capacity to tolerate her expressions of anger and aggression. It will be important for the therapist to be alert to the operation of projective identification in the relationship and to interpret it consistently. The masochistic trends in her interpersonal functioning are probably a manifestation of the projective identification of her own rage at abandonment. The sequence is likely to be that she cannot tolerate her own rage, projects it into another, and by seductive behavior winds up becoming involved in a masochistic relationship with the one into whom she has projected her own aggression. At the same time she expiates her guilt for having caused the abandonment in the first place. This dynamic will undoubtedly be played out again and again in her psychotherapy. As Brenman (1952) pointed out, the manifestations of desexualized masochism in the psychotherapeutic situation can be extremely subtle, taking the form, for example, of a light banter in which the patient is typically the "teasee." Such patterns are actually complex transference phenomena that need to be consistently interpreted.

We may also anticipate that the intensity of her affects will lead her to have periodic brief psychotic transference reactions. At such times, it is imperative for the therapist to keep in mind that she is likely to reconstitute quickly once the triggering conflict is resolved and a consistent interpretive stance is maintained.

If the therapy is successful, we may also anticipate that she will need to endure a period of significant depression as she confronts her primitive experience of loss and abandonment. A successful early period of treatment should enable her to bear the experience of depressive affect without decompensation or resort to primitive defenses. The capacity to experience depression must be considered a developmental achievement. As Pontalis (1981) pointed out, the experience of psychic pain (as opposed to the translation of one's painful experiences into somatic experience) implies the existence of a secure psychic space in which to experience it. This depression is likely to have a substantially different feel to it from the "lows" that she has been experiencing heretofore. Again, a consistent interpretive stance is likely to be the most successful in helping her weather this. Despite the severity of her pathology, Eva stands a reasonably good chance of making significant gains if she is able to commit to a long-term therapeutic endeavor.

REFERENCES

American Psychiatric Association. (1994). *Diagnostic and statistical manual of mental disorders* (4th ed.). Washington, DC: Author.

Beizman, C. (1967). Considérations sur différentes modalités d'apprehénsion des réponses intermaculaires [Thoughts on the different kinds of dread seen in the white space response]. *Bulletin de la Societe Française du Rorschach et des Methodes Projectives, 10,* 21-31.

Blatt, S. J., & Ford, R. Q. (1994). *Therapeutic change: An object relations perspective.* New York: Plenum.

Brenman, M. (1952) On teasing and being teased: And the problem of moral masochism. *Psychoanalytic Study of the Child, 7,* 264-285.

Exner, J. E. (1993). *The Rorschach: A comprehensive system: Vol. 1. Basic foundations* (3rd ed.). New York: Wiley.

Fried, R. (1980). Rorschach and Icarus. In J. S. Kwawer, H. Lerner, P. Lerner, & A. Sugarman (Eds.), *Borderline phenomena and the Rorschach test* (pp. 107-132). New York: International Universities Press.

Gacono, C. B., & Meloy, J. R. (1994). *The Rorschach assessment of aggressive and psychopathic personalities.* Hillsdale, NJ: Lawrence Erlbaum Associates.

Jagger, M., & Richards, K. (1967). Ruby Tuesday. On *Flowers* [compact disc 509; Originally released on London Records]. New York: Abkco.

Kernberg, O. (1975). *Borderline conditions and pathological narcissism.* New York: Aronson.

Lerner, P. (1991). *Psychoanalytic theory and the Rorschach.* Hillsdale, NJ: The Analytic Press.

Lerner, P., & Lerner, H. (1980). Rorschach assessment of primitive defenses in borderline personality structure. In J. Kwawer, H. Lerner, P. Lerner, and A. Sugarman (Eds.), *Borderline phenomena and the Rorschach test* (pp. 257-274). New York: International Universities Press.

Merceron, C., Husain, O., & Rossel, F. (1988). A specific category of borderline conditions: Perverse personality organizations and the Rorschach. In H. Lerner & P. Lerner (Eds.), *Primitive mental states and the Rorschach* (pp. 377-402). Madison, CT: International Universities Press.

Murray, H. (1955). An American Icarus. In A. Burton (Ed.), *Clinical studies of personality* (pp. 615-641). New York: Harper.

Ogden, T. (1989). Playing, dreaming, and interpreting experience: Comments on potential space. In M. Fromm & B. Smith (Eds.), *The facilitating environment: Clinical applications of Winnicott's theory* (pp. 255-278). Madison, CT: International Universities Press.

Pechoux, R., & Harmand, M.-F. (1967). Deux problems: l'opposition, les détails blancs [Two problems: Oppositionalism, the white space]. *Bulletin de la Societe Français du Rorschach et des Methodes Projectives, 10,* 51-57.

Phillips, L., & Smith, J. (1953) *Rorschach interpretation: Advanced technique.* New York: Grune & Stratton.

Pontalis, J.-B. (1981) *Frontiers of psychoanalysis: Between the dream and psychic pain.* New York: International Universities Press.

Rapaport, D. (1967). The theory of attention cathexis. In M. Gill (Ed.) *The collected papers of David Rapaport* (pp. 778-794). New York: Basic Books. (Original work published 1959)

Rorschach, H. (1942). *Psychodiagnostics.* Berne, Switzerland: Hans Huber.

Schwartz, F., & Lazar, Z. (1979). The scientific status of the Rorschach. *Journal of Personality Assessment, 43*, 3-11.

Smith, B. (1991). Theoretical matrix of interpretation. *Rorschachiana, 17*, 73-77.

Smith, B. L. (1990). Potential space and the Rorschach: An application of object relations theory. *Journal of Personality Assessment, 55*, 756-767.

Smith, B. L. (1994). Object relations theory and the integration of empirical and psychoanalytic approaches to Rorschach interpretation. *Rorschachiana, 19*, 61-77.

Spitz, R. (1957). *No and yes: On the genesis of human communication.* New York: International Universities Press.

Sugarman, A. (1979) The infantile personality: Orality and the hysteric revisited. *International Journal of Psycho-analysis. 60*, 501-513.

Sugarman, A. (1991). Where's the beef? Putting personality back into personality assessment. *Journal of Personality Assessment, 56*, 130-144.

Wechsler, D. (1981). *Wechsler Adult Intelligence Scale–Revised.* New York: The Psychological Corporation.

Weiner, I. (1994). The Rorschach Inkblot Method (RIM) is not a test: Implications for theory and practice. *Journal of Personality Assessment, 62*, 498-504.

Winnicott, D. (1971). *Playing and reality.* London: Tavistock Books.

I

1. (10") I see this female figure. Do you want to know why? She sort of has her arms up and she has sort of an omnipotent air—like this (gestures with her arms). [laugh]

2. 4 ghost-like figures. I could go on and on.

3. On top of the shoulders are 2 hawk-like birds perched on the shoulders. There's more but it's boring.

II

This looks a lot more organic to me. Several things.

4. 30" First thing I saw—2 huge bear-type figures. Mammoth-sized, huge. Sort of touching each other. Boy, there's a lot of stuff on the bottom!

5. The lower part looks like a vagina. It does! That's what it looks like.

6. It also looks like a butterfly—a monarch.

7. Up on top—it looks like jungle masks. Not delicate—very barbaric. You can see eyes, nose, mouth.

8. In between the bears—it looks like a pool hall light, like above a pool table.

9. I see something else. If you look in a completely different way, it is a face—The red on top is his eyes, the lamp is his nose, the vagina or butterfly is the mouth and the bears are the cheeks.

III

How are these made? Random?

10. I see these 2, I would call them female figures—it looks like high heels, it looks like breasts, although the faces look more like bird's faces—the beak.

11. In the middle I see sort of a bow tie.

12. Lots of birds here. 2 eagles flying thru the air, carrying something in their mouth. Reminds me of the dove and the story of Noah's ark. That's the main thing, lots of other things, but . . .

(?)Right in the center. (?) Just a fact . . . it looked like a dress on—a long dress the way it's formed, it's a woman. Probably more than anything, it's the dress.

(?) Under the arms and around the waist—2 on each side. Not upright. (?) completely white and they look like they're robed—like a sheet over them, a long sheet. Not very distinct features.

(?) Above the shoulders; beak and wings. They're also huge—as big as she is.

(?) large and black. (?) furry-looking and stocky, furry legs and a huge body and furry arms. Shape looked like a silhouette of a bear.

(?) The red part. The body of the butterfly is the vagina. It was red. Bloody red; female menses. (?) The shape is just like it: openings and so on.

(?) 2 sides were . . . it looked like a monarch butterfly with a few speckles. (Monarch?) Monarch is the closest, especially the top part.

(?) In the red. They're barbaric—not very defined. The eyes are black, the mouth is whitish. Carvings like a totem mask.

(?) Between the 2 bears. White. The shape of it and the tassel hanging.

(?) If you look at it completely different way, the whole instead of parts. The other picture (Card I) looks a lot more like a cardinal than a hawk—much more, in fact.

(?) 2 black areas. (?) High heels and protuberances in the chest area. Not very feminine faces—a beak.

(?) It just does.

The white area. It could be a dove because it could have something in the mouth.

13. I see sort of (inaudible) shape—sort of the shape of a bulldog. The area from the nose down. Not the eyes, but wearing a bow like a poodle. Puffy and wrinkled cheeks.

14. Oh wow! The two on the side look like 2 dead rats falling from the sky.

(?) In the center you can see eyes, you can see a fleshy face, mouth, and a flat nose. It looks like a ribbon on the head. The cheeks, nose, mouth chin (points).

(?) The two red on the top. Tails and they look like they already came out of a mousetrap. The bodies are mangled and red and bloody—just perched up there. It looks like they're falling because the hair on the back stuck out.

IV

15. It looks like a giant monster with a tiny, tiny face of an anteater. The rest is huge. Huge legs and feet. Very masculine, but not too threatening because of the tiny, tiny face. It's big, but it doesn't look dangerous. That's all. Anything else is boring.

(?) The whole thing. (?) Mammoth size. An anteater's face. You can't see the eyes. You can see the long nose. It's very masculine. Gentle, not threatening at all. This [D] is probably a penis; that's what made me think of a male.

V

I can see this several different ways.

16. It looks like a bat if you look at the whole thing.

17. The white underneath the wing—2 reclining figures look like they're reading what looks like a notebook in their hand. It looks like they're very wise, ancient figures, like Bedouins, robed, not facing one another, facing away from one another. Well . . .

18. 2 faces—actually sillhouette. Kind of bewitched-looking; big crooked nose, scraggly beard, ugly face. Kind of like a dunce's face, a stupid ugly face.

(?) Wing span and legs sticking out from the bottom. It looks like it just took off in flight.

(?) Sitting, it looks like they're not leaning on a post, their backs aren't touching the post. Reclining as if almost leaning against a tree. They look like ancient figures. Look like ancient wisemen.

The top of the bat's wing, at an angle of 45°. Nose, mouth, scraggly beard, they look pathetic, the kind you'd feel sorry for.

VI

19. The 1st thing I see if I look at it as a whole is . . . like a dead cat. Actually the skin of a dead cat as if somebody had emptied out the insides and laid it open for mounting 'cause you can see whiskers at the top and 4 legs—split open. Yucch!

20. Again, it looks like female anatomy, also.

Lots of little things, but if I stretch my imagination I could make up stories, but I don't think I will.

(?) Like the skin of a cat, actually. Guts removed and opened flat as if to study it or hang it on a wall. The head is fairly small; you can see whiskers. If you split a cat open, I suppose that's what it would look like—4 legs—right?

Right in the center. (?) Features aren't exactly . . . sort of reminds you of it at a glance.

VII

[looks at back of Card]

21. The middle kind of looks like a ballerina past her time; an old woman wearing a ballerina's tutu. You can't see the face, but the body's out of shape, wearing a ballerina's costume.

(?) The white in the center. It looks old because the breast part is sort of misshapen, not like a young, taut ballerina would be. I don't see legs, just the trunk.

(continued)

22. I see 6 different faces. Maybe . . . I'll say 6 distinct . . . 2 are looking toward each other.

It looks like feathers coming out of their heads—they look like Indian kids.

23. 2nd set sort of look like pigs with noses and mouth—facing away.

They look more like pigs' heads, but sort of shark's mouth—chin receding. Nose of a pig; mouth of a shark.

24. The bottom faces . . . like an Impressionist painter painting something, and he didn't like it and went [gestures with arm].

Smudgy as if the artist didn't like what he painted. You can still detect eyes and the form of the head. Barely there, but you can still see it.

25. Again the same female parts. Smaller. They don't look the same, but . . . well, they don't actually look the same anyway. Weird pictures.

At the bottom, the small area. (?) Just the way it looked. They're not the same as the last one. But none of them are the same, anyway.

VIII

Lots of things here.

26. 1st intuitive . . . animals in the forest. The top sort of looks like a forest—it's green. Very fertile-looking.

The green at the top part. Also it looked like trees. An evergreen forest. Very fertile.

27. These 2 look like ground animals. The legs aren't very long. They don't look like they have wings.

On the sides. I can't really tell what kind. They're not dog-like, not lizard-like, pretty nondescript.

28. There's a butterfly . . . but it's . . . kinda deformed.

(?) At the bottom—the red and orange. The wings weren't exactly like a butterfly.

The impression I get is very, like forest. Animals. Bunch of stuff you can see here if you really want to make things up.

29. A bird, as if you were looking at it from behind. You could make up lots of stuff, but it's going to get boring, so I will let it go.

(?)The wings. You can't see the head . . . it could be an eagle, too, because of the wing span.

30. If you stretch the imagination, it looks like an X-ray painted over in color.

You can see lungs and the stomach and esophagus. The colors remind me of human insides. Red and greenish and purple.

IX

31. This part looks like an urn or a vase.

In the center. (?) Just the shape. It looks like . . .

32. Looks like a couple of witches—Halloween witches—deformed faces and bodies. Bunch of stuff here, but nothing seems to . . . bunch of separate things.

On the top. It was the color. Orange. More than that, the tall triangular hats and deformed faces and long robe and arms and mangled and ugly looking.

33. Faces on the bottom . . . look like maybe a kid's face, but the features aren't defined at all. Horizontal, you can only see up to the chest. Looks like they're looking up. Maybe gazing up at clouds—blue clouds, and letting their imaginations go. Imagining witches or something. Like kids dreaming—kids, infants, fetuses—features aren't distinct.

Pinkish faces. Look like they're gazing up. Eye and nose. Very indistinct,very babyish.

X

I see a whole bunch of animals, all different kinds.

34. The blue kinda looks like a crab. Or even a scorpion. Part looks like a scorpion.

(?) Tentacles. It looks like a combination. Crab body because it's round. Scorpion because you could see it with longer body and tentacles.

35. 2 green on top look like rabbits. At least 40 other things.

I see ears and a face and so on.

36. Could be a miniature horse. Two in the middle with a tail; actually more like a lion now that I look at the body.

The yellow part. (?) like a cat: tail, color, shape.

37. Green in the middle looks like a grasshopper.

Looks like the face of a grasshopper—green.

38. 2 on the sides look like birds perched on a tree limb. Ground animals, birds, crawling animals, even termites.

The two around the middle. (?) It just did. The wings were out.

39. 2 termites at the top.

They were gray, and the faces looked like termites' faces.

40. White stands out. It looks like a type of ornament you find on a religious type mosque; elaborate type designs you find on a mosque or, I don't know . . . I see all sorts of things; you can make up stuff.

You know, it just does.

41. If this is to be a face, the grasshopper is a moustache.

Cheeks. You can sort of make it up. It's more or less symmetrical.

APPENDIX B
Sequence of Scores

Card	No.	Loc.	#	Determinant(s)	(2)	Content(s)	Pop Z	Special Scores
I	1	Do	4	Mpo		H, Cg, Hx		AB
	2	DdSo	26	C'Fo	2	(H), Cg		
	3	D+	7	FMpo	2	A	4.0	
II	4	D+	1	FMa.FC'.FTo	2	A	P 3.0	
	5	Ddo	24	FCo		An, Bl		MOR
III	6	Do	3	FYo		A		
	7	Do	2	FYo	2	A		AB, CP
	8	DSo	5	F+		Hh		
	9	WS+	1	F–		Hd	4.5	
III	10	Do	1	Fo	2	H, Cg, Sx, Ad	P	INC
	11	Do	3	Fo		Cg		
	12	DdSo	23	FMau	2	A, Ay		ALOG
	13	DdS+	99	F–		Ad, Art	4.5	
	14	Do	2	FMa.FCo	2	A, Bl		MOR
IV	15	Wo	1	Fo		A, Ad, Sx	2.0	INC
V	16	Wo	1	FMao		A	P 1.0	
	17	DdS+	99	Mpu	2	H, Hh, Ay, Bt	2.5	
	18	Ddo	35	Fo	2	(Hd)		MOR
VI	19	Wo	1	Fo		Ad	P 2.5	MOR
	20	Do	12	Fu		An, Sx		
VII	21	DSo	7	Fu		Hd, Sx, Cg		MOR
	22	D+	1	Mpo	2	Hd, Ay	P 1.0	
	23	Do	3	FMpo	2	Ad		INC
	24	Ddv	23	YF–	2	Hd, Art		
	25	Do	6	Fo		An, Sx		PSV
VIII	26	Do	6	CF–		Ls		
	27	Do	1	Fo	2	A	P	DV
	28	Do	2	FCo		A		MOR
	29	DdSo	32	Fo		A		
	30	W+	1	CF–		Xy	4.5	
IX	31	DSo	8	Fo		Hh		
	32	Do	3	CFo	2	(H), Cg	P	MOR
	33	D+	4	Mp.CFo	2	Hd, Cl	4.5	FAB
X	34	Do	1	Fo	2	A	P	INC
	35	Do	12	F–	2	A		
	36	Do	2	FCo	2	A		
	37	Do	10	FC–		A		
	38	D+	15	FMpo	2	A, Bt	4.0	
	39	Do	8	FCo	2	A		
	40	DdSo	99	Fu		Art, Ay		
	41	Dd+	22	F–		Hd	4.5	

Summary of Approach

I:D.DdS.D	VI:W.D
II:D.Dd.D.D.DS.WS	VII:DS.D.D.Dd.D
III:D.D.DdS.DdS.D	VIII:D.D.D.DdS.W
IV:W	IX:DS.D.D.
V:W.DdS.Dd	X:D.D.D.D.D.D.DdS.Dd

APPENDIX C
Rorschach Structural Summary

LOCATION FEATURES	DETERMINANTS		CONTENTS	S-CONSTELLATION
	BLENDS	SINGLE		NO..FV + VF + V + FD > 2
			H = 3,0	NO..Col-Shd Bl>0
Zf = 13	FM.FC'.FT	M = 3	(H) = 2,0	YES..Ego<.31,>.44
ZSum = 42.5	FM.FC	FM = 5	Hd = 6,0	YES..MOR>3
ZEst = 41.5	M.CF	m = 0	(Hd) = 1,0	NO..Zd > ± 3.5
		FC = 5	Hx = 0,1	YES..es>EA
W = 5		CF = 3	A = 17,0	NO..CF+C>FC
(Wv = 0)		C = 0	(A) = 0,0	YES..X+%<.70
D = 26		Cn = 0	Ad = 3,2	YES..S>3
Dd = 10		FC' = 0	(Ad) = 0,0	NO..P<3 or >8
S = 10		C'F = 1	An = 3,0	NO..Pure H <2
		C' = 0	Art = 1,2	NO..R<17
DQ		FT = 0	Ay = 0,4	5.....TOTAL
.........(FQ-)		TF = 0	Bl = 0,2	
+ = 10(4)		T = 0	Bt = 0,2	SPECIAL SCORINGS
o = 30(3)		FV = 0	Cg = 1,5	Lv1 Lv2
v/+ = 0 (0)		VF = 0	Cl = 0,1	DV = 1x1 0x2
v = 1 (1)		V = 0	Ex = 0,0	INC = 4x2 0x4
		FY = 2	Fd = 0,0	DR = 0x3 0x6
		YF = 1	Fi = 0,0	FAB = 1x4 0x7
		Y = 0	Ge = 0,0	ALOG = 1x5
FORM QUALITY		Fr = 0	Hh = 2,1	CON = 0x7
		rF = 0	Ls = 1,0	SUM6 = 7
FQx FQf MQual SQx		FD = 0	Na = 0,0	WSUM6 = 18
+ = 1 1 0 1		F = 18	Sc = 0,0	
o = 28 11 3 4			Sx = 0,5	AB =2 CP = 1
u = 5 3 1 4			Xy = 1,0	AG =0 MOR = 7
– = 8 4 0 2			Id = 0,0	CFB =0 PER = 0
none = 0 – 0 0		(2) = 20		COP =0 PSV = 1

RATIOS, PERCENTAGES, AND DERIVATIONS

R = 41	L = 0.78		FC:CF+C =6:4	COP = 0	AG = 0
			Pure C =0	Food	= 0
EB = 4:7.0	EA = 11.0	EBPer = 1.8	SumC':WSumC =2:7.0	Isolate/R	= 0.12
eb = 7:6	es = 13	D = 0	Afr =0.64	H:(H)Hd(Hd)	= 3:9
	Adj es = 11	Adj D = 0	S =10	(HHd):(AAd)	= 3:0
			Blends:R =3:41	H+A:Hd + Ad	= 22:12
FM = 7 C' = 2 T = 1			CP =1		
m = 0 V = 0 Y = 3					
		P = 8	Zf =13	3r+(2)/R	= 0.49
a:p = 4:7	Sum6 =7	X+% = 0.68	Zd =+1.0	Fr+rF	= 0
Ma:Mp = 0:4	Lv2 =0	F+% = 0.61	W:D:Dd =5:26:10	FD	= 0
2AB+Art+Ay = 11	WSum6 = 18	X–% = 0.20	W:M =5:4	An + Xy	= 4
M– = 0	Mnone = 0	S–% = 0.25	DQ+ =10	MOR	= 7
		Xu% = 0.12	DQv =1		

SCZI = 2	DEPI = 5*	CDI = 2	S-CON = 5	HVI = No	OBS = No

14

Borderline Personality Organization, Psychopathy, and Sexual Homicide: The Case of Brinkley[1]

Carl B. Gacono
U.S. Department of Justice

Perhaps no other area of psychological study has the power to both attract and abhor as predatory murder. Large audiences at movies such as *Manhunter* and *Silence of the Lambs* (based on novels by Harris, 1981, 1988), and a plethora of paperbacks (Bugliosi & Gentry, 1974; Graysmith, 1976; Larsen, 1980; O'Brien, 1985) speak to the American public's fascination with the subject. With the exception of forensic experts who study these killers, the law enforcement community, or the unfortunate families of their victims, Americans remain psychologically detached from murders whose motives elude rational explanation (Brown, 1991). Even mental health professionals have great difficulty accepting the possibility that certain individuals "enjoy killing people" (Dietz, 1986, p. 487).

Psychodynamic theory concerning borderline personality organization and severe narcissism adds to our understanding of one subtype of predatory murderer, the sexual psychopath (Gacono & Meloy, 1994; Liebert, 1985; Meloy, 1988; Podolsky, 1965). Early frustration of libidinal drives, often through actual physical and sexual abuse, creates the template of borderline personality structure. Overwhelmed by aggression, the developing ego does not mature to a neurotic level but instead remains reliant on splitting and related primitive defense mechanisms (Kernberg, 1975). During arousal the

---

[1]This chapter is a revised version of "A Rorschach Case Study of Sexual Homicide" (1992), reprinted with permission of the *British Journal of Projective Psychology*. The views in this chapter are solely mine and may not reflect the views of the Federal Bureau of Prisons or United States Department of Justice.

fragile and ill-defined boundary (maintained by splitting) separating libidinal and aggressive drives is easily disrupted, wherein the drives are linked.[2]

Primitive defenses underlie and interact with narcissistic object relations. The defensive use of fantasy (grandiosity) and identification with the aggressor (Freud, 1936/1966; Ressler, Burgess, & Douglas, 1988) help the child compensate for neglect and deprivation. Power and pleasure are gained through the imaginary control and sadistic treatment of the frustrating object.

The classical pairing of libidinal and aggressive drives in childhood may create a template for operant sexual violence in adolescence and adulthood (Meloy, 1988). Histories of sexual murderers typically include pernicious escalation of violence toward others. Their behaviors can be traced through successive approximation to the inevitable sexual murder (i.e., childhood cruelty toward animals, breaking and entering accompanied by affective exhilaration, date rape, choking partner during intercourse), and rehearsal fantasies that increase in violent content (Prentky et al., 1989) and behavioral expression (Gacono & Meloy, 1994). The first murder may occur as a by-product of a sexually stimulating situation when the perpetrator is intoxicated, depressed, and aggressively aroused. After the initial sexual murder, the act begins to serve an intrapsychic regulatory function helping to restore narcissistic equilibrium and stabilize affect (Bluestone & Travin, 1984; Gacono & Meloy, 1988, 1994; McCarthy, 1978; Meloy, Gacono, & Kenney, 1994; Rappaport, 1988; Revitch, 1965). "After committing the first murder and not being caught, he is surprised; after committing the second murder, he is amazed; and after the third murder he is omnipotent" (Gacono & Meloy, 1994, p. 286).

Primitive defensive mechanisms (Kernberg, 1975, 1984) such as splitting, projective identification, dissociation, devaluation, idealization, and primitive denial operate during all phases of the murder (stalking, murder, dumping of the body; Dietz, 1986; Gacono & Meloy, 1988, 1994; MacCulloch, Snowdon, Wood, & Mills, 1983; Rappaport, 1988). Idealization sometimes occurs during the stalking phase as victim choice may match an internalized part object.[3] When reality intrudes on the grandiose fantasies of the perpetrator, aggressive drive derivatives as well as the devalued part object are projected *into* the initially idealized victim. Devaluation of the victim protects the idealized representations within the grandiose self-structure (Kernberg, 1975), whereas the transfer of aggressive drive derivatives through projective identification

---

[2]The following sexual murderer's description of his thinking and affective experience preceding and during one of several murders illustrates this process, "I began to think of killing her . . . but even as I did think of this, every time my sexual desire crept in the thought of killing her disappeared, until the thought or fear of being identified by her flashed into my thought, then I'd think of killing her again, only to subside back to the intense desire I had to have her sexually. So the two thoughts never came together until the instant of the murder itself" (Gacono, 1992, p. 2).

[3]This "goodness of fit" (Meloy, 1988) was most prominent with Theodore Bundy's victims who bore striking similarities in appearance (Larsen, 1980).

transforms the victim into a threatening object. The victim now "deserves" to be subjected to sadistic sexual acts intended to control and hurt (Klein, 1946; Shapiro, 1981), thereby allowing the murderer to rationalize the heinous acts. For the sexual psychopath, hurt and control are not sufficient. The murder allows annihilation of the hated part of the self (Rappaport, 1988), thereby purging the malevolent self-representations that are not reintegrated (Goldstein, 1991). Dissociation complements the other defensive operations and allows the victim to be further depersonalized,[4] although this perceptual illusion is not specific to sexual homicide.

The Rorschach of a man whom I call Brinkley is presented to illustrate the primitive defenses, narcissistic object relations, identity diffusion, and impaired reality testing that contribute to one subtype of sexual homicide. Brinkley could be classified as a hedonistic (Holmes & DeBurger, 1988) and sexually sadistic psychopathic murderer (Dietz, 1986; Rappaport, 1988) whose first sexual homicide revealed crime scene elements of a mixed pattern (Ressler et al., 1988).

BRINKLEY: A SEXUAL MURDERER

Historical Data

Brinkley was a 31-year-old, White male, interviewed and tested as part of two dissertation research projects studying psychopathy in inmate populations (Gacono, 1988; Heaven, 1988). He presented as a muscular male with glasses and thinning brown hair. Although we introduced ourselves by last names, Brinkley quickly made the interview less formal by shaking hands, and with a wide grin stated, "Carl, you can call me Brinkley." At the time of our interview, Brinkley had served 5 years of a 25-year sentence for the sexual murder of a female stranger.

Brinkley's developmental history was similar to other murderers (Lewis et al., 1988; Ressler et al., 1988). It included a family history of alcoholism and psychiatric problems, physical and mental abuse, instability of residence with his father leaving in early adolescence, negative relationships with other male caretaker figures, a negative relationship with a dominant biological mother, perceptions that he had been unfairly treated, and the absence of an older sibling role model. Childhood abuse or neglect is a frequent occurrence in histories of particularly violent murderers (Lewis et al., 1988; Ressler et al., 1988), and some histories contain both.

---

[4]These patterns (absent the homicide) are readily observable within a hospital milieu. One sexual psychopath "targeted" an idealized female and fraudulently obtained her home phone, sent her cards, and wrote poetry to her. When confronted, he reacted with rage and later was observed glaring in an intimidating fashion and disparaging manner (devaluation) toward the once idealized female.

Brinkley reported a history of violence toward both males and females. The aggression took a sexual form toward females, including several instances of oral sex with a neighbor girl at age 10, employment as a prostitute in his early 20s, and a "date rape" at age 23. Typical of his rationalization of sexually aggressive behavior, Brinkley jokingly stated, "The devil made me do it." Aggression toward males involved fighting, sometimes with weapons such as a knife or a sap.

Brinkley reported a history of depression and believed he was depressed at the time of the instant offense. A history of depression in sexual murderers is consistent with previous research (Reinhardt, 1973), although not expected in severe psychopaths (Meloy et al., 1994). He previously remarked, "I had planned to kill myself on that day, but after I picked the girl up I killed her instead." On another occasion he remarked, "I was going to punish someone for what was done to me" (referring to his being abused as a child). As with some sexual psychopaths, Brinkley's affective dysregulation in part motivated his sexual aggression, because rage and erotic arousal temporarily dissipated his depression (Meloy et al., 1994).

Brinkley's victim was a stranger female whom he approached at a party. Like many other sexual murderers, he was intoxicated at the time of the offense (Ressler et al., 1988). Brinkley enticed her into his car, strangled, and then raped her. Because she survived the initial strangulation and rape, he killed (strangulation) her after the rape. He transported the body to his home, stuffed her under his bed, and 2 days later deposited her in a garbage dumpster. Despite an occasional glimmer of insight, Brinkley tended to rationalize the murder in a typical criminal fashion (Gacono & Meloy, 1988): "It was like a mercy killing. I thought that if she lived she would be a veg."

Brinkley reported rehearsal fantasies (Brittain, 1970; MacCulloch et al., 1983; Prentky et al., 1989; Ressler et al., 1988; Revitch, 1965) involving rape and strangulation that increased in frequency over a 2-week period prior to the murder. Although Brinkley's victim was strangled and raped, sexual homicide in other cases has been suggested by victim attire, exposure of sexual parts, body positioning, insertion of foreign objects into body cavities, evidence of sexual intercourse, evidence of autoerotic activity or sadistic fantasy (Ressler et al., 1988), mutilation (including evisceration and/or strangulation; Simonsen, 1989), head injuries from behind, or multiple stab wounds (Gee, 1988).

Psychological Assessment Data

Brinkley completed the Shipley Institute of Living Scale (Shipley, 1940; Zachary, 1986), Minnesota Multiphasic Personality Inventory (MMPI; Hathaway & McKinley, 1951), Millon Clinical Multiaxial Inventory (MCMI; Millon, 1983), Self-Focus Sentence Completion Test (SFSC; Exner, 1969, 1973), Rorschach Psychodiagnostic Test (Rorschach, 1942), and a semistructured interview designed to complete the Hare Psychopathy Checklist–Revised (PCL–R; Hare, 1991). His correctional files were studied. The Shipley revealed intellectual functioning at the high end of the average range (Wechsler Adult Intelligence Scale–Revised equivalent = 110; Wechsler, 1981). His MMPI profile evidenced a 4–5 high-point pair (*Pd* Scale 4 = 85 *T* score). His SFSC score of 21 was greater than the mean score (*M* = 15.20) Exner (1973) reported for an offender sample. MCMI elevations on Scales 5 (antisocial) and D (depression) provided further empirical support for the presence of antisocial disturbance.

Similar to the Cleckley (1941/1976) psychopath, Brinkley exhibited egocentricity, a callous lack of empathy, poor control of anger, and a lack of remorse. He also fit Hare's empirical conceptualization of psychopathy (PCL–R; Hare, 1991), showing elevations on both factors: aggressive narcissism (selfish, callous, and remorseless use of others) and a chronic antisocial lifestyle (Hare, 1991). His PCL–R (Hare, 1991) total score was 34, placing him in the severe range of psychopathy (≥ 30). Brinkley also met the *Diagnostic and Statistical Manual of Mental Disorders* (3rd., rev. [*DSM–III–R*]; American Psychiatric Association [APA], 1987) criteria for all of the four cluster B personality disorders: Antisocial, Borderline, Narcissistic, and Histrionic.

Brinkley's Rorschach Protocol

Analysis of Comprehensive System (CS) data (Exner, 1993) alone greatly limits the Rorschach's usefulness for differential diagnosis. A combined methodology is particularly helpful in elucidating the nuances of character style (Gacono, Meloy, & Berg, 1992). In some cases content analysis (Lane, 1984; Lerner, 1991; Lindner, 1946, 1947), in conjunction with CS data, provides added insight into the perpetrator dynamics and can aid in differentiating the psychopath from the sexual psychopath (Gacono & Meloy, 1994; Meloy et al., 1994).

Brinkley's protocol was scored with the Exner (1993) CS. The structural summary (see Appendix A) was formulated with the Rorschach Interpretation Assistance Program, Version 3 (Exner, 1994). The protocol was also scored for psychoanalytic indices including primitive modes of relating (Kwawer, 1980), primitive defenses (Cooper, Perry, & Arnow, 1988; Lerner & Lerner, 1980) and aggressive content (*AgC*), aggressive potential (*AgPot*), aggressive past (*AgPast*), & sadomasochism (*SM*; Gacono, 1990; Meloy, 1988; Meloy & Gacono, 1992a) and impressionistic responses (*IMP*; Gacono, 1990; Gacono, Meloy, & Heaven, 1990). Two licensed clinical psychologists and several clinical psychology graduate-level Rorschach seminar students rescored these indices for reliability. For the reader's benefit, select Rorschach indices are highlighted within the context of individual responses (see Appendix B).

Brinkley's protocol is valid (*Lambda* = .18) but constricted (*R* = 13). Characterological constriction is suggested (Gacono & Meloy, 1992). Brinkley's attempt to maintain imaginary control over all aspects of the blot

(*W:R* = 8:13), his defensiveness (*PER* = 9), and grandiosity (*W:M* = 8:3; *Fr* = 3; *3r+(2)/R* = 1.08) result in low *R*. Despite limited responses the protocol is complex (*Blends/R* = 6:13) and impulse driven (*FM* = 4, *Sx* = 3, *Bl* = 1; *AG* = 1). The press of unmet needs (*FM* = 4, *m* = 1) causes a severe thought disorder (*WSum6* = 71). The interplay of psychopathic character and sexual homicide psychodynamics is suggested because significant elevations for total responses (*R*) would be expected in sexual homicide perpetrators, but not so in nonsexually offending psychopaths (*p* < .0058; Meloy et al., 1994). In this case psychopathy constricts the total *R*, but neither prevents unwanted ideational noise (*FM* = 4) nor the cognitive slippage apparent in other sexual homicide perpetrators (Meloy et al., 1994).

Similar to many antisocial personality disorders (40%) and sexual homicide perpetrators (40%; Gacono & Meloy, 1994), but unlike nonpatient males (23%; Exner, 1990), Brinkley is an ambitent. His controls (*D* = 0, *AdjD* = 0) and available resources (*EA* = 7.5) are normative. Considering the reduced number of responses, Brinkley perceptually organizes more than normals (*Zf* = 10). Although he is not positive on the hypervigilant index (HVI), his overincorporative style (*Zd* = +4.0), 9 personals (*PER*), and a *W:M* ratio near the 3:1 threshold (8:3) suggest a grandiose and paranoid style. Brinkley actively scans the environment both to protect himself (potential victim) and to hunt (potential prey).

He is chronically angry (*S* = 3), yet affectively avoidant (*Afr* = .30). His avoidance may have developed in response to difficulties modulating emotions (*FC:CF+C* = 2:3, *PureC* = 1), a tendency to be explosive (*PureC* = 1), and the disruptive effects of impulses on his cognitive functioning (*WSum6* = 71). Given the obvious perceptual distortions concerning interactions with others (*3Ms* = M.C, M.Fr.CF, M.Fr), Brinkley's interpersonal isolation (*Isolate/R* = .23) is not surprising. Despite having an expectation of interpersonal cooperativeness (*COP* = 3, all spoiled), he neither desires nor has the capacity for affectional relationships (*T* = 0). His four whole human responses (*H*) should be interpreted within the context of pathological narcissism (*3r+(2)/R* = 1.08; *Fr* = 3; *PER* = 9) and spoiled COPs. His interest in others relates to his overincorporative style, that is, to act out his sadistic fantasies (to prey on) or to prevent being preyed on.

Response 1 is paradigmatic of Brinkley's intrapsychic functioning. It illustrates the primitive defenses that regulate borderline personality organization (Gacono et al., 1992; Kernberg, 1976; Kohut, 1971), the failure of higher level defenses, and the sequence of defenses that are hypothesized to operate during the sexual murder sequence. Splitting occurs throughout Brinkley's record (Responses 1, 4, 8, 10, 12, 13) and operates in Response 1, as the insect is first devalued/tarnished (ugly insect) and then, in wish, turned into its opposite, an idealized "cute little lady bug or butterfly." As higher level defenses such as intellectualization and isolation fail, Brinkley intrapsychically regresses to more primitive defensive operations. Envy toward the idealized object results in a failure to internalize its potentially soothing properties and wished-for destruction (primitive sadism), "If only you could crush them." Brinkley's victim was initially idealized in fantasy, later devalued: "This is how dumb the broad was, I told her I was too drunk to start my car, so she got in and started it for me," and eventually sadistically raped. A vista/X-ray (*FV*) response followed by aggression supports a pattern of aggressive acting out (sadism) in response to painful emotions. He ends Response 1, as he does on several others (4, 6, 8, 10, 11), by offering a bland and unconvincing rationalization.

Defensive detachment is indicated by $T = 0$, $Afr = .30$ (see Appendices A and C), and a reliance on the use of devaluation. Unable to maintain higher level defenses, Brinkley cannot tolerate the ambivalence surrounding both needing and dreading the hurtful, idealized object (Meloy, 1988; Moberly, 1985), "cute little lady bug." Instead, defensive sadism and projective identification facilitate object destruction. Three reflections produced without *Y* or *T* suggest narcissistic detachment and developmental issues (the need for mirroring) different from the psychotic sexual psychopath who manifests sadism within the context of symbiotic relating and fears of engulfment (Meloy & Gacono, 1992b).

Both unconscious and conscious devaluation are insidious in antisocial personality disorders, psychopaths (Gacono, 1990; Gacono & Meloy, 1992), and sexual homicide perpetrators (Gacono & Meloy, 1994). Devaluation, the most frequently produced defense in all three groups, serves to protect the grandiose self structure (Kernberg, 1975). It is often dramatically expressed in statements of killers such as Angelo Buono, "Some girls don't deserve to live" (O'Brien, 1985, p. 117). This defense occurs throughout Brinkley's protocol (1, 3, 4, 5, 7, 10, 12, 13), and in Response 10, in which devaluation is combined with a reflection response (*Fr*), it may correlate with Brinkley's attitude toward women and his hatred of his own femininity/passivity. The "elderly" woman may represent Brinkley's devalued and hated maternal object whom he described as, "Not a good mother, physically and mentally abusive." This response may capture a symbolic link between maternal object and victim, which is further supported by the presence of "bug" imagery (1, 7) with its hypothetical relationship to a destructive mother figure and attitudes of superiority that protect or shield affective needs (Phillips & Smith, 1953).

Providing an avenue for sadistic impulses, projective identification is inherent in sexual homicide (Dietz, 1986; Gacono & Meloy, 1988; Rappaport, 1988). This defense (1, 6, 7, 11, 12, 13) regulates and maintains a malevolent internal self and object world. Frequently coupled with *AgC*, *AgPot*, and/or *AgPast* responses (Meloy & Gacono, 1992a), it suggests both predator self-identifications and self-representations that have been subjected to damage and aggression. Projective identification creates malevolent transformations in which benign Rorschach percepts or idealized victims are transformed into potential aggressors. This occurs on Response 1 when an insect is transformed into an intimidating Goliath bug (*AgPot*) armed with pincers (*AgC*), and on

Response 7 where a normally benign object (most people see a bat on Card V) is transformed into a "winged demon with claws." Through projective identification the unwanted externalized predatory object intrapsychically returns to haunt the self; the sexual murder attempts to annihilate it (Rappaport, 1988). The experience of pleasure/exhilaration (sadism) accompanies the purging and control of the malevolent object through projective identification.

Projective identification coupled with the frequent use of personal responses (PER = 9) indicate the operation of omnipotent control. As the object world is externalized, omnipotent control becomes a motivating factor in predation and of concern during testing. Within the testing it serves a defensive function (Exner, 1993), protecting Brinkley from projected "all bad" self-representations placed into the examiner (Gacono et al., 1990). Omnipotent control is evident in this statement by Theodore Bundy, a serial sexual murderer: "What really fascinated (the killer) was the hunt, the adventure of searching out his victims, and . . . possessing them physically as one would possess a potted plant, a painting, or a Porsche; Owning, as it were, this individual" (Michaud & Aynesworth, 1983).

The defensive use of dissociation, common both in borderline pathology (Kernberg, 1975) and sexual psychopathy (Lancaster, 1978; Meloy, 1988; Tanay, 1969), is suggested by three impressionistic responses (IMP; Responses 2, 5, 11), a FC:CF+C ratio of 2:3 (1 PureC; see Appendix A) and a color projection (CP) special score. Although quite rare, the CP response is significantly more likely to occur in sexual homicide perpetrators (15%) than antisocial males (2%), psychopaths (3%; Gacono & Meloy, 1994), or nonpatient males (.5%; Exner, 1990). Impressionistic responses are frequently produced by individuals with borderline personality organization such as sexual homicide perpetrators (50%), psychopaths (41%; Gacono & Meloy, 1994), and outpatient borderline males (89%; Gacono et al., 1992). Sometimes dissociative states are evident through reported amnesia or, in Brinkley's case, derealization: "It was like watching a film in slow motion." Frequently enhanced through the ingestion of alcohol or drugs, severe dissociation, along with the projective identification of self-representations, may account for primitive, psychoticlike behaviors during the sexual murder. "Splitting off" affect and "splitting" of the internalized object world are exhibited throughout this protocol.

Projective identification and dissociation provide the vehicle for sexual murder, whereas narcissistic rage (Kohut, 1971), "an all-consuming need for revenge or need to undo a hurt by whatever means, by those who have suffered a narcissistic injury" (Bluestone & Travin, 1984; p. 150), provides the fuel. On Response 2, "broken mirror" and "crushed apples" shed light on the failure of an early maternal object relation to protect and mirror (McDevitt, 1983) and aggressive oral dependency turned into sadistic rage. The violent symbiosis, separation, and reunion responses (Kwawer, 1980) on Responses 5 and 13, narcissistic mirroring responses (Kwawer, 1980) on 3, 5, and 10, and the combination of aggression and food on 2 and 13 also point to an early maternal object as the source of narcissistic injury and the genesis of narcissistic object relations. Response 6 (Card IV, paternal associations), which combines a *PER* with *AgPot* ("about to get trampled") and *AgC* (vulture, cobra, monster), may symbolize his very real "childhood nightmare monster," an abusive father. During childhood Brinkley was the helpless victim of physically abusive parents.[5] As a sexual murderer, however, he has become the powerful aggressor (Freud, 1936/1966).

A narcissistic orientation is suggested by a SFSC score of 21, 3 reflection responses and an egocentricity ratio of 1.08 (as noted in Appendix A). The choice of a Goliath bug on Response 1 symbolically highlights Brinkley's narcissistic vulnerability. Although the largest beetle in Africa, its body is extremely sensitive to touch and consequently easily damaged (Hutchins, 1966; Stanek, 1969). The female lays its eggs in rotting wood (Fanning, 1965), not unlike Brinkley's childhood environment. The association of a "size that is intimidating but no real strength" (1) is an expression of his narcissistic vulnerability. Projective identification underlies Brinkley's ability to externalize and rationalize responsibility for the most heinous behaviors (see Appendix B; rationalization).

Identity disturbance has been associated with borderline personality organization (Kernberg, 1976), borderline personality disorder (APA, 1987), and sexual murderers (Rappaport, 1988). Statements such as, "Gives an illusion" (1), "Just something about it" (3), "As if" (4), "Gives the illusion" (6), "Reminds me of . . . just the image" (7), and, "nothing fits together . . . disintegrates into nothing" (8) reveal the "as if" quality (Deutsch, 1942) of Brinkley's Rorschach. Brinkley's elevated MMPI Scale 5 suggests a departure from a traditional male sex role and may indicate anxieties about sexual identification. Uncertain identity is also suggested by a confused reflection response (3), "If one was looking down into a pool you would see *themselves*, not a reflection" (Gacono et al., 1990, p. 276), and the fusion of masculine and feminine sexual parts within one figure (4). A metamorphosis and transformation response (5) and two boundary disturbance responses (1, 8) suggest an identity in developmental transition, but not yet crystallized.

Pervasive thought disorder, the effects of primary process on cognitive functioning (Kernberg, 1976), is suggested by Special Scores occurring throughout the record and a *WSum6* of 71 (see Appendix A). When Brinkley's perceptual accuracy, $X+\% = 77$, $F+\% = 100$, $X-\% = 0$, is compared to normals, $X+\% = 79$, $F+\% = 71$, $X-\% = 7$, character disordered (Exner, 1990), $X+\% = 58$, $F+\% = 59$, $X-\% = 20$, psychopaths, $X+\% = 54$, $F+\% = 56$, $X-\% = 22$, sexual homicide perpetrators (Gacono & Meloy, 1994), $X+\% = 51$, $F+\% = 53$, $X-\% = 20$, or schizophrenic subjects (Exner, 1990), $X+\% = 40$, $F+\% = 42$, $X-\% = 37$, it does not appear severely distorted. Rather, nine *PERs*

---

[5]Brinkley was unable to recall being sexually abused. This could not, however, be ruled out.

and a $WSum6 = 71$ comprised of egocentric deviations ($DR = 13$) and idiosyncratic combinations ($INC = 2$) reflect severe impairment in conceptual rather than perceptual accuracy (Meloy, 1985; associated with narcissistic pathology).

Abuse of fantasy is suggested by a $M^a:M^p$ ratio of 1:2, and on Response 5 the combination of M^p, DR^2, self focus (Fr), and H, Bl, and Sx content suggest the primitive sexual nature of these fantasies. In conjunction with sexual aggression, $M^p > M^a$ has been hypothesized to suggest rehearsal fantasy (Meloy, 1988; Prentky et al., 1989) and given a history of violence, may indicate the planning of predatory violence (Gacono & Meloy, 1994; Meloy & Gacono, 1992a). Rehearsal fantasy and intrusive, obsessive thoughts ($FM = 4$, $V = 1$) are consistent with Brinkley's self-reported real-world behavior.

Sadism is evident throughout the record, and on Responses 5 and 13 surfaces in the form of sadomasochistic (SM) responses. "Abortion" is first suggested on Response 3; however, Brinkley initially constrains, then expresses, the sadistic impulse (Response 5). Relief rather than anxiety accompanies its expression. This pattern indicates ego syntonic sadism, and the externalization, devaluation, and control of predatory self-representations. "Okay . . . A woman that's had an abortion and she is having difficulty dealing with regrets afterwards (laughs). This is great (SM)." Laughter coupled with an $AgPast$ and reflection response (5) may indicate the fusion of aggressive drive derivatives within the grandiose self-structure and resultant characterological sadism (Kernberg, 1982). Subsequently, the externalization of sadistic superego components (Lerner, 1991) is suggested by the use of projective identification on the subsequent response (6).

Sexual responses are less frequently produced by nonpatient males (4%; Exner, 1990) than antisocial personality disordered males (45%; Gacono & Meloy, 1992). Brinkley produced three sexual content (Sx) responses (3, 4, 5; see Appendix C), and although their form quality was adequate, severe cognitive slippage resulted ($Lv2$). On Response 3 sexual content is produced with narcissistic mirroring, a personal, devaluation, and a deviant response ($DR2$). This pattern of scores indicates the disruptive effects of sexual impulses, and may symbolize the nonempathic, controlling, ruthless quality Brinkley has demonstrated in sexual interactions.

Brinkley's final response (13) reveals a dramatic and fluid display of ego-syntonic aggression. It contains a variety of primitive defenses, such as idealization, splitting, projective identification and omnipotence (Cooper et al., 1988), and all the aggressive scores—Ag, AgC, $AgPot$, $AgPast$, and SM. It also demonstrates the presence of characterological sadism (Kernberg, 1982), a complete absence of empathy, and a strong identification with aggressive and predatory self-representations (Freud, 1936/1966; Meloy, 1988). This final response reveals the predatory nature of his object world and is reminiscent of a statement from the "Zodiac" (a serial killer who terrorized the San Francisco Bay area in the late 1960s): "This is the Zodiac speaking. I like killing people because it is so much fun. It is more fun than killing wild game in the forest because man is the most dangerous animal of all" (Graysmith, 1976, p. 54).

SUMMARY

Although some sexual murderers produce rather empty "borderline" or typically constricted "psychotic" protocols, others produce Rorschachs with striking similarities to Brinkley's (see Gacono & Meloy, 1994, pp. 117–140). Brinkley's Rorschach, despite low R, exhibits all the components expected in borderline personality organization (Acklin, 1993), psychopathy, and sexual homicide (Gacono & Meloy, 1994). Specific ego weakness (Knight, 1953), general instability of psychic functioning, and easily provoked regression are all present. These patterns are consistent with the borderline and antisocial traits associated with murderers (Yarvis, 1990) and are not expected in the record of a smooth-functioning psychopath.

The reader is struck by a rawness that manifests in both affective and content spheres (Acklin, 1993). Human percepts range from cooperative to malevolent. Primitive modes of relating (Kwawer, 1980) are prevalent ($N = 7$). Responses vacillate between rapid deterioration and recovery and evidence a loss of distance from the blots, emotional lability, unusual (u form $= 3$) over minus form (– form $= 0$), boundary and identity disturbance, a reliance on primitive defenses, pervasive deficits in reality testing, and themes of pregenital aggression and sadism (Kernberg, 1976).

Brinkley is positive for five of our six (Gacono & Meloy, 1994) empirically postulated psychodynamics of sexual homicide: chronic anger ($S = 3$), entitlement and grandiosity ($Fr = 3$; $3r+(2)/R = 1.08$), abnormal bonding ($T = 0$), formal thought disorder ($WSum6 = 71$), and obsessional thoughts ($FM = 4$). Brinkley's T-less, Y-less protocol, with an egocentricity ratio of 1.08, nine $PERs$, D and adjusted D scores equal to 0 (see Appendix A), and seven primitive modes of relating (Kwawer, 1980), is consistent with our previous findings (Gacono et al., 1990; Gacono & Meloy, 1991, 1992) and indicative of an emotionally ($Afr = .30$) and interpersonally ($T = 0$; $Isolate/R = .23$) detached psychopath. These Rorschach findings are convergent with his MCMI, MMPI, and $DSM–III–R$ (APA, 1987) diagnosis of Antisocial Personality Disorder and a PCL–R clinical assessment of severe psychopathy (PCL–R ≥ 34).

The Rorschach holds a "pre-eminent place in the diagnostician's tool box . . . for assessing and displaying the underlying structural, affective, and representational features of the borderline's inner world" (Acklin, 1993, p. 338), the nuances of personality disorders (Gacono et al., 1992; Murray, 1993; Peterson, 1993), and in the case of Brinkley, the dynamics of a psychopathic sexual homicide perpetrator. When asked how he would avoid future incarceration, Brinkley adamantly replied, "I am not a criminal!" Brinkley was eligible for parole in 1993.

REFERENCES

Acklin, M. (1993). Psychodiagnosis of personality structure II: Borderline personality organization. *Journal of Personality Assessment, 61*, 329–341.

American Psychiatric Association. (1987). *Diagnostic and statistical manual of mental disorders.* Washington, DC: Author.

Bluestone, H., & Travin, S. (1984). Murder: The ultimate conflict. *The American Journal of Psychoanalysis, 44*, 147–167.

Brittain, R. (1970). The sadistic murderer. *Medical Science and the Law, 10*, 198–207.

Brown, J. (1991). The psychopathology of serial sexual homicide: a review of the possibilities. *American Journal of Forensic Psychiatry, 12*(1), 13–21.

Bugliosi, V., & Gentry, C. (1974). *Helter skelter.* New York: Bantam.

Cleckley, H. (1976). *The mask of sanity.* St. Louis, MO: C.V. Mosby. (Original work published 1941)

Cooper, S., Perry, J., & Arnow, D. (1988). An empirical approach to the study of defense mechanisms: I. Reliability and preliminary validity of the Rorschach defense scales. *Journal of Personality Assessment, 52*, 187–203.

Deutsch, H. (1942). Some forms of emotional disturbance and their relationships to schizophrenia. *Psychoanalytic Quarterly, 11*, 301–321.

Dietz, P. (1986). Mass, serial and sensational homicides. *Bulletin of the New York Academy of Medicine, 62*, 477–491.

Exner, J. E. (1969). Rorschach responses as an index of narcissism. *Journal of Projective Techniques and Personality Assessment, 33*, 324–330.

Exner, J. E. (1973). The Self-Focus Sentence Completion: A study of egocentricity. *Journal of Personality Assessment, 37*, 437–455.

Exner, J. E. (1990). *A Rorschach workbook for the Comprehensive System* (3rd ed.). Asheville, NC: Rorschach Workshops.

Exner, J. E. (1993). *The Rorschach: A comprehensive system: volume 1: Basic foundations* (3rd ed.). New York: Wiley.

Exner, J. E. (1994). *Rorschach interpretation assistance program, Version 3.* Asheville, NC: Rorschach Workshops.

Fanning, E. (1965). *Insects from close up.* New York: Thomas Crowel.

Freud, A. (1966). *The ego and the mechanisms of defense* (Rev. ed.) New York: International Universities Press. (Original work published 1936)

Gacono, C. B. (1988). *A Rorschach analysis of object relations and defensive structure and their relationship to narcissism and psychopathy in a group of antisocial offenders.* Unpublished doctoral dissertation, United States International University, San Diego, CA.

Gacono, C. B. (1990). An empirical study of object relations and defensive operations in antisocial personality disorder. *Journal of Personality Assessment, 54*, 589–600.

Gacono, C. B. (1992). A Rorschach case study of sexual homicide. *British Journal of Projective Psychology, 37*(1), 1–21.

Gacono, C. B., & Meloy, J. R. (1988). The relationship between cognitive style and defensive process in the psychopath. *Criminal Justice and Behavior, 15*, 472–483.

Gacono, C. B., & Meloy, J. R. (1991). A Rorschach investigation of attachment and anxiety in antisocial personality disorder. *Journal of Nervous and Mental Disease, 179*, 546–552.

Gacono, C. B., & Meloy, J. R. (1992). The Rorschach and the *DSM–III–R* antisocial personality: A tribute to Robert Lindner. *Journal of Clinical Psychology, 48*, 393–406.

Gacono, C. B., & Meloy, J. R. (1994). *The Rorschach assessment of aggressive and psychopathic personalities.* Hillsdale, NJ: Lawrence Erlbaum Associates.

Gacono, C., Meloy, J. R., & Berg, J. (1992). Object relations, defensive operations, and affective states in narcissistic, borderline, and antisocial personality disorder. *Journal of Personality Assessment, 59*, 32–49.

Gacono, C. B., Meloy, J. R., & Heaven, T. (1990). A Rorschach investigation of narcissism and hysteria in antisocial personality disorder. *Journal of Personality Assessment, 55,* 270–279.

Gee, D. (1988). A pathologist's view of multiple murder. *Forensic Science International, 38,* 53–65.

Goldstein, W. (1991). Clarification of projective identification. *American Journal of Psychiatry, 148,* 153–161.

Graysmith, R. (1976). *Zodiac.* New York: Berkeley.

Hare, R. (1991). *The Psychopathy Checklist–Revised manual.* Toronto, Canada: Multihealth Systems.

Harris, T. (1981). *Red dragon.* New York: Bantam.

Harris, T. (1988). *The silence of the lambs.* New York: St. Martin's.

Hathaway, S., & McKinley, J. (1951). *Minnesota Multiphasic Personality Inventory (Revised).* Minneapolis: University of Minnesota Press.

Heaven, T. (1988). *Relationship between Hare's Psychopathy Checklist and selected Exner Rorschach variables in an inmate population.* Unpublished doctoral dissertation, United States International University, San Diego, CA.

Holmes, R., & DeBurger, J. (1988). *Serial murder.* Newbury Park, CA: Sage.

Hutchins, R. (1966). *Insects.* Englewood Cliffs, NJ: Prentice-Hall.

Kernberg, O. (1975). *Borderline conditions and pathological narcissism.* New York: Aronson.

Kernberg, O. (1976). *Object relations theory and clinical psychoanalysis.* New York: Aronson.

Kernberg, O. (1982). An ego psychology and object relations approach to the narcissistic personality. In *Psychiatry: Annual review* (pp. 510–523). Washington, DC: American Psychiatric Association.

Kernberg, O. (1984). *Severe personality disorders: Psychotherapeutic strategies.* New Haven, CT: Yale University Press.

Klein, M. (1946). Notes on some schizoid mechanisms. *International Journal of Psycho-Analysis, 27,* 99–110.

Knight, R. (1953). Borderline states. *Bulletin of the Menninger Clinic, 17,* 1–12.

Kohut, H. (1971). *The analysis of self.* New York: International Universities Press.

Kwawer, J. (1980). Primitive interpersonal modes, borderline phenomena and Rorschach content. In J. Kwawer, A. Sugarman, P. Lerner, & H. Lerner (Eds.), *Borderline phenomena and the Rorschach test* (pp. 89–105). New York: International Universities Press.

Lancaster, N. (1978). Necrophilia, murder and high intelligence. *British Journal of Psychiatry, 132,* 605–608.

Lane, R. (1984). Robert Lindner and the case of Charles: a teen-age sex murderer: "Songs my mother taught me." *Current Issues in Psychoanalytic Practice, 1*(2), 65–83.

Larsen, R. (1980). *Bundy: The deliberate stranger.* New York: Pocket Books.

Lerner, P. (1991). *Psychoanalytic theory and the Rorschach.* Hillsdale, NJ: The Analytic Press.

Lerner, P., & Lerner, H. (1980). Rorschach assessment of primitive defenses in borderline personality structure. In J. Kwawer, P. Lerner, H. Lerner, & A. Sugarman (Eds.), *Borderline phenomena and the Rorschach Test* (pp. 257–274). New York: International Universities Press.

Lewis, D., Piricus, J., Bard, B., Richardson, E., Prichep, L., Feldman, M., & Yeager, C. (1988). Neuropsychiatric, psychoeducational, and family characteristics of 14 juveniles condemned to death in the United States. *American Journal of Psychiatry, 145,* 584–589.

Liebert, J. (1985). Contributions of psychiatric consultation in the investigation of serial murder. *International Journal of Offender Therapy and Comparative Criminology, 29,* 187–199.

Lindner, R. (1946). Content analysis in Rorschach work. *Rorschach Research Exchange, 10,* 121–129.

Lindner, R. (1947). Analysis of the Rorschach Test by content. *Journal of Clinical Psychopathology and Psychotherapy, 8,* 707–719.

MacCulloch, M., Snowden, P., Wood, P., & Mills, H. (1983). Sadistic fantasy, sadistic behavior and offending. *British Journal of Psychiatry, 143,* 20–29.

McCarthy, J. (1978). Narcissism and the self in homicidal adolescents. *The American Journal of Psychoanalysis, 38,* 19–29.

McDevitt, J. (1983, June). *Emergence of hostile aggression and its modification during the separation-individuation process.* Paper presented to the Seattle Psychoanalytic Society.

Meloy, J. R. (1985). Concept and percept formation in object relations theory. *Psychoanalytic Psychology, 2,* 35–45.

Meloy, J. R. (1988). *The psychopathic mind: origins, dynamics and treatment.* Northvale, NJ: Aronson.

Meloy, J. R., & Gacono, C. B. (1992a). The aggressive response and the Rorschach. *Journal of Clinical Psychology, 48,* 104–114.

Meloy, J. R., & Gacono, C. B. (1992b). A psychotic (sexual) psychopath: "I just had a violent thought . . . ." *Journal of Personality Assessment, 58,* 480–493.

Meloy, J. R., Gacono, C. B., & Kenney, L. (1994). A Rorschach investigation of sexual homicide. *Journal of Personality Assessment, 62,* 58–67.

Michaud, S., & Aynesworth, H. (1983). *The only living witness.* New York: New American Library.

Millon, T. (1983). *Millon Clinical Multiaxial Inventory (3rd. ed.).* Minneapolis, MN: Interpretive Scoring Systems, Division of National Computer Systems.

Moberly, E. (1985). *The psychology of self and other.* New York: Tavistock.

Murray, J. (1993). The Rorschach search for the borderline holy grail: An examination of personality structure, personality style, and situation. *Journal of Personality Assessment, 61,* 342–357.

O'Brien, D. (1985). *Two of a kind: The Hillside stranglers.* New York: Signet.

Peterson, C. (1993). A borderline policeman: Aka, a cop with no cop. *Journal of Personality Assessment, 62,* 374–393.

Phillips, L., & Smith, J. (1953). *Rorschach interpretation: Advanced techniques.* New York: Grune & Stratton.

Podolsky, E. (1965). The lust murderer. *Medio-Legal Journal, 33,* 174–178.

Prentky, R., Burgess, A., Rokous, F., Lee, A., Hartman, C., Ressler, R., & Douglas, J. (1989). The presumptive role of fantasy in serial sexual homicide. *American Journal of Psychiatry, 146,* 887–891.

Rappaport, R. (1988). The serial and mass murderer: Patterns, differentiation, pathology. *American Journal of Forensic Psychiatry, 9,* 39–48.

Reinhardt, J. (1973). The dismal tunnel: Depression before murder. *Journal of Offender Therapy and Comparative Criminology, 17,* 246–249.

Ressler, R., Burgess, A., & Douglas, J. (1988). *Sexual homicide: Patterns and motives.* Lexington, MA/Toronto, Canada: D.C. Heath.

Revitch, E. (1965). Sex murder and potential sex murderer. *Diseases of the Nervous System, 26,* 640–648.

Rorschach, H. (1942). *Psychodiagnostics.* New York: Grune & Stratton.

Shapiro, D. (1981). *Autonomy and rigid character.* New York: Basic.

Shipley, W. C. (1940). A self-administering schedule of measuring intellectual impairment and deterioration. *Journal of Psychology, 9,* 371–377.

Simonsen, J. (1989). A sadistic homicide. *The American Journal of Forensic Medicine and Pathology, 10,* 159–163.

Stanek, V. (1969). *Pictorial encyclopedia of insects.* New York: Hamlyn.

Tanay, E. (1969). Psychiatric study of homicide. *American Journal of Psychiatry, 125,* 1252–1258.

Wechsler, D. (1981). *Wechsler Adult Intelligence Scale–Revised.* New York: The Psychological Corporation.

Yarvis, R. (1990). Axis I and Axis II diagnostic parameters of homicide. *Bulletin of the American Academy of Psychiatry and the Law, 18,* 249–269.

Zachary, R. (1986). *Shipley Institute of Living Scale: Revised manual.* Los Angeles: Western Psychological Services.

Rorschach Structural Summary

LOCATION FEATURES	DETERMINANTS BLENDS	CONTENTS SINGLE	S-CONSTELLATION

LOCATION FEATURES	DETERMINANTS		CONTENTS		S-CONSTELLATION
	BLENDS	SINGLE			NO..FV + VF + V + FD > 2
		H $\quad$ = 4,0			NO..Col-Shd Bl>0
Zf $\quad$ = 10	M.C	M $\quad$ = 0	(H) $\quad$ = 0,0		YES..Ego<.31,>.44
ZSum = 35.0	FM.Fr	FM $\quad$ = 1	Hd $\quad$ = 0,0		NO..MOR>3
ZEst $\quad$ = 31.0	M.Fr.CF	m $\quad$ = 1	(Hd) = 0,1		YES..Zd > ± 3.5
	M.Fr	FC $\quad$ = 1	Hx $\quad$ = 0,0		NO..es>EA
W $\quad$ = 8	FM.CF	CF $\quad$ = 0	A $\quad$ = 3,0		YES..CF+C>FC
(Wv $\quad$ = 0)	FM.FC	C $\quad$ = 0	(A) $\quad$ = 4,0		NO..X+%<.70
D $\quad$ = 5		Cn $\quad$ = 0	Ad $\quad$ = 0,1		NO..S>3
Dd $\quad$ = 0		FC' $\quad$ = 0	(Ad) = 0,0		NO..P<3 or >8
S $\quad$ = 3		C'F $\quad$ = 0	An $\quad$ = 0,0		NO..Pure H <2
		C' $\quad$ = 0	Art $\quad$ = 1,0		YES..R<17
DQ		FT $\quad$ = 0	Ay $\quad$ = 1,2		4.....TOTAL
.........(FQ–)		TF $\quad$ = 0	Bl $\quad$ = 0,1		
+ $\quad$ = 7 (0)		T $\quad$ = 0	Bt $\quad$ = 0,1		SPECIAL SCORINGS

LOCATION FEATURES			CONTENTS			SPECIAL SCORINGS		
o $\quad$ = 6 (0)			FV $\quad$ = 1	Cg $\quad$ = 0,1			Lv1	Lv2
v/+ = 0 (0)			VF $\quad$ = 0	Cl $\quad$ = 0,0		DV	= 0x1	0x2
v $\quad$ = 0 (0)			V $\quad$ = 0	Ex $\quad$ = 0,0		INC	= 0x2	2x4
			FY $\quad$ = 0	Fd $\quad$ = 0,1		DR	= 5x3	8x6
			YF $\quad$ = 0	Fi $\quad$ = 0,0		FAB	= 0x4	0x7
			Y $\quad$ = 0	Ge $\quad$ = 0,0		ALOG	= 0x5	
FORM QUALITY			Fr $\quad$ = 0	Hh $\quad$ = 0,0		CON	= 0x7	
			rF $\quad$ = 0	Ls $\quad$ = 0,0		SUM6	= 15	
	FQx $\quad$ FQf $\quad$ MQual $\quad$ SQx		FD $\quad$ = 1	Na $\quad$ = 0,1		WSUM6	= 71	

	FQx	FQf	MQual	SQx							
+	= 1	0	0	0	F $\quad$ = 2	Sc $\quad$ = 0,0					
o	= 9	2	1	3		Sx $\quad$ = 0,3	AB $\quad$ =1		CP $\quad$ = 1		
u	= 3	0	2	0		Xy $\quad$ = 0,0	AG $\quad$ =1		MOR = 2		
–	= 0	0	0	0		Id $\quad$ = 0,0	CFB $\quad$ =0		PER $\quad$ = 9		
none	= 0	–	0	0	(2) $\quad$ = 5		COP $\quad$ =3		PSV $\quad$ = 0		

RATIOS, PERCENTAGES, AND DERIVATIONS

R $\quad$ = 13	L $\quad$ = 0.18			FC:CF+C $\quad$ =2:3	COP = 3	AG = 1
				Pure C $\quad$ =1	Food	= 1
EB $\quad$ = 3:4.5	EA = 7.5	EBPer = N/A		SumC':WSumC =0:4.5	Isolate/R	= 0.23
eb $\quad$ = 5:1	es = 6	D = 0		Afr $\quad$ =0.30	H:(H)Hd(Hd)	= 4:1
	Adj es = 6	Adj D = 0		S $\quad$ =3	(HHd):(AAd)	= 1:4
				Blends:R $\quad$ =6:13	H+A:Hd + Ad	= 11:2
FM = 4	C' = 0	T = 0		CP $\quad$ = 1		
m $\quad$ = 1	V = 1	Y = 0				
			P = 3	Zf $\quad$ =10		3r+(2)/R $\quad$ = 1.08
a:p	= 3:5	Sum6 $\quad$ =15	X+% = 0.77	Zd $\quad$ = +4.0		Fr+rF $\quad$ = 3
Ma:Mp	= 1:2	Lv2 $\quad$ =10	F+% = 1.00	W:D:Dd $\quad$ =8:5:0		FD $\quad$ = 1
2AB+Art+Ay = 6		WSum6 $\quad$ = 71	X–% = 0.00	W:M $\quad$ =8:3		An + Xy $\quad$ = 0
M–	= 0	Mnone $\quad$ = 0	S–% = 0.00	DQ+ $\quad$ =7		MOR $\quad$ = 2
			Xu% = 0.23	DQv $\quad$ =0		

SCZI = 1	DEPI = 4	CDI = 3	S-CON = 4	HVI = No	OBS = No

I.

1. An insect... an ugly insect (**devaluation**).

E: (Rpts S's response)
S: Because I've always, even as an adult, hated bugs. Anything that had a large shell-like structure. You ever see a Goliath bug? (**intellectualization**) Always hated them, except cute little lady bugs (**splitting**) or butterflies (**pollyannish denial**).
E: Bug?
S: The obvious torso, wings, and pinchers. Gives an illusion (**isolation**) of being able to see the inner spine structure, x-ray effect, the lighter and darker shades. If only you could crush the damn things. Big bugs always frighten me especially if they could fly (**agitated mania**).
E: Inner spine?
S: Depth. The size is intimidating (**projection**) but no real strength (**rationalization**). It's fragile, like I know I'm being silly being afraid of it (**rationalization**). It looks intimidating (**projective identification**).

Comprehensive scoring: *Wso FVo A 1.0 PER,DR2*
Aggression scoring: *AgC, AgPot*
Primitive modes of relating: Boundary disturbance
Defenses coded: Devaluation, intellectualization, splitting, pollyannish denial, isolation, projection, rationalization, projective identification

II.

2. Hmm (laughs) Probably saw too much cartoons as a kid. Two mice on Christmas Eve. They're hanging stockings (**pollyannish denial**).

E: (Rpts S's response)
S: I almost said something else. Taking it apart bit by bit. Two animated cartoon mice (**distancing**). Red giving it a Christmas look (**pollyannish denial, dissociation**).
E: You said red?
S: Yea red always meant Christmas to me (**regression**). I never wear red except during holidays. The upper red is like two hands curled around a pear-shaped object. Like a mirror that seems broken. You can see a face. You can see only the eyes. The bottom red figure, I see two apples that got crushed (**projection**). Someone stepped on them and slid. There's definitely two apples. That's too much (**omnipotence**).

Comprehensive scoring: *W+ Ma.Cu 2 (A) 5.5 COP,DR2,AB,PER*
Aggression scoring: None
Primitive modes of relating: None
Defenses coded: Pollyannish denial, dissociation, regression, projection, omnipotence

III.

3. Hmm..a male gorilla watching his reflection in a pool.

E: (Rpts S's response)
S: The slumped-over posture. The obvious chest. The thick upper limbs and slim waist. I thought male because of the genitalia. The

232

outer part struck me as an abortion. I saw it in a picture (isolation). It makes me feel like an idiot (devaluation) talking about Christmas. The red in the middle I don't get anything from that (denial). Just something about it (repression). Yea, that's interesting. If one was looking down into a pool you would see *themselves,* not a reflection. I still see water in the middle. Something about it (repression). Here I get water, a pool or stream.

Comprehensive scoring: *D+* 1 *FMp.Fr+ A,Sx,Na* 3.0 *DR2,PER*
Aggression scoring: None
Primitive modes of relating: Narcissistic mirroring
Defenses coded: Isolation, devaluation, denial, repression

4. This one's a puzzle. It puzzles me because of the human shapes. You see not really human (devaluation). To guess, seem more hermaphroditic with respect to genitals (splitting). I keep wanting to say abortion.

E: (Rpts S's response)
S: Keep seeing a breast and a phallus (primitive denial). Gee that's not fair. Of course, I realize not everyone would see that (rationalization).

Comprehensive scoring: *Do* 1 *Fo* 2 *H,Sx DR1,INC2*
Aggression scoring: None
Primitive modes of relating: None
Defenses coded: Devaluation, splitting, primitive denial, rationalization

5. Okay. A woman that's had an abortion (devaluation) and she is having difficulty dealing with regrets afterwards (laughs). This is great!

E: (Rpts S's response)
S: As if suddenly they looked in the mirror and saw themselves. Felt sorry for themselves. They realize it takes two to tango.
E: What makes it look like an abortion?
S: The red figures (dissociation). The little bloody fetus. I don't get anything at all from the red in the middle (denial). Interesting (omnipotence).

Comprehensive scoring: *D+* 1 *Mp.Fr.CFo H,Bl,Sx P* 4.0 *MOR,DR2*
Aggression scoring: *AgPast,* SM
Primitive modes of relating: Narcissistic Mirroring, Violent Symbiosis, Separation & Reunion, Metamorphosis and Transformation
Defenses: Devaluation, dissociation, denial, omnipotence
IV.

6. That's too easy (omnipotence). I won't say it (reaction formation). Yes I will. Your basic 10-story childhood nightmare monster (regression). It gives the illusion (isolation) of great height and size.

E: (Rpts S's response)
S: Yea, cause I don't know what to call it (repression). A cross between a vulture and a cobra (primitive denial). Like looking up 20, 30, 40, or 100 feet (dissociation). Brought back childhood nightmares. They're about to get trampled (projective identification). Nothing they can do about it, it's so high (rationalization).

Comprehensive scoring: *Do* 7 *FDo* (*A*) *DR2,PER,INC2*
Aggression scoring: *AgC, AgPot*
Primitive modes of relating: None
Defenses coded: Omnipotence, reaction formation, regression, isolation, repression, primitive denial, dissociation, projective identification, rationalization.

(continued)

233

V.

7. Hm...Bad vibes. A winged demon about to take flight, real negative looking (**projection**), intimidating.

E: (Rpts S's response)
S: I watch too much science fiction (**projection**). I knew I would be sorry for watching all those horror movies. I see the head of the figure. The old insect fright paranoia. I saw an English film where a space ship had crashed in London. Reminds me of a body with claws and wings. Really intimidating (**projection**). Maybe 3 or 4 feet tall greenish, slanty eyes. Wouldn't have to be physically real strong, just image would be intimidating to me (**projective identification**). I have a hang up about ugly things (**devaluation**).

Comprehensive scoring: *Wo FMpo (A)* 1.0 *DR2,PER,CP*
Aggression scoring: *AgC, AgPot*
Primitive modes of relating: None
Defenses coded: Projection, projective identification, devaluation

VI.

8. Oh my (laughs). This is great (**repression**). You got an interesting job. An Indian shrine honoring a great warrior (**idealization**). How about that (**omnipotence**).

E: (Rpts S's response)
S: Feathered cross. Are you familiar with Indian artifacts? (**intellectualization**) I've traveled through the southwest. I see a stretched puma hide with Indian beadwork—woven, covered with feathered trim. Nothing fits together (**isolation**). You have a cross with an adobe base disintegrating into nothing. All of a sudden a puma skin.
E: What makes it look stretched?
S: That would draw everything together. If it were lying flat it would just end with skin. All this sounds strange, but that's your business (**rationalization**). This is amusing but hard work.

Comprehensive scoring: *W+ mpo Ay,Ad* 2.5 *DR1,PER*
Aggression scoring: None
Primitive modes of relating: Boundary disturbance
Defenses coded: Repression, idealization, omnipotence, intellectualization, isolation, rationalization.
*Defensive splitting (Cooper, Perry, & Arnow, 1988) as a devalued percept (#7) precedes an idealized one (#8).

VII.

9. And here's the Indians.

E: (Rpts S's response)
S: I've always been attracted to Indians. I'm part Indian. I saw feathers and a headdress.

Comprehensive scoring: *Do 2 Fo 2 H,Ay,Cg P DR1*
Aggression scoring: None
Primitive modes of relating: None
Defenses coded: None

10. It's funny how things come to you. A woman, an old woman, in her seventies. The pioneer era, America, 1860s. Doing nothing in particular. Brings to mind Norman Rockwell (**intellectualization**; **idealization**).

E: (Rpts S's response)
S: Jolly woman with ill-fitting dentures (**devaluation**). In fact she doesn't have them in. It seems like when they get into their 70s or 80s they get that go to hell attitude. The chin

extends. . . . She's looking at her reflection, looking at herself and seeing how terrible she looks without her dentures. She doesn't care **(rationalization, splitting)**.

Comprehensive scoring: *W+ Mp.Fru H* 2.5 *DR1*
Aggression scoring: None
Primitive modes of relating: Narcissistic Mirroring
Defenses coded: Intellectualization, idealization, devaluation, splitting, rationalization
VIII.

11. Well I see two animals unlike any animals I have ever seen. I'd say a pair of animals out hunting. They climbed through a rocky canyon and it's too late for them to do anything about it **(rationalization)**. You can title this one 'uh-oh' **(omnipotence)**. Interesting.

E: (Rpts S's response)
S: Pink figures are animals. The size of a cougar again. Nothing like I've ever seen. Four legs. The red and orange reminded me of desert **(dissociation)**. Like I said I've done alot of traveling. They are getting into the greenery, the pines. They see something they never saw before; another big creature. With their simple animal brains they made a mistake. It's about to get them by the throat **(projective identification)**. They won't know what hit them. I've seen "Alien" too much **(rationalization)**. I really believe in extraterrestrial life.

Comprehensive scoring: *Ws+ FMa.CFo* 2 *A,Bt P* 4.5 *COP,PER,DR1*
Aggression scoring: *AgPot, AgC*
Primitive modes of relating: None
Defenses coded: Rationalization, omnipotence, dissociation, projective identification
IX.

12. Oh, what the hell. A Chinese mask.

E: (Rpts S's response)
S: No only because I couldn't see anything else **(repression)**. But I saw the eye holes. I saw an exhibition of Chinese art at the one in Pasadena. Norman Simon **(idealization)** exhibition in LA **(intellectualization)**. I was fascinated with them. They looked so evil **(projective identification)**. Coloring is wrong. Chinese never use green and orange.
E: Eyes?
S: Basic tools, poorly defined as head, nose, and mouth **(devaluation, splitting)**. It fits. It was easy **(omnipotence)**.

Comprehensive scoring: *Wso FCo Art,(Hd),Ay* 5.5 *PER,DR2*
Aggression scoring: None
Primitive modes of relating: None
Defenses coded: Repression, idealization, intellectualization, projective identification, devaluation, splitting, omnipotence

(continued)

X.

13. I have a busy one here. Ever hear of an artist called Frank Stella? (**intellectualization**) I think he did this (**idealization**). Oh boy (**repression**). Two little creatures who have caught a large creature for game (*AgPast*; **projection, splitting**). Who is being threatened (*AG*) to have their catch taken away from them by crab like creatures (*AgPot*; **projective identification**), real predators (*AgC*). On the hunting trip. I feel like a voyeur. Crab creatures offed them (*AgPast*), not knowing their buddy had ate it. They don't know these crab creatures are going to lop their head off (*AgPot*; **projective identification**) (laughs). That's a Rorschach original (**omnipotence**). It's fun (*SM*).

E: (Rpts S's response)
S: They're in each other's face, familiar sight in prison life. The red figure is in their grip. Game is the capture. Blue are the crab creatures. They have big pinchers (*AgC*) to take their heads off and take the game away. These two are dead (*AgPast*). The two buddies died while carrying the other end of the red (**projection**).

Comprehensive scoring: *W* + *FMa.FCu* 2 (*A*),*Fd* 5.5 MOR,COP,DR2,AG,PER
Aggression scoring: *AgPast, AgPot, AG, AgC, SM*
Primitive modes of relating: Violent Symbiosis, Separation, Reunion
Defenses coded: Intellectualization, idealization, repression, projection, splitting, omnipotence

Sequence of Scores

Card	No.	Loc.	#	Determinant(s)	(2)	Content(s)	Pop Z	Special Scores
I	1	WSo	1	FVo		A	1.0	PER, DR2
II	2	W+	1	Ma.Cu	2	(A)	5.5	COP, DR2, AB, PER
III	3	D+	1	FMp.Fr+		A, Sx, Na	3.0	DR2, PER
	4	Do	1	Fo	2	H, Sx		DR, INC2
	5	D+	1	Mp.Fr.CFo		H, Bl, Sx	P 4.0	MOR, DR2
IV	6	Do	7	FDo		(A)		DR2, PER, INC2
V	7	Wo	1	FMpo		(A)	1.0	DR2, PER, CP
VI	8	W+	1	mpo		Ay, Ad	2.5	DR, PER
VII	9	Do	2	Fo	2	H, Ay, Cg	P	DR
	10	W+	1	Mp.Fru		H	2.5	DR
VIII	11	WS+	1	FMa.CFo	2	A, Bt	P 4.5	COP, PER, DR
IX	12	WSo	1	FCo		Art, (Hd), Ay	5.5	PER, DR2
X	13	W+	1	FMa.FCu		(A), Fd	5.5	MOR, COP, DR2,
					2			AG, PER

Summary of Approach

I:WS	VI:W
II:W	VII:D.W
III:D.D.D	VIII:WS
IV:D	IX:WS
V:W	X:W

15

Revisiting the Rorschach of Sirhan Sirhan

J. Reid Meloy
University of California, San Diego

It has been said that one act by one unknown individual may change, on occasion, the course of history. Such may have been the case when Sirhan Bishara Sirhan, a 24-year-old Palestinian immigrant, assassinated Democratic presidential aspirant Robert F. Kennedy on June 5, 1968.

Kennedy had just won the California Democratic Primary and finished his victory speech when he entered a poorly lit food service corridor leading from the Embassy Ballroom in the Los Angeles Ambassador Hotel. It was 12:15 a.m. Sirhan stepped from behind a food tray rack and pointed his .22 caliber Iver-Johnson revolver within an inch of the back of Kennedy's head. The first and fatal Mini-Mag hollow point bullet shattered his right mastoid bone and lodged in the right hemisphere of his cerebellum. The second and third bullets entered the back of his right armpit. Five other rounds were rapidly fired. There were 77 people in the pantry. Six of them, including Kennedy, became victims. Sirhan was wrestled onto a steam table, where police handcuffed him and immediately took him from the hotel. Kennedy died 25 hours later (Clarke, 1982; Kaiser, 1970).

During the summer and fall of that year, the defendant underwent unprecedented psychiatric and psychological examination by eight different clinicians. The defense team included Bernard Diamond, MD, Eric Marcus, MD, Martin Schorr, PhD, and Roderick Richardson, PhD. Steven Howard, PhD, and William Crain, PhD, consulted with the defense doctors. The prosecution team included Seymour Pollack, MD, Georgene Seward, PhD, George De Vos, PhD, and Leonard Olinger, PhD.

Sirhan Sirhan was administered the Rorschach on two occasions, first by Richardson and then by Schorr. The Rorschach test data were entered into evidence at trial and discussed in detail. The first Rorschach protocol, including miniature inkblots and location scoring, was published in Kaiser (1970). The second Rorschach protocol was administered several months later by Schorr in the presence of a team of deputies, an attorney, a writer, and a legal assistant. It was not published.

The purpose of this study was to generate and test clinical hypotheses from the first Rorschach protocol through the use of reliable and valid interpretative systems unavailable in 1968. Although an idiographic study does not substantially contribute to nomothetic scientific knowledge, this individual's psychology does find importance in the historical event of the Robert F. Kennedy assassination, given the small number of American assassins that are available for study in any one generation.[1]

METHOD

The Rorschach protocol posed three difficulties (Appendix A). First, the examiner did not limit the number of responses, yielding a protocol with 63 responses. This tends to disproportionately increase the number of D and Dd location responses, and $X+\%$ may be lower than average due to a higher frequency of unusual answers (Exner, 1986a). Second, the examiner failed to inquire on 19 (30%) of the responses. Ritzler and Nalesnik (1990) found that with no inquiry, color and shading determinants are reduced, *pure F* is therefore inflated, and blends decrease. Special Score (Exner, 1986a) categories measuring formal thought disorder are also difficult to determine. All of these scores would affect several composite scores, including distortion of EB in the introversive direction, the attenuation of EA and es, and increased *Lambda*. The Suicide Constellation, Depression Index, and Schizophrenia Index (Exner, 1986a) would also be less sensitive to pathology. Ritzler and Nalesnik (1990) concluded, "subjects whose protocols have no inquiry may appear more introverted, less emotionally expressive, more rigid and controlled, less suicidal and depressed, and/or less psychotic" (p. 652). They also found, however, that only 6 of 33 essential Comprehensive System indices demonstrated significant differences without inquiry across four groups of subjects. I addressed this problem by applying the Ritzler and Nalesnik (1990) liberalized scoring rules to the responses without inquiry. I assumed this application would restore the validity of overall scoring for these responses, except for Special Scores. The inability to ferret out vista (V) from form dimension (FD) responses with the liberalized scoring rules would also obscure the former and increase the latter. The third problem was a "testing of the limits" for sex and texture done by the examiner to response Number 44 (Card VI). Although both a sex response and implied texture response were elicited, I did not score them, and subsequent responses did not yield a sex content or texture determinant.

---

[1]Clarke (1982) noted 16 actual assassination attempts between 1835, when Richard Lawrence failed to kill President Andrew Jackson, and 1981, when John Hinckley, Jr., wounded President Ronald Reagan. All of these attempts were directed against nationally prominent political figures, 7 of whom died as a result of their wounds.

The protocol was scored using the Exner (1986a) Comprehensive System, and interpretive hypotheses were generated with the Rorschach Interpretation Assistance Program, Version 2 (Exner, 1990). Interrater agreement was determined by a second independent scoring of the protocol. The protocol was also scored for defense mechanisms (Cooper & Arnow, 1986; Cooper, Perry, & Arnow, 1988), primitive (borderline) object relations (Kwawer, 1980), and Mutuality of Autonomy (MOA) responses (Urist, 1977). Our aggression scores (Meloy & Gacono, 1992) and Gacono's (1990) impressionistic response were also scored. The Rorschach was then compared to results of a study by Miner and De Vos (1960) concerning Algerian males and the Rorschach acculturation hypotheses of Meyers (in press). The question of malingering was also considered. Rorschach data were then compared to psychiatric and psychological diagnoses at the trial, major developmental events in the childhood and adolescence of Sirhan Sirhan, and his behavior around the time of the assassination.

RESULTS

Psychostructural Data

The Comprehensive System (Exner, 1990) sequence of scores and structural summary for the Sirhan protocol are listed in Appendix B and Appendix C. Interrater agreements for five scoring categories were: 98% for developmental quality, 83% for determinants, 100% for form quality, 87% for content, and 87% for special scores ($M = 91\%$). Differences were resolved through discussion between Erdberg and me, the independent raters. The protocol was positive for both the Depression Index (Score 7) and the Suicide Constellation (Score 8).

The Rorschach Interpretation Assistance Program, Version 2 (Exner, 1990) generated 43 hypotheses, which are summarized according to each psychological operation.

Affect.   Characteristics common to those who have attempted or effected suicide, frequent and intense experience of affective disruption, probable major affective or dysthymic disorder, tendency to merge feelings and thinking during trial-and-error problem solving, serious emotional modulation problems, conveys impressions of impulsiveness, less mature psychological organization for age, tendency to avoid emotional stimuli, currently experiencing distress or discomfort, excessive introspection focusing on negative features, irritated by testing, confused and intense feelings experienced, and difficulty bringing closure to emotional situations.

Capacity for Control and Stress Tolerance.   Unusually good capacities for control, considerable tolerance for stress, pervasive stabilization, and readily able to formulate and give direction to behaviors.

Situational Stress.   Significant increase in stimulus demands due to situational stress, some decisions and behaviors may not be as well organized as usual, potential for impulsiveness is considerable, vulnerable to disorganization in complex situations, and added psychological complexity and confused feelings are results of current stress condition.

Self-Perception.   Regards himself as less favorable when compared to others, engages in more introspection than is customary, focuses on perceived negative features of the self-image, frequent painful feelings concerning negative self-value, which is largely based on imaginary rather than real experience, issues of self dealt with in a detached and overly intellectualized manner that tends to distort reality, unusual body concern and preoccupation.

Interpersonal Perception and Relations.   Does not experience needs for emotional closeness; maintains distance and safety in relations, but prefers dependency on others, creating conflict; normatively interested in others; takes a passive, but not necessarily submissive, role in relationships; insecure about personal integrity, and will tend to be authoritarian when relations appear to challenge the self; regarded by others as rigid or narrow and will have difficulty maintaining relations; likelihood of forceful and aggressive behaviors, but may not be obvious or direct because of passive tendencies; less involved in social interactions, probably due to timidity.

Information Processing.   A marked tendency to narrow or simplify stimulus fields, a form of psychological economizing that can create a potential for behaviors that do not coincide with social demands or expectations, a preference for less complex stimulus fields, and little effort made to organize and integrate fields of information in a complex or sophisticated manner.

Cognitive Mediation.   Likelihood of less conventional responses and behaviors; may reflect individualism, social alienation, or more serious mediational or affective modulation problems; will likely result in a strong orientation to distance from an environment that is perceived as threatening, demanding, and ungiving; a tendency to overpersonalize stimuli; perceptual inaccuracy and mediational distortion.

Ideation.   Thinking is usually merged with feelings during problem solving, which may give rise to more elaborate patterns of thought and acceptance of imprecise or ambiguous logic systems. Feelings can be put aside in favor of an ideational approach; ideational sets and values are well fixed; chronic and higher than expected levels of ideational activity outside the focus of attention; excessive use of fantasy to deny reality and avoid responsibility in decision making, creating a self-imposed helplessness; a long-standing pattern of limited concentration and interruptions in deliberate thinking; intellectualization is a major defense in affectively stressful situations; vulnerable to disorganization during intense emotional experiences because this pseudo-intellectual process becomes less effective; there is a presence of seriously disturbed thinking, marked by flawed judgment, conceptualization, and disorganized patterns of decision making; and this promotes distortions of reality and a marked predisposition toward pathology.

In summary, the Comprehensive System interpretive hypotheses suggest that Sirhan Sirhan, at the time of testing, was suicidal and profoundly dysphoric, confused by intense and painful affective disruptions. His considerable stress tolerance and control were being tested by intense and complex situational demands that created a potential for impulsiveness. His self-perception was negative, and although he maintained a rigid distance from others, he preferred dependency. His cognitive processing was characterized by simplification, major impairments in reality testing marked by the perception of personal threat, and seriously disturbed thought organization suffused with unpleasant affect.

Psychodynamic Data

The Cooper et al. (1988) Rorschach Defense Scale scoring is listed in Table 15.1. The Sirhan protocol evidenced 35 scorable responses. According to the categorizing of their 15 defenses as neurotic, borderline, or psychotic (Cooper et al., 1988; Kernberg, 1984), there were 12 (34%) neurotic defenses utilized, the most common being isolation; 21 (60%) borderline defenses utilized, the

TABLE 15.1
Rorschach Defense Scale Scoring of Sirhan Protocol

Level of Personality Organization	Defense	Frequency	%
Neurotic	Higher level denial	1	
	Intellectualization	1	
	Isolation	7	
	Reaction formation	0	
	Repression	0	
	Rationalization	0	
	Pollyannish denial	3	
	Total neurotic		34
Borderline	Devaluation	4	
	Omnipotence	0	
	Primitive idealization	5	
	Projection	5	
	Projective identification	2	
	Splitting	5	
	Total borderline		60
Psychotic	Hypomanic denial	0	
	Massive denial	2	
	Total psychotic		6
Total scored		35	100

Note. Adapted from Cooper and Arnow (1986).

most common being primitive idealization, projective identification, and splitting; and 2 (6%) psychotic defenses utilized. There were no apparent trends in the sequential use of the grouped defenses across the time of examination. For instance, isolation, a neurotic defense, was used on Card I and Card VII (Example, Card 1: "Cliffs. [Inquiry] This reminds me of cliffs looking far away. The space is the water"). Projection, a borderline defense, was used on Card II and Card IX (Example, Card II: "A face of a person. Glass. [Inquiry] Profile. It projects no feeling to me. (?) Madness (?) anger—the teeth are showing, they look more like women than men").

There was only one scorable primitive (borderline) object relations response (Kwawer, 1980) to Card X: "This whole color. It throws me off! Monsters! It's really about all on this one? It's frightening. It frightens me. They all seem the same. Wickedness! Too many entanglements!" Inquiry: "It's a cacophony of colors, a hodgepodge. All those legs. This here looks like some kind of rat. No, not a rat, it flies, a bat. The whole thing looks like monstrosities. It's more vulgar, I'd avoid it. Everybody wants to catch on to you, with all those legs! The minute you're within reach you're in their clutches" (Kaiser, 1970, p. 608). This would be categorized as engulfment (Kwawer, 1980). MOA (Urist, 1977) scoring yielded five scorable responses, with a most adaptive score of 1 (reciprocal acknowledgment) to Card III—"A couple of dancers. [Inquiry] A jovial bunch of Negro drum players—Watusi—although up here—this much looks like foxes—more animal than human—looks like a werewolf (sex?). Oh, men"—and a most pathological score of 5 (coercion, hurtful influence, or threat) to three responses (Card VII: "Bears. Stuffed bears. [Inquiry] A bear's head. The expression is wicked, mean, mad"). The average MOA score was 3.6.

The aggression scores (Exner, 1986a; Gacono, 1990) and impressionistic score (Gacono, Meloy, & Heaven, 1990) are listed in Table 15.2. These Sirhan protocol scores are descriptively compared to data from a small sample of borderline personality disordered outpatient males ($N = 18$) previously described in Gacono, Meloy, and Berg (1992). The protocol yielded 11 scorable aggression responses and one impressionistic response: the same Card X response (62) scored with the Kwawer (1980) criteria (the impressionistic response is scored when a chromatic or achromatic color determinant and abstraction special score occur together). The most common aggression score was aggressive content (Gacono, 1990), followed by aggression (Exner, 1986a), and aggressive potential (Gacono, 1990).

Cultural Data

The protocol was compared to the Rorschach data provided by Miner and De Vos (1960) and De Vos and Boyer (1989) on Algerian males and the Rorschach cultural adaptation hypotheses of Meyers (in press). Miner and De Vos (1960) reported Rorschach data collected in 1950 from 64 Algerian Arab males between the ages of 20 and 50. They divided the group into "oasis" and "urban" samples. The proportion of unpleasant content was significantly higher among

TABLE 15.2
Comparison of Aggression Response and Impressionistic Response Frequencies of
Sirhan Protocol to Male Borderline Personality Disordered (N = 18) Protocols

Category	Sirhan Protocol	Male BPD Patients		
		Mean	SD	Frequency
Aggression (Exner, 1986)	4.0	1.39	1.33	13
Aggressive content	6.0	2.89	1.88	18
Aggressive past	0	.83	1.46	8
Aggressive potential	1.0	.89	2.16	6
Impressionistic	1.0	1.78	1.35	16

the urban Arabs, most notably content indicative of body preoccupation and hostility. Two patterns of adjustment were frequent in the urbanized Arabs: greater rigidity and internalization of aggression, suggested by anatomical responses; or a more complex, flexible ego that perceived the external environment as hostile and dangerous. Human figures were rarely seen and were usually not moving or engaged in positive activity. When movement was perceived, it was attributed to foreign or supernatural figures. Often humans were incomplete or mutilated, and the latter responses usually involved a reference to the genitals. The Arab men were also loath to see women; only 12 of the entire 82 human percepts in all the Rorschachs were female. They were not perceived to move, and attention was focused on their sexual organs. Human figures were usually attached to each other in a passive and immobile manner.

Most of these findings are consistent with the Sirhan protocol (see Appendices A, B, and C). There were no Pure H responses and a paucity of (H), Hd, or (Hd) responses. There was one sex (female) response, six anatomy responses, and three blood responses. Of the five human movement (M) responses, one had no human content (46). Unlike the Arab sample, the Sirhan protocol evidenced no human figures either passively attached to each other or mutilated.

Meyers (in press) contended that the Rorschach is a useful predictor of cross-cultural adaptability and hypothesized a number of Rorschach variables that measure the lack of flexibility and openness (*Lambda* and *EB*), poor perceptual acuity ($X+\%$, $X-\%$, Zd), decreased personal autonomy (T, *FD*, *Egocentricity Ratio*, *Morbid*, *Vista*), and decreased emotional resiliency (*FC:CF* + C, *Afr, S, Blends, Adjusted D*) as predictive markers of pathological adjustment to a new culture. The Sirhan protocol is generally consistent with Meyers' predictions, except for adjusted D.

Malingering

The question of malingering was considered and ruled out during the initial phases of this study for the following reasons: (a) throughout the trial, Sirhan

Sirhan adamantly opposed the use of a mental disability defense and did not want to be labeled as mentally ill (Kaiser, 1970); (b) despite his objections, he cooperated with psychological and psychiatric procedures and produced other valid test data (the Minnesota Multiphasic Personality Inventory, Wechsler Adult Intelligence Scale, Thematic Apperception Test, and Bender–Gestalt); and (c) he met only one (medicolegal setting) of the four contexts for suspected malingering, according to the *Diagnostic and Statistical Manual of Mental Disorders* (3rd ed., rev. [*DSM–III–R*]; American Psychiatric Association, 1987), and (d) a reduction in *R* appears to be the most prominent finding in the Rorschach malingering literature, despite the overall inconsistent and inconclusive results (Perry & Kinder, 1990).

DISCUSSION

The Sirhan Rorschach protocol, when analyzed with technology unavailable in 1968, strongly suggests a depressed and suicidal individual whose personality is predominately organized at a borderline level (Kernberg, 1984), with some adaptive neurotic, and occasionally psychotic, defenses. The protocol presents a mixed characterological picture with hysterical, paranoid, and dependent features all evident.

To what degree are the Rorschach findings of this study consistent with historical data concerning Sirhan Sirhan? A review of psychiatric findings at the trial, significant developmental events in the childhood and adolescence of Sirhan, and his behavior around the time of the assassination should answer this question.

Psychiatric and Psychological Opinion at Trial

All of the psychologists independently evaluated the Sirhan Rorschach protocol and agreed, except for one, with a diagnosis of paranoid schizophrenia. Olinger dissented and rendered a diagnosis of pseudoneurotic schizophrenia (Kaiser, 1970).

The Rorschach data in this study, however, do not support a schizophrenic diagnosis. The Comprehensive System (Exner, 1990) Schizophrenia Index (*SCZI*) score of 3 suggests the unlikelihood of such a mental illness. Only 18% of Exner's (1990) normative inpatient schizophrenic sample scored less than 4 on this index. There is likewise a 13% false positive rate for borderline personality disorder on the *SCZI* (Exner, 1986b). The Cooper and Arnow (1986) defenses also do not support a psychotic diagnosis, but rather a personality organized at a borderline level of psychopathology (P. Lerner, 1990; see Table 15.1). H. Lerner, Albert, and Walsh (1987) found that the Cooper and Arnow defenses of splitting, devaluation, and omnipotence had the most power in discriminating borderline from schizophrenic patients. Both the

Kwawer (1980) and Urist (1977) measures also suggest a borderline level of pathology. Blatt, Tuber, and Auerbach (1990) found the MOA scale a better measure of psychopathology than interpersonal relations.

Nevertheless, the defense team, led by Diamond, concluded that Sirhan Sirhan had paranoid schizophrenia and had killed Robert Kennedy in a dissociative state, a self-induced trance brought on by the lights and mirrors in the Ambassador Hotel lobby. His political views were considered delusional fantasies (Kaiser, 1970). Diamond later found his own testimony an "absurd and preposterous story, unlikely and incredible" (*People v. Sirhan*, 1969, p. 6998).

The prosecution team, led by Pollack, disagreed. In his February 5, 1969 report, he diagnosed the defendant as "borderline schizophrenia with paranoid and hysterical features, but I do not believe that he was clinically psychotic" (1969a, p. 3). He also noted the complete absence of any hallucinations or delusions. He wrote, "Sirhan's motivation in killing Senator Kennedy was entirely political, and was not related to bizarre or psychotic motivation or accompanied by peculiar and highly idiosyncratic reasoning" (p. 3). In a March 21, 1969 supplemental report, Pollack considered the defendant a "developing paranoid personality whose assassination of Senator Robert Kennedy was motivated by political reasons which were highly emotionally charged" (1969b, p. 1). These Rorschach findings are consistent with Pollack's diagnosis of borderline schizophrenia and Olinger's diagnosis of pseudoneurotic schizophrenia, terms that described what we today would consider borderline personality disorder (Stone, 1980).

Developmental Events

The childhood and adolescent pathogenesis of Sirhan's personality was shaped by two psychological themes, trauma and loss. He was born into a large Arab family in Jerusalem on March 19, 1944, and by the age of 5 had experienced a number of traumatic events during the war-torn prelude to Israel's statehood: He witnessed a bomb explosion at the Damascus Gate which left mutilated Arab corpses in the street, observed his older brother run over and killed by a Zionist truck trying to avoid sniper fire, discovered the body of an Arab neighbor, observed portions of a British soldier's body dangling from a church tower, and fled from a driverless truck which then exploded. At the age of 5 his family left their home in the middle of the night and moved into a 15 × 30 ft room in the Old Walled City of Jerusalem (Clarke, 1982).

His Christian mother refused to let the children play in the street, and his father's hostility resulted in physical abuse of the children, including Sirhan. Sirhan attended a Lutheran school from age 7 to 12 and was described as mature beyond his years (Kaiser, 1970). On December 14, 1956, he emigrated with his family to the United States. He was 12 years old. They settled in a lower middle class neighborhood in Pasadena, but resisted acculturation. One year later, Sirhan's father abandoned the family and returned to Jordan. Neighbors described him as a mean and self-centered man (Clarke, 1982). Sirhan, however, appeared to make a good adjustment. He learned English quickly, received above average grades, and graduated from John Muir High School. He was not reclusive, joined the officer cadet corps, and was elected to the student council. He was viewed as cooperative and enthusiastic (Kaiser, 1970).

At the age of 20, however, his object world began to fall apart. His sister, Aida, whom he revered, died of leukemia. Two of his brothers were arrested. He was dismissed from Pasadena City College for not attending classes. He tried to pursue a career as a jockey, but fell from a galloping horse when he was 22 at a ranch in Corona. His blurred vision and pain complaints were compensated through a settlement that paid him $2,000. In March 1968, at age 24, he quit his job at a health food store 3 months before the assassination (Clarke, 1982).

Sirhan had fostered his identity as an Arab throughout his adolescence and was quite vocal in his hatred of the Zionists, whom he equated with Nazis. Following the Six Day War, which began June 5, 1967, he often repeated his belief that the wealthy American Jews controlled the politicians and the media. His conscious hatred of the Jews is captured in this *DR* response to Card VIII: "I don't know, it's a desert plant. Grows very tall—not a cactus. I don't know the name." Inquiry: "The colors shock me, no, l don't know, l feel very jittery. l can't hold still. It stirs me. l read this magazine article on the 20th anniversary of the State of Israel. It was in color—that color—I hate the Jews. There was jubilation. I felt that they were saying in the article, we beat the Arabs. It burns the shit out of me, there was happiness and jubilation."

The repetitive developmental experiences of trauma and loss condensed into a conscious hatred (Terr, 1991) for the perceived aggressor, the (father) Zionists, which was then generalized to all Jews. Structural characteristics of his depression (*S–CON, DEPI, MOR, Isolate/R, Egocentricity, V, Y, T*) and aggression (*Ag, Ag Content, Ag Potential, S, Pure C*) are amply evident in the Rorschach data (see Appendix B). The inference that pathological mourning accounts for the depression is reasonable, given the plethora of his actual object losses: brother, first Jerusalem home, Palestinian cultural milieu (Levy-Warren, 1987), father, sister, career opportunity, freedom after arrest, and Robert Kennedy as a persecutory object. Sirhan's depression is considered anaclitic, rather than introjective (Blatt, 1974), and the psychopathology is primarily oral aggressive with feelings of helplessness, weakness, and depletion in the face of a continual abandonment threat or a more annihilatory intent by the object.

Psychological trauma is also linked to mourning (Krystal, 1984) and begs the question of the presence of posttraumatic stress disorder (PTSD; American Psychiatric Association, 1987) in Sirhan at the time of the examination. Two studies of inpatient and outpatient Vietnam veterans with PTSD (Hartman et al., 1990; Swanson, Blount, & Bruno, 1990) provide some comparative Rorschach data. Both studies indicate that the Sirhan protocol is more different than similar to the average PTSD Rorschach. Similarities include tenuous reality testing (*X–%*), high suicide risk (*S–CON*), devaluation of self (*MOR*), little interest in others as whole and real objects (*Pure H*), and a simplistic problem-solving style (*Lambda*). In contrast to the PTSD subjects (combined *N* = 91), the Sirhan protocol shows much more formal thought disorder (*WSum6*), an extratensive style (*EB*), no stimulus overload (*Adj D*), severe depression (*DEPI*), no pathological narcissism (*Rf*), and high aggression (*Ag, S*). However, comparison of an immigrant Arab who was subjected to combat as a child to indigenous soldiers subjected to combat as adults is only suggestive.

Other authors (Herman & van der Kolk, 1987) have seen a similarity between PTSD and borderline personality disorder (BPD) and have argued for the importance of assessing for actual childhood trauma in all borderline patients. Despite the organization of the Sirhan data at a borderline level of personality (Kernberg, 1984), the differences, once again, are greater than the similarities when his Rorschach is compared to a sample (Exner, 1986b) of male and female borderline personality disordered patients. The Sirhan protocol is similar to this sample (*N* = 84) in poor modulation of affect (*FC:CF + C*), extratensive problem solving (*EB*) and impaired reality testing (*X–%*). It is different from the BPD patients in the absence of stimulus overload (*Adj D*), severe formal thought disorder (*WSum6*), abuse of fantasy (*Ma:Mp*), negative self-worth (*Egocentricity Index*), and avoidance of affect (*Afr*).

The hysterical character pathology of Sirhan is suggested by a number of Rorschach indices. The computer-based test interpretation hypotheses (Exner, 1990) emphasize the merging of thinking and affect and intense affective disruption. These hypotheses are based on the variables of *EB, eb, Y, FC:CF + C, Afr, Pure C, V, S*, and three blends that have no form, two of which are *C.Y.* These latter blends infer the experience of unmodulated affect followed by anxiety. The Cooper and Arnow (1986) defenses of denial and primitive idealization (31% of the scorable defenses) are also consistent with hysterical character (Shapiro, 1965). The impressionistic response suggests affect that is rapidly split off through the use of symbolization (Gacono et al., 1990). And the first and last responses to the Rorschach are food ambivalence responses (P. Erdberg, personal communication, May 7, 1991), perhaps regressive traces of early dependency frustrations and consequent oral rage. Card I: "I've seen it before. I still don't know. Looks like the back part of a chicken. You fry a chicken. That's the only thing I can—" Inquiry: "It's the whole thing, this being the center. I've eaten some chicken. I never used to like that part, if I could avoid it. It's very bony." And the last response to Card X: "Blood!" Inquiry: "I seem to associate the whole thing negatively with blood. It looks like liver to me—some kind of meat. I'd rather not even discuss it."

Hysterical character has historically been linked with dissociation (American Psychiatric Association, 1987; Breuer & Freud, 1893–1895/1957), and egodystonic dissociative states are found in BPD (Kernberg, 1975), perhaps as a result of childhood trauma (Terr, 1991). Sirhan was easily hypnotized on several occasions by Dr. Diamond and abreacted his traumatic childhood experiences in Jerusalem (Kaiser, 1970).

Despite the differences between the Sirhan protocol, the BPD sample, and the PTSD samples, the Rorschach data are somewhat consistent with the theme of psychic trauma; very consistent with the theme of recurrent loss and pathological mourning; and validate a characterological distrust and hatred of, yet hysterical dependence on, the object world. The witnessing of extreme violence outside his home and physical abuse by father in his home would disrupt the safety necessary for autonomous striving, the normative flowering of grandiosity, and the rapprochement subphase of separation–individuation (Mahler, Pine, & Bergman, 1975) during his pre-Oedipal years. Hence, the predominance of borderline level defenses and object relations and the absence of object constancy.

Predation and Assassination

On January 9 and 10, 1968, the *New York Times* ("Report on a Meeting," 1968; Witkin, 1968) reported Kennedy's proposed sale of 50 Phantom Jet fighter–bombers to Israel. Sirhan was enraged; an idealized paternal object for whom he hungered was shattered. Evidence suggests that he made the conscious decision to kill Kennedy on January 31, when he wrote in his diary, "RFK must die" (Kaiser, 1970, p. 549). He had joined the Ancient Mystical Order of the Rosae Crucis that month and repeatedly used his diary as a form of self-hypnosis. As he later testified, "how you can install a thought in your mind and how you can have it work and become a reality if you want it to" (*People v. Sirhan*, 1969, p. 4905). The defense considered this automatic writing.

When Kennedy announced his candidacy and President Lyndon Johnson announced his decision to not seek another term, Sirhan began practice shooting. On April 6, a few days after the Martin Luther King assassination, he told a Black trash collector that he was going to shoot Kennedy. He wrote in his diary on May 18, "my determination to eliminate RFK is becoming . . . more of an unshakeable obsession" (*People v. Sirhan*, 1969, People's Exhibit 71). He vowed to complete the act before June 5, the day after the California primary and the first anniversary of the Six Day War.

There were probably four stalking attempts to assassinate Kennedy before the actual June 5 killing. On May 20, he was seen with a woman at Robbie's Restaurant in Pomona where Kennedy was dining and speaking. On May 24, he was observed at a Kennedy rally at the Los Angeles Sports Arena. On Saturday, June 1, he purchased two boxes of .22 caliber hollow points and practiced shooting. On Sunday, June 2, he practiced shooting again and then went to a Kennedy campaign rally at the Ambassador Hotel. And on Monday, June 3, he travelled to San Diego to see Kennedy speak at the El Cortez Hotel and returned that night (Clarke, 1982).

The day of the assassination, Sirhan practiced rapid fire shooting at the San Gabriel Valley Gun Club and left the range at 5 p.m. He ate at Bob's Big Boy, went to the Ambassador Hotel, and had four alcoholic drinks over several hours. He then asked two people if the Kennedy bodyguards were with him all the time and if he would be coming through the kitchen pantry. Just before he shot Kennedy, he was heard to say, "Kennedy you son of a bitch" (Clarke, 1982; Kaiser, 1970).

The assassination of Robert F. Kennedy was a paranoid condensation of hatred for the Jews onto an object with whom Sirhan projectively identified, a previously idealized, and then homicidally devalued, introject (Meloy, 1988b). Kennedy was not only a projective vehicle, but also a malevolent object by whom Sirhan felt increasingly controlled and threatened. The operation of projective identification as a defense in Sirhan's object world is captured in the two Cooper and Arnow (1986) projective identification responses to Cards VIII and X (Responses 56 and 62) already noted. The degree to which these Rorschach percepts both carry malevolent objects and are felt to control the subject is evident. In the Sirhan protocol, projective identification is used as a borderline, rather than psychotic, defense, because the object, rather than the self, representation is being projected and controlled and the boundary between self and other is maintained (Goldstein, 1991; Meloy, 1991).

Although the motivation to assassinate Kennedy was suffused with intense affect, the stalking and killing closely fit the criteria for a predatory mode of violence (Meloy, 1988a). The act was planned, purposeful, carried out over the course of 5 months, and involved rehearsal in both fantasy and deed.

Certain structural characteristics of the Rorschach data support this capacity for predatory violence. Both the elevated *Lambda* (1.10) and *Adj D* (+ 1) suggest an individual who was highly defended against his own affect with better than average stress tolerance and control, despite a proneness toward unmodulated affective outbursts ($FC < CF + C$). The absence of T suggests a chronic emotional detachment that would attenuate any feelings of empathy toward the proposed victim. The absence of *Pure H* responses would also facilitate the representation of others as part objects suffused with imaginary, in this case grandiose, malevolent, and overpersonalized, characteristics.

The $Ma < Mp$ ratio in the Sirhan protocol is also suggestive of a capacity for rehearsal fantasy prior to an act of predation (Meloy, 1988a). Instead of an abuse of fantasy (Exner, 1986a), this passive ideational mode, which found its real-world correlate in the repetitive diary writings, may have facilitated the practicing of the assassination in fantasy. Sirhan's hysterical propensity to self-hypnotize, a voluntary form of dissociation learned from the Rosicrucians, may also have facilitated this process.

Content analysis is also suggestive of predatory violence. Objects of violence (Card VI: "a rocket," Card VIII: "guns–mortars") comprise several of his aggressive content; his one aggressive potential response (Card IV: "very dark—serpents (grimaces). Looks ready to strike") is consistent with our finding in Rorschach protocols of psychopaths who are prone to predatory violence (Meloy & Gacono, 1992). Is the Sirhan protocol psychopathic? None of the Rorschach variables that discriminate between psychopathic and nonpsychopathic criminals, other than an absence of T, are present (Gacono & Meloy, 1991; Gacono et al., 1990).

CONCLUSION

The archival study of a Rorschach protocol of an American assassin yields a wealth of data when subjected to current technology. The structural and psychodynamic characteristics of the Sirhan Sirhan protocol, although not supportive of the majority of psychiatric and psychological opinion at his trial, are quite consistent with known historical information concerning his development and the assassination of Robert F. Kennedy.

ACKNOWLEDGMENTS

A portion of this chapter was first presented at the Midwinter Meeting of the Society for Personality Assessment, New Orleans, March 8, 1991. It is dedicated to the memory and work of Seymour Pollack, MD, and Bernard Diamond, MD.

I thank Drs. Carl Gacono, Judith Meyers, and Nancy Kaser-Boyd for their help during the preparation of this study and Dr. Phil Erdberg for the interrater agreement scoring.

The views expressed are my own, and do not necessarily reflect those of the University of California, San Diego, Department of Psychiatry.

REFERENCES

American Psychiatric Association. (1987). *Diagnostic and statistical manual of mental disorders* (3rd ed., rev.). Washington, DC: Author.

Blatt, S. J. (1974). Levels of object representations in anaclitic and introjective depression. *The Psychoanalytic Study of the Child, 29,* 107–157.

Blatt, S., Tuber, S., & Auerbach, J. (1990). Representation of interpersonal interactions on the Rorschach and level of psychopathology. *Journal Of Personality Assessment, 54,* 711–728.

Breuer, J., & Freud, S. (1957). *Studies on hysteria*. New York: Basic Books. (Original work published 1893–1895)

Clarke, J. (1982). *American assassins*. Princeton, NJ: Princeton University Press.

Cooper, S., & Arnow, D. (1986). An object relations view of the borderline defenses: A Rorschach analysis. In M. Kissen (Ed.), *Assessing object relations phenomena* (pp. 143–171). Madison, CT: International Universities Press.

Cooper, S., Perry, J., & Arnow, D. (1988). An empirical approach to the study of defense mechanisms: I. Reliability and preliminary validity of the Rorschach defense scales. *Journal of Personality Assessment, 52,* 187–203.

De Vos, G., & Boyer, L. B. (1989). *Symbolic analysis cross-culturally*. Berkeley: University of California Press.

Exner, J. (1986a). *The Rorschach: A comprehensive system. Vol. 1: Foundations* (2nd ed.). New York: Wiley.

Exner, J. (1986b). Some Rorschach data comparing schizophrenics with borderline and schizotypal personality disorders. *Journal of Personality Assessment, 50,* 455–471.

Exner, J. (1990). *Rorschach interpretation assistance program, Version 2*. Asheville, NC: Rorschach Workshops.

Gacono, C. (1990). An empirical study of object relations and defensive operations in antisocial personality disorder. *Journal of Personality Assessment, 54,* 589–600.

Gacono, C., & Meloy, R. (1991). A Rorschach investigation of attachment and anxiety in antisocial personality disorder. *Journal of Nervous and Mental Disease, 179,* 546–552.

Gacono, C., Meloy, R., & Berg, J. (1992). Affect states, defenses, and object relations in borderline, narcissistic, and antisocial personality disorder. *Journal of Personality Assessment, 59,* 32–49.

Gacono, C., Meloy, R., & Heaven, T. (1990). A Rorschach investigation of narcissism and hysteria in antisocial personality disorder. *Journal of Personality Assessment, 55,* 270–279.

Goldstein, W. (1991). Clarification of projective identification. *American Journal of Psychiatry, 148,* 153–161.

Hartman, W., Clark, M., Morgan, M., Dunn, V., Fine, A., Perry, G., Jr., & Winsch, D. (1990). Rorschach structure of a hospitalized sample of Vietnam veterans with PTSD. *Journal of Personality Assessment, 54,* 149–159.

Herman, J., & van der Kolk, B. (1987). Traumatic antecedents of borderline personality disorder. In B. van der Kolk (Ed.), *Psychological trauma* (pp. 111–126). Washington, DC: American Psychiatric Press.

Kaiser, R. (1970). *"R.F.K. must die!"*. New York: Dutton.

Kernberg, O. (1975). *Borderline conditions and pathological narcissism*. New York: Aronson.

Kernberg, O. (1984). *Severe personality disorders*. New Haven, CT: Yale University Press.

Krystal, H. (1984). Psychoanalytic views on human emotional damages. In B. van der Kolk (Ed.), *Post-traumatic stress disorder: Psychological and biological sequelae* (pp. 1–28). Washington, DC: American Psychiatric Press.

Kwawer, J. (1980). Primitive interpersonal modes, borderline phenomena and Rorschach content. In J. Kwawer, P. Lerner, H. Lerner, & A. Sugarman (Eds.), *Borderline phenomena and the Rorschach test* (pp. 89–109). New York: International Universities Press.

Lerner, H., Albert, C., & Walsh, M. (1987). The Rorschach assessment of borderline defenses. *Journal of Personality Assessment, 51,* 344–354.

Lerner, P. (1990). Rorschach assessment of primitive defenses: A review. *Journal of Personality Assessment, 54,* 30–46.

Levy-Warren, M. (1987). Moving to a new culture: Cultural identity, loss, and mourning. In J. Bloom-Feshbach & S. Bloom-Feshbach (Eds.), *The psychology of separation and loss* (pp. 300–315). San Francisco: Jossey-Bass.

Mahler, M., Pine, F., & Bergman, A. (1975). *The psychological birth of the human infant*. New York: Basic Books.

Meloy, R. (1988a). *The psychopathic mind: Origins, dynamics, and treatment.* Northvale, NJ: Aronson.

Meloy, R. (1988b). Violent and homicidal behavior in primitive mental states. *Journal of the American Academy of Psychoanalysis, 16,* 381–394.

Meloy, R. (1991). The "blurring" of ego boundary in projective identification [Letter to the editor]. *American Journal of Psychiatry, 148,* 1761–1762.

Meloy, R., & Gacono, C. (1992). The aggression response and the Rorschach. *Journal of Clinical Psychology, 48,* 104–114.

Meyers, J. (in press). Assessing cross-cultural adaptability. *Journal of Personality Assessment.*

Miner, H., & De Vos, G. (1960). *Oasis and Casbah: Algerian culture and personality in change.* Ann Arbor: University of Michigan Press.

People v. Sirhan, No. 14026 (Los Angeles County Superior Court, State of California, 1969).

Perry, G., & Kinder, B. (1990). The susceptibility of the Rorschach to malingering: A critical review. *Journal of Personality Assessment, 54,* 47–57.

Pollack, S. (1969a). Psychiatric report to the Honorable Evelle J. Younger, District Attorney, February 5, 1969, *People v. Sirhan,* Peoples Exhibit 111.

Pollack, S. (1969b). Supplemental psychiatric report to the Honorable Evelle J. Younger, District Attorney, March 21, 1969, *People v. Sirhan,* Peoples Exhibit 111.

[Report on a meeting between Senator Robert Kennedy and Premier Eshkol]. (1968, January 10). *New York Times,* p. 14.

Ritzler, B., & Nalesnik, D. (1990). The effect of inquiry on the Exner Comprehensive System. *Journal of Personality Assessment, 55,* 647–656.

Shapiro, D. (1965). *Neurotic styles.* New York: Basic Books.

Stone, M. (1980). *The borderline syndromes.* New York: McGraw-Hill.

Swanson, G., Blount, J., & Bruno, R. (1990). Comprehensive System Rorschach data on Vietnam veterans. *Journal of Personality Assessment, 54,* 160–169.

Terr, L. (1991). Childhood traumas: An outline and overview. *American Journal of Psychiatry, 148,* 10–20.

Urist, J. (1977). The Rorschach test and the assessment of object relations. *Journal of Personality Assessment, 41,* 3–9.

Witkin, R. (1968, January 9). [Report on a Robert Kennedy speech at Manhattan Community College]. *New York Times,* p. 25.

I.

1. I've seen it before. I still don't know. Looks like the back part of a chicken. You fry a chicken. That's the only thing I can . . .

1. It's the whole thing, this being the center. I've eaten some chicken. I never used to like that part, if I could avoid it. It's very bony.

2. A butterfly in flight.

2. The body is here and here are the wings.

3. A frog.

3. Looks like the internal dissection of it. From the little of what I remember, this looks like the cloaca.

4. Two birds—doves.

4. (Top dd.) (How does it appear?) as though they have just landed.

5. Coastline.

5. From a top view like from an airplane. Looks like both a photo and an aerial view could be either. I can see islands.

6. Mountains.

6. Looking down from a plane, the darker areas.

7. Clouds.

7. Is very dark. Just about ready to start to rain. Dark clouds.

8. Cliffs.

8. This reminds me of cliffs looking far away. The space is the water.

9. A bowl

9. It looks like the top of a bowl, like it's curved here.

II.

10. A crown.

10. It's in the space here, a crown for a queen or a king.

11. A diamond.

11. It looks like a diamond or the top of a mosque. A minaret up here. It's the same space, the cut of it.

12. A satellite, you know, space.

12. It's the same area, you know, just the shape of it.

13. A blood smear on a microscope thing.

13. In here looks like blood smeared around. (Red shading in the dark area, lower right.)

14. A cross.

14. It's at the top, a Rosicrucian cross is the way I think of it.

15. Blood! (Looks intently at the blot.)

15. All of the red especially here (lower D) looks like mixed with other liquids (W).

16. A face of a person. Glass.

16. Profile (red, at top). It projects no feeling to me. (?) Madness (?), anger—the teeth are showing, they look more like women than men.

17. An elephant or a bear.

17. The GOP elephant (popular area). Maybe it could be just a bear.

III.

18. A couple of dancers

18. A jovial bunch of Negro drum players—Watusi—although up here—this much looks like foxes—more animal than human—looks like a werewolf (sex?). Oh, men.

(continued)

19. Lungs.

19. (Center D lower.) Looks like a cauliflower really. I see all the fine edges—the edge of it looks like a cauliflower. Also looks like the trachea, leading to bronchial tubes.

20. Cauliflower.

21. Sternum. This is the sternum, isn't it. (Long pause.)

22. A rooster.

22. (Side d.) Maybe a turkey—Red made me think of it.

IV.

Hell!

23. Underwater plantations—plant life—kelp (grimace).

23. Looks like seeing through kelp, this depth thing here. I see it? Looking through it all. (Additional comment.) Now I feel like saying it looks like a casket to me. It represents death.

24. A medieval castle, abandoned.

24. (Top dd.)

25. An X-ray of the chest (grimace).

25. Well, going down the center here (top 1/3) in the shading it looks like the muscles around the neck.

26. (Points at own stomach.) I see these muscles, the abdominal muscles.

26. (Center line just above center). The shading in here looks like the abdominal muscles. (Additional comment.) This much here is way out beyond. It goes beyond. I can't describe it.

27. Very dark—serpents (grimacing). (Blinks.) (?) Looks ready to strike.

28. An animal on hind legs.

28. (Center D) Say a penguin.

29. The hoof of an animal.

29. (dd at the bottom of D.)

V.

30. A bird. A big eagle like. Flying head-on

30. (W, FM, A, P.)

31. A chicken leg. Fried chicken.

31. You know these advertisements for fried chicken. Some old man has all these franchises for fried chicken.

32. Horns, look like the ears of a kangaroo.

32. Looks like horns and ears of a kangaroo, looking straight at me. Right in here.

33. A ballet dancer.

33. The legs are here, the skirt and all that floating around. (Gestures.) Just the legs and standing on the toes. Just the center bottom legs.

34. A seal.

VI.

35. A cat.

35. (Just the tip of the top d.) Eyes, whiskers.

36. This chicken comes in here again.

36. No inquiry.

37. A lamp.

37. It's the brightest spot in the blot. (dd on center line.)

256

38. A rocket.

38. (The center line, lower 2/3, F+)

39. An owl.

39. No inquiry.

40. I have a feeling of high altitude.

40. From the cliffs. Very high. Looks like looking very high and from a high altitude.

41. The bust of a female from the chest up.

41. (Tip of outer top extension dd.)

42. The claws of an eagle or predatory bird

42. Just these claws here.

43. Walking in a very dense forest, a lot of foliage.

43. Looks like an aerial view what you might see around the equator. (Center, both sides in shading.)

44. Vertebrae.

44. No inquiry. (Limits.) Can you find anything of a sexual nature in this particular blot? "Yeah, you mean this being the vagina?" What about an animal skin or a hide that's often seen on this card? "Oh, yeah, the whole thing. That's beautiful. Looks like the fur side—" Again this foliage.

VII.

45. Monkey with tail.

45. Heads, playful. The heads and the tails (tail is the usual ear).

46. Bears. Stuffed bears.

46. A bear's head. The expression is wicked, mean, mad.

47. A jigsaw puzzle.

47. A jigsaw puzzle (W no inquiry).

48. A dam.

48. A dam. Inquiry—a canal, more like in Egypt.

49. A canal.

50. A map of Egypt, you know the boundaries.

50. (One side of lower D.)

51. The Delta River, no, a delta, a river.

52. Towers (very ruminative, here).

52. The towers very distant. (At top of the center.) Very mountainous—might be a church on a cliff.

VIII.

53. The California bear.

53. D, F, A, P.

54. Flags.

54. (Blue area.) Is that blue or green—like the United Nations flags at the top of the buildings.

55. The spine. The vertical column. Is it vertical?

55. The spine, the center line—the spinal column.

56. I don't know, it's a desert plant. Grows very tall—not a cactus. I don't know the name.

56. Patient suddenly verbalizes—"The colors shock me—no—I don't know—I feel very jittery—I can't hold still,—it stirs me. I read this magazine article on the 20th anniversary of the State of Israel. It was in color—that color—I hate the Jews. There was jubilation—I felt that they were saying in the article, we beat the Arabs—it burns the shit out of me, there was happiness and jubilation."

(continued)

257

57. Guns—mortars.

58. Boats.

IX.

59. In school class—in biology—plant life under a microscope—I don't remember the name of this plant.

59. The smear of a botanical slide (W). The color clashes—I am not used to it—too many of them at the same time—it confuses me. It just increases in degrees.

60. Apples.

61. Fire. It's weird, (shakes head). Whew! It has depth—it's too deep. Whew!

X.

62. This whole color—it throws me off! Monsters! (60-second interval.) It's really about all on this one? (You seem upset.) It's frightening—it frightens me—they all seem the same—wickedness! Too many entanglements!

62. It's a cacophony of colors, a hodgepodge. All those legs! This here looks like some kind of rat (brown area). No, not a rat—it flies—a bat. The whole thing looks like monstrosities. It's more vulgar—I'd avoid it. Everybody wants to catch on to you—with all those legs! They minute you're within reach you're in their clutches.

63. Blood! (Grimace, puts card away quickly.)

63. (What about the blood?) I seem to associate the whole thing negatively with blood. (What about the red area?) It looks like liver to me—some kind of meat. (Grimace.) I'd rather not even discuss it—I'd rather not even discuss it. All those legs.

Card	No.	Loc.	#	Determinant(s)	(2)	Content(s)	Pop Z	Special Scores
I	1	Wo	1	Fu		Fd	1.0	PER
	2	Wo	1	FMao		A	P 1.0	
	3	Do	4	F–		A, An		
	4	Ddo	28	FMp–	2	A		
	5	Ddv	99	FDu		Ls, Sc		
	6	Ddo	99	FD.YF–		Ls		
	7	Ddv	99	Y		Cl		
	8	DdSo	32	FDu		Na	3.5	
	9	Ddo	99	Fu		Hh		
II	10	DSo	5	Fu		Art		
	11	DSo	5	Fu		Art	4.5	
	12	DSo	5	Fo		Sc		
	13	Ddv	99	C.Y		Bl		
	14	Do	4	Fu		Art		
	15	Wv	1	C.Y		Bl		
	16	Do	2	Mp–	2	Hd, Hx, Art		AG
	17	Do	1	Fo		(A), Art	P	
III	18	D+	1	Mpo	2	(H), Ay	P 3.0	INC2, COP
	19	Do	7	F–		An		
	20	Do	7	Fu		Fd		
	21	Do	8	Fu		An		
	22	Do	2	CFo		A		
IV	23	Ddv	99	FV–		Bt		AB, MOR
	24	Ddo	21	Fu		Ay		
	25	Ddo	99	FYu		Xy		
	26	Ddo	99	FYu		An		PER
	27	Do	4	FY.FMao	2	(A)		
	28	Do	1	FMp–		A		
	29	Ddo	99	Fu		Ad		
V	30	Wo	1	FMao		A	1.0	
	31	Do	1	Fo		Fd		DR
	32	Do	6	FMpo		Ad		INC
	33	W+	1	Ma.mpo		Hd, Cg	2.5	
	34	Wo	1	F–		A	1.0	
VI	35	Ddo	99	Fu		Ad		
	36	Ddo	99	F–		A		PSV
	37	Ddo	32	Fu		Hh		
	38	Do	12	Fu		Sc		
	39	Do	3	F–		A		
	40	Ddv	99	FDu		Ls		
	41	Ddo	25	Fu		Hd, Sx		
	42	Ddo	21	Fo		Ad		
	43	Wv	1	FD.YFu		Ls		
	44	Do	5	Fo		An		
VII	45	Do	1	FMpu	2	A		
	46	Do	3	Mpo	2	(Ad)		AG, INC
	47	Wv	1	Fu		Id		
	48	Do	4	Fu		Ls, Sc		
	49	Ddo	99	Fu		Ls, Sc		
	50	Ddo	23	Fu		Ge		
	51	Wv	1	Fu		Na		
	52	Do	8	FDu	2	Ls, Sc		
VIII	53	Do	1	Fo		(A), Art	P	
	54	Do	5	FCo	2	Art		
	55	Ddo	21	Fo		An		
	56	Wo	1	FCo		Bt	4.5	DR2
	57	Ddo	99	Fu	2	Sc		
	58	Wo	1	F–	2	Id	4.5	

(continued)

259

Card	No.	Loc.	#	Determinant(s)	(2)	Content(s)	Pop Z	Special Scores
IX	59	Wv	1	CF.YFu		Bt, Sc		PER, DR
	60	Do	6	Fo	2	Fd		
	61	Dv	3	C.V		Fi		
X	62	Wo	1	CF.Mp–		(H), Hx, A	5.5	AB, AG, DR2
	63	Wv	1	C		Bl, Fd		MOR, DR

Summary of Approach

I:W.W.D.Dd.Dd.Dd.Dd.DdS.Dd

II:DS. DS.DS.Dd.D.W.D.D.

III:D.D.D.D.D.

IV:Dd.Dd.Dd.Dd.D.D.Dd

V:W.D.D.W.W

VI:Dd.Dd.Dd.D.D.Dd.Dd.Dd.W.D

VII:D.D.W.D.Dd.Dd.W.D

VIII:D.D.Dd.W.Dd.W

IX:W.D.D

X:W.W

APPENDIX C
Rorschach Structural Summary

LOCATION FEATURES	DETERMINANTS BLENDS	SINGLE	CONTENTS	S-CONSTELLATION
				YES..FV + VF + V + FD > 2
		H = 0,0		YES..Col-Shd Bl>0
Zf = 11	FD.YF	M = 3	(H) = 2,0	YES..Ego<.31,>.44
ZSum = 32.0	C.Y	FM = 6	Hd = 3,0	NO..MOR>3
ZEst = 34.5	C.Y	m = 0	(Hd) = 0,0	NO..Zd > ± 3.5
	FY.FM	FC = 2	Hx = 0,2	YES..es>EA
W = 14	M.m	CF = 1	A = 10,1	YES..CF+C>FC
(Wv = 6)	FD.YF	C = 1	(A) = 3,0	YES.X+%<.70
D = 27	CF.YF	Cn = 0	Ad = 4,0	YES..S>3
Dd = 22	C.V	FC' = 0	(Ad) = 1,0	NO..P<3 or >8
S = 4	CF.M	C'F = 0	An = 5,1	YES.Pure H <2
		C' = 0	Art = 4,3	NO..R<17
DQ		FT = 0	Ay = 1,1	8.....TOTAL
.........(FQ–)		TF = 0	Bl = 3,0	
+ = 2 (0)		T = 0	Bt = 3,0	SPECIAL SCORINGS
o = 49(11)		FV = 1	Cg = 0,1	Lv1 Lv2
v/+ = 0 (0)		VF = 0	Cl = 1,0	DV = 0x1 0x2
v = 12 (1)		V = 0	Ex = 0,0	INC = 2x2 1x4
		FY = 2	Fd = 4,1	DR = 3x3 2x6
		YF = 0	Fi = 1,0	FAB = 0x4 0x7
		Y = 1	Ge = 1,0	ALOG = 0x5
FORM QUALITY		Fr = 0	Hh = 2,0	CON = 0x7
		rF = 0	Ls = 7,0	SUM6 = 8
		FD = 4	Na = 2,0	WSUM6 = 29

	FQx	FQf	MQual	SQx	FD	Contents	
+	= 0	0	0	0	F = 33	Sc = 3,5	
o	= 18	8	3	1		Sx = 0,1	AB =2 CP = 0
u	= 28	19	0	3		Xy = 1,0	AG =3 MOR = 2
–	= 12	6	2	0		Id = 2,0	CFB =0 PER = 3
none	= 5	–	0	0	(2) = 11		COP =1 PSV = 1

RATIOS, PERCENTAGES, AND DERIVATIONS

R = 63		L = 1.10		FC:CF+C =2:7		COP = 1	AG = 3
				Pure C =4		Food	= 5
EB = 5:10.0	EA = 15.0		EBPer = 2.0	Afr =0.21		Isolate/R	= 0.27
eb = 8:11	es = 19		D = –1	S =4		H:(H)Hd(Hd)	= 0:5
	Adj es = 11		Adj D = +1	Blends:R =9:63		(HHd):(AAd)	= 2:4
				CP =0		H+A:Hd + Ad	= 16:8
FM = 7	C' = 0	T = 0					
m = 1	V = 2	Y = 9					
			P = 4	Zf =11		3r+(2)/R = 0.17	
a:p = 4:9	Sum6 =8		X+% = 0.29	Zd =–2.5		Fr+rF = 0	
Ma:Mp = 1:4	Lv2 =3		F+% = 0.24	W:D:Dd =14:27:22		FD = 6	
2AB+Art+Ay = 13	WSum6 = 29		X–% = 0.19	W:M =14:5		An + Xy = 7	
M– = 2	Mnone = 0		S–% = 0.00	DQ+ =2		MOR = 2	
			Xu% = 0.44	DQv =12			

SCZI = 3	DEPI = 7*	CDI = 3	S-CON = 8*	HVI = No	OBS = No

III

NEUROTIC PERSONALITY
ORGANIZATION

16

Psychodiagnosis of Personality Structure: Neurotic Personality Organization

Marvin W. Acklin
Honolulu, HI

This chapter applies Kernberg's psychostructural framework of neurotic personality organization (Acklin, 1992, 1993) to the Rorschach Test. The focus of this contribution is the "highest" level in Kernberg's framework, the neurotic range of personality organization (Kernberg, 1976). Using Rorschach resources derived from the integration of nomothetic approaches (data derived from Exner's Comprehensive System) and idiographic approaches (derived from classical and contemporary psychoanalysis), the goal of this chapter is an elucidation of neurotic functioning for the practicing psychodiagnostician using the inkblot test.

A focus on the more "severe pathologies" based on concepts of developmental deficit—the borderline and narcissistic disorders—has characterized clinical theorizing over the past 15 years (Blanck & Blanck, 1974). The integration of sign and theory approaches to the Rorschach has occurred as a result of the widening scope of psychoanalysis and its interest in borderline disorders.

The term *neurotic* has disappeared from the official diagnostic nomenclature (Bayer & Spitzer, 1985; Vaillant, 1984). The term has been criticized as lacking specificity and as being pejorative in tone and inconsistent with the atheoretical tone of the *Diagnostic and Statistical Manual of Mental Disorders* (3rd ed. [*DSM–III*]; American Psychiatric Association, 1980). *DSM–III* subsumed neurotic disorders broadly into the heterogeneous anxiety disorders with a focus on descriptive symptomatology, divorcing anxiety from its underlying origins and causes. The psychostructural approach, in contrast, understands neurotic functioning based on the viewpoints of psychoanalytic theory—the structural, economic, dynamic, genetic, and adaptive points of view (Rapaport & Gill, 1959)—or in ego psychological terms with a focus on ego structure and functioning (Bellak, 1989). To quote one commentator (C.

Peterson, personal communication), "Where have all the neurotics gone?".
Despite the apparent lack of fashionability of the concept of neurosis, it is this
writer's contention, and that of other writers whose cases follow, that the
concept of neurosis continues to offer useful, even critical insights, into the
functioning of large segments of the clinical population.

Kernberg's tripartite psychostructural framework of personality organization—psychotic, borderline, and neurotic—delineates broad ranges of personality functioning, based on prominent defenses, integration of identity and
object relations, and anxiety tolerance and affect management, based on
structural–developmental theory. In his highly influential proposals for the
classification of character pathology, Kernberg (1976) attempted

> (1) to establish psychoanalytic criteria for differential diagnoses among different
> types and degrees of character pathology; (2) to clarify the relationship between
> a descriptive characterological diagnosis and a metapsychological, especially
> structural analysis; and (3) to arrange subgroups of character pathology according
> to their degree of severity. (p. 139)

Table 16.1 presents Kernberg's criteria, derived from ego psychology and
object relations theories, for the differential diagnosis of personality organization.

Kernberg (1984) identified three primary criteria for differential diagnosis
of personality organization—identity integration, types of defenses habitually
employed, and capacity for reality testing. To quote Kernberg:

> I propose that neurotic personality structure, in contrast to borderline and
> psychotic personality structures, implies an integrated identity. Neurotic per-
> sonality structures present a defensive organization centering on repression and
> other advanced or high-level defensive operations. Reality testing is maintained
> in neurotic and borderline organization but is severely impaired in psychotic
> organization. These structural criteria can supplement the ordinary behavioral
> or phenomenological descriptions of patients and sharpen the accuracy of the
> differential diagnosis of mental illness, especially in cases that are hard to classify.
> (1984, pp. 5–6)

Despite the establishment of a secure inner/outer and self/other boundary,
the achievement of object constancy, and the maintenance of reality testing,
the neurotic individual demonstrates conflict-based inhibition of drive-laden
fantasy in the face of castration and moral anxiety. The primary organizer of
the neurotic range of functioning is the Oedipus complex, the successful
resolution of which is the establishment of a gendered and generationally
identified identity. "The perpetuation of the oedipal–parricidal or oedipal–in-
cestual experience of objects via repression (or related defense maneuvers)
constitutes the core of neurosis" (Hedges, 1983, p. 31). The Oedipus complex
may be viewed as a developmental period or task, in terms similar to the earlier
stages of separation–individuation posited by Mahler and other developmental

TABLE 16.1
Kernberg's Differential Diagnosis of Personality Organization

Area	Neurotic	Borderline	Psychotic	Diff
Ego development	High	Moderate	Low	N/B/P
Reality testing	Generally intact	Good in distant relations, poor in intimate relations	Generally poor	N/B/P
Defenses	Predominantly high level	Predominantly low level	Predominantly low level	N/B
Affect	Modulated, stable, appropriate	Unmodulated, intense, unstable, inappropriate	Unmodulated, intense, unstable, inappropriate	N/B
Impulsivity	Highly selective, infrequent	Moderately selective, frequent	Unselective, frequent	N/B/P
Anxiety tolerance	High	Low	Low	N/B
Sublimatory channels	Yes	No	No	N/B
Superego integration	Contemporary, integrated, depersonified	Archaic, personified, unintegrated	Archaic, personified, unintegrated	N/B
Dynamics	Oral, anal, phallic, genital	Oral aggressive	Oral aggressive	N/B
Object relations	Contemporary, depersonified, abstract	Archaic, personified, concrete	Archaic, personified, concrete	N/B
Object constancy	Constant	Inconstant	Inconstant	N/B
Self–other differentiation	Good in most relations	Good in superficial relations	Poor in most relations	N/B/P
Identity	Intact	Diffusion likely	Diffusion	N/B/P
Interpersonal relationships	Stable with symptoms, anxiety inhibitions	Superficially stable, intimate relations chaotic	Unstable in all relations	N/B/P

Note. Adapted from Kernberg (1975, 1976, 1980). Diff = relevant differential diagnosis. N/B/P = neurotic, borderline, and psychotic personality organization, respectively.

theorists (Chodorow, 1978; Hedges, 1983). Neurosis, then, implies a structured ego and depersonified superego, intact but conflict-driven object relations, and the achievement of object constancy. Consequently, neurotic individuals are capable of forming organized and stable transference reactions (Greenson, 1968) in contrast to the rapid, affectively charged, and unstable transferences noted in borderline individuals (Kernberg, 1992). In neurotic personality organization, object relations are triadic, focused on the self in a system (Johnston, 1991) of relations, in contrast to the dyadic focus of preoedipal organization. Although the superego in neurotics is typically depersonalized, it may be harshly critical in the face of temptations for instinctual gratification, namely the expression of predominantly oedipal libidinal or aggressive fantasies and behaviors (compare Kernberg, 1984: "Most of these patients present no specific superego pathology other than an unconscious dominance of infantile morality linked with a fixation on oedipal prohibitions and demands," p. 288). Individuals who suffer from neurotic conflicts typically demonstrate problems in the areas of "love and work." A symptomatic picture of conflict, anxiety, and inhibition is typically noted. They commonly split their loving and sexual feelings and have difficulties in healthy competition and self-assertion. Because of the "return of the repressed" and "compulsion to repeat," neurotic conflicts are rarely quiescent but require constant dynamic management through impulse defense configurations. Emphasizing the active aspects of neurotic functioning, Shapiro (1965) noted that the "neurotic person does not simply suffer neurosis, as, essentially, one suffers tuberculosis or a cold, but actively participates in it, functions, so to speak, according to it, and, in ways that sustain its characteristic experiences" (p. 20). Although neurotic individuals may be highly conflicted in their love and work situations, their overall level of social adaptation, in contrast to borderline and psychotic levels of organization, is not seriously impaired.

Classical psychoanalytic theory delineates between the symptom and character neuroses (Fenichel, 1945; Gitelson, 1963; Yorke, Wiseberg, & Freeman, 1989), although contemporary theorists have criticized a simple dichotomy (Shapiro, 1989: "all neurosis is characterological"). One of Freud's chief contributions was understanding symptom formation as a "compromise formation" between id-derived drives—organized by the pleasure principle—and the strictures of the ego and superego along lines similar to dream formation. The symptom neuroses (conversion hysteria, phobias, and obsessional neurosis) present with well-circumscribed, ego alien symptomatology, typically related to anxiety management.

The psychoanalytic conceptualization of character has made a rich contribution to clinical theory and psychodiagnostic assessment. Combining views of Freud, Reich, and Fenichel, Moore and Fine (1968) defined character as

> that aspect of personality . . . which reflects the individual's habitual modes of bringing into harmony his own inner needs and the demands of the external world. It is a constellation of relatively stable and constant ways of reconciling conflicts between the various parts of the psychic apparatus to achieve adjustment in relation to the environment. Character therefore has a permanent quality that affects the degree and manner of drive discharge, defenses, affects, specific object relationships, and adaptive functioning in general. (p. 25)

The character neuroses, or more appropriately, "neurotic disorders of character" (Yorke et al., 1989, p. 72), in contrast to the symptom neuroses, demonstrate the inhibiting effects of habitually utilized character defenses (typically based on repression and reaction formation) in relation to conflictual needs. In the neurotic character disorders, the ego is "hardened . . . defenses are consolidated into chronic attitudes, into chronic, automatic modes of reaction" (Reich, 1949, p. 156). Kernberg's psychostructural framework is especially useful in assessing the range and severity of personality style and diagnosis; for example, the more severe personality disturbances, such as paranoid personality, are found only in the lower levels of character organization. For example, Kernberg (1976) noted that most hysterical, obsessive–compulsive, and depressive–masochistic characters are organized at the higher (neurotic) level of personality organization.

In a fashion predating Kernberg's framework, character structure was described in two broad ranges of functioning: pregenital/preoedipal (characterized by part object relations, failure to integrate love and hate, predominance of the pleasure principle in coping and adaptation, and the use of omnipotent modes of conflict resolution; Josephs, 1992) and genital/oedipal (characterized by whole object relations, integration of sexual and aggressive feelings, and ascendancy of the reality principle; Josephs, 1992). Neurotic defenses—typically "higher" level defenses (repression, intellectualization, reaction formation, isolation, undoing, and rationalization)—are deployed in relation to warded-off and threatening impulses and their associated representations and affects (Kernberg, 1980a). These ego-defense configurations and their associated conflicts are the primary issues in the neurotic personality functioning and psychotherapeutic treatment.

In clinical practice, one may see individuals with pure symptom neuroses with well-circumscribed classical symptoms, such as generalized anxiety or phobias, symptom neuroses with characterological features, or nonsymptomatic individuals with a neurotic character organization. In the following three Rorschach case studies, neurotic functioning is exemplified in a symptomatic individual with neurotic character features ("A Neurotic Lawyer: AIDS or Oedipus"), a criminal motivated by the sense of guilt (Freud, 1916/1957) demonstrating a more purified case of a neurotic character disorder ("A Neurotic Criminal: I've learned my lesson . . ."), and a complex case of a teenager functioning "on the neurotic border" (Grinker, Werble, & Drye, 1968) with borderline personality organization.

Rapaport, Gill, and Schafer (1968) noted the Rorschach's prominence in the test battery in the diagnosis of neurotic conditions (p. 528). The typical neurotic Rorschach demonstrates notable ego-limiting mechanisms—constriction, conventionality, and inhibition of drive-laden material (Rapaport et al., 1968, p. 526; Schafer, 1948). In contrast to the more severe pathologies, one has the sense that taking the test is generally not as upsetting to the neurotic patient; there is less dysphoria and an absence of morbidity and fragmentation—evidence of ego weakness and malignant regression—in the record. In general, one observes less primary process "leakage," aptly referred to as "psychic bleeding" by Stern (1938), than in the borderline cases. The raw drive-laden content of the borderline Rorschach, typically revealed in morbid sex and anatomy responses, passively received aggression indicating feelings of damaged victimization (cf. the Aggressive Past score; Meloy & Gacono,

1992), and fabulized combinations reflecting boundary disturbances (Acklin, 1993) are absent.

Emerging conceptualization of borderline personality disorder views the disorder as a variant of posttraumatic stress disorder. In contrast to the borderline Rorschach in which the test seems to provoke an experience of retraumatization, neurotic regressions, revealed in lowered form quality and the emergence of special scores, are well circumscribed with good recovery and commonly focused on specific conflict-arousing material. The record is indicative of signal rather than traumatic anxiety (Blanck & Blanck, 1974). In fact, "indications of extreme anxiety or utter inability to express anxiety seen in the Rorschach test . . . are usually accurate in pointing to the presence of a maladjustment justifiably labeled neurotic," (Rapaport et al., 1968, p. 525). The borderline record is less evident in demonstrating borderline struggles around object constancy, sudden and deep regression, boundary disturbance, or malevolent traumatization.

Rigidity or flexibility of defensive functioning is a central issue in the psychodynamic assessment of neurotic functioning. Schafer, whose 1954 classic offers an encyclopedic overview of defensive processes on the Rorschach, wrote that "insofar as operations are defensive, they seek to obstruct discharge of rejected impulses totally; insofar as operations are adaptive, they facilitate discharge of accepted impulses, although they may also greatly delay, refine, and limit expression of these accepted impulses" (p. 163). Bellak's (1989) and Holt's frameworks (Holt & Havel, 1960) are particularly valuable in assessing the quality and flexibility of neurotic defensive functioning in the expression of primary process material, defensive functions, adaptive regression, and object relations. When drive-laden material is noted, the examiner may see, in relatively healthy neurotics, a flexible repertoire of defensive functioning and, in some cases, adaptive regression in service of the ego (Schafer, 1954). In less healthy neurotic individuals, constriction, inhibition, avoidance ("shock"), or focal regression are noted. Nevertheless, these regressions are well circumscribed and recovery is typically rapid.

Sign approaches to the diagnosis of neurosis "represent a brief and inglorious chapter in Rorschach research" (Goldfried, Stricker, & Weiner, 1971, p. 252) because of the vagueness of neurosis as a criterion variable and of "inadequately conceived and inappropriately constructed test indices" (p. 287). In terms of nomothetic data derived from the Comprehensive System (Exner, 1978), guided by a conceptual approach, one might expect the neurotic record to be characterized by banality (high Populars, high Intellectualization Index) without elevation of validity indicators (*Lambda*), affective overcontrol (reflected in the predominance of FC responses in the Color Balance), generally adequate reality testing (X+% and F+%), and immaturity (predominance of *FM* over M, Human Movement associated with Animal content, and Color Projection).

The Rorschach is particularly useful in illuminating not only the broad range of neurotic functioning, but also the stylistic features that distinguish the cognitive, perceptual, and emotional style of neurotic functioning (Shapiro, 1965). For example, in his discussion of the white space response, Fonda (1960) noted "the endless exceptions, qualifications, and occasions for undoing that are so beloved by the obsessive personality" (p. 98). Current psychoanalytic characterology using the Rorschach understands the diagnostic process as an explication of the underlying structural organization of the personality—whether psychotic, borderline, or neurotic—and the more stylistic features that characterize thinking, affect management, and interpersonal relations—hysterical, narcissistic, obsessional, depressive (Acklin, 1992). Thus, an individual demonstrating narcissistic character features (arrogance, grandiosity, egocentricity) may function at a neurotic or a borderline level with obvious differences in the overall quality of adaptation. As a sample of behavior, the Rorschach provides an unparalleled opportunity to observe the stylistic features of the neurotic individual in action.

Atheoretical or sign-based approaches to Rorschach data, as noted here, have not been particularly useful in delineating neurotic personality features. Theory-saturated approaches are necessary to meaningfully organize and interpret complex clinical material into a meaningful personality description. Despite the disappearance of neurosis from the official diagnostic nomenclature (and with it psychodynamic modes of clinical theorizing), the term continues to be useful in delineating a broad range of human functioning based on intrapsychic conflict and of critical value in providing a multidimensional theoretical framework for the integration of Rorschach test data.

ACKNOWLEDGMENTS

A version of this chapter was the introduction to the symposium "Neurotic Personality Organization: Through the Looking Glass III," presented at the Midwinter Meeting of the Society for Personality Assessment in San Francisco, California, on March 19, 1993.

REFERENCES

Acklin, M. W. (1992). Psychodiagnosis of personality structure: Psychotic personality organization. *Journal of Personality Assessment, 58,* 454–463.

Acklin, M. W. (1993). Psychodiagnosis of personality structure II: Borderline personality organization. *Journal of Personality Assessment, 61,* 329–341.

Bayer, R., & Spitzer, R. (1985). Neurosis, psychodynamics, and DSM–III: A history of the controversy. *Archives of General Psychiatry, 42,* 187–196.

Bellak, L. (1989). *Ego function assessment (EFA): A manual.* Larchmont, NY: C.P.S., Inc.

Blanck, G., & Blanck, R. (1974). *Ego psychology: Theory and practice.* New York: Columbia University Press.

Chodorow, N. (1978). *The reproduction of mothering: Psychoanalysis and the sociology of gender.* Berkeley: University of California Press.

Exner, J. E. (1978). *The Rorschach: A comprehensive system: Vol. 2. Current research and advanced interpretation.* New York: Wiley.

Fenichel, O. (1945). *Psychoanalytic theory of neurosis.* New York: Norton.

Fonda, C. S. (1960). The white space response. In M. A. Rickers-Osviankina (Ed.), *Rorschach psychology* (pp. 80–105). New York: Wiley.

Freud, S. (1957). Some character types met with in psychoanalytic work. In J. Strachey (Ed. and Trans.), *The standard edition of the complete psychological works of Sigmund Freud* (Vol. 14, pp. 309–333). London: Hogarth. (Original work published 1916)

Gitelson, M. (1963). On the problem of character neurosis. *Hillside Journal of Clinical Psychiatry, 12*, 3–17.

Goldfried, M. R., Stricker, G., & Weiner, I. B. (1971). *Rorschach handbook of clinical and research applications*. Englewood Cliffs, NJ: Prentice-Hall.

Greenson, R. R. (1968). *The theory and practice of psychoanalysis*. New York: International Universities Press.

Grinker, R., Werble, B., & Drye, R. C. (1968). *The borderline syndrome*. New York: Basic Books.

Hedges, L. E. (1983). *Listening perspectives in psychotherapy*. New York: Aronson.

Holt, R., & Havel, J. (1960). A method for assessing primary and secondary process in the Rorschach. In M. A. Rickers-Ovsiankina (Ed.), *Rorschach psychology* (pp. 255–279). New York: Wiley.

Johnston, S. (1991). *The symbiotic character*. New York: Norton.

Josephs, L. (1992). *Character structure and the organization of the self*. New York: Columbia University Press.

Kernberg, O. (1975). *Borderline conditions and pathological narcissism*. New York: Aronson.

Kernberg, O. (1976). A psychoanalytic classification of character pathology. In O. Kernberg (Ed.), *Object relations and clinical psychoanalysis* (pp. 139–160). New York: Aronson.

Kernberg, O. (1980a). *Internal world and external reality*. New York: Aronson.

Kernberg, O. (1980b). Neurosis, psychosis, and the borderline states. In A. M. Freeman, H. I. Kaplan, & B. J. Sadock (Eds.), *Comprehensive textbook of psychiatry* (Vol. 3). Baltimore: Williams & Wilkins.

Kernberg, O. (1984). *Severe personality disorders: Psychotherapeutic strategies*. New Haven, CT: Yale University Press.

Kernberg, O. (1992). *Aggression in personality disorders and perversions*. New Haven, CT: Yale University Press.

Meloy, R., & Gacono, C. (1992). The aggression response and the Rorschach. *Journal of Clinical Psychology, 48*, 104–114.

Moore, B. E., & Fine, B. D. (1968). *A glossary of psychoanalytic terms and concepts* (2nd ed.). New York: American Psychoanalytic Association.

Rapaport, D., & Gill, M. (1959). The points of view and assumptions of metapsychology. *International Journal of Psychoanalysis, 40*, 153–162.

Rapaport, D., Gill, M., & Schafer, R. (1968). *Diagnostic psychological testing* (rev. ed.; R. Holt, Ed.). New York: International Universities Press.

Reich, W. (1949). *Character analysis*. New York: Orgone Institute Press.

Schafer, R. (1948). *The clinical application of psychological tests: Diagnostic summaries and case studies*. New York: International Universities Press.

Schafer, R. (1954). *Psychoanalytic interpretation in Rorschach testing: Theory and application*. New York: Grune & Stratton.

Shapiro, D. (1965). *Neurotic styles*. New York: Basic Books.

Shapiro, D. (1989). *Psychotherapy of neurotic character*. New York: Basic Books.

Stern, A. (1938). Psychoanalytic investigation of and therapy in the borderline group of neuroses. *Psychoanalytic Quarterly, 7*, 467–489.

Vaillant, G. E. (1984). A debate on DSM–III: The disadvantages of DSM–III outweigh its advantages. *American Journal of Psychiatry, 141*, 542–545.

Yorke, C., Wiseberg, S., & Freeman, T. (1989). *Development and psychopathology: Studies in psychoanalytic psychiatry*. New Haven, CT: Yale University Press.

17

A Neurotic Lawyer: AIDS or Oedipus?

Charles A. Peterson
Department of Veterans Affairs, Minneapolis Medical Center
and University of Minnesota

In 1947, Henry Murray offered four reasons to explain the paucity of case histories in the psychological literature:

1) Every life, swift to the self as it may be, is long and complicated to the psychologist, and many hours are required for explorations of a few portions of it. 2) Man's power to recall his past is, at best, deficient, and, at worst, radically subverted by the devious devices of his vanity. 3) Man is a reputation guarding animal who bristles with defenses when the cool eye of scientific scrutiny is cast on a crucial area of his secret life. 4) The psychologist's conscience, acknowledging that every man is entitled to his privacy, forbids unscrupulous intrusions. (Murray, 1947/1955, p. 15)

Another reason must be added to this already impressive and inhibiting list. Just as an author reveals something about him-or herself in his or her work, the publication of a case history reveals something about both subject and author: Hugo's long-winded, digressive oratory and romantic fascination with the downtrodden betrays a depressive position unsuccessfully covered with rosy, hypomanic denial; Hemingway's terse prose and combative content reveals vulnerability covered with an illusory veneer of macho and self-sufficiency. Similarly, the psychologist is a fallible human, equally given to vulnerability and vanity, fearful of revealing him- or herself in the countertransference that shapes and limits each case publication or presentation. Although progressively desensitized to the glaring eye of public scrutiny every time we write a psychological test report, the psychodiagnostician is particularly vulnerable to what R. D. Laing (1965) called "petrification anxiety," namely the belief that the Other's gaze will penetrate our defenses and freeze our essence with cool, critical comprehension. When the Rorschach clinician publishes or presents a case, the test data are right there; the

Structural Summary is the petard on which we might be hoisted, as it invites the Other to scrutinize the professional and private Self, perhaps reinterpreting the data with a vengeance, while we long for admiration and affirmation. Although I should own this vulnerability, I believe that this is a collective anxiety. How else can we explain the paucity of case material in the *Journal of Personality Assessment (JPA)*? If we survey the 12 issues composing the 1991–1992 *JPA*, we find 4 case studies amidst 190 articles. Surely, this suggests that somebody is anxious and, not surprisingly, avoidant. Rather than identify with the scientist reluctant to leave the laboratory, I prefer to join the literary biographer, striving for "the faithful portrayal of a soul in its adventures through life." With Henry Murray (1947/1955), I believe that "dissecting the intricate plexus of forces at the core of a single personality can be scientifically rewarding" (pp. 5–6).

But what about our focus on neurosis? In an era when "deprivation and deficit" is the banner regnant, in an era when many clutch the atheoretical *Diagnostic and Statistical Manual of Mental Disorders* (3rd ed., rev.; American Psychiatric Association, 1987), in an era when the word neurosis has passed from the index of our Bible (Exner, 1986), we may justifiably wonder "Where have all the neurotics gone?" Is this diagnosis passé? The psychoanalytically oriented clinician, following the guidance of Freud, Fenichel, and Kernberg, believes that the term neurosis continues to explain considerable variance in the misery of the human condition. If we transit autism and hallucinatory gratification, we are rewarded with drive-based frustration and conflict with the environment, as well as a frightening awareness of our awful instinctual potential.

MR. Y: A NEUROTIC LAWYER

Mr. Y was a handsome thirty-something lawyer who could have found a home in the script of *L.A. Law*. He was an ambitious, promising, junior member of a large firm, anxiously poised on the cusp of partnership. He worried that he would not be promoted to partner, a status that would rescue him from the humiliation he repeatedly experienced (imagined?). However, he was most anxious that he would acquire AIDS in his sexual relations with whatever woman about whom he was currently and fearfully inflamed. Despite several negative tests for the AIDS virus and multiple consultations with prestigious internists and infectious disease specialists, Mr. Y could not be reassured, leading to two brief supportive psychotherapies, each lasting approximately 9 months. The psychodiagnostic consultation on which this chapter is based occurred about halfway in the second psychotherapy.

Mr. Y felt considerably more secure during a rosy, two-parent, suburban childhood. He was the older of two children, a sister trailing him by a couple of years. His earliest memory? "Riding in a toy car, in back of our apartment building." This phallic exuberance is only slightly spoiled by the fact that "my sister had one, too," possibly signaling the beginning of his concern with sexual differences. His mother was a commercial artist, "a good person, hard working, sympathetic, understanding, never judgmental . . . I just about tell her everything," the present tense suggesting some strands of overinvolvement rather than the necessary disidentification from mother (Greenson, 1968). His father was a social worker, "a good person, down to earth, more passive (than mom), laid back . . . supportive, concerned." He wasn't quite comfortable with his description of his parents' relations: "Mom wears the pants; Dad's henpecked." He describes his relations with them as good, close, although "Mom may have spoiled me too much. My parents paid for my college and law school; I never worked, never made my bed and had dinner in front of the TV whenever I wanted." His earliest memory of his mother involved her crying after her mother's (his grandmother's) death. His earliest memory of his father involved a "wallop for minor misbehavior like straying from the yard or blowing out the candles on my sister's birthday cake." In general he described childhood as a time free from worry, with no responsibilities, where he was safe and protected. With certain relevance for an understanding of his ambition and attendant anxiety, his scariest early memory finds him "caught up in a tree; I couldn't get down; I'm not really phobic of heights, just don't like 'em." He states that he was "a terrible student, getting lousy grades, smoking pot, dropping ludes." He says he had "real long hair, a kind of a punky kind of guy. I read a lot and that probably saved me from a life as a garage mechanic." Rather than take responsibility for his dalliance, he wishes that his mother and father had pushed and threatened him more.

He began dating in high school and first had sex in college. Because of a fear of pregnancy, he and his girlfriend relied almost exclusively on oral sex. Even though he professed considerable affection for this woman, he was uncomfortable with the mix of sex and love and he cheated on her. After graduation from a state university, he attended law school, eventually taking a position with his current high-pressure firm. He began to date a woman he described as "very sexy but cold and aloof," a constellation he excitedly regarded as whorish. After being fellated by a prostitute some months before his wedding and again on the night of his bachelor party, his anxiety began to mount, so much so that on his honeymoon he had anxiety about mounting. He could not perform sexually. He says: "I was afraid I'd hurt her," but with blustery pseudomasculinity, he alibied to her that the steroids he had used with weight-lifting had robbed his libido. After a year of no marital sex, but some extramarital sex, they were divorced. He began dating a woman he had known since childhood, a physician, a "good woman" approved by his parents. He described her as "affectionate, caring, very supportive." However, he was decidedly ambivalent about her, unable to marry her: On the one hand, he was somewhat aroused, not by her, but by her sexual history. He reasoned that other men had found her desirable; therefore, she was desirable. On the other hand, that same sexual history made him worry that she might give him AIDS. He said, "I'm crazy about her, but she doesn't turn me on all the way. I still get the desire to screw other women; I'm just a horny toad." His AIDS anxiety peaked after a sexual escapade with a female coworker; again, his anxiety was disproportionate to the risk. He had kissed and digitally stimulated this woman, his finger never entering her vagina. He was firmly convinced that the AIDS virus had entered his body through a hangnail. Another round of tests and medical consultations followed but did not allay his mounting anxiety.

Against a background of little actual risk for acquiring HIV, that is, relatively few sexual partners, no unprotected sex, no passive anal sex, no IV drug abuse, no homosexual sex, the alert clinical listener will have begun to suspect that other factors may have contributed to Mr. Y's assessment of his risk. His psychiatrist called the "expert diagnostic consultant" (Weiner, 1972), who entered Mr. Y's world as a theory-guided participant–observer to empathically and appreciatively comprehend his experience of risk. Was it AIDS or Oedipus?

THE PSYCHODIAGNOSIS OF NEUROTIC PERSONALITY STRUCTURE

Previous efforts to diagnose neuroses with the Rorschach have focused unproductively on a "sign" approach (e.g., Harrower-Erickson, 1942; Miale & Harrower-Erickson, 1940; Munroe, 1941). The diagnostician would inspect a Rorschach protocol and compare it against a checklist of signs, and if a fixed cutting score was exceeded, a neurotic diagnosis was assigned. This approach has been justifiably criticized for the inattention to cross-validation and subsequent shrinkage, failure to adjust cutting scores for differential base rates, and the typically haphazard, hodgepodge atheoretical vision that cannot animate, organize, and integrate the test data (Goldfried, Stricker, & Weiner, 1971). By contrast, Weiner (1977) advocated a conceptual approach: (a) The practitioner or researcher should draw on extant theory to indicate the personality variables that account for the syndrome or diagnosis in question; (b) The tester then indicates what aspects of the Rorschach or the test battery that best assess those variables.

Freud, Fenichel, and Kernberg shall point the way. According to Freud (1924/1959), "Neurosis is the result of a conflict between the ego and its id. . . . [The conflict] originates from the ego's refusing to accept a powerful instinctual impulse . . . and denying it motor discharge, or disputing the object towards which it is aimed." According to Fenichel (1945), the drives have an "urging energy . . . a provocative character," and clamor for satisfaction. The ego, by contrast, represents delay, "the mediation between the organism and the outer world. . . . It is the consideration of reality that keeps the ego from complying with the discharge of the impulses" (pp. 16–18). This caution initiates the sequence of repression and compromise, resulting in the symptom, which is housed, per Kernberg (1980, 1981), within an intact, integrated identity. Reality testing is preserved, with the exception of conflict-specific distortion (Abend & Porder, 1983). Relations with the Other are stable but often plagued by anxious inhibition.

RESULTS

The Rorschach was administered according to the Comprehensive System (Exner, 1986), nondirective inquiry following the final free association to Card X. The results of the Rorschach are presented in Appendix A (the Free Association and Inquiry), Appendix B (Sequence of Scores), and Appendix C (Structural Summary). Per Weiner's (1977) guidelines for the conceptual point of view, each section of the discussion that follows first dogmatically states the experience distant postulates/expectations that can organize our thinking about neurosis, and then translates them into palpable guidelines for the working Rorschacher.

DISCUSSION

Reliability and Validity

The avoidant and repressive tendencies of a personality organized at the neurotic level are reflected in marginally acceptable indices of test reliability. The tester–patient interaction is structured in a manner consistent with a neurotic level transference, that is, with no significant misalliance or misperception of the therapist.

Although *R* (number or responses) is low, this is a reliable, valid, and interpretively useful record. Beyond the simple question of reliability and validity, what can a low *R* and low *lambda* (percentage of pure form responses) tell us about Mr. Y? Clinical theory must transform mere numbers into meaningful descriptors. Consistent with his presenting problem, the low *R* may suggest a phobic involvement with the stimuli, an avoidant response to the anxiety of involvement, fearing he might catch something from the "dirty pictures." However, the low *lambda* signifies some overinvolvement with the stimuli, an inability to stay detached. A low *lambda* suggests imprecise, uneconomical, issue-ridden involvement with the stimuli, driven by unfulfilled needs, conflicts, and emotions. Maybe a better phrase is an unhealthy involvement with stimulation, a lack of autonomy from inner and outer stimulation, which is how Mr. Y described himself, goaded by his sexual drives, and erratically over- and underreactive to specific sexual stimuli.

With regard to the quality of the interaction, Mr. Y was appropriately focused on and invested in the testing, engaged in a dutiful collaboration with the tester. With the exception of the Draw-A-Person, which prompted transient regression to prepubertal latency, his behavior was appropriate and did not involve the tester in any misalliance or misperception. His narrative revealed conflictual self-images, on the one hand, an earnest, hard-working, ambitious young man on the way up or, on the other hand, a fearful, insecure, gland-driven Peter Pan who did not want to grow up.

Thought Organization

To make a neurotic level diagnosis, it is imperative to rule out any psychotic thinking or alteration of reality that would be indicated by indices of disturbed ideation or cognitive mediation: The lid must be on the id.

In a previous article, I opined that "If ideation is testimony to existence, then the nature of that thought is divinatory of the diagnostic level of existence" (Peterson, 1992, p. 465). This is, in other words, a crucial branch on the diagnostic decision tree, as the diagnostician makes a tentative assignment to psychotic, borderline, or neurotic level of thinking. Mr. Y shows no sign of a psychotic thought process. The *WSUM6* (weighted sum of special scores) is 2 and the *SCZI* (a set of decision rules indicative of schizophrenia) index is 0. Rather than simply note the Special Score (indicator of disturbed thinking), the psychoanalytically minded tester will wonder what provoked the cognitive slippage. An inspection of the *WSUM6* reveals two level 1 *DV*s (deviant verbalization): The first occurs on Response 4, in which an odd word choice follows his perplexity about the simultaneous presence of breasts and penises. Thanks to the pioneering work of Rapaport (Rapaport, Gill, & Schafer, 1945–1946), Friedman (1953), and Watkins and Stauffacher (1952), we know that deviant thought on the Rorschach is indicative of an earlier mode of cognition, here time transporting the examiner to a time in Mr. Y's life when the mystery of the sexual differences often activates castration anxiety in the young boy. The second *DV* follows on the high heels of the first, signaling some conflict-inspired slippage, again provoked by some phallic insecurity. His $X + \%$ (percentage of good form responses) is low, but an inspection of the Sequence of Scores and response content indicates that the transient perceptual regression, that is, two *FQ*– (minus Form Quality) responses, occurred in conjunction with conflict-relevant imagery, most likely vaginal stimuli. Neither of those two responses were accompanied by deviant verbalizations or resulted in malignant regressions, suggesting that problems with reality testing are dynamically circumscribed and not structural deficits. This conflict-tainted judgment is exacerbated by a fuzzy, uncritical cognitive style that neglects critical information, reflected in the following structural variables: The disproportionate number of lazy Whole (use of the entire inkblot) responses, the lopsided *W:M* (ratio of whole responses to Human Movement responses) ratio, the low number of *DQ*+ (developmental quality) responses, and a *Zd* (a measure of organizational activity/ability) score of –7.0. A Bright Normal Wechsler Adult Intelligence Scale score with minimal scatter, no leakage, and reasonably faithful reproduction of the Bender Gestalt Test stimuli further attest to an intact ego structure, even if anxiety does impair attention and concentration.

Affective Factors and Security Operations

At the neurotic level, affects are not absent or unneutralized or inappropriate. Affects, specifically anxiety and depression, are tolerated but may lead to conflict and inhibition, which are contained with repression and other higher level defense mechanisms. The Experience Balance of 2:0.5 and corresponding Experience Actual indicate a generalized coarctation of resources, particularly in the affective realm. Although the $FC:CF + C$ ratio would not suggest control/discharge problems, this may represent marginal control, achieved through overcontrol, inhibition, and avoidance, signaled by a very low Affective Ratio of .27, which bears brief comment. Just as no symptom should ever be considered apart from its characterological context, Rorschachers should not look at this—or any other score—in isolation. An examination of the sequence of content usually proves instructive. Prior to his encounter with the three chromatic cards, which often stimulate productivity, Mr. Y produced vaginal stimuli on Card VII. It looks as if his conflictual preoccupation with the vagina leads to poignant despair (indicated by a color shading blend) and regression (indicated by two successive FMs, or Animal Movement, and some implied food content) on the next two cards, a sequence isomorphic to his interaction with women and their parts.

The positive $DEPI$ (depression index) would suggest that Mr. Y is depressed, which is puzzling given his interview claim that "I'm not depressed and can't ever recall being depressed." An inspection of the $DEPI$ and pairing the signs with the actual content of the responses will help the diagnostician to resolve this dilemma. His Vista (shading used for dimensionality) response, an FV (form dominant use of shading for dimensionality) occurs on Card I, the perception of depth occurring in an area often experienced as a woman's hips or pelvis. Perhaps the juxtaposition of "sinister fangs, claws and pincers" with a "transparent abdomen" heralds the *vagina dentata*, the nemesis of the Oedipal neurotic. The second positive $DEPI$ sign, a color shading blend, that occurred on Card VIII, Response 12, was discussed *supra*. The next $DEPI$ sign is a low Egocentricity Index (ratio of pairs and reflection responses to total responses) signaling low self-esteem, a Barnum descriptor not specific to depression. The next $DEPI$ sign, a low Affective Ratio and a low incidence of Blends (i.e., one) is suggestive of simple, perhaps sluggish cognitive operations and affective inhibition, problems not peculiar to depression, but certainly compatible with phobic constriction. The last positive $DEPI$ sign is an absence of cooperative human interaction, again, a problem not restricted to depression. It may be that MOR (Morbid) content is necessary for the experience of sadness or the display of dysthymia, all of which were absent in Mr. Y.

Are there Rorschach variables that address his anxious presentation? The positive Coping Deficit Index does not comment specifically on his anxiety, but individuals with such deficits will likely display anxiety in their maladaptive response to inner need or environmental press. The *D* (measure of stress tolerance) and *Adjusted D* (stress tolerance adjusted for situational variables) scores also reflect this deficit. Mr. Y's *An* + *Xy* (sum of anatomy and X-ray contents) score of 0 surprisingly does not capture the reported anxiety about his body. One of his two *FY* (form dominant use of general shading) scores occurs on Card VIII, Response 12, and most likely occurred in sequential regression after the threatening vaginal content on Card VII. Normatively, the single *FT* (form dominant use of shading for texture) response on Card IV may say little, other than some capacity for—and anxious concern about the nature of—attachment and relatedness. Idiographically, however, there is much more to glean: Because a single texture response is typically given to Card VI, the presence of texture here attests to the specificity of the drive and the attendant anxiety, particularly because it overwhelms some of his ego functions, witnessed in the *FQ*– and the Deviant Verbalization. Might this suggest an anxious estrangement from a secure representation of his father?

The structural summary is witness to an absence of Aggression: There is no *Ex* (explosion) content. There is no *AG* (aggressive) movement. Meloy and Gacono's (1992) expanded scoring system for aggressive responses does capture some aggression on Responses 8 and 12. "Stingray" and "Lions [or] panthers" would be scored as Aggressive Content. However, these derivatives are safely distant from his aggressive drive and would suggest that Mr. Y is intolerant of, or, at best, has a reluctant ownership of his aggression. Still, there may be some preconscious discomfort in Response 12, conveyed in the retroflected kinesthesia "hunched." Further, the impulse is carried but disowned in a Passive Animal Movement. In the end, we may conclude that Mr. Y, per Freud's (1924/1961b) guidelines on neurosis, attempts to reject instinctual reality.

Security Operations

The neurotic level of personality organization will show a relative emphasis on higher level defenses, such as repression, and a relative absence of lower level defenses, such as splitting and devaluation.

We will be brief here. The repressive and phobic aspects of the protocol have already been mentioned. The coarctation described earlier also serves to dampen the felt intensity of his affective experience. The Music content following the "stingray" suggests that intellectualization is employed in response to the mobilization of aggression. Six Popular responses in 14 total responses suggests defense by conventionalization, best described by Schachtel (1959) in his classic *Metamorphosis*. The *PER* (personalized) content suggests insecurity obscured by an evidential appeal to experience. Potentially threatening affects are denied: "Lions" transmute as harmless "squirrels or small creatures." The *a:p* (ratio of active to passive movement) score of 2 to 5 is indicative of an unproductive flight into fantasy in response to unpleasant situations. Unlike a psychosis, this is not "a loss of reality," but as Freud (1924/1961a) noted, "a substitute for reality." Most importantly, there is an absence of the more primitive defenses associated with lower levels of psychopathology. This is consistent with Haan's (1964) research, indicating that when *FM* exceeds *M* (Human Movement), neurotic level defenses, such as regression, intellectualization, and rationalization, are likely. Before moving on we must note that the presence of higher level defenses and the absence of lower level defenses does not guarantee effective management of troublesome thoughts and affects. For example, when *FM* exceeds *M*, consciousness is often disrupted by unwelcome drive-based thoughts, consistent with Mr. Y's pressured rumination about sex.

Self and Others

A neurotic level identity is essentially intact/cohesive, temporally continuous, with some evidence of immaturity but without deterioration or fragmentation of the basic personality. Object constancy has been attained, and affective ambivalence has been integrated but may be conflictual in relation to the significant Other. The superego is contemporary and depersonified. Relations with the Other are stable but often plagued by conflict and inhibition.

Mr. Y's record shows evidence of immaturity. Like preadolescent children, Mr. Y produced more Animal than Human Movement responses. The four *PER* (use of personal experience to justify/explain a response) content scores speak to a rigidity, defensively covering low self-esteem and insecurity, the latter betrayed by his low Egocentricity Index of .29. Normatively Mr. Y shows an *H* (human content) deficiency, even if the presence of a Form-Texture response suggests that he has the hard-wired capacity for attachment. His only pure *H* occurs on the powerfully compelling Card III. Two Human Detail responses, one of which is an *M–*, that convey interpersonal distortion and mystification, are given on Card VII. Witness how his relations with the Other are colored by the focal power of his conflicts: The people in Response No. 4 "could be anything, monkeys"; the "person's profile . . . looks more like an animal." The poorly differentiated figures have both "breasts [and] penises." The verbalized uncertainty within the response is a carrier of conflict: At first he is uncertain about the breasts, but then he is less certain about "what's meant to be a penis." Might this be a representation of the phallic mother, the fantasy about her penis protecting him from castration anxiety? He is unable to produce a strong masculine representation on Card IV, activating some disorganizing longing, reflected in the *FT–* and the attendant *DV.* Given the referral question, his responses to Card VII inform us about his relations with women: He actively avoids the Popular whole person or persons in location *D2,* the *FQ–* in the response nicely documenting the drive-based distortion. He reduces the whole women to part objects, that is, vaginas. The second response to Card VII even manages to perceive the vagina as disembodied from the woman. Obviously, relations with the part object other are sexualized; all H/Hd content is associated with Sex content. There is, however, no Cooperative Human Movement, implying an inability to work cooperatively toward the satisfaction of his need for satisfaction. Two unconnected statements in his Rorschach Interpretive Assistance Program interpretive narrative say it well, if wryly: "This subject appears to have a marked sexual preoccupation. . . . This subject appears to have little interest in people!" Such are the dilemmas of need and relatedness. An atheoretical perspective cannot meaningfully resolve or integrate such potentially discrepant descriptors. The atheoretical tester would be limited to the ever-banal "approach–avoidance conflict." Psychoanalytic theory can do better than that.

Freud (1912/1957) discussed a problem familiar to the everyday therapist: psychic impotence, which, notwithstanding the misplaced nominative case suggesting the phallus has a mind of its own, Freud described as "a refusal on the part of the sexual organs to execute the sexual act." Because the problem occurs with some but not all women, Freud observed that the man concludes "that the disturbance of his masculine potency is due to some quality in the sexual object," even though Freud's statement should be corrected to read *fantasies about the sexual object*. The afflicted, like Mr. Y, is unable to bring about the necessary confluence of tender, affectionate, and erotic feelings, which remain split and attached to separate part objects, the mother and the whore. With compelling prescience, Freud could have been describing Mr. Y: "Where such men love, they have no desire and where they desire, they have no love." Mr. Y could have sex with strangers, prostitutes, even his girlfriends, but was psychically impotent and disinterested when his whorish girlfriend became his loving wife. His next girlfriend, whom he loved for her maternal soothing of his friable nerves, did not arouse him at all. In the midst of his relationship with this maternal woman, he completed the sentence completion stem *I SECRETLY* with "like X-rated films." Only the sexy stranger, the part object, excited him. His fixation on his mother—with whom he remained incestuously (not literally, Fromm, 1964) involved—prevented the sensual from uniting with the affectionate. Again, Freud (1912/1957): "In order to keep their sensuality out of contact with the objects they love, they seek out objects whom they need not love." But after Mr. Y sought out a sex object he didn't love, he was stricken with great anxiety. In the end his so-called AIDS anxiety really amounted to a wish/fear conflict about—and punishment for having an erotic interest in—Oedipal objects. This is consistent with Fenichel's (1944) comments: "Most frequently [the phobia] combines an unconscious temptation with an anticipation of punishment" (p. 313).

Murray commented on how hard it is for the psychologist–biographer to do justice to someone's life. Indeed, many issues have been neglected in this discussion, prominent among them the relationship between the sexual confusion on Card III and his homophobia, his ambition, and the potential for a sibling transference to affect his perception of women. Before a brief epilogue satisfies the reader's desire to know how the story turns out, his last response, the so-called signature response, bears comment as it carries a hopeful sign. Response 14, "Spiders dancing around": Animal Movement or Human Movement with Animal Content? Do spiders dance around? That is the question. Do they jump about, move quickly and nimbly? I think they do. Do they do the Jitterbug? I think not. What to do? Assuming, for the moment, an experienced Rorschacher, a scoring dilemma, the experience of uncertainty, may represent a successful projective identification, an interactional communication, here helping the tester/scorer sample Mr. Y's uncertainty about relatedness. The scorer's momentary uncertainty is momentarily isomorphic with Mr. Y's uncertainty. At some level he might wish for cooperative human interaction, but he is defending against it, knowing he will spoil it, as he did on this response. The analysis of this conflict may help both tester and therapist experience the optimism necessary to sustain the journey toward a higher level of relatedness.

EPILOGUE

Mr. Y terminated therapy several months after the completion of the diagnostic testing on which this chapter was based. Although he did report a mild reduction in his anxiety, it was eventually discovered that he had been "cheating" on his psychiatrist, obtaining Xanax from his motherly, physician girlfriend. In the end we discovered that Mr. Y, like many neurotics, did suffer from "AIDS," that is, *Aversion to Insight Disorder*, a condition best combatted with a combination of nomothetic and theory-driven idiographic approaches to the Rorschach.

ACKNOWLEDGMENTS

This chapter was part of a symposium entitled "Neurotic Personality Organization: Through the Looking Glass III" presented at the Midwinter Meeting of the Society for Personality Assessment in San Francisco on March 20, 1993.

I thank the other members of the symposium, especially Dr. Marvin "Cap'n" Acklin, for their mutual stimulation, Dr. Fred Schick for access to case data, and the Department of Veterans Affairs for supporting this research. This article is dedicated to Dr. Murray Tieger, my first supervisory hero, and an "expert diagnostic consultant" incarnate.

REFERENCES

Abend, S. M., & Porder, M. A. (1983). *Borderline patients: Psychoanalytic perspectives* (Kris Study Group Monograph, B. Fine, Ed.). New York: International Universities Press.

American Psychiatric Association. (1987). *Diagnostic and statistical manual of mental disorders* (3rd ed., rev.). Washington, DC: Author.

Exner, J. E. (1986). *The Rorschach: A comprehensive system* (2nd ed.). New York: Wiley.

Fenichel, O. (1944). Remarks on common phobias. *Psychoanalytic Quarterly, 13,* 313–326.

Fenichel, O. (1945). *The psychoanalytic theory of neurosis.* New York: Norton.

Freud, S. (1957). On the universal tendency towards debasement in the sphere of love. In J. Strachey (Ed. and Trans.), *Standard edition of the complete psychological works of Sigmund Freud* (Vol. 11, pp. 179–190). London: Hogarth. (Original work published 1912)

Freud, S. (1959). Neurosis and psychosis. In J. Riviere (Ed. and Trans.), *Collected papers of Sigmund Freud* (Vol. 2, pp. 250–254). New York: Basic Books. (Original work published 1924)

Freud, S. (1961a). Loss of reality in neurosis and psychosis. In J. Strachey (Ed. and Trans.), *Standard edition of the complete psychological works of Sigmund Freud* (Vol. 19, pp. 183–187). London: Hogarth. (Original work published 1924)

Freud, S. (1961b). Neurosis and psychosis. In J. Strachey (Ed. and Trans.), *Standard edition of the complete psychological works of Sigmund Freud* (Vol. 19, pp. 149–153). London: Hogarth. (Original work published 1924)

Friedman, H. (1953). Perceptual regression in schizophrenia: An hypothesis suggested by the use of the Rorschach. *Journal of Projective Techniques, 17,* 171–185.

Fromm, E. (1964). *The heart of man.* New York: Harper & Row.

Goldfried, M. R., Stricker, G., & Weiner, I. B. (1971). *Rorschach handbook of clinical and research applications.* Englewood Cliffs, NJ: Prentice-Hall.

Greenson, R. R. (1968). Disidentifying from mother: Its special importance for the boy. *International Journal of Psycho-Analysis, 49,* 370–374.

Haan, N. (1964). An investigation of the relationships of Rorschach scores, patterns and behaviors to coping and defense mechanisms. *Journal of Projective Techniques and Personality Assessment, 28,* 429–441.

Harrower-Erickson, M. R. (1942). The value and limitations of the so-called "neurotic signs." *Rorschach Research Exchange, 6,* 109–114.

Kernberg, O. (1980). Neurosis, psychosis, and other borderline states. In A. M. Freedman, H. L. Kaplan, & B. J. Saddock (Eds.), *Comprehensive textbook of psychiatry, Vol. III* (3rd ed., pp. 1079–1092). Baltimore: Williams & Wilkins.

Kernberg, O. (1981). Structural interviewing. *Psychiatric Clinics of North America, 4,* 169–195.

Laing, R. D. (1965). *The divided self.* New York: Penguin.

Meloy, J. R., & Gacono, C. (1992). The aggression response and the Rorschach. *Journal of Clinical Psychology, 48,* 104–114.

Miale, F. R., & Harrower-Erickson, M. R. (1940). Personality structure in the psychoneuroses. *Rorschach Research Exchange, 4,* 71–74.

Munroe, R. L. (1941). Inspection techniques. *Rorschach Research Exchange, 5,* 166–191.

Murray, H. A. (1955). Introduction. In A. Burton & R. Harris (Eds.), *Clinical studies of personality* (Vol. 1, pp. 4–17). New York: Harper & Row. (Original work published 1947)

Peterson, C. A. (1992). A psychotic gynemimetic: I just had a pregnant thought. *Journal of Personality Assessment, 58,* 464–479.

Rapaport, D., Gill, M., & Schafer, R. (1945–1946). *Diagnostic psychological testing.* Chicago: Year Book.

Schachtel, E. G. (1959). *Metamorphosis: On the development of affect, perception, attention, and memory.* New York: Basic Books.

Watkins, J. G., & Stauffacher, J. C. (1952). An index of pathological thinking on the Rorschach. *Journal of Projective Techniques, 16,* 276–286.

Weiner, I. B. (1972). Does psychodiagnosis have a future? *Journal of Personality Assessment, 36,* 534–546.

Weiner, I. B. (1977). Approaches to Rorschach validation. In M. A. Rickers-Ovsiankina (Ed.), *Rorschach psychology* (2nd ed., pp. 575–608). Huntington, NY: Krieger.

APPENDIX A
Rorschach Protocol

I.

1. Looks like a bat.

(?) Wings, bat-shaped, fangs, claws, almost see-through skeletal structure, kind of transparent. (?) Outer is lighter, inner darker, the abdomen. (?) Sinister (?) fangs, pincers.

2. Maybe a butterfly.

(?) Wings, a winged creature, more bat-ish.

II.

3. Looks like a cat's face.

(?) Eyes, nose, whiskers, cheeks. (?) no. (?) Would be the whites.

III.

4. Two people leaning over, could be anything, monkeys or people; a table, ouija board?

(?) Head, arms reaching down, torso arched over, buttocks, what might be breasts, penises, wearing high heels, on person's coffee table. (breasts & penises?) A bit of an anachronism, huh? Person's profile, breasts and what's meant to be a penis; head looks more like animal, a jutting jaw.

IV.

5. Looks like a fly's head.

(?) Mandibles, forgot the term, a tongue type apparatus, head kind of furry (touches and rubs card), hairy, shaded in, less defined, diffuse.

V.

6. (Laughs) Looks more like a bat in flight.

(?) Really, got to tell you, if you've seen it, that's what it looks like; wings, hindquarters, head.

7. Maybe a bird.

(?) Or a flying squirrel; if you've seen one in flight, it looks about like that.

VI.

8. Could be a stingray.

(?) If you've seen one in the water. Body, long narrow tail with barbs.

9. A violin.

(?) Stem, base, forget what this is called (?) The darkness, wood grain is darker in the center, lighter elsewhere.

VII.

10. A woman's legs in the air.

(?) Vagina, buttocks, legs in the air. (?) Vagina is slightly spread. Do you see that?

11. A vagina.

(?) Right here.

VIII.

12. Two lions hunched up on an evergreen tree, or small creatures like squirrels, hunched up on a tree.

(?) Creature, head, ears, leg, tail, looks like eating from tree. I was in Africa, saw animals doing that. The darker stem of the tree, delta shape of the evergreen. (?) Top color is green. (Lions? Squirrels?) More like a panther, cougar, the small creatures I saw in Africa.

(continued)

IX.

13. (>60 sec) Nothing comes to mind (repeat instruction). Two crabs or shrimp touching, claws, antennae, tentacles.

(?) On top of something (?) Coral, rock, head of shrimp, body (?) Generally where shrimp hang around, jagged shape.

X.

14. Looks like several spiders dancing around.

(?) Small creatures, insects, dancing around.

(Card you like the most?) III is the most interesting (?) Can't quite tell what they're doing. Staring at each other. Don't know if men or women, or both. (Card you dislike the most?) IX, crabs or shrimp, doesn't say anything to me; it's my most creative answer, like modern art; flash it on and that's what you get.

APPENDIX B
Sequence of Scores

Card	No.	Loc.	#	Determinant(s)	(2)	Content(s)	Pop Z	Special Scores
I	1	Wo	1	FVo		A	P 1.0	
	2	Wo	1	Fo		A	P 1.0	
II	3	WSo	1	F–		Ad	4.5	
III	4	D+	1	Mpo	2	H, Sx, Hh	P 3.0	DV
IV	5	Wo	1	FTo		Ad	2.0	DV
V	6	Wo	1	FMao		A	P 1.0	PER
	7	Wo	1	FMpo		A	1.0	PER
VI	8	Wo	1	Fu		A	2.5	PER
	9	Wo	1	FYu		Id	2.5	
VII	10	Wo	1	Mp–		Hd, Sx	2.5	
	11	Do	6	Fo		Hd, Sx		
VIII	12	W+	1	FMp.FC.FYo	2	A, Bt	P 4.5	PER
IX	13	Wv/+	1	FMpu	2	A, Na	5.5	
X	14	Do	1	FMao		A	P	
					2			

	Summary of Approach	
I:W.W		VI:W.W
II:WS		VII:W.D
III:D		VIII:W
IV:W		IX:W
V:W.W		X:D

Rorschach Structural Summary

LOCATION FEATURES	DETERMINANTS BLENDS	SINGLE	CONTENTS	S-CONSTELLATION
			H = 1,0	NO..FV + VF + V + FD > 2
				YES..Col-Shd Bl>0
Zf = 12	FM.FC.FY	M = 2	(H) = 0,0	YES..Ego<.31,>.44
ZSum = 31.0		FM = 4	Hd = 2,0	NO..MOR>3
ZEst = 38.0		m = 0	(Hd) = 0,0	YES..Zd > ± 3.5
		FC = 0	Hx = 0,0	YES..es>EA
W = 11		CF = 0	A = 8,0	NO..CF+C>FC
(Wv = 0)		C = 0	(A) = 0,0	YES..X+%<.70
D = 3		Cn = 0	Ad = 2,0	NO..S>3
Dd = 0		FC' = 0	(Ad) = 0,0	NO..P<3 or >8
S = 1		C'F = 0	An = 0,0	YES.Pure H <2
		C' = 0	Art = 0,0	YES..R<17
DQ		FT = 1	Ay = 0,0	7.....TOTAL
.........(FQ–)		TF = 0	Bl = 0,0	
+ = 2 (0)		T = 0	Bt = 0,1	SPECIAL SCORINGS

					Lv1	Lv2
o = 11(2)		FV = 1	Cg = 0,0			
v/+ = 1 (0)		VF = 0	Cl = 0,0	DV = 2x1		0x2
v = 0 (0)		V = 0	Ex = 0,0	INC = 0x2		0x4
		FY = 1	Fd = 0,0	DR = 0x3		0x6
		YF = 0	Fi = 0,0	FAB = 0x4		0x7
		Y = 0	Ge = 0,0	ALOG = 0x5		
FORM QUALITY		Fr = 0	Hh = 0,1	CON = 0x7		
		rF = 0	Ls = 0,0	SUM6 = 2		

	FQx	FQf	MQual	SQx	FD = 0	Na = 0,1	WSUM6 = 2
+	= 0	0	0	0	F = 4	Sc = 0,0	
o	= 9	2	1	0		Sx = 0,3	AB =0 CP = 0
u	= 3	1	0	0		Xy = 0,0	AG =0 MOR = 0
–	= 2	1	1	1		Id = 1,0	CFB =0 PER = 4
none	= 0	–	0	0	(2) = 4		COP =0 PSV = 0

RATIOS, PERCENTAGES, AND DERIVATIONS

R = 14   L = 0.40

			FC:CF+C =1:0	COP = 0	AG = 0
			Pure C =0	Food	= 0
EB = 2:0.5	EA = 2.5	EBPer = N/A	Afr =0.27	Isolate/R	= 0.21
eb = 5:4	es = 9	D = –2	S =1	H:(H)Hd(Hd)	= 1:2
	Adj es = 8	Adj D = –2	Blends:R =1:14	(HHd):(AAd)	= 0:0
			CP =0	H+A:Hd + Ad	= 9 4

FM = 5   C' = 0   T = 1

m = 0   V = 1   Y = 2

			P = 6	Zf =12	3r+(2)/R = 0.29
a:p	= 2:5	Sum6 = 2	X+% = 0.64	Zd =–7.0	Fr+rF = 0
Ma:Mp	= 0:2	Lv2 = 0	F+% = 0.50	W:D:Dd =11:3:0	FD = 0
2AB+Art+Ay = 0		WSum6 = 2	X–% = 0.14	W:M =11:2	An + Xy = 0
M–	= 1	Mnone = 0	S–% = 0.50	DQ+ =2	MOR = 0
			Xu% = 0.21	DQv =0	

SCZI = 0	DEPI = 5*	CDI = 4*	S-CON = 7	HVI = No	OBS = No

Incomplete Sentences

1. I LIKE — to lift weights.
2. THE HAPPIEST TIME — of my life was in college.
3. I WANT TO KNOW — if UFOs exist.
4. BACK HOME — my parents are happy.
5. I REGRET — not going to medical school.
6. AT BEDTIME — I often fight the urge to stay up.
7. MEN — smoke cigars.
8. THE BEST — friends are old friends.
9. WHAT ANNOYS ME — is my own impatience.
10. PEOPLE — live lives of quiet desperation.
11. A MOTHER — can always be trusted.
12. I FEEL — like my future is about to be decided.
13. MY GREATEST FEAR — is not making partner.
14. IN SCHOOL — I did not realize my full potential.
15. I CAN'T — seem to become a shining star at work.
16. SPORTS — are generally boring to watch.
17. WHEN I WAS A CHILD — I loved to watch television.
18. MY NERVES — could be stronger.
19. OTHER PEOPLE — think I am intense.
20. I SUFFER — from anxiety.
21. I FAILED — to do as well as I could in school.
22. READING — is more fun for pleasure than for work.
23. MY MIND — may not be suited for the law.
24. THE FUTURE — looks bright.
25. I NEED — to get organized.
26. MARRIAGE — is something I am not ready for.
27. I AM BEST WHEN — I am not anxious.
28. SOMETIMES — I want to live my life as a bachelor.
29. WHAT PAINS ME — is my fear of failure.
30. I HATE — when partners don't think I'm a good lawyer.
31. THIS PLACE — is very competitive.
32. I AM VERY — hard-working.
33. THE ONLY TROUBLE — with the law is its lack of stability.
34. I WISH — I were back in high school.
35. MY FATHER — is a good man.
36. I SECRETLY — like X-rated films.
37. I — wish I was a physician.
38. DANCING — is not something I enjoy.
39. MY GREATEST WORRY — is not making partner.
40. MOST WOMEN — want to be married.

Note. Stems are in capital letters.

18

A Neurotic Criminal: "I've learned my lesson . . ."

J. Reid Meloy
University of California, San Diego

Carl B. Gacono
U.S. Department of Justice

In 1916, Freud speculated that the majority of criminals might be motivated by a sense of guilt and a need to rationalize it by behaving criminally. Nietzsche (1883/1969) called this neurotic fellow the "pale criminal" (p. 65). Freud left it "to future research to decide how many criminals are to be reckoned among these 'pale' ones" (1916/1957, p. 333; see also Alexander, 1930a, 1930b, 1935). We sadly report, nearly 80 years later, that there seem to be very few.

Despite the apparent rarity of the neurotic criminal in our time, we have managed to identify one such feckless and hapless individual and would like to present his case and Rorschach. This is the fourth study in a series (Gacono, 1992; Meloy & Gacono, 1992b; Meloy & Gacono, 1993) that investigates psychopathic character at various levels of personality organization (Kernberg, 1984). We think this case provides idiographic support for Meloy's (1988) hypothesis that the neurotic psychopath, per se, does not exist; yet a person organized at a neurotic level could, for a variety of reasons, do criminal things.

CASE STUDY

David is a 42-year-old caucasian man born and raised in an intact, Greek, Roman Catholic, middle-class family. He has two older brothers. His mother was a housewife, and his father was a store manager until his death from a heart attack when David was 31.

He describes his childhood as confusing.

> Father invalidated me in every aspect of my personality. I was a fuck-up unless he was there. When I hit puberty I began to assert myself. In school I rebelled. Academically I was at the bottom, but on the SATs I was at the top.

David was neither physically nor sexually abused as a child, but he does have potent early memories of his father: "Explosive scenes. I had no warm times with him. He told me what a shit I am. He'd scream, holler like a madman." He characterized his mother as emotionally withdrawn. He summarizes his childhood as a time of fear, unhappiness, and confusion. His mother would explain that his father was "sacrificing" for him when he got "crazy." There is no history of conduct disorder as a child and no history of alcoholism, criminality, or psychiatric disorder in the family. His lifetime medical history was insignificant except for pneumonia in the first grade.

David met his wife in college; they married after she became pregnant, and three sons were subsequently born. He describes his marriage: "When I met Susan, my self-esteem was very low. Hers was too. Our interaction was minimal for seven years. Emotionally our relation was retarded. We were meeting our goals, but not taking care of the relationship."

Meanwhile, David graduated from business school, worked briefly as a county auditor, and then entered private practice as a financial investor. After 7 years of marriage, David and Susan separated. He began dating another woman and was introduced to gambling by a client.

> I started winning. I became preoccupied with gambling and finding time. I tried to maintain the status quo and not make choices. Freeze it, rather than choose, it was an escape. Dad made all my choices up 'til then. I'd rationalize, run over to Las Vegas and gamble by myself. My denial was rampant. . . . I was making lots of money, and it accelerated the gambling. I'd cover my lines of credit within two weeks and no one knew. My ongoing rationale was I'd get even and quit. I borrowed money from a client. When my father died, I became reckless, I affirmed my father's opinion that I would fuck-up without him there.

Three years after he began gambling, David was borrowing money from client trust accounts, abusing alcohol, lying to his clients, missing appointments, and owed approximately $600,000 to various individuals and institutions. He sought treatment from a psychiatrist during this time but was not hospitalized until he was arrested and charged with conspiracy to obtain, distribute, manufacture, and possess illegal drugs. He describes his criminal activity: "Most compulsive gamblers will [commit crimes]. The opportunity was there. The meth [methamphetamine] manufacturing was part of my self-destruction. I knew I was being surveilled by the police five weeks before I did the lab." When asked if he feels guilt, he said, "I feel shame. I feel like a bad person. I was raised a Catholic and a Christian. I was lying, manipulating, breaking the law, not telling the truth."

David eventually pled guilty to three separate, nonviolent crimes, including theft and tax evasion, and was sentenced to 5 years in prison. He was released to a halfway house after 7 months and successfully completed his parole 2 years later. David became an active member of Gamblers Anonymous after his hospitalization and continues to participate in that self-help group. He is also in individual psychotherapy. This evaluation was prompted by his attempt to be licensed in another state so that he could, once again, practice financial investing. The purpose of the evaluation was to aid the court in determining whether David had been sufficiently rehabilitated and had the moral character to practice as a licensed financial investor.

At the time of testing, David was not on any prescribed medications. He did have a positive drug abuse history, however, for alcohol, cocaine, amphetamine, and cannabis. He was administered the MCMI–II, the MMPI–2, and the Rorschach. He produced a two point 4(T69) 5(T68) MMPI–2 profile and a histrionic personality pattern (BR78) MCMI–II profile.

RESULTS

The Rorschach protocol is presented in Appendix A, the sequence of scores in Appendix B, and the structural summary in Appendix C. The Rorschach was analyzed using the Rorschach Scoring Program Version 2 (Exner, 1990). Table 18.1 is the scoring for defenses (Cooper, Perry, & Arnow, 1988), and Table 18.2 is the aggression scoring (Meloy & Gacono, 1992a).

DISCUSSION

Kernberg (1984) theorized that neurotic personality organization would evidence (a) sharply delimited, yet whole self and object representations; (b) repression and higher level defenses that would protect the patient from intrapsychic conflict; and (c) preserved reality testing that contributes to the realistic and meaningful evaluation of self and others. The Rorschach of David generally supports these theoretical premises and validates our hypothesis that he is organized at a neurotic level, and furthermore, is not a psychopathic character.

Self and Object Representations

The object world of David suggests a normative interest in others (All H = 5) and the expectation of cooperativeness in his interpersonal life (COP = 2). Despite an imaginative propensity not to represent others as whole, real, and meaningful objects ($H:(H) + Hd + (Hd)$ = 1:4), none of his human content or movement responses indicate loss of contact with reality. Likewise, he is neither isolative (*Isolate/R* = .09) nor dependent (Fd = 0). His aggressive response (Ag = 1) is normative for nonpatient male subjects (M = 1.17, SD = 1.10; Exner, 1990), and there is no suggestion of a paranoid elaboration of his internal objects ($H + A:Hd + Ad$ = 6:1). Most importantly, and unlike antisocial personality disordered male subjects (Gacono & Meloy, 1992), he has a normative capacity to form attachments to others (T = 1).

TABLE 18.1
Defense Scale Scoring of a Neurotic Criminal (Cooper, Perry, & Arnow, 1988)

Defense	Response	Frequency	Percentage
Neurotic			
Higher level denial	(13)	1	
Intellectualization	(1, 2, 6, 11, 12, 15, 18, 20, 23)	9	
Isolation	(3, 9, 10, 15, 18, 23)	6	
Reaction formation		0	
Repression	(7, 19, 20, 21, 22)	5	
Rationalization	(12)	1	
Pollyannish denial		0	
			76%
Borderline			
Devaluation		0	
Omnipotence		0	
Primitive idealization	(1, 6, 10, 15, 16)	5	
Projection	(5, 7)	2	
Projective identification		0	
Splitting		0	
			24%
Psychotic			
Hypomanic denial		0	
Massive denial		0	
			0%
Total scored		29	100%

Note. Several defenses may appear in one response.

TABLE 18.2
Aggression Scoring of a Neurotic Criminal (Meloy & Gacono, 1992a)

Category	Frequency	
Ag	1	(17)
AgC	1	(5)
AgPast	0	
AgPot	0	
SM	0	
Ag denial	1	(13)

David's self-perception is also what we would expect in a neurotic individual who may be experiencing shame and guilt concerning bad deeds. He compares himself negatively to others (Egocentricity ratio = 0.22), which generates painful, dysphoric feelings ($V = 1$), the latter finding unusual in nonpatient male subjects (17%; Exner, 1991). Despite this difficult introspective process, predicted during psychotherapy, he does not evidence an abnormal sense of self-injury ($MOR = 1$) or a pathologically narcissistic grandiosity ($Rf = 0$). David's expectations of himself are also realistic ($W:M = 10:6$). All of these indices bode well for psychotherapeutic success. The only negative indicator is a plethora of personal ($PER = 6$) responses, suggesting in this clinical context an intellectualized ($2AB + Art + Ay = 10$) rigidity when challenged, rather than self-aggrandizement (Gacono, Meloy, & Heaven, 1990).

Repression and Higher Level Defenses

David's neurotic defenses (76%) predominate over his borderline defenses (24%), and there is a complete absence of psychotic defenses (see Table 18.1). These findings sharply contrast with the defensive operations of the psychotic and borderline psychopath (Meloy & Gacono, 1992b, 1993). The proportionate distribution of defenses is consistent with neurotic personality organization but captures the dynamic shifts that occur among defenses and between levels of personality during the Rorschach process itself.

Idealization, scored in the Cooper, Perry, and Arnow system (1988) at the borderline level, is used by David in an adaptive manner consistent with his history. This defense is generally absent in psychopaths (Gacono, 1990; Gacono & Meloy, 1992), and, when it does appear, is devoid of human content. In this case, 60% of the idealizing responses contain human content (Responses 6, 10, 15), which identify artistic figures (Bernstein, Max, and Lautrec).

Intellectualization is most commonly employed at the neurotic level, followed by isolation, repression, rationalization, and higher level denial. These defenses generally work well to manage both sexual and aggressive impulses, and derivative emotions.

Sexual impulses do not appear in the record ($Sx = 0$), consistent with 96% of nonpatient male subjects (Exner, 1991), and are only suggested in a sublimated form in Response 20 (Card IX): "brass balls on a spring." Aggressive impulses are also denied or sublimated in the service of maintaining attachment. Card VI: "A pelt, a dry pelt. I know nothing about hunting. (?) Shading—hide would look like." When directly expressed (Card VIII: "A woman's corset being torn apart."), aggression disorganizes him, reality testing is momentarily lost (Responses 17 and 18), and the impulse is turned inward to render a sense of self-injury (MOR on Response 18). Aggressive impulse is ego dystonic for David and infrequently articulated when scored using our more detailed indices (Gacono & Meloy, 1994; Meloy & Gacono, 1992a; see Table 18.2).

The derivative emotions of his instinctual life are also well managed by his higher level neurotic defenses. There is less defense against internal emotion ($lambda = 0.28$) and more avoidance of external emotional stimuli ($Afr = .53$) than expected. However, affect is modulated most of the time in a normative manner ($FC:CF + C = 3:2$) with an occasional unmodulated lapse ($C = 1$). This latter response is extremely unusual in an introversive like David (expected in 1% of introversives; Exner, 1991) but is consistent with a histrionic character style in which affective flooding will often occur (Shapiro, 1965). Nevertheless, stress tolerance and control are better than average ($AdjD = + 1$), and affect appears to help with perceptual accuracy ($F+\% = 20, X+\% = 61$). Constraint of affect is normative ($C' = 1$), and Vista ($V = 1$) in a neurotic context is likely to suggest introjective rather than anaclitic depression (Blatt, 1974; Meloy, 1992), a finding consistent with David's articulated remorsefulness.

Preserved Reality Testing

David's reality testing, although idiosyncratic ($X+\% = 61$), is not impaired ($X-\% = 9$). This is an unusual and welcome finding in a criminal subject (Gacono & Meloy, 1991). Furthermore, he shows no $M-$ responses, a pathognomonic indicator of ideational distortion, particularly around object relations, and no clinically significant formal thought disorder ($WSum6 = 7$, Level 2 = 0). Ideational helplessness, however, is contributing to perceptual distortion ($m = 3$), and this state variable, in the absence of anxiety ($Y = 0$), may be measuring his sense of controllable stress (McCown, Fink, Galina, & Johnson, 1992). This variable's elevation is predicted given David's choice to seek relicensure and the consequent attack upon his character that he knew would occur.

The most striking cognitive abnormality is the underincorporative style ($Zd = -6.0$). This information processing characteristic, most prevalent in young children, is present in only 10% of introversives and 5% of nonpatient male subjects (Exner, 1986). It predicts what Exner called "stimulus neglect," a haphazard scanning of the environment, but can be easily altered through treatment (Exner, 1986, p. 361).

Psychopathic Character

Does David have a psychopathic character, even if it is organized at a neurotic level? We think not. Weiner (1991) proposed four measures of core psychopathic deficits (superego impairments): $T = 0$, Pure $H < 2$, $COP = 0$, and $S > 2$. These variables infer an emotionally detached, disinterested, uncooperative, and chronically angry individual. David's Rorschach is only positive for the second criterion, and his total human content is normative. Our research (Gacono et al., 1990; Gacono & Meloy, 1991, 1992, 1994; Meloy, 1988) suggested that five variables distinguished psychopathic from nonpsychopathic criminals: $T = 0$, $Rf > 0$, Egocentricity > 0.45, $PER > 2$, $Y = 0$. David is positive for the latter two variables. Unlike our psychopathic samples, however, his use of personals was not juxtaposed with the borderline defenses of projective identification or omnipotence (Meloy & Gacono, 1993), but instead appeared with intellectualization, isolation, and repression. We think the absence of Y, found in 58% of normal male subjects (Exner, 1986), was due to the absence of uncontrollable stress (McCown et al., 1992).

CONCLUSIONS

The Rorschach data suggest an individual organized at a neurotic level of personality with compulsive, histrionic, and antisocial character traits. He is not psychopathic. Although our test results do not speak directly to his criminal motivation, they are consistent with an individual whose low self-esteem and wish to avoid some serious life stressors made gambling an exciting and novel outlet (Galski, 1987). When money was needed, criminal activity followed, and with the death of father, the unconscious wish to be caught resulted in his arrest and prosecution. If he had only not listened to his dad. "Of all terrors of conscience speak to me, but do not speak to me of my father!" (from the opera *Don Carlos*, quoted in Reik, 1961, p. 268). David, our neurotic criminal, "was equal to his deed when he did it; but he could not endure its image after it was done" (Nietzsche, 1883/1969, p. 65).

ACKNOWLEDGMENTS

An earlier version of this chapter was presented at a symposium entitled, "Neurotic Personality Organization: Through the Looking Glass III" at the Midwinter Meeting of the Society for Personality Assessment, March 20, 1993, San Francisco, California.

We thank Marilyn Clarke for the excellent preparation of this article.

REFERENCES

Alexander, F. (1930a). The neurotic character. *International Journal of Psycho-Analysis, 11*, 292–313.

Alexander, F. (1930b). *Psychoanalysis of the total personality* (B. Glueck & B. D. Lewin, Trans.). New York: Nervous and Mental Disease Publications. (Original work published 1923)

Alexander, F. (1935). *Roots of crime*. New York: Knopf.

Blatt, S. (1974). Levels of object representation in anaclitic and introjective depression. *The Psychoanalytic Study of the Child, 29*, 107–157.

Cooper, S., Perry, J., & Arnow, D. (1988). An empirical approach to the study of defense mechanisms: I. Reliability and preliminary validity of the Rorschach defense scales. *Journal of Personality Assessment, 52*, 187–203.

Exner, J. (1986). *The Rorschach: A comprehensive system: Vol. 1. Basic foundations* (2nd ed.). New York: Wiley.

Exner, J. (1990). *Rorschach Scoring Program version 2*. Asheville, NC: Rorschach Workshops.

Exner, J. (1991). *The Rorschach: A comprehensive system: Vol. 2. Interpretation*. (2nd ed.). New York: Wiley.

Freud, S. (1957). Criminals from a sense of guilt. In J. Strachey (Ed. and Trans.), *The standard edition of the complete psychological works of Sigmund Freud* (Vol. 14, pp. 332–333). London: Hogarth. (Original work published 1916)

Gacono, C. (1990). An empirical study of object relations and defensive operations in antisocial personality disorder. *Journal of Personality Assessment, 54*, 589–600.

Gacono, C. (1992). A Rorschach case study of sexual homicide. *British Journal of Projective Psychology, 37*, 1–21.

Gacono, C., & Meloy, R. (1991). A Rorschach investigation of attachment and anxiety in antisocial personality disorder. *Journal of Nervous and Mental Disease, 179*, 546–552.

Gacono, C., & Meloy, R. (1992). The Rorschach and the DSM–IIIR antisocial personality: A tribute to Robert Lindner. *Journal of Clinical Psychology, 48*, 393–405.

Gacono, C., & Meloy, R. (1994). *The Rorschach assessment of aggressive and psychopathic personalities*. Hillsdale, NJ: Lawrence Erlbaum Associates, Inc.

Gacono, C., Meloy, R., & Heaven, T. (1990). A Rorschach investigation of narcissism and hysteria in antisocial personality disorder. *Journal of Personality Assessment, 55*, 270–279.

Galski, T. (1987). *The handbook of pathological gambling*. Springfield, IL: Thomas.

Kernberg, O. (1984). *Severe personality disorders*. New Haven, CT: Yale University Press.

McCown, W., Fink, A., Galina, H., & Johnson, J. (1992). Effects of laboratory-induced controllable and uncontrollable stress on Rorschach variables m and Y. *Journal of Personality Assessment, 59*, 564–573.

Meloy, R. (1988). *The psychopathic mind: Origins, dynamics, and treatment*. Northvale, NJ: Aronson.

Meloy, R. (1992). *Violent attachments*. Northvale, NJ: Aronson.

Meloy, R., & Gacono, C. (1992a). The aggression response and the Rorschach. *Journal of Clinical Psychology, 48*, 104–114.

Meloy, R., & Gacono, C. (1992b). A psychotic (sexual) psychopath: "I just had a violent thought . . . " *Journal of Personality Assessment, 58*, 480–493.

Meloy, R., & Gacono, C. (1993). A borderline psychopath: "I was basically maladjusted . . . " *Journal of Personality Assessment, 61*, 358–373.

Nietzsche, F. (1969). *Thus spoke Zarathustra*. New York: Penguin. (Original work published 1883)

Reik, T. (1961). *The compulsion to confess: On the psychoanalysis of crime and punishment*. New York: Grove Press.

Shapiro, D. (1965). *Neurotic styles*. New York: Basic Books.

Weiner, I. (1991). Conceptual issues in the Rorschach assessment of criminality and antisocial personality. *Rorschachiana, XVII*, 31–38.

I

1. Something flying, an airplane.

Looking down on plane, wing look to it. Howard Hughes after WWII—outline.

2. A flying insect.

Same thing. Wing structure is irregular in design—different motion, how I saw it.

3. Shape of a woman in here.

Like in antique shop—the shape—made with wire.

4. A pumpkin, jack-o-lantern.

Opening—mouth, eyes.

5. I see something more carnivorous, a wolf.

Ears, Jowls, shape, coming down. Openings here.

6. I can see a conductor, the Philadelphia orchestra, reminds of Leonard Bernstein.

Hands (holds up)—like Stravinsky.

7. An inkblot.

Seen my son's work—looks like ink.

II

8. Two rabbits playing Pattycake.

Ears, heads up, hands.

III

9. Two waiters serving a table at a restaurant.

An artist, cartoonist used to . . . in New Yorker, reminds me of that (?) heads, torso, arms, legs, looks like waist jacket.

IV

10. Looking up at a giant standing in front of a tree—angle of some one tall.

Feet here, tree trunk, cause of color, depth perception. Peter Max could have done it in the 60s.

V

11. Ballet, a dance.

Shape—abstract, grace, fluid. "Dance of butterflies."

12. A butterfly.

In a theatrical sense, not a real butterfly.

VI

13. A pelt, a dry pelt. I know nothing about hunting.

Shading—hide would look like.

14. A bass fiddle.

The blackness, image of a fiddle.

VII

15. Two Moulin Rouge dancers looking at each other.

Reminds me of a Lautrec poster—two heads, headpieces, way he'd draw girls.

VIII

16. It's pretty. Two gophers.

Legs, on a seal, a state seal somehow.

17. A woman's corset being torn apart.

Lives in here—opened up.

18. Skeleton of a bizarre fish.

Just does. In a museum like New York—old skeletons. Looking down on it.

IX

19. The colors—no images.

20. A German clock—like we had as a kid in our house.

Brass balls on a spring, rotating back and forth.

X

21. Two crabs.

Bizarre, colorful crabs—I've seen on PBS.

22. Yellow flowers—cotton or something.

Covering—irregularity of when cotton blooms.

23. Rest looks like art work my son abhors.

I've looked at modern art that looks like this. Colors, pastels. Visually exciting to me.

Card	No.	Loc.	#	Determinant(s)	(2)	Content(s)	Pop Z	Special Scores
I	1	Wo	1	mau		Sc	1.0	
	2	Wo	1	FMao		A	1.0	
	3	Ddo	99	Fu		(H)		
	4	DdSo	99	Fu		Art	3.5	
	5	WSo	1	FMao		A	3.5	
	6	Do	1	Mpo		H		
	7	Wv	1	Fu		Art		PER
II	8	D+	6	Mao	2	A	3.0	FAB, COP
III	9	D+	1	Mao	2	(H), Hh, Art, Cg	P 3.0	COP, PER
IV	10	W+	1	Mp.FVo		(H), Bt	P 4.0	DR
V	11	Wv	1	Mao		Hx, A		AB
	12	Wo	1	Fo		(A)	P 1.0	
VI	13	Wo	1	FTo		Ad	P 2.5	
	14	Ddo	99	FC'u		Sc, Art		
VII	15	D+	1	Mpo	2	(Hd), Art	P 3.0	PER
VIII	16	D+	1	FCo		(A), Art	P 3.0	
	17	Do	5	mp–		Cg		AG
	18	Do	4	F–		An, A		MOR
IX	19	Wv	1	C		Art		
	20	Do	6	mau		Sc		PER
X	21	Do	1	FCo	2	A	P	PER
	22	Do	15	FCo	2	Bt		
	23	Wv	1	CFo		Art		PER

Summary of Approach

I:W.W.Dd.DdS.WS.D.W	VI:W.Dd
II:D	VII:D
III:D	VIII:D.D.D
IV:W	IX:W.D
V:W.W	X:D.D.W

298

LOCATION FEATURES	DETERMINANTS BLENDS		CONTENTS	S-CONSTELLATION
		SINGLE		NO..FV + VF + V + FD > 2
			H = 1,0	NO..Col-Shd Bl>0
Zf = 11	M.FV	M = 5	(H) = 3,0	YES..Ego<.31,>.44
ZSum = 28.5		FM = 2	Hd = 0,0	NO..MOR>3
ZEst = 34.5		m = 3	(Hd) = 1,0	YES..Zd > ± 3.5
		FC = 3	Hx = 1,0	NO..es>EA
W = 10		CF = 1	A = 4,2	NO..CF+C>FC
(Wv = 4)		C = 1	(A) = 2,0	YES..X+%<.70
D = 10		Cn = 0	Ad = 1,0	NO..S>3
Dd = 3		FC' = 1	(Ad) = 0,0	NO..P<3 or >8
S = 2		C'F = 0	An = 1,0	YES.Pure H <2
		C' = 0	Art = 4,4	NO..R<17
DQ		FT = 1	Ay = 0,0	4.....TOTAL
.........(FQ–)		TF = 0	Bl = 0,0	
+ = 5 (0)		T = 0	Bt = 1,1	SPECIAL SCORINGS

DQ				FORM QUALITY						

									Lv1	Lv2
+ = 5 (0)				T = 0	Bt = 1,1					
o = 14(2)				FV = 0	Cg = 1,1			DV	= 0x1	0x2
v/+ = 0 (0)				VF = 0	Cl = 0,0			INC	= 0x2	0x4
v = 4 (0)				V = 0	Ex = 0,0			DR	= 1x3	0x6
				FY = 0	Fd = 0,0			FAB	= 1x4	0x7
				YF = 0	Fi = 0,0			ALOG	= 0x5	
				Y = 0	Ge = 0,0			CON	= 0x7	
FORM QUALITY				Fr = 0	Hh = 0,1			SUM6	= 2	
				rF = 0	Ls = 0,0			WSUM6	= 7	
	FQx	FQf	MQual	SQx	FD = 0	Na = 0,0				
+	= 0	0	0	0	F = 5	Sc = 3,0				
o	= 14	1	6	1		Sx = 0,0		AB =1		CP = 0
u	= 6	3	0	1		Xy = 0,0		AG =1		MOR = 1
–	= 2	1	0	0		Id = 0,0		CFB =0		PER = 6
none	= 1	–	0	0	(2) = 5			COP =2		PSV = 0

RATIOS, PERCENTAGES, AND DERIVATIONS						
R = 23	L = 0.28			FC:CF+C =3:2	COP = 2	AG = 1
				Pure C =1	Food	= 0
EB = 6:4.0	EA = 10.0	EBPer = 1.5		Afr =0.53	Isolate/R	= 0.09
eb = 5:3	es = 8	D = 0		S =2	H:(H)Hd(Hd)	= 1:4
	Adj es = 6	Adj D = +1		Blends:R =1:23	(HHd):(AAd)	= 4:2
				CP =0	H+A:Hd + Ad	= 12:2
FM = 2	C' = 1	T = 1				
m = 3	V = 1	Y = 0				
			P = 7	Zf =11	3r+(2)/R = 0.22	
a:p = 7:4	Sum6 = 2		X+% = 0.61	Zd =-6.0	Fr+rF = 0	
Ma:Mp = 3:3	Lv2 = 0		F+% = 0.20	W:D:Dd =10:10:3	FD = 0	
2AB+Art+Ay = 10	WSum6 = 7		X-% = 0.09	W:M =10:6	An + Xy = 1	
M– = 0	Mnone = 0		S-% = 0.00	DQ+ =5	MOR = 1	
			Xu% = 0.26	DQv =4		

SCZI = 0	DEPI = 4	CDI = 1	S-CON = 4	HVI = No	OBS = No

19

The Rorschach and Diagnosis of Neurotic Conditions in Children and Adolescents: A Case Study

James F. Murray
Knoxville, TN

Psychoanalytically informed thinking about psychopathology has increasingly come to employ a model involving two different levels of personality organization that serve to identify personality features that cluster and suggest a general etiological framework (Kernberg, 1975, 1976, 1984; Stone, 1980). These models focus on a structural approach that identifies internal mental structures (or intrapsychic structures) enduring across conditions and over time (Kernberg, 1980). Psychodiagnosis has come to focus on two basic levels of analysis: a structural diagnosis involving identification of a level of personality organization, and a stylistic dimension, identifying preferred patterns of cognition, affect experience and expression, and defense processes (Murray, 1993). The first aspect of personality identifies a level of personality organization (psychotic, borderline, or neurotic). The second dimension of personality functioning involves personality style reflecting preferred type or modes of adaptation. This stylistic dimension cuts across different levels of personality organization (although important aspects of defensive functioning may vary across levels of personality organization). Acklin (1992) outlined the role of these theories in providing a framework for the use of the Rorschach in the psychodiagnostic process.

This chapter focuses on the use of the Rorschach to identify neurotic-level pathology in children and adolescents. It is a particularly difficult diagnostic process with children and adolescents. The accurate diagnosis of neurotic functioning in children requires an understanding of the two major components within the concept of *neurosis*. Neurosis is defined by two interrelated features: conflict and defense. Freud's great discovery was tracing neurotic symptomatology to the Oedipus complex—the conflictual situation in which unacceptable sexual and aggressive wishes are directed toward parental figures and are then dealt with by various defensive maneuvers (Freud, 1900/1974a,

1916–1917/1974b). In his investigation of the Oedipus complex, Freud identified sexual wishes toward the parent of the opposite sex and aggressive impulses toward the parent of the same sex as the root of neurotic symptoms. Neurotic symptoms are seen as defenses against these wishes.

Neurotic symptoms are acute or emergent defensive structures (compromise formations) that are attempts to manage internal conflict. Freud and his followers (e.g., Abraham, 1954; Fenichel, 1931) have pointed out how the oedipal conflict has important organizing influences not just in the formation of neurotic symptoms but in the structuring of character. Kernberg has gone even further, noting the structuralizing function of the oedipal experience in developing the capacity for repression-based defenses (for Kernberg the defining feature of a neurotic level of personality organization) as well as the capacity for mature love relations (1976, 1980).

Thus, a neurotic level of personality organization is marked by the presence of a particular type of dynamic experience (the oedipal conflict), and the management or resolution of this experience serves to structure major aspects of the personality. In an individual organized on a neurotic level, one finds neurotic structures linked to the oedipal experience. This linkage is important because neurotic symptoms are often found in individuals with severe character pathology, but, as Kernberg (1975) noted, the linkage to the oedipal experience is not present. In addition, components of the oedipal experience are present in individuals with severe character pathology although the oedipal experience is fragmented, incomplete, or "contaminated" by preoedipal pathology. This condition is not seen as a "full" or "true" oedipal experience because it is not the central, organizing, and structuralizing feature of the personality.

Diagnostic issues are complicated further in working with children and adolescents. Particularly in young children, the exact level of personality organization may not as yet have been established. Similarly, a well-synthesized and integrated personality style and pattern of defenses may not be fully crystallized. Consequently, the defensive functioning of children and adolescents can be more erratic, haphazard, and vulnerable to disruption. In the face of stress or trauma, children and adolescents are vulnerable to rapid and fairly intense regressions. During these regressions, relatively mature and well-organized defensive capabilities are lost or relinquished, and far more primitive and disorganized (or disorganizing) defenses are substituted. The extent to which these losses are temporary depends on the nature, severity, and duration of the stress or trauma as well as the personality resources of the child.

In addition to or in combination with stress-induced regression, normal developmental demands can contribute to regression-like experiences. Difficulty dealing with developmental demands can induce defensive reactions or shape defensive orientations that mimic defensive processes consistent with more severe character pathology. As with stress-induced regressions, in some circumstances these defenses can crystallize into defenses consistent with particular levels of pathology.

When attempting to identify neurotic level of personality organization in children or adolescents, one must consider developmental issues related to: (a) incomplete development of personality structures, (b) the vulnerability of existing structures or functions to disruption by trauma or stress (along with the potential for fairly rapid recovery when stress decreases), and (c) the potential for developmental demands to induce stress or combine with other stressors to exacerbate defensive operations, making them relatively more primitive, inflexible, or temporarily maladaptive. Thus, even more than when diagnosing adults, the diagnosis of neurotic level of personality organization in children requires a sophisticated understanding of the total personality functioning of the individual. The mere presence or absence of *neurotic defenses* can be misleading. The presence of neurotic defenses can be misleading if they are imbedded or cover more primitive defenses and personality organization. Similarly, one cannot rule out neurotic organization merely given the presence of *nonneurotic defenses* because more primitive defenses may come to the fore if the individual experiences stress or developmental demands that induce regression.

Astute diagnosticians must understand the personality and defensive operations within the individual and the function they serve. For the diagnosis of neurotic personality organization this requires first an identification of the centrality of the oedipal experience as an organizing feature of the personality, and second, a predominance of neurotic-level defenses (or the likely potential for that level of development in a younger child). Seen in Freudian terms, one must identify both the conflict (the oedipal experience) and the defense (the structural elements signifying neurotic-level defenses or personality organization).

CASE PRESENTATION

When presenting cases illustrating a diagnostic approach or identifying a particular level or type of pathology, it is tempting to present a case that is severe in nature, clear-cut, or obvious. Although there is much to be learned from these more "pure" cases, in real-life diagnostic work one often meets with cases that are less than pure and are complex, not obvious, or contradictory. This case has been selected because it allows for an examination of the complex interaction of developmental issues, family dynamics, situational stressors or crises, character style, and level of personality organization. Careful consideration of the interaction of these factors is particularly important in assessment work with children and adolescents given the potential fluidity of personality functioning and change, as well as the impact of family and developmental pressures.

To illustrate this complex interaction, a case history is provided. This is followed by two Rorschachs from the patient: the first taken at the very onset of treatment during a period of crisis and significant regression, the second approximately 1½ years into treatment. The structural variables from the two

Rorschachs are examined using the Weiner and Exner (1991) measures of personality characteristics related to changes in psychotherapy. The contents of individual responses are also examined because they are quite compelling. Finally, material from her psychotherapy is presented to help illustrate the major issues she faces and her efforts at growth, compromise, and conflict resolution.

History

Karen is a tall, thin, attractive adolescent. She was 15 years of age at the time of the first testing. Her mother has a doctorate and works as the head of a large service agency. The patient's father also has an advanced degree and has functioned as a university dean. Karen was brought in for treatment by her mother, who reported that Karen had displayed recurrent deep sadness that at times was incapacitating and led to hours of crying and regressive behavior. Karen would at times be found wrapped in an old quilt, holding an old teddy bear and crying. On one occasion she took her teddy bear to school. In the initial session Karen admitted to being quite depressed and feeling "young" during periods of stress. She stated that she had been thinking of hurting herself, gave vague thoughts involving guns or knives, and noted that she had cut on her wrist in sixth grade when depressed but stopped because it scared her.

Karen is the youngest of three children; she has two brothers who are 5 and 7 years older. They are superstars academically, attend distinguished universities, and are progressing to prestigious graduate training. Both have been very active and competitive in sports. Karen has always been very attached to her brothers, especially the younger of the two brothers. She describes herself as never playing with little children's toys and especially never playing with girl toys (I once made a joking reference to her playing with Barbies and with an icy stare she replied that she never played with Barbies). From a very early age her life focused on attaching to, pleasing, and imitating her older brothers and father. Both Karen and her mother (her mother with a sense of disappointment) stated that Karen would never do "girl things" with her mother or by herself. Karen discussed how she would pound, kick, or scream and cry at her brothers' door to be let in and allowed to hang around with her brothers and their friends. Even though there was a large age difference she would accompany her brothers when they went out with friends and even on dates. She described herself, with some disdain, as being very emotional as a child and prone to temper outbursts. During one particularly memorable outburst directed at her parents, her brother attempted to calm or reassure her and, in a fit of temper, she started throwing things around the room. An object struck him in the eye, and Karen was terrified that she may have put his eye out. No permanent damage was done, but she resolved to be more like the rest of her family and keep her emotions under control and to herself.

Karen was very active in school: a mostly A student, class president, and on several sports teams. Her only trouble in school manifested in her sarcastic irreverence to the more rigid or authoritarian teachers and her tendency to get into trouble for vociferously defending students she felt were being treated unfairly.

In the family, the father was idealized and fairly dominant. He was very active and sometimes intrusive or disruptive in watching the children's sports activities and serving as a backseat coach. He also set high standards for academic achievement and social conduct. Karen described her mother as distant and maintained they were never close.

With the advantage of hindsight, it is easy to see that the immediate difficulties began a little over a year before the patient presented for treatment. Karen was in a distant foreign country on a summer exchange program. Her parents had been talking about having to move because her father was seeking a new position. Suddenly, the regular letters from home stopped, and just as Karen began to worry, she received a letter from her father stating that he would be moving to a distant city but that she and her mother would remain at home; no further information or explanation was offered. Karen assumed that her parents were divorcing because she viewed them as distant and they fought frequently.

Karen returned home, and upon seeing her parents, was distraught. They were puzzled and surprised to learn of her concerns about a divorce. To Karen the message from her parents was "What's the big deal . . . nothing's wrong, no divorce, no problems, your father is just moving away for 2 years, he'll still be around some weekends." Although Karen showed little overt reaction at this point, it is clear the loss of her two brothers to college followed by the loss of her father began to weigh on her.

In looking at her periods of regression, it became apparent that the angry/regressive episodes occurred or worsened during father's weekends at home. As she began to talk in therapy, she would describe her father as distant, not knowing how to relate to the family, and acting "fake." She noted that he was increasingly self-absorbed and would ignore Karen's attempts to talk about her life, while focusing on discussions of the important people he met or worked with and the expensive restaurants he ate in every night. Karen began to become vaguely aware of her anger toward her father but feared expressing it out of concern that he would react with disapproval or further withdrawal and lack of availability. Consequently, she began to withdraw into her room alone to cry or arrange to be out with friends and unavailable to father.

To condense a year of treatment, I highlight the major issues:

1. Exploration of identification with brothers and father.

2. Exploration of a sense of distance from and lack of identification with mother—although, as we explored this issue, her increasing disillusionment with father and mother's increased sensitivity and responsiveness led to more enjoyment of mother and increased identification with her.

3. Exploration of how the intensity and richness of her emotional experience made her different from her family—how this emotionalism seemed to

be frowned upon by her family, and how family members tend to deny, avoid, or inhibit emotional expression, and how Karen followed suit.

4. The relationship with her father completely fell apart as he became increasingly more distant and self–absorbed, then finally announced that he had been having an ongoing affair since moving, planned a permanent life with this married woman, and intended to function as a father-figure for this woman's daughters. Karen's anger and alienation increased as father would repeatedly voice surprise at the family's anger—he had expected them to be happy that he had found a new life that made him happy.

Rorschach Analysis

Karen's Rorschach is examined using the Rorschach measures of personality characteristics related to changes in psychotherapy developed by Weiner and Exner (1991) and employed previously for case analysis (Murray, 1993). Weiner and Exner identified Rorschach variables reflecting changes in psychotherapy that cluster in the following groups:

1. Stress
2. Problems With Experience of Self
3. Comfort in Interpersonal Relations
4. Problems in Modulating Affect
5. Ideational Difficulties

The Rorschach of Karen taken at the onset of treatment is compared with the testing approximately 1½ years into therapy. The analysis involves primarily the features as reflected in the Weiner and Exner categories (see Table 19.1), but content on selected responses is also examined because the changes in this area are particularly telling. Comparisons to normative samples employ Exner's (1990) tables.

Stress

Probably the most striking factor here is that she fails to trip any of the indicators in the Stress category. This is particularly remarkable in the first testing given her overt depression, her periods of regression, and her angry outbursts or withdrawal. In fact D and CDI are not even close to reaching significant levels in either of the two testings. The main reason for this is evident in No. 3. EA in the first testing is 16.5, which is greater than 2 standard deviations above the age mean. The EA in the second testing was 12.0, which is greater than 1 standard deviation above the age mean.

Clearly, Karen has significantly more personality resources than the average adolescent her age. Although she certainly has her vulnerabilities, her ability to maintain a nearly straight A average at a competitive school, function

TABLE 19.1
Rorschach Measures in First and Second Testing: Rorschach Measures of Personality Characteristics Related to Changes in Psychotherapy

Characteristic	First Testing	Second Testing
Stress		
1. $D < 0$: subjectively felt stress resulting from inadequate resources to meet demands	$D = +1$ –	$D = 0$ –
2. *Adj D* = –3: persistently felt distress extending beyond transient or situational difficulties in meeting demands	$Adj\ D = +2$ –	$Adj\ D = +1$ –
3. $EA < 7$: limited resources for implementing deliberate problem-solving strategies	$EA = 16.5$	$EA = 12.0$
4. $CDI > 3$: general deficit in capacities for coping with demands of daily living	$CDI = 2$ –	$CDI = 1$ –
Difficulty dealing effectively with experience		
1. Ambitent: lack of commitment to a cohesive coping style, resulting in a sense of uncertainty	$EB = 12:4.5$ –	$EB = 12:1$ –
2. $Zd < -3.0$: inattention to nuances of one's experience, superficial scanning hastily drawn conclusions	$Zd = +0.5$ –	$Zd = +7.0$ –
3. $Lambda > .99$: narrow, limited frames of reference; overly simplistic response	$L = .36$	$L = .38$
4. $X+\% < 70$: inability/disinclination to perceive objects and events as most people would	$X+\% = 63\%$ +	$X+\% = 68\%$ +
5. $X-\% > 20$: inaccurate perception and faulty anticipation of consequences	$X-\% = 20\%$ +	$X-\% = 18\%$ –
Problems with experience of self		
1. $Fr + rF > 0$: narcissistic glorification and externalization of blame	$r = 1$ +	$r = 1$ +
2. $3r + (2)/R > .43$: excessive self-focusing and self-preoccupation	$EI = .40$ –	$EI = .55$ +
3. $3r = (2)/R < .33$: low regard for self in comparison with others	–	–
4. $FD > 2$: unusual extent of introspection	$FD = 4$ +	$FD = 2$ –
Comfort in interpersonal relations		
1. $p > a + 1$: passivity and avoidance of initiative and responsibility	$a{:}p = 9{:}12$ +	$a{:}p = 17{:}5$ –
2. $T = 0$: lack of expectation or seeking of close, intimate, nurturant, mutually supportive relationships	$T = 0$ +	$T = 1$ –
3. $T > 1$: unmet needs for closeness and comfort, leading to feelings of loneliness and deprivation	–	–
4. Pure $H < 2$: disinterest in and/or difficulty identifying with others	$H = 6$ –	$H = 4$ –
5. $H < [(H) + Hd + (Hd)]$: uneasiness in relatedness with real, live, fully functional people	6:9 +	4:10 +
Problems in modulating affect pleasurably and sufficiently		
1. $SumSh > FM + m$: negative emotional experience: dysphoria, loneliness, helplessness, and/or self-denigration	3:9 –	8:6 +
2. $DEPI = 5$: depressive concerns	$DEPI = 4$ –	$DEPI = 2$ –
3. $DEPI > 5$: likelihood of diagnosable depressive disorder		
4. $Afr < .50$: avoidance of emotional interchange and lack of involvement in affect-laden situations	$Afr = .36$ +	$Afr = .38$ +
5. $CF + C > FC + 1$: overly itense feelings and unreserved expression of affect	3:3 –	0:1 –

(continued)

TABLE 19.1 *(Continued)*

Characteristic	First Testing	Second Testing
Ideational difficulties		
1. *Sum6 Sp Sc* > 6: loose and arbitrary thinking	*Sum6* = 4	*Sum6* = 3
2. *M–* > 0: strange conceptions regarding human experience	*M–* = 2 −	*M–* = 3 −
3. *Mp* > *Ma*: excessive escapist fantasy substituted for constructive planning	+ 8:4 +	+ 3:10 −
4. *Intellect* > 5: excessive reliance on intellectualization	+ *Intel* = 4 −	*Intel* = 1 −

Note. + signifies presence of variable at pathological level. − signifies absence of variable at pathological level. Form adapted from Weiner and Exner (1991).

actively and successfully in social settings, and compete in two varsity sports seem to be genuine accomplishments and probably well-integrated capacities rather than some narcissistic shell in the form of a facade or false self-configuration.

There is a second factor as well. Given her positive *HVI*, the weighting of *EA* so heavily toward the *M* side, and her low *Afr*, it is reasonable to conclude that she is someone who is quite guarded affectively and interpersonally. She is probably fairly contained or constricted most of the time, and particularly when she is being defensive and defenses are not overwhelmed. This kind of hypercontrol allows for few avenues for venting of anxiety, dysphoria, and anger. Consequently, stress is likely to be contained for long periods of time and then will trigger regression rather than behavioral dyscontrol in the form of socially conflictual behavior. This pattern is further evidence of a neurotic level of personality organization because it reflects a neurotic style of inhibition rather than impulse-ridden action.

Difficulty in Dealing Effectively With Experience

The first item in this category is the Ambitent measure, and there is no problem here because she has developed a sophisticated and consistent coping style that is heavily weighted to the ideational side. Although the *EB* ratio of 12:1 in the second testing raises some concern about affective constriction and possible defensive inflexibility, a close examination of both protocols reveals considerable emotional richness.

The second measure, *Zd*, is also not positive, indicating that she is not inattentive to her internal and external world. In fact, her positive *HVI* in the first testing and her second testing *Zd* of + 7.0 suggests that she is somewhat hyperattuned to the world. In addition, Measure 3, *Lambda*, is also not positive: She is clearly not a simplistic or concretely self-focused individual.

Measures 4 and 5 involve $X+\%$ and $X-\%$. The $X+\%$ measure is positive in both the first and the second testings. In the first testing $X+\% = 63\%$, in the second $X+\% = 68\%$. Although these are not outstanding levels, she gave 30 responses in the first testing, and increases in R tend to decrease $X+\%$; and in the second testing $X+\% = 68\%$, just under the limit.

The $X-\%$ was positive in the first testing, and this was of some concern given the diagnostic question of suicide potential. However, there was evidence of a decreased tendency for severe perceptual distortion with the negative finding in the second testing. The major clue regarding the first testing lies in the number of blends. In the first testing she had 9 blends out of 30 responses, with 3 blends of 3 or more determinants. In the second testing she had 12 blends in 22 responses, with 2 blends of 3 or more determinants. Clearly, Karen has a lot on her mind and a great deal pressing her. This tends to make things inordinately complex, and, as a result, she sometimes has a hard time viewing things simply and accurately.

Problems With Experience of Self

This area is obviously a very important category for Karen. She has or approaches reflection responses in both testings. Although these may not technically be reflection responses (she describes two people "mirroring each other" or "playing the mirror game"), the cognitive–perceptual process and the underlying process appear to be the same. As Peterson has noted, often when a determinant is on the borderline of scorability, it indicates that the patient is struggling at the border of the personality process associated with that determinant. To look at the issue of narcissistic or self issues, it is helpful to examine the content of a sequence of responses over the two testings (see Appendixes E and F). This helps to flesh out our understanding of her sense of self and others.

Karen's responses to Cards I and II across the two testings are quite powerful in describing her experience of self and others, and very revealing of a process of change. She is strikingly consistent in the themes and images across Card I and across her responses to Card II.

In the first testing, she sees the two figures disappearing, going away, fading away off into space, and a body that was once there but is going off into space. One sees here a repeated description of dissolution and the loss of a sense of self. She seems to equate loss or separation ("going away") with dissolution of self.

In the second testing, one sees a similar response but without this sense of dissolution or loss of self. Ego boundaries are firmer, but one still sees peculiar or somewhat primitive thoughts about people and relationships. She sees angels—implying fantasy-based images of people—and she notes that two figures are connected in some unspecified fashion. The transition in this sequence of responses suggests that she remains fairly primitive or immature in her conceptualization of people, continues to be highly sensitive to separations, but that these issues no longer grossly intrude on or impair her sense of self.

Her first response to Card II is essentially the same response across both testings. It is a very intriguing response and, although it may not technically be a reflection response, it is treated as such because if it is not, it is about as close as one can get. The narcissistic element of mirroring is clearly delineated here by the patient herself. There is great attention to the dress, detail, and posturing of the people. In addition, the relatedness of the two figures takes place in the context of a game in which people observe, imitate, and blur identities.

Looking at the second measure in this category reveals an elevated Egocentricity Index. It is close to significant in the first testing and is positive in the second. This is no surprise because Karen remains very intensely focused on herself. The nature of this focus and changes in this focus through psychotherapy appear elsewhere.

Moving on to the fourth measure ($FD > 2$), it is positive in the first testing ($FD = 4$), and there is also a Vista (V) response. This elevation in FD and the presence of a V response reflects an intense, painful, and probably disruptive self-focus and self-preoccupation. However, in the second testing, the FD declines to 2 (below the pathological level) and the V drops out. This suggests that the patient's self-focus has become much less depressive and disruptive.

In looking at the section on Experience of Self, it is clear that Karen remains quite focused on herself, and she does tend to regulate self-esteem through the reactions of or via identifications with others. However, neither the Rorschach data nor history/therapy material suggest that she views others as what Self Psychologists would term *selfobjects*. There is not the dehumanizing aspect in her relatedness: She consistently sees others as full and complete objects, and by far the most pathological relatedness occurs in the context of her relationship with her father.

Comfort in Interpersonal Relations

The first measure in this category is $p > a + 1$. This measure is positive in the first testing and reflects Karen's sense of helplessness, her passivity, her high level of dependency, and consequently her vulnerability to regression.

This tendency is also reflected in Measure 3 in the Ideational Difficulties section: the $Mp > Ma$. This measure reflects excessive escapist fantasy substituted for constructive planning. In the first testing her performance on this measure trips the "Snow White Syndrome" interpretation (Exner, 1991), suggesting:

1. An abuse of fantasy in the service of denying reality.
2. A self-imposed helplessness that induces dependency on others.
3. A vulnerability to dependency-induced manipulation of and by others.

4. A particular vulnerability to this passive–dependent–avoidant style given her highly ideational orientation.

In the second testing, both of these measures are negative, and this appears to be the most significant product of her psychotherapy. With a direct focus on her developmental experience with her family, its impact on her, and a focus on her own understanding/experience of events as well as her own resources, her sense of self has been firmed up to a large extent independent of her immediate relatedness with her parents. She is now much more active, capable, confident, and competent.

The second variable in this cluster involves the Texture response $(T = 0)$. In the first testing she was quite guarded in her emotional attachments or involvements, largely in defense of her sense of vulnerability due to dependency. In fact, early on in treatment she spoke of breaking up with a boyfriend who was warm and supportive because she feared getting too dependent on him. The $T = 0$ measure was negative in the second testing, indicating she is relatively more comfortable with emotional involvement with others, although she waited until her last response to give a rare texture response on Card X.

Variable 4 in this cluster is negative; she is in fact quite interested in and identifies quite easily with others. However, Variable 5 (*Pure H* < *Non-Pure H*) is positive over both testings, indicating that although she is interested in people, this interest is often immature and tends to be somewhat regressively based on fantasy or wish.

Problems in Modulating Affect

The first variable (*SumSh* > *FM* + *m*) is negative in the first testing, suggesting that even though she is in some pain, it is not overwhelming, and furthermore that the dysphoria that does exist is probably circumscribed to areas of self and identity. This is also supported by the finding that the *DEPI* = 5 variable is negative in both testings, although somewhat elevated in the first. Overall test results suggest that depressive experience is associated mainly with self-esteem and object loss issues.

The *Afr* < .50 measure is positive in both testings and reflects her affective guardedness. She is very careful about emotional displays, and control or denial of emotion is highly valued. Further understanding of her handling of emotion is revealed in the fifth variable in this cluster, *CF* + *C* > *FC* + 1. One can see by this measure that she is quite constricted and appears to become more emotionally constricted over the course of treatment.

Ideational Difficulties

The first measure in this category is negative because she manifests no problems in logical reasoning and conceptualization. However, the second measure ($M-> 0$) is positive in both testings, reflecting her potential for distorted or confused thinking about people. It is of some concern that she retains the vulnerability to distorted thinking at the time of the second testing. This is probably associated with the third variable in this cluster, $Mp > Ma$. Karen is oriented to more passive and dependent involvements that often involve fantasy or fantasized identifications. As discussed previously, this measure probably reflects her relationship with her father and secondarily her brothers, and also helps to explain her distorted thinking about people. The last measure, $Intellect > 5$, is not positive on either testing because this is not her preferred defensive style.

Recent Psychotherapy Sessions

In one recent session, Karen described an episode in which she publicly humiliated her father. They were at one of her games and father had the nerve to sit with the other parents of the team members and act as if he was just being a good father and nothing was wrong. This is a tight-knit group, and many of her father's friends and colleagues were there. Within earshot of this group Karen confronted her father and once again berated him for what he had done. She spoke loudly and was crying, which created quite a scene. Karen's father anxiously eyed the other parents and repeatedly asked her to go somewhere private to discuss things. Karen refused, stating they were going to talk right then and there. Karen recalled a similar occurrence some years back while in junior high school. On that occasion (again a scene in school and in front of other parents) she was struck at the time by her father's sense of vulnerability to what others thought about him and her sense of power in using this against him. In session she went on to talk about how she is hurt that father was upset not by what she thought about him (he had disappointed, rejected, and abandoned her) but by what others might think of him (he might get embarrassed).

Through interpretive comments, I noted the following:

1. Her apparently accurate reading of father's narcissistic vulnerability.
2. Her sensitivity to that in father being based on similar features within her.
3. She is like father in that she feels humiliated by father's rejection/abandonment.
4. She wanted to show father what public humiliation felt like, essentially to do to him what she perceived him doing to her.

In a subsequent session, she talked about her concern over the destructiveness of her anger, her fear that she would drive him away. She tearfully stated that she loves him because he's been so important to her, yet hates him because he won't acknowledge that he's hurt her. Crying she stated, "Yet he's the only father I'll ever have . . . I'll never have another . . . I don't want to lose him."

In a later session, she talked about how her father always presented a perfect and moral image, how she "fell for it" (i.e., she attempted to live up to this standard); suddenly it's gone (father's perfect and moral image), and she doesn't know what's real and what's "fake–image." She notes that her father hasn't seen her or called in a long time; her anger has driven him away, she misses him, and maybe this is what she deserves for being such a bad daughter.

I made the following series of interpretations to her: There seemed to be some validity to her statement about father promoting an image. This idealized image seemed to have served a number of functions. First, it was the image of father, and father was lovable because he was or lived up to that image. Second, she loved her father by attempting to live up to that image (i.e., by identifying with father). Third, she was lovable (to father) to the extent that she lived up to that idealized image. Finally, she was good or lovable to herself to the extent that her sense of self lived up to that image and tied in with father. Consequently, the loss of father's idealized image threatened the loss of father, the loss of a positive image of father, her sense of being lovable to father, and her own sense of self.

This interpretation begins to set the stage for future interpretations along more oedipal lines. Karen's difficulties consist of a condensation of oedipal and narcissistic pathology. In essence, Karen appears to have had a mother she experienced as somewhat distant or unavailable. This led to a premature and overly intense investment in father (and by displacement onto brothers). This began a contamination of narcissistic issues with oedipal issues. Karen's father was a highly narcissistic individual who promoted or exacerbated this process, and ultimately the crisis occurred in early to middle adolescence—just when identity issues are at the fore. So we see a combination of family constellation factors, possible individual pathology within parents, developmental pressures, and personality features combining to create this condensation of oedipal and narcissistic disturbance. From working with Karen in therapy, I believe that narcissistic pathology is largely a reaction to father, a result of developmental forces, and increasingly a defense against oedipal wishes. It does not seem deeply entrenched in her personality functioning, and Rorschach analysis helps point that out.

This case illustrates the need for the psychodiagnostician to understand personality functioning (from research and theoretical perspectives) as well as the Rorschach. It is imperative that diagnosticians and therapists place Rorschach interpretation in the context of an overall understanding of personality dynamics. A simple sign or pattern approach is not likely to be successful in more complex or demanding cases. A dialectic between the empiricism of the Comprehensive System and theoretical approaches to understanding personality creates a natural process of checks and balances. This type of approach is particularly necessary for the diagnosis of neurotic states in children and adolescents given the complicated interaction between personality and development.

REFERENCES

Abraham, K. (1954). Character-formation on the genital level of libido-development. In K. Abraham (Ed.), *Selected papers of Karl Abraham* (pp. 407–417). New York: Basic Books. (Original work published 1925)

Acklin, M. (1992). Psychodiagnosis of personality structure: Psychotic personality organization. *Journal of Personality Assessment, 58,* 454–463.

Exner, J. E. (1990). *A Rorschach workbook for the comprehensive system* (3rd ed.). Asheville, NC: Rorschach Workshops.

Exner, J. E. (1991). *The Rorschach: A comprehensive system: Vol. 2. Interpretation* (2nd ed.). New York: Wiley.

Fenichel, O. (1953). Specific forms of the Oedipus complex. In H. Fenichel & D. Rapaport (Eds.), *The collected papers of Otto Fenichel: First series* (pp. 204–220). New York: Norton.

Freud, S. (1974a). The interpretation of dreams. In J. Strachey (Ed. and Trans.), *The standard edition of the complete psychological works of Sigmund Freud* (Vols. 4 & 5, pp. 1–627). London: Hogarth. (Original work published 1900)

Freud S. (1974b). Introductory lectures on psychoanalysis (rev. ed.). In J. Strachey (Ed. and Trans.), *The standard edition of the complete psychological works of Sigmund Freud* (Vols. 15 & 16, pp. 1–483). London: Hogarth. (Original work published 1916–1917)

Kernberg, O. (1975). *Borderline conditions and pathological narcissism.* New York: Aronson.

Kernberg, O. (1976). *Object relations theory and clinical psychoanalysis.* New York: Aronson.

Kernberg, O. (1980). *Internal world and external reality.* New York: Aronson.

Kernberg, O. (1984). *Severe personality disorders.* New Haven, CT: Yale University Press.

Murray, J. F. (1993). The Rorschach search for the borderline Holy Grail: An examination of personality structure, personality style, and situation. *Journal of Personality Assessment, 61,* 342–357.

Stone, M. (1980). *The borderline syndromes: Constitution, personality, and adaptations.* New York: McGraw-Hill.

Weiner, I. B., & Exner, J. E. (1991). Rorschach changes in long-term and short-term psychotherapy. *Journal of Personality Assessment, 56,* 451–465.

Card	No.	Loc.	#	Determinant(s)	(2)	Content(s)	Pop Z	Special Scores
I	1	W+	1	Mp.mpo		Hd, Cg	4.0	
	2	WSo	1	Fo		(Hd), Art	1.0	
	3	Wo	1	Fo		A	P 1.0	
II	4	W+	1	Fr.Ma.FCo		H, Cg	4.5	COP
	5	WSo	1	Mp.mp–		Hd	4.5	MOR
III	6	WS+	1	CF.mp–		Hd, Bl	5.5	MOR
	7	D+		Mao	2	H	P 3.0	COP
	8	Do		FCo		Cg		
IV	9	Wo	1	FD–		Ad, Art, Sc	2.0	PER
	10	W+	1	Mpo		H, Cg	P 4.0	
	11	Do		FMa.FD–	2	Ad		
V	12	Wo	1	Fo		A	P 1.0	MOR
	13	W+	1	Mpo		H, Cg	2.5	
	14	W+	1	Mp.FMao	2	H, A	5.0	AG
VI	15	Wo	1	Fo		(A)	P 2.5	MOR, DV
	16	Wo	1	Fo		(Ad), Hh	P 2.5	
	17	W+	1	FD–		A, Id	2.5	DV
	18	Do		Fo		Ay, Art		
VII	19	W+	1	Mpo	2	(Hd)	P 3.0	
	20	W+	1	Mao	2	H	P 3.0	
	21	WSv	1	mpu		Id		
	22	Do		Fu	2	Hh		
VIII	23	W+	1	CF.C'Fo		Fi, Hh	4.5	
	24	W+	1	FMao		A, Ls	P 4.5	
IX	25	D+		Mao	2	(H), Cg	P 4.5	COP, AG
	26	DS+		Mp.VF.FD.CFu		Hd, (Hd), Id	4.5	
X	27	Do		Mp–		(Hd)		DR
	28	D+		FMa.FC.FC'u	2	A	P 4.5	INC
	29	Do		Fu	2	A		
	30	Do		FMao		A		

Summary of Approach

I:W.WS.W	VI:W.W.W.D
II:W.WS	VII:W.W.WS.D
III:WS.D.D	VIII:W.W
IV:W.W.D	IX:D.DS
V:W.W.W	X:D.D.D.D

315

APPENDIX B
First Testing Rorschach Structural Summary

LOCATION FEATURES	DETERMINANTS BLENDS	SINGLE	CONTENTS	S-CONSTELLATION
				YES..FV + VF + V + FD > 2
			H = 6,0	YES..Col-Shd Bl>0
Zf = 22	M.m	M = 7	(H) = 1,0	NO..Ego<.31,>.44
ZSum = 74.0	Fr.M.FC	FM = 2	Hd = 4,0	YES..MOR>3
ZEst = 73.5	M.m	m = 1	(Hd) = 3,1	NO..Zd > ± 3.5
	CF.m	FC = 1	Hx = 0,0	NO..es>EA
W = 19	FM.FD	CF = 0	A = 7,1	NO..CF+C>FC
(Wv = 1)	M.FM	C = 0	(A) = 1,0	YES..X+%<.70
D = 11	CF.C'F	Cn = 0	Ad = 2,0	YES..S>3
Dd = 0	M.VF.FD.CF	FC' = 0	(Ad) = 1,0	YES..P<3 or >8
S = 5	FM.FC.FC'	C'F = 0	An = 0,0	NO..Pure H <2
		C' = 0	Art = 0,3	NO..R<17
DQ		FT = 0	Ay = 1,0	6.....TOTAL
.........(FQ–)		TF = 0	Bl = 0,1	
+ = 15(2)		T = 0	Bt = 0,0	SPECIAL SCORINGS
o = 14(4)		FV = 0	Cg = 1,5	Lvl Lv2
v/+ = 0 (0)		VF = 0	Cl = 0,0	DV = 2x1 0x2
v = 1 (0)		V = 0	Ex = 0,0	INC = 1x2 0x4
		FY = 0	Fd = 0,0	DR = 1x3 0x6
		YF = 0	Fi = 1,0	FAB = 0x4 0x7
		Y = 0	Ge = 0,0	ALOG = 0x5
FORM QUALITY		Fr = 0	Hh = 1,2	CON = 0x7
		rF = 0	Ls = 0,1	SUM6 = 4
FQx FQf MQual SQx		FD = 2	Na = 0,0	WSUM6 = 7
+ = 0 0 0 0		F = 8	Sc = 0,1	
o = 19 6 9 1			Sx = 0,0	AB =0 CP = 0
u = 5 2 1 2			Xy = 0,0	AG =2 MOR = 4
– = 6 0 2 2			Id = 1,2	CFB =0 PER = 1
none = 0 – 0 0		(2) = 9		COP =3 PSV = 0

RATIOS, PERCENTAGES, AND DERIVATIONS

R = 30	L = 0.36	FC:CF+C =3:3 COP = 3 AG = 2	
		Pure C =0 Food = 0	
EB = 12:4.5	EA = 16.5 EBPer = 2.7	Afr =0.36 Isolate/R = 0.03	
eb = 9:3	es = 12 D = +1	S =5 H:(H)Hd(Hd) = 6:9	
	Adj es = 9 Adj D = +2	Blends:R =9:30 (HHd):(AAd) = 5:2	
		CP =0 H+A:Hd + Ad = 16:11	
FM = 5	C' = 2 T = 0		
m = 4	V = 1 Y = 0		
		P = 11 Zf =22 3r+(2)/R = 0.40	
a:p = 9:12	Sum6 = 4	X+% = 0.63 Zd = +0.5 Fr+rF = 1	
Ma:Mp = 4:8	Lv2 = 0	F+% = 0.75 W:D:Dd =19:11:0 FD = 4	
2AB+Art+Ay = 4	WSum6 = 7	X–% = 0.20 W:M =19:12 An + Xy = 0	
M– = 2	Mnone = 0	S–% = 0.33 DQ+ =15 MOR = 4	
		Xu% = 0.17 DQv =1	
SCZI = 2	DEPI = 4	CDI = 2 S-CON = 6 HVI = Yes OBS = No	

APPENDIX C
Second Testing Sequence of Scores

Card	No.	Loc.	#	Determinant(s)	(2)	Content(s)	Pop Z	Special Scores
I	1	W+	1	Ma–po	2	(H), H, Cg	4.0	
	2	WSo	1	Fo		(Hd)	1.0	
II	3	W+	1	Ma.Fro		(H)	4.5	COP
	4	DdSo		F–		Hd	4.5	
	5	DdSo		Ma.FD–		Hd	4.5	
III	6	W+	1	Ma.mpo	2	H, Cg, Hh	P 5.5	FAB
	7	DdSo		FC'.FY.Mp–		(Hd), Art	4.5	
IV	8	W+	1	Mp.FYo		H, Cg	P 4.0	
	9	W+	1	Mao		H, Id	P 4.0	
V	10	Wo	1	Fo		A	P 1.0	
	11	W+	1	Fma.Mau	2	(H), A	5.0	INC, COP
VI	12	Wo	1	Fo		A	P 2.5	
	13	Wo	1	Fo		(A)	2.5	
	14	W+	1	FMa.FDu		A, Na	2.5	
VII	15	W+	1	Ma.YFo	2	H, Na, Cg	P 2.5	
	16	WS/	1	Fu		Id	4.0	
VIII	17	D+		FMao	2	A	P 3.0	
	18	D+		ma.CFo		Sc, Fi	3.0	
	19	D+		FMa–po	2	A	P 3.0	COP
IX	20	D+		Ma.mao	2	(H)	P 4.5	AG, COP
	21	DdSo		Ma.YF–	2	Hd	5.0	
X	22	W+	1	Ma.FMa.FTo	2	(A)	P 5.5	COP, FAB

Summary of Approach

I:W.WS	VI:W.W.W
II:W.DdS.DdS	VII:W.WS
III:W.DdS	VIII:D.D.D
IV:W.W	IX:D.DdS
V:W.W	X:W

APPENDIX D
Second Testing Rorschach Structural Summary

LOCATION FEATURES	DETERMINANTS BLENDS	SINGLE	CONTENTS	S-CONSTELLATION
			H = 3,1	NO..FV + VF + V + FD > 2
Zf = 22	M.Fr	M = 2	(H) = 5,0	NO..Col-Shd Bl>0
ZSum = 80.5	M.FD	FM = 2	Hd = 3,0	YES..Ego<.31,>.44
ZEst = 73.5	M.m	m = 0	(Hd) = 2,0	NO..MOR>3
	FC'FY.m	FC = 0	Hx = 0,0	YES..Zd > ± 3.5
W = 14	M.FY	CF = 0	A = 5,1	YES..es>EA
(Wv = 0)	FM.M	C = 0	(A) = 2,0	YES..CF+C>FC
D = 4	FM.FD	Cn = 0	Ad = 0,0	YES..X+%<.70
Dd = 4	M.YF	FC' = 0	(Ad) = 0,0	YES..S>3
S = 6	m.CF	C'F = 0	An = 0,0	YES..P<3 or >8
	M.m	C' = 0	Art = 0,1	NO.Pure H <2
DQ	M.YF	FT = 0	Ay = 0,0	NO..R<17
..........(FQ–)	M.FM.FT	TF = 0	Bl = 0,1	7.....TOTAL
+ = 13(0)		T = 0	Bt = 0,0	
o = 8 (4)		FV = 0	Cg = 0,4	SPECIAL SCORINGS

							Lv1		Lv2
v/+ = 1 (0)				VF = 0	Cl = 0,0	DV	= 0x1		0x2
v = 0 (0)				V = 0	Ex = 0,0	INC	= 1x2		0x4
				FY = 0	Fd = 0,0	DR	= 0x3		0x6
				YF = 0	Fi = 0,1	FAB	= 2x4		0x7
				Y = 0	Ge = 0,0	ALOG	= 0x5		
FORM QUALITY				Fr = 0	Hh = 0,1	CON	= 0x7		
				rF = 0	Ls = 0,0	SUM6	= 3		
	FQx	FQf MQual	SQx	FD = 0	Na = 0,2	WSUM6	= 10		
+ = 0	0	0	0	F = 6	Sc = 1,0				
o = 15	4	8	1		Sx = 0,0	AB =0		CP = 0	
u = 3	1	1	1		Xy = 0,0	AG =1		MOR = 0	
– = 4	1	3	4		Id = 1,1	CFB =0		PER = 0	
none = 0	–	0	0	(2) = 9		COP =5		PSV = 0	

RATIOS, PERCENTAGES, AND DERIVATIONS

R = 22	L = 0.38		FC:CF+C =0:1	COP = 5	AG = 1
			Pure C =0	Food	= 0
EB = 12:1.0	EA = 13.0	EBPer = 12.0	Afr =0.38	Isolate/R	= 0.18
eb = 8:6	es = 14	D = 0	S =6	H:(H)Hd(Hd)	= 4:10
	Adj es = 9	Adj D = +1	Blends:R =12:22	(HHd):(AAd)	= 7:2
			CP =0	H+A:Hd + Ad	= 17:5
FM = 5	C' = 1	T = 1			
m = 3	V = 0	Y = 4			
			P = 10	Zf =22	3r+(2)/R = 0.55
a:p	= 17:5	Sum6 = 3	X+% = 0.68	Zd = +7.0	Fr+rF = 1
Ma:Mp	= 10:3	Lv2 = 0	F+% = 0.67	W:D:Dd =14:4:4	FD = 2
2AB+Art+Ay = 1		WSum6 = 10	X–% = 0.18	W:M = 14:12	An + Xy = 0
M–	= 3	Mnone = 0	S–% = 1.00	DQ+ =13	MOR = 0
			Xu% = 0.14	DQv =0	

SCZI = 2	DEPI = 2	CDI = 1	S-CON = 7	HVI = No	OBS = No

First testing

1. S: It ll 2 peo with a . . . in the center and they're kinda disappearing off to the side. . . . Kinda going away

1. S: 2 hnds raised abv thr hds & bodies coming down & thrs a skirt & ths part. Thy're in thr but thy're fading away . . . off into space—going away.
E: Going away?
S: Disappearing bc u cnt see all the body tht was once thr body its going off into space.

Second testing

1. S: ll 2 peo here—mb angels bc thy hv wings—and 2 more peo in the center && thy're kinda pulling thm away.

1. E: here are 2 peo on the outside, angels & have wings on the end—peo in the center hnds are up—Thy'd b wmn, thy hv skirts. Thy're connected & ll thy're (angels) going away.

First testing

1. S: Ths ll 2 peo dressed in costumes sitng @ a tbl—ll thy're mirroring eo—Tht little game whr u sit across frm eo &

1. S: These are 2 peo—hds, bodies, & ft—ll costume bc dnt normally c red headed peo—here's arms & thy're alike & arms togthr going (gestures).

Second testing

1. S: Ths ll 2 mimes sitng. Thy're across frm eo playing tht mirror game—Thy imitate eo.

1. S: Th hds, costumes, legs together—ll came whr thy sit across frm eo & thy do it simultaneously bc thr faces ll thy hav the same expression on thm.

20

Bulimia As a Neurotic Symptom: A Rorschach Case Study

James H. Kleiger
Menninger Clinic, Topeka, Kansas

Over the last 25 years, diagnosticians have shifted attention and interest away from the assessment of classical neuroses to the study of more primitive types of personality formation. The Rorschach literature has captured this shift in a number of works that have focused almost exclusively on structural aspects of the borderline and narcissistic personality (Acklin, 1993; Kwawer, Lerner, Lerner, & Sugarman, 1980; Lerner & Lerner, 1988), or the psychotic level of personality organization (Acklin, 1992; Holzman, Shenton, & Solovay, 1986; Johnston & Holzman, 1979; Smith, 1983). Certainly the apparent disappearance of neurotic conditions from the Rorschach literature reflects the "retirement" of this term from official diagnostic classification (American Psychiatric Association, 1980). However, the scrapping of the label has also led to a tendency to ignore, or worse, deinvent, the concept of neurosis or neurotic level of functioning. This unfortunate tendency has led diagnosticians to view almost all psychopathology through the lenses of primitive defenses and internalized object relations, deficits in self-cohesion, or weaknesses in the structure of the ego. Such conceptual and diagnostic pigeon-holing may lead clinicians to overlook dynamic conflicts and ego strengths that have implications for making informed treatment decisions about a particular patient. Assessing treatment implications has always been part of psychodiagnostic work; however, in an era of shrinking mental health insurance benefits, it is even more critical to know which patients may be capable of utilizing an aggressive, fast-paced, short-term dynamic psychotherapy or tolerating the intensity of a long-term psychoanalysis.

Earlier applications of the Rorschach to the study of psychoneurosis appeared in the literature in the 1940s, 1950s, and 1960s (Rapaport, Gill, & Schafer, 1968; Schafer, 1948, 1954). Schafer (1948), in particular, applied psychoanalytic ego psychology to the study of several types of neurotic conditions. Although somewhat outdated by today's diagnostic nomenclature, his diagnostic summaries and case studies provide a useful conceptual frame

321

for making test-based inferences about the structural and dynamic characteristics of classical neurotic conditions. More recently, Acklin (1994), Peterson (1994), Meloy and Gacono (1994), and Murray (1994) resurrected the
neurotic concept, as viewed by the Rorschach, by placing it in the context of
a contemporary psychoanalytic diagnostic framework (Kernberg, 1976, 1984)
and by utilizing a psychodiagnostic strategy that integrates idiographic and
nomothetic approaches to assessment. Their studies on the neurotic level of
personality organization will hopefully lead to a revival of interest in this
frequently overlooked realm of personality functioning and encourage users
of the Rorschach and other psychological tests to employ a similar integrative
strategy that combines structural, object relational, and dynamic perspectives
in diagnostic work.

What follows is a Rorschach case study of an eating disordered patient with
an underlying neurotic structure, whose ego strengths and dynamic conflicts,
identified in the testing, alerted treaters to the fact that she could tolerate a
brief expressive psychotherapy process. Following a presentation of the patient's clinical background, conceptually meaningful characteristics of neurotic
level functioning are reviewed in the context of this individual's Rorschach.
After reviewing the structural dimensions of neurotic functioning, the content
and sequence of the patient's responses are examined for relevant psychological themes and areas of conflict.

CASE STUDY

A 32-year-old fashion designer and the mother of two young children, Mrs. A.
had suffered for many years with symptoms of depression and an eating
disorder. She was admitted to an inpatient unit in the context of increasing
suicidal thoughts, social withdrawal, and a pattern of food restriction and
overexercise. Episodically, she induced vomiting at those times that she felt
most out of control; although her mood was frequently depressed, she suffered
as often from crippling anxiety and constant feelings of guilt. In her background, Mrs. A. described an early family history characterized by verbal
abuse. She was the oldest of three children and experienced a great deal of
pressure to conform to her parents' expectations that she be a "good" and
responsible child. Her parents were strict, moralistic, and quite intolerant of
complaints or needs, which they typically viewed as selfish or childish. In
particular, Mrs. A. learned from her parents that all sexual, as well as aggressive
feelings, were considered "bad" and unacceptable. Mrs. A. strived to control
her emotions and present a pleasing and compliant image to her parents and
the world in general. She struggled to ward off underlying resentment and
rebellious impulses by becoming overly solicitous and caretaking. Furthermore, she worked to become everything that her mother was not. In her eyes,
her mother was overly critical and selfish. Thus, she tried to be generous and

selfless. She viewed her mother as negative, sour, and pessimistic; and as a result, Mrs. A. became a rose-colored optimist to the point of being pollyannish. In viewing her mother's quickness to anger and violent displays of temper, Mrs. A. stifled her negative feelings and worked, instead, to always find something positive to say to others.

Mrs. A. was a bright and academically successful student who completed college and received some graduate training in the field of Art History. In her late 20s, she met a man several years older than herself, fell in love, and got married. Only later did she disclose to her treatment team the extent of her husband's alcoholism and abusive behavior. Although she had hoped to find peace and fulfillment in her marriage, she ended up marrying a man who was demanding, controlling, and perfectionistic. She struggled to ward off rage at her husband for attempting to control her sexually. On several occasions, she felt that he had forced her to have sex and that one of these incidents resulted in a pregnancy. Because of her early family experiences, she feared an open confrontation with her husband because she was certain that he, like her parents, would not tolerate her anger. Instead, she gradually withdrew from him, began restricting her eating, and became preoccupied with exercise and controlling her weight. Her husband, angered by her precipitous weight loss, appeared to lose interest in her and withdrew into his work. Although she gained much of her weight back, Mrs. A. continued purging and became more severely depressed.

Mrs. A.'s testing battery consisted of a Minnesota Multiphasic Personality Inventory–2 (MMPI–2; Hathaway & McKinley, 1989), Millon Clinical Multiaxial Inventory–II (MCMI–II, Millon, 1987), Personal History Questionnaire, Early Memories Test, Sentence Completion Test, Thematic Apperception Test (TAT), and eight cards of the Rorschach. She was given an abbreviated Rorschach because she was included as a subject in a clinical investigation into the diagnostic implications of using shortened forms of the Rorschach. Mrs. A. was given Cards II, IV, VII, and X, followed by Cards III, VI, I, and IX. Both card sets were established by previous research on abbreviated forms of the Rorschach (Carpenter et al., 1983), which found that certain 4-card sets were equivalent to the standard 10-card sets in yielding composite indices of thought disorder as measured by the Thought Disorder Index (TDI; Johnston & Holzman, 1979). Mrs. A.'s Rorschach was administered and scored according to the Comprehensive System (Exner, 1993). Her Rorschach responses on free association and inquiry are included in Appendix A, her sequence of scores is presented in Appendix B, and her structural summary is presented in Appendix C.

Mrs. A.'s MMPI–2 Welsh Code (New) was 3**21*78"6'+04–/95:F+LK/, and her MCMI–II Personality and Syndrome Codes were 327**8B1*–+5"46A6B8A"//–**–*// and AD**–*//–**CC*//, respectively. Her MMPI–2 profile captured her struggle with depression and anxiety. The interpretive report depicted her as a guilt-ridden and overly controlled woman who uses a great deal of denial and repression to deal with strong emotion and conflict (Butcher, 1991). The MCMI–II interpretive report highlighted Mrs. A.'s dependent and intropunitive nature that enables her to appear pleasant and calm despite experiencing a strong undercurrent of anxiety, sadness, and guilt (Millon, 1987). One or both of the interpretive reports indicated that her profiles were consistent with Axis I diagnoses of Dysthymia, Major Depression, or Generalized Anxiety Disorder and suggested that she may also have a Dependent, Avoidant, and/or Obsessive-Compulsive Personality Disorder on Axis II.

The following section outlines structural aspects of the Rorschach that characterize neurotic functioning and includes features of Mrs. A.'s Rorschach that reflect these different categories of functioning. Following a review of the structural aspects of Mrs. A.'s Rorschach, the content and sequence of her responses are examined.

NEUROTIC LEVEL RORSCHACH VARIABLES

Acklin (1994) looked toward Kernberg's (1976, 1984) tri-level model of personality functioning as a basis for attempting to operationalize those aspects of neurotic functioning that can be assessed psychodynamically. Acklin offered suggestions about scoring aspects of the Comprehensive System that would seem to provide face valid measures of the Rorschach components of neurotic level functioning. Amplifying the Rorschach characteristics proposed by Acklin, one could construct a more comprehensive outline of neurotic level Rorschach variables that are consistent with both a theory of neurotic functioning, on the one hand, and also with what is known empirically about certain Rorschach scores, on the other. Each variable is reviewed against the backdrop of Mrs. A.'s Rorschach responses and structural summary scores.

General Measures of Ego Strengths

Although Schafer (1954) did not limit the focus of his work to neurotic conditions per se, he identified six general aspects of a Rorschach response that indicate success or failure of defensive and adaptive operations. These features include: (a) emotional tone of the response; (b) emphasis on articulated form (form domination); (c) accurate form level; (d) integration of scores, images, and attitudes; (e) thematic moderation and an absence of primitive imagery; and (f) no evidence of formal thought disorder. Taken together, an individual's success or failure on each of these scoring dimensions provides valuable information about the relative strength or weakness of his or her ego. We would expect a neurotically organized individual to adhere to most of these criteria with some measure of success. An examination of Mrs.

A.'s responses and structural Rorschach summary indicates that she generally meets each of the criteria laid down by Schafer. Because it is reasonable to view these dimensions as a collective measure of ego-strength, we may infer that Mrs. A.'s Rorschach responses and structural data reflect a higher level of ego-functioning.

In attempting to construct an empirical measure of ego-strength versus ego-weakness, Perry and Viglione (1991) developed the Ego Impairment Index (EII) using a combination of theoretical and empirical methods. The EII samples domains of critical ego-functions and provides a summary measure of the relative weakness (or conversely, strength) of the ego. The six variables that make up the EII include sum *FQ*– (minus form level responses); derepressed content (including anatomy, blood, explosion, fire, food, sex, X-ray, and aggressive movement responses); *WSum6* (sum of special scores); and *Sum M*– (minus form level human movement responses). Additionally, Perry and Viglione constructed two new variables to assess object relations including the "good human experience" score (*GHX*) and the "poor human experience" scores (*PHX*). Several studies have demonstrated that the EII is a reliable and valid measure of ego impairment that shows promise in differentiating higher from lower functioning patient groups (Perry & Viglione, 1991; Perry, Viglione, & Braff, 1992; Resnick, 1994). Perry and Viglione's (1991) beta-weighted formula to measure ego impairment is as follows:

EII = .136 (*sum FQ*–) + .050 (*Wsum6*) + .068 (derepressed contents) + .208 (*M*–) + .108 (*PHX*) – .160 (*GHX*) – .062 *R* – .049 [constant]

Resnick (1994) developed an index that he termed the Conceptual Ego-Strength Index (CESI) made up of four variables that he scored as follows: (a) accurate versus inaccurate form level (*FQ*+, *FQo* = +1; *FQu* = 0; *FQ*– = –1); (b) form dominant versus nonform dominant color and shading responses (form-dominant = +1; form secondary = 0; formless = –1); (c) the absence versus presence of primitive contents (*AN, BL, EX, FI, FD, SX, XY contents* and *AG* and *MOR* Special Scores; none = +1; one or more = –1); and (d) the absence versus presence of special thought disorder scores (none = +1; Level 1 Special Score = 0; Level 2 Special Score, *ALOG* or *CONTAM* = –1). By comparing the CESI from a sample of psychotic, borderline, and nonpsychotic, nonborderline patients (neurotic characters?), Resnick found that he could make significant discriminations between the latter group and the two former groups on several key components of the CESI. Resnick also used the EII in an attempt to compare the two ego measures in distinguishing three levels of personality organization characterized by his three patient groups. Resnick found that both measures performed equally well. The EII and CESI can be viewed as two broad measures of ego-functioning that can be clinically useful in identifying patients who function at a neurotic level.

Mrs. A. performed well on these three broad measures of ego-functioning. Seventy-one percent of her responses satisfied Schafer's six criteria for successful defensive and adaptive functioning. Her EII score was –.957, which is well in the direction of less ego-impairment (greater ego-strength) compared to the patient groups in previous studies (Perry & Viglione, 1991; Perry et al., 1992), and her CESI score of 1.46 is similar to (and slightly greater than) the nonpsychotic, nonborderline group in Resnick's study (1994). Table 20.1 summarizes Mrs. A.'s performance on these measures of ego strength and impairment.

Finally, one might expect to find a greater degree of resiliency in the Rorschach records of neurotic patients. Although not captured in any one summary score or index, a neurotic patient's ego-resiliency should be reflected in the capacity to recover more quickly following the breakthrough of warded off impulses. Thus, we might expect dips in form level or the intrusion of drive derivatives in the response content to be followed by responses of better form quality and conventionality. This is exactly what we see in Mrs. A.'s protocol. Three of her four responses of minus form level are followed by quick recovery as evidenced by responses of more adequate form level.

Reality Testing and Thought Organization

Accurate perception of form on the Rorschach has long been taken as a measure of reality testing. Although it might not be possible to establish a precise cutoff to distinguish neurotic from borderline or psychotic reality testing, Exner's norms for nonpatient adults indicate means for $X+$ percentage and $F+$ percentage greater than 70 (Exner, 1986). Despite the similarities between neurotic and normal ego functioning, we would expect the neurotically organized individual to demonstrate isolated dips in reality testing (primarily FQu along with occasional $FQ-$ responses) when confronted with a conflict

TABLE 20.1
Measures of Ego Strength and Impairment

	Mrs. A.	Perry and Viglione (1991)	Resnick (1994)
Ego Impairment Index (EII)	–.957	0 (Melancholic Depressives)	.243 (Nonborderlines)
Conceptual Ego Strength Index (CESI)	1.46	—	1.29 (Nonborderline)
Percentage of responses satisfying Schafer's six criteria for successful defensive and adaptive functioning	71%	—	—

situation. In their case studies of neurotically organized patients, Peterson (1994), Meloy and Gacono (1994), and Murray (1994) all documented form level in the low- to mid-60s. Furthermore, Exner's (1986) norms for inpatient depressives indicate mean form levels in the low 50s, whereas the norms for character disorder patients were in the high 50s. We might assume that these largely heterogeneous groups of depressive and character disordered patients were comprised of individuals organized at both a borderline as well as neurotic psychostructural level. Thus, it may be reasonable to expect that a neurotically organized patient would achieve a slightly higher summary form level ($X+\%$ between 60 and 70) than Exner's two patient samples and a somewhat lower form level than Exner's normals. Mrs. A. achieved an $X+$ of 67% and an $F+$ of 63%, placing her squarely within this hypothetical range of neurotic functioning and at a level consistent with previously studied neurotic patients.

Thought organization pertains to a variety of formal aspects of thinking including the capacity to use thoughts and fantasy in the service of delaying and selecting appropriate action (presence or absence of good human movement responses); rigidity or flexibility in ideational sets (a balance or imbalance between active and passive movement responses); and the degree and style of integrative capacity (reflected in the Zf and Zd scores). Additionally, the presence or absence of deviant verbalizations and strained logic, suggesting formal thought disorder, is a key component in assessing thought organization. With these separate functions in mind, we would expect to find an appropriate level of thought organization in the neurotic patient's Rorschach as measured by several high Level M responses (accurate form level, cooperative movement, and absence of special scores or primitive content). The presence of either an elevated or depressed Zf and Zd score might suggest the effect of defensive processes on ideation. For example, the overideational obsessive patient may engage in excessive scanning, hypercritical attention to details, and intellectual striving resulting in an elevated Zf and Zd score, whereas an impressionistic, histrionic patient who perceives the world in a more capricious and global manner would achieve lower scores on these two indices.

The absence of special scores indicates that Mrs. A.'s thinking is governed by secondary process and attuned to the demands of external reality (Meloy & Singer, 1991). Although she is solidly extratensive, she produced two adequate human movement responses suggesting that she has the capacity to employ ideation in the service of adaptation. Her emotionality and external focus of attention (as reflected by her extratensive style) may be associated with a repressive orientation and her attempt to distract herself from painful thoughts and feelings. However, her cognitive style is not generally global, impressionistic or repressive. Her slightly elevated organizational scores (Zf = 13 and Zd = +2.0) suggest an obsessional quality to her style of thinking. She is a cautious and detail-oriented woman who may get caught up in attempting to weigh all sides before responding. Her careful, calculated efforts to consider all of her observations before responding are consistent with her marked tendency to present a carefully managed external appearance to the world, and may be a by-product of learning to survive in a hypercritical and judgmental early environment. Additionally, an elevated Zd score may reflect ideational "wheel-spinning" and indecisiveness, which were characteristic of Mrs. A.'s approach to problem solving.

Management of Affects and Impulse Life

Affect tolerance, differentiation, integration, and regulation are important components of ego-functioning. In the neurotic structure, affects are better tolerated and can be used as signals for defensive and adaptive action. Likewise, the neurotic individual is better able to discriminate different feeling states and integrate words and ideas into emotional experience. Finally, we expect the neurotically intact ego to be more capable of regulating affect and controlling its discharge. Thus, we would expect the neurotic-level Rorschach to contain measures of both emotional arousal as well as reasonably effective containment.

All types of color and shading responses might be present, with a predominance of form-dominated, accurately perceived, non-thought-disordered responses expected. Kleiger (1992) suggested that traditional approaches to the Rorschach would view form dominated shading responses (*FY, FC', FV,* and *FT*) as indicative of more controlled and integrated experiences of anxiety and unpleasant affect. Although standard interpretation of the Comprehensive System holds that the aggregate of shading scores, regardless of the variables of form quality, form domination, content, or special scores, is generally understood to reflect the impingement of poorly organized affects that drive an individual toward uncontrolled behavior, Kleiger described how psychoanalytic theories of affect can contribute to a conceptual understanding of accurately perceived form-dominated shading responses. Despite their painful content, such higher level shading responses suggest a capacity for tolerating and using different kinds of affect as signals for adaptive and defensive purposes.

An examination of Mrs. A.'s color and shading scores indicates that her capacity to tolerate and modulate her expression of affect is basically intact. Her *FC* is greater than *CF* + *C*, she has no pure *C* responses, and five of her seven color scores are *FQo* or *FQ+*. Mrs. A.'s seven shading scores indicate that she experiences private agony in the form of painful anxiety, depression, and guilt. Her *D* score of −2 tells us that her subjective distress is significantly interfering with her functioning. However, six of her seven shading responses are either ordinary or excellent form level; five of the seven are form-dominated; and there are no Special Scores associated with any of these responses. Thus we find additional evidence that Mrs. A.'s ego has some capacity to contain painfully distressing feelings that although producing subjective anguish, should not disorganize her.

Success or failure in affect regulation is also qualitatively reflected in the types of defensive processes employed. For example, combinations of formal scores, response content, and aspects of the patient–examiner interaction might converge in a manner representative of a particular type of defensive process. Schafer (1954) detailed how the confluence of formal scores, thematic imagery, and test-taking behavior could reflect a variety of neurotic level defenses including repression, pollyannish denial, isolation of affect, intellectualization, and undoing. More recently, researchers developed Rorschach content scales to assess different types of defensive processes (Cooper, Perry, & Arnow, 1988; Lerner & Lerner, 1980). Meloy and Gacono (1994) used the defense scales developed by Cooper et al. (1988) to evaluate the defensive functioning of the neurotic patient they studied. Cooper et al's defense scales can also be employed to evaluate Mrs. A.'s defensive functioning reflected in her Rorschach responses. Table 20.2 summarizes findings from this analysis. Of the 20 scorable defenses on Mrs. A's Rorschach, 15 of these, or 75%, fell within the neurotic range; they mostly represented examples of pollyannish denial (35%), repression (20%), or higher level denial (15%). Responses such as, "pretty spring flowers" (Card X), "the colors are pretty" (Card IX), "[the girls] had a happy look" (Card VII), and rabbits had their hands together "like playing pattycake or London Bridge" (Card II), symbolically capture the process of pollyannish denial. Additionally, her frequent use of color projection, seen in particular on Card VII in which she attempted to infuse bright and cheerful colors into the grayness of the blot, also reflects her tendency to turn from the presence of painful or dysphoric experience and imagine something pleasant, nonthreatening, or innocent instead. Finally, her elevated Intellectualization Index $(2AB + Art + Ay = 4)$ suggests that Mrs. A. may use this additional neurotic level defense in attempting to manage emotional arousal.

Internalized Object Relations

The Rorschach assessment of object representation has traditionally involved an examination of human movement (M) and human content scores $(H, Hd,$

TABLE 20.2
Mrs. A's Defense Scale Scoring (Cooper, Perry, & Arnow, 1988)

Defense	Response	Percentage
Neurotic Defenses		
Higher Level Denial	VII–1, VII–2, X–1	15%
Pollyannish Denial	II–2, VI–2, VII–1, IX–1, X–1, X–2, X–2	35%
Repression	II–4, III–4, IV–3, VI–1	20%
Isolation	VII–1	5%
Borderline Defenses		
Devaluation	I–1, II–3, VII–1, VII–3	20%
Splitting	VII–1/2	5%

[*H*], and [*Hd*]). Neurotically organized individuals are expected to have more integrated, benign, and differentiated internalized representations of people. It follows that accurately perceived, non-thought-disordered human movement responses would occur more frequently in the records of neurotically organized individuals. Additionally, percepts of humans, alone or interactive, that have a cooperative, as opposed to aggressive, malevolent, or sadomasochistic quality would be expected. Mrs. A.'s Rorschach contains two non-thought-disordered *M* responses, one of ordinary (Card III) and one of excellent (Card VII) form level. Both responses reflect humans involved in either neutral or benign interactions (*COP*).

The quality of internalized relationships can also be systematically examined from a developmental perspective. Two well-researched scales have potential relevance for distinguishing object representations of neurotics from less well-organized patients (Blatt, Brenneis, Schimek, & Glick, 1976; Urist, 1977). Blatt et al. developed a scoring system that applied developmental principles of differentiation, articulation, and integration (Werner, 1940/1957) to the study of human responses on the Rorschach. Differentiation refers to the degree of wholeness or realistic nature of the figures perceived (*H, Hd,* [*H*], and [*Hd*]). Articulation refers to the number and various types of characteristics that an individual attributes to a human figure. Finally, integration includes the degree of internality of the action of the figure, the degree of integration of the human figure and its action, and the degree of integration with another object. Human responses are also scored along a qualitative dimension of benevolence versus malevolence. Blatt et al. (1976) found a progressive increase in the number of well-differentiated, articulated, and integrated human responses in normal patients as they mature developmentally. Furthermore, they found a significant increase in the degree to which human figures were seen in constructive interactions. In contrast, Blatt's group found that seriously disturbed inpatients had a significantly greater number of human responses scored at lower developmental levels (e.g., human responses that were either quasi-human, inaccurately perceived, incongruous, passive, unmotivated, or malevolent). Interestingly, however, the more disturbed patients produced responses at lower developmental levels primarily on accurately perceived responses, whereas their developmentally more advanced responses occurred chiefly on inaccurately perceived human responses.

Blatt and Lerner (1983) applied the Concept of the Object Scale to a variety of different patient groups and found that a group of patients diagnosed as hysteric produced human figures that were accurately perceived, well-differentiated, and highly articulated. However, the elaborations of the human figures involved superficial physical details as opposed to internal attributes. Furthermore, there was little internal sense of motivation or interaction between figures. Another neurotic-level group comprised of suicidal patients with introjective depressive features produced human responses that vacillated between high developmental levels, on the one hand, and isolated responses in which there were impaired representations of humans in which the activity was either destructive or malevolent, on the other.

Each of Mrs. A.'s full human responses is accurately perceived, reasonably well-differentiated, and highly articulated. On Card III, for example, she sees "two people facing each other, leaning back or maybe sitting on something." This is a popular full human response that she then expands by identifying a number of physical characteristics and external details. She notes that the figures have "prominent chins," that they look "large busted," and that they appear to be wearing skirts. However, the degree of interaction is minimal, and the figures are doing little other than sitting down and facing each other. Her first response to Card VII is even more illustrative of her tendency to perceive accurate, differentiated, highly articulated, and conventional human figures that are generally lacking in motivated activity or more complex internal or interpersonal features. Her accurately perceived response of "two girls' faces" is highly embellished with attention to facial features and physical characteristics. However, once again, the figures are involved in parallel, noninteractive activity with little attention paid to the internal state of either figure.

In 1977, Urist developed the Mutuality of Autonomy Scale (MOAS) to assess degree of separation between self and other. In some respects, Urist's scale has broader application than Blatt et al.'s (1976) Concept of the Object Scale because it can be applied to any response in which there are two figures or objects involved in some degree of interaction. The lower end of Urist's scale applies to Rorschach responses that reflect a lack of differentiation or a degree of fusion between the objects, animals, or human figures. The highest point on the scale is applied to those responses that depict a clear separation between two distinct objects or figures. Urist believes that responses of this type are associated with more advanced levels of self–other differentiation associated with a capacity for object constancy and empathy. A number of studies have provided validation for the MOAS and demonstrated its utility in assessing qualitative differences of object relations among different diagnostic groups (Ryan, Avery, & Grolnick, 1985; Tuber, 1983; Urist, 1977; Urist & Shill, 1982). These studies have consistently demonstrated a strong relationship between scores on the MOAS and severity of psychopathology.

Mrs. A. has five responses that can be scored on the MOAS (one response on Card II; two responses on Cards III and VII). Each of these responses reflects a high degree of separateness between the figures or objects involved and would, thus, receive scores of 1 or 2 on Urist's 7-point scale. Lower scores on this scale (1 or 2) are associated with more developmentally mature object relations. Even though Mrs. A.'s responses are scored at the higher functioning end of the MOAS, the nature of interactions between figures remains simple and passive. Thus, both Blatt et al.'s Concept of the Object Scale and Urist's MOAS provide useful measures of Mrs. A.'s neurotic-level object relations and the histrionic quality of her perceptions of self and others.

Superego Organization

In assessing levels of personality organization, the nature of superego function-ing is frequently overlooked. Distinguishing neurotic from borderline or psychotic structures depends, in part, on the integrity and maturity of super-ego. Superego functioning in neurotic patients, although possibly harsh and unbending, should be more integrated and depersonified. Greater integration implies the absence of incongruent elements. For example, one would not expect to see the simultaneous presence of primitively punitive superego introjects in the context of psychopathic trends. Similarly, the neurotic level superego should not be characterized by intense sadomasochistic needs to either suffer or inflict pain. Although the neurotic patient may suffer painful symptoms of superego origin such as feelings of inadequacy, shame, and guilt, the more neurotically intact ego provides a greater capacity to tolerate these painful feelings and use them as signals for defensive or adaptive action.

Neurotic patients may reveal a great deal of painful affect on the Rorschach but also give evidence of a capacity to tolerate such painful feelings. Kleiger (1992) raised questions about whether accurately perceived, non-thought-dis-ordered, form-dominated shading responses might reveal something about an individual's capacity to tolerate painful affects. Kleiger suggested that an accurately perceived and well-integrated $FV+$ response might indicate a capacity to tolerate painful, self-directed aggression such as shame or guilt. Viewed in this way, $FC'+$ responses could signal the capacity to tolerate or contain depression. The capacity to tolerate depressive affect leads the way to a capacity for concern (Winnicott, 1963), which is a prerequisite for more intact superego functioning.

Inferences about superego functioning are frequently based on an analysis of thematic content. Schafer (1954) provided a detailed list of categories of thematic content that could reflect aspects of superego pathology. In a similar vein, Holt (1977) developed a primary process scoring system for the Ror-schach. In his system, he identified several varieties of primitively aggressive responses that included sadistic aggression, masochistic victimization, and the aftermath or results of aggression. More primitive superego functioning may be reflected in Rorschach imagery that combines morbid and aggressive themes in the same score.

Inferences about Mrs. A.'s superego functioning are based primarily on an examination of structural features of her Rorschach responses. For example, despite evidence that she is experiencing a great deal of subjective pain and emotional discomfort, Mrs. A.'s accurately perceived and form-dominated vista and achromatic color responses suggest some capacity to tolerate painful feelings of shame, guilt, and inadequacy. Nonetheless, these shading scores, together with her low egocentricity index (0.17) and her one Morbid response, suggest an experience of extreme self-dissatisfaction and inadequacy. Self-criticism and feelings of inadequacy can easily be understood as expressions of a harsh superego or a failure to measure up to one's ego ideal. This was certainly the case for Mrs. A. who experienced frequent pangs of guilt and worthlessness resulting from her failure to measure up to her unrealistically high ideals and the intrusions of warded off sexual and aggressive impulses that made her feel like she was "bad."

ANALYSIS OF THEMATIC CONTENT AND SEQUENCE OF RESPONSES

Symbolic and representational inferences based on the sequence of Mrs. A.'s responses yield a number of dynamic themes that provide windows into her conflicted internal experience. Integrating scores and content as they unfold in a sequence of responses highlights dynamic themes that emerge on a number of cards.

Card II

Intense dependency needs (lipstick that reminded her of her mother) are associated with emotional arousal (FC) that she is unable to ignore. Mrs. A. may try to ward off this uncomfortable experience in a regressive childlike manner (her next response of "bunny rabbits"); however, what eventually emerges is a painful sense of deprivation and loss (a heart that is disintegrating and falling apart) that compromises her functioning (FC–). The painful experience of loss and deprivation gives way to urges to avoid and take flight (a "jet") but she may be left with the rumbling of well-controlled aggressive impulses (an accurately perceived arrowhead) that are not consciously available to her (her white space response might suggest that the stirring of negativistic or rebellious feelings is not well-integrated or consciously available).

Card III

Mrs. A. seems capable of presenting an adequate social facade (the initial impression is that she has produced a popular human movement response—"looks like two people facing each other, leaning back or maybe sitting on something. It looks like two ladies"). However, she emphasized surface characteristics of the figures (prominent chins, large busts, and skirts) and essentially described them as passive figures with little sense of internal direction or motivation. This initial appearance of meaningful social interaction is followed by a sense of being off balance (she emphasized how the figures could not be standing on their own) and vulnerable (two anatomy responses, one of which is an F–).

Card VII

Mrs. A.'s sequence of responses to Card VII provides support for the inferences made on Card III. Again, we can see that the patient tries to maintain a happy, cheerful facade in her interpersonal transactions. Although she may be socially adept and attuned to superficial nuances, she tends to keep her distance ([*H*]) and relates to others in a superficial and stylized manner. Her sequence of responses to Card VII suggests that despite her attempt to view the world through rose-colored lenses (her playful image of two cartoonlike girls with a great deal of color injected into the gray inkblot), she is troubled by depressing and negatively tinged images of herself as a needy and unattractive person (ugly faces of rats with open mouths).

Card IV

Mrs. A.'s four responses to Card IV suggest an anxious quality to her needs for attachment. Her two *FT* responses are of unusual form level, suggesting that her dependency needs, although well-controlled, may leave her feeling awkward and out of step. The stirring of needs for closeness and nurturance may evoke a phobic reaction (her following response of "scary creatures") together with a painful sense of worthlessness (*FV*).

Card IX

Mrs. A.'s two responses to Card IX reflect the impact of emotional arousal on her defensive functioning. Despite her initial effort to paint the world with pretty colors ("the colors are pretty"), she may struggle to contain diffuse and pressing aggressive impulses (her first response of "fire" scored as *CF.ma*) and worry about the destructive impact of her intense anger ("melted crayons," *CF.YF*). Mrs. A.'s story to Card 18 GF of the TAT vividly captured her struggle to fend off her rage by becoming depressed or engaging in unsuccessful reaction formation.

> Somebody is sick, hurt, or . . . I don't know. The taller one looks either sad or angry; I don't know which. I'm going to say sad. She looks like this is her mother. Her mother is maybe going to die or dying and she's very upset and is trying to help her . . . or she may hate her and is choking her to death. Unless of course she is catching her from falling.

FINAL FORMULATION

Aided by the testing, Mrs. A.'s therapist was able to formulate a comprehensive dynamic understanding of areas of neurotic conflict and earlier experiences of emotional deprivation and trauma. Empathic failures by her parents, who viewed her needs and impulses as selfish and unacceptable, not only gave rise to a sense of falseness and inauthenticity, but also set the stage for lifelong conflict between intense neediness and starvation for nurturance on the one hand, and extreme self-denial and guilt over wanting and needing anything on the other. Essentially, Mrs. A. warded off her need for close and comforting relationships by attempting to be self-sufficient. After her husband forced her to have sex, which resulted in a pregnancy, Mrs. A. became overrun by intense affects and impulses that threatened to break through her defenses. Gesensway (1988) discussed how pregnancy can stir oedipal conflicts that may trigger regression to oral and anal fixations. In the wake of this unexpected and unwanted pregnancy, Mrs. A. became confronted with distant memories of abuse and also felt the dangers of her sexual and aggressive impulses. She tried to silence these forbidden impulses by displacing them onto food. Not eating represented her efforts to disgorge guilt feelings and gain control over these intrapsychic threats.

Mrs. A.'s eating disorder became a physical expression of internal conflicts and served a number of related intrapsychic functions. Not eating and losing weight protected Mrs. A. against the dangers of sexuality, pregnancy, and rage. Essentially, not eating was both an expression of rage at her husband (her loss of weight annoyed her husband and eventually kept him away) and a defense against open expression of her anger (her loss of weight led to weakness and depression, which made it extremely difficult for her to openly confront her husband with her anger). Furthermore, self-starvation and extreme self-denial served Mrs. A.'s harsh superego and provided ample opportunity for self-punishment. Finally, Mrs. A.'s eating disorder was a compromise formation that expressed both her starvation for safe and nourishing relationships and her self-denial and associated sense of badness for needing and wanting things for herself.

DISCUSSION

There is a great deal of research suggesting that eating disorder patients have significant ego impairment (Kaufer & Katz, 1983; Small, Teango, Madero, Gross & Ebert, 1982; Struber & Goldenberg, 1981; Van-Der Keshet, 1988) and are organized at a borderline level (Garfinkel & Gardner, 1982; Johnson, Lewis, & Hagman, 1984; Lerner, 1991; Piran, 1988; Sugarman, Quinlin & Devenis, 1982; Swift & Stern, 1982). It was a surprise to find that key aspects of Mrs. A.'s personality organization, as depicted by the Rorschach, were not consistent with those found in eating disorder patients organized at a borderline level. Mrs. A.'s reality testing was superior to that of borderline-level eating disorder patients (Piran, 1988; Van-Der Keshet, 1988); she demonstrated an absence of thought disorder (Piran, 1988; Small et. al., 1982); the vast majority of her defenses were not primitive in nature (Piran, 1988; Piran, Lerner, Garfinkel, Kennedy, & Brouillette, 1988); and her level of object relations was developmentally more advanced than is typically found in borderline patients who have eating disorders (Brouillette, 1987; Piran, 1988; Sugarman et al., 1982).

Mrs. A.'s unexpected ego strengths confirm Aronson's (1986) finding that eating disorders, bulimia in particular, should be viewed as a cluster of symptoms associated with differing levels of psychic organization such as neurosis, borderline personality, or psychosis. Aronson presented data that demonstrated that higher and lower level bulimics could be differentiated on the Blatt Assessment of Qualitative and Structural Dimensions of Object Representations Scale (Blatt, Chevron, Quinlan, & Wein, 1981). Aronson's findings bolster a growing body of research that describes the structural and dynamic diversity of bulimic patients and moves away from focusing on the veneer of bulimic symptoms and concluding, in a circular manner, that the patient must be borderline (Lacy, 1982; Mintz, 1982; Wilson, 1983; Yudkovitz, 1983).

Awareness of Mrs. A.'s neurotic level of object representations, her dynamic conflicts, and lack of significant ego weaknesses helped her therapist feel confident in structuring a more expressive psychotherapy process that ultimately allowed her to identify key aspects of her underlying emotional turmoil, clarify the conflictual nature of her relationship with her husband as it emerged in the transference, and help her begin to develop healthier ways of expressing her feelings and getting her needs met.

Although Mrs. A.'s Rorschach data identified ego resources and helped treaters understand her bulimia as a neurotic compromise formation, the single-case nature of this report and the atypical use of the Rorschach (8 cards vs. 10) may raise questions about the validity and generalizibility of the findings. The fact that Mrs. A. was administered an abbreviated Rorschach with the cards out of standard sequence may present potential difficulties in terms of calculating key indices and using normative data for comparison purposes. It could even be argued that because Mrs. A. was not administered the Rorschach in the standard manner, use of normative databases is unwarranted. If true, this would present a serious limitation to this case study.

On the other hand, the use of short forms of the Rorschach is nothing new in clinical practice; and in at least one study (Carpenter et al., 1993), select 4-card sets yielded acceptably high interrater reliabilities for categories of the TDI when compared to TDI scores from the standard 10-card set. One might make the argument that achieving high interrater reliabilities when attempting to score complex phenomena like deviant thought processes would suggest that more easily scored determinants and locations would yield similarly high levels of reliability between different card sets and the standard 10-card set. Furthermore, the fact that key ratios in the Structural Summary are based on the total number of responses and not the number of cards provides additional support for the use of the structural data from Mrs. A.'s Rorschach. Her R for 8 cards was 24, quite comparable with Exner's norms for nonpatient adult 10-card records (Exner, 1986).

Because the diagnostic understanding and treatment recommendations concerning Mrs. A. were based on a convergence of data from a variety of sources, and not on the Rorschach alone, it is unlikely that the primary conclusions regarding her dynamic conflicts and structural organization would have changed appreciably if she had been given a 10-card, instead of an 8-card

Rorschach. For example, Mrs. A.'s MMPI–2 3-point code of 321 is consistent with a neurotic level of functioning and significantly different from the 284 profiles of typical anorectics and the 4,278 profiles found among bulimics (Norman & Herzog, 1983), both frequently associated with borderline phenomena. Nonetheless, as rational as this and other arguments may seem, the actual impact of using a shortened form of the Rorschach on the diagnostic understanding of Mrs. A. cannot be known, and the widespread utility of abbreviated Rorschach records is a question that should be empirically answered.

REFERENCES

Acklin, M. W. (1992). Psychodiagnosis of personality structure: Psychotic personality organization. *Journal of Personality Assessment, 58,* 454–463.

Acklin, M. W. (1993). Psychodiagnosis of personality structure II: Borderline personality organization. *Journal of Personality Assessment, 61,* 329–341.

Acklin, M. W. (1994). Psychodiagnosis of personality structure III: Neurotic personality organization. *Journal of Personality Assessment, 63,* 1–9.

American Psychiatric Association. (1980). *Diagnostic and statistical manual of mental disorders* (3rd ed.). Washington, DC: Author.

Aronson, J. K. (1986). The level of object relations and severity of symptoms in the normal weight bulimic patient. *International Journal of Eating Disorders, 5,* 669–681.

Blatt, S. J., Brenneis, C. B., Schimek, J., & Glick, M. (1976). Normal development and the psychopathological impairment of the concept of the object in the Rorschach. *Journal of Abnormal Psychology, 85,* 264–273.

Blatt, S., Chevron, E., Quinlan, D. M., & Wein, S. (1981). *A manual for the assessment of qualitative and structural dimensions of object representations.* New Haven, CT: Yale University Press.

Blatt, S., & Lerner, H. (1983). The psychological assessment of object representation. *Journal of Personality Assessment, 47,* 7–28.

Butcher, J. (1991). *The Minnesota Report: Adult clinical system interpretative report.* Minneapolis: Regents of the University of Minnesota.

Carpenter, J. T., Coleman, M. J., Waternaux, C., Perry, J., Wong, H., O'Brian, C., & Holzman, P. S. (1983). The Thought Disorder Index: Short form assessments. *Psychological Assessment, 5,* 75–80.

Cooper, S., Perry, J., & Arnow, D. (1988). An empirical approach to the study of defense mechanisms: I. Reliability and preliminary validity of the Rorschach defense scales. *Journal of Personality Assessment, 52,* 187–203.

Exner, J. E. (1986). *The Rorschach: A comprehensive system: Vol. 1. Basic foundations* (2nd ed.). New York: Wiley.

Exner, J. E. (1993). *The Rorschach: A comprehensive system: Vol. 1. Basic foundations* (3rd ed.). New York: Wiley.

Garfinkel, P., & Gardner, D. (1982). *Anorexia nervosa: A multidimensional perspective.* New York: Brunner/Mazel.

Gesensway, D. B. (1988). A psychoanalytic study of bulimia and pregnancy. In H. J. Schwartz (Ed.), *Bulimia: Psychoanalytic treatment and theory* (pp. 299–346). New York: International Unversities Press.

Hathaway, S., & McKinley, J. (1989). *MMPI-2 scoring and administration manual.* Minneapolis: University of Minnesota Press.

Holzman, P., Shenton, M., & Solovay, M. (1986). Quality of thought disorder in differential diagnosis. *Schizophrenia Bulletin, 12,* 360–371.

Holt, R. R. (1977). A method for assessing primary process manifestations and their control in Rorschach responses. In M. A. Rickers-Ovianskina (Ed.), *Rorschach psychology* (2nd ed., pp. 375–420). New York: Robert Krieger.

Johnson, C., Lewis, C., & Hagman, J. (1984). Bulimia: Review and synthesis. *Psychiatric Clinics of North America, 7,* 247–273.

Johnston, M. H., & Holzman, P. S. (1979). *Assessing schizophrenic thinking.* San Francisco: Jossey-Bass.

Kaufer, J., & Katz, J. (1983). Rorschach responses in anorectic and non-anorectic women. *International Journal of Eating Disorders, 3,* 65–74.

Kernberg, O. (1976). *Object relations and clinical psychoanalysis.* New York: Aronson.

Kernberg, O. (1984). *Severe personality disorders: Psychotherapeutic strategies.* New Haven, CT: Yale Unversities Press.

Kleiger, J. H. (1992). A conceptual critique of the EA:es comparison in the Comprehensive Rorschach System. *Psychological Assessment, 4,* 288–296.

Kwawer, J., Lerner, H., Lerner, P., & Sugarman, A. (1980). *Borderline phenomena and the Rorschach test.* New York: International Universities Press.

Lacy, J. H. (1982). The bulimic syndrome at normal body weight: Reflections on pathogenesis and clinical features. *International Journal of Eating Disorders, 2,* 59–66.

Lerner, H., & Lerner, P. (1980). Rorschach assessment of primitive defenses in borderline personality structure. In J. Kwawer, H. Lerner, P. Lerner, & A. Sugarman (Eds.), *Borderline phenomena and the Rorschach test* (pp. 257–274). New York: International Universities Press.

Lerner, H., & Lerner, P. (1988). *Primitive mental states and the Rorschach.* New York: International Universities Press.

Lerner, P. M. (1991). *Psychoanalytic theory and the Rorschach.* Hillsdale, NJ: The Analytic Press.

Meloy, J. R., & Gacono, C. B. (1994). A neurotic criminal: "I've learned my lesson . . ." *Journal of Personality Assessment, 63,* 27–38.

Meloy, J. R., & Singer, J. (1991). A psychoanalytic view of the Rorschach Comprehensive System "Special Scores." *Journal of Personality Assessment, 56,* 202–217.

Millon, T. (1987). *Millon Clinical Multiaxial Inventory II interpretive report.* Minneapolis, MN: National Computer Systems.

Mintz, N. E. (1982). Bulimia: A new perspective for clinical social work. *Clinical Social Work, 10,* 289–301.

Murray, J. F. (1994). The Rorschach and diagnosis of neurotic conditions in children and adolescents: A case study. *Journal of Personality Assessment, 63,* 39–58.

Norman, D. K., & Herzog, D. B. (1983). Bulimia, anorexia nervosa, and anorexia nervosa with bulimia: A comparative analysis of MMPI profiles. *International Journal of Eating Disorders, 2,* 43–52.

Perry, W., & Viglione, D. J. (1991). The Ego Impairment Index as a predictor of outcome in melancholic depressed patients treated with tricyclic antidepressants. *Journal of Personality Assessment, 56,* 487–501.

Perry, W., Viglione, D. J., & Braff, D. (1992). The Ego Impairment Index and schizophrenia: A validation study. *Journal of Personality Assessment, 59,* 156–175.

Peterson, C. A. (1994). A neurotic lawyer: AIDS or Oedipus? *Journal of Personality Assessment, 63,* 10–26.

Piran, N. (1988). Borderline phenomena in anorexia and bulimia. In H. Lerner & P. Lerner (Eds.), *Primitive mental states and the Rorschach* (pp. 363–376). New York: International Universities Press.

Piran, N., Lerner, P., Garfinkel, P., Kennedy, S., & Brouillette, C. (1988). Personality disorders in anorexic patients. *International Journal of Eating Disorders, 7,* 589–600.

Rapaport, D., Gill, M., & Schafer, R. (1968). *Diagnostic psychological testing.* (Rev ed.; R. Holt, Ed.). New York: International Universities Press.

Resnick, J. D. (1994). *Rorschach assessment of ego functioning: A compairson of the EII and CESI.* Unpublished masters thesis, Loyola University, Chicago.

Ryan, R., Avery, R., & Grolnick, W. (1985). A Rorschach assessment of children's mutuality of autonomy. *Journal of Personality Assessment, 49,* 6–12.

Schafer, R. (1948). *Clinical application of psychological tests.* New York: International Universities Press.

Schafer, R. (1954). *Psychoanalytic interpretation of Rorschach testing.* New York: Grune & Stratton.

Small, A., Teango, L., Madero, J., Gross, H., & Ebert, M. (1982). A comparison of anorexics and schizophrenics on psychodiagnostic measures. *International Journal of Eating Disorders, 1,* 49–57.

Smith, K. (1983). Object-relations concepts applied to the psychotic range of ego functioning. *Bulletin of the Menninger Clinic, 47,* 417–439.

Struber, M., & Goldenberg, J. (1981). Ego boundary disturbance in juvenile anorexia nervosa. *Journal of Clinical Psychiatry, 37,* 433–438.

Sugarman, A., Quinlan, D., & Devenis, L. (1982). Ego boundary disturbance in anorexia nervosa. *Journal of Personality Assessment, 46,* 455–461.

Swift, W. J., & Stern, S. (1982). The psychodynamic diversity of anorexia nervosa. *International Journal of Eating Disorders, 2,* 17–36.

Tuber, S. (1983). Children's Rorschach scores as predictors of later adjustment. *Journal of Consulting & Clinical Psychology, 51,* 379–385.

Urist, J. (1977). The Rorschach Test and the assessment of object relations. *Journal of Personality Assessment, 41,* 3–9.

Urist, J., & Shill, M. (1982). Validity of the Rorschach Mutuality of Autonomy Scale: A replication using excerpted responses. *Journal of Personality Assessment, 46,* 451–454.

Van-Der Keshet, Y. (1988). *Anorexic patients and ballet students: A Rorschach analysis.* Unpublished doctoral dissertation, University of Toronto.

Werner, H. (1957). *The comparative psychology of mental development.* New York: International Universities Press. (Original work published 1940)

Wilson, C. P. (1983). *Fear of fat.* New York: Aronson.

Winnicott, D. W. (1963). The development of the capacity for concern. *Bulletin of the Menninger Clinic, 27,* 167–176.

Yudkovitz, E. (1983, November–December). Bulimia: Growing awareness of eating disorders. *Social Work,* 472–479.

I.

1. Oh I know . . . I'm thinking of a skeleton. Looks like shoulders, ribs, and vertebrae.

INQ: Shoulders, maybe the collar bone; one, two, three ribs and these are vertebrae (?) The holes here look like spaces between the ribs and I can imagine the discs in between.

II.

2. I don't know . . . I think of lipstick. Do you mean what the shape might be?

INQ: It's shaped kinda like lips. At top made me think of lipstick because of the red of course but it also reminds me of the way my mother used to blot her lipstick on tissue. Its kinda open like a mouth would be in the middle.

3. I don't know, maybe two animals, rabbits maybe, that's their knees and hands or front paws together, I guess, and here's their ears.

INQ: The shapes of the animals in the black; the way they're arranged looks like rabbits crouched down, no sitting upright. You could see their knees; do bunny rabbits have knees? (laughs). I could see their little cotton tails and ears going straight up.

4. The red at the bottom almost looks like a heart.

INQ: The shape and sorta the color I guess. The bottom was not connected to a point but was kinda disintegrating, falling apart or chipping away (?) Because it didn't come to a point.

5. I think of a jet.

INQ: It sorta had the shape; it was pointed at the top.

6. or an arrowhead.

INQ: Just the shape of it. (The rabbits had their hands together as if?) Oh like they were playing patty cake or London Bridge.

III.

7. Looks like two people facing each other, leaning back or maybe sitting on something. Looks like two ladies.

INQ: The heads, bodies, legs (sitting?) or maybe about to sit down. They have prominent chins and they look large busted and this part looks like a skirt. I don't see how they could be standing that way without falling over.

8. I can see kidneys.

INQ: They're equal in size and shape.

9. The red thing in the middle looks like a bowtie.

INQ: The shape and color of it.

10. It almost looks like a hip bone. Looks like a section of a skeleton that includes the upper part of the hip.

INQ: The thigh bone fits in here. The pelvis is what I'm thinking of because of the way it's shaped.

IV.

11. I think of the head of a furry or fuzzy insect.

INQ: The whole thing looks like the head, like it was big, magnified (furry/fuzzy?) The dark and light in the gray areas.

12. or a moth, something that has a lot of texture.

INQ: The whole thing. Butterfly's wings are thin and this looked thick and furry (?) Same reasons as the other one.

13. I see a scary creature with a cape on.

INQ: He had like a batman type head and the shape made it just look scary (cape?) Just the outline brought that to mind.

14. V Maybe a bat.

INQ: It had its wings fold over. The shape of the whole thing. (?) The wings flopped over (?) A section of light which folded over the dark part was like a shadow under the wing.

VI.

15. The bottom part looks like a bearskin rug.

INQ: The shape.

16. Something about the patterns—the co-ors and grays—makes me think of an indian pattern.

INQ: The top part. The fringes along the edges and the patterns of shading. Some kind of indian art.

17. V This way it looks like an iris, a flower.

INQ: Petals high in the middle and the sides droop down and the stem is there too. Its rich grays make me think of rich purple and this could be the yellow middle.

VII.

18. Looks like two girls' faces and they have pony tails and they're going straight up . . . more cartoon like and they might be sitting on some kind of rocking horse or see-saw. I can even imagine that the girl's hair is blonde, thick and curly. She has real rosy cheeks.

INQ: The top part on each side looks like the girls. The pony tail is the part sticking up and the neck section beneath and the body is underneath—really the body is pretty much of a blob (?) Well it's a profile view. It had a real turned up nose and mouth and nose were close together. They had big foreheads and bangs coming down from the hairline. Kinda like 50s looking (?) They way they look. Maybe pony tails are high on their heads and they're real bouncy like at a sock hop. (blonde hair?) I guess I was trying to color it in my mind and it looked like a yellow-blonde color (anything about the inkblot itself?) It wasn't real dark, lighter I guess (curly?) The outside edges (rosey cheeks?) The color was darker around the mouth and cheeks and lighter where the eyes and hair were, so I imagined she'd have light eyes and a light complexion and their faces might be even dirty but they were having fun (?) They had a happy look (See-saw?) It had the shape of some kind of rocking thing they were on.

19. The girls seem so clear I'm not sure I see anything else . . . Oh . . . ugly faces, a rat or something. I see eyes, nose and mouth but that's just a tiny fraction of the big picture.

INQ: It's where the girls' bodies were. The noses are pointing to the outside (?) The shape of their noses and the wrinkles (?) The darker ink in the creases made it look like wrinkles (Ugly?) Well the mouth was open and it had tiny beady eyes. It was definitely gray.

IX.

20. Colors are pretty . . . I see fire, a flame in the middle, but you usually don't see all those colors in a fire.

INQ: The flame in the center is blue and yellow and it looks warm; warm colors around the flames and I get the feeling it's moving up.

21. It looks like something hot, melting; maybe like melted crayons.

INQ: It looks like a painting or melted wax (?) The light and dark of each color is like when wax melts, it gets so hot and just melts. The colors concentrate in the center and the edges are more transparent.

(continued)

X.

22. V Looks like flowers, pretty spring flowers.

INQ: The colors and the thing at the bottom could be a glass vase.

23. I see the Eiffel Tower with a garden in front of it or maybe fireworks going off.

INQ: A perfect shape for the Eiffel Tower and it's gray, arched and the colors of the flowers (fireworks?) The blue streaks could have been fireworks going off.

24. These two yellow things look like they could be eyes.

INQ: If you take the two eyes and come down a little it looks like it could be a mouth at the bottom (?) Just the shapes.

Sequence of Scores

Card	No.	Loc.	#	Determinant(s)	(2)	Content(s)	Pop Z	Special Scores
I	1	WSo	1	F–		An	3.5	
II	2	Do		FCu		Hd		
	3	D+		FMpo	2	A	3.0	
	4	Do		FC.ma–		An		MOR
	5	DSo	1	Fo		Sc	4.5	
	6	DSo		Fo		Ay	4.5	
III	7	D+		Mpo	2	H	P 4.0	
	8	Ddo		F–		An		
	9	Do		FCo		Cg		
	10	Do		Fo		An		
IV	11	Wo	1	FTu		Ad	2.0	
	12	Wo	1	FTu		A	2.0	
	13	Wo	1	Fo		(H)	P 2.0	
	14	Wo	1	FVo		A	2.0	
VI	15	Do		Fo		Ad	P	
	16	Do		YFo		Art		
	17	Wo	1	FYu		Bt	2.5	CP
VII	18	W+	1	Ma.FY+	2	(H)	P 2.5	CP, COP
	19	Do		FC'.FVo	2	Ad		
IX	20	Wv	1	CF.mao		Fi		
	21	Wv	1	CF.YFo		Art		
X	22	W+	1	CFo		Bt	5.5	
	23	W+	1	FC.FD.ma+		Art, Bt, Fi	5.5	
	24	Ddo		F–		Hd		

Summary of Approach

I:WS	VI:D.D.W
II:D.D.D.DS.DS	VII:W.D
III:D.Dd.D.D	VIII:*Rejection*
IV:W.W.W.W	IX:W.W
V:*Rejection*	X:W.W.Dd

LOCATION FEATURES	DETERMINANTS	CONTENTS	S-CONSTELLATION
	BLENDS	SINGLE	YES..FV + VF + V + FD > 2

LOCATION FEATURES	DETERMINANTS BLENDS	DETERMINANTS SINGLE	CONTENTS		S-CONSTELLATION
		H	= 1,0		YES..Col-Shd Bl>0
Zf = 13	FC.m	M = 1	(H)	= 2,0	YES..Ego<.31,>.44
ZSum = 43.5	M.FY	FM = 1	Hd	= 2,0	NO..MOR>3
ZEst = 41.5	FC'.FV	m = 0	(Hd)	= 0,0	NO..Zd > ± 3.5
	CF.m	FC = 2	Hx	= 0,0	YES..es>EA
W = 11	CF.YF	CF = 1	A	= 3,0	NO..CF+C>FC
(Wv = 2)	FC.FD.m	C = 0	(A)	= 0,0	YES..X+%<.70
D = 11		Cn = 0	Ad	= 3,0	NO..S>3
Dd = 2		FC' = 0	(Ad)	= 0,0	NO..P<3 or >8
S = 3		C'F = 0	An	= 4,0	YES..Pure H <2
		C' = 0	Art	= 3,0	NO..R<17
DQ		FT = 2	Ay	= 1,0	6.....TOTAL
.........(FQ–)		TF = 0	Bl	= 0,0	
+ = 5 (0)		T = 0	Bt	= 2,1	SPECIAL SCORINGS
o = 17(4)		FV = 1	Cg	= 1,0	Lvl Lv2
v/+ = 0 (0)		VF = 0	Cl	= 0,0	DV = 0x1 0x2
v = 2 (0)		V = 0	Ex	= 0,0	INC = 0x2 0x4
		FY = 1	Fd	= 0,0	DR = 0x3 0x6
		YF = 1	Fi	= 1,1	FAB = 0x4 0x7
		Y = 0	Ge	= 0,0	ALOG = 0x5
		Fr = 0	Hh	= 0,0	CON = 0x7
FORM QUALITY		rF = 0	Ls	= 0,0	SUM6 = 0
		FD = 0	Na	= 0,0	WSUM6 = 0
FQx FQf MQual SQx		F = 8	Sc	= 1,0	
+ = 2 0 1 0			Sx	= 0,0	AB =0 CP = 2
o = 14 5 1 2			Xy	= 0,0	AG =0 MOR = 1
u = 4 0 0 0			Id	= 0,0	CFB =0 PER = 0
– = 4 3 0 1					COP =1 PSV = 0
none = 0 – 0 0		(2) = 4			

RATIOS, PERCENTAGES, AND DERIVATIONS

R = 24	L = 0.50	FC:CF+C =4:3	COP = 1	AG = 0
		Pure C =0	Food	= 0
EB = 2:5.0	EA = 7.0 EBPer = 2.5	Afr =0.26	Isolate/R	= 0.13
eb = 4:9	es = 13 D = –2	S =3	H:(H)Hd(Hd)	= 1:4
	Adj es = 8 Adj D = 0	Blends:R =6:24	(HHd):(AAd)	= 2:0
		CP =2	H+A:Hd + Ad	= 6:5
FM = 1	C' = 1 T = 2			
m = 3	V = 2 Y = 4			
		P = 4 Zf =13	3r+(2)/R = 0.17	
a:p = 4:2	Sum6 = 0	X+% = 0.67 Zd =+2.0	Fr+rF = 0	
Ma:Mp = 1:1	Lv2 = 0	F+% = 0.63 W:D:Dd =11:11:2	FD = 1	
2AB+Art+Ay = 4	WSum6 = 0	X–% = 0.17 W:M = 11:2	An + Xy = 4	
M– = 0	Mnone = 0	S–% = 0.25 DQ+ =5	MOR = 1	
		Xu% = 0.17 DQv =2		

SCZI = 1	DEPI = 7*	CDI = 4*	S-CON = 6	HVI = No	OBS = No

21

Personality Factors in Chronic Fatigue Syndrome: Psychological Assessment

Robert Lovitt
Cynthia A. Claassen
The University of Texas Southwestern Medical Center

Psychodiagnostic evaluation and consultation is a prized and important skill for psychologists practicing in medical-surgical settings (Lovitt 1984, 1987; Lovitt & Weiner, 1980). Cases in which patients do not respond to traditional medical therapies or in which symptomatic complaints exceed what can be inferred from medical-psychiatric evaluation are perplexing to medical personnel and expensive and frustrating for patients. The ability of psychologists to provide diagnostic and treatment recommendations in such cases has been well described in the Minnesota Multiphasic Personality Inventory (MMPI) literature (Graham, 1993). In its original conception, MMPI (Hathaway & McKinley, 1940) scales were constructed to identify patients who developed physical symptoms in response to psychic stressors (Dahlstrom & Welsh, 1960). Rorschach work with medical patients has been less thoroughly documented, and interest in hysterical and psychophysiological processes had a more indirect and limited impact on this test's construction. Therefore, the Rorschach has had a more limited role in the assessment of somaticizing conditions than it has had with other psychiatric groups. In addition, there are limited empirical data and few helpful models are available to the practicing clinician (Lovitt 1987).

The biopsychosocial model (Engel, 1980) provides the most comprehensive understanding of patients' illness behavior. The model asserts that a patient's behavioral response to disease is determined by an interaction of biological (e.g., a virus, specific organ system being affected), psychological (e.g., level of ego organization, personality style), and social-environmental factors (e.g., family support). The interaction between these factors transforms biological pathology into a highly subjective psychological experience resulting in a unique pattern of illness behavior. Illness behavior differs from cellular and physiological disease. *Disease* may be understood as the underlying physio-chemical process operating at the cellular level and impacting organ systems. *Illness behavior* is a reflection of the patient's emotional equilibrium secondary to processing the feelings precipitated by disease. Individuals with similar disease processes behave differently due to their unique personality functioning.

Illness behavior is dependent on a host of psychological variables that become the major focus of the psychodiagnostic evaluation. Patients who cope most successfully with the biological aspects of their disease are those with a good social support system who successfully grieve the loss of health secondary to disease and who improvise techniques for altering their lifestyles. In facilitating the development of successful coping behavior, psychologists must keep in mind that losses associated with chronic disease invariably have unique symbolic significance to patients. Their symbolic meaning is dependent on the patient's history, intrapsychic life, and social environment. Thus, patients must discover new sources of reward and gratification and come to terms with the personality disruption generated by psychological regression secondary to the disease.

This discussion presents an example of how to evaluate the quality of a patient's psychological response (or "illness behavior") to a disease of unknown etiology. A conceptual-empirical orientation (Weiner, 1986) to data analysis is used. We demonstrate use of the Rorschach and MMPI in combination—the most powerful and justifiable set of instruments available to assess patients' illness behavior.

CHRONIC FATIGUE SYNDROME (CFS)

CFS is a debilitating disorder in which the exact etiology remains unknown. Research suggests four potential etiologies for CFS: (a) infectious, (b) immunological, (c) psychological, and (d) musculoskeletal deconditioning. The syndrome is often reported following acute illness caused by a variety of infectious agents (Summergrad, Rauch, & Neal, 1993).

The central symptom of CFS is disabling fatigue that impairs patients' routine lifestyles, particularly social and occupational activities. Typical complaints include persistent, severe fatigue lasting 6 months or more and reduced activity below 50% of premorbid functioning. For the diagnosis to be made, a full medical evaluation must rule out other possible causes of fatigue. Additional typical complaints are feelings of feverishness, tender or enlarged lymph nodes, recurrent sore throat, depressed mood, and cognitive impairment (attention and concentration). Many of the complaints are subjective and often difficult to objectively replicate (Summergrad et al., 1993).

No persistent infection or cause has been found as an etiology for CFS and it is felt that additional research needs to be done in order to clearly determine the potential role of infectious agents. It has also been suggested that psychological factors play an important role in precipitating and maintaining the illness in a significant number of patients.

CASE HISTORY

L. is a 43-year-old White woman who has been diagnosed with CFS. She is seen in conjunction with a psychiatric and medical workup requested by her primary care physician. She complains of symptoms of fatigue, pain, decreased concentration, and sleeping problems. She describes pain in her joints and lymph nodes and reports that she is not able to engage in fine motor behavior. The symptoms began after a flulike illness when the patient was 38 years old. She was never well after that time and suffered from chronic exhaustion. At age 40, reportedly as a result of her physical condition, she became depressed and suicidal and was admitted to a psychiatric hospital for a 2-week stay. She was treated for depression with medications and a 16-month course of intensive outpatient psychotherapy. Symptoms of depression were resolved, although there has never been a change in the complaints of fatigue.

L. graduated from college, having done well in course work and having participated in a broad range of extracurricular activities. She worked successfully as an attorney with a series of law firms until age 38. After college she maintained an active personal life engaging in several sports and social activities. She had been employed at a major law firm since age 35 and had worked as a trial attorney. She was promoted with increased corporate-legal responsibilities and was able to maintain her career until about 10 months after she became ill. At that time, she had to assume increasingly less demanding responsibilities until she was essentially unable to work. At the time of evaluation she denied symptoms of depression but stated that it required a lot of effort not to become depressed again. L. denied medical difficulties before the onset of her illness.

L. is the youngest of five children. Her parents died shortly after her birth. They were killed in a motor vehicle accident. The children were sent to different family members and had minimal contact with each other. L. was raised by a paternal uncle who never married. She remained with this uncle whom she described as being very critical and perfectionistic toward her and everyone else with whom he came in contact. L. basically looked after herself. The patient recalls being fearful that she would be abandoned by her uncle and responded by becoming a perfectionistic, driven, active achiever. She was in a number of honor societies, and was very active in high school sports and numerous social and extracurricular activities. She did well in high school, college, and law school. She describes herself as having been very unhappy on the inside while functioning well and being able to overcome these internal difficulties. "I turned anger and misery into a strength; I used misery positively." She was married at age 31 and stated she was drawn toward her husband's stable and solid family. She was divorced at age 37 and had another close relationship with a man that broke up a couple of months before her psychiatric hospitalization. The initial flulike illness developed shortly after the finalization of her divorce.

A focused psychological consultation follows an articulation of pertinent referral questions. The referral questions direct our attention to specific test indices that allow us to understand our patient's illness behavior. We wish to determine:

1. Is there a syndrome of psychologically based symptoms producing or aggravating illness behavior? Do these symptoms intensify the experiences of physical distress?
2. What are the patient's coping strategies and pathological conflicts?
3. What is the psychological etiology of these symptoms?
4. What are pertinent treatment and management recommendations?

MMPI INTERPRETATION

Diagnostically, a relevant *behavioral* description characterizing illness behavior begins with a pertinent MMPI interpretation. In Fig. 21.1 the mean profile pattern of a group of 25,723 female medical patients who had a broad range of diagnoses (Severson, Pearson, & Osborne, 1973) is compared to the typical MMPI–2 profile that we have found in patients with severe chronic disease. The typical MMPI–2 profile is derived from the authors' experience and the literature. (See, e.g., profile of seriously ill patients, Kurland & Hammer, 1968; of end-stage renal failure patients, Osberg, Meares, McKee, & Burnett, 1982; and of chronic obstructive pulmonary emphysema patients, DeCencio, Leschner, & Leshner, 1968). These are cases in which there is widespread disruption of biopsychosocial functioning secondary to disease process affecting multiple organ systems. Significant elevations on scales *1, 2,* and *3* are typically found. These elevations reflect genuine somatic distress (*1* and *3*) and depressive experiences. It is generally assumed that marked elevations on scales *1* and *3* ($T > 80$) suggest significant factors impacting on physical functioning (Graham, 1993). MMPI findings of L. are represented in Figs. 21.2 and 21.3. Significant differences in the profiles are apparent. L. has significantly higher scores on scales *1, 2,* and *3*. The valley at scale *2,* the major elevation of scale *3,* and the elevation of the right side of the profile are noteworthy.

Based on the MMPI, L. may be described as extraordinarily preoccupied with a broad range of distressing physical symptoms that preclude her being able to attend to and become involved in work-related and pleasurable activities. She spends much of her time being worried and apprehensive about her health and well-being. Her life centers around the sick role. She is not

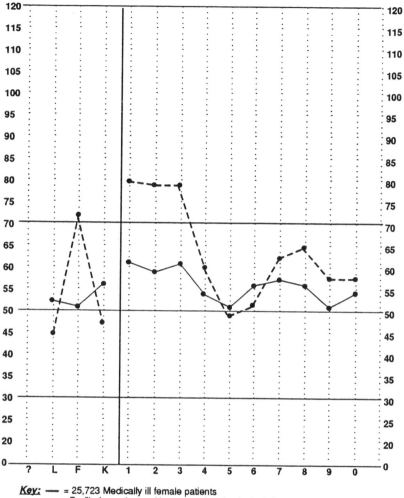

FIG. 21.1.   Mean MMPI profile of medically ill female patients with a variety
of different disorders. Medically ill female profile source: Swenson, W.,
Pearson, J., & Osborne, D. *An MMPI Source Book*. Minneapolis: University
of Minnesota Press, 1973. Reproduced by permission of Mayo Clinic and the
University of Minnesota Press. MMPI template source: Minnesota Multiphasic Personality Inventory (MMPI) Profile for Content Scales. Copyright ©
1989 the Regents of the University of Minnesota. All rights reserved. "MMPI"
and "Minnesota Multiphasic Personality Inventory" are trademarks owned
by the University of Minnesota. Reproduced by permission of the University
of Minnesota Press.

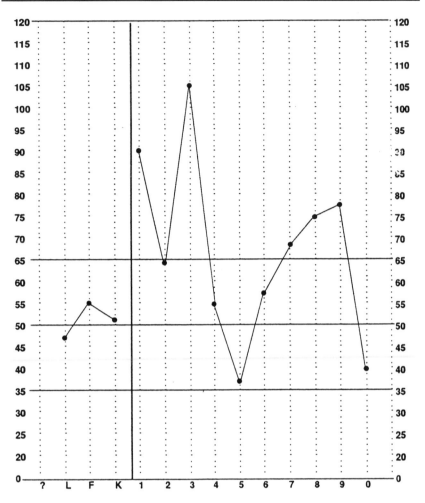

FIG. 21.2. T-Scores for L.'s MMPI–2 Validity and Clinical scale scores. MMPI template source: Minnesota Multiphasic Personality Inventory (MMPI) Profile for Content Scales. Copyright © 1989 the Regents of the University of Minnesota. All rights reserved. "MMPI" and "Minnesota Multiphasic Personality Inventory" are trademarks owned by the University of Minnesota. Reproduced by permission of the University of Minnesota Press.

likely to experience enduring relief from these symptoms in response to medical intervention. She probably experiences extensive symptom formation secondary to psychic stressors (e.g., the height and position of scale 3). Psychic stressors are poorly processed and inadequately attended to by L. She has difficulties being able to directly confront conflictual ideas and affects; she experiences increased fatigue and physical distress as a result of not directly confronting psychological conflict. Therefore, an adequate intervention for L. intended to target complaints of fatigue needs to address psychological contributions to symptom formation.

A critical stage in our consultation is to understand the etiology of this dysfunctional behavior by selective Rorschach interpretation. Precise understanding of etiology will lead to focused treatment planning.

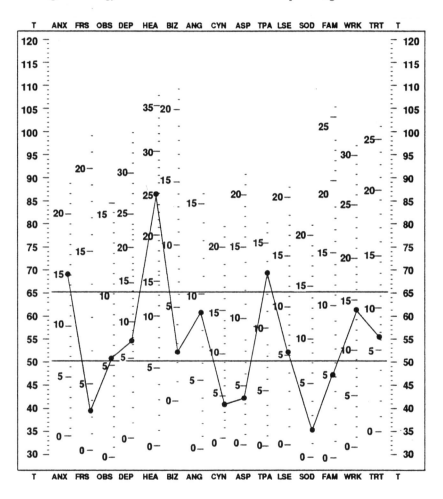

FIG. 21.3. MMPI–2 Content scales profile for L. MMPI template source: Minnesota Multiphasic Personality Inventory (MMPI) Profile for Content Scales. Copyright © 1989 the Regents of the University of Minnesota. All rights reserved. "MMPI" and "Minnesota Multiphasic Personality Inventory" are trademarks owned by the University of Minnesota. Reproduced by permission of the University of Minnesota Press.

For clinically relevant MMPI–Rorschach integration to take place, a series of data analysis strategies are undertaken. These steps do not occur in a sequential manner but characterize the general interpretive approach.

1. Interpret MMPI features relevant to referral issues.
2. Interpret Rorschach features relevant to referral issues.
3. Identify areas of MMPI–Rorschach consistency.
4. Reaffirm and/or modify statements generated from initial MMPI review after Rorschach review.
5. Identify areas of MMPI–Rorschach inconsistency; offer explanations regarding inconsistencies and their clinical meaning.
6. Integrate test-derived hypotheses with historical information.
7. Effect a transition from nomothetic-level hypotheses to idiographic, clinically pertinent statements.

RORSCHACH AND HISTORICAL INTERPRETATION

The approach to interpretation when combining the Rorschach and MMPI is different than when utilizing either instrument by itself. Emphasizing an interpretive approach that thoroughly, scientifically, and parsimoniously addresses patient referral issues is utilized.

Use of structural summary data (Exner, 1993) has been employed with an informal clinical approach to selective content analysis. In this case this type of analysis of these databases provides the most efficient basis for interpretation.

L's Rorschach responses are found in Appendix A, with response scores and structural summary profile in Appendices B and C. L. experiences intense and disruptive depressive symptoms ($DEPI = 5$) that create widespread adaptive difficulties. She engages in excessive self-examination (FD, FV) in which she experiences self-reproach and disappointment with herself. Her affective life is dysphoric (right side $eb = 10$) with intense episodes of agitating depression ($FV.FY$) and a generalized sense of dissatisfaction and anxiety experienced in the presence of others ($S = 5$, $Y = 4$, color-shading blends). She has become socially isolated (Isolation index $= .37$).

These experiences are easily aroused and desperately denied ($R1$). Despite a variety of defensive maneuvers she begins and terminates her Rorschach protocol with graphic testament to her depressive burden (R 26 and 27). $R26$, "The pink and purple area reminds me of bruised human tissue," reflects a joining of depressive ideation with a somatic defense (An) in the presence of regressed (DQv) and faulty processing and mediation.

We have found apparent contradictions between Rorschach and MMPI data to be singularly important in revealing crucial information about patients. We suspect more adequately integrated patients have a close correspondence between their verbalizations (MMPI) and their experiences and performance (Rorschach). Those less adequately integrated have a greater discrepancy between what they say to themselves and others as opposed to how they function. L. has significant discrepancies between Rorschach and MMPI indices of depression. These discrepancies are central to understanding psychic contributions to her physical complaints. She is not able to verbally articulate depressive experiences to herself or to those involved in her care (MMPI depression scales, clinical examination).

L. constructed a lifestyle centering around energized competition and success in social and vocational roles. Her lifestyle was superimposed on experienced parental abandonment and neglect and abuse by caretakers. Although "extremely unhappy" on the inside, she was competent, intelligent, attractive, and performed well. A failed marriage and loss of a family support system at age 38 probably stimulated fears of abandonment and preceded her protracted illness. She became seriously ill for the first time in her life and suffered a depressive illness. Her major defensive and adaptational strategies (i.e., energized activity) became unavailable during this period and she developed an extended flu and depression. In the presence of these multiple losses she was less able to protect herself from intrapsychic conflicts that she previously defended against.

L.'s conflicts around relationships are related to significant attachment pathology reflected in a variety of Rorschach indices. The presence of four texture responses suggests painful loneliness and affective hunger reflecting her sense of deprivation. Her ambivalent attitude toward attachment is indicated by the content and context within which these responses are offered. Disembodied and artificial (R7) and "rough bark" (R8) suggests affective hunger accompanied by shallow and negative expectations. Affective hunger (R12, R13) stimulates fears of disappointment defended against by efforts to appear confident and optimistic (Color Projection). The outcome of this inadequate denial is a defensive failure with morbid ideation and agitating anxiety (R14).

L.'s ambivalence surrounding her attachment needs is reflected in several domains of functioning. She has a generally negative affective set toward her environment (S = 5). She becomes anxious and apprehensive when interacting with others (color-shading blends = 2). Although she is intensely involved and interested in others (M = 4, H = 5), this interest occurs in the context of energized accomplishment in which she "struts her stuff" (R 3, 6, 10, 20). A loss of ability to perform and to satisfy attachment needs while performing (MMPI-elevated 9) leaves her vulnerable to conflicted expectations about what she can hope for from others when she is not performing. Previously repressed affects of self-doubt (V = 3) and confusion about her own identity (R1, 9) were probably reenergized subsequent to the breakup of her marriage and loss of her husband's family; this likely stimulated unresolved feelings of loss, perhaps secondary to the loss of her parents. She was made even more vulnerable by the loss of her major adult identification (career) and major defensive strategy of compulsive, energized achievement. (She was unable to work, perform, and achieve.) Therefore, the biopsychosocial stressors preceding and accompanying the CFS may be summarized as: (a) the biological stressors: likely viral infection that may or may not be continuous; (b) psychological stressors: depression and regression with a reenergizing of previously repressed conflicts and a probable use of somaticizing defenses; and (c) social stressors: loss of marriage, career, and adult social roles.

At this time L. is not able to verbalize to herself or others an accurate representation of these losses and her attendant psychic experience. Synthesizing MMPI–Rorschach differences allows us to conclude that she denies having depressive affects and cognition. Instead she transforms the depressive experiences (that she demonstrates to us on the Rorschach) so that they are experienced and understood as arising from physical fatigue and dysfunction (MMPI code 1 2 3, scale 3 elevation). Further Rorschach review and interpretation of pertinent historical events allows us to more fully understand the nature of the specific depressive pattern.

Early life deprivation and trauma are often reacted to with more primitive defenses than losses occurring at later stages of life. Denial during L.'s early years may have been important in shielding her from intense feelings of being unworthy of having parents. This sense was reinforced by a harsh and demanding uncle who filled the caretaking role, but was minimally involved in nurturing and care-taking activities. The loss of her higher level defenses and coping patterns (i.e., intellectualization, competitive achievement, and accomplishment) and adult identity roles provoked a regression to the previously repressed conflicts and defenses that emerged in the psychological testing.

L.'s current use of denial is excessive and self-defeating. It interferes with her ability to appropriately deal with losses and frustrations associated with her disease and illness. She "makes believe" and acts as though her psychic pain and embitterment do not exist (CP). She has limited insight into the psychic meaning of her discomfort ($D = 0$). She nevertheless carries an exhausting and painful psychological burden ($es = 14$). Avoiding but yet being subjected to $es = 14$ drains her energy and her morale. She feels demoralized and exhausted doing this but understands the exhaustion as being secondary to a CFS virus (MMPI 1–3 code). L. subjects herself to an extraordinary psychic burden by relying so heavily on denial. It is a strenuous psychic task to transform so much pain and shame into a positive attitude of psychic tranquility and harmony. The psychic pain does not disappear. It continues to act on her and drain her energy. The defense of denial allows her to maintain the belief that the source of her pain and fatigue is secondary to a physical illness and not secondary to psychic frustrations and disappointments. The burden of this transformation leaves her with little energy to attend to other tasks.

Inspection of response sequences allows us to understand how L.'s pattern of conflict, defense, and impairment originate. We avoid using jargonistic technical terms whenever feasible to describe this process. Instead we describe the process in nontechnical language. We have found that using nontechnical descriptive terms significantly enhances our ability to provide feedback to patients and laypersons. We may expect to see patients who function at differing developmental (age), psychological (level of sophistication), or intellectual levels. Effective feedback is correlated with the ability to translate technical concepts into everyday language employed by patients.

L. begins her Rorschach (*R1*) with a response combining Color Projection, Vista, and identity confusion. In one response she summarizes the psychic structure underlying her reaction to her losses: severe self-doubt accompanied by negative affects that she is unable to acknowledge directly and come to terms with. She attempts to convince herself "all is well" and in the process "makes believe" everything is going well in her life except for her health. This make-believe effort creates a barrier to accurate self-examination and makes it difficult for others to understand her. It also interferes with her ability to deal with her actual psychic state. The barriers to self-examinations are partially successful (*R2*). She achieves momentary psychic relief by assuming a detached intellectual posture (*FD*). This posture is largely self-protective rather than open and engaging, and will be experienced by others as rigidly maintained (*S, PER*). She broods about her condition (*FD* = 4, *FV* = 3) in a rigid intellectualizing manner. (Wouldn't anyone react this way with her type of illness?) L.'s respect for reality and capacity for good object relations are grossly intact. She is not psychotic. However, L's ability to think clearly and to maintain her previous level of functioning has been clearly compromised. She has a situationally generated stress reaction (*Y* = 4, *m* = 2). She manifests considerable thinking difficulties (*M–* = 3, *X+%* = 48, *X–%* = 26) and a deterioration from a previous high level of functioning. Wherever possible she employs her ambition (*Zf* = 17, *R* = 27, *DQ+* = 13) and energized needs to perform (*R3*, 6, 11) to avoid acknowledging her underlying dysphoria.

Patients who react to physical illness with depression manifest behavioral changes complicating the clinical picture of the illness (Rodin & Vashart, 1986). Physiological sequelae of depression are manifested in wide-ranging somatic symptoms that can affect multiple organ systems. The depression response may cause changes in usual patterns of behavior that include withdrawal with loss of energy in social and interpersonal areas. However, loss of self-esteem and dysphoric mood are understood by L. not in psychic terms (*CP*), but secondary to the disease.

FEEDBACK

Historical events have generally had a beneficial and profound impact on the growth of assessment practice (e.g., aftermath of World War II and the need to provide additional psychological services to veterans, innovations in the

French school system, and the development of the Binet Tests at the beginning of the century). Today cultural values are exerting a restrictive impact on psychological practice and specifically on assessment. For Rorschach practice to retain its place in the assessment battery, it is imperative that we pay attention to the pressures of health care economics. It is important to demonstrate that our formulations translate into recommendations that have concrete, practical, efficient, and demonstrable beneficial outcomes for patients. Formulations that are psychodynamically elegant and that invariably lead to recommendations of long-term, insight-oriented psychotherapy are increasingly out of step with reimbursement patterns. Therefore, feedback and output regarding treatment and management recommendations need to be tailored to demonstrate that contemporary Rorschach assessment is consistent with current health care economics and good clinical practice.

We begin by providing feedback to patients and referral sources in which we articulate major conclusions. Treatment intervention begins by viewing the patient and referral sources (including managed care entities) as informed, critical consumers. This permits patients (and managed care entities) to immediately experience how testing (MMPI–2 and Rorschach) ensures that pertinent diagnostic questions are addressed. It also illustrates how test results lead to interventions addressing dysfunctional behaviors. We have found a direct relationship between patients' level of ego organization and their capacity to make use of feedback from psychological testing. Patients at higher levels of organization are able to make more constructive use of extensive feedback than patients at lower levels of organization. Patients at higher levels are able to process and make use of more extensive and threatening material than are patients who are more limited and impaired in their functioning. Despite L.'s regression and her extensive use of denial, she has considerable personality strengths and the ability to make constructive use of the findings from the current evaluation. The following is a narrative reflecting the types of constructs and the specific language we would employ to explain pertinent findings to L. (and managed care entities) and that we would include in a report:

Because of the death of your parents and your uncle's demanding behavior, you had a difficult early life in which you had limited support, affection, and attention. This is very hard for a child to bear; you probably responded with feelings of loneliness, dejection, and perhaps a sense of unworthiness. Because these are difficult feelings to tolerate they ordinarily stimulate children in two ways. One way children respond is by developing strategies to get away from these feelings (defenses). The other way children respond is by developing skills and talents to prove to themselves that they are indeed worthy (adaptation). You specifically responded by not paying attention (denial) to feelings of dejection and proving to yourself and others that you were capable and worthy. You became a high-level achiever to protect yourself from these feelings and to go on with your life. These strategies were necessary for your development when you were a vulnerable child. Despite the deprivation you had considerable talent. You were able to develop skills in many areas, but you were probably never able to totally free yourself from feelings of dejection and unworthiness. You described your uncle as critical and perfectionistic and you learned that if you performed well you were able to retain his love and approval and he would not abandon you. You stated that you were extremely unhappy on the inside but functioned well. In other words, you "turned your anger and misery into strength" and that was an admirable and courageous effort on your part. That strategy worked for you, particularly in the world of work, until you became ill and things fell apart.

You had learned to avoid those feelings of loneliness and dejection by working hard for long hours in order to become successful in many different areas. Although you were able to avoid these feelings, they did not disappear. As long as you were successful and the feelings were avoided you were able to continue to perform.

Your marriage was an effort to enrich your life with experiences of intimacy you had not had before. A successful and enduring marriage is usually one in which a person's weaknesses and vulnerabilities are exposed. Even though the marriage failed, your intense need for unconditional acceptance and love probably became more apparent to you through that experience. It is likely that you were more emotionally vulnerable at that time. The failure of a marriage is considered a major adult life stressor and you were particularly vulnerable to this stressor because of your history of experienced rejection. Subsequent to the coincidental merging of the divorce, increased vulnerability, and flulike illness, you needed to relinquish selected work and achievement-related activities that partially served as self-protective devices (defenses) for you. One outcome of this life dilemma was that you developed a severe depression, which was probably a result of your struggles subsequent to the divorce and achievement-oriented losses.

A person's health is determined by an interaction of biological, psychological, and social factors. At this time we do not clearly understand the nature of the specific biological underpinnings of CFS. As medical research progresses, this will undoubtedly become easier to understand. What we can do now is describe very precisely to you your psychological reaction to a disease of unclear etiology and how it fits in with your life history.

You have become incapacitated by feelings of fatigue and a worried despondency about your health. In addition, worries and fears that had been largely set aside have reemerged and are intensifying whatever biological factors exist that produce your current sense of fatigue.

You are experiencing emotions of loneliness, dejection, and unworthiness and you expend considerable energy to avoid acknowledging these feelings. This is an exhausting burden! People with your pattern of test results are extremely sensitive to being threatened by events in their lives that stimulate those things they are most afraid of. You spent a great deal of your life proving to yourself and others you were a worthy and lovable person. When you are stimulated by fears of being unworthy and unlovable, a number of things happen. Your negative and confused feelings become intensified. Your self-protective denial increases. At the same time you feel worse, more dejected, and hopeless, but are unaware of the situations in your life or in your imagination that stimulate this reaction. You focus on the physical component of your distress, not the ideas or fears, and you understand this as part of your CFS.

We find it helpful to think about your improvement as being divided into things that can be done immediately and activities that need to be attended to over a longer period of time. There are steps that you can take to bring your self immediate relief.

You currently have intense needs for personal contact. You are preoccupied with and long for social contact and you have become socially isolated. Some of your feelings of demoralization come from feelings of deprivation in this area.

We will work with you to develop increased social participation at a level consistent with your physical stamina. One place you might start is by doing volunteer work in a nursing home or children's hospital. This would allow you to perform socially involved tasks and give you the opportunity to develop social relationships with residents and other volunteers. It would also allow you to rekindle your sense of purpose through action, which remains an important need for you. Our initial intervention will focus on providing you with counsel and support to get you going in this area. We anticipate you will feel immediate relief as we put this plan into operation (supportive psychotherapy).

To complicate matters, you have several negative expectations about how rewarding social contact will be when it occurs outside of a work or competitive setting. These feelings may interfere with your ability to establish rewarding personal relations in purely social situations when you are not performing or competing with others. This is probably due to early expectations about being lovable only when you were competent and successful.

Wishes for emotional closeness and cynicism about whether these needs will be met create tension and mixed feelings in many of your current relationships. This may have created difficulties for you in establishing new relationships after your divorce. As stressors accumulated for you—divorce, extended flu, loss of job responsibilities—you began to rely more heavily on the self-protective measures (defenses) you had used when you were a vulnerable child. A major strategy was to try to make believe everything was really just fine with your relationships and your feelings, and that the only problem you had was that you were physically ill. You came to believe that any negative feeling that you had was due to your illness and not how you were appraising your life situation. Because of this it appears that your loss of energy, fatigue, and demoralization are actually depressive experiences and treatable by a combination of lifestyle changes and attitudinal changes (psychotherapy). The lifestyle changes can begin with some immediate modifications in how you spend your free time. The attitudinal changes about yourself and your relationships will occur more slowly. A course of psychotherapy to examine feelings and ideas will involve considerable effort and dedication.

CONCLUSION

What are the implications of this case for a contemporary personality assessment? Effective Rorschach use coincides with an appreciation of strengths and limitations of the instrument. L. is a patient not able to verbally articulate the nature and extent of her despair. She has been vigorously committed to a pattern of self-deception that is clearly unmasked through Rorschach examination. L.'s deceptions require that a massive amount of energy be devoted toward convincing herself she is psychologically at peace with herself—an exhausting process. Despite the fact that she has performed well she has areas of significant intrapsychic vulnerability, the most notable being intense and ambivalent attachment needs.

In medical-surgical settings involving psychodiagnostic consultation the Rorschach is most productively used as part of a test battery. A self-report instrument such as the MMPI that has extensive validity data regarding somatization disorders should regularly be paired with the Rorschach.

Use of the Rorschach leads us directly toward focused treatment planning. Our clinical experience indicates that patients achieve significant relief when receiving feedback from psychological testing. Finn's (1994) work provides objective support for the therapeutic impact of feedback.

More specific feedback can be provided to L.'s psychotherapist concerning treatment goals and potential resistances. We anticipate L. will achieve immediate gains from this feedback and support focused on helping her reestablish interpersonal networks via charitable activities. Longer term treatment targets would be directed toward treating the depressive and conflictual attitudes. The treatment can be conceptualized as having two components: a supportive set of interventions that will generate fairly immediate benefits and longer term interventions that are necessary to maintain therapeutic gains.

We anticipate that steps to help L. reestablish limited areas of energized accomplishments, such as involvement in a part-time charitable activity, would help her move out of her regressed state.

Finally, as this chapter illustrates, close collaboration with treating physicians and psychotherapists can facilitate heightened sensitivity regarding psychic contributions to disease processes.

ACKNOWLEDGMENT

We wish to extend our appreciation to Kaye Starr Woolery for her assistance in the preparation of this manuscript.

REFERENCES

Dahlstrom, W. G., & Welsh, G. S. (1960). *An MMPI handbook: A guide to use in clinical practice and research*. Minneapolis: University of Minnesota Press.

DeCencio, D. V., Leshner, M., & Leschner, B. (1968). Personality characteristics of patients with chronic obstructive pulmonary emphysema. *Archives of Physical Medicine and Rehabilitation, 49,* 471–475.

Engel, G. (1980). The clinical application of the biopsychosocial model. *American Journal of Psychiatry, 137,* 535–544.

Exner, J. (1993). *The Rorschach: A comprehensive system: Vol. 1. Basic foundations* (3rd. ed.). New York: Wiley.

Finn, S. (1994). Therapeutic aspects of psychological assessment. *Society for Personality Assessment Exchange, 4,* 2.

Graham, J. (1993). *MMPI-2: Assessing personality and psychopathology*. New York: Oxford University Press.

Hathaway, S. R., & McKinley, J. C. (1940). A multiphasic personality schedule: I Construction of the schedule. *Journal of Psychology, 10,* 249–254.

Kurland, H. D., & Hammer, M. (1968). Emotional evaluation of medical patients. *Archives of General Psychiatry, 19,* 72–78.

Lovitt, R. (1984). Rorschach interpretation in a multidisciplinary hospital setting. *Professional Psychology: Research and Practice, 15,* 244–250.

Lovitt, R. (1987). A conceptual model and case study for the psychological assessment of pseudoseizures with the Rorschach. *Journal of Personality Assessment, 5,* 207–219.

Lovitt, R., & Weiner, M. (1980). Conservation-withdrawal: A Rorschach case study. *Journal of Personality Assessment, 44,* 460–464.

Osberg, L. W., Meares, G. L., McKee, D. C., & Burnett, G. B. (1982). The MMPI as a measure of the emotional correlates of chronic hemodialysis: A review. *Journal of Personality Assessment, 46,* 268–278.

Rodin, G., & Vashart, K. (1986). Depression in the medically ill: Overview. *American Journal of Psychiatry, 143,* 696–705.

Severson, W., Pearson, J., & Osborne, D. (1973). *An MMPI source book*. Minneapolis: University of Minnesota Press.

Summergrad, P., Rauch, S., & Neal, R. (1993). Human Immunodeficiency Virus and other infectious disorders affecting the central nervous system. In A. Stoudemire & B. Fogel (Eds.), *Psychiatric care of the medical patient* (pp. 1–50). New York: Oxford University Press.

Weiner, I. (1986). Conceptual and empirical perspectives on the Rorschach assessment of psychopathology. *Journal of Personality Assessment, 50,* 472-479.

I.

1. A cross between an insect and a butterfly; a moth and a butterfly.

(Q) Body and wings. Is distorted because there are shadows on top of it. Dark shadows over parts which make parts look farther away and parts closer. I can see greens, oranges and yellows. White part would be designs. Body of moth and wings of butterfly.

2. Aerial view of lakes, like when I flew into Montana.

(Q) Different coves. White looks like islands, road going across the lake. I've seen lakes like this way up from an airplane.

II.

3. Two Russian dancers with red hats and shoes on.

(Q) They're kicking together and hitting their hands, body, feet, and they're in motion.

4. A space shuttle. You're from above looking down like this is the ground and it's coming in for a landing.

(Q) Black part is the ground and shuttle above it. It's coming down because it's covering up part of the ground.

5. Birds' heads.

(Q) Beaks, mouth, neck.

III.

6. Two men playing bongo drums, the Desi Arnez type of drum with musical notes.

(Q) Head, upper torso, arms, legs and shoes. These are the drums, these are musical notes or a rough sketch of a guitar to denote the music. It looks like a guitar and it's representing the playing of music.

IV.

7. It is laying flat on its back. Looks like a costume of some type.

(Q) You're looking at it from the bottom perspective cause the head is smaller. Feet, legs, shoulders looks like costume cause it has a lot of texture to it. The dark and light.

8. Huge tree.

(Q) Like a redwood where you drive through spaces in the trees. These are limbs and it looks like it's going way up in the air into infinity. Rough texture like bark because of the different shades.

V.

9. It looks like the body of a butterfly but not the wings.

(Q) Tail of a butterfly, butterfly body but wings don't go with the body. It looks like something is covering the wings up so I can't see the wings of the butterfly. Looks like wings are darker than the head which makes it look like something is covering it and it looks like head is farther away.

10. Someone's feet in a ballet slipper.

(Q) Foot and slipper.

11. Looks like the LaCosta alligator.

(Q) Head—the Izod alligator head.

VI.

12. An Indian heritage—like a weave or blanket pattern.

(Q) Feathers. Darker section looks light and dark like weave. Also looks like there are many different colors. I like, see greens, blues, oranges, and yellow.

(continued)

13. Animal skin.

(Q) Got texture with Indian like feathers. The darks and the lights.

14. An aerial view like flying over Salt Lake City. All of a sudden you see a road going through it.

(Q) I've never seen anything uglier than Salt Lake City. It is very barren. It looks dark on the edges. Like a road in the middle because it's darker.

VII.

15. Looks like busts of two little old ladies facing one another with funny hats on and these look like the backs of rocking chairs.

(Q) Profiles, nose, hair, hats with plumes, and this is the curved back of a rocking chair. Busts facing each other.

VIII.

16. Looks like two bears climbing rocks and trees.

(Q) Their heads, legs. Pink looks like rocks. The colors are mixed and overlapping each other and it almost makes it look like a water-color painting.

17. Something at the bottom reminds me of a racoon though I don't clearly see the shape.

(Q) Stripes and the tail and body. Looks like dark and light.

IX.

18. A seed that's opening at the edge of the ground before it blooms into something. The different layers of the earth.

(Q) It's cracking open and something wants to sprout. These are layers of the earth, the orange is up by the sun which makes it appear warm. The ground there would be warm to the touch.

X.

19. Things underwater in the ocean. Blue looks like crabs.

(Q) Body and claws.

20. Scuba divers.

(Q) Leg and their flippers and their bodies and they have tanks on and it looks like they are swimming.

21. Sea horses.

(Q) Just the curve of the body.

22. Coral formations and stuff.

(Q) Thin and wide and pink.

23. Two little creatures—fictional that are talking. They look angry.

(Q) Legs, tails, amoeba-like body, eyes, antenna.

24. Eiffel Tower.

(Q) Shape.

25. These two don't look as mean as those two but they appear to have horns and guns.

(Q) Heads, snout, horns, look like guns. Look like they are holding a gun.

26. The pink and purple area reminds me of bruised human tissue.

(Q) I saw some gross picture on TV, the internal flesh. It gets dark purple.

27. All the yellow gives it a bright sunny effect and with all the colors and stuff I keep trying to make it into a flower garden but it won't work.

(Q) Just the yellow. I like the color and yellow is bright and optimistic.

Sequence of Scores

Card	No.	Loc.	Determinant(s)	(2)	Content(s)	Pop Z	Special Scores
I	1	DdS+	FVu		A	4.0	CP, INC1
	2	WS+	FDu		Ls	3.5	PER
II	3	W+	Ma.FCo	2	H, Cg	4.5	COP
	4	DS+	FD.mao		Sc, Ls	4.5	
	5	Ddo	F–	2	Ad		
III	6	D+	Ma+	2	H, Cg, Sc	P 4.0	AB, COP
IV	7	Do	FD.FTo		H, Ad		
	8	WS+	FT.FDo		Bt	5.0	
V	9	W+	FVu		A	2.5	
	10	D+	Fu		Hd, Cg	2.5	
	11	Do	Fo		Ad, Art		
VI	12	Wo	FTo		Ad, Ay	P 2.5	CP
	13	Wo	FTo		Ad	P 2.5	
	14	Wo	FV. FYu		Ge	2.5	MOR, PER
VII	15	D+	Fu	2	Hd, Hh	P 3.0	
VIII	16	W+	FMa.CF.YFo	2	A, Ls	P 4.5	
	17	Ddo	FY–		A		
IX	18	W+/v	ma.CF–		Na	5.5	
X	19	Do	Fo	2	A	P	
	20	D+	Ma–	2	H, Cg	4.0	
	21	Do	Fo	2	A		
	22	Do	CFo	2	Ls		
	23	DS+	Ma–	2	(H)	6.0	AG
	24	Do	Fo		Ay		
	25	D+	Mp–	2	H	4.5	
	26	Dv	CF.YF–		An		MOR, PER
	27	Dv	C		Na		AB

APPENDIX C
Rorschach Structural Summary

LOCATION FEATURES	DETERMINANTS BLENDS	SINGLE	CONTENTS	S-CONSTELLATION
			H = 5,0	YES..FV + VF + V + FD > 2
			(H) = 1,0	YES..Col-Shd Bl>0
Zf = 17	M.FC	M = 4	Hd = 2,0	NO..Ego<.31,>.44
ZSum = 65.5	FD.ma	FM = 0	(Hd) = 0,0	NO..MOR>3
ZEst = 56.0	FD.FT	m = 0	Hx = 0,0	YES..Zd > ± 3.5
	FT.FD	FC = 0	A = 6,0	YES..es>EA
W = 9	FV.FY	CF = 1	(A) = 0,0	YES..CF+C>FC
(Wv = 0)	FM.CF.YF	C = 1	Ad = 5,0	YES..X+%<.70
D = 15	m.CF	Cn = 0	(Ad) = 0,0	YES..S>3
Dd = 3	CF.YF	FC' = 0	An = 1,0	NO..P<3 or >8
S = 5		C'F = 0	Art = 1,0	NO..Pure H <2
		C' = 0	Ay = 2,0	NO..R<17
DQ		FT = 2	Bl = 0,0	7.....TOTAL
.........(FQ-)		TF = 0	Bt = 1,0	
+ = 10(1)		T = 0	Cg = 4,0	SPECIAL SCORINGS

		Lvl	Lv2
DV	= 0x1		0x2
INC	= 1x2		0x4
DR	= 0x3		0x6
FAB	= 0x4		0x7
ALOG	= 0x5		
CON	= 0x7		
SUM6	= 1		
WSUM6	= 2		

				CONTENTS	
o = 15(4)		FV = 2	Cl = 0,0		
v/+ = 1 (1)		VF = 0	Ex = 0,0		
v = 2 (1)		V = 0	Fd = 0,0		
		FY = 1	Fi = 0,0		
		YF = 0	Ge = 1,0		
		Y = 0	Hh = 1,0		
		Fr = 0	Ls = 4,0		
		rF = 0	Na = 2,0		

FORM QUALITY

	FQx	FQf	MQual	SQx			
+	= 1	0	1	0	FD = 1	Sc = 2,0	AB =2 CP = 2
o	= 14	5	2	0	F = 7	Sx = 0,0	AG =1 MOR = 2
u	= 4	1	0	0		Xy = 0,0	CFB =0 PER = 3
−	= 7	1	3	0		Id = 0,0	COP =2 PSV = 0
none	= 1	−	0	0	(2) = 11		

RATIOS, PERCENTAGES, AND DERIVATIONS

R = 27	L = 0.35		FC:CF+C =1:5	COP = 2	AG = 1
			Pure C =1	Food	= 0
EB = 5:6.0	EA = 11.0	EBPer = N/A	Afr =0.80	Isolate/R	= 0.37
eb = 3:10	es = 14	D = −1	S =5	H:(H)Hd(Hd)	= 5:3
	Adj es = 10	Adj D = 0	Blends:R =8:27	(HHd):(AAd)	= 1:0
			CP =2	H+A:Hd + Ad	= 12:7

FM = 1	C' = 0	T = 4			
m = 2	V = 3	Y = 4			
			P = 6	Zf =17	3r+(2)/R = 0.41
a:p	= 7:1	Sum6 = 1	X+% = 0.48	Zd =+9.5	Fr+rF = 0
Ma:Mp	= 4:1	Lv2 = 0	F+% = 0.57	W:D:Dd =9:15:3	FD = 4
2AB+Art+Ay	= 7	WSum6 = 2	X−% = 0.26	W:M = 9:5	An + Xy = 1
M−	= 3	Mnone = 0	S−% = 0.14	DQ+ =13	MOR = 2
			Xu% = 0.22	DQv =2	

SCZI = 3	DEPI = 5*	CDI = 1	S-CON = 7	HVI = No	OBS = No

22

A Rorschach Child Single-Subject Study in Divorce: A Question of Psychological Resiliency

Donald J. Viglione, Jr.
Janet Kates
California School of Professional Psychology, San Diego

Psychological research findings and developmental theories outline the grave consequences of childhood stress and trauma (Barahal, Waterman, & Martin, 1981; Emery, 1982; Long, Slater, Forehand, & Falber, 1988; Rutter, 1983; Wallerstein, 1991). Only recently have we begun to study the ways in which children survive and even thrive in the most inhospitable of environments (Garmezy, 1974, 1983; Murphy & Moriarty, 1976; Rutter, 1979a, 1979b). This work has stimulated a gradual shift in some child research from vulnerability and pathology to coping and resiliency. Nonetheless, psychological resiliency, particularly at the individual level, is poorly understood. In addition, research has not focused on the ways in which resilient responses in children are manifested on the Rorschach. For example, we are just beginning to learn that a well-adapted child, undergoing a stressor but effecting a resilient response, may produce contradictory and confusing data, which may induce us to overdiagnose psychopathology (Viglione, 1990).

Recognizing the limitations of resiliency research and the marked variation in children's responses to adversity, researchers have called for studies of the interplay of processes in childhood resiliency (Compas, 1987; Rutter, 1987; Seifer & Someroff, 1987). In response to this call, this work presents a research case study of a child who has undergone psychological stress but continues to function well. It is offered as an adaptation of the single-case research design. We propose that such a longitudinal design, involving multiple measurements, independent validity criteria, and instruments that access behavioral and emotional problems (Luthar & Zigler, 1991) and the internal world (Perry & Viglione, 1991; Viglione, 1990) can illuminate the processes involved in childhood resiliency.

Accordingly, we have two goals—one substantive and one methodological. The first goal is to increase our understanding of psychological resiliency in cases of divorce, particularly as it plays out over time on the Rorschach. The second goal is to propose a methodological advancement by demonstrating the utility of a single case, multiple measurements, longitudinal design with independent validity criteria combining repeated measures, and case-dependent hypothesis formulation and testing. Before introducing the case, we first briefly summarize pertinent resiliency, divorce, and Rorschach literature while the child literature contributes to understanding the struggle with adversity. The Rorschach is an ideal instrument for this study because it illuminates the internal world (Viglione & Perry, 1991), is related to stress, trauma, and divorce (Exner, 1994; Spiegelman & Spiegelman, 1991; Viglione, 1990), and has predictive validity over long periods (Ingham, 1994; Perry & Viglione, 1991).

RESILIENCY

Rutter (1985, 1987) viewed resiliency as a process or a characteristic of a prolonged reaction or behavior, rather than as a fixed trait. He agreed with Murphy and Moriarity (1976) that children can develop protective mechanisms from mastering adversity. Garmezy (1985) referred to this as a *steeling effect*, and observed it in children who are made stronger by their encounter with adversity. Rutter (1985) discussed the life course of such resilient responses as an "adaptive trajectory." One might also posit a "maladaptive trajectory," when adversity results in self-defeating behavioral and emotional patterns, vulnerability to related stresses, and excessive rigidity that represent characterological malformation (Terr, 1991; Viglione, 1990). Along these lines, Luthar and Zigler (1991) suggested that children, who may be called resilient as a result of their lacking behavior disturbances, may nonetheless suffer from emotional distress and disturbances. Accordingly, trauma and its aftermath may function as negative crystallizing personality experiences. Indeed, minor variants of such rigidities may be the cost of resiliency in the face of hardship. In other words, adaptive, defensive, or coping tactics that allowed one to maintain adequate adjustment during and after a trauma may be rigidly applied long after the trauma in a maladaptive fashion.

Many who have researched coping (e.g., Compas, 1987; Dohrenwend, 1979; Folkman & Lazarus, 1980; O'Grady & Metz, 1987; Rutter, 1987) have emphasized the child's active participation in the resilient coping response. For example, in the case of social support, the child may actively employ coping and problem-solving skills. In doing so, the child recognizes the need for, arranges for, and elicits emotional and social support and task assistance from others. Children are then active reorganizers of their environments in the resiliency process.

Presuming a biological basis emerging in infancy, Chess and Thomas (Chess & Thomas, 1984; Thomas & Chess, 1977; Thomas, Chess, & Birch, 1968) identified activity level, approach and adaptability to new situations, positive mood, expressiveness, sociability, and regularity of biorhythms as basic components of psychological adjustment. One would expect that these factors play out in the psychological and emotional domains with older children, rather than just in the physical arena as they might in infants. Applying Chess and Thomas' "goodness of fit" perspective, a positive temperament might allow one to induce positive support and care from the environment, even in the midst of a difficult reaction to trauma.

Emphasizing intrapsychic rather than biological development, object relations and attachment theorists arrive at similar conclusions. Basic trust, positive, well-organized internalization of early relationships, or a secure attachment allow one to induce support from others, maintain relationships in difficult times, and thus sustain internal growth.

Children may effectively respond to adversity by attempting to rework trauma through regression, fantasy, and play (Waelder, 1933), as well as dreams and daydreams (Schafer, 1954). Kris (1952) labeled these phenomena as regression in the service of the ego. Since that time, the term *adaptive regression* has been widely used. It involves a temporary, partial regression with increased illogical, associative (primary) processes aimed at increasing adaptive functioning. Primary process and primitive drive-related contents are stimulated but are reintegrated through logical, reality-oriented concerns (secondary processes). Optimal functioning is resumed with an increased insight, understanding, internal capacity, and flexibility (Schafer, 1958). Thus, in adaptive regression, threatening experiences are transformed through a temporary, contained disorganization largely confined to content related to the stressor. Resilient responses might manifest as a contained regression in the Rorschach severity of disturbance indicators accompanied by projective contents symbolizing the stressor (Carr, 1984; Viglione, 1990). True adaptive regression among adults can be a fairly well-organized and integrated process, but among children, particularly as represented on the Rorschach, such organization might not readily appear.

Risk research has focused on identifying stable, enduring characteristics of resilient children and their environments (Compas, 1987). Three broad resiliency factors have emerged from this research: (a) positive traits, including temperament, internal locus of control, and self-esteem; (b) family cohesion and warmth; and (c) supportive models (Garmezy, 1983). Unfortunately, these risk studies have not explained considerable variation in individual responses to stress and adversity (Rutter, 1985, 1987).

Kobasa (1979), in his stress research, developed the concept of *hardiness.* His research paradigm employs laboratory methods, self-report measurement, retrospective designs, and psychosomatic phenomena. According to this position, hardy persons tolerate adversity well and are characterized by control, commitment, and challenge. The notion of challenge is consistent with problem-focused coping (Folkman & Lazarus, 1984), psychoanalytic understandings of progressive versus regressive response to stress (Nagera, 1963), and Dweck and Wortman's (1982) work in an achievement context.

DIVORCE

Divorce is accompanied by detrimental effects on children and adolescents both in the short and long term (Guidubaldi, 1988; Hetherington, 1984; Wallerstein, 1991; Wallerstein & Kelly, 1980). For example, in the Wallerstein studies initial reactions by young latency-age children to the divorce were of grief and fear leading to psychological disorganization, feelings of deprivation, yearning for the departed parent, inhibition of aggression toward noncustodial fathers, anger at the custodial mother, fantasies of responsibility and reconciliation, and loyalty conflicts. Also, this work has suggested that divorce consists of a complex set of stressors, including predivorce conflict, parental remarriage, and birth of half-siblings. Children fantasize in response to these stressors. For example, they imagine parental reconciliation, contacts with the absent parent, and intact and loving families especially where children take care of other children.

Wallerstein and Kelly (1980) found that adjustment at 5 years postdivorce for girls, who were 7 or 8 at the time of the divorce (our subject's age at the first testing), is enhanced by secure, stable, reliable, and predictable relationships with both parents and peers. These findings suggest that the capacity to sustain relatedness, to induce and to maintain others' interest, are critically important determinants of resiliency. More recent work (Wallerstein, 1987, 1991) identified a 10-year sleeper effect among those that originally adapted well but eventually succumbed to depression, adolescent alienation, and self-defeating behavior 10 years after the separation. Recent work with the Rorschach has suggested lingering, depressive, and aggressive intrapsychic reactions even among nonpatient divorced children (Spiegelman & Spiegelman, 1991).

The Wallerstein studies and others have been criticized on methodological grounds. On the other hand, better designed studies (Guidubaldi, 1988; Hetherington, 1984) focus on external and behavioral factors at the expense of exploring how emotional disturbances and internal processes interact with external realities to foster resilient outcomes. These emotional disturbances, covert during childhood, may manifest more prominently in adolescence and adulthood (Luthar & Zigler, 1991).

THE RORSCHACH AND RESILIENCY

In a previous case study paper on adaptive response to trauma (Viglione, 1990), it was proposed that resiliency might emerge from internal disorganization without sustained deficits both in behavior and in environmental–behavioral interaction. Thus, the resilient child maintains environmental support and positive feedback. Examples would include continuing to meet the challenge of school, maintaining relationships and activities, or continuing to relate positively to supportive adults. Within the Rorschach, as representative of the internal world, we would expect some evidence of disturbance, accompanied by symbols or references to the trauma, as evidence of its being reworked in fantasy and mastered. During this phase, the resilient individual maintains a satisfactory external adaptation, even if there are temporary disruptions. This external adaptation allows environmental inputs to further internal growth. Resiliency is seen as a pattern of adaptation incorporating internal, behavioral, environmental, and biological processes (Viglione, 1990; Viglione & Perry, 1991), rather than solely an internal or enduring disposition. Of course, one must keep in mind that resiliency and psychopathology are intertwined patterns. It is probably too simplistic to assert that that which is not adaptive is probably self-defeating and potentially pathological. Resiliency may entail coping with a trauma and preservation of one's adaptation and environmental support, yet be achieved at the expense of developing certain rigidities and vulnerabilities.

FIRST EXAMINATION

The case we introduce to explore the issues of divorce and resiliency we call Linda. She was initially selected because she appeared to be functioning well despite her parents' recent divorce. She was first evaluated at 7 years, 7 months; this was about 2 years after her parents separated. According to the mother, marital conflict and the father's drinking contributed to her choosing to dissolve the marriage. As part of a more intensive initial study of this child (Viglione, van den Daele, Brager, Zambianco, & Perry, 1988), Linda was interviewed, as was her mother, and administered a Rorschach. The interviewer and test administrators had no knowledge about the subject except that the subject was reportedly functioning well after a conflictual and stressful separation and divorce. Our goal was exploratory at that time, to collect data regarding background, present states, behavior, adaptation, and internal processes to relate it to processes of divorce stress and resiliency.

The developmental history interview revealed that Linda had the temperament of an "easy" baby (Chess & Thomas, 1984; Thomas & Chess, 1977) and was securely attached. She was expressive, active, and sociable. Her mother was enamored with her, and she was well-liked by others. She was also very close to her father, who spent a year at home while on disability when Linda was 3. Growing up, Linda always had a best friend and was very close to her younger brother.

According to her mother, Linda took the divorce very hard and had been angry with her mother for divorcing her father. Since the separation, she had maintained a good relationship with her mother and had not regressed in any significant way. She saw her father only twice a month. After a difficult start in kindergarten, she did well academically.

Our operational definition of resiliency was conservative, verifiable, and quantifiable. We defined resiliency as having undergone a significant stress and adjusting to it so that one continues to meet age-appropriate life demands and maintains psychological health, rewarding interpersonal relationships, and adaptational competencies. Such a definition could allow for the internal disorganization hypothesized by LaBarbera and Cornsweet (1985) and included in adaptive regression. We selected measures to address both external behavior and internal states. Certainly, temporarily, less well-adapted behavioral responses may occur within what ultimately is a resilient pattern. To address issues of cross-situational specificity, we also followed the recommendation (Achenbach, McConaughy, & Howell, 1987) to collect data in multiple environments. Thus, resiliency was operationally defined as well-adapted behavior across a number of different environments, including the "internal environment," with a number of different methods.

Consistent with the aim of obtaining independent validity data, Linda's mother was administered the Vineland Adaptive Behavior Scale (Sparrow, Balla, & Cicchetti, 1984) and Achenbach's Child Behavior Checklist (CBCL; Achenbach & Edelbrok, 1983). Interviews of both the mother and child provided information about Linda's level of adjustment and were not conducted by the author. Linda's teacher also completed a Teacher's Report form (TRF) of the CBCL and the Health Resources Inventory (HRI; Gesten, 1976) to address competencies and psychological resources.

The results revealed no significant behavioral, social or emotional problems at school or at home (T-scores for the Internal, External, and Total Problem Scales were less than 55, and all narrow band and competency scales were in the normal range). The HRI revealed a sociable, assertive child who follows rules, cooperates with authority, and maintains satisfactory frustration tolerance and appropriately asserts herself. Because of the possibility that these clearly normal reports by Linda's mother and teacher were subject to socially desirable response sets, interview results from both mother and child were also reviewed. Of particular note was Linda's communicating to her teacher that she was unhappy with her mother for divorcing her father. The independent interviewer (Zambianco, 1988) found that Linda was an essentially normal, engaging, and verbally and emotionally expressive child.

A number of concerns emerged from the data and were formulated as hypotheses to guide the second examination. These may reflect the "costs" and emotional distress associated with resiliency and presage possible personality rigidity or vulnerability. First of all, a number of factors suggested some depression, not obviously manifest in behavior. Indeed, the optimal reaction to the loss of her father would be some sadness. In addition, the depressive experiences as well as other problems (addressed later in this chapter) appeared to coalesce around references to her father. There was also some concern about Linda's apparent ingratiating, interpersonally hungry, overly conforming attitude at home, school, and in the examination and interview. Along with the concern with possible overconformity was that of perfectionism. The teacher, mother, and interviewers offered observations about perfectionism and "hyper-mature" attitudes. Linda herself voiced some concerns about not being able to be herself with her father as exemplified by her not wanting to let her father know that she had cried. Nonetheless, after the extensive clinical interview, the examiner was not overly concerned with her being falsely mature and conforming, so as to sacrifice her individuality. Furthermore, the HRI items suggested autonomy in that she both questioned authority and her peers on occasions when she felt that she was being treated unfairly, and also expressed her needs and feelings.

In reviewing structural summary information for the first Rorschach (see Appendix A), one might first notice that the record is short (R), but $Lambda$ is in the acceptable range so that the record would be considered valid for normative comparisons. Such short records are common among young children, but lead to more cautious interpretations. Nonetheless, one cannot attribute evidence of pathology or personalized responses to this general lack of productivity. On the contrary, one must consider them seriously, even in shorter records.

Given this contextual interpretation issue, one might first address the evidence of distorted fantasy $(M-)$, which is, surprisingly, more passive $(a{:}p, Ma{:}Mp)$ than one would expect. In other words, she may withdraw from more realistic problem solving and mull over or gratify herself through personalized and idiosyncratic fantasy. Reality testing, judgment, and conventionality were also compromised $(X-\%, X+\%, P)$. In this context, evidence of cognitive complexity $(DQ+, Z$, one 4-determinant blend) probably constitute confusion, or the malevolent bloom that Schafer (1954) described. Presumably, the continuing divorce stress and defensive or coping processes are undermining her reality testing and appreciation of conventionality. These findings suggest that there are some ideational disturbances and idiosyncratic understandings of the world. They do not appear to be manifest in overt behaviors. It may be related to an internal preoccupation and regression and the stimulation of primary processes. On the other hand, LaBarbara and Cornsweet (1985) associated such scores with positive therapeutic outcomes among inpatient children.

There is strong evidence of discomfort with feelings (Afr). The elevated $DEPI$ suggests the presence of depressive feelings, possibly manifested only internally, and not in clinically relevant, overt, depressive behavior. One might interpret the lack of shading and Afr as fleeing discomfort, so that relieving depression may be a primary motivator of behavior and decisions. Depression is also evident among the self-image data. The low $3r + (2)/R$ suggests a negative self-image. Linda apparently is internalizing some of her disappointment and feelings of responsibility about the family breakup as a damaged self-concept and inadequacy.

As far as the interpersonal data, Linda gives no pure *H*, and her *Good* to *Poor H* (Perry & Viglione, 1991) suggests misunderstanding of others. The *ISO* (Isolation) index is grossly elevated, and in the context of only four human contents suggests social isolation and distancing despite active social behavior. In addition, the lack of texture responses suggests discomfort with closeness and intimacy.

There is an enormous amount of empirical, quantitative data indicating that the contents, descriptions, images, and verbalizations offered on the Rorschach test are valid for a variety of crucial interpretive purposes. For example, these include human interpersonal representations and characterizations (e.g. Blatt, Brenneis, Schimek, & Glick, 1976; Kates, 1994; Mayman, 1967; Perry & Viglione, 1991; Picker, 1984; Urist, 1977), sexual contents (Morgan & Viglione, 1992), aggressive contents (Elizur, 1949; Exner, 1993a; Gacono & Meloy, 1994; Holt, 1977), anatomy (Exner, 1989), and trauma-related contents (Armstrong & Loewenstein, 1990; Wycoff, 1993). These data are supplemented by many case reports of the personal relevancy of some Rorschach responses (see Carr, 1984, and Viglione, 1990, for examples of personalized Rorschach stress responses). Based on this evidence, if one respects the distinction between "projective" and "nonprojective" responses (Exner, 1989, 1993a), and if one uses content analysis as elaboration of basic hypotheses derived from the structural summary and other data, qualitative analysis is justified and rests on a sound empirical foundation.

Linda's words elaborate on previously identified themes related to resiliency, her personal stresses, depression and self-image, cognitive confusion, and interpersonal difficulties. (Please see Appendix B for responses to representative cards.) Linda offers fantastic, frightening, and dangerous images ("monster face," Card I; "skeleton," III; "cliffs," VII) that are reiterated in various references to heights and helplessly hanging; devouring and aggressive creatures (X), damaged, old, and devalued images as evident in the three MOR, and elaborations of percepts as "small" and "little," "yucky" and "dirty" (I), and "pigs" (VII); and confused images of creature's consuming others (X). Quite revealing of her self-image is a "magic wand" that later is a "yucky wand that got thrown away" (VI). On the positive side is the complement to the cliffs and dangling theme, that of climbing, and particularly "tigers" (VIII) suggesting mastery strivings. Images of strength, stability, and sturdiness resonate in repeated images of "rocks," and an "old oak tree" (III), and in her elaboration of other responses. The "magic wand," "lady bug" (VI), and cartoon characters suggest an adaptive, hopeful outlook and playfulness. Also evident is an orientation to authority and status ("crown," III; "castle," IX), in rather incongruous contexts, which might be related to the concerns about conformity.

Is she resilient? Looking at the behavioral data, one might answer affirmatively. She has suffered and continues to endure a significant stressor, yet is adapting at home, school, and with her peers. However, the projective data reveal a withdrawal into personalized fantasy involving a struggle to persist, overcome, and stay strong despite perceptions of being discarded and damaged. They also reveal idiosyncratic translations of external stimuli that are not directly observable in behavior. Can this be called an adaptive regression that will resolve? Is it the beginning of the psychological costs of resiliency, or a forerunner of significant maladjustment?

In the sense that this disturbance is largely maintained inside and seems to contain some references to her predicament, it might be adaptive. Also, social, assertive, mastery striving, and cooperative competencies are consistent with characterizing it as adaptive. Like previous descriptions (Fitzgerald, 1966; LaBarbara & Cornsweet, 1985; Schachtel, 1959; Viglione, 1990) of good prognostic indicators and adaptive responses to trauma, there is a certain openness to experiencing disorganization and an active, internal, reworking while sustaining growth-promoting relationships with the world. Outside of trauma, and even considering the temporal inconsistency of some of the severity of disturbance variables in childhood, one might worry about more serious psychopathology in the future.

Another obvious concern was the possibility of an underlying depression contained by both emotional constriction and a pleasing external persona. Together they bring up the specter of character pathology, and of rigid, false self and as-if personality developments (Deutsch, 1942; Gardner & Wagner, 1986). In a more general way, they may be the precursors to neurotic character development with inhibition, constriction, and fantasy serving as the basis of symptomatic developments and defensive processes. Nonetheless, one would expect that if such pathology existed that it would "leak through" into one of the environmental contexts (home, school, or peers) or measurement contents. Furthermore, she is not hiding her feelings with important others, except with her father. She easily communicated them to her mother, her teacher, and to our interviewer (Zambianco, 1988). In that light, she continued to access the environment to meet her needs and is not alienating it through acting out or withdrawal (Viglione, 1990). Thus she affords herself the opportunity of further emotional and social growth. She may be effecting a resilient response, or undergoing a resilient process (Rutter, 1985, 1987), by maintaining herself in a growth-promoting psychological "space." As in a previous study of a child's adaptive response (Viglione, 1990), confining the pathological response to the internal world may be adaptive, and one must explore psychopathology and resiliency in tandem under conditions of environmental trauma. However, although competencies emerge, whether this is a case of resiliency cannot be answered with only a single assessment.

SECOND EXAMINATION

As a part of our proposed methodological advancement, we selected instruments to address the hypotheses derived from the first examination and repeated other measures. Accordingly, Linda's mother was recontacted, and Linda was retested at 10 years and 1 month, some 2 years and 7 months after the first examination. The Child Depression Inventory (ChDI; Kovacs, 1979) was added to address the suggestions of depression, and we prepared structured questions to add other relevant information. The possibility of anxiety was addressed through the State Trait Anxiety Inventory for Children (STAI–C; Spielberger, 1973). Subscales from the CBCL and teacher's version (TRF) added additional information about these issues from the point of view of Linda's mother and school. Target questions were also designed to address the issue of an overly compliant or conforming self-presentation and the possibility of an as-if persona. An updated version of the HRI, and the Teacher's Child Rating Scale (TCRS; Hightower & Dirk, 1986) offered a subscale measuring assertive skill, a characteristic inconsistent with overcompliance. The CBCL, TRF, and TCRS again offered information about the overall level of adaptation, and the Rorschach allowed us once again to explore the internal processes involved in this possibly resilient reaction. The examiner at the second examination was blind to the nature and purpose of the study and data collection.

At the time of the second examination, Linda was seeing her father, who had since remarried, only twice a year. Linda's mother reported that Linda was hurt and angry about this situation and sometimes expressed dislike for her stepmother. The relationships between Linda and her mother and between Linda and her brother were still good. Although occasionally still upset, Linda was crying much less frequently and not overtly distressed as she had been 2½ years ago. Despite her initial distress, she had received no psychological treatment, and indeed received no treatment after this second examination. Linda voiced her concern about her father to her mother, but did not express her negative feelings to her father. Her mother contended that Linda was very unnatural around her father and "tries to keep the peace at all costs." Thus the underlying depression and overcompliance appeared most clearly in her relationship with her father.

Linda was excelling academically and athletically. Physically, she had grown a great deal since the first examination. Both her mother and teacher reported that Linda had good peer relationships. The teacher reported precocious interest in boys, her only concern about Linda's psychological development.

In response to the predetermined questions designed to address the issue of a false self or as-if presentation, Linda's mother and teacher produced considerable relevant data. Most of the data were inconsistent with this notion. Both attributed leadership potential to Linda, and Linda reportedly spoke her mind and often dominated in small groups. There was no convincing evidence of adopting different persona to please others, or of excessive imitation or complementing what she might assume is asked of her. In larger groups she did look to others for cues for acceptable behavior and conformity, rather than risk disapproval. Further data concerning these issues came from the selected subscale of the TCRS in which Linda scored high on the subscale measuring assertive social skill. Once again the CBCL and TRFs collected from her mother and teacher revealed no problem behaviors and above-average behavioral adjustment and competence. The findings did not confirm a depressed mood. The ChDI, STAI–C, and the relevant subscales on the CBCL and TRF were all in the normal range.

In summary, Linda again emerged as an attractive, bright, engaging child, who displayed above-average adaptation across a variety of circumstances. Extending Achenbach's (Achenbach et al., 1987) notion, we now see well-adapted behavior across time and across environments. Accordingly, this complex of factors diminishes the probability of psychopathology and essentially meets the behavioral definition of resiliency.

An inspection of the Rorschach data in Appendix A reveal that this second recorded protocol is short (*R*) but reasonably rich (*Lambda*), as was the first record. Nonetheless, a dramatic improvement is evident, so that one might speculate that the constriction (*R*) now adaptively allows her to control the expression of problems. Her ideational confusion has greatly diminished and places her in the normal range (*Sum6, Wsum6, M–*). The levels of disturbance data are also greatly improved (*SCZI, EII*). More adaptive cognitive complexity has superseded the confusion on the first examination (*DQ+, Z, Blends*). In contrast to traumatic responses, primitive ideas are not evident in awareness (Derepressed Contents—the sum of more primitive contents—*An, Bl, Ex, Fd, Fi, Sx, Xy, MOR, AG*; Perry & Viglione, 1991; Viglione, 1990). In fact, the low score for Derepressed Contents might suggest constriction. Other data (*X–%, X+%, P*) clearly indicate that fantasy and primitive material, along with the defensive struggle to control it, no longer undermine her reality testing.

However, it does appear that emotional constriction (*FC:CF + C, Afr*) may limit her opportunities for emotional gratification. The lack of shading is again interpreted as consistent with the affective constriction as a fleeing from distress and conflict. Other self-image data, on the other hand, have improved (*MOR, 3r + (2)/R*).

Interpersonal relatedness data have also improved (*Pure H, Sum H, Good:Poor H, AG*). Nonetheless, a lack of interpersonal intimacy and depth, with excessive interpersonal distancing, persists (*T, COP, Iso*). As in the first examination, passive fantasy and passive orientation (*Ma:Mp, a:p*) again are inconsistent with behavioral data and literature on resiliency, and suggest a withdrawal into fantasy. It may be that such activation of the inner life (*EB*) aids adaptation through providing internal comfort. Linda's images on the second examination (see Appendix C) are similar to those on the first examination, but are depicted in more constrained, less devalued ways without the crass confusion and disturbance previously evident. On Card I, she now reports a comical and less threatening "mean cat" instead of the frightened monster. The skeleton response is now the second response, rather than the first on III and, accordingly less compelling. The dangerous cliff is now not so foreboding and it replaces the devouring, convoluted, disturbed, aggressive images on X. Indeed, there is more identification with aggressive images and power and effectiveness, rather than being victimized by them as was evident previously. The orientation to authority is still evident but not so disorganized (temple door, II; ruler, VI). Negative, self-image themes are less prominent (trashed, mean cat, I; ugly globs, IV; donkeys, VII). Big (II, IV, V, VI, VIII) rather than small (II) elaborations predominate, and the helplessness theme is diminished (only reference is "falling," X). Sturdy rocks are again evident (II, VI, X) and the most positive, aspiring response is on VIII with two tigers climbing out of a pit. One might conclude that resilient, striving themes are solidifying while the internal perturbation diminishes.

At age 10, 2½ years after the first exam, Linda continues to adapt well. Overall, it appears that her response to the divorce is resilient in that she is continuing to adapt to life demands, doing well in many areas, and inducing appropriate environmental support. From a temporal perspective we see considerable improvement in Rorschach evidence of psychological distur-bance, so that it appears that her initial disruption was contained internally, rather than expressed in behavior and alienation from supports. Thus, it does appear that her original internal disturbance might be considered to be an adaptive, regressive process. We also see what appears to be the "costs" of this resiliency. She is rather affectively constricted, so that she may suffer in the form of rigidity and lack of flexibility in new situations. On the other hand, as-if or false-self features do not appear. The problematic references to the father, precocious heterosexual interest, and interpersonal distancing, along with the depression, suggest some concern about the potential for the delayed "sleeper-effect" outlined by Wallerstein (1987, 1991).

Thus, there is considerable improvement in the internal world data and Linda has maintained a relatively strong external, behavioral adaptation (Viglione & Perry, 1991). However, it would be premature to conclude that hers is a resilient reaction. Rorschach data differ too much from normative expectations (*FC:CF* + *C, Afr, T, COP, ISO, CDI*) and suggest significant internal distress that might eventually manifest as depression, character problems, or self-defeating behaviors as found in other research (e.g., Waller-stein, 1991; Waters & Sroufe, 1983). On the other hand, continued psycho-logical development, as a result of staying in contact with a growth-promoting environment, is also a possibility. To address the question of whether or not this was a resilient response and how to understand the "costs" of her resilient adaptation, we examined Linda a third time.

EPILOGUE

As in the previous exams and consistent with single-case methodology, the third examiners were once again blind to the nature of the case and research question. Indeed, at the time of the third exam, we were running a research program that provided a standard battery of tests including the Rorschach,

CBCL, ChDI, and scales under development to assess Axis V from the *Diagnostic and Statistical Manual of Mental Disorders* (3rd ed., rev. [*DSM–III–R*]; American Psychiatric Association, 1987). These tests allowed us to address the remaining issues.

Our goals in this exam were simpler than in the previous two, for we focused on the question of whether or not Linda's overall reaction was resilient and whether or not there were costs involved in her adaptation. In other words, if she was clearly adjusting well at age 12 years, 3 months, we would conclude that her response was resilient. More specifically, we were worried that affective constriction, object representational, or interpersonal schema distortions might conspire during her adolescence to undermine her adaptation under the pressure of intimacy, as was the case with Wallerstein's (1991) "sleeper effect." In developmental terms, like Wallerstein's subjects, Linda might not be ready for important tasks of adolescence like the initiation of intimacy and the reemergence of sexuality.

The CBCL (all scales again in the normal range), structured questions, and the *DSM–III–R* Axis V scale ($GAS = 80$) indicated that Linda continued to adapt quite well with family, friends, and at school, despite her mother's remarriage and having a baby. An examination of the Rorschach data in Appendix A reveals continued improvement over the third exam in a richer, more adaptive record. Overall then, there is no convincing evidence of a "sleeper effect" and we feel more certain in concluding that hers is a resilient process. The internal disturbance among Rorschach data has largely dissipated. Interpersonal data are also improved.

A number of minor negative indicators remain. Notable, but not "clinical range," elevations in the ChDI (16) and the Anxious/Depressed CBCL scale ($T = 60$) suggest distress and the promise of some depression as indicated by the first Rorschach. The lack of color responses ($FC:CF + C$) in this context reveals characterological, affective constriction and rigidity. It appears then that her affective constriction has set in as an emotional style that helps her to suppress dysphoric feelings. The elevated $Xu\%$, and low P suggest some idiosyncracies but not reality distortions. The elevation in M (Viglione, 1990) in the context of little behavioral disturbance suggests that much of the coping with life's difficulties and the divorce stress is worked out, and contained in this child's private thoughts and images. Indeed, these thoughts might be unrealistic at times ($M-$). Such negative indicators should be understood as a rigidity that has crystallized as a "cost" or resiliency. Appendix D contains responses from the same cards presented from earlier testings.

CONCLUSIONS

Through data derived from a single-case, longitudinal research design with repeated measures in multiple environments, we conclude that Linda's response to the family upheaval was resilient in the sense that it allowed for continued emotional growth for eventual recovery from an adaptive regression and internal disturbance. A pathological response, on the other hand, would probably manifest in behaviors that disrupt ongoing psychological development. The initial internal disruption and its gradual resolution suggest that we should understand resiliency as an interactive process rather than a trait (Rutter, 1985, 1987). In this process, success in staving off internal disorganization, as evident in the Rorschach but not in observable behavior or self-report so as not to manifest the disturbance in behavior, may be a strength or a sign of resiliency. Under conditions of psychological stress, evidence of such internal disorganization may not indicate structural personality deficits, particularly with young children. This hypothesis is also supported by a previous child case in which considerable Rorschach disturbance followed a significant stressor but was diminished at later examinations (Viglione, 1990). As found in the resiliency literature, verbal expressiveness, active coping, sociability and maintaining interpersonal supports, mastery strivings, temperamental factors, behavioral style, and suppression of distress might be associated with resilient responses to trauma. In this case, the "cost" of resiliency is reflected in some affective constriction and rigidity, apparently stabilized as characterological mechanisms to ward off subjective depression. This rigidity might express itself in the pressure to avoid situations that might simulate depressive experiences. The possibility also remains that this feature might become an internalizing problem in adulthood.

In regard to the methodological goals of this work, we believe we have demonstrated that such a single-case, longitudinal research design offers unique insights into the resiliency process. Unlike many case studies, our collecting data from independent sources allows a relatively unbiased exploration. Selecting instruments and formulating research questions to test specific hypotheses increases precision and relevance of data as it might in a quantitative study. Using multiple measurements, some repeated, from different "environments" with empirically based instruments, including the Comprehensive Rorschach System (Exner, 1990, 1993b), allows a comprehensive and objective picture to emerge. The longitudinal design and the respect for both internal and external processing and projective and objective tests are key factors in illuminating the richness of the dynamic process and interplay of factors in resiliency over time. In this case the early disruption and distress were contained internally and eventually dissipated, but also gradually crystallized in depressive features and affective constriction. Insights from such an in-depth case study deepen our understanding of the processes of stress and resiliency over time.

As in this case, resiliency and psychopathology must be understood in the entire configuration of internal, behavioral, environmental, and biological factors, rather than solely in the internal world or behavior (Rutter, 1987; Viglione, 1990; Viglione & Perry, 1991). Contributions from future case study research might be increased by using independent validity data, multiple measurements incorporating repeated measures, and hypothesis testing.

ACKNOWLEDGMENTS

Many thanks are extended to Robert Brager, Leland van den Daele, Deborah Zambianco, and William Perry for their contributions to the first symposium on the first examination of this subject at the California Psychological Association Convention (Viglione et al., 1988). Parts of the current chapter were presented at the California Psychological Association's annual meeting in 1991 and at the Society for Personality Assessment annual meeting in 1991 (Viglione & Kates, 1991a, 1991b). Thanks also to Jo Clare Sullivan for her expert editing, and to Karen Martin and Jennifer Miller for help with manuscript preparation.

Thanks to reviewers of previous versions of this chapter for helping us to articulate these issues.

REFERENCES

Achenbach, T. M., & Edelbrok, C. S. (1983). *Manual for the Child Behavior Checklist and Revised Child Behavior Profile*. Burlington: University of Vermont, Department of Psychiatry.

Achenbach, T. M., McConaughy, S. M., & Howell, C. T. (1987). Child/adolescent behavioral and emotional problems: Implications of cross-informant correlations for situational specificity. *Psychological Bulletin, 101*, 213–232.

American Psychiatric Association. (1987). *Diagnostic and statistical manual of mental disorders* (3rd ed. Rev.). Washington DC: Author.

Armstrong, J., & Loewenstein, R. (1990). Characteristics of patients with multiple personality and dissociative disorders on psychological testing. *The Journal of Nervous and Mental Disease, 178*, 448–454.

Barahal, R. M., Waterman, J., & Martin, M. P. (1981). The social-cognitive development of abused children. *Journal of Consulting and Clinical Psychology, 49*, 508–516.

Blatt, S., Brenneis, C., Schimek, J., & Glick, M. (1976). Normal development and psychopathological impairment of the concept of the object on the Rorschach. *Journal of Abnormal Psychology, 85*, 364–373.

Carr, A. (1984). Content interpretation re: Salley and Teillings, "Dissociated rage attacks in a Vietnam veteran. A Rorschach Study." *Journal of Personality Assessment, 48*, 420–421.

Chess, S., & Thomas, A. (1984). *Origins and evolution of behavior disorders: From infancy to adult life*. New York: Bruner-Mazel.

Compas, B. E. (1987). Coping with stress during childhood and adolescence. *Psychological Bulletin, 101*, 393–403.

Deutsch, H. (1942). Some forms of emotional disturbance and their relationship to schizophrenia. *Psychoanalytic Quarterly, 11*, 301–331.

Dohrenwend, B. P. (1979). Stressful life events in psychopathology: Some issues of theory and method. In J. E. Barrett (Ed.), *Stress and mental disorder* (pp. 1–15). New York: Raven.

Dweck, C. S., & Wortman, C. B. (1982). Learned helplessness and reinforcement responsibility in children. *Journal of Personality and Social Psychology, 38*, 441–452.

Elizur, A. (1949). Content analysis of the Rorschach with regard to anxiety and hostility. *Journal of Projective Techniques, 13*, 247–284.

Emery, R. E. (1982). Interparent conflict and the children of discord and divorce. *Psychological Bulletin, 92*, 310–330.

Exner, J. E., Jr. (1989). Searching for projection in the Rorschach. *Journal of Personality Assessment, 53*, 520–536.

Exner, J. E., Jr. (1990). *The Rorschach: A Comprehensive System: Vol. 2* (2nd ed.). New York: Wiley.

Exner, J. E., Jr. (1993a). *The Rorschach: A Comprehensive System: Vol. 1* (2nd ed.). New York: Wiley.

Exner, J. E., Jr. (1993b). *The Rorschach: A Comprehensive System: Vol. 1* (3rd ed.). New York: Wiley.

Exner, J. E., Jr. (1994). *The Rorschach: A Comprehensive System: Vol. 3. Assessment of children and adolescents* (2nd ed.). New York: Wiley.

Fitzgerald, E. T. (1966). Measurement of openness to experience: A study of regression in the service of the ego. *Journal of Personality and Social Psychology, 4,* 655–663.

Folkman, S., & Lazarus, R. S. (1980). An analysis of coping in a middle-aged community sample. *Journal of Health and Social Behavior, 21,* 219–239.

Gacono, C. B., & Meloy, J. R. (1994). *The Rorschach assessment of aggressive and psychopathic personalities.* Hillsdale, NJ: Lawrence Erlbaum Associates.

Gardner, C. S., & Wagner, S. (1986). Clinical diagnosis of the personality disorder. *Bulletin of the Menninger Clinic, 50,* 135–147.

Garmezy, N. (1974). Children at risk: The search for the antecedents of schizophrenia. Part I. Conceptual models and research methods. *Schizophrenic Bulletin, 8,* 14–90.

Garmezy, N. (1983). Stressors of childhood. In N. Garmezy & M. Rutter (Eds.). *Stress, coping and development in children* (pp. 43–84). New York: McGraw-Hill.

Garmezy, N. (1985). Stress-resistant children: The search for protective factors. In J. Stevenson (Ed.) *Recent research in development psychopathology* (pp. 62–93). New York: Pergamon Press.

Gesten, E. L. (1976). A health resources inventory: The development of a measure of the personal and social competence of primary grade children. *Journal of Consulting and Clinical Psychology, 44,* 775–786.

Guidubaldi, J. (1988). Differences in children's divorce adjustment across grade level and gender: Report from the NASP–Penn State Nationwide Project. In S. A. Walchik & P. Karoly (Eds.), *Children of divorce: Empirical perspective on adjustment* (pp. 203–225). New York: Gardner.

Hetherington, C. M. (1984). Stress in coping with children in families. In A. Doyle, D. Gold, & D. S. Moskowitz (Eds.), *Children in families under stress* (New directions for child development No. 24, pp. 7–33). San Francisco: Jossey-Bass.

Hightower, A., & Dirk, R. (1986). The Teacher-Child Rating Scale: A brief objective measure of elementary children's school problem behavior and competencies. *School Psychology Review, 15,* 393–409.

Holt, R. R. (1977). A method for assessing primary process manifestations and their control in Rorschach responses. In M. A. Rickers-Ovsiankina (Ed.), *Rorschach Psychology* (2nd ed., pp. 375–420). New York: Krieger.

Ingham, M. (1994). *Predicting adaptation to spousal separation with the Ego Impairment Index. A Rorschach study with navy wives.* Unpublished doctoral dissertation, California School of Professional Psychology, San Diego.

Kates, J. (1994). *A construct validity study of the Rorschach Ego Impairment Index.* Unpublished doctoral dissertation, California School of Professional Psychology, San Diego.

Kobasa, S. C. (1979). Stressful life events, personality, and health: An inquiry into hardiness. *Journal of Personality and Social Psychology, 37,* 1–11.

Kovacs, M. (1979). Rating scales to assess depression in school-aged children. *Acta Paedopsychiatrica, 46,* 305–315.

Kris, E. (1952). *Psychoanalytic explorations in art.* New York: National Universities Press.

LaBarbera, J. D., & Cornsweet, C. (1985). Rorschach predictors of therapeutic outcome in a child psychiatric inpatient service. *Journal of Personality Assessment, 49,* 120–124.

Long, N., Slater, E., Forehand, R., & Falber, R. (1988). Continue high or reduced interparental conflict following divorce. *Journal of Consulting and Clinical Psychology, 56,* 457–469.

Luthar, S. S., & Zigler, E. (1991). Vulnerability and competence: A review of research on resilience in childhood. *American Journal of Orthopsychiatry, 61,* 6–22.

Mayman, M. (1967). Object-representations and object relationships in Rorschach responses. *Journal of Projective Techniques, 31,* 17–25.

Morgan, L., & Viglione, D. (1992). Sexual disturbances, Rorschach sexual responses, and mediating factors. *Psychological Assessment, 4,* 530–536.

Murphy, L. B., & Moriarity, A. E. (1976). *Vulnerability, coping and growth: From infancy to adolescence.* New Haven, CT: Yale University Press.

Nagera, H. (1963). The developmental profile. *Psychoanalytic Study of the Child, 18,* 511–540.

O'Grady, D., & Metz, J. R. (1987). Resilience in children at high risk for psychological disorder. *Journal of Pediatric Psychology, 12,* 3–23.

Perry, W., & Viglione, D. J. (1991). The Rorschach Ego Impairment Index as a predictor of outcome in melancholic depressed patients treated with tricyclic antidepressants. *Journal of Personality Assessment, 56,* 487–501.

Picker, W. R. (1984). Object relations theory and the Rorschach: An examination into impaired perceptions of humanness (Doctoral dissertation, Oklahoma State University). *Dissertation Abstracts International, 43.* (University Microfilms No. 8504375)

Rutter, M. (1979a). Maternal deprivation, 1972–1978: New findings, new concepts, new approaches. *Child Development, 50,* 283–305.

Rutter, M. (1979b). Protective factors from children's responses to stress and disadvantage. In M. W. Kent & J. E. Rolph (Eds.), *Social confidence in children* (pp. 49–74). Hanover, NH: University Press of New England.

Rutter, M. (1983). Stress, coping, and development: Some issues and some questions. In N. Garmezy & M. Rutter (Eds.), *Stress, coping, and development in children* (pp. 43–84). New York: McGraw-Hill.

Rutter, M. (1985). Resilience in the face of adversity: Protective factors and resistance to psychiatric disorder. *British Journal of Psychiatry, 47,* 598–611.

Rutter, M. (1987). Psychosocial resilience and protective mechanisms. *American Journal of Orthopsychiatry, 57,* 316–331.

Schachtel, E. (1959). *Metamorphosis.* New York: Basic Books.

Schafer, R. (1954). *Psychoanalytic interpretation in Rorschach testing.* New York: Grune & Stratton.

Schafer, R. (1958). Regression in the service of the ego: The relevance of a psychoanalytic concept for personality assessment. In G. Lindzey (Ed.), *Assessment of human motives* (pp. 23–52). New York: Grove Press.

Seifer, R., & Someroff, A. J. (1987). Multiple determinants of risk and invulnerability. In E. S. Anthony & B. J. Cohler (Eds.), *The invulnerable child* (pp. 51–69). New York: Guilford.

Sparrow, S. S., Balla, D. A., & Cicchetti, D. V. (1984). *Expanded form manual for the Interview Edition of the Vineland Behavior Scales.* Circle Pines, MN: American Guidance Service.

Spiegelman, A., & Spiegelman, G. (1991). Indications of depression in divorce and non-divorce children reflected by the Rorschach test. *Journal of Personality Assessment, 57,* 120–129.

Spielberger, C. (1973). *Manual for the State-Trait Anxiety Inventory for Children.* Palo Alto, CA: Consulting Psychologists Press.

Terr, L. (1991). Childhood traumas: An outline and overview. *American Journal of Psychiatry, 148,* 10–20.

Thomas, A., & Chess, S. (1977). *Temperament and development.* New York: Bruner-Mazel.

Thomas, A., Chess, S., & Birch, H. G. (1968). *Temperament and behavior disorders in children.* New York: New York University Press.

Urist, J. (1977). The Rorschach Test and the assessment of object relations. *Journal of Personality Assessment, 41,* 3–9.

Viglione, D. J. (1990). Severe psychopathology versus stress induced adaptive reaction: A Rorschach child case study. *Journal of Personality Assessment, 55,* 281–295.

Viglione, D. J., & Kates, J. (1991a, February). *A child case study in psychological resiliency.* Symposium conducted at the meeting of the California Psychological Association, San Diego.

Viglione, D. J., & Kates, J. (1991b, March). Resilience and coping: Adaptive response to trauma. In N. Kaser-Boyd (Chair), *Trauma and personality functioning.* Symposium conducted at the meeting of the Society for Personality Assessment, New Orleans, LA.

Viglione, D. J., & Perry, W. (1991). A general model for psychological assessment and psychopathology applied to depression. *British Journal of Projective Psychology, 36,* 1–16.

Viglione, D. J., van den Daele, L., Brager, R., Zambianco, D., & Perry, W. (1988, February). *A case study in psychological health and resilience.* Symposium conducted at the meeting of the California Psychological Association, San Diego.

Waelder, R. (1933). The psychoanalytic theory of play. *Psychoanalytic Quarterly, 2,* 208–224.

Wallerstein, J. S. (1987). Children of divorce: Report of a ten-year follow-up of early latency-age children. *American Journal of Orthopsychiatry, 57,* 199–211.

Wallerstein, J. S. (1991). The long term effects of divorce on children: A review. *Journal of the American Academy of Child Psychiatry, 30,* 349–360.

Wallerstein, J. S., & Kelly, J. B. (1980). *Surviving the Breakup.* New York: Basic Books.

Waters, E., & Sroufe, L. A. (1983). Social competence as a developmental construct. *Developmental Review, 3,* 79–97.

Werner, E. E. (1989). High-risk children in young adulthood: A longitudinal study from birth to 32 years. *American Journal of Orthopsychiatry, 59,* 72–81.

Wycoff, A. (1993). *Sexually abused and nonabused borderlines: Differentiating groups through psychological testing.* Unpublished doctoral dissertation, California School of Professional Psychology, San Diego.

Zambianco, D. (1988, February). Clinical point of view. In D. J. Viglione (Chair), *A study of psychological health and resiliency.* Symposium conducted at the meeting of the California Psychological Association, San Diego.

Rorschach Structural Summary Data for Three Examinations

Variable	First	Second	Third
Age	7 years 7 months	10 years 1 month	12 years 3 months
Validity and complexity			
R	14^b	15^b	24
L	.75	.67	.60
Cognition			
EB	4:3	$4:0.5^b$	$8:1.0^b$
eb	4:1	3:1	6:1
Sum6	7	3	2
Wsum6	16	8	8
Level 2	0	0	0
M^-	2^a	0	2^a
m	1	0	3
DQ+	5	8	11
Zf	11	12	14
$M^a:M^p$	2:2	1:3	8:4
a:p	3:4	3:5	10:4
Reality testing			
X–%	$.29^a$	.13	.17
X+%	$.50^b$	.60	.54
Xu%	.21	$.27^a$	$.29^a$
Severity of disturbance			
SCZI	3^a	1	2
EII^c	1.4	–.6	–.6
Derepressed contents	6^c	2	3
Affect			
FC:CF + C	2:2	$1^a:0^a$	$0^a:1^a$
Afr	$.27^b$	$.25^a$	.60
C'	1	0	1
Y	0	1	0
DEPI	5^a	3	2
Self-perception			
$3r + (2)\backslash R$	$.21^b$	.47	.42
MOR	3	1	0
V	0	0	0
Interpersonal perception			
$Gd:Poor\ H^c$	1:3	4:2	6:4
ISO	$.50^a$	$.27^a$	.21
Pure H	2	3	7
Sum H	3	6	10
T	0	0	0
COP	1	0	3
AG	2	0	2
CDI	3	4^a	1

[a]More than 2 standard deviations above mean and median of age data (Exner, 1993b) or above cutoff for indicated index. [b]More than 2 standard deviations below mean and median of age data (Exner, 1993b). [c]Normative data not available.

I.

Before Examiner presents Card I:

S: Do you know what they are?

E: It's up to you, tell me what they look like to you.

1. 2" I think it's a headed, a monster face .
. .

1. ER

E: If you look at it a little longer . . .

S: Nope, all I see is a monster face! Oh with two little crosses on the top of him, I don't know what . . . (S keeps card, not looking for R's) . . .

E: When you are finished you can hand it back.

$WS + M^P. FC'u (Hd) 4.0 AG, DV H-^a$

S: Here his, with eyes, his nose, and here's his yucky mouth and he's putting them together so that they look that way and there are two humps on his head and this looks like two crosses this one picture as his ears.

E: His mouth is yucky?

S: Because he has all that stuff and he has dirty, dirty teeth, and that's why he put he put them together to look yucky and mean.

E: What makes them look dirty?

S: Even his teeth look dirty . . . cuz it's black and that's all the pictures on this picture.

VI.

1" You already showed me this one. (E repeats "What might this be?")

9. ER

S: Because I thought it was the same one as the other one but looking at it upside down, thought it was a wand.

9. 2" I told you it was a tree

Wo FDo Bt 2.5

E: You also said it was a tree.

S: These are all the leaves (points to the middle) going up the tree and here's the roots down here.

E: Help me to see the leaves.

S: Oh, bet there's, nice and puffy, they all stick together (points to the middle)

E: What about the inkblot make the leaves look puffy?

S: Oh, because the sticking out parts.

10. ^,v, It really doesn't look like a tree upside down. It looks like a wand with a little lady bug's head sticking out of the top.

$W + F- Id, Ad 2.5 MOR$

10: ER

S: This is the way it looked (v) upside down, see the little tiny lady bug, its head is there.

E: Help me to see the wand.

S: Wands are like stars and this is like a star, this is a yucky wand, that got thrown because it has parts that are coming off and parts sticking out and not pointed and stuff like that.

VII.

11. Looks like oh . . . 4" I think it might be rocky cliffs that you climb up.

11. ER

S: I don't know to explain. There's a sign (not a part of percept), it says "Dangerous cliffs, don't climb up." But they wanted to climb up. There right there. And see the people who climbed up, right there? They're going down.

384

W v/+ M^{P}o Ls,H 2.5 DR H+

E: Cliffs?

S: Because, yes I think there's a sign that say that there, pretty dangerous rocks look pretty weird, specially going up.

E: Rocks

S: Rocks are hard and sturdy and this 11 hard and sturdy, pretty . . . , and that's all (2 dimensional, points and protrusions)

E: Ppl

S: They really 11 pigs . . . IDK . . . I can't really see, it's 11 a little kid or s.t. Little teeny ppl standing up.

X

14. 1" Look this looks like goats (D12) climbing and these are pincher bugs (D1) and this are, this (D11) is making the rock sticking apart, and these are two bad, bad guys (D6) who are trying to creep up on the two goats to eat them and these guys (D2) are trying to creep up on the bad guys and these are two headed dragons (D10) (bottom green)

14. ER

S: Oh, cuz the face and goats have legs like that here's the tail.

E: Faces?

S: See the eyes are, cuz eyes are round and there's a clear place in that's round.

E: Pincher bugs?

S: Pincher bugs have lots of legs, no they only have two, and two goats are clashing because one goat like one person and the other goat like the other person. And this guy looks like plain old yucky guys. I don't know what makes these guys look like dragons.

WS+ Fm^a.M^a.CF.m^P– 2 A, Ls, (A), H 6.0
AG, FAB, DV, COP H–

E: Help me to see the bad guys.

S: They have two feet in front of them, why two bad bugs or something are trying to get up there to defeat these goats.

E: Two headed dragons?

S: Dragons have two things, this and two faces and they are green. They're sturdy because they have people on them.

E: Different rocks, with something sticking them apart?

S: Because it looks like rock, there and there the shapes, its different colored rocks. See there, there, and there. This part keeps them apart.

[a]*H+* = Good Human; *H–* = Poor Human (Perry & Viglione, 1991).

I.

1. 2" Okay, uh looks like a mean cat that has teeth all right there and not right there it looks like a cat that just came out of the trash can.

WSo FDo Ad 3.5 *MOR, DV*

1. ER
S: There's the ears and here's the forehead and here's two bumps on its head and it looks like it's all trashed up. And here its eyes, the nose and this is all covered which makes it look like teeth.
E: What about the blot makes it look covered?
S: It's like its covered and then this part isn't
E: Trashed up?
S: The side and stuff, it's all worn out and stuff like that.

VI.

10. 14" (grins) Looks like there's a ruler up here and this big rock underneath him. That's about it.

W+ M^{p}u 2 *H, Ls* 2.5 *H+*

ER
S: Here's the ruler right there and here's the big rock (outlines)
W: A Ruler?
S: You know, one of those people who stand up like they rule a city or stuff. He's standing up like he's all powerful or something.

VII.

11. 2" This looks like two people facing this way and they're both looking at each other facing this way, with feathers on their heads.

W+ M^{p}u 2 *H, Ad* 2.5 *H+*

ER
S: Here's the head and there's the feather, their bodies are going this way and their heads are going this way, looking at each other.
E: It might look like a feather?
S: Well, it's, I guess I just imagined it there Because I don't know what else it would be.

12. It also looks like two donkeys I don't see anything else. (D3 + Dd 23)

Ddo FM^p- 2 *A*

ER
S: Here's one of the donkeys right there. Just cut off that part, one right there and one right there.
E: It might look like donkeys?
S: Right here is the ear, mouth, eye, and right here they're laying down sort of in a body shape.

X.

15. 3" (smiles) Two insects on two rocks and there are a whole bunch of other insects falling off the rocks. That's it.

W + FM^{p}o 2 *A, Ls* 5.5

ER
S: Here's all the insects falling off the rocks and here's the two insects on the rocks and here's these two pink things and looks like rocks.
E: Help me to see it as you do.
S: This is like where the antennas will be and then the mouth and stuff like that. It's like a cliff, it's going down and then off.

I.

1. A cat?

WSo Fo Ad 3.5

1. ER
S: 'Cause this is like the eyes right here and the ears and this is like the mouth.

2. Kind of like a bat, kind of.

WSo FC'o A 3.5

2. ER
S: Really the same thing. These look like eyes, kind of like. It's black, kind of scary.

3. Kind of like somebody is laying down with their legs out right there.

Do M^p u H H+

3. ER
S: Right here, their face and their feet going out right here and their hands are folded.

VI.

12. [v] This looks like a tree

Wo Fo Bt 2.5

12. ER
S: Here's the trunk and the leaves coming out right here.

13. [v] This looks like two people punching outwards.

Do4 M^a u 2 H AG H−

13. ER
S: Here's their heads and their fists coming out.

VII.

14. This is two Indians, like . . .

W+ Fu 2 H, Art 2.5 *H+*

14. ER
S: 'Cause the feathers going up and the face like a face and the hands going out.
E: Could you show me the outline? S Points to half of blot, (*Dd22*).

15. [v] This looks like two girls dancing or something.

W+ M^a o 2 H 2.5 *COP H+*

15. ER
S: Their hair, hands going right there and then feet coming down.

X.

21. [>] This looks like a crab or a lobster.

Do 1 *Fo A P*

21. ER
S: Here's their legs coming out all over the place.

22. This looks like two insects fighting

D+ 8 *FM^a o 2 A* 4.0 *AG H−*

22. ER
S: Right here. Looks like they have mean looks on their faces, looks like they're fighting or something.

23. This looks like a guy's face with a moustache.

DdSo99 F− Hd H−

23. ER
S: Here's his eyes and looks like a moustache coming down right there.

24. This looks like a seahorse, kind of.

Do9 Fu A

24. ER
S: Their nose right there and then it comes down like that, kind of seahorse.

[a]No reaction times were collected in the third testing.

387

23

An Old Neurosis in an Old Neurotic: "I shouldn't have played with it"

Charles A. Peterson
Cynthia Lindman Port
Department of Veterans Affairs, Minneapolis Medical Center

Although dangerously near 50 himself, and just beginning to approach his most creative period, Freud (1905b) once offered the puzzling opinion that anyone over the age of 50 was unsuitable for psychoanalytic intervention. The developmental narrative was too lengthy for efficient comprehension. The older patient lacked the mental elasticity needed for this type of self-observation. The defenses were encrusted. The libido was both stuck and waning. In sum, Freud felt it was better to devote the limited resources of psychoanalysis to patients who might be capable of change. Abraham (1919), acting the Oedipal upstart to an authoritarian Laius, amended Freud's pessimism, noting that it was the age of the neurosis, not the age of the neurotic, that counted. Cases of relatively late onset psychopathology in the elderly were as amenable to psychoanalytic scrutiny and intervention as were comparable youthful cases. An old neurotic with a relatively more acute neurosis could learn new tricks.

Meanwhile, psychoanalysis was deemphasizing discovery and abreaction and turning its attention to the issues of resistance and relatedness. The analytic patient was no longer pressured for hypnotic confession, but was invited to look inward at the roadblocks to instinctual expression and outward at the repetition of infantile modes of relatedness. If psychoanalysis was slow to turn its attention away from the oedipal paradigm and toward the dawn of attachment and relatedness, the appreciation of the other end of life was even more delayed. After awakening from a hypnotic nap that would rival Rip Van Winkle, psychoanalysis began to map the vicissitudes of adult development (e.g., Butler, 1963; Eissler, 1955; Erikson, 1950; Erikson, Erikson, & Kivnick, 1986; Grotjahn, 1951; Gutmann, 1981, 1987; Levinson, 1978; Valliant, 1977). Viewed from this perspective, the spontaneous reminiscence of narrative identity, which is the elder's dominant ego modality (Molinari & Reichlin,

1984–1985), served the psychotherapy task of telling stories about one's life. The older patient was welcomed into the psychoanalytic consulting room (Griffin & Grunes, 1990; Muslin, 1992). Not surprisingly, the problem of the aging analyst has only been addressed recently and sparingly (Eissler, 1973), but is not addressed here.

The Rorschach assessment of the elderly followed a somewhat different intellectual course. Rorschach (1921) and Klopfer (1946) were relatively optimistic about the utility of the *procedure* with older adults, if not the older patient, and suggested the Rorschach was age-irrelevant. However, the seminal normative work by Ames, Metraux, Rodell, and Walker (1950/1973) threw a wet blanket on the Rorschach diagnosis of the older patient. Ames et al. offered the bleak opinion that the inner world of the older adult as revealed by the Rorschach was, in general, quite barren, coarcted, perceptually compromised, affectively impoverished, and interpersonally detached. Why bother wondering about the older patient's inner life? This study has been criticized on conceptual, attitudinal, methodological, and clinical grounds (Peterson, 1991). Furthermore, clinical experience should remind clinicians that coarctation (e.g., a young obsessive-compulsive) and impoverishment (e.g., a young schizoid personality disorder) are, once again, age-irrelevant, more a function of psychopathology (whether drive/defense/conflict or deficit) than age. Still, there is no denying that an old neurosis in an old neurotic would present a formidable challenge to both diagnostician and psychotherapist.

MR. G.: AN OLD NEUROTIC WITH AN OLD NEUROSIS

Mr. G. was an old neurotic with an old neurosis, clearly a tough case. For many years his misery had remained refractory to both medication and electroconvulsive therapy (ECT), and so he was referred for exploratory psychological testing. Perhaps the "expert diagnostic consultant" (Weiner, 1972) could shed some light on an inner world ignored by previous medicators and shockers.

The expert diagnostic consultant had a wish to empathically comprehend the patient; this wish was made incarnate with an invitation to Mr. G. to take the Rorschach Inkblot Test and to discuss his memories. It is argued here that both the elderly and the Rorschach are best understood using a combination of nomothetic and idiographic approaches, the former guided by Exner's (1986) atheoretical work, the latter guided by a developmental psychoanalytic approach organized within Kernberg's (1980, 1981) psychostructural levels and the Freudian theory of neurosis (cf. Fenichel, 1945). The Rorschach record of an old neurosis in an old neurotic is presented and discussed in a manner similar to previously published work (Peterson, 1992, 1993, 1994; elsewhere in this volume).

The Rorschach was administered first, and served to guide the developmental and sexual anamnesis, ultimately helping the psychoanalytic listener appreciatively construct a narrative (Schafer, 1979) and assisting in the restoration of the narrative continuity of the self. However, in accordance with traditional case study methodology, the history is presented first.

Mr. G. (identifying details have been altered to protect confidentiality) presented to a midwestern VA hospital with complaints of guilt, sadness, lethargy, and sexual rumination. This episode of depression flared up after he sold his farm and purchased a lot in a nearby city on which he planned to build a house. Not only did he lose the link to the bucolic place where he had spent the most happy and peaceful time in his life, he coincidentally lost another sustaining object. His lifelong guilty dysphoria had been made barely tolerable with a first generation monoamine oxidase (MAO) inhibitor. With the advent of new, less toxic, easier to manage medication, his medication was no longer manufactured. The loss of both familiar comforts, his farm and his medication, added a desperate, lonely quality to his depression.

He was admitted to an inpatient psychiatry ward. Initially he was treated with no medication. The attending staff, either colluding in perseverating on the hope embodied in his former medication or unwittingly empathically attuned to his transitional needs, made heroic efforts to find a lab that would synthesize the formula for his old medication. During his inpatient stay, he was treated in a partial hospitalization program that offered him containment, support, structure, validation, and understanding (Gunderson, 1978). He was seen in daily psychoanalytic group psychotherapy, in which he was reflective, expressive, productive, and generative. When facing many of the painful, existential issues raised by a despairing group, he spoke with the ego-integrity that befit someone (Erikson, 1950) facing the inevitable *Torschlusspanik* (German, translated as "panic at the closing of life's door"; Butler, 1963). His issues focused on loss of farm and medication, uncertainty about how to approach his much younger wife for both comfort and sex, fearful wonder about the quality of remaining years, and tormented puzzlement surrounding his life-long guilt over sexuality, past and present. As memory composes identity, he was organized around and full to his narrative brim with memories of exciting, dirty, guilty sex.

Mr. G. was born in the early 1920s, the only son of six children. He lived with his religious parents on a dairy farm in Nebraska until the age of 9, when his family resettled on another farm in Wisconsin. He describes his childhood as "good," but there are hints of discontent. His father is described as stern and unaffectionate, but reasonable. His mother is described as intelligent and controlling. He recalls his mother as being quite intolerant of any expression of anger or sexuality. He experiences her memory as an alive, vigilant, forebidding, repressive, and regulatory presence yet today. When he recalls her condemnation, the memory replays her voice, and he feels the guilt in his viscera. This is consistent with the role of the auditory sphere in the formation and day-to-day activity of the superego that was discussed by Isakower (1939).

Early memories find him nestled in an intact but affect-intolerant family. His earliest memory involves his mother's tyrannical attitudes toward sexuality: "I was a little child, sitting on the floor, playing with my penis, examining my penis, the rough edge underneath. She told me not to do that. I learned that it was a no-no. I stopped." A more accurate statement might be he tried to stop. His earliest memory of his father is embedded in a setting of never-ending chores: "We worked hard from dawn till dusk, even when I was quite young." He was helping his father with chores and recalls "feeling bad over spilling an entire evening's collection of cream." Could this be a screen memory for a parent's wrath and his subsequent guilt over yielding to his urges and spilling his "cream" in masturbation? Other early memories include playing hide-and-go-seek with his sisters in the dark, and playing tag on the way home from school with a neighbor boy: "We'd try to touch each other last." Both of these animated memories may again reflect or carry sexual anxieties, the former involving heterosexuality, the latter homosexuality. He also recalls that:

My two sisters and I slept in the same bed. My older sister and I were pressing against each other sexually. The youngest sister told my parents at the supper table. My other sister and I started crying. We were ashamed. I was four or five years old. They changed me to another room. I remember it as a big, lonely room.

Sexuality, it seemed, led to problems and punishment.

Other memories jump to a postpubertal adolescence. "I was always quite prudent about sexuality." Does he mean "prudish"? Either way the memories suggest a sexual character that is modest, proper, cautious, and sober. "The fact that I couldn't continue it [masturbation] in adolescence caused me a lot of anxiety." He recalls:

some hired men working on a car, talking about girlfriends. I picked up some things from them. At one point they asked me, "Did you know that your dad lays on top of your mother?" I was upset about that. I was upset because I didn't think they'd do that kinda thing. I told my mother and she was upset that they told me. That started me thinking about what adults did sexually.

Not only was he troubled about his parents' sexuality, he was tortured about his own sexual development, "especially masturbation. I was always trying to stop myself." His father, reinforced by the testimony of a neighbor, told him that

one kid died, had fits or something from playing with himself too much. I was afraid I was going to lose my mind. But the urge was stronger than I was. I still masturbated about once a week. I was gonna tell my mother. She said, "Don't stop in the middle (of masturbating); if you have to do it, do it all the way."

Such advice would surely contribute to an interesting repressive calculus involving the hydraulics of instinctual pressure and guilt.

Many of his adolescent memories center on masturbation and guilt.

> I had one defeat after another. I had a lot of guilt. I used rags to tie my hands to the bedstead to keep me from waking up and doing it. One time my dad was sleeping in my room with me but he didn't comment on the fact my hands were tied down. He didn't say anything. It didn't work. I did that for about one year.

Naturally, the tester wondered how he could have tied up his own two [!] hands. The distortion and illogic (primary process contaminates secondary process) in this memory makes it clear that he remains tortured about his sexuality. Again, such an exciting, guilty memory of bondage in the proximity of another man might prefigure his later anxiety regarding homosexuality. He reports postmasturbation guilt, stating "I'd be depressed in the morning. I'd work my way out of it over the day, but it built up over time." Reminiscent of Abraham's (1910, p. 123) observation that "the neurotic often has recourse to onanism as a consolation—to remove depressive spirits," he knew that masturbation felt good, but he felt awful afterward. This postmastubation guilt contributed to his overall nervousness: "I got nervous. One time in high school I had pain in my stomach. I think I was giving myself an ulcer. I felt I had sinned and was not a good person. I felt God would forgive my sins." In high school he

> went with a girl. I never really liked her. We just did some kissing and fondled her breasts. I didn't do anything more due to my morals. I didn't date much in high school. I felt quite inadequate because I was a farm kid and all the girls I liked were town children. They looked down on us.

After high school Mr. G. left home and moved to a larger town where he worked in a factory and lived in a boarding house. He describes this experience as unsettling, as he lived in a bad neighborhood and was exposed to the seamy side of life. At dinner other boarders often talked about sex with prostitutes. He recalls being shocked and disgusted to hear one man describe his sexual exploits by saying "I had so much fun I drank her piss." He states that he struggled to ignore these men and the juicy memories they bequeathed him.

At the age of 21 he enlisted in the Navy and spent 3 years on active duty without any physical injury. Psychologically he was shocked by witnessing the homosexual activity of other servicemen, including his close friend and roommate (recall the potentially pathogenic mystery about being tied up and sleeping with his father = roommate). He had ambivalent feelings about his exposure to homosexuality. He states that he was surprised and disgusted, but he accepted this and remained friends with his roommate. He was pressured by his buddies to go to brothels. On one occasion, thinking he was going to a "bullfight" he accompanied other sailors to a whorehouse. He states that he was shocked: "I felt sorry for the girls." He did not participate in the tawdry ritual of manhood and was thereafter taunted by his fellow soldiers, no doubt accusing him of homosexuality, a taunt/accusation dangerously close to some of his fantasies and fears. As the memory moves from "bullfight" to the whorehouse, note that aggression is associatively connected with sexuality. Why pair aggression and sexuality in the same memory? Such a linking signals that adult sexuality is likely linked to fantastic memories and reworkings of the aggression in the primal scene observed in childhood, as well as to the homosexuality excitedly perceived in the adjacent cot in his barracks. His story to Card 18BM of the Thematic Apperception Test (TAT; Appendix A; Murray, 1943) finds both pleasure and its denial in a possible homosexual scene.

Following discharge from the Navy he started forestry school at a large midwestern university. His first "nervous breakdown" occurred while he was in school. He was in love "for the first time." He had met this girl at a college dance and was quite taken with her. One night as he prepared for sleep, he thought about this girl, but suddenly found himself thinking about homosexuality. He states that his attempt to suppress the homosexual thoughts caused his mind to snap. In his own words, "I repressed that and that caused something to short circuit in my mind. . . my mind just snapped. I felt that click in my mind." He notes that he awoke the next morning and descended into a depression that was followed by his dropping out of school, subsequent hospitalization, and returning to live with his parents for the next year.

He never felt "well enough" to return to school, but joined a forestry camp. Somewhat later he had his second "nervous breakdown," which occurred during an unbearably anxious evening awaiting a visit from the woman who was then his fiancée. He had his first experience of intercourse with this woman: "It was not very satisfying. We did it a number of times. I didn't feel a lot. I withheld my feelings. My doctor at the time said I should be more free with sex but I couldn't." He noted the omnipresence of sexual guilt: "I got sick again right afterward [sex]. I had both feelings then, yes and no." He describes a similar onset: "I went to bed and woke up depressed." He was hospitalized for 2 months, culminating in the severance of his engagement. Commenting directly on his perceived level of psychosocial support, but speaking to his object constancy, he states "my family was there when I needed them."

After a course of ECT, he left the hospital and went home for 6 months. He moved to Arizona and again worked in the forestry services. A promotion was followed by a fourth depression. Again, the bewildering experience of waking up depressed, this time aphonic, resulted in his hospitalization. He was hospitalized for 18 months. Upon his discharge he worked a variety of odd jobs and lived in a room over a bar. He tried to minimize expenses by moving in and living with another man, but could only tolerate 1 month of this arrangement. He was hospitalized, treated with ECT, and transferred to a VA hospital near his home for 1 year's convalescence. He recalls a period of "great inner tension, pressure in my head, in my whole body." Thorazine helped to reduce his tension, which might also mean that it suppressed his libido. He lived for a short time at a cousin's farm and eventually settled comfortably on his parents' farm, where he lived for the next 15 years. The simple, single life on the farm was good for him. The structure was organic (e.g., milk cows have a predictable cycle of engorgement and lactation). The grounding was elemental. The impingement was minimal. The inevitable challenge to this happy embeddedness came, not from within, but from his family, when they encouraged and funded the purchase of his own farm. He states: "I sorta got pushed out of the home; it was good for me."

After 2 solitary years on his own farm, he met and married his wife. She is younger by about 2 decades, and has three children from a previous marriage. They eventually created their own child. Although life on the farm was generally good for him, the years are clouded by a period when he was "angry." His temper was "extremely short," with angry spillover to his family. The 4 years of anger remain a mystery to Mr. G.: "It arrived and it left." Compare Card 14 (Appendix A) of the TAT in which he explains the character's affective experience by saying "It came out of a void." This lacunae, this pseudostupidity, this mental evasion of responsibility for his aggression, is reminiscent of the amnesia-filled history that embodies and accompanies neurotic disturbance (Freud, 1905a). Still, Mr. G. describes the time on his farm as the most peaceful and happy time of his life. The decision to sell the farm and move to the city was difficult, painful, and was of issue in the depression preceding this consultation.

There was also another issue troubling him at the same time. He complained that when he was home from the hospital, his wife often wanted to have sex in the morning, and this left him anxious beforehand and guilty afterward. Speaking to the diurnal dawn of despair known to most depressives, he stated, "I never have sex in the mornings. . . . My wife can't understand why I can't have sex in the morning and all that." Repetition is at work here. He used to masturbate at night and was guilty in the morning. Now his wife wanted sex at a time when he frequently awoke feeling guilty.

He accrued some temporary, compensatory esteem in discussing, no doubt revising, his current sexual life. "I was very active sexually when I would come home from [the hospital]. We would have intercourse and I would get depressed." If true, the reward still was guilt. Or this part of the story may be more wish than reality. Most recently he admitted to impotence. Of course, the impotence may be guilty retribution for the wish to be sexual. It is clear that guilt hovers ever near. He is visited by guilt-laden nightmares: "Things like Bosnia, like I'm responsible."

Although civilization may be founded on the suppression of the sexual instinct (Freud, 1908a, 1930), there are psychic costs, as the case of Mr. G. surely illustrates. Presciently writing as if he had Mr. G.'s repressive development in mind, Freud (1908a) stated, "The strict training which tolerates no sort of expression of this precocious sexual state lends support to the forces of suppression, and the conflict at this [early] age contains all the elements needed to cause lifelong neurosis" (p. 97).

If one adds original sin to the etiological equation, Mr. G. has been guilty from the cradle to the precipice before the grave.

RESULTS

The Rorschach was administered according to the Comprehensive System (Exner, 1986), nondirective inquiry following the final free association to Card X. The results of the Rorschach are presented in Appendix B (free association and inquiry), Appendix C (sequence of scores), Appendix D (structural summary), and Appendix E (testing the limits for sex). Appendix A presents the results of the TAT following Murray's (1943) instructions; however, the cards are presented in the developmental order advocated by Peterson (1990). These data serve as the basis for a determination of the test's reliability and validity, and an exploration of the patient's thought organization, affect organization, security operations, and interpersonal modes.

DISCUSSION

Reliability and Validity

Stung by decades of psychometic criticism of the Rorschach, the Comprehensive System (Exner, 1986) attempts to address the issue of reliability and validity in a two-step process. Mr G.'s R (total number of responses) is 36, which is well above average, and therefore provides an adequate sample of his responses to the inklot stimuli. On the other hand, the second reliability indicator, *Lambda* (ratio of pure form responses to responses with all other determinants) is 1.77. This is higher than desired, and raises the possibility of an overly simplistic or defensive misuse of the stimuli. The high L in this case likely represents a personality style variable and not defensiveness. Although it is tempting to cling simply and rigidly to the false security of numbers, an atheoretical stance will have difficulty resolving this and other apparent contradictions. Schactel (1996, chap. 12) looked past numbers to persuasively argue that the way in which the responses are delivered represents another source of data on the patient's involvement with the Rorschach situation. How the responses are delivered must matter nearly as much as the data themselves. Schafer (1954) said it simply: "The ['autocratic'] tester wants responses" (p. 14). The patient who hastily expells the required number of responses may be submitting to and bombarding the powerful toilet-training parent who demands a product, a "dutiful and submissive delivery of internal products" (Schafer, 1954, p. 44). The psychoanalytic clinician (not the psychometric examiner!) will look past the numbers to the behavioral nature of the parent's relationship to the task and the cards themselves. Mr. G. was clearly involved with the inkblots and his responses. For example, Mr. G. would variously stare, ponder, sigh, grimace, and smile hopefully, obviously immersing himself in the inkblots. One final indicator is the internal experience of the tester. Just as the therapist waits to feel the interactional pressure of the patient's communication (Tansey & Burke, 1989), the receptive tester empathically felt the affective signal announcing the interactional pressure of Mr. G.'s communication as he grappled with the inkblots.

Further, not all form responses are created equal. Pure form responses are often thought to represent the conflict-free sphere of the ego, a more or less realistic affect-free response to the adaptive demands of the stimuli. Again, Schachtel (1966) took us deeper. Some form responses are delivered with obvious derivatives of unconscious conflict, signified by affect-laden (often psychosexual) words. Schactel referred to such responses as "dynamic form responses" that carry the "implication, however slight and tentative, that the subject 'lives' in a certain dynamic relationship to the form perceived" (Schactel, 1966, p. 125). To illustrate: "a butterfly" (inquiry: "body, wings") is likely affect/conflict-free whereas "testicles" (inquiry: "the pouch, definitely two of 'em") is likely freighted with personal meaning. Many of Mr. G.'s pure F responses are obvious carriers of interpretively significant material.

Another indicator of meaningful, conflictual involvement with the stimuli may be found in the form quality of the pure form responses. Ordinary form quality may be just that—ordinary, minimal involvement with and registration of the stimuli. The "+" or "superior-overelaborated" form quality indicates a deep involvement with and enrichment of the stimulus. Likewise, a "−" or "minus" form quality likely represents a conflict-stimulated distortion of the blot. For that matter, a "+" or "synthesized" developmental quality scoring indicates that the test subject has critically examined the stimuli and rearranged them in line with some personal choice. All of these subtleties are lost in the *Lambda* ratio. Perhaps more than other testers, the Rorschach clinician wants to get closer to the individual phenomenology of the patient. This goal requires that the clinician get closer to the patient's raw data (responses) rather than focus on the more experience distant numbers and ratios. For the theory-sustained, receptive clinician, as opposed to the rule-driven tester, this is a reliable, valid, interpretively useful, idiographically rich protocol.

Thought Organization

A *SCZI* Index (a set of decision rules that addresses psychotic ideation/functioning) of 2 suggests that Mr. G. is not psychotic. A *Raw Sum6* (sum of variables measuring disordered thinking) of 5 and a *Weighted Sum6* (sum of variables weighted for severity of disturbed thinking) of 18 do, however, suggest that Mr. G. will show some disordered thinking, likely under the pressure of particular affects based on conflicts with instinctual drives. His $X+\%$ (the ratio of good and bad form level of all determinants) and $F+\%$ (the ratio of good and bad form level on the pure form determinant only) are strongly suggestive of impaired reality testing. However, in clinical interviews, Mr. G. has never reported or demonstrated any fragmentation products, such as hallucinations or delusions. This is confirmed by other Rorschach scores.

There are no M– (human movement with grossly distorted form quality) responses that often signal the presence of delusions about Self and Other. Further, there are no CONTAM (contamination or fusion of two or more images in one perceptual space) responses that indicate a primary ego weakness or a breakdown of psychological boundaries. Nearly all of his poor form quality (i.e., u or –) responses are associated with sexual, or less frequently, aggressive derivatives. For example, of his first four responses, the two responses with sexual material are associated with impaired reality testing or instances of minor cognitive slippage (e.g., response numbers 4, 5, and 7, etc.). Instinctual material clashing with internalized (conscience) standards is the hallmark of neurotic level disturbance (Freud, 1924b).

The adequate number of P or *Popular* (common responses appearing in one of every three records) clearly indicates that he can respond to obvious consensual reality. Mr. G.'s location choice is noteworthy. He differs from most severe depressives in that his *W:D ratio* (ratio of Whole vs. Common Detail) is disproportionately weighted in favor of D. Rather than make the Barnum claim that Mr. G. has a defective or unusual "set" or evidences "disorganization" (Exner, 1986, p. 359), it is preferable to look to Rorschach (1921), who explained the D response as reflecting a person's ability to respond to the most obvious aspects of their environment. The high number of D may suggest that Mr. G. cannot escape a banal, leaden reality, the mimicry of death that is depression (Becker, 1973). On the other hand, it could be said that the numerous easy Ds represent simplicity and economy in service of conservation withdrawal. The paucity of *Blends* (responses with more than one determinant), that is, 1 *Blend*, offers another indicator of a cognitive style that eschews complexity. His few W responses are used up in the first five cards (I, IV, and V) that pull for such lazy-easy W responses. A glance at his TAT (Appendix A) finds the same leaden, economical approach to a stimulus field. Most of his TAT stories stick closely to the concrete details and evidence palpable reluctance to enter an uncertain unstructured future. The Zd score (a measure of organizational activity/effort/style) of +1.0 suggests a balanced approach to stimulus demand, neither neglecting nor frantically connecting (too many) stimuli. In sum, Mr. G. does not demonstrate undue slowing of perceptual or associational processes. He prefers to keep it simple, turning compulsively, but inefficiently, toward a leaden reality, an attention cathexis that diverts him away from unwelcome, insistent, and disorganizing instinctual material. For Mr. G., sex rears its ambivalent (little) head and troubles/distorts what is in his (big) head.

Affective Factors and Security Operations

The *DEPI* Index (a set of decision rules that address depressive affect and ideation) is a mere 3, likely a false negative given the current hospitalization for the (chronic) guilty dysphoria and the recent hospitalization. How does a clinician make sense of two discrepant realities; that is, a relatively conspicuous misery felt by Self and displayed to Other, and a presumptively different level of experience manifested on and captured in Rorschach scores such as the *DEPI?* An overreliance on signs and rules prevents the clinician from heeding Schafer's (1954) trenchant advice: "No matter how helpful a clinical tool it might be, no psychological test does its own thinking" (p. xii). Theory helps the clinician do the thinking that is necessary to animate, organize, and interpret the numerous numbers that collide in the Structural Summary. Weiner (1977) pointed out that a conceptual approach to the Rorschach is more likely to make sense to the clinician and be validated by the researcher.

Although it is not clear what exactly *DEPI* measures (Kaiser, Futch, & Williamson, 1996), an analysis of its component parts may prove useful. The relatively high number of responses is indicative of above-average energy, consistent with his uneasy, almost pressured rumination about sexuality. The absence of *V* (shading used for depth perception) responses is quite interesting, particularly when they most likely would have appeared on his several vagina responses (2, 4, 12), or his anus response (18). Not seeing, or not reporting, the shading associated with the perception of depth may represent ambivalence and a defense against entering the "hard" castrating vagina or the "hard" homosexual anus. If it is "hard," it could not be entered. Because there is clinical evidence of anguished rumination, the absence of *FD* (dimensionality based on the form of the blot) on the Rorschach shows indirect evidence that he defends against such painful introspection lest he spiral down into guilty sexual preoccupation. This is consistent with his TAT stories, where he appears equally hesitant to vicariously introspect regarding the feelings of the characters. Although his depression will be passive, the number of responses in the record indicates that he will not likely be abulic. There is an absence of the stubborn oppositionality (as measured by the number of white space responses) often associated with depression (Coyne, 1976). The *Afr* (affective ratio) suggests that he will approach affective material and will likely be quite reactive to emotional stimuli. Furthermore, the *FC/CF* + *C* ratio (a measure of adaptive or maladaptive use of color/affect) of 1:5 indicates his affects press for discharge, often in maladaptive ways, overwhelming his cognitive response to reality demands. In a man his age, this is likely to be affective instability, not impulsivity. Some of Mr. G.'s *CF*s (e.g., numbers 4 and 24) are feebly justified in the inquiry as if the shape was first and foremost. Despite these weak justifications, it is clear that color is most influential. This, along with the unusual form quality, indicates that he struggles to order, control, and regulate the affect. This thin layer of judgment does not work very effectively. In the face of such a challenge to his autonomous ego functions, he has simplified his cognitive style (1 *Blend* and few *DQ+*; an indicator of sophisticated analysis and synthesis of external stimuli) in service of conservation-withdrawal. According to the Comprehensive System, he shows no formal, structural indicators of anxiety such as shading or achromatic color. Clinically, however, it is clear that he is anxious, albeit mostly about sexual issues, as revealed in the massing of the Sx, easily the most striking feature in the protocol. A few of these sexual responses (e.g., numbers 4 and 5) are insufficiently neutralized (Holt, 1977), indicating a failure of repression and a breakthrough of sexual material and attendant anxiety.

Aggression is more securely contained by Mr. G.'s repressive barrier. Admittedly, the absence of any AG (aggressive movement) responses might speak to his relative inability to comfortably assert himself, because assertion often has both aggressive and libidinal (striving and thrusting) roots (Freud, 1916). However, the absence of aggression may be iatrogenic to the Comprehensive System, which is fairly limited in its sensitivity to the vicissitudes of aggression and the layers of defense against its expression. The supplementary scoring system of Meloy and Gacono (1992) identifies four Aggressive Content responses (numbers 3, 20, 28, and 33). Apparently Mr. G. successfully prevents his aggressive tendencies from being expressed, which would have been manifest in the AG (aggressive movement response). He is equally hesitant to own and express his aggression in his TAT stories. For example, on Card 8BM he says "I see the gun as something unrelated to the picture." As a result, the inevitable, omnipresent "readiness to aggress" (Freud, 1937) is likely retroflected or turned against the self, as well as projected (likely on to the frightening female genital). An atheoretical approach would have sadly concluded that there is no evidence of aggression; guided by theory, the clinician justly wonders how the aggression has been denied. Overall, Mr. G. could be doing worse. He has a negative CDI (Coping Deficit Index) and an *Adjusted D* (an indicator of resources for control and stress management) score of $+1$, showing some reasonable capacity for adaptation, even though he is situationally stressed at present. The negative CDI notwithstanding, the 4 m (inanimate movement) responses suggest that there will be times when he will feel helpless, out of control, and temporarily buffeted by powerful forces. Two of the m responses occur on Card III where he may have been agitated by his sexual concerns. The third m occurs in anxious concert with castration concerns on a not-so-cohesive Card X. Given the relative absence of positive depressive signs, it is possible to suggest that he suffers from an incapacity to bear depression (Zetzel, 1965), leaving him intrapsychically unprepared (i.e., poorly structured) to tolerate life's necessary sadness, and for guilt.

It is diagnostically and prognostically affirming to note an absence of lower-level defenses such as splitting, idealization-devaluation, and psychotic denial. His efforts at suppression and repression, particularly of sexuality, are obvious if not totally successful. It is clear that he makes efforts to avoid and block out aggression. Retroflection or turning aggression against the Self is obvious, as are guilt and its undoing. Further, he evidences a variant of repression, pseudostupidity, where the intellectually lazy and defensively profound "I don't know" serves to block awareness and inquiry. There are also flagging efforts to cover pressing affect with a thin layer of intellectualization.

Self and Other

As measured by the *Egocentricity Index* (the weighted sum of pair and reflection responses divided by the total number of responses), his self-esteem is surprisingly high; that is, assuming he can keep the guilt at bay. The absence of *COP* (cooperative interaction in a movement response) and the deficient single *H* response (human content) point to a relative avoidance of or withdrawal from sustaining human relationships. This is consistent with the desperately lonely tinge to his depression. Just as he does not appreciate the *H* content in the cards, he does not comfortably approach human relationships in his everyday world. When he approaches a person, he finds that certain issues anxiously cloud his perceptions. The exaggerated number of *Hd* (human detail content), almost all of which are delivered with poor form and paired with *Sx* content, reveals that his human relationships are filled with distortion born in sexual conflict (Freud, 1912). Many of his TAT (Appendix A) stories involve the combination of sexuality and distortion. His story to Card 7GF goes so far as to depict a character who wishes to avoid and cannot quite fathom the facts of life. The *H* + *A* : *Hd* + *Ad* ratio (proportion of whole human and animal to part human and part animal) content convergently suggests a wariness or hesitance in relationships. Again, many of his TAT stories depict uncertainty about and a defensive disinterest in relationships. The *T* (shading used for texture) deficiency points to a hesitance or caution to get attached, again most likely because his fantasy-laden sexual drives distort even his anaclitic objects. Exciting-but-guilty sexuality continues to invade his consciousness, likely resulting in his generalized avoidance of the verdure of relationships (his wife being the exception). A whore–wife conflict typical of a neurotic level of development (Freud, 1912) appears in his relationship with his wife as depicted on Card 4 of the TAT (Appendix A). It is possible to speculate that the absence of articulated texture may be reminiscent of his early recollection of being forbidden to touch the rough ridge on the underside of his penis. Exploratory sexual play was forbidden then and it is affectively forbidding now.

The prevalence of passive ideation ($p = 5$) suggests that he will spend time in unproductive fantasy, likely sexually focused. Card 13 of the TAT (Appendix A) illustrates this with a young (he hints that the child may be preschool) boy lost in sexual fantasy, apparently enjoying the wish to be big and have the privileges that come with growing up (Freud, 1909). While engaging in sexual fantasy, the boy is simultaneously sucking his thumb, indicating that the dialectic between sexuality and comfort is an old one, and the personalization of the story leaves no doubt that the conflict is indeed Mr. G.'s. Passive fantasy leads to passive behavior that may invite others to benevolently dominate him.

Some Rorschach variables are interpreted depending on their presence and frequency whereas others are notable by their absence. The white space response may be a case in point. The absence of *S* (white space) location choice indicates a passive-submissive stance in his relationships. An emphasis on white space could be interpreted along a developmental line (Freud, 1965). For example, it can suggest primitive negativism (if the white space is poor form, or accompanied by *WSum6* scores) or a feisty assertiveness in the service of autonomy (if the white space is accompanied with good form and healthy content). In the end he passively wishes that his needs will be passively met. However, it is clear that interpersonal relations are tainted by his sexual conflicts that leave him too guilty and fearful to approach the Other.

Sequence Analysis

Beck, Beck, Levitt, and Molish (1961) offered a de facto apology for scoring, stating "nature seldom follows textbooks" (p. 32). Said differently, a collection of mostly nominal and ordinal variables cannot isomorphically represent a stream of experience. Of course, this does not mean that we should abandon scoring. It does mean that the structural summary is, unavoidably, an experience-distant attempt to codify and categorize human experience. By contrast, an analysis of the sequence of responses facilitates a more experience-near immersion in the world of the other. Empathy and phenomenology are siblings.

Mr. G. begins with a familiar, hyperconventional response. It soon becomes apparent that the "bat" *Popular* is a facade of normality, covering some sexual preoccupation. Rather than see the whole woman (D4), he sees the hole of the woman, which, when followed by the "horns" response, promises danger, and perhaps injury. Card II continues with a "vagina with blood." The outside of the vagina is, surprise, "hard," the barrierlike attribute possibly indicating that the vagina is well-defended. His sexual anxiety continues on Card III. The often-perceived humans (D9) are degraded as birds (birds or chicks as slang for women?). The breast is noted first but the castration anxiety prompts him to add a penis, creating an avian she-male. Castration anxiety diminishes if the female has a penis, too. Likewise, his story to TAT Card 12F (Appendix A) involves a character that is "half woman, half man." The *m* on the next response signals that powerful forces have been unleashed, indicating that Mr. G. feels goaded rather than guided by his sexual affects.

This insecurity is fairly clear in the next response. Not only are bags "holding the testicles," but "hands are holding the testicles," fearfully protecting them and him from the powerful phallic female encountered psychic moments before. Response #9 indicates that the man is not safe: dysphoric affect accompanies his perception of men, "hanging upside down . . . sort of Christ-like." Mr. G. associates the picture with "the old days," reminiscent of the guilty moments when he was tied up, hanging from his bed-posts in a defense against the "sin" of masturbation. On Card IV, which may pull for representations of the father, he reacts sharply to "something evil," a poorly seen face, the impact of the blot (an anxious denial of the shading) overwhelming the autonomous function of reality testing. It is easy to imagine him imagining an evil, scary face regulating him in the darkness. He rests on the first response on Card V: The "butterfly" indicates that he can put a temporary lid on the libido that threatens from within. Based solely on the "crack in the middle," he confabulates a "woman's vagina," the near redundancy and the poor form revealing, once again, the preoccupation that overwhelms internal functions and external reality. The next response, the poorly articulated "round things, part of the [butterfly from two responses prior] wing, sinister," indicates that he has not recovered from the vaginal content *supra.*

Card VI, which often promises a glimpse at the perceiver's sexuality, does not disappoint. He begins with a "penis" with "feather-like projections on the side." Although he reassures himself that the penis is "hard," the feathered penis is pause for thought. Is the decorated penis an object of childhood worship, part of his masculine identity? Or will the feathered penis take wing and leave him castrated, the punishment for a young boy's prideful, pleasurable, preoccupation with the external badge of masculinity? The next two responses, "a woman's vagina" and "ovaries," are both delivered to the center of the card, often a repository for a sense of self (Schachtel, 1966). These suggest that his masculinity is waning per the sexual bimodality of later life and his late life identity is increasingly feminine (Gutmann, 1981, 1987). His first response to Card VII is a "woman's face," appropriate to a card that pulls for feminine, maternal representations. Several hypotheses leap to mind: the infant's first object (not counting the thumb, which can be discovered in Dd21) is its mother's face, at which the infant gazes during nursing. At that point in developmental time the infant's attachment is anaclitic, a nonsexual tender dependency. That the attachment is nonsexual is made clear by the phrase, "from the neck down disconnected." The regression continues on the next response, "the anus"; the anus is "hard" while the "cheeks" are "soft." A "hard anus"? Is this an impaction of later life? Is it a defense against entering the homosexual anus? Or more consistent with the earlier maternal representation, is it an infantile theory (Freud, 1908b) involving the anal birth of a sibling?

He clings to a somewhat higher level of functioning with the first response to Card VIII, "lizards," an unambitious *Popular.* The "lizards," however, are "stuck," speaking to an uncertain outcome in the struggle against regression to an earlier fixation point (Schafer, 1978). The next two responses are ill-formed, first something bony, sharp, and hard, then something "soft and jelly like." Might this mean that some crabbiness and irascibility (bony anatomy; Phillips & Smith, 1953) cover a sense of vulnerability? Card IX, a difficult, amorphous, regressive stimulus, prompts a surprising productivity. Most of the responses involve an aqueous theme. Among those that bear special comment are the fragile seahorses (#23) who have "bony sharp projections" that are presumably protective, perhaps from the "devilish-like figures" that probably represent projections of his own guilt-laden sexual bedevilment. The "ocean water" response must obviously be color affect driven, yet he claims that first the "shape," and then the color "blue" prompted the percept. This sequence indicates that intellect will prove inadequate to support judgment's struggle with affect. He then attempts to escape some of the regressive pull (Greenson, 1968) by expressing himself in a masculine manner, anchoring himself with stereotypically phallic imagery, namely a "fountain . . . going up in here" and a "worm." Although "worm" is clearly phallic, Mr. G. cannot account for his "worm." On inquiry he looks at the card and says "Don't know," the perplexity response expressive of sexual impotence. Card X involves continued regression, despite the *Popular* on the first response. We can note that Cards IX and X begin in similar ways, something hard, bony, and ambivalently aggressive followed by something "devilish," that is, phallic assertion followed and equated with bedevilment (Did he learn that masturbation was the work of the devil?). He takes pains to mention the crab's "pincher" and, a few responses later, skittish seahorses improbably share a "pincher." Both creatures have a soft and edible interior, but here are armed and ready to defend themselves. More "devilish-like creatures" further confirm guilty retribution for yielding to the impulses with which he has been tempted. Card 13MF of the TAT (Appendix A) involves great regret for unspecified but clearly sexual and aggressive misdeeds. Response #30 is quite unique, and likely telling about Mr. G. He sees a "penis . . . a fake penis, pointing down." He no longer has a penis—instead he has a prosthesis! No longer is the penis triumphantly erect; it is "pointing down." He could be speaking about his waning sexual powers, and a self representation that is increasingly feminine, having been castrated for the sexual "crimes" of playing with himself, as well as watching and wondering about homosexuality. Many of his TAT (Appendix A) stories involve curiosity and observation. Two of his last responses, numbers 34 and 35, ride the regression to a lower, anal level. Witness poorly articulated creatures expelling (presumably fecal) "waste." The final response is a strange one: "birds . . . beak pointing to the seahorses"; the poor form is in good company with the five other poor form responses following the "fake penis" response. Phillips and Smith (1953, p. 120) offered a hunch quite congruent with Mr. G.'s record and history: "bird" content reflecting "men who are immature and inept sexually."

Formulation

In looking at this nonpsychotic, nonborderline case, the ten Sx responses quickly seize the examiner's attention (surprisingly the Rorschach Interpretive Assistance Program, Version 3 neglected this supersalient bit of data!). An atheoretical perspective could really only conclude there were too many Sx responses. An examination of both the specific content and the manner (both specific to the Rorschach and nonspecific psychological processes) with which it was delivered will deepen our understanding of Mr. G.'s sexual concerns. Lest the Rorschach be understood and reported in an awkward, artificial "Rorschach-ese" (the RIAP3 output comes to mind here), Rorschachers need what Freud called "metapsychology" (Freud, cited in Strachey, 1957); that is, they need the theoretical superstructure from a more general psychology, where numbers are enriched with a theoretical superstructure.

One crucial reminder: Rorschach content is mediated by both unconscious and conscious factors, and this includes the test subject's concern for social approval (Draguns, Haley, & Phillips, 1967; Haley, Draguns, & Phillips, 1967). At a minimum, an abundance of Rorschach Sx content indicates clearly that Mr. G. is preoccupied with sexuality. However, it is apparent that the sexual material is not simply "there"; it is dynamically alive. Mr. G.'s repression barrier could no longer contain the instinctual, conflictual material, leaking the libidinous material into consciousness. Further, there is the question of personal ownership of the material. The Rorschach instruction uses the subjunctive mood (Peterson & Schilling, 1983) to invite the test subject to modify "suggestive" stimuli (Rorschach, 1921), encouraging the test subject to create and project a response into potential space (Smith, 1990; Willock, 1992). All projection, indeed all creation, pays toll to reality (Freud, 1922), yet carries the unique signature of the "projector," in this instance, Mr. G.'s lingering, inadequately defended sexual conflicts.

His relationship to the Sx content may be further understood by employing an infrequently used procedure, namely "testing the limits for sex" (TTLS; Shaw, 1948; Appendix E). Developed at a time when both patient and diagnostician might have been hesitant to talk directly about sexuality, TTLS asks the test subject to "take a look at the inkblots [and] please point to anything that might be sexual anatomy, or sexual body parts." At first glance this might be considered a "permissive instruction" (Morgan & Viglione, 1992). However, the invitation "What might this be?" is more open, not restricting the test subject to any particular content; by contrast, the TTLS instruction more narrowly focuses on (potentially anxiety-engendering) sexuality. When compared with a normative list of "sex populars" (Pascal, Ruesch, Devine, & Suttell, 1950; Shaw, 1948), it is possible to make inferences about the test subject's sexual comfort, discomfort, and fixation or preoccupation.

On Card I the testee begins by noting testes. He places "testicles" in an area more conducive to (i.e., more typically seen as) breasts or buttocks, perhaps avoiding the former because of guilt over heterosexual sex, and the latter because of guilt over homosexual sex. His second response is a "person here with penis." Although the instructions clearly ask for "sexual anatomy," he includes the "person" along with the "penis." It is as if he tries to prevent castration by refusing to note a disembodied "penis." On Card II, he reports a sex popular, namely a "vagina," but adds bloody injury to the insult of castration. The penis is hastily replaced with his next response to Card II. Mr. G. notes "breasts" on Card III but reassures himself by noting the "penis on each side." He disidentifies with powerful thrusting sexuality by failing to report a phallus on Card IV. Mr. G. rests on Card V. On Card VI he finds a "penis" and then adds the "gonads." Both "testicles" on Card I and the "gonads" on Card VI are highly unusual and therefore suggest preoccupation; these responses are reminiscent of response #7 on the free association: "Hands holding the testicles." A sexually anxious, guilty man, he periodically reassures himself by either noting the presence of—or clutching, holding and protecting—his genitals. Card 13 of the TAT (Appendix A) witnesses an anxious preschool-age boy comforting himself with sexual fantasy (or potential potency!). No doubt the sensations in his erogenous zone reassure him of the presence of his penis. He avoids all sexuality on Card VII, the "Mother Card." The incest taboo is respected. On Card VIII he finds nothing. After this brief latency (stage?), he finds a very distorted "penis" in the D5 area of Card IX. Delivered to the very center of the card, an area occasionally associated with a geyser or fountain, this response suggests how clearly he identifies with his penis. On Card X, which by now he knows will be his last card, he leaves his sexual signature, "animals carrying a penis." This rich response is surely overdetermined. Once again, sexual material is accompanied by cognitive slippage (*FABCOM*). Furthermore, the animal content indicates the regressed nature of the response, perhaps reminiscent of times in childhood when the discovery of his penis carried him away nightly. Finally, isomorphic with the content, his life is witness to his animalistic desires carrying him away and producing the feared castration—a punishment fitting his guilt. Guilt plus *lex talionis* equals castration equals impotence. The weight of this conclusion is highlighted by the fact that Card X hosts similar content/themes on both the free association and the testing of the limits for sex. Although one is a fake penis and the other a disembodied (castration) penis carried away by animals, both highlight one of the classic danger situations that accompanies being male (young or old), namely castration.

What awaits him psychologically? What are the developmental demands that challenge him? What are his options? Diagnostically, the absence of a thought disorder or fragmentation products suggests that he is not organized at the psychotic level of development. That his identity is intact removes him from the borderline level of development. He has been able to love and work, with palpable if ambivalent affect in his relationship with his wife, and a measure of peace in his work close to the land. He has a conflict between the desire for instinctual expression and the barriers of civilization and (guilty) conscience. This has been a long-standing conflict. Change will be difficult but he does deserve understanding and relatedness as well as medication. This collaboration between sufferer and expert diagnostic consultant is a promising beginning to attachment, understanding, and change. Well into his 70s, he must face his mortality and the accompanying *Torschlusspanik*. Just as he is late in his life, he produces his only two *symbiosis* scores (Kwawer, 1980) late in the sequence of scores on Card X of the Rorschach. This symmetry alerts the expert diagnostic consultant to interpretive significance. Although those scores suggest some ambivalence, he may be ready to give up and lay down and die, returning to the symbiotically enfolding arms of Mother Earth. Dissolution and dust await us all.

He must face separation from the hospital and thrust toward the future. If the past predicts the future, he may return to the shortlived buoyancy he has experienced on previous discharges. Perhaps the confinement and previous ECT represented sufficient punishment so that he could go forth and thrust again (Freud, 1924a). Or, because Mr. G. has never been aggressively treated with a developmentally driven psychotherapy, we can reserve some hope for a better prognosis. His story to Card 12M of the TAT (Appendix A), the so-called "therapy card," suggests a neurotic level transference, finding some comfort and forgiveness within a "professional relationship." Might we recall Mr. G.'s abortive *shading* responses, the efforts to control and dampen his *Color* responses, and the near *M* responses? Schafer (1978) discussed such patients as Mr. G. who struggle to recover from and resist regression. He stated:

> Those who are the most promising candidates for successful readjustment give Rorschach responses that can *almost* be scored M, FC, and FCh [the shaded responses in the Comprehensive System] but cannot be so scored owing to the lack of spontaneous reference to movement, color and shading and a similar lack in response to inquiry. . . . This struggling type of patient may be said to be playing it safe with regard to freedom of fantasy and of involvement with others, even though some potential and readiness for those ventures can be identified. (p. 567)

Mr. G. must become more comfortable with his sexuality. The one memory he retained from an earlier psychiatric visit involved encouragement to loosen up sexually. This was clearly good advice then, and is good advice now. More specifically, Mr. G.'s therapist will have to help him tolerate the developmentally expectable "castration" associated with the sexual bimodality of later life (Gutmann, 1981, 1987). At the same time his therapist, taking the role assigned his wife in the first story told on the TAT (Card 10, Appendix A), must "hold" and metabolize the nagging guilt associated with masturbation. Like the good-enough mother who releases and affirms spontaneous genital play (Spitz, 1962; Spitz & Wolf, 1949), the good-enough therapist may help him feel good, for the first—and last—time, about playing with it.

ACKNOWLEDGMENTS

The Department of Veterans Affairs has supported this research. I wish to thank my grandparents, and David Gutmann and Jerome Grunes, the former for introducing me to, and the latter for teaching me the psychoanalytic appreciation of, the inner world of the older adult. Special gratitude is also due Reid Meloy for his affirming patience during a miserable time of life in which I aged considerably. This chapter is dedicated to my daughter Stacy who did not get to live long enough to be both buffeted and sustained by the passions of later life.

REFERENCES

Abraham, K. (1910). Hysterical dream-states. In Selected papers on psycho-analysis (Vol. 1, pp. 90–124). New York: Brunner-Mazel.

Abraham, K. (1919). The applicability of psycho-analytic treatment to patients at an advanced age. In Selected papers on psycho-analysis (Vol. 1, pp. 312–317). New York: Brunner-Mazel.

Ames, L. B., Metraux, R. W., Rodell, J. L., & Walker, R. N. (1973). Rorschach responses in old age (2nd ed.). New York: Brunner-Mazel. (Original work published 1950)

Beck, S. J., Beck, A. G., Levitt, E. E., & Molish, H. B. (1961). Rorschach's test I. Basic processes. New York: Grune & Stratton.

Becker, E. (1973). The denial of death. New York: The Free Press.

Butler, R. N. (1963). The life review: An interpretation of reminiscence in the aged. Psychiatry, 26, 65–76.

Coyne, J. C. (1976). Toward an interactional model of depression. Psychiatry, 40, 28–40.

Draguns, J. G., Haley, E. M., & Phillips, L. (1967). Studies of Rorschach content: A review of the research literature. Part I: Traditional content categories. Journal of Projective Techniques and Personality Assessment, 31, 3–32.

Eissler, K. R. (1955). The psychiatrist and the dying patient. New York: International Universities Press.

Eissler, K. R. (1973). On the possible effects of aging on the practice of psychoanalysis. Journal of the Philadelphia Association of Psychoanalysis, 3, 138–152.

Erikson, E. H. (1950). Childhood and society. New York: Norton.

Erikson, E. H., Erikson, J. M., & Kivnick, H. Q. (1986). Vital involvement in old age. New York: Norton.

Exner, J. E., Jr. (1986). The Rorschach: A comprehensive system: Vol. 1. Basic foundations (2nd ed.). New York: Wiley.

Fenichel, O. (1945). The psychoanalytic theory of neurosis. New York: Norton.

Freud, A. (1965). Normality and pathology in childhood. New York: International Universities Press.

Freud, S. (1905a). Fragment of an analysis of a case of hysteria. In Standard edition of the complete psychological works of Sigmund Freud (Vol. 7, pp. 3–122). London: Hogarth Press.

Freud, S. (1905b). On psychotherapy. In Standard edition of the complete psychological works of Sigmund Freud (Vol. 7, pp. 257–270). London: Hogarth.

Freud, S. (1908a). "Civilized" sexuality and modern nervous illness. In Standard edition of the complete psychological works of Sigmund Freud (Vol. 9, pp. 177–204). London: Hogarth.

Freud, S. (1908b). On the sexual theories of children. In Standard edition of the complete psychological works of Sigmund Freud (Vol. 9, pp. 205–226). London: Hogarth.

Freud, S. (1909). Family romances. In Standard edition of the complete psychological works of Sigmund Freud (Vol. 9, pp. 235–244). London: Hogarth.

Freud, S. (1912). On the universal tendency toward debasement in the sphere of love. In Standard edition of the complete psychological works of Sigmund Freud (Vol. 11, pp. 179–190). London: Hogarth.

Freud, S. (1916). Some character types met with in psycho-analytic work. In Standard edition of the complete psychological works of Sigmund Freud (Vol. 14, pp. 311–336). London: Hogarth.

Freud, S. (1922). Some neurotic mechanisms in jealousy, paranoia and homosexuality. In Standard edition of the complete psychological works of Sigmund Freud (Vol. 18, pp. 221–233). London: Hogarth.

Freud, S. (1924a). The economic problem of masochism. In Standard edition of the complete psychological works of Sigmund Freud (Vol. 19, pp. 157–172). London: Hogarth.

Freud, S. (1924b). Neurosis and psychosis. In Standard edition of the complete psychological works of Sigmund Freud (Vol. 19, pp. 149–153). London: Hogarth.

Freud, S. (1930). Civilization and its discontents. In *Standard edition of the complete psychological works of Sigmund Freud* (Vol. 21). London: Hogarth.

Freud, S. (1937). Why war? Letter from Einstein. Letter from Freud. In *Standard edition of the complete psychological works of Sigmund Freud* (Vol. 22, pp. 197–218). London: Hogarth.

Greenson, R. R. (1968). Disidentifying from mother: Its special importance for the boy. *International Journal of Psycho-Analysis, 49*, 370–374.

Griffin, B. P., & Grunes, J. M. (1990). A developmental approach to psychoanalytic psychotherapy with the aged. In R. A. Nemiroff & C. A. Colorusso (Eds.), *New dimensions in adult development* (pp. 267–287). New York: Basic Books.

Grotjahn, M. (1951). Some analytic observations about the process of growing old. In G. Roheim (Ed.), *Psychoanalysis and the social sciences* (Vol. 3, pp. 301–312). New York: International Universities Press.

Gunderson, J. G. (1978). Defining the therapeutic process in therapeutic milieus. *Psychiatry, 41*, 327–335.

Gutmann, D. L. (1981). Psychoanalysis and aging: A developmental view. In S. I. Greenspan & G. R. Pollock (Eds.), *The course of life: Adulthood and the aging process* (Vol. 3, pp. 489–517). Adelphi, MD: U.S. Department of Health and Human Services.

Gutmann, D. L. (1987). *Reclaimed powers.* New York: Basic Books.

Haley, E. M., Draguns, J. G., & Phillips, L. (1967). Studies of Rorschach content: A review of research literature: II. Non-traditional uses of content indicators. *Journal of Projective Techniques and Personality Assessment, 31*, 3–38.

Holt, R. R. (1977). A method for scoring primary process manifestations and their control in Rorschach responses. In M. A. Rickers-Ovsiankina (Ed.), *Rorschach psychology* (2nd ed., pp. 375–420). Huntington, NY: Krieger.

Isakower, O. (1939). On the exceptional position of the auditory sphere. *International Journal of Psycho-Analysis, 20*, 340–348.

Kaiser, R., Futch, G., & Williamson, D. (1996, March). *What is the DEPI?* Paper presented at the Midwinter Meeting of the Society of Personality Assessment, Denver, CO.

Kernberg, O. (1980). Neurosis, psychosis, and the borderline states. In A. M. Freedman, H. I. Kaplan, & B. J. Saddock (Eds.), *Comprehensive textbook of psychiatry* (Vol. 3, 3rd ed., pp. 1079–1092). Baltimore: Williams & Wilkins.

Kernberg, O. (1981). Structural interviewing. *Psychiatric Clinics of North America, 4*, 169–195.

Klopfer, W. G. (1946). Personality patterns in old age. *Rorschach Research Exchange, 10*, 145–166.

Kwawer, J.S. (1980). Primitive interpersonal modes, borderline phenomena and Rorschach content. In J. S. Kwawer, H. Lerner, P. Lerner, & A. Sugarman (Eds.), *Borderline phenomena and the Rorschach test* (pp. 89–105). New York: International Universities Press.

Levinson, D. J. (1978). *The seasons of a man's life.* New York: Knopf.

Meloy, J. R., & Gacono, C. B. (1992). The aggression response and the Rorschach. *Journal of Clinical Psychology, 48*, 104–114.

Molinari, V., & Reichlin, R. (1984–1985). Life review and reminiscence in the elderly: A review of the literature. *International Journal of Aging and Human Development, 20*, 81–92.

Morgan, L., & Viglione, D. J. (1992). Sexual disturbances, Rorschach sexual responses, and mediating factors. *Psychological Assessment, 4*, 530–536.

Murray, H. A. (1943). *Thematic Apperception Test manual.* Cambridge, MA: Harvard University Press.

Muslin, H. (1992). *The psychotherapy of the elderly self.* New York: Brunner-Mazel.

Pascal, G., Ruesch, H., Devine, D., & Suttell, B. (1950). A study of genital symbols on the Rorschach Test: Presentation of method and results. *Journal of Abnormal and Social Psychology, 45*, 285–289.

Peterson, C. A. (1990). Administration of the Thematic Apperception Test: Contributions of psychoanalytic psychotherapy. *Journal of Contemporary Psychotherapy, 20*, 191–200.

Peterson, C. A. (1991). Reminiscence, retirement and Rorschach responses in old age. *Journal of Personality Assessment, 57,* 531–536.

Peterson, C. A. (1992). A psychotic gynemimetic: I just had a pregnant thought. *Journal of Personality Assessment, 58,* 464–469.

Peterson, C. A. (1993). A borderline policeman: AKA, a cop with no COP. *Journal of Personality Assessment, 61,* 374–393.

Peterson, C. A. (1994). A neurotic lawyer: AIDS or Oedipus? *Journal of Personality Assessment, 63,* 10–26.

Peterson, C. A., & Schilling, K. M. (1983). Card pull in projective testing. *Journal of Personality Assessment, 47,* 265–275.

Phillips, L., & Smith, J. G. (1953). *Rorschach interpretation: Advanced technique.* New York: Psychological Corporation.

Rapaport, D., Gill, M. M., & Schafer, R. (1945–1946). *Diagnostic psychological testing* (Vols. 1 & 2). Chicago: Yearbook Publishers.

Rorschach, H. (1921). *Psychodiagnostics.* New York: Grune & Stratton.

Schachtel, E. G. (1966). *Experiential foundations of Rorschach's test.* London: Tavistock.

Schafer, R. (1954). *Psychoanalytic interpretation of Rorschach testing.* New York: Grune & Stratton.

Schafer, R. (1978). Psychological test responses manifesting the struggle against decompensation. *Journal of Personality Assessment, 42,* 562–571.

Schafer, R. (1979). The appreciative analytic attitude and the construction of multiple histories. *Psychoanalysis and Contemporary Thought, 2,* 3–24.

Shaw, B. (1948). "Sex populars" in the Rorschach test. *Journal of Abnormal and Social Psychology, 43,* 466–470.

Smith, B. L. (1990). Potential space and the Rorschach: An application of object relations theory. *Journal of Personality Assessment, 55,* 756–757.

Spitz, R. A. (1962). Autoeroticism re-examined: The role of early sexual behavior patterns in personality formation. *Psychoanalytic Study of the Child, 17,* 283–315.

Spitz, R. A., & Wolf, K. M. (1949). Autoeroticism: Some empirical findings and hypotheses on three of its manifestations in the first year of life. *Psychoanalytic Study of the Child, 3,* 85–120.

Strachey, J. (1957). Papers on metapsychology. Editor's introduction. In *Standard edition of the complete psychological works of Sigmund Freud* (Vol. 14, pp. 105–110). London: Hogarth.

Tansey, M. J., & Burke, W. F. (1989). *Understanding countertransference.* Hillsdale, NJ: The Analytic Press.

Valliant, G. E. (1977). *Adaptation to life.* Boston: Little, Brown.

Weiner, I. B. (1972). Does psychodiagnosis have a future? *Journal of Personality Assessment, 36,* 534–546.

Weiner, I. B. (1977). Approaches to Rorschach validation. In M. A. Rickers-Ovsiankina (Ed.), *Rorschach psychology* (2nd ed., pp. 575–608). Huntington, NY: Krieger.

Willock, B. (1992). Projection, transitional phenomena, and the Rorschach. *Journal of Personality Assessment, 59,* 99–116.

Zetzel, E. R. (1965). Depression and the incapacity to bear it. In M. Schur (Ed.), *Drives, affects, behavior* (Vol. 2, pp. 243–274). New York: International Universities Press.

APPENDIX A
Thematic Apperception Test

Card 10

They're a married couple, elderly, married quite a while, and something happened that brought them to this instant here. He feels compassionate towards her. He's the aggressive person that started this, kissing her. Something she had done made him feel that way about her. A couple alone in their home, living alone, married a long time. He wants to show how he feels about whatever happened. She has her hand on his chest. *What led up to it?* Maybe something has happened to the children. Something being resolved and they're feeling good about it. Her hand, as if she were going to hold his penis later on.

Card 7GF

I see this as a case where a young girl is setting on a love seat and the maid or servant is talking to her about the child in her arms, explaining something to her about the baby. She's in a state of shock. I think the maid is trying to make her understand something she can't quite fathom, such as having and caring for the baby. *What is going to happen?* In the future? I don't know. She's undecided whether she'll keep the baby or not.

Card 6BM

This is my dad and he's quite serious looking. The woman is some relation of his. He looks quite as if he's going to or has told her something and I have a feeling he's not gonna stay and she doesn't want him to stay. My dad is quite handsome. Looks a lot like my dad in pictures. He's quite tense, holding his hat. His fingers look quite tense. *What is going to happen?* A country home, a wooded part through the window the old lady is looking out through. Took place in an earlier time, not at the present. *What is going to happen?* Something very solemn, so many possibilities.

Card 7BM

I see this as sort of a sinister picture, both of them looking quite foreboding or evil, talking about some unlawful thing. The older one is talking to the younger one. The older one is quite shrewd. The younger man looks quite corrupt or outside of the law. *What are they talking about?* I haven't any idea what they're talking about.

Card 13

I see this back in the early days of log cabins. The young boy sitting in the doorway, could be like myself, sucking on his thumb or chewing his finger, his hands clasped. It's a rural scene back in pioneer days. The door is out of alignment. The sun is shining. *What is the story?* Boy's just sitting and thinking, all so solitaire. *What is he thinking?* He's gonna grow up. *What is he feeling?* Being a man, sexually active and having girlfriends and going to school. *What is feeling?* Hope for the future.

Card 8BM

I see this, a dead man there, and the boy in the foreground is detached from the rest of them. The ones in back holding a knife are gonna perform an autopsy. They're physicians. The man with the knife is gonna put a lot of pressure on the knife. *What led up to this?* Looks like a prison, bars in the back. I see the gun as something unrelated to the picture. The boy is just detached from the picture, looks intelligent, a moral type of boy. His thoughts are on religion. There's a beam of light on him. *Can you tell me a story?* I did.

Card 9BM

These men have been working in a field. They just came in for dinner and they're relaxing after dinner. By their poses, they're good friends, one on the other's back, the other with his body close to the other man. The one without the hat is a younger man, sort of detached from the rest of them as if he were questioning why they were laying there. He's wanting them to go back to work. *What is he feeling?* He's feeling he doesn't have much effect on what the other fellas are feeling.

(continued)

Card 2
I feel the man by the horse is working in the field. The woman off to the side is his wife. She's pregnant. Her bosoms filled out, stomach swelled out like she were pregnant. The younger girl is a school girl. She might be infatuated with the man without his shirt as if she were waiting for him. He has his back turned as if he were not interested.

Card 17BM
A naked man, very powerful, hanging onto a rope that doesn't have any connection to anything. Yet he's not falling. He's looking at something he's real curious about. *What is he looking at?* The whole picture puzzles me. *What is he feeling?* Curiosity.

Card 4
I see a young woman infatuated with this man, trying to talk him into giving her his attention. He's more interested in something behind her, maybe another woman, like this one in the back. He's very intent on what he sees and he's not paying any attention to the woman who is trying to get his attention. The picture seems to have two parts. A woman in part of a house, and a man at a house of prostitution. She's a wife, she's a prostitute. She's his wife. He's more interested in the prostitute. *What are they feeling?* He's feeling desire. She's feeling left out or abandoned. *What's going to happen?* Yet to be found out. I guess I don't know.

Card 13MF
I see a woman. She's dead, her breasts are exposed. This man is very remorseful that he had something to do with her death. He can't bring himself to look at her. He's covering his eyes with his arm. On the table there there's a book, a Bible on top. I see this as a domestic scene; it happened in her home. *How did she die?* He discovered she was dead. He's feeling remorse. *Why is he feeling remorse?* He discovered her dead. He's feeling remorse about her being dead.

Card 18BM
I see this as a homosexual scene. The man that's behind this other man, his hand on his arm and shoulder. The man in front is fully clothed. I can't see how there can be activity going on. He has a gratifying look as if enjoying some sensual pleasure. I don't understand the one arm there, one arm sticking out, that shouldn't be there. *What will happen?* I don't know.

Card 14
A black room, no light in it at all. The man going to the window with it open, looking out at the light. Not much meaning to me. *What will happen?* Nothing; he's just looking. *What is he thinking?* He's glad to see the light. *What led up to it?* It came out of a void.

Card 12F
I see the older woman as being very evil, evil face and some kind of a robe, very sinister looking. The person in front is half woman, half man. She's looking at something different than the other woman. *What is she feeling?* Just curiosity I guess.

Card 12M
The young man is dead, lying on a sofa or couch. This man has his hand out over the top of his head. He's saying a prayer over him. He's giving off a holy light, an older man, balding. *What led up to it?* The boy died peacefully, whatever the situation was. *What is he thinking?* Of God and his prayer. *What is he feeling?* Looks professional about it.

I.

1. I see a bat, the eyes here and the wings.   The configuration. (?) No

Wo Fo A P 1.0

2. And maybe a woman's vagina here   Just the crack and the position

Ddo Fu Hd, Sx CONFAB (Position)[1]

3. Horns here, hard horns   Hard. (?) No I just felt that way

Do Fo 2 Ad (AgContent)[2]

II.

4. Woman's vagina with blood here, this   The shape (?) Red, shape (?) Don't know
outside being hard, hard points here, the dark   (?) Don't know
part, hard here, this being soft here

Wv/+ Cfu Hd, Sx, Bl 4.5

III.

5. I see these heads as being birdlike crea-   The shape
tures, breast here, and penis here, arms here.

Do Fo 2 (A), Sx INCOM-2

6. Separate from them here, them holding   Just the way it looks
it, a whirling thing, a stake holding a whirling
thing.

Do m(a)u Sc (Relationship)[1]

7. Like bags here, holding the testicles.   The shape
Hands holding the testicles

D+ M(p)o 2 Hd, Sx 3.0

8. Red thing sort of like a butterfly, wings   Just when I looked at it
held together by something elastic here.

Do m(p) o A, Sc

9. A man upside down, as if he's hanging   Sort of Christ-like to me
there, for some reason, I don't know, sort of a
gruesome picture I have of these two men here
upside down, having a pointed beard and a
tunic like the old days, arms, legs, and feet.
These birdlike creatures and men hanging, the
whole thing is gruesome.

Do M(p)o 2 H, CG, MOR (Relationship)[1]

IV.

10. Something evil, with these as the eyes,   The shape (?) Just the general aspect of it.
the ears here, the whole thing, a face, nose,
beard on the face or cheeks.

Wv F– Hd AB

V.

11. A bat or butterfly   More like a butterfly shape, antennas, swal-
                                                     lowtail

Wo Fo A P 1.0

12. Woman's vagina here   Crack in the middle

Ddo F– Hd, Sx CONFAB

(continued)

13. Round things, part of the wing, sinister.　　Markings (?) The whole whole thing is sinister

Do Fu 2 Ad MOR (Relationship)[1]

VI.

14. This I see as a penis, featherlike projec-　　Just the way it looks
tions on the side, soft, this being hard, the penis

D+ Fo Hd, Sx 2.5 FABCOM-2

15. Woman's vagina, hard part on the out-　　Can't explain it, you just get an impression
side, the whole thing hard

Do Fu Hd, Sx

16. The ovaries here　　Shape, look soft to me

Ddo F– 2 Hd, Sx

VII.

17. Women's face, hair in the air, neck right　　Nose, eyes, hair, mouth, pigtail. From neck
here. These parts seem disconnected, not part　　down disconnected (points)
of the picture

Do Fo 2 Hd P

18. This I see as the anus, that being hard,　　Connected. (?) No
projection out here being the cheeks, soft
cheeks.

Do F– Hd, Sx

VIII.

19. More colorful, lizards here, tails here.　　Head, tail, body, feet are stuck

Do FM(p)o 2 A P (Affective)[1]

20. I see a division in here. I can't identify　　Yeah. Shape
what that is. Like fishlike things and a sharp
beak. These is ribs and the back backbone,
some kind of connection.

Ddo F– A DV (AgContent)[1]

21. Something soft and jelly-like.　　Don't know.

Dv Fu A

IX.

22. Seahorses, bony sharp projections here.　　(points) Same part.

Do F– 2 A (AgContent)[2]

23. Devilish-like figures on the side with　　Here.
this being the head.

Do Fo 2 (H)

24. Ocean water.　　Shape, blue.

Dv Cfu Na

25. Coral here.　　Being pink, part of the water

Dv Cfo Na (Relationship)[1]

26. And a water fountain-like thing going　　Just the way it looks
up in the middle

Do m(a) u Sc

27. With something green and long here　　Don't know
like a worm

Ddo FCo A

414

X.

28. Crablike creatures, green appendages with a pincher on the end

Just look like crabs, look hard (?) Shape, they're soft

D+ Fo 2 A P 4.0 (AgCont)[2]

29. Devlish-like creatures all on the side here

These here, just eyes and shape

Dv Fu 2 (A)

30. A penis only not really, sort of a fake penis, pointing down

Fake (?) It doesn't look realistic (?) No

Do m(p)u (Hd), Sx, Sc (Castration)[1]

31. Islands, coral islands here, connected by water.

Pink, water blue, hard (pointing at pink D9)

Dv/+ Cfu Ls 4.5 (Separation-division)[2]

32. Semaphore flags here.

Just looks like a signal, upside down though

Do Fu 2 Sc

33. Green things, upside down seahorses with a little white pincher in the middle

(points) No.

D+ Fu 2 A INCOM-1 (AgContent[2], Symbiotic merging[3]) 4.0

34. Devlish-like creatures exhausting something yellow

Exhaust. (?) Coming out tail end

Dv/+ CF.FM(a)u 2 (A) FABCOM-1 4.0

35. Waste from the seahorses

Out the end

Dv Fu 2 Ad (Relationship)[1]

36. Birds with an eye there, bird with his beak pointing toward the seahorses.

There (points)

Do F-2 A (Relationship).

Note. Scorings in parentheses belong to (1) Rapaport, Gill, and Schafer (1945–1946), (2) Meloy and Gacono (1992), or (3) Kwawer (1980).

[1] "Affective" verbalizations involve unsolicited comments on the color/affect embodied in and evoked by the inkblot; these verbalizations indicate a certain lability, a failure to contain or manage affect. "Castration" verbalizations include responses that have something missing or incomplete, occasionally with reference to disfigured, dysfunctional anatomy. It may indicate castration anxiety and/or a feeling of insufficiency. "Position" responses resemble *ALOG* responses and involve strained, predicate logic based on the shape/position of the response within the inkblot; these responses indicate cognitive slippage. "Relationship" responses involve a connection posited between responses within or across cards; they indicate a tendency toward overinclusive/referential thinking.

[2] "AgC" (Aggression Content) responses involve imagery popularly perceived as aggressive.

[3] "Symbiotic merging" responses involve fantasies of and primitive processes of merger, fusion, denial of separation. Separation-division responses indicate ambivalence or conflict regarding separation and reunion.

Card	No.	Loc.	#	Determinant(s)	(2)	Content(s)	Pop Z	Special Scores
I	1	Wo	1	Fo		A	P 1.0	
	2	Ddo		Fu		Hd, Sx		CFB
	3	Do		Fo	2	Ad		
II	4	W/	1	CFu		Hd, Sx, Bl	4.5	
III	5	Do		Fo	2	(A), Sx		INC2
	6	Do		mau		Sc		
	7	D+		Mpo	2	Hd, Sx	3.0	
	8	Do		mpo		A, Sc		
	9	Do		Mpo	2	H, Cg		MOR
IV	10	Wv	1	F–		Hd		AB
V	11	Wo	1	Fo		A	P 1.0	
	12	Ddo		F–		Hd, Sx		CFB
	13	Do		Fu	2	Ad		MOR
VI	14	D+		Fo		Hd, Sx	2.5	FAB2
	15	Do		Fu		Hd, Sx		
	16	Ddo		F–	2	Hd, Sx		
VII	17	Do		Fo	2	Hd	P	
	18	Do		F–		Hd, Sx		
VIII	19	Do		FMpo	2	A	P	
	20	Ddo		F–		A		DV
	21	Dv		Fu		A		
IX	22	Do		F–	2	A		
	23	Do		Fo	2	(H)		
	24	Dv		CFu		Na		
	25	Dv		CFo		Na		
	26	Do		mau		Sc		
	27	Ddo		FCo		A		
X	28	D+		Fo	2	A	P 4.0	
	29	Dv		Fu	2	(A)		
	30	Do		mpu		(Hd), Sx, Sc		
	31	D/		CFu		Ls	4.5	
	32	Do		Fu	2	Sc		
	33	D+		Fu	2	A	4.0	INC
	34	D/		CF.FMau	2	(A)	4.0	FAB
	35	Dv		Fu	2	Ad		
	36	Do		F–	2	A		

Summary of Approach

I:W.Dd.D	VI:D.D.Dd
II:W	VII:D.D
III:D.D.D.D.D	VIII:D.Dd.D
IV:W	IX:D.D.D.D.Dd
V:W.Dd.D	X:D.D.D.D.D.D.D.D

416

APPENDIX D
Rorschach Structural Summary

LOCATION FEATURES	
Zf	= 9
ZSum	= 28.5
ZEst	= 27.5
W	= 4
(Wv	= 1)
D	= 27
Dd	= 5
S	= 0

DQ	..........(FQ–)
+	= 4 (0)
o	= 23(6)
v/+	= 3 (0)
v	= 6 (1)

FORM QUALITY

	FQx	FQf	MQual	SQx
+	= 0	0	0	0
o	= 14	8	2	0
u	= 15	8	0	0
–	= 7	7	0	0
none	= 0	–	0	0

DETERMINANTS

BLENDS	SINGLE	
CF.FM	M	= 2
	FM	= 1
	m	= 4
	FC	= 1
	CF	= 4
	C	= 0
	Cn	= 0
	FC'	= 0
	C'F	= 0
	C'	= 0
	FT	= 0
	TF	= 0
	T	= 0
	FV	= 0
	VF	= 0
	V	= 0
	FY	= 0
	YF	= 0
	Y	= 0
	Fr	= 0
	rF	= 0
	FD	= 0
	F	= 23
	(2)	= 17

CONTENTS	
H	= 1,0
(H)	= 1,0
Hd	= 10,0
(Hd)	= 1,0
Hx	= 0,0
A	= 11,0
(A)	= 3,0
Ad	= 3,0
(Ad)	= 0,0
An	= 0,0
Art	= 0,0
Ay	= 0,0
Bl	= 0,1
Bt	= 0,0
Cg	= 0,1
Cl	= 0,0
Ex	= 0,0
Fd	= 0,0
Fi	= 0,0
Ge	= 0,0
Hh	= 0,0
Ls	= 1,0
Na	= 2,0
Sc	= 3,2
Sx	= 0,10
Xy	= 0,0
Id	= 0,0

S-CONSTELLATION

NO..FV + VF + V + FD > 2
NO..Col-Shd Bl>0
YES..Ego<.31,>.44
NO..MOR>3
NO..Zd > ± 3.5
NO..es>EA
YES..CF+C>FC
YES..X+%<.70
NO..S>3
NO..P<3 or >8
YES..Pure H <2
NO..R<17
4.....TOTAL

SPECIAL SCORINGS

	Lv1	Lv2
DV	= 1x1	0x2
INC	= 1x2	1x4
DR	= 0x3	0x6
FAB	= 1x4	1x7
ALOG	= 0x5	
CON	= 0x7	
SUM6	= 5	
WSUM6	= 18	

AB	=1	CP	= 0
AG	=0	MOR	= 2
CFB	=2	PER	= 0
COP	=0	PSV	= 0

RATIOS, PERCENTAGES, AND DERIVATIONS

R = 36	L = 1.77		
EB = 2:5.5	EA = 7.5	EBPer = 2.8	
eb = 6:0	es = 6	D = 0	
	Adj es = 3	Adj D = +1	
FM = 2	C' = 0	T = 0	
m = 4	V = 0	Y = 0	

FC:CF+C	=1:5	COP = 0	AG = 0
Pure C	=0	Food	= 0
SumC':WSumC	=0:5.5	Isolate/R	= 0.14
Afr	=1.00	H:(H)Hd(Hd)	= 1:12
S	=0	(HHd):(AAd)	= 2:3
Blends:R	=1:36	H+A:Hd + Ad	= 16:14
CP	=0		

				P = 5	Zf	=9	3r+(2)/R	= 0.47
a:p	= 3:5	Sum6	= 5	X+% = 0.39	Zd	=+1.0	Fr+rF	= 0
Ma:Mp	= 0:2	Lv2	= 2	F+% = 0.35	W:D:Dd	=4:27:5	FD	= 0
2AB+Art+Ay	= 2	WSum6	= 18	X–% = 0.19	W:M	= 4:2	An + Xy	= 0
M–	= 0	Mnone	= 0	S–% = 0.00	DQ+	=4	MOR	= 2
				Xu% = 0.42	DQv	=6		

SCZI = 2 DEPI = 3 CDI = 2 S-CON = 4 HVI = No OBS = No

Card I

   1. Testicles (Dd22)

   2. Person here with penis (D2)

Card II

   1. Vagina, blood coming out (D3)

   2. Penis (D4)

Card III

   1. Breasts (Dd27)

   2. Penis on each side (Dd26)

Card IV: Nothing

Card V: Nothing

Card VI

   1. Penis (D6)

   2. Gonads (Dd32)

Card VII: Nothing

Card VIII: Nothing

Card IX

   1. Penis (D5)

Card X

   1. Animals carrying a penis there (D11)

IV

SPECIAL APPLICATIONS

24

Vitamin C or Pure C: The Rorschach of Linus Pauling

Carl B. Gacono
U.S. Department of Justice

Clifford M. DeCato
Virginia Brabender
Widener University

Ted G. Goertzel
Rutgers University

Linus Pauling was one of the most distinguished scientists of the 20th century. He was a pioneer in applying quantum theory to the study of complex molecules and founded the science of molecular biology. A charismatic speaker and effective political activist, he campaigned successfully against atmospheric nuclear testing and resisted the pressures of McCarthyism during the 1950s. He was the only person to win two unshared Nobel Prizes (Goertzel & Goertzel, 1995).

He became committed, at the age of 65, to orthomolecular medicine, particularly the advocacy of megadoses of Vitamin C as a treatment or preventative for cancer, the common cold, and many other diseases. Admirers were puzzled by his commitment to a cause that went beyond his field of expertise and put him in conflict with most specialists working in the area.

Pauling was an extremely intelligent, creative, and intuitive thinker, for whom original ideas came spontaneously. He contrasted himself with very capable scientists who got new ideas by "fiddling with the equations." "I've never made a contribution that I didn't get just by having a new idea. Then I would fiddle with the equations to help support the new idea" (Kauffman & Kauffman, 1994, p. 523).

He utilized two different strategies for channeling ideas. One involved comparing a carefully tested hypothesis against empirical data. Within the scientific method, he was receptive to modifying or abandoning ideas that were

421

not supported by data. His contributions to chemistry utilized this approach. He was at his best when he was solving scientific puzzles with little emotional involvement. In a second approach he became emotionally committed to ideas, selectively seeking out supportive evidence and minimizing or discounting contradictory evidence (Goertzel & Goertzel, 1995).

Comfortable with intellectual pursuit, Pauling found emotional life troublesome, and tended to avoid situations that involved emotionally charged interactions. Once he achieved success with his theory of the chemical bond, however, he allowed himself involvement in issues that were affectively charged. Pauling deemphasized personal or family life. He was more at ease in the public arena, which provided avenues for his skill as a speaker and writer and offered prestige as a scientist.

Pauling participated in two psychological studies concerning scientists' personalities (Eiduson, 1962; Roe, 1953). Both studies used the Rorschach as a method for comparing subjects. The researchers, unfortunately, were not experienced Rorschachers. Roe (1953), for example, had no formal training other than learning how to administer the test in preparation for her study. This contributed to the poor quality of the Pauling protocol, particularly with regard to the inquiry (see Appendix A).[1] Despite these limitations the Pauling protocol offers unique insights into the personality of this scientific genius. This chapter contains the Rorschach from the Roe (1953) study.

LINUS PAULING'S RORSCHACH

Consistent with the intent of this book we, along with others (Acklin, 1992, 1993, 1994; Erdberg, 1993; Gacono, 1992; Gacono & Meloy, 1992, 1994; Meloy & Gacono, 1992, 1993, 1994; Murray, 1992, 1993, 1994; Peterson, 1992, 1993, 1994; Weiner, 1995a), espouse an integrated method for interpreting the Rorschach. From the interpersonal testing situation (Lerner, 1991; Schachtel, 1966) through structural scoring (Exner, 1991), scoring of primary process, object relations (Kwawer, 1980; Urist, 1977), and defensive operations (Cooper, Perry, & Arnow, 1988; Lerner & Lerner, 1980; Schafer, 1954), no one system quantifies every nuance of an individual protocol. Each system adds another piece to understanding the individual assessed.

We analyzed the Pauling protocol with several systems: Perceptanalytic method (DeCato, 1993a, 1993b; Piotrowski, 1957, 1982), Comprehensive System (Exner, 1991), expanded aggression scoring (Gacono & Meloy, 1994;

---

[1]Reduced means for Developmental Quality-vague (*DQv*), Form Quality-unusual (*FQu*), sum of color responses (*SumC*), sum of shading responses (*Sum Shading*), weighted thought disorder (*WSum6*), and an increased percentage of pure form responses (*F*) have been found in protocols scored without inquiry (Ritzler & Nalesnik, 1990). Although we do not believe the inadequate inquiry from the Pauling protocol significantly affected scoring or interpretation, we note this limitation.

Meloy & Gacono, 1992), object relations (Kwawer, 1980), and defensive operations (Cooper, Perry, & Arnow, 1988; Lerner & Lerner, 1980).

Appendix A presents Linus Pauling's Rorschach protocol; Appendix B shows the structural summary; Appendix C shows the sequence of scores (both generated by Rorschach Scoring Program, Version 3; Exner & Tuttle, 1994); and Appendix D presents select defensive operations (Cooper et al., 1988).

PERCEPTANALYTIC INTERPRETATION[2]

This Rorschach gives the impression of an adult man who is intellectually very bright and has acquired a wide array of information through reading, education, or experience. He attempts to make his adaptation to the world through the use of intelligence in a rapid-response fashion ($IRT = 3.9$"; $T/R = 27$"). That is, he is often quick to respond without taking the time to review the situation in depth.

He is quite capable of using visual imagery and fantasy; indeed he would be expected to engage in abstraction and fantasy to a greater degree than average ($^\wedge R$, range of scores and contents, quality of abstractions). He has formed a sense of identity, a core sense of who he is and how to cope with important human relationships, which is less secure than that of the average adult (M content). This sense of self is not always reality-based and tends to be generated from an excessive reliance on fantasy ($M = 9$, $Ma = 1$, $M- = 2$, $(h) = 7$, $h = 1$). Interpersonal relations may be difficult to understand and negotiate as they are approached with preconceptions rather than based on the nuances of the specific interpersonal interaction ($Ma = 1$, $M = 2$, $(h) = 7$, $h = 1$). Because dialogue with others and subsequently the ability to accurately assess are important for maintaining ongoing close relationships, this trend could lead to interpersonal difficulties. At times his judgment can become idiosyncratic, although much of the time he manages to form views that might be similar to others ($M- = 2$, $FC- = 2$, $FC+ = 5$, $P = 7$, $P = 3$). Overall, his approach is very passive, suggesting that he wishes to avoid responsibility for important decisions and allow much of life's direction to be decided by others or by his own inactions and indecision. There is a strong trend suggesting a passive-dependent style. On a superficial level he exhibits traits that make casual relationships less problematic (*Populars*, the ability to achieve common views).

This individual is quite sensitive to emotional cues from others and at times may appear to be overexcitable ($SumC = 9.5$, $CF = 6$, $FC = 7$, $Sumc:SumC = 4:9.5$). He has difficulty managing an overabundance of emotions. His

[2]Dr. DeCato provided the Pauling Rorschach protocol for analysis in this chapter. The perceptanalytic interpretation originated from his blind analysis and stemmed from principles articulated in the *Perceptanalytic Method* (DeCato, 1993a, 1993b, 1994; DeCato, Cicocca, DelConte, & Piotrowski, 1984/1992; DeCato & Piotrowski, 1977; Piotrowski, 1957, 1982). Dr. DeCato knew only that the subject was a 48-year-old "famous man."

response style alternates between thinking before reacting and acting impulsively without first considering the needs, rights, and/or feelings of others ($CF = 6, FC = 7, M{:}SumC = 9.5$). There is a strong trend in emotional organization toward being "oversocialized," that is, feeling guarded around emotional expression ($FC+ = 5, FC- = 2$). Most of the time he can realistically assess the emotional cues from others; however, there are times when the intentions of others are misjudged. At times he participates in less forethought, which may make him appear egocentric, insensitive, or emotionally impulsive ($CF = 6, IRT = 3.9$"). High elevations of fantasy use coupled with emotional sensitivity suggest that others may view him as somewhat unpredictable, not having a consistent mode for interacting, or perhaps being moody (at times even appearing to have a manic component with pressured and driven ideas and actions). Depression, mood swings, anxiety, and self-doubt are present in greater degrees than for most people ($Sumc = 4.0, ColShad = 2, MOR = 4, Blood = 2$).

Chronic anger and hostility, perhaps expressed through oppositionalism or stubbornness, are suggested ($S = 6$). Individuals with this trait can sometimes accomplish outstanding achievements by refusing to give in and by insisting on following their principles or convictions no matter what the cost to themselves or others.

There is evidence of frequent and intermittent disruptions in reality testing that result in misjudgments ($F+\% = 73, ExtF+\% = 70, RPT = 4, M- = 2$). Unrealistic and distorted thinking occur in many contexts, such as when emotionally aroused ($CF = 6, FC- = 2$) or when evaluating interpersonal nuances and environmental stimuli ($M- = 2, F- = 8$). Disrupted thinking occurs suddenly, unpredictably, and frequently. Such regressions are usually followed by rapid recovery (sequence analysis).

The protocol suggests a lifelong tendency toward being somewhat "different" or perhaps odd or eccentric. In a properly structured and supportive environment that would reward thinking aberrations, these patterns could result in regression in service of the ego with potentially creative outcomes (sequence analysis; rapid recovery after regressions). A passive-dependent style (M) combined with high intelligence and the ability to superficially adapt ($P = 7, F+\% = 73$) would permit him to function in some work environments without revealing his underlying thinking difficulties. In other words, it is quite possible that environments that drew on strengths and did not overly stress his cognitive weaknesses would permit him to function in an apparently normal fashion. At the time of testing he was experiencing considerably heightened environmental stress similar to individuals who feel very helpless and intensely threatened ($Sumc = 4, Sumc' = 0.5, m = 6$, content analysis).

Perceptanalysis Summary

This man presents some intriguing and challenging material for Rorschach blind analysis. A personality picture emerges of an intelligent man whose social adjustment relies on a passive-dependent style with emphasis on conventionality in everyday relationships. Behind this adaptive mode of conventionality lies a very complex man who is fantasy-oriented and easily emotionally aroused. He struggles constantly with tendencies toward unrealistic perceptions and judgments that are kept under control in more superficial situations, but nevertheless are revealed in odd ideas and associations, leaps and breaks in logic, distortions in self and other perceptions, and emotional misjudgments. Under structured conditions (conventional interpersonal interactions) that accentuate the use of his intelligence he would be perceived as bright but perhaps, at times, a bit eccentric or odd. Under ideal circumstances his peculiar ideation could result in creativity.

STRUCTURAL INTERPRETATION: COMPREHENSIVE SYSTEM

Pauling's Rorschach yielded 65 responses, a valid but inflated protocol (see Appendix B). The protocol's expansiveness must be considered during the interpretive process as response frequency accounts for much of Rorschach variance and significantly impacts ratios, constellations, and subsequent inferences (Meyer, 1992, 1993).

When R is elevated or restricted an explanation is always warranted (Gacono & Meloy, 1992, 1994). In this case expansiveness stems from emotional and cognitive processes. Pauling is not avoidant of affective stimuli ($Afr = .67$). He experiences press ($FM = 7$) from physiological (nonvolitional) need states ($es = 24$) that dominate his internal world. Some need states are situationally induced ($D = -2, AdjD = 0$), whereas others are likely chronic.[3] He is both pushed and pulled to produce responses during the Rorschach process.

Overincorporation (tendency toward, $Zd = +3.5$) and heightened attention to detail ($Dd = 14$) may contribute to the obsessive elevation of R.[4] Impulse and affect, however, disrupt cognitive processes ($WSum6 = 90$).

Pauling is extratensive ($EBPer = 1.6; EB = 7:11.5$); that is, he relies on environmental interaction for problem solving. An extratensive style is not generally problematic; however, when incoming information is filtered through unconventional ($Xu\% = 43$), distorted ($X+\% = 31, F+\% = 35, X-\%$ $= 25; M- = 2$), and idiosyncratic ($PER = 6$) lenses, interpersonal cues are frequently misinterpreted. This process would be exacerbated by preconceived ideas of interpersonal interactions based more on wish and fantasy than

---

[3]Interpersonal interactions both stimulate affect and create additional affect. For Pauling affect is predominantly dysphoric ($V = 5, Y = 2, S - Con = 8$) or unpleasant ($TF = 1, m = 8$).

[4]Although Dd is a structural variable highly influenced by R ($>R$, $>Dd$), 78% of Pauling's Dd responses occur in highly idiosyncratic areas ($Dd99$). Pauling did not merely exhaust W and D areas but demonstrated a predilection for carving out his own perceptual sanctuary.

reality ($Mp > Ma$; (H) = 5, H = 1) and it is unlikely that Pauling was receptive to modifying his ideas (S = 7).

Pauling's passive ($Mp > Ma$, 5:2) dependent (TF = 1, Fd = 1) reliance on others (EB = 7:11.5) results in feelings of frustration (S = 7) and a sense of helplessness (m = 8). Although he hungers for (TF = 1),[5] depends on (Fd = ?), and expects cooperative human interactions (COP = 3), they are not satisfying (all COPs are spoiled). Interpersonally he misinterprets, yet, at the same time, he feels misunderstood (m = 8). This may be one source of his brooding (V = 5) as stubbornness (S = 7) counters any ability to change.

Pauling has difficulty modulating emotions ($FC:CF + C$ = 4:8) and at times can be explosive ($PureC$ = 3). High levels of hostility and frustration (S = 7) might contribute to angry outbursts. Although the depression index is not positive ($DEPI$ = 4), a major mood disorder cannot be ruled out as Pauling experiences an abundance of dysphoric emotions and needs (C' = 1, m = 8, V = 5, Y = 2, Sx = 3, TF = 1, Fd = 1, $S - Con$ = 8).

Pauling does not compare himself favorably to others ($EgoC$ = 0.29; V = 5). He may view himself as damaged (MOR = 3), perhaps the target of other's aggression or envy ($AgPast$ = 2). Uncertainty about self contributes to and is exacerbated by interpersonal difficulties. As a result he is likely to be defensive (PER = 6) and sensitive to criticism, perhaps at times withdrawing from the source of his discomfort, interpersonal interactions. Further elucidation of the defensive and object relations implications await sequence and content analysis.

INTERPRETATION OF SCORING SEQUENCE

Sequence analysis (Schafer, 1954) provides a hypothetical model for understanding (a) the nature of impulse (emotion) and defense (coping strategies; primitive or mature), (b) the prevalence of each, (c) intrapsychic and interpersonal stimuli that are likely to provoke impulse and activate defense, and (d) the stability of defensive operations. A predominance of impulse over defense is suggested by a mere 31% of all form quality achieving o or + (see Appendix B). The tenuous nature of Pauling's defenses is evidenced by poor recovery throughout the protocol (80% of the cards evidence – or u form quality on their final response). Even though Cards V and VII end with adequate form (20%), both produce final responses spoiled by mild to severe cognitive slippage (Response 38 = $ALOG$).

Card I is paradigmatic of Pauling's response to ambiguous, emotionally provoking, perhaps interpersonal stimuli. Shock (a mild special score) gives way to quick recovery as perceptual accuracy is maintained until Response 3.

---

[5]Use of the modified scoring method for partial or absent inquiry (Ritzler & Nalesnick, 1990) would allow for scoring 1 or more additional texture responses along with this unmodulated T.

The stimulus field is simplified in an attempt to cope (*Dd*, Response 3), and despite the presence of higher level defenses (intellectualization, denial), vague (*v*) developmental quality and *u* form suggest failed defenses. Ambiguity (loss of control) stimulates hostility (*S*), while coping is only partially successful (*u* form and a *DR*). Narrowing of the stimulus field (*Dd*), intellectual distancing, and devaluation (*Sc*; Response 4) follow with recovery through Response 6 (aided by a popular; conventionality). Card I ends with an unsuccessful *Dd* (*u* form, a *DV*; Response 7). The three *Dd*s on Card I suggest a coping style through which narrowing the stimulus field is used in an attempt to manage affect and need.

Card II shows the powerful effect of strong, easily provoked, hard to constrain emotion (C.C'F) on thinking (*Wv+*, *u*, *ALOG*). Simplifying the stimulus field (*D*, *Dd*), intellectual distancing (*Art*, *Sc*), and conventionality (*P*) are unsuccessfully employed to manage impulse (*Bl*, *Sx*, *FM*, *Mp*). Card II ends with poor recovery, and provides cues to idiosyncratic thinking (*Mpu*, *FAB*) and the manner in which an unusual fantasy life exists, even in the presence of conventionality (*P*, Response 12).

Card III follows a similar pattern. Initially intellectualization, isolation, and a popular (Response 13) aid in maintaining perceptual accuracy. However, interpersonal issues are stimulated (*Mpo*, *H*, *Mp–*, (*H*)), physiological needs press for expression (*FMp–*), and ultimately a sense of frustration (*S*; Responses 14 and 15), helplessness (*mp–*), and circumstantial thinking (*DR2*; Response 16) result (as noted in Appendix B). Projection is used with little success on Response 14.

Painful introspection (*VF*) and a sense of being victimized are stimulated by Card IV. Subsequent responses continue to evidence a similar dysphoric emotional experience (Response 21; *FMp.mp.VFo*). Already familiar coping strategies reappear. Intellectual pursuits or intellectual distancing (*Sc* = 3, Responses 18, 19, and 23) are unsuccessfully employed to compensate for painful emotional and interpersonal issues. Frustration and passivity lead to a sense of helplessness (*m* = 3) and feelings of victimization (*AgPast*, Response 22). Cards V and VI display similar interactions.

The protocol's only texture response (*T*) is produced on Response 37. Form is secondary (*TF*) and minus (–) form quality. Affectional relatedness (*TF–*) is first avoided (*Sc*; Response 36), then experienced (Response 37), and finally distanced from (*Ls*, Response 38). This poorly modulated *T* response is combined with aggressive content suggesting ambivalence in relation to the soft, libidinal aspects of intimacy. Minus (–) form and distorted thinking (*ALOG*, Response 38) suggest the disruptive effects of emotional desires. Card VIII further highlights difficulties with affect modulation (C, CF–, CF.YF). The press of needs (*FMpo*) disrupt thinking (*INC2,FAB*).

Card IX is impulse laden (*Hx*, *An*, *Bl*, *Fi*). The use of isolation (Response 45), aided by a popular, helps to briefly control affect. It quickly gives way to

---

[6]In fact 70% of the cards evidence one or more *Dd* responses.

impulse as subsequent responses vividly display their impact on perceptual accuracy (only 25% of the responses evidence adequate form). Poor affect modulation is combined with intense dysphoria (2 ColShading blends; $S = 2$). An Fd response (Response 49), coupled with a complex and unmodulated V ($FC.VFu$; Response 52), suggests frustrated needs ($S = 2$) that result in brooding ($V = 2$) and thoughts of helplessness ($m = 2$). Rigid controls ($Dd = 3, An = 1$) are intertwined with painful affect.

Card X contains all of the COPs in the record (as noted in Appendix B). Generally viewed in a positive manner, all three are, unfortunately, spoiled either by their imaginary quality ((H)), (Responses 55 and 56); (A), (Response 58), poor form (Responses 55 and 56), or distorted thinking (Mpu, FAB, $INC2$, Response 56). Devaluation (54, 55, 56, 60, 64) and isolation (61, 63) predominate over higher level defenses, perhaps as a final effort to ward off painful affect. An expectation of interpersonal cooperativeness remains only a fantasy based, inchoate wish ($FMp-$, Response 65).

CONTENT ANALYSIS

Pauling's morbid, movement, and highly elaborated responses are particularly revealing concerning the characteristics of his self- and object-representations.

Self-Perception

Pauling produces three MOR responses, the first of which (Response 22; scored $AgPast$) conveys a sense of exposure and vulnerability to others' aggressive acts: "A carcass of an animal spread open . . . I must have seen a butcher cleave one open" (see Appendix A). A second MOR response (44), "the central structure of a landscape in which there has been a lot of erosion by rain," reflects concern about some deterioration in capacities. The pairing of a morbid response with m (Response 48): "water is dripping, perhaps blood dripping down. . . . The color . . . ," suggests a current stressor stimulating helpless, pessimistic thinking. The progression from benign to bloody suggests failed defense and perhaps developmental fears of himself as he will be in the future.[7]

Among his M responses, a perception of "two rabbits sitting down with forepaws up in the air in an attitude of supplication" (Response 12; see Appendix A) provides a hint of the wish to idealize or be idealized. The fact that this behavior is engaged in by animals may suggest some mockery or criticalness of the wish. Similar ambivalence is noted in Response 29 where the idealized figure "Icarus" is combined with devalued content, "legs . . . that

---

[7]Pauling's daughter, Mrs. Pauling-Kamb, indicated that he suffered from Bright's disease, at one period coming close to death. The illness resulted in severe dietary restrictions and its impact on latent Rorschach content has not been determined.

look funny."[8] The oral-receptive aspect of such content (Responses 12 and 14) also corroborates the passive trend in his personality (e.g., $Ma:Mp$ ratio = 2:5; see Appendix B). However, other responses point to exhibitionistic and grandiose trends (Response 13: "The Joo's dancers facing each other . . . the dance of the diplomats around a table")[9] as well as hypomanic trends (Response 35: "animal faces laughing hilariously").

Although passivity pervades most of his movement responses ($a:p$ = 2:20), animal responses lie at the boundary of visible activity and inertness (e.g., "wings spread" on Response 6, "cat vanishing" on Response 15 and "cow lying down" on Response 59). If animal movement responses are interpreted as representing less conscious elements of personality than human movement responses, this pattern suggests passive trends that are more ego-dystonic and less fully in conscious awareness.

An element of grandiosity is seen in Response 21: "I also have a sort of gorilla-like impression as though a gorilla was standing there illuminated by a bright light." Choosing a gorilla as the object of the illumination may suggest some criticalness or reflectiveness in relation to this personality feature.

The inanimate movement responses (m) for the most part have the limp quality that Pauling ascribes to the "Dali watches" (Response 18). Possibly he sees in himself a lack of vitality. Response 20, "A penis hanging at the wrong end of a pelt," suggests that this impotent pattern may extend to the sexual arena as inanimate movement is combined with sexual content (Sx). Sexual responses are infrequently produced (4% of nonpatients; Exner, 1991); Pauling's delivery of three indicates a sexual preoccupation. The other two sexual responses are of female sexual organs and do not have the lifeless quality ascribed to the male organ.

Taken together, the movement responses suggest a person who, on the one hand, has a strong tendency toward passivity and sees himself as lacking vitality and wholeness, and on the other, is active, self-exalting, and exhibitionistic. A more speculative hypothesis is that each trend may serve at times as a defense against the other or as traits exhibited at different times and circumstances.

Equivocation and obsessive self-doubt are suggested by Pauling's response elaborations. They often serve to negate or diminish the percept that was initially presented (devaluation). For example, in Response 4, after saying that "the two little central humps at the top suggest a sine curve" he adds, "it's a poor sine curve because the top part of the arc is too much." Throughout the

---

[8]The choice of Icarus is symbolically interesting. As the myth goes, Icarus and his father constructed wings in an attempt to escape from captivity (on an island). Feathers were fastened to a frame with wax. During the escape Icarus became fascinated with the beauty of the sun, subsequently flying too close. Heat from the sun melted the wax, his wings disintegrated, and he fell to his death. The price of focusing on a dream (Mpu) at the expense of reality (Mao) ultimately led to his death.

[9]It should be noted that these exhibitionistic trends surface after the initial presentation of a more formal, stilted, passive orientation, "waiters . . . formal dress."

protocol, he searches for symmetry that he rarely finds, possibly reflecting a compulsive yet disappointing search for order in his own psychological life. Or perhaps he was never fully satisfied by his accomplishments (devaluation), but continued to strive for greater achievements (motivated by idealization, expressed throughout his protocol).

Interpersonal Perception

M responses with pairs and Human responses particularly reveal a subject's self-perceptions of his object world. Pauling's answers are frequently characterized by a formal, stilted, nonspontaneous mode of interaction. Examples of these (see Appendix A) are Responses 12, "rabbits . . . in an attitude of supplication" and 13, the formally-attired "Joo dancers." When figures interact in a less stylized fashion, it is with complete abandon (Response 35: "animal faces . . . laughing hilariously"). Object relations, as reflected in his paired Human Movement perceptions, alternate between extreme constraint or dyscontrol.

Only one of Pauling's human percepts contains Pure H. This paucity may suggest interpersonal understanding that is based more on fantasy than actual experience. Several percepts involve devalued content ("gnomes; paunches with pendulous abdomens"). These characters are distinguished by their mischief. Their inclusion may suggest a hidden worry about others' aggression and the use of devaluation to ward off the threat. They also suggest an effort to respond to worry with humor and playfulness (reaction formation).

Kwawer's (1980) primitive interpersonal modes of relating provide additional insights into Pauling's object relational world (see Appendix A). Although there were several of these scores, they account for a relatively small percentage (6%) of his total number of responses. Two Boundary Disturbance responses (22 and 48) and one Symbiotic Merging response (41) suggest some tension in relation to the issue of separation and fusion, an expected finding given the conflict between dependency and separateness noted earlier. The frequency and quality of Pauling's scores, however, are not within the range of the severe character pathologies such as Antisocial Personality Disorder (Gacono & Meloy, 1994).

Defensive Operations

An evaluation of Pauling's defensive operations, based on the Cooper et al. (1988) system, reveals that neurotic defenses (53%; see Appendix D) predominate over borderline (47%) or psychotic (0%) defenses. Intellectualization (Responses 3, 4, 13, 16, 23, 29, 41, 43) is the most commonly occurring defense. The importance of intellectualization in Pauling's defensive repertoire is also supported by his score of 10 on the Intellectualization Index, based on weighted Abstract, Anthropology, and Art contents. According to Exner

(1991), this elevation is particularly common in persons with an extratensive coping style (such as Pauling's) who immerse themselves in their feelings but then become uncomfortable with them. This formulation is congruent with the manner in which Pauling introduces intellectualization into his responses. Typically, his *Art* and *Ay* scores occur relatively late in the response, almost as an afterthought, suggesting an attempt to bind whatever disturbing affects were stimulated by the primary content of the response. The quality of the intellectualization responses provides added insight. Four out of eight have minus form quality, one occurs with a *FAB* and *INC2*, whereas two have *ALOGs*, a most serious form of cognitive slippage (Meloy & Singer, 1991). Additionally, the presence of this defense (Response 29; noted in Appendix D), concurrent with lower level defenses (all borderline), suggest that for Pauling intellectualization is not a wholly functional defense.

The ineffectiveness of intellectualization appearing on early responses leads to a prevalence of isolation on later ones (Responses 13, 45, 61, 63). Instances of higher level denial (Responses 3, 33), reaction formation (Response 12) and repression (Response 22) were also observed.

Among the borderline defenses, devaluation plays the most significant role, both in the order of its emergence and its frequency (see Appendix D; responses 4, 20, 28, 29, 54, 55, 56, and 60). As discussed, devaluation is likely a defensive activity that Pauling extended not only to his evaluation of others, but also to himself and his accomplishments, a hypothesis consistent with his low Egocentricity Index (as noted in Appendix B). Devaluation mediated through higher level defenses such as intellectualization could exhibit (sublimation) in socially acceptable behavior (i.e., critical review) rather than what would be expected in severe character pathology (behavioral aggression). Less prominent is his use of primitive idealization (Responses 21 and 29). The adaptive attributes of this defense have been previously discussed (Lerner, 1991) and linked to the capacity for creating and pursuing goals (Gacono & Meloy, 1992). The fact that one of these occurred in the context of a Vista response suggests that the effort to idealize either the self or the other is aimed at warding off feelings of shame or guilt. The failure of such a defensive effort is seen in the second idealization response (29) where the grandness of Icarus is diminished (devalued) by legs that "look funny." Both of the splitting responses (Responses 21, 29) occur in the presence of this devaluation–idealization cycle. A single instance (Response 14) of projection occurred, revealing Pauling's capacity to externalize blame when pressed, a hypothesis consistent with his 7 *PER* responses.

CONCLUSION

Personality analysis based on the Rorschach method often leaves the untrained student confused, especially concerning the issue of manifest, observable behavior versus latent behavior, underlying traits, and organizing personality structure. For example, the person who smiles while emotionally angry may have a personality structure that inhibits overt actions involving the expression of angry feelings. Overtly, they appear as never angry, "laid-back," meek, even mild-mannered. Perhaps consciously unaware of these feelings, they are nevertheless chronically angry, even rageful. Their Rorschach imagery parallels interpersonal patterns and allows for inferences concerning unexpressed underlying anger. Similarly, a person may have the capacity to regress into momentary fantasy that is highly illogical and unrealistic and still be able to monitor this reaction, not allowing direct influence on conscious decisions and behavior. To others they appear rational, reasonable, and in control, despite their underlying tendency to occasionally engage in highly illogical, unrealistic thinking that subtly colors relationships and contributes to the formation of ideas and decisions in a manner not directly observable.

Pauling exhibited many of these complex dilemmas in his Rorschach. He could engage in illogical and unrealistic thinking at times, quickly recover, and then reflect and act on those ideas that were most conforming to reality or scientific investigation. Pauling "generated many ideas and threw away the bad ones." He was aware of his ability to permit regression while maintaining control over the progression of his scientific work. Many similar apparent discrepancies between what his Rorschach suggests (personality) and how he appeared to others can be understood by comparing manifest behavior to underlying personality structure and functioning.

Pauling's Rorschach suggests a creative and intelligent individual internally driven to achieve, yet due to exceedingly high standards (self-depreciation) and less than anticipated acceptance in the more controversial areas of his research, was never fully satisfied with his accomplishments. A sensitive man, Pauling was more comfortable with intellectual pursuit and less so with emotions and interpersonal relations. Pure science offered a vehicle for avoiding and distancing from emotional experience and the slings and arrows of interpersonal interaction. Pauling was at his best during the early and middle phases of his career, first when he was applying quantum mechanics to chemistry, ushering in the development of modern chemistry, and later when he made his contributions to molecular biology (Goertzel & Goertzel, 1995).

The Rorschach suggests interpersonal difficulties. Although he relied on others, Pauling's preconceptions and tendency to misinterpret interpersonal cues would inhibit emotionally satisfying relationships. Stubbornness, which within scientific pursuit (tenacity) served him well, would interfere with assessing emotionally laden interpersonal situations. The Rorschach suggests resultant emotional dissatisfaction, frustration, and a tendency to ruminate. In fact, Pauling was described as uncomfortable around people, sometimes sitting by himself at social functions and saying very little to others (Goertzel & Goertzel, 1995). With aging the Rorschach predicts a tendency toward emotional isolation and guardedness.

Although Pauling's Rorschach results are largely confluent with historical data, several aspects provide seeming contradictions that allow for fine-tuning hypotheses. For example, how might the intensely passive trend in Pauling's personality be reconciled with his pioneer status as a scientist, his willingness to "go out on a limb" without, at times, support from the scientific community? Although Pauling's personality may have had a passive dimension, his relationship to passivity was egodystonic (see Content Analysis). By engaging in thinking that was contrary to common scientific belief (*Mpu*), Pauling concealed his passivity while giving direct expression to another prominent personality trend, his oppositionalism. One might also wonder whether his insistence that the ingestion of a food substance, Vitamin C, might be a cure for a range of physical problems (an insistence that many perceived to be at odds with the existing data) may have been intellectualized expression of a dependency trend. Perhaps, in areas less critical to his career identity, Pauling allowed the passive aspect of his personality more direct expression. Indeed, he was reported to have relied heavily on his wife for organizing everyday matters related to household and family (Goertzel & Goertzel, 1995).

In reviewing the major scoring systems, we are struck by the high levels of interpretive convergence between the Piotrowski and Comprehensive Systems. As Weiner (1995b) noted:

> There is no good reason to anticipate that differences in theoretical orientation will lead *competent* Rorschach examiners to draw widely different conclusions. . . . To the contrary, the Rorschach Inkblot Method has considerable power to transcend theoretical differences and allow skilled hands to paint similar pictures of subjects' personality characteristics. (p. 2)

Scoring with the Comprehensive or Piotrowski systems provides a foundation for interpretation. The examiner uses scoring to identify and organize "building blocks" of personality (P. Erdberg, personal communication, March 1995). Analysis of sequence, defense, content, and object relations aid in fine tuning hypotheses and understanding relationships between the personality's component parts.

Rorschach mastery, however, places far greater demands on the novice than proficiency with scoring. Rorschach administration, scoring, and interpretation are intimately linked in a manner unique to the test. Understanding the meaning of individual variables, such as determinants, guides inquiry, whereas a full inquiry results in valid scoring. Knowledge of Rorschach literature and personality functioning (theoretical as well as clinical) allows specific variables and constellations to be linked to behavioral patterns—all necessary to the interpretive process. In the hands of a skilled clinician, the Rorschach method provides a valuable tool for understanding psychopathology, and in the case of Linus Pauling, creative genius. The Rorschach should never be dismissed prematurely by those not proficient in its use.

REFERENCES

Acklin, M. W. (1992). Psychodiagnosis of personality structure: Psychotic personality organization. *Journal of Personality Assessment, 58*, 454–463.

Acklin, M. W. (1993). Psychodiagnosis of personality structure II: Borderline personality organization. *Journal of Personality Assessment, 61*, 329–341.

Acklin, M. W. (1994). Psychodiagnosis of personality structure III: Neurotic personality organization. *Journal of Personality Assessment, 63*, 1–9.

Cooper, S., Perry J., Arnow, D. (1988). An empirical approach to the study of defense mechanisms: I. Reliability and preliminary validity of the Rorschach defense scale. *Journal of Personality Assessment, 52*, 187–203.

DeCato, C. M. (1993a). On the Rorschach M response and monotheism. *Journal of Personality Assessment, 60*, 362–378.

DeCato, C. M. (1993b). Piotrowski's enduring contributions to the Rorschach: A review of Perceptanalysis. *Journal of Personality Assessment, 61*, 584–595.

DeCato, C. M. (1994). Toward a training model for Rorschach scoring revisited: A follow-up study on a training system for interscorer agreement. *Perceptual and Motor Skills, 78*, 3–10.

DeCato, C. M., Cicocca, J. V., DelConte, G., & Piotrowski, Z. A. (1992). *Rorschach scoring: A workbook for the perceptanalytic system* (Rev. ed.). Chester, PA: Widener University Graphic Arts. (Original work published 1984)

De Cato, C. M., & Piotrowski, Z. A. (1977). *A concise manual for Rorschach interpretation.* Cherry Hill, NJ: Post Graduate International.

Eiduson, B. (1962). *Scientists: Their psychological world.* New York: Basic Books.

Erdberg, P. (1993). The U.S. Rorschach scene: Integration and elaboration. *Rorschachiana, 18*, 139–151.

Exner, J. (1991). *The Rorschach: A comprehensive system: Vol. 2. Interpretations* (2nd ed.). New York: Wiley.

Exner, J. E., Jr., & Tuttle, K. (1994). *Rorschach scoring program, Version 3.* Odessa, FL: Psychological Assessment Resources.

Gacono, C. (1992). A Rorschach case study of sexual homicide. *British Journal of Projective Psychology, 37*(1), 1–21.

Gacono, C., & Meloy, J. R. (1992). The Rorschach and the *DSM–III–R* antisocial personality: A tribute to Robert Lindner. *Journal of Clinical Psychology, 48*, 393–405.

Gacono, C., & Meloy, J. R. (1994). *The Rorschach assessment of aggressive and psychopathic personalities.* Hillsdale, NJ: Lawrence Erlbaum Associates.

Goertzel, T., & Goertzel, B. (1995). *Linus Pauling: A life in science and politics.* New York: Basic Books.

Kauffman, G. B., & Kauffman, L. (1994, November). Linus Pauling: Reflections. *American Scientist, 82*, p. 523.

Kwawer, J. (1980). Primitive interpersonal modes, borderline phenomena and Rorschach content. In J. Kwawer, P. Lerner, H. Lerner, & A. Sugarman (Eds.), *Borderline phenomena and the Rorschach test* (pp. 89–109). New York: International Universities Press.

Lerner, P. (1991). *Psychoanalytic theory and the Rorschach.* Hillsdale, NJ: The Analytic Press.

Lerner, P., & Lerner, H. (1980). Rorschach assessment of primitive defenses in borderline personality structure. In J. Kwawer, P. Lerner, H. Lerner, & A. Sugarman, (Eds.), *Borderline phenomena and the Rorschach test* (pp. 257–274). New York: International Universities Press.

Meloy, R., & Gacono, C. (1992). A psychotic sexual psychopath: "I just had a violent thought..." *Journal of Personality Assessment, 58*, 480–493.

Meloy, R., & Gacono, C. (1993). A borderline psychopath: "I was basically maladjusted. . ." *Journal of Personality Assessment, 61*, 358–373.

Meloy, R., & Gacono, C. (1994). Assessing the psychopathic personality. In J. Butcher (Ed.), *Clinical personality assessment* (pp. 410–422). New York: Oxford University Press.

Meloy, R., & Gacono, C. (1994). A neurotic criminal: "I've learned my lesson. . . " *Journal of Personality Assessment, 63*, 10–26.

Meloy, R., & Singer, J. (1991). A psychoanalytic view of the Rorschach Comprehensive System "Special Scores." *Journal of Personality Assessment, 56*, 202–217.

Meyer, G. (1992). Response frequency problems in the Rorschach: Clinical and research implications with suggestions for the future. *Journal of Personality Assessment, 58*, 231–244.

Meyer, G. (1993). The impact of response frequency on the Rorschach constellation indices and on their validity with diagnostic and MMPI-2 criteria. *Journal of Personality Assessment, 60*, 153–180.

Murray, J. (1992). Toward a synthetic approach to the Rorschach: The case of a psychotic child. *Journal of Personality Assessment, 58*, 494–505.

Murray, J. (1993). The Rorschach search for the borderline Holy Grail: An examination of personality structure, personality style, and situation. *Journal of Personality Assessment, 61*, 342–357.

Murray, J. F. (1994). Children and adolescents: A case study. *Journal of Personality Assessment, 63*, 39–58.

Peterson, C. A. (1992). A psychotic gynemimetic: I just had a pregnant thought. *Journal of Personality Assessment, 58*, 464–479.

Peterson, C. A. (1993). A borderline personality: AKA, A cop with no COP. *Journal of Personality Assessment, 63*, 374–393.

Piotrowski, Z. (1957). *Perceptanalysis.* New York: Macmillan.

Piotrowski, Z. (1982). Unsuspected and pertinent microfacts in personology. *American Psychologist, 37*, 190–196.

Ritzler, B., & Nalesnick, D. (1990). The effect of inquiry on the Exner Cmprehensive System. *Journal of Personality Assessment, 55*, 647–656.

Roe, A. (1953). *The making of a scientist.* New York: Dodd, Mead.

Schachtel, E. (1966). *Experiential foundations of Rorschach's test.* New York: Basic Books.

Schafer, R. (1954). *Psychoanalytic interpretation in Rorschach testing.* New York: Grune & Stratton.

Urist, J. (1977). The Rorschach test and the assessment of object relations. *Journal of Personality Assessment, 41*, 3–9.

Weiner, I. B. (1995a). Implications for theory and practice. *Journal of Personality Assessment, 62*, 498–504.

Weiner, I. B. (1995b). Speaking Rorschach: Let not theory come between us. *Rorschachiana, 20*, 1–7.

I.

1) That looks like a pelvis.

E: (Rpts S's response)
S: There is a duplication on the pelvis but this looks like a sacrum.

Structural Scoring: *Wo Fo An* 1.0 *DV*
Piotrowski Scoring: *W F+ at*
Aggression Scores: None.
Primitive Modes of Relating: None.
Defenses Coded: None.

2) Reminds me of an insect, too.

E: (Rpts S's response)
S: Like a specimen.

Structural Scoring: *Wo Fo A* 1.0
Piotrowski Scoring: *W F+ a Mp*
Aggression Scores: None.
Primitive Modes of Relating: None.
Defenses Coded: None.

3) It suggests to me a repeating figure in that, there is enough symmetry between the two pairs of white spots to indicate there might be a symmetrical translation that might produce an infinitely long figure but I see the upper pair is not identical so I have to abandon this.

E: (Rpts S's response)
S: It's the repetition of a unit with a symmetrical operation.

Structural Scoring: *DdSv* 29 *Fu* 2 *Id DR*
Piotrowski Scoring: *WS F+/-* repeating figures *Mp*
Aggression Scores: None.
Primitive Modes of Relating: None.
Defenses coded: Higher Denial, Intellectualization.

4) The two little central humps at the top suggest a sine curve starting to the right and reflecting off the vertical line but not a, it's a poor sine curve because the top part of the arc is too much . . .

E: (Rpts S's response)
S: (Not recorded)

Structural Scoring: *Ddo* 22 *Fu Sc DR*
Piotrowski Scoring: *D F+* sine wave
Aggression Scoring: None.
Primitive Modes of Relating: None.
Defenses Coded: Devaluation, Intellectualization.

5) The two little adjacent protuberances look like lobster claws.

E: (Rpts S's response)
S: (Not recorded)

Structural Scoring: *Do* 1 *Fo* 2 *Ad*
Piotrowski Scoring: *D F+ ad*
Aggression Scoring: *AgC*
Primitive Modes of Relating: None.
Defenses Coded: None.

6) A suggestion of bat wing about the whole thing and I looked for the little hooks a bat uses to hang by but they are not visible.

E: (Rpts S's response)
S: Wings Spread.

Structural Scoring: *Wo FMpo A P* 1.0
Piotrowski Scoring: *W F+ a P*
Aggression Scoring: None.
Primitive Modes of Relating: None.
Defenses Coded: None.

436

7) Now I notice a lack of symmetry because a little white line on the left is not there on the right and some of the other details are unsymmetrical.

Structural Scoring: *Ddo* 99 *Fu Ad DV*
Piotrowski Scoring: *d F+ ad*
Aggression Scoring: *AgC*
Primitive Modes of Relating: None.
Defenses Coded: None.

II.

8) This reminds me of blood and the black of ink, carbon and the structure of graphite.

Structural Scoring: *Wv+ C.C′Fu Bl,Art,Id* 4.5 *ALOG*
Piotrowski Scoring: *W Fc′+/–.CF* blood,ink,graphite
Aggression Scoring: None.
Primitive Modes of Relating: None.
Defenses Coded: None.

9) Of course a vulva like appearance, all along in fact.

Structural Scoring: *Do* 3 *Fo Hd,Sx DV*
Piotrowski Scoring: *D F+* sex
Aggression Scoring: None.
Primitive Modes of Relating: None.
Defenses Coded: None.

10) A pair of butterflies with wings vertical, at the top facing each other.

Structural Scoring: *Dd+* 99 *FMpu* 2 *A* 5.5
Piotrowski Scoring: *d FM+ a*
Aggression Scoring: None.
Primitive Modes of Relating: None.
Defenses Coded: None.

11) The upper figure is a pair of sharp-nosed pliers.

Structural Scoring: *Do* 2 *F– Sc*
Piotrowski Scoring: *D F–* pliers
Aggression Scores: None.
Primitive Modes of Relating: None.
Defenses Coded: None.

12) I get an impression of two rabbits sitting down with fore paws up in in the air in an attitude of supplication.

Structural Scoring: *Do* 1 *Mpu* 2 *A P FAB*
Piotrowski Scoring: *D Ma+ P*
Aggression Scores: None.
Primitive Modes of Relating: None.
Defenses Coded: Reaction Formation.

E: (Rpts S's response)
S: A little claw there. I could go on and on is that enough?

E: (Rpts S's response)
S: Structure, because I was thinking of carbon and I always think of structure. The straight lines in the little central figure are puzzling, because the general impression is curvature.

E: (Rpts S's response)
S: (Not recorded)

E: (Rpts S's response)
S: (Not recorded)

E: (Rpts S's response)
S: (Not recorded)

E: (Rpts S's response)
S: (Not recorded)

(continued)

III.

13) Well, these look like two men perhaps waiters. Suggestion of formal dress, facing each other. Perhaps they are Joo's dancers or some other pair of male dancers.

E: (Rpts S's response)
S: Usual. Joo's dancers the ones who did the dance of the diplomats around a table.

Structural Scoring: *W+ Mpo* 2 *H,Cg P* 5.5 *PER*
Piotrowski Scoring: *W M+ h P*
Aggression Scores: None.
Primitive Modes of Relating: None.
Defenses Coded: Isolation, Intellectualization.

14) Down below I get the impression of a crab as though the men were each holding one of the big claws and there is a central body and other legs underneath.

E: (Rpts S's response)
S: I'm reminded of Picasso because the two white spots suggest two eyes looking out . . . the contour generally is like the profile. I thought the protuberance is the nose rather than the chin and these are long heads, oligocephalic, look as though handkerchiefs in the pockets of the men.

Structural Scoring: *DdS+* 99 *Mp–* 2 *(H),(A),Art,Cg* 3.0
Piotrowski Scoring: *DS M– (h),(a),Art*
Aggression Scores: None.
Primitive Modes of Relating: None.
Defenses Coded: Projection.

15) I got a sort of feline impression momentarily as though the whole structure except for the heads was the face of a cat and whiskers down below, just this flash, not exactly Cheshire appearing in a tree and vanishing, not quite so evanescent.

E: (Rpts S's response)
S: (Not recorded)

Structural Scoring: *DdSo* 99 *FMp– (A) PER,ALOG*
Piotrowski Scoring: *dS FM– (a)*
Aggression Scores: None.
Primitive Modes of Relating: None.
Defenses Coded: None.

16) The red blotches not so much but in the center one the Bible is standing open perhaps as I saw it at Balliol.

E: (Rpts S's response)
S: You need a big book, the leaves are hanging down. I might have thought of a dictionary but they are usually on a stand and flat.

Structural Scoring: *Do* 2 *mp– Ay PER,DR2*
Piotrowski Scoring: *D m–* bible
Aggression Scores: None.
Primitive Modes of Relating: None.
Defenses Coded: Intellectualization.

IV.

17) This gives the impression of a pelt that has been skinned off an animal and spread out to some extent. It looks as though looking on the skin side and to some extent at the fur side.

E: (Rpts S's response)
S: I keep getting an impression of skins, even of a pile of skins, one above the other.

Structural Scoring: *Wv+ VFo Ad* 4.0
Piotrowski Scoring: *W Fc+ ad P RPT*
Aggression Scores: *AgPast*
Primitive Modes of Relating: None.
Defenses Coded: None.

18) I'm reminded of Dali's watches by the two arms at upper right and left that seem to hang over in that limp manner, and the fact that the form is about like.

Structural Scoring: *Wo mp– Art,Sc* CFB
Piotrowski Scoring: *W M+ (h),art*
Aggression Scores: None.
Primitive Modes of Relating: None.
Defenses Coded: None.

E: (Rpts S's response)
S: (Not recorded)

19) This is a spigot that iron comes out of. A cupola, perhaps is indicated up at the top by this figure, just a little bit at at the top.

Structural Scoring: *Do 3 Fu Sc*
Piotrowski Scoring: *D F+* spigot
Aggression Scores: None.
Primitive Modes of Relating: None.
Defenses Coded: None.

E: (Rpts S's response)
S: The cupola is the whole furnace, it doesn't show here, just the spigot.

20) Also looks sort of sexual in nature. Perhaps testicles and penis hanging there below at the wrong end of the pelt.

Structural Scoring: *Do 3 mp– Sx,Ad*
Piotrowski Scoring: *D F–* sex
Aggression Scores: None.
Primitive Modes of Relating: None.
Defenses Coded: Devaluation.

E: (Rpts S's response)
S: Same structure for the spigot.

21) I also have a sort of gorilla like impression as though a gorilla was standing there illuminated by a bright light close behind his back causing him to cast shadows that stand out radiating to the right and left.

Structural Scoring: *DdS+ 99 FMp.mp.VFo A,Id* 4.0
Piotrowski Scoring: *DS FM+.m+.Fc'+/–* vista
Aggression Scores: None.
Primitive Modes of Relating: None.
Defenses Coded: Idealization, Splitting (between responses).

E: (Rpts S's response)
S: Omitting center bottom. Heavy side, boots are shadows.

22) A carcass of an animal spread open. I seem to see a cleaver, not in the picture but the act of cleaving is suggested to me. I must have seen a butcher cleave one open.

Structural Scoring: *Wv Fu An* PER,MOR,DR
Piotrowski Scoring: *W F+* art vista *Mp*
Aggression Scores: *AgPast*
Primitive Modes of Relating: Boundary Disturbance.
Defenses Coded: Repression.

E: (Rpts S's response)
S: Through the insides.

23) A little group of very small dots that remind me of the spots on a Laue photograph that makes me think of a 2-dimensional lattice, of course a great number of ideas go thru my head as a result of that.

Structural Scoring: *Ddo 99 Fu Sc* PER,DR2
Piotrowski Scoring: *d F+/–* dots vista
Aggression Scores: None.

E: (Rpts S's response)
S: Laue was the one who got the Nobel prize for discovering X-Ray diffraction by crystals.

(continued)

Primitive Modes of Relating: None.
Defenses Coded: Intellectualization.

V.

24) This looks batty to me, too, that's the first thing I think of.

E: (Rpts S's response)
S: The symmetry makes me think of static objects. If there were less symmetry there would be more motion.

Structural Scoring: *Wo Fo (A) P* 1.0 *DR1*
Piotrowski Scoring: *W FM+ a P*
Aggression Scores: None.
Primitive Modes of Relating: None.
Defenses Coded: None.

25) A swallow tailed butterfly or somewhat related moth is suggested by the structure of the bottom part of the median region.

E: (Rpts S's response)
S: Not really the whole.

Structural Scoring: *Ddo* 99 *Fu A*
Piotrowski Scoring: *d F+ a → P*
Aggression Scores: None.
Primitive Modes of Relating: None.
Defenses Coded: None.

26) The upper part rather indicates for some reason a deer. I think deer. I think of horns of a deer in the velvet, these blunt structures seem fuzzy although their contour is well defined.

E: (Rpts S's response)
S: The velvet is the bluntness of the ends.

Structural Scoring: *Do* 6 *Fo Ad*
Piotrowski Scoring: *D F+ a*
Aggression Scores: None.
Primitive Modes of Relating: None.
Defenses Coded: None.

27) A suggestion of a nutcracker, the little protuberances towards the center, they would be handles.

E: (Rpts S's response)
S: The nut would go here.

Structural Scoring: *Do* 6 *Fu Hh*
Piotrowski Scoring: *D F+–* nutcracker
Aggression Scores: None.
Primitive Modes of Relating: None.
Defenses Coded: None.

28) I now see a little picture of a man with a derby hat. Just below the horns which suggests he is cuckolded but not the forms that artists usually indicate for that purpose.

E: (Rpts S's response)
S: (Not recorded)

Structural Scoring: *Ddo* 30 *Fu Hd,Cg ALOG*
Piotrowski Scoring: *d F– hd,clg,(ad)*
Aggression Scores: None.
Primitive Modes of Relating: None.
Defenses Coded: Devaluation.

29) I think of Icarus. A flyer but rather of pictures I have seen of early flyers with wings attached to a man's arms. Like DaVinci's drawing. The legs look funny of course. I don't know why, perhaps as though wearing skis foreshortened.

E: (Rpts S's response)
S: (Not recorded)

Structural Scoring: *W+ Fu (H),Id* 5.0 *INC,PER*
Piotrowski Scoring: *W F+ (h)* Icarus *Mp*
Aggression Scores: None.
Primitive Modes of Relating: None.
Defenses Coded: Idealization, Devaluation, Splitting (within card), Intellectualization.

30) The extremities of the wings look like alligator heads, characteristic shape to the mouth and lower jaw, bulging above the eyes and even the contour of the nose.

E: (Rpts S's response)
S: You can even see the two eye bulges.

Structural Scoring: *Do* 10 *Fo* 2 *Ad DV*
Piotrowski Scoring: *D F+ ad*
Aggression Scores: None.
Primitive Modes of Relating: None.
Defenses Coded: None.

VI.

31) This gives a sort of totem pole effect, plus..

E: (Rpts S's response)
S: The top looks like the stylized wings that are sometimes portrayed with feathers carved on poles, and these are cat's whiskers here although that's something I've never seen on a totem pole.

Structural Scoring: *Do* 3 *Fo Ay,Ad INC1*
Piotrowski Scoring: *D F+* totem pole
Aggression Scores: None.
Primitive Modes of Relating: None.
Defenses Coded: None.

32) The same sort of skin as before here at the bottom.

E: (Rpts S's response)
S: (Not recorded)

Structural Scoring: *Dv* 1 *Fo Ad P*
Piotrowski Scoring: *D F+ ad → P Mp*
Aggression Scores: None.
Primitive Modes of Relating: None.
Defenses Coded: None.

33) This structure makes me interested in the question of embryological development and that arises from the ridge down the middle which is like the medial ridge in a human or animal body.

E: (Rpts S's response)
S: It has a sort of vulva like significance, too. I have the impression for some reason I'm not able to understand, that this should be colored and should be orange. I don't know why, not uniformly but some parts should be colored orange . . . Maybe it made me think of marine life.

Structural Scoring: *Ddo* 99 *Fu Hd,Sx DV2*
Piotrowski Scoring: *d Fc–* sex embryo *CP*
Aggression Scores: None.
Primitive Modes of Relating: None.
Defenses Coded: Higher Denial.

VII.

34) This gives sort of an insect impression, perhaps the antennae or some mouth parts of an insect are suggested.

E: (Rpts S's response)
S: (Not Recorded)

Structural Scoring: *Wo F– Ad* 2.5
Piotrowski Scoring: *W F– ad*
Aggression Scores: None.

(continued)

Primitive Modes of Relating: None.
Defenses Coded: None.

35) The two top structures also remind me of animal faces and heads, like the funny papers, or cartoons, like that.

E: (Rpts S's response)
S: . . . at each other. I think of them as laughing hilariously.

Structural Scoring: *D*+ 1 *Mau* 2 (*Ad*) 3.0
Piotrowski Scoring: *D Ma* (*a*)
Aggression Scores: None.
Primitive Modes of Relating: None.
Defenses Coded: None.

36) Suggestion of a hinge at the central part at the bottom, some special sort of structure, perhaps like that on a bivalve.

E: (Rpts S's response)
S: (Not recorded)

Structural Scoring: *Do* 6 *Fo Sc*
Piotrowski Scoring: *D F*+ *ad* bivalve hinge
Aggression Scores: None.
Primitive Modes of Relating: None.
Defenses Coded: None.

37) The texture generally does suggest crustaceans, or lobster claws.

E: (Rpts S's response)
S: Not the form so much its shell like because of the texture.

Structural Scoring: *Wo TF– Ad* 2.5
Piotrowski Scoring: *W Fc– ad*
Aggression Scores: *AgC*
Primitive Modes of Relating: None.
Defenses Coded: None.

38) If it were not for the symmetry I might have had suggested to me the appearance of islands from the air, but the symmetry tends to remove that because no tropical island would occur in pairs like that.

E: (Rpts S's response)
S: (Not recorded)

Structural Scoring: *Wo Fo* 2 *Ls* 2.5 *ALOG*
Piotrowski Scoring: *W F– na* vista
Aggression Scores: None.
Primitive Modes of Relating: None.
Defenses Coded: None.

VIII.

39) Well these are nice colors.

E: (No Inquiry)

Structural Scoring: *Wv C Id*
Piotrowski Scoring: -------
Aggression Scores: None.
Primitive Modes of Relating: None.
Defenses Coded: None.

40) This looks sort of skeletal, too.

E: (Rpts S's response)
S: The upper part does indicate a spinal column of a fish and ribs coming out from that with something similar attached.

Structural Scoring: *DSo* 3 *Fu An* 4.0
Piotrowski Scoring: *DS F*+ *at*
Aggression Scores: None.
Primitive Modes of Relating: None.
Defenses Coded: None.

41) It seems to me there are a couple of animals right and left sort of but not exactly beaver like, tails to the bottom climbing up. Reminds me of a Dutch painter, Breughel? Maybe. They do remind me both of Breughel and of Bosch, Hieronymus Bosch and of some of his portrayals of fanciful animals. The temptation of St. Anthony involved trumpets in the noses and in this case, tail suggests an adhesive organ, like the placenta.

E: (Rpts S's response)
S: Animals seem to be stuck to the bottom part. Movement not strong.

Structural Scoring: D+ 1 *FMpo* 2 *(A),Art* P 3.0 *INC2,FAB*
Piotrowski Scoring: *D FM–* (*a*),sex *FABC*
Aggression Scores: None.
Primitive Modes of Relating: Symbiotic Merging.
Defenses Coded: Intellectualization.

42) That and the color suggest that the bottom looks rather like a liver.

E: (Rpts S's response)
S: Partly the color, just the brownish part.

Structural Scoring: *Dv* 7 *CF– An*
Piotrowski Scoring: *D FC– at*
Aggression Scores: None.
Primitive Modes of Relating: None.
Defenses Coded: None.

43) The whole upper part strongly suggests one of those Breughel imaginary animals. Animals.

E: (Rpts S's response)
S: The upper part there not clear, may have been a carryover. Later it looked like a lobster but not an imaginary one.

Structural Scoring: *Do* 4 *Fu (A),Art*
Piotrowski Scoring: *D F+* (*a*)
Aggression Scores: None.
Primitive Modes of Relating: None.
Defenses Coded: Intellectualization.

44) I get the impression from the central structure of a landscape in which there has been a lot of erosion by the rain.

E: (Rpts S's response)
S: The bluish part. I was thinking of sand, of a blue clay soil like in the desert.

Structural Scoring: *Dv* 5 *CF.YFu Ls MOR*
Piotrowski Scoring: *D CFc Na*
Aggression Scores: None.
Primitive Modes of Relating: None.
Defenses Coded: None.

IX

45) Well . . . here . . . that's Punch two, Punches at the top with pendulous abdomens, arms not visible.

E: (Rpts S's response)
S: It was chiefly the abdomens that suggested it. These punches, the faces remind me of some other character that seems familiar, perhaps a funny paper, from my early days, a little suggestion of Happy Hooligan about them.

Structural Scoring: *Do* 3 *Fo* 2 *(H),Hx* P *AB,PER*
Piotrowski Scoring: *D M+* (*h*) → *P*
Aggression Scores: None.
Primitive Modes of Relating: None.
Defenses Coded: Isolation.

(continued)

46) Impression again of insects.

E: (Rpts S's response)
S: All but the lower pink.

Structural Scoring: *Do 2 F– 2 A*
Piotrowski Scoring: *D F– a RPT*
Aggression Scores: None.
Primitive Modes of Relating: None.
Defenses Coded: None.

47) The green structure is like the pelvic bones from this view.

E: (Rpts S's response)
S: Anterior view, form and symmetry. The central part like the pelvis the holes. I don't know if the pelvic bones have those holes or not but it seems proper.

Structural Scoring: *DdSo 99 F– An 5.0*
Piotrowski Scoring: *D F– at*
Aggression Scores: None.
Primitive Modes of Relating: None.
Defenses Coded: None.

48) In the central part there is a suggestion that water is dripping, perhaps blood dripping down. The color suggests that.

E: (Rpts S's response)
S: As though oozing out.

Structural Scoring: *Ddv 99 mp.Cu Bl MOR*
Piotrowski Scoring: *d m+/–.CF Na,blood*
Aggression Scores: None.
Primitive Modes of Relating: boundary Disturbance.
Defenses Coded: None.

49) Vague impression of some peaches or similar fruit. Four of them arranged in a row at the base.

E: (Rpts S's response)
S: It's the shape and structure more than the color, it shows that ridge. If it had been the color I would have said plum.

Structural Scoring: *Do 6 FCo Fd*
Piotrowski Scoring: *D F+/– food*
Aggression Scores: None.
Primitive Modes of Relating: None.
Defenses Coded: None.

50) I think of flame produced from a central structure at the top.

E: (Rpts S's response)
S: As though a tube up here and something burning and a general impression of a flame in the blue background.

Structural Scoring: *Dv+ 5 mp.CF.VFu Fi 4.5*
Piotrowski Scoring: *D m+/–.CF fire*
Aggression Scores: None.
Primitive Modes of Relating: None.
Defenses Coded: None.

51) The holes closer into the center remind me of the holes of the metal cylinder into which the glass globe of a kerosene lamp would fit and the bottom structure might be the container for the lamp.

E: (Rpts S's response)
S: (Not recorded)

Structural Scoring: *DdSo 99 Fu Hh 5.0*
Piotrowski Scoring: *ds F+ lamp Mp*
Aggression Scores: None.
Primitive Modes of Relating: None.
Defenses Coded: None.

52) I got the impression of two pigs' heads in the green structure here, dark green end of snout and I can see here the jowls, quite a porcine indication.

E: (Rpts S's response)
S: Texture gives the impression of fatness.

Structural Scoring: *Do* 1 *FC.VFu* 2 *Ad DV*
Piotrowski Scoring: *D FCc ad*
Aggression Scores: None.
Primitive Modes of Relating: None.
Defenses Coded: None.

X.

53) This gives me a sort of wish bone impression.

E: (Rpts S's response)
S: (Not recorded)

Structural Scoring: *Do* 7 *F– An*
Piotrowski Scoring: *D F+* food
Aggression Scores: None.
Primitive Modes of Relating: None.
Defenses Coded: None.

54) Also the governor of a locomotive by the little central structure of 3 ellipses attached together by arms; it seems to be dynamically unsatisfactory because I would expect the two outer to be swung out.

E: (Rpts S's response)
S: Same location. I have feeling of rotation.

Structural Scoring: *Do* 3 *mpu Sc DR1*
Piotrowski Scoring: *D m+* governor
Aggression Scores: None.
Primitive Modes of Relating: None.
Defenses Coded: Devaluation.

55) I get the impression to the right and left of dancing gnomes. Two on right and two on left. The fatter one with arms and the thinner holding up a green structure which isn't heavy.

E: (Rpts S's response)
S: Pale blue is fat and darker blue the thin one.

Structural Scoring: *D+* 1 *Ma.FC.YFu* 2 *(H),Id* 4.0 COP
Piotrowski Scoring: *D M+.FC+ (h)*
Aggression Scores: None.
Primitive Modes of Relating: None.
Defenses Coded: Devaluation.

56) Two similar gnomes holding up, perhaps a candle stick in the center at the top and I am reminded by them . . . some little insect colorless, water nymph. I think, of some sort. These little fellows have three legs.

E: (Rpts S's response)
S: (Not recorded)

Structural Scoring: *D+* 8 *Mpu* 2 *(H),Hh,A* 4.0 *FAB,INC2,*COP
Piotrowski Scoring: *D M– (h),a* candle,nymphs *FABC*
Aggression Scores: None.
Primitive Modes of Relating: None.
Defenses Coded: Devaluation.

(continued)

57) This blue in the middle gives a sort of pelvis effect to me again although much different in nature I don't know why I see that so often.

E: (Rpts S's response)
S: (Not recorded)

Structural Scoring: *Dv* 6 *F– An DR*
Piotrowski Scoring: *D f– at RPT*
Aggression Scores: None.
Primitive Modes of Relating: None.
Defenses Coded: None.

58) At the bottom a rabbit being held up by two caterpillars.

E: (Rpts S's response)
S: Alice-in-Wonderland effect. Just the rabbit's face.

Structural Scoring: *D+* 10 *FMpo* 2 *(A)* 4.0 COP
Piotrowski Scoring: *FM–.FC– (a) P FABC*
Aggression Scores: None.
Primitive Modes of Relating: None.
Defenses Coded: None.

59) Nice yellow sea shells, not exactly conch shells.

E: (Rpts S's response)
S: The opening into the interior is important and some sea shells are spiny, so that is right too.

Structural Scoring: *Do* 2 *CF.FVu Ad*
Piotrowski Scoring: *D CF* sea shells vista
Aggression Scores: None.
Primitive Modes of Relating: None.
Defenses Coded: None.

60) The red is like sea horses, but the tails are bent in the wrong way

E: (Rpts S's response)
S: They have an Irish appearance, too, the nose, and there is something hanging from both upper and lower lips, mouth open, it's ectoplasmic.

Structural Scoring: *Do* 9 *Mp.mp–* 2 *A,Id,Ay INC2,FAB*
Piotrowski Scoring: *D Ma–.m– a,(h) FABC, CL*
Aggression Scores: None.
Primitive Modes of Relating: None.
Defenses Coded: Devaluation.

61) The California peninsula, geographical coastal contour.

E: (Rpts S's response)
S: Also the pink, the one on the right. Topographical map, one of the old colored ones.

Structural Scoring: *Do* 9 *CFu* 2 *Ge*
Piotrowski Scoring: *D FC+ geo*
Aggression Scores: None.
Primitive Modes of Relating: None.
Defenses Coded: Isolation.

62) Out to the right it suggests the floats that hold kelp up on the surface.

E: (Rpts S's response)
S: And attached to that is a sweet pea, not quite open.

Structural Scoring: *Dv+* 7 *F– Bt* 4.0 *FAB*
Piotrowski Scoring: *D FC+ bt mp*
Aggression Scores: None.
Primitive Modes of Relating: None.
Defenses Coded: None.

446

63) On the lower left is Madagascar, the right not.

E: (Rpts S's response)
S: Clear general contour and orientation enough but the right there is no suggestion of that sort.

Structural Scoring: *Dv* 7 *Fu Id*
Piotrowski Scoring: *D F+ geo*
Aggression Scores: None.
Primitive Modes of Relating: None.
Defenses Coded: Isolation.

64) This green thing looks like a locust, a sort of fat locust.

E: (Rpts S's response)
S: (Not recorded)

Structural Scoring: *Do* 12 *FCo A*
Piotrowski Scoring: *D FC+ a*
Aggression Scores: None.
Primitive Modes of Relating: None.
Defenses Coded: Devaluation.

65) It might also be a cow lying down.

E: (Rpts S's response)
S: On both sides.

Structural Scoring: *Do* 12 *FMp–* 2 *A*
Piotrowski Scoring: *D FM+ a*
Aggression Scores: None.
Primitive Modes of Relating: None.
Defenses Coded: None.

APPENDIX B
Rorschach Structural Summary

LOCATION FEATURES	DETERMINANTS BLENDS	SINGLE	CONTENTS	S-CONSTELLATION
				YES..FV + VF + V + FD > 2
			H = 1,0	YES..Col-Shd Bl>0
Zf = 26	C.C'F	M = 5	(H) = 5,0	YES..Ego<.31,>.44
ZSum = 91.5	FM.m.VF	FM = 6	Hd = 3,0	NO..MOR>3
ZEst = 88.0	CF.YF	m = 4	(Hd) = 0,0	NO..Zd > ± 3.5
	m.C	FC = 2	Hx = 0,1	YES..es>EA
W = 14	m.CF.VF	CF = 2	A = 10,1	YES..CF+C>FC
(Wv = 2)	FC.VF	C = 1	(A) = 5,1	YES..X+%<.70
D = 37	M.CF.YF	Cn = 0	Ad = 11,1	YES..S>3
Dd = 14	CF.FV	FC' = 0	(Ad) = 1,0	NO..P<3 or >8
S = 7	M.m	C'F = 0	An = 7,0	YES..Pure H <2
		C' = 0	Art = 1,4	NO..R<17
DQ		FT = 0	Ay = 2,1	8.....TOTAL
.........(FQ–)		TF = 1	Bl = 2,0	
+ = 10 (1)		T = 0	Bt = 1,0	SPECIAL SCORINGS
o = 42(12)		FV = 0	Cg = 0,3	Lv1 Lv2
v/+ = 4 (1)		VF = 1	Cl = 0,0	DV = 4x1 1x2
v = 8 (2)		V = 0	Ex = 0,0	INC = 2x2 3x4
		FY = 0	Fd = 1,0	DR = 7x3 2x6
		YF = 0	Fi = 1,0	FAB = 5x4 0x7
		Y = 0	Ge = 1,0	ALOG = 3x5
FORM QUALITY		Fr = 0	Hh = 2,1	CON = 0x7
		rF = 0	Ls = 2,0	SUM6 = 27
	FQx FQf MQual SQx	FD = 0	Na = 0,0	WSUM6 = 90
+ = 0 0 0 0		F = 34	Sc = 6,1	
o = 20 12 1 1			Sx = 0,3	AB =1 CP = 0
u = 28 15 4 3			Xy = 0,0	AG =0 MOR = 3
– = 16 7 2 3			Id = 3,5	CFB =1 PER = 6
none = 1 – 0 0		(2) = 19		COP =3 PSV = 0

RATIOS, PERCENTAGES, AND DERIVATIONS

R = 65	L = 1.10	FC:CF+C =4:8 COP = 3 AG = 0	
		Pure C =3 Food = 1	
EB = 7:11.5	EA = 18.5 EBPer = 1.6	SumC':WSumC =1:11.0 Isolate/R = 0.06	
eb = 15:9	es = 24 D = –2	Afr =0.67 H:(H)Hd(Hd) = 1:8	
	Adj es = 16 Adj D = 0	S =7 (HHd):(AAd) = 5:7	
		Blends:R =9:65 H+A:Hd + Ad = 23:16	
FM = 7	C' = 1 T = 1	CP =0	
m = 8	V = 5 Y = 2		
		P = 7 Zf =26 3r+(2)/R = 0.29	
a:p = 2:20	Sum6 = 27	X+% = 0.31 Zd = +3.5 Fr+rF = 0	
Ma:Mp = 2:5	Lv2 = 6	F+% = 0.35 W:D:Dd =14:37:14 FD = 0	
2AB+Art+Ay = 10	WSum6 = 90	X–% = 0.25 W:M = 14:7 An + Xy = 7	
M– = 2	Mnone = 0	S–% = 0.19 DQ+ =10 MOR = 3	
		Xu% = 0.43 DQv =9	

| SCZI = 3 | DEPI = 4 | CDI = 2 | S-CON = 8* | HVI = No | OBS = No |

Card	No.	Loc.	#	Determinant(s)	(2)	Content(s)	Pop	Z	Special Scores
I	1	Wo	1	Fo		An		1.0	DV
	2	Wo	1	Fo		A		1.0	
	3	DdSv	29	Fu	2	Id		3.5	DR
	4	Ddo	22	Fu		Sc			DR
	5	Do	1	Fo	2	Ad			(AgC)
	6	Wo	1	FMpo		A	P	1.0	
	7	Ddo	99	Fu		Ad			DV (AgC)
II	8	W/	1	C.C'Fu		Bl, Art, Id		4.5	ALOG
	9	Do	3	Fo		Hd, Sx			DV
	10	Dd+	99	FMpu	2	A		5.5	
	11	Do	2	F–		Sc			
	12	Do	1	Mpu	2	A	P		FAB
III	13	W+	1	Mpo	2	H, Cg	P	5.5	PER
	14	DdS+	99	Mp–	2	(H), (A), Art, Cg		3.0	
	15	DdSo	99	FMp–		(A)		4.5	DR
	16	Do	2	mp–		Ay			PER, DR2
IV	17	W/	1	VFo		Ad		4.0	(AgPAST)
	18	Wo	1	mp–		Art, Sc			CFB
	19	Do	3	Fu		Sc			
	20	Do	3	mp–		Ad, Sx			
	21	DdS+	99	FMp.mp.VFo		A, Id		4.0	
	22	Wv	1	Fu		An			PER, MOR, DR (AgPAST)
	23	Ddo	99	Fu		Sc			PER, DR2
V	24	Wo	1	Fo		(A)	P	1.0	DR
	25	Ddo	99	Fu		A			
	26	Do	6	Fo		Ad			
	27	Do	6	Fu		Hh			
	28	Ddo	30	Fu		Hd, Cg			ALOG
	29	W+	1	Fu		(H), Id		5.0	INC, PER
	30	Do	10	Fo	2	Ad			(AgC)
VI	31	Do	3	Fo		Ay, Ad			INC
	32	Dv	1	Fo		Ad	P		
	33	Ddo	99	Fu		Hd, Sx			DV2
VII	34	Wo	1	F–		Ad		2.5	
	35	D+	1	Mau	2	(Ad)		3.0	
	36	Do	6	Fo		Sc			
	37	Wo	1	TF–		Ad		2.5	(AgC)
	38	Wo	1	Fo	2	Ls		2.5	ALOG
VIII	39	Wv	1	C		Id			
	40	DSo	3	Fu		An		4.0	
	41	D+	1	FMpo	2	(A), Art	P	3.0	INC2, FAB
	42	Dv	7	CF–		An			
	43	Do	4	Fu		(A), Art			
	44	Dv	5	CF.YFu		Ls			MOR
IX	45	Do	3	Fo	2	(H), Hx	P		AB, PER
	46	Do	2	F–	2	A			
	47	DdSo	99	F–		An		5.0	
	48	Ddv	99	mp.Cu		Bl			MOR
	49	Do	6	FCo		Fd			
	50	D/	5	mp.CF.VFu		Fi		4.5	
	51	DdSo	99	Fu		Hh		5.0	
	52	Do	1	FC.VFu	2	Ad			DV
X	53	Do	7	F–		An			
	54	Do	3	mpu		Sc			DR
	55	D+	1	Ma.FC.YFu	2	(H), Id		4.0	COP
	56	D+	8	Mpu	2	(H), Hh, A		4.0	FAB, INC2, COP
	57	Dv	6	F–		An			DR
	58	D+	10	FMpo	2	(A)		4.0	COP

(continued)

449

Card	No.	Loc.	#	Determinant(s)	(2)	Content(s)	Pop Z	Special Scores
	59	Do	2	CF.FVu		Ad		
	60	Do	9	Mp.mp–	2	A, Id, Ay		INC2, FAB
	61	Do	9	CFu	2	Ge		
	62	D/		F–		Bt	4.0	FAB
	63	Dv	7	Fu		Id		
	64	Do	12	FCo		A		
	65	Do	12	FMp–	2	A		

Summary of Approach

I:W.W.DdS.Dd.D.W.Dd

II:W.D.Dd.D.D

III:W.DdS.DdS.D

IV:W.W.D.D.DdS.W.Dd

V:W.Dd.D.D.Dd.W.D

VI:D.D.Dd

VII:W.D.D.W.W

VIII:W.Ds.D.D.D.D

IX:D.D.DdS.Dd.D.D.DdS.D

X:D.D.D.D.D.D.D.D.D.D.D.D

450

APPENDIX D
Defense Scoring for the Pauling Protocol (Cooper, Perry, & Arnow, 1988)

Defense	Response(s)	Frequency	Percentage
Neurotic			
Higher-level Denial	3,33	2	
Intellectualization	3,4,13,16,23,29,41,43	8	
Isolation	13,45,61,63	4	
Reaction Formation	12	1	
Repression	22	1	
Rationalization	—	0	
Pollyannish Denial	—	0	
Total		16	53%
Borderline			
Devaluation	4,20,28,29,54,55,56,60,64	9	
Omnipotence	—	0	
Primitive Idealization	21,29	2	
Projection	14	1	
Projective Identification	—	0	
Splitting	21,29	2	
Total		14	47%
Psychotic			
Hypomanic Denial	—	0	
Massive Denial	—	0	
Total		0	0%
Total Scored		30	100%

25

He-She-It: The Construction and Destruction of an Illusory Identity

Marvin W. Acklin
Diana E. Wright
Honolulu, Hawaii

Arnold R. Bruhn
Bethesda, Maryland

Theorists and clinicians typically resort to structural metaphors in understanding and describing personality organization and functioning. Freud (1923), of course, established the early foundations of structural theory. Psychoanalytic theory became more completely organized around structural and developmental constructs based on the contributions from ego psychology (Blanck & Blanck, 1975), nonpsychoanalytic structural developmental theories (Loevinger, 1976; Werner, 1957), Erikson's (1950) epigenetic theory, object relations theories (Kernberg, 1976, 1992), and self-psychology (Kohut, 1971; Mahler, 1968; Mahler, Pine, & Bergman, 1975; Pine, 1990; Stolorow & Lachmann, 1980). Structural theories of personality focus on the cohesive organization of personality functioning, level of complexity and hierarchical organization, defensive organization, range and quality of adaptive functioning, and response to conflict and stress. The concept of developmental lines has made a major contribution to the multidimensional description and assessment of personality functioning (Blanck & Blanck, 1975; Freud, 1963). From Freud's simple tripartite structural theory, a contemporary approach to structural developmental processes integrates structural theory, attachment theory and developmental psychology, and cognitive psychology in defining and understanding internalized mental structures (Blatt, 1995).

Two broad approaches to personality structure, based on deficit or conflict theories, form the traditional foundation of psychoanalytic developmental theory (Gedo & Goldberg, 1973). The delineation of these theories as deficit- or conflict-based is admittedly arbitrary and is modeled on ideal types. The Oedipal period of development is traditionally viewed as the point where the fundamental structuralization of personality, in the context of triadic object relations, is achieved (Kernberg, 1976). The foundation for a stable sense of gendered identity and a generational identification is the result. Conflict-based theory assumes a structuralization of the personality where psychopathology derives from nonintegration. Broadly speaking, psychopathology that derives from conflict is viewed as organized in the neurotic range (Acklin, 1994; Kernberg, 1976). Deficit theories focus more on the pre-Oedipal period of development. In deficit theories, psychopathology is understood to represent either the direct behavioral or subjective expressions of deficient structuralization or maladaptive efforts to compensate or defend against these effects (Acklin, 1992; Kernberg, 1976). Psychopathology that is deficit-based is viewed as organized in the borderline, or in more severe conditions, the psychotic range of functioning (Acklin, 1992, 1993; Kernberg, 1976). In the real world, using a differentiated theory of developmental lines and object relations theory, psychopathology can best be understood as combining elements of both deficit and conflict theory. Structural developmental theory, then, plays a significant role in psychodiagnosis of personality organization and in understanding functional responses to growth and development, stress, and trauma (Kernberg, 1992).

Continuing the structural metaphor, stress or strain on structural components of personality may be associated with psychological symptoms, subjective distress, and loss of adaptive functioning. Trauma may be of sufficient intensity to actually "destructure" personality organization, shattering the sense of cohesiveness and organization that forms the core sense of self (Ulman & Brothers, 1988). Personality decompensation represents the most dramatic clinical presentation of psychological turmoil and distress. Commonly, the clinician may observe not only the overt turmoil of psychological decompensation, but also efforts at personality restabilization or reconstitution (Kohut, 1971). Acute reconstitutive efforts may range from simple withdrawal and reduction of stimulation, on the more benign end, to regression and the emergence of primitive defensive processes and the reorganization of the sense of reality, for example, in delusional formation. In the worst case scenario, the complete disintegration of personality is possible, revealed in disorganized, psychotic states. Most often the clinical effects of psychological trauma are the combined product of the nature and intensity of trauma, the unique structural features (ego strength, characterological defenses, modes of relatedness) of the victim, and the type of social support or therapeutic intervention available following the trauma. Most commonly, the response to trauma opens up previously experienced traumatic experiences, synergizing the emotional impact of the instant trauma but also providing an opportunity to address earlier issues. Depending on the intensity and nature of the trauma, the premorbid integrity of the personality structure, and the availability of therapeutic support, trauma may be an opportunity for personality growth and development based on mastery and integration of the traumatic experience

(McCann & Pearlman, 1990). A less desirable, and more common outcome, especially in trauma experiences that are catastrophic—serious, life-threatening, or disfiguring—is the permanent ingraining of traumatic stigmata and chronic, maladaptive reconstitutive efforts, represented in character deformation ("psychic scarring") and loss or compromise of adaptive functioning (Krystal, 1978). Such pathological alterations of the self-schema create the foundation for continuing psychological instability.

Projective techniques, especially the Rorschach Test, because of their access to both structural and thematic features of personality functioning, make a unique contribution to the assessment of personality organization, trauma, and "primitive" mental states (Lerner & Lerner, 1988; Van der Kolk & Ducey, 1989). Themata are accessed by means of narratives such as the Thematic Apperception Test (TAT); Early Memories (Bruhn, 1989, 1990; Mayman, 1968; Mayman & Faris, 1960); spontaneous descriptions, including parental descriptions (Blatt, D'Affliti, & Quinlan, 1976); the history or "anamnesis"; dreams; and responses to projective techniques (Krohn & Mayman, 1974). Themata may best be understood as issues that reflect dynamically based wishes or unfinished business expressed as relationship paradigms (Acklin, Bibb, Boyer, & Jain, 1991; Aronow & Reznikoff, 1976; Luborsky, 1984; Mayman & Faris, 1960). Structural issues in personality organization are favorably illuminated by the Inkblot Test. The combination of the Rorschach, which accesses both structural and thematic techniques, and other projective techniques, provides a rich approach to personality assessment and psychodiagnosis.

CASE MATERIAL

This chapter presents the case of R. B., a 55-year-old male-to-female transsexual who was seriously beaten and sexually assaulted in her Waikiki apartment in late 1988. Marvin W. Acklin has seen R. B. in outpatient psychotherapy since the time of her assault. Of Dutch-Chinese-Indonesian ancestry, she was born in Indonesia and raised in both Indonesia and Europe. She was born in an upper class home. Her father was a musician, a band leader and "very handsome," and her mother was described as both "cruel" and "very beautiful." Her parents divorced when she was a young child. As a child, she described herself as an effeminate boy who was rejected by her mother and her more masculine male relatives and frequently punished for her precocious (homo)sexuality. She recalls being conflicted about her sex assignment and role as a young child and probably meets Stoller's designation as a male primary transsexual. Prior to her surgery in the early 1960s, she was a practicing homosexual, primarily in passive-receptive modes. She was a nonsurgical transsexual (gynemimetic) for several years prior to her sex change operation. During the late 1960s and 1970s, she was a successful and well-known entertainer in Europe, and her talents included singing, dancing, and modeling. Her presentation at this time was in the mode of a hyperexaggerated and theatrical feminine allure with opulent gowns, hair styles, and lap dogs. Although she denies that she was ever a prostitute, sexuality was her stock in trade.

In late 1988, an unknown assailant attacked her in her apartment, and she was severely beaten and sexually assaulted. Her jaw was broken in three places and her breasts disfigured, requiring several surgeries to repair. Aside from her physical injuries, she experienced an almost complete dissociation during the beating and sexual assault, and an amnesia for the face of her assailant who was never identified or apprehended. Over a period of months and then years following the assault, she suffered from a severe posttraumatic stress disorder, including life-threatening depression, pain complaints due to injury-induced neuropathy in her jaw, and periodic episodes of dissociation and emergence of multiple personalities. The three alter egos that emerged in the course of her treatment were more or less present since her childhood years, and especially so in the stage personifications she adopted in her career as a "show girl," model, and professional seductress.

Her assault would be defined as a "catastrophic trauma" in Krystal's (1978) terms, in which trauma completely overwhelms personality functioning. She experienced frequent episodes of derealization, depersonalization, episodic freezing (Krystal, 1978), psychic numbing, and nightmares. She often complained of being unable to feel, to which her reactions ranged from indifference to perplexity. Her cognitive and affective constriction and intensification of somatized affects are consistent with trauma-induced alexithymia and commonly observed in trauma victims (Acklin, 1991; Acklin & Alexander, 1988; Krystal, 1988). She was constantly preoccupied with suicidal thoughts but rejected killing herself for fear of "messing up my face." Through early crisis intervention and supportive, and then later, expressive psychotherapeutic interventions, she started to master the trauma and reintegrate. Her defenses, however, remained fragile and brittle and her social adaptation deeply compromised. Central themes in her therapy concerned the reactivation of earlier traumata, including feelings of being punished for her childhood sexual behavior that seemed oriented, in retrospect, to securing the love and affection of males. These themes pervaded her reactions to the assault. The traumatic abandonment by her father and her mother's rejection of her sexuality, and finally her effeminate masculinity, seemed to illuminate some of her underlying motives for a sex change. Her use of her feminine wiles and sexual allure, with which she both attracted and controlled men, was seen by her as the "cause" for the rape and assault, a sort of payback for decades of titillation and sexual control (Frazier, 1990). She remains socially phobic, severely obsessive-compulsive (e.g., continuously washing her hands and feet and taking as many as 12 showers a day because she feels "dirty"), "psychosomatic" (Waigandt & Miller, 1986), and often experiences a borderline psychotic state in which she feels that she can talk to and experience emotions with trees. She frequently hears a voice calling her at night and on the street and sees "faces" in shadows and in the bark of trees. Whenever she inadvertently found herself in close quarters with a strange man, she would panic, struggle for breath, and in demonstrating her reactions would grasp her neck with both hands in a choking movement. Efforts at systematic desensitization were unsuccessful in reducing her paralyzing conditioned fear responses to men, primarily because it forced her to relinquish stringent controls that rekindled traumatic recollections and panic episodes.

Prior to her assault, she described an apparently stable life, with many friends and employment in a clothing store for women. She continues to be seen on a twice-monthly basis by Marvin W. Acklin, is maintained on antidepressant medications that have reduced her showering to about five times daily, and has assumed the lifestyle of a "nobody" and "old woman" (Lebowitz, Harvey, & Herman, 1993). She obtained a score of 46 on the Dissociative Experiences Scale (DES). A score of 30 or greater is highly suggestive of dissociative or posttraumatic stress disorder (Saxe, Van der Kolk, Berkowitz, & Chinman, 1993). Her highest DES factor score was for Depersonalization/Derealization (M = 64.5), a finding that was highly consistent with descriptions of her daily life. R. B. had many spontaneous recollections, some of which reflected confusion in her sense of reality. She recalled a vivid "memory" of sitting on a beautifully tiled porch in sea side Pompeii, the ancient Italian city that was destroyed in 79 A.D. by a volcanic eruption. She frequently complained of deadness or feeling as good as dead: "I'm not alive." Reflecting what appears to be a permanently dissociated state, she refers to the "old woman" and her body as "her" or a "doll": "It's not me anymore" and "I dress her . . . I bathe her." She describes herself as "wanting to grow together and be one" and trying "to get closer to the body." Her "old woman" routine seems to be a sort of camouflage or security operation that effaces visible signs of her femininity. By imagining that she is old, unattractive, and invisible, she somewhat superstitiously wards off her fears of retraumatization (Mayr & Price, 1989).

This case study focuses on psychological test material obtained in two examinations, including her initial MMPI in January 1989 and a full battery administered almost 2 years later, including Minnesota Multiphasic Personality Inventory (MMPI; Hathaway & McKinley, 1970), Rorschach, TAT, Human Figure Drawings, and Early Memories. The focus of this chapter is on the projective techniques rich in thematic and structural data, in particular the Rorschach and the Early Memories Procedures (Acklin et al., 1991; Bruhn, 1989, 1992a, 1992b), their integration, and unique contribution in elucidating the dynamics of traumatization and reconstitution. The framework for approaching the Rorschach relies on a contemporary method based on the Comprehensive System for the Rorschach developed by Exner (1991, 1993; Exner & Weiner, 1995) augmented by content-analytic approaches that emphasize idiographic and dynamic processes (Acklin & Wright, 1997; Blatt, Brenneis, Schimek, & Glick, 1976; Blatt & Lerner, 1983; Coonerty, 1986; Cooper & Arnow, 1986; Cooper, Perry, & Arnow, 1988; Cooper, Perry, & O'Connell, 1991; Gacono & Meloy, 1994; Holt, 1970; Holt & Havel, 1960; Kwawer, 1979, 1980; Lerner, 1986, 1990, 1991; Lerner, Albert, & Walsh, 1987; Lerner & Lerner, 1980; Lerner & St. Peter, 1984; Meloy & Gacono, 1992; Urist, 1977, 1980). A contemporary, integrative approach to Rorschach interpretation requires attention to scores, indices, percentages, and ratios as well as content (Acklin, 1995).

R. B.'s initial MMPI, administered soon after her assault, is presented first. It is followed by her complete Early Memory Procedure (Bruhn, 1995) administered 2 years later in 1991. Her Rorschach protocol follows with interpretive commentary. The appendices present the Rorschach sequence of scores, structural summary, and tables summarizing content-analytic codes. Ancillary test data, including a second MMPI, are introduced and described as appropriate.

R. B.'S FIRST MMPI

Within a month of her assault and hospitalization, R. B. took an MMPI as part of her intake at the outpatient clinic of a large, urban medical center. All of her validity and clinical scales were extremely high. Her Welsh code for the profile was 48**2*61''370'9/5: L/F*K:. The interpreter (Marvin W. Acklin) wrote,

> R. B. is experiencing a high level of psychological distress and raising a cry for help . . . the overall impression is of a person who is struggling hard to maintain a sense of psychological intactness in the face of a great deal of distress. It appears that she has been severely traumatized by the attack she suffered . . . consistent with the diagnosis of Post-Traumatic Stress Disorder.

R. B.'s earliest recollections were organized and collected using the Early Memory Procedure (see Appendix A).

SUMMARY AND SYNTHESIS OF EM ISSUES

Even a cursory examination of R. B.'s early memories reveals the rich themata that organized her identity and perceptions of others. From her comments, it is clear that R. B. is profoundly affected by her past experiences. Her basic coping style, however, is fundamentally neurotic: she tries to suppress bad feelings (denial) and "forget" unpleasant memories (repression). Her attempt to suppress feelings from such experiences has made her tight as an emotional drum and highly reactive to present experiences that resonate with what she has suppressed. Although R. B. is capable of reflection and introspection, she is not psychologically minded. She tends to blame herself almost by reflex, consistent with what she did in *EM* 6 (her clearest most important memory), rather than understanding what may have motivated particular events in her life, especially those involving how she was treated by others. This pattern provides a breeding ground for resentment as well as splitting and reenactment in relationships—from her standpoint either one likes her and treats her well or one does not and treats her poorly (see Memory of Mother). Such perceptions make it difficult for her to understand subtleties in relationships or changes in the other that may situationally or transiently impact her relationship with the other. Her polarized, all-or-nothing perceptions, reflecting splitting security operations, reduce the need for conflict resolution skills as the other either likes you or does not.

Intrapsychically and developmentally, R. B.'s meta-issue involves issues of trust/abandonment. Throughout the Early Memory Procedure, we find highlighted problems involving separation/abandonment/loss, beginning with *EM* 1 (rated as 1–5, her clearest and most negative memory along with *EM* 6). Historically, she seems to have handled this issue by remaining strongly attached to a figure in her life (father) who seems wonderful only in contrast to her mother. The latter is drawn as severe, aloof, angry, judgmental, hypersensitive/overreactive, unpredictable in her reactions, rejecting and capricious—in addition to being totally unaccepting of her sexuality and abusive (physically and emotionally).

Father disappears and reappears periodically as a white knight who rescues her and protects her from the abuse she suffers, only to disappear again and leave her vulnerable and unprotected. Nevertheless, he remains as a fantasy figure who may yet reemerge in her life to save her from the annihilation she fears, much as the Major (mother's boyfriend) plays a similar role in her memory of an inappropriate sexual experience—the man who will love her and make everything right. Her transsexualism, which transforms her Pygmalion-like into a beautiful and desirable woman, offers a resolution for a number of painful issues: reunion with father/men, eroticized control of men, rejection of her unwanted and rejected male child-self, and triumph over a cruel mother.

She may not be aware of it, but she is very much her mother's daughter. Like her mother, she probably remains emotionally aloof, although she probably makes extremely fast (but superficial) connections with those she senses like her. She probably finds others confusing in their actions, unpredictable, and in the end, disappointing, much as her mother did in her relationships. A major problem for her now is her need to be secretive regarding anything she believes may cause her to be rejected or suffer retraumatization. This secretiveness accompanies a pattern of avoidance that compromises her ability to form the kind of relationships with others that might enable her to work through the traumas that she has experienced in the past.

Intrapsychically, she has not learned to accept herself; her sexuality is a prime example. She has internalized her mother's reactions, especially in light of her sexual assault, and as a result, feels dirty and "bad" about her sexuality. There is a high probability that R. B. was sexually abused, possibly before age 6 if her dates are accurate. As a child, she was needy and "clingy." She wanted to be loved by a man (see Memory of an Inappropriate Sexual Experience). She slept with her father. We know that she suppresses unpleasant memories, so memories in this category would be excellent candidates for repression. In any case, her relationships are deeply ambivalent and highly eroticized.

The Early Memory Procedure demonstrates its power in elucidating themes that organize R. B.'s experience of her issues, conflicts, and perceptions of self and others. After considering her second MMPI, we will now turn to her Rorschach as an independent source of information about R. B.'s personality organization and structure.

R. B.'S SECOND MMPI

R. B.'s second MMPI was given at the same time in late 1991 as her Early Memories Procedure and Rorschach. Her profile yielded a Welsh Code of 862*74''103'9-5: $F*L/K$:. The T-score for the F scale of 98 continued to reflect intense psychological distress and turmoil. Similarly, R. B.'s profile revealed significant elevations on the Paranoia and Schizophrenia scales (T scores of 102 and 106, respectively). The picture was of a deeply paranoid, probably psychotic individual who was severely depressed, angry, and socially withdrawn.

RORSCHACH INTERPRETATION

Review of Structural Data

A preliminary review of R. B.'s Rorschach structural summary (see Appendices B, C, and D), with a special interest in various signs, indices, ratios, and percentages, reveals a brief 14-response record with a relatively low *Lambda* of .27. Exner's search sequence (Exner, 1993), based on positive key variables, yields the following order for data interpretation: self-perception, interpersonal perception, controls, ideation, processing, mediation, and affect. The protocol includes a card rejection at Card IX. The low *Lambda* suggests that although the record is short, it is not overly dominated by form, and is therefore unlikely to reflect conscious efforts at avoiding the task. As further evidence of complexity and potential richness, the record has six blends, all of which involve human movement. Surprisingly, none of the special indices (*DEPI*,

SCZI, CDI, or *S-CON*) are positive. The record reflects a highly introversive (*EB* = 7: 1.0) personality type with affect minimized and strictly controlled (*FC:CF* + *C* = 2:0, *Afr* = .40, Card IX rejection). Consistent with her clinical presentation, the Rorschach data reveal a person whose range of affectivity is severely constricted. Three of R. B.'s seven human movement responses are minus form quality, indicating significant problems in thinking, although she obtains seven populars, reflecting an intact capacity for conventionality. This finding is strengthened by the *X*+% of .43, *F*+% of .33, and *X*–% of .21. In this context, she may appear socially functional from an observer's perspective, but on closer examination the quality of her reasoning and judgment is quite poor. Three of her human responses (*M*) are good form quality, one is unusual, and three are minuses. Two of her *M*– responses are passive, likely reflecting thought disorder, probably of a delusional nature. Her *WSUM6* of 13 is moderately noteworthy, but her Contamination on Card IV is critical. The structural features of this percept indicate a rapid, regressive shift in mental functioning characterized by boundary disturbance and a malevolent transformation. She tends to be an isolated (*Isolate/R* = .50), alienated (*S* = 4), passive (*Ma:Mp* = 3:4), and self-involved person (*3r* + *(2)/R* = 0.64 and *FD* = 1). Despite the significant emotional turmoil she experiences, evidence of situational stress or problems in self-control is mostly absent from the record (*m* = 1; *Y* = 0; right side of *eb* = 2; *es* = 6; and *D* and *Adj D* = 0). Nor does the record contain much evidence of mood disturbance (*DEPI* = 4; *MOR* = 1; *es* = 6), a finding that contradicts her self-report and observable behavior. Stylistically, she is positive on the Hypervigilance Index, maintaining a denial of felt needs for closeness and a mistrustful attitude, which, in combination with her passivity, affective withdrawal, and social isolation, strengthens the impression that she is alienated from ordinary social relations. Turning to content categories, the record is notable for the amount of human content, over half of which is *Hd* or parenthesized. These latter findings suggest that her human relations are organized around part-object or need-driven motivations that interfere with mature perception and interaction. Derepressed contents (*An, Bl, Sx,* etc.), common indicators of trauma, are mostly absent (*An* = 1). The record, on the other hand, has six Clothing (*Cg*) responses, some of which are associated with exhibitionistic human movement (Responses 1, 5, 12). Exhibitionistic human movement is often emphasized in individuals who perform, such as models and dancers. Issues of appearance and being covered seem especially salient.

   In a record as rich in human movement as this one, particularly in light of the poor form quality, one might expect evidence of projection-laden material. This expectation is confirmed in examining individual responses. The "female blowing in the wind" and "face of a monster" (Card I), "women in the time of Toulouse Lautrec" (Card II), "skinny man looking in the mirror trying to pose" (Card III), "witch" (Card IV), "women in veils" (Card VI), "house with an evil spirit" (Card VII), and "woman with a blue bra and feather stoles"

(Card X) all seem rich in projective content. The Contamination response, as mentioned earlier, associated with an uncanny, malevolent transformation on Card IV, reflects the condensation of numerous dynamic elements and an associated severe regression in thought processes.

In summarizing the Rorschach data from the Comprehensive System point of view, R. B.'s record is quite revealing—despite the fact that the record is brief—pointing up her introversion, disturbance in thinking, suppressed affectivity, heightened self-involvement, heightened capacity for regression and recovery, and guarded, alienated social relations.

Content-Analytic Data

In contrast to the sign approach, content analytic approaches derived from psychoanalytic theory significantly augment the interpretive yield. Integrating a "four psychologies" approach (Pine, 1990), content analytic approaches allow for an assessment of the nature and quality of drive expressions, effectiveness of defensive operations, intactness and stability of ego boundaries, and prototypical object relations, including self- and object-representations with their associated affects.

Despite the brevity of the record ($R = 14$), viewed from the Holt scoring of primary process manifestations, R. B.'s record is rich with libidinal and aggressive drive expressions, all of which are at the more benign Level 2 score. Most of her control and defense scores, which reflect defensive operations in the face of drive-laden ideation, are based on remoteness operations (shift of the percept to other contexts): avoidance based on displacement. Generally speaking the effectiveness of her defenses is marginal, as reflected in her Drive Demand × Drive Effectiveness score of –9.5. Responses 6 (the evil woman transforming herself into an orchid) and 10 (house with spirits) reflect thorough defensive failure in the face of intrusive primary process ideation.

Similarly, R. B.'s defensive operations, illustrated in the various Rorschach content scales, are predominantly in the lower or more primitive range (Acklin, 1992; Kernberg, 1976), ranging from Pollyanna-type denial (Response 4), use of remoteness (Responses 3 and 5), and narcissistic mirroring and sexualized exhibitionism (Responses 3, 4, 5, 12), to heavy emphasis on splitting and projective defenses (Responses 2, 6, 10). Responses 1, 6, 9, and possibly 10 are marked by dissociative analogues that have been shown to occur in the records of individuals with dissociative tendencies (Labott, Leavitt, Braun, & Sachs, 1992). Responses 2, 6 and 10 find the self endangered by fear of annihilation, with terror as the accompanying affect. The Lerner and Kwawer scales highlight the degree of splitting, engulfment, and boundary disturbance that characterizes R. B.'s experience of self and others, reflecting functions that are consistent with borderline personality organization.

What is perhaps most interesting is the absence of affective turmoil that is often seen in the records of individuals suffering from psychological trauma (Arnow & Cooper, 1984). It appears that in R. B.'s case, the trauma-induced alterations of her personality functioning, in the context of a highly introversive personality type, have made their impact on her reality testing, perceptions of self and other, and perception of her world. It seems likely that these areas of functioning are infiltrated by delusional thought processes. She seems to have based, and continues to struggle to locate her self-organization around sexual appearance and attractiveness, reflecting narcissistic and hysterical tendencies. These rather fragile and brittle defenses readily decompensate away when triggered, provoking panic-stricken regression where she perceives herself as a target of malevolent, annihilating attack. The perceptions of her mother as an annihilating introject have become fused with elements of her physical and sexual assault. It appears that R. B.'s trauma has been ingrained and internalized as psychic structure, fusing developmental-genetic and posttraumatic elements.

CASE SUMMARY

As this case amply demonstrates, the combination of earliest recollections and Rorschach data enriches the interpretive task by elucidating the narrative themes that organize meanings in R. B.'s life. Structural and dynamic forces illustrate her troubled efforts at maintaining self-organization, narcissistic equilibrium (Stolorow & Lachmann, 1980), and a capacity for adaptation. In R. B.'s case, her early memories point out her early life attachment problems with both parents, her disavowal of both her personhood and masculinity by an obviously troubled mother, and the precocious erotization of her self-image and interpersonal relations as a means of compensating for early loss and capturing the love and attention of men. Her response to her adult rape and assault echoes and recapitulates an early life episode where she was beaten for child sex games. R. B.'s transsexualism seems to have functioned, in part, as a compromise solution for the dynamic conflicts of her childhood: loss of father, a rejected and then disavowed masculine identity, and competition and triumph over mother through her Pygmalion-like self-transformation where she herself became a beautiful and desirable "woman." The structural deficits in her gender identity, despite years of compensation when she seems to have convinced herself and others that she was a real "woman," and the nagging reminders that she could not bear children created the brittle and fault-ridden foundation of her posttraumatic response. Similar to Marilyn Monroe, another sexual goddess with an unstable identity, the desire and adoration she elicited in men consolidated her sense of power, warded off feelings of being an unwanted, motherless child, and allowed her to maintain the illusion that she was "surrounded by love and affection" (Chessick, 1983). Nevertheless, also like Marilyn Monroe, R. B.'s inability to be a "real woman," that is, to have a baby "was a dagger at her ego" (Rosten, 1973, p. 46). In a sense, her masquerade has a delusional quality. As a woman, R. B. lived in a perfect dream-world, a sort of escape from reality, until she was assaulted. Aside from the focus on trauma, many issues in R. B.'s therapy reflected the vicissitudes of narcissism in late midlife (Kernberg, 1975), where loss of attractiveness and allure provokes a sense of painful absence. The role of aggression in R. B.'s psychic economy is particularly interesting inasmuch as it is bound to eroticism: control of men, competition and triumph over mother, and finally, punishment for the dream of being self-made, complete, and goddesslike in sexual beauty, perfection, and allure. Sexuality for R. B. had the dual function of obtaining the love of a lost father, simultaneously expressing revenge obtaining and control.

What seems clear, after having reviewed and integrated the rich yield of data in this case, is the fact that nomothetic and idiographic, as well as structural and thematic data, complement and enrich each other in broadening and deepening a personological investigation. The malevolent quality of her object relations reflected in her early memories, with themes of both annihilation and abandonment, suggest correlative problems in structure and organization. Conversely, given the nature of the structural problems noted in the Rorschach, one should not be surprised that the thematic material should reflect primitive dangers and anxieties.

With respect to her current functioning, the data reflect both primitive themes of attack as well as a fluid, fragile, and easily destabilized array of defensive adaptations. Analyses of structural, content, and defensive operations suggest that R. B.'s personality organization at the time of the 1991 assessment falls into the borderline range of personality organization (Gacono, Meloy, & Berg, 1992) with an array of ineffective, hysteroid, and sometimes psychotic defenses.

To describe R. B. as a shattered self would be no understatement. Her bold ambition to rise above the ashes of childhood defeat and refashion herself, Pygmalion-like, into a goddess, recalls figures of Greek mythology who heroically but tragically challenged divine necessity.

REFERENCES

Acklin, M. W. (1991). Alexithymia, somatization, and the Rorschach response process. *Rorschachiana, 17*, 180–187.

Acklin, M. W. (1992). Psychodiagnosis of personality structure: Psychotic personality organization. *Journal of Personality Assessment, 58*, 454–463.

Acklin, M. W. (1993). Psychodiagnosis of personality structure II: Borderline personality organization. *Journal of Personality Assessment, 61*, 329–341.

Acklin, M. W. (1994). Psychodiagnosis of personality structure III: Neurotic personality organization. *Journal of Personality Assessment, 63*, 1–9.

Acklin, M. W. (1995). Integrative Rorschach interpretation. *Journal of Personality Assessment, 64*, 235–238.

Acklin, M. W., & Alexander, G. (1988). Alexithymia and somatization: A Rorschach study of four psychosomatic groups. *Journal of Nervous and Mental Disease, 176*, 343–350.

Acklin, M. W., Bibb, J. L., Boyer, P., & Jain, V. (1991). Early memories as expressions of relationship paradigms: A preliminary investigation. *Journal of Personality Assessment, 57*, 177–192.

Acklin, M. W., & Wright, D. (1997). *Rorschach content analysis.* Manuscript in preparation.

Arnow, D., & Cooper, S. (1984). The borderline patient's regression on the Rorschach test. *Bulletin of the Menniger Clinic, 48*, 25–36.

Aronow, E., & Reznikoff, M. (1976). *Rorschach content interpretation.* New York: Grune & Stratton.

Blanck, G., & Blanck, R. (1975). *Ego psychology: Theory and practice.* New York: Columbia University Press.

Blatt, S. (1995). Representational structures in psychopathology. In D. Cicchetti & S. L. Toth (Eds.), *Rochester symposium on developmental psychopathology: Vol. VI. Emotion, cognition, and representation* (pp. 1–33). Rochester, NY: University of Rochester Press.

Blatt, S., Brenneis, C., Schimek, J., & Glick, M. (1976). *A developmental analysis of the concept of the object on the Rorschach.* Unpublished manuscript, Department of Psychology, Yale University, New Haven, CT.

Blatt, S., D'Affliti, J. P., & Quinlan, D. M. (1976). Experiences of depression in normal young adults. *Journal of Abnormal Psychology, 85*, 383–389.

Blatt, S., & Lerner, H. (1983). The psychological assessment of object representation. *Journal of Personality Assessment, 47*, 20–28.

Bruhn, A. R. (1989). *The early memories procedure.* Bethesda, MD: Arnold R. Bruhn.

Bruhn, A. R. (1990). *Earliest childhood memories: Vol. 1: Theory and application to clinical practice.* New York: Praeger.

Bruhn, A. R. (1992a). The Early Memories Procedure (Part I): A projective test for autobiographical memory. *Journal of Personality Assessment, 55*, 1–15.

Bruhn, A. R. (1992b). The Early Memories Procedure (Part II): A projective test of autobiographical memory. *Journal of Personality Assessment, 58*, 326–346.

Bruhn, A. R. (1995). Early memories in personality assessment. In J. Butcher (Ed.), *Clinical personality assessment: Practical approaches* (pp. 278–301). New York: Oxford University Press.

Burgess, A. (1983). Rape trauma syndrome. *Behavioral Sciences and the Law, 1*, 97–113.

Chessick, R. D. (1983). Marilyn Monroe: Psychoanalytic pathography of a preoedipal disorder. *Dynamic Psychotherapy, 1*, 161–176.

Coonerty, S. (1986). An exploration of separation-individuation themes in the borderline personality disorder. *Journal of Personality Assessment, 50*, 501–511.

Cooper, S., & Arnow, D. (1986). An object relations view of the borderline defenses: A Rorschach analysis. In M. Kissen (Ed.), *Assessing object relations phenomena* (pp. 143–171). Madison, CT: International Universities Press.

Cooper, S., Perry, J., & Arnow, D. (1988). An empirical approach to the study of defense mechanisms: I. Reliability and preliminary validity of the Rorschach defense scale. *Journal of Personality Assessment, 52*, 187–203.

Cooper, S., Perry, J., & O'Connell, M. (1991). The Rorschach defense scales: II. Longitudinal perspectives. *Journal of Personality Assessment, 56*, 191–201.

Erikson, E. H. (1950). *Childhood and society.* New York: Norton.

Exner, J. E., Jr. (1991). *The Rorschach: A comprehensive system: Vol. II. Interpretation.* (2nd ed.). New York: Wiley.

Exner, J. E., Jr. (1993). *The Rorschach: A comprehensive system: Vol. I. Basic foundations* (3rd ed.) New York: Wiley.

Exner, J. E., Jr., & Weiner, I. B. (1995). *The Rorschach: A comprehensive system: Vol. III. Assessment of children and adolescents.* New York: Wiley.

Frazier, P. A. (1990). Victim attributions and post-rape trauma. *Journal of Personality and Social Psychology, 59,* 298–304.

Freud, A. (1963). The concept of developmental lines. *Psychoanalytic Study of the Child, 18,* 245–265.

Freud, S. (1923). The ego and the id. *Standard Edition, 19,* 3–66.

Gacono, C., & Meloy, J. R. (1994). *The Rorschach assessment of aggressive and psychopathic personalities.* Hillsdale, NJ: Lawrence Erlbaum Associates.

Gacono, C., Meloy, J. R., and Berg, J. (1992). Object relations, defensive operations, and affective states in narcissistic, borderline, and antisocial personality disorder. *Journal of Personality Assessment, 59,* 32–49.

Gedo, J., & Goldberg, A. (1973). *Models of the mind: A psychoanalytic theory.* Chicago: University of Chicago Press.

Hathaway, S., & McKinley, J. (1970). *The Minnesota Multiphasic Personality Inventory.* Minneapolis: University of Minnesota Press.

Holt, R. (1970). *Manual for the scoring of primary process manifestations in Rorschach responses* (10th ed.). New York: New York University, Research Center for Mental Health.

Holt, R., & Havel, J. (1960). A method for assessing primary and secondary process in the Rorschach. In M. Rickers-Ovsiankina (Ed.), *Rorschach psychology* (pp. 263–315). New York: Wiley.

Kernberg, O. (1975). *Borderline conditions and pathological narcissism.* New York: Aronson.

Kernberg, O. (1976). *Object relations in clinical psychoanalysis.* New York: Aronson.

Kernberg, O. (1992). *Aggression in personality disorders and perversions.* New Haven, CT: Yale University Press.

Kohut, H. (1971). *The analysis of the self.* New York: International Universities Press.

Krohn, A., & Mayman, M. (1974). Object-representations in dreams and projective tests. *Bulletin of the Menninger Clinic, 38,* 445–466.

Krystal, H. (1978). Trauma and affects. *The Psychoanalytic Study of the Child, 33,* 81–116.

Krystal, H. (1988). *Integration and self healing: Affect, trauma, alexithymia.* Hillsdale, NJ: The Analytic Press.

Kwawer, J. (1979). Borderline phenomena, interpersonal relations, and the Rorschach test. *Bulletin of the Menninger Clinic, 43,* 515–524.

Kwawer, J. (1980). Primitive interpersonal modes, borderline phenomena and Rorschach content. In J. Kwawer, P. Lerner, H. Lerner, & A. Sugarman (Eds.), *Borderline phenomena and the Rorschach test* (pp. 89–109). New York: International Universities Press.

Labott, S. M., Leavitt, F., Braun, B. G., & Sachs, R. S. (1992). Rorschach indicators of multiple personality. *Perceptual and Motor Skills, 75,* 147–158.

Lebowitz, L., Harvey, M., & Herman, J. (1993). A stage-by-dimension model of recovery from sexual trauma: Special Issue: Research on treatment of adults sexually abused in childhood. *Journal of Interpersonal Violence, 8,* 378–391.

Lerner, H. (1986). An object representation approach to Rorschach assessment. In M. Kissen (Ed.) *Assessing object relations phenomena* (pp. 127–142). Madison, CT: International Universities Press.

Lerner, H. D., & Lerner, P. M. (1988). *Primitive mental states and the Rorschach.* New York: International Universities Press.

Lerner, H., Albert, C., & Walsh, M. (1987). The Rorschach assessment of borderline defenses: A concurrent validity study. *Journal of Personality Assessment, 51,* 334–348.

Lerner, H., & St. Peter, S. (1984). The Rorschach response and object relations. *Journal of Personality Assessment, 48,* 345–350.

Lerner, P. (1990). Rorschach assessment of primitive defenses: A review. *Journal of Personality Assessment, 54,* 30–46.

Lerner, P. (1991). *Psychoanalytic theory and the Rorschach.* Hillsdale, NJ: The Analytic Press.

Lerner, P., & Lerner, H. (1980). Rorschach assessment of primitive defenses in borderline personality structure. In J. Kwawer, P. Lerner, H. Lerner, & A. Sugarman (Eds.), *Borderline phenomena and the Rorschach test* (pp. 257–274). New York: International Universities Press.

Loevinger, J. (1976). *Ego development: Conceptions and theories.* San Francisco: Jossey-Bass.

Luborsky, L. (1984). *Principles of psychoanalytic psychotherapy.* New York: Basic Books.

Mahler, M. (1968). *On human symbiosis and the vicissitudes of individuation.* Madison, CT: International Universities Press.

Mahler, M., Pine, F., & Bergman, A. (1975). *The psychological birth of the human infant.* New York: Basic Books.

Mayman, M. (1968). Early memories and character structure. *Journal of Projective Techniques and Personality Assessment, 32,* 303–316.

Mayman, M., & Faris, M. (1960). Early memories as expressions of relationship paradigms. *American Journal of Orthopsychiatry, 30,* 507–520.

Mayr, S., & Price, J. (1989). The Io syndrome: Symptom formation in victims of sexual abuse. *Perspectives in Psychiatric Care, 25,* 36–39.

McCann, I. L., & Pearlman, L. A. (1990). *Psychological trauma and the adult survivor: Theory, therapy, and transformation.* New York: Brunner/Mazel.

Meloy, J. R., & Gacono, C. (1992). The aggression response and the Rorschach. *Journal of Clinical Psychology, 48,* 104–114.

Pine, F. (1990). *Drive, ego, object, and self: A clinical synthesis.* New York: Basic Books.

Rosten, N. (1973). *Marilyn: An untold story.* New York: Signet.

Saxe, G., Van der Kolk, B., Berkowitz, R., & Chinman, G. (1993). Dissociative disorders in psychiatric inpatients. *American Journal of Psychiatry, 150,* 1038–1042.

Stolorow, R., & Lachmann, F. (1980). *Psychoanalysis of developmental arrest.* New York: International Universities Press.

Ulman, R. B., & Brothers, D. (1988). *The shattered self: A psychoanalytic study of trauma.* Hillsdale, NJ: The Analytic Press.

Urist, J. (1977). The Rorschach test and the assessment of object relations. *Journal of Personality Assessment, 41,* 3–9.

Urist, J. (1980). The continuum between primary and secondary process thinking: Toward a concept of borderline thought. In J. Kwawer, P. Lerner, H. Lerner, & A. Sugarman (Eds.), *Borderline phenomena and the Rorschach test* (pp. 257–274). New York: International Universities Press.

Van der Kolk, B. A., & Ducey, C. P. (1989). The psychological processing of traumatic experience: Rorschach patterns in PTSD. *Journal of Traumatic Stress, 2,* 259–274.

Waigandt, C., & Miller, D. A. (1986). Maladaptive responses during the reorganization phase of rape trauma syndrome. *Response to the Victimization of Women and Children, 9,* 20–21.

Werner, H. (1957). *Comparative psychology of mental development.* New York: International Universities Press.

EM 1:

I am about (+/−) 1 year old. It's dark, raining, and my mother carries me in her arms, talking with my father. All of the sudden he slaps her face—she loses her balance. Daddy is screaming, taking me away from her. She's in pain, she cries, and daddy slapped her once more. She runs into the rainy night, crying. I cry . . . am afraid. Mommy, mommy. She's gone!

Daddy let me sleep in their big bed and is so nice but I want my mommy and I cry. In the morning my mommy is there all by herself. I start to cry again, she helps me to get me out of the big bed.

Clearest Part: My mother walking into the rain and darkness, leaving me alone.

Strongest Feeling: Daddy talking so sweet and nice to me when he was mean to Mommy a minute ago.

Changes: Not to have this memory at all or daddy hugging Mommy and let me sleep between them in that big bed.

Age: One year or 11 months.

Precis: Dad is mean one minute and nice the next *or* my parents fought and my mother abandoned me.

Perception of Self: Upset and afraid when mom leaves and Dad is screaming.

Perception of Others: (Mother): Abandons her to Dad; (Father) labile mood, which is difficult to predict.

Perception of World: Unpredictable, unstable, frightening.

Major Issues: 1) Attachment issues; 2) Trust (cannot predict Dad's moods); 3) Abandonment anxiety.

Comment: She seems most concerned about predictability/dependability—being able to count on others and depend on them for security/protection.

EM 2:

Granny is taking care of my little brother and me. I have no parents. Mom is in another room waiting for divorce papers. Daddy comes only now and then. He lives in the same street and my Mommy is walking my brother and me every day past his house. I see him kissing the other woman and Mommy saying she is a bad woman.

I am sick and daddy comes to see me with presents. I am so happy and never, never want to let him go. Granny is taking me out of the room and when we are back daddy is gone, I cry. Was he there or not?

Clearest Part: Hugging and kissing him and holding him so close.

Strongest Feeling: He left me alone.

Changes: Daddy would bring Mommy home and he would live in our house.

Age: 3 years

Precis: Daddy came to visit me and brought me presents but abandoned me.

Perception of Self: Abandoned.

Perception of Others: (Father): Disloyal (kissing other woman), unreliable (leaves her).

Major Issues: 1) Attachment issues (abandoned by *both* parents in this memory); 2) Self and object constancy and reality testing (was Dad there or did I just want him to be?—abandonment appears to cause sufficient stress that reality testing becomes problematic).

Process Interpretation: Ambivalent, anxious attachment is the common element in both EMs. If anything, this theme is stronger in the EM 2, as she is abandoned by both mother and father and "dumped" for father's girlfriend. The kissing element in this memory makes me wonder if she tends to sexualize relationships as a way of holding on, which is a major problem for her in a primary relationship ("I am so happy and never want to let him go").

EM 3:

My auntie, Mom's sister, was dancing in a ballet show. Her son and husband took me with them. I am excited to see those beautiful girls in those beautiful costumes. In the intermission, suddenly daddy comes. He was playing in the band from that show. I am so happy and excited, but he says "Jackie, don't ruin my jacket." I was eating candy! My uncle took me and said "look there is auntie." I look, then I want to say some things to Daddy but he's gone again. I am sad and in pain. I look down at the floor watching the bare feet of the dancers, they were dirty.

Clearest Part: The dirty feet of my auntie, they danced the ballet without shoes.

Strongest Feeling: The surprise of seeing my father. I told my cousin, "You see, I have a daddy too like you."

Changes: Daddy picking me up. Running away with me home to mommy.

Age: 3 or 4 years.

EM 4:

I cry a lot. My favorite aunt is the sister of granny. I adore her. She always smells like violet flowers. She often put me to sleep in her bed and wait till I fall asleep. I adore and love her my whole life. I cry again one evening. A brother of my mother comes into the room. He shakes me, tells me to be quiet and for the first time I feel a slap on my face. I am in shock. I stopped crying, but my aunty screams at him. "Not the face, don't slap the face."

Clearest Part: The fresh smell of her flower perfume.

Strongest Feeling: The slap in my face.

Changes: 'Til today I wish I could give this back to that man. I never forget the slap.

Age: 4 years.

Precis: After I unexpectedly saw my Daddy, he criticized me for being dirty and left me again.

Perception of Self: Abandoned and "bad" in some way—dirty.

Perception of Others (Father): Critical, distancing, rejecting ("Don't ruin my jacket").

Major Issue: Attachment issues, preoccupation with abandonment and reunion.

Process Interpretation: The repetition of content themes between EMs 1, 2, and 3 is unusual in a set of spontaneous EMs. R. B. is fixated on having been abandoned, on not being able to count on others. The one *new element* in this memory is that she wonders if she had a role in her being abandoned (she was messy from having eaten candy). That her aunt had dirty feet makes me wonder if she is not having problems with herself as a woman: "women are unclean." This theme pervades her current obsessive-compulsive preoccupations with showering and removing her feelings of being dirty, especially her feet.

Precis: When I am upset and need TLC, I expect men to be impatient and unsympathetic, or even angry with me.

Perception of Self: Easily upset.

Perception of Others (Uncle): Impatient, unsympathetic, rejecting. (Auntie): Enfolding in feminine warmth and fragrance.

Major Issue: Security/soothing/protection.

Process Interpretation: This memory almost exactly repeats the form of EM 1—except that she is slapped by her uncle versus her mother is slapped by her father. The message appears to be that she (women) cannot expect much sympathy and understanding from men and they are punished somehow.

Comment: We see some signs of splitting in relationships—there is the favorite aunt who is sensitive to her feelings and needs, and there is her uncle who is impatient and unsympathetic. It is becoming very apparent that she has problems with male relationships.

(continued)

EM 5:

Mommy is living with another man. I hate him! He always, when we were noisy or fighting, took our feet and put our heads into the lavatory. My brother is sometimes red in his face. So long he kept us that way with our heads dangling into the lavatory. I hate him! I hate him! One day all of a sudden Daddy comes. I am so happy, and this time I do not let go of him. I hold him when he eats or sits or whatever. He is my Daddy. When that other man comes home, I feel secure for the first time because Daddy's presence. I sleep with him in the bed close. I adore my father.

Clearest Part: Sitting on my father's knee when he (that man) comes into the house and feel not afraid because my Daddy is *there.*

Strongest Feeling: Holding my father close to me.

Changes: My father beating up that man. Mommy was so in love with him. I hated him!

Age: 6 years.

Precis: 1) When I did anything wrong, I was threatened with annihilation; 2) When I feel threatened, I look for someone to protect me (probably male) and try to fuse with this person ("this time I do not let go of him"). Attachment to men is ephemeral, reflecting problems in object constancy.

Perception of Self: Severely punished when naughty/bad; clingy and dependent with those who seem protective/caring.

Perception of Others: (Mother's Boyfriend): Threatening, not in control of his anger, lacking in judgement; (Father) Protective and evanescent.

Major Issues: 1) Separation; 2) Security/protection/trust.

Process Interpretation: This memory introduces a new element to her by now well-established concerns about attachment and security: her tendency to fuse with a significant other (male) when she feels threatened. As we scan her previous EMs, we find that father is represented as a volatile (EM1) and undependable man who is nice one minute and absent the next. Once she feels threatened, however, other feelings/concerns are set aside, and she fuses with father, with significant eroticized overtones. The last part is extremely disquieting—she goes to bed with him. This makes me wonder if her concerns about security/annihilation (being flushed down the toilet) have not left her vulnerable to being sexually abused. Specifically, she may have bartered an inappropriate sexual relationship in exchange for security/protection. [This is exactly what happened in her childhood relations with other boys. See below.]

EM 6:

It's afternoon and we children are in a room alone. We are playing doctor. My brother, cousin and me. All of a sudden we play cow and I start to lick his penis. His mother comes into the room, calling my mother. I am afraid. She closes the door and has a bamboo stick in her hand. "You filthy, dirty, rotten child," she said. "Why didn't I kill you at birth?" She beats me over my body, legs and face. I scream. I beg her to stop. I crawl over the floor and she beats my whole body 'til the bamboo breaks in parts. I am a mess. She leaves the room.

Precis: I associate sexual urges, which bring others, especially males, close to me with being bad/dirty and with deserving punishment.

Perception of Self: Having strong sexual drive/interests, driven by attachment issues, and feeling dirty and punished as a result.

Perception of Others: (Mother): Extraordinarily hostile about sexual matters. Overly severe and inappropriate in her role as disciplinarian—lacking in judgement and self-restraint and disowning the child's right to exist.

Clearest Part: The beating and screaming of my mother without stopping. The merciless look and all the frustrations she had about life for which I pay dearly.

Strongest Feeling: The beating with the bamboo stick. And the red, blue and purple streams (sic)on my face, body and legs.

Changes: I wish I never had done this to my cousin—never had the urge to do it.

Age: 6 or 7 years.

Additional Memory

Strange enough, there will be two more similar situations like this with my cousin! Another cousin, another schech (sic)! This time my mother didn't touch me but told me that she will "sell me to someone" and she means it! I beg her "please to forgive." She rejects me in all I try to do to please her. She is so cold and looks at me, saying all the time, "Why, why, why?!!!" I crawl to her and beg for mercy. But she is cold as ice, and I feel hopeless, rotten, dirty.

Clearest Part: The coldness of my mother's face—her rejection.

Strongest Feeling: The empty lonely feeling to be alone and "ashamed" about myself.

Changes: Not to have those feelings of playing "cow" or doctor with my cousins.

Age: 7 years.

Major Issues: 1) Security/protection/trust; 2) Sexuality.

Process Interpretation: Our concerns about sexual abuse (EM 5) are strengthened. Where did she learn to "play cow"? Throughout this series of EMs, we find issues with judgement and appropriateness on the part of several authority figures (see especially EMs 4,5) where she is slapped by an uncle (mother's brother) and threatened with being flushed down the toilet by mother's boyfriend. Now mother herself brutally beats her. Throughout, we observe evidence of pathological object relations in which others are perceived in polar terms: as desirable sources of comfort or malevolently punishing and abandoning. What appears increasingly evident is a pattern of over-reactions to minimal or questionable misconduct on her part. These experiences mirror a difficulty on her part to adequately assess the appropriateness of her actions. As a result she probably experiences intense anxiety, panic, depression, rage and guilt, depending on how much she blames herself and how much she blames others.

[See memory 6. Memories with the same form, as this one well illustrates, reinforce our beliefs that the issues involved are highly significant. There is no question in my opinion that sexuality is a major issue. She feels intense guilt about gratifying her sexual needs. Put in baldest terms, she feels like a whore and, due to her experiences with her mother, may act out her mother's image of her in a manner that compulsively repeats what she has described in Memory 6.]

(continued)

Summary of EM Affect and Clarity Rating

EM	*Affect Rating	**Clarity Rating
1	1	5
2	2	3
3	3	5
4	2	5
5	3	2
6	1	5

* 1 = very negative; 5 = very positive
** 1 = very unclear; 5 = exceptionally clear

Most Significant Memories (Client Rated)

Primary significance: EM1
Secondary significance: EM6
Tertiary significance: EM4

Note: The affect and clarity ratings allow for a more differentiated assessment of specific memory features. Memories that are high on affect, and clarity, especially when they are rated as significant, are indicative of highly salient emotional issues that have continuing relevance.

Q: Why are these memories important to you?
A: They are important, but still feel the pain and nervousness when I think back or when some similar situation happens. The first impressions of life now seemed to have an impact on my whole being! My mind and feelings.

Q: Why do you think you recall these from all your childhood experiences?
A: I was so young when confronted with those situations. I don't know why they are engraved in me since those times are so far away but so clear in my mind! I always become hysterical when a man and woman start fighting in front of me. Or a TV special when he beats her around and she screams. I always check and become nervous watching these situations.

EMP Part 2—Selected Memories

A Memory of Mother:

Her strange possessive love—her cursing, rude language. Her glamorous looks, her "I don't care" attitude.

Clearest Part: Her always saying: "Do not cry . . . never cry . . . Stop crying."

Strongest Feeling: We (my brother) and I always had our hands and arms over our heads when she called us to come to her—afraid for a sudden beating.

Changes: "Mommy, Mommy, don't curse me. Don't you use His name in vain . . . please."

Age: 8, 9, or 10 years.

Comment: This is a pattern (repeated event) memory or a description, not a single event memory. The description follows in the same vein as her rendition of her previous two memories. Trust and safety are major issues—for example, "we . . . always had our hands and arms over our heads when she called us to come to her" and "her strange possessive love" and "her 'I don't care' attitude." Such an erratic and unpredictable object is impossible to bond to appropriately. As a negative pattern memory, it clearly represents her meta-issue—trusting and bonding to her primary object.

A Memory of Father:

The war is over. We are back in B. again. One day we were having lunch at home, Mommy, my brother and little step-brother baby. The maid brings in a man. He is darker, older. My brothers don't know who he is. And suddenly I see my Daddy. He smiles, he looks at me and I see tears. He holds me up close to him. Daddy's home. I love him. I love him so much. He found us. I wished. I hoped. I prayed.

Clearest Part: The man standing in the doorway smiling at us.

Strongest Feeling: Back again with us. He is my Daddy.

Changes: My mother was sarcastic and he was married to another woman. Oh, how I wished they could be together like a family again.

Age: 12 years.

Happiest Memory:

The year 1973. We were having a great birthday party for my mother and stepbrother. All the family were there (about 80 people). I was rich, a woman, an artist and beautiful. . . . That night we had a 1/2 stage over the swimming pool. The pool was pink with flowers and candles, and I danced for them in the traditional way. The spirits of my grandparents and aunt were there. They all were melted and I felt like in heaven.

Clearest Part: To enter the garden, going on stage with all the candles and flowers in the pool.

Strongest Feeling: The tears from women, men (big strong guys) while I danced for the first time as a woman for them! My mother's and brother's tears.

Changes: I cannot! This was my life and I was I. I am who I am. Honest. A woman and loved by them.

A Traumatic Memory:

The day . . . I got raped, beaten and almost killed. My whole face, body and womanhood was destroyed. All I have worked for, suffered for, wished for, were gone by this stranger. This is also the part of a woman (sic), being raped and sexually assaulted.

Precis: Out of nowhere came my father, but he had remarried so he was therefore inaccessible and my parents could not be together again.

Comment: This memory virtually repeats the form of EM 2, her attempt to undo the effect of EM 1, her most significant memory.

Precis: I was happiest as a woman when my family was around me, I was the center of attention and through dance and my extravagant femininity I found a way to get what I need.

Comment: This must have been a powerful healing experience for she was accepted in a manner that reversed the rejection she experienced in Memory 6 and the Additional Memory. It seems to capture a compromise that forms the basis for her adult character.

(continued)

Clearest Part: My trembling two dogs while he was raping and beating my body. I was afraid for them. Not even me.

Strongest Feeling: I had no feelings of pain and it was like watching a stage or TV.

Changes: The day/night is a bad dream and does not exist.

Age: 53 years.

An Incident That Made You Feel Ashamed:

A returning feeling of shame all my adult life was when women or sometimes men telling their friends: "she's not a woman but a man" and them looking at me like a freak or disgusting piece of meat.

Clearest Part: The pain of rejection.

Strongest Feeling: Not to belong in society and always being an outcast!

Changes: Was born a normal woman who could have a baby.

Age: 28 years.

A Memory of Being Physically or Emotionally Abused:
[EM 4 and EM 6]

A Memory of An Inappropriate Sexual Experience:

Right after the second world war. Mommy met a major of the army. Strong, tall, handsome and nice. She and he lived like man and wife. I liked him alot. Later they separated. We met him again a couple of years [later] and I feel a strange attraction for him. At night he slept in my brother's bed and my brother in Mom's rooms—she had gone away for two days to her future husband. He asked me, "Are you asleep?" I said "No." He said goodnight and bowed over me naked as he was (sic). Suddenly we were on the floor making love.

Clearest Part: The wonderful feeling of being desired and loved for myself.

Strongest Feeling: His strong body and his completely enjoying of me in our sexual act.

Age: 12 years.

perience largely undoes what she gained from her previous memory, that is, the solution to her problems by sex change.

Comment: Again, this is not a single event but a recurring situation (pattern memory) that highlights her sense of being an outcast and a reject, which have deep roots for her—e.g., being abandoned (EM 1) and being severely punished (EM 6, Additional Memory). Her infertility provides "objective" evidence that there is something wrong with her, that she truly is not normal. Her sex change, while a compromise to the rejection of her masculinity and a solution to abandonment by father—comes with a heavy cost.

Comment: My strongest impression is how vulnerable she must be to such experiences, considering her own need to be loved and wanted, her experience of being abandoned by men and rejected, and her own apparently strong libido. It is interesting that her mother's apparent problems with judgement and self-control are reflected in the Major. Her eroticized reaction to the Major carries overtones of a father-daughter relationship.

A Fantasy Memory:

This fantasy memory was part of my wishes that I had when I was all that makes a woman: beautiful, rich, adored, free of pain sometimes, and not remembering my childhood memories any more! Living my own life far away from Mommy and all the family! When I was with the man I loved more than life itself. Where we talked of adopting a baby, marriage and traveling around the world when I was 45 years. When all was so beautiful.

Comment: The fantasy memory usually functions to gratify the individual's strongest unmet need. Her fantasy memory confirms all that we have said about R. B.—that she has considerable difficulty with her self image, especially with herself as a woman.

I.

1. It's a person, a female who throws open her coat and the wind's blowing and her coat is blowing in the air and her hands are up in the air and this is her body. She's in the sea and all the little pieces of sand are falling down. It's a large coat.

S: This is the body, this is her hands, and she throws her large cape open, blowing by the wind, and this is part of the coat, and all the little shells and sand fall off.
E: (?)
S: Because of the wind, when you throw something it goes open like that.

Structural Scoring: W+ Ma.mao H,Cg,Na ZA
Holt Score: Fu 4 L2E–V O–beh DD = 2 DE = 1.5 DDXDE = 3
Aggression Scores: None
Primitive Modes of Relating: Engulfment
Defenses: None

2. It's the face of a monster, the eyes are terrible . . . the teeth.

E: (Rpts S's response)
S: Here are the eyes, the teeth are outside. The whole face is disfigured and maybe looks like a type of devil.

Structural Scoring: WSo Fu (Hd) ZW MOR
Holt Score: Fu 2 L2O–Ag Ag2A Ag2R Rficn O–exp DD = 3 DE = –1 DDXDE = –3
Aggression Scores: Aggressive Potential
Primitive Modes of Relating: Engulfment
Defenses: Devaluation, Projection, Projective Identification

II.

3. Two women with red hair in the time of Toulouse Lautrec, the painter, giving . . . clap . . . kneeling and giving one hand and holding something in the other. They are excited.

E: (Rpt's S's response)
S: This is the hair, up, these are the faces, the one hand held out, they are kneeling, these are the feet, I put one hand like this, and the other clapping their hands, this part is their coat.

Structural Scoring: W+ Ma.FCo 2 H,Cg,Hx,Ay ZW AB COP
Holt Score: Fu 3 L2S L2H VP2 O–beh O–exp R–time:me Cx–C DD = 2 DE = +1.5 DDXDE = 3.0
Aggression Scores: None
Primitive Modes of Relating: Symbiotic merging, Mirroring
Defenses: Isolation, Intellectualization, Splitting, Pollyannish denial

4. I see two dogs, two very cute dogs sniffling a bone.

E: (Rpt's S's response)
S: This is a dog, and this is a dog, this is their mouth and this is the bone, feet very cute, they're holding their noses to the bone. Ears.

Structural Scoring: D+ FMpu 2 A,Fd P ZA DV1
Holt Score: Fu 1 L2O–ag VP2 R–am o–beh; DD = 2 DE = .5 DDXDE = 1.0
Aggression Scores: None
Primitive Modes of Relating: None
Defenses: Idealization, Pollyannish denial

III.

5. I always see double . . . it's from Toulouse Lautrec, this is a dancer, a very skinny man looking in the mirror trying to pose.

E: (Rpt's S's response)
S: This is his face, this is his jacket, legs and bottom, and shoes, sharp pointed shoes.

Structural Scoring: D+ Mp.Fro H,Cg,Ay P ZD DV1
Holt Score: Fo 3 L2E–V R–time; Refl DD = 2 DE = 1.5 DDXDE = 3.0
Aggression Scores: None

Primitive Modes of Relating: Narcissistic mirroring
Defenses: Isolation, Intellectualization

IV.

6. Oh God, it's an evil woman, it's a witch. She has . . . she can change herself into anything, she has a large collar around her face and she can change her coat into boots and walk and run away. She's a evil woman. She can change if she wants to, into a porcelain flower, like an orchid.

E: (Rpts S's response)
S: Here is the face of the woman, here is a kind of heart or an organ, this is the coat and she's very slender, very tall, this is the body of the woman.
E: (?)
S: She can change herself, it's a flower, just only here, and the coat she can change into boots.

Structural Scoring: W+ Fu (H),Cg,An, Hx P 4.0 AB, CONTAM
Holt Score: Fu 4 Ag2A Cinl 1 Dchain 1 Trans 1 AvEl2 R–fic n
O–pot Va– DD = 5 DE = –3 DDXDE = –1.5
Aggression Scores: Aggressive Content
Primitive Modes of Relating: Engulfment, Boundary disturbance, Malignant internal processes
Defenses: Devaluation, Splitting, Hypomanic Denial, Projective Identification

V.

7. It's a bat . . . animal . . . he's flying away.

E: (Rpt's S's response)
S: This is his feet, head and wings
E: (?)
S: Because he's stretched.

Structural Scoring: Wo FMao A P 1.0
Holt Score: Fo 1 L20–Ag (wk)R–an O–beh DD = 1 DE = .5 DDXDE = .5
Aggression Scores: None
Primitive Modes of Relating: None
Defenses: None

VI.

8. It's a door that cannot be opened, a long hallway.

E: (Rpt's S's response)
S: This is the door, see it's so close, it's a long hallway. The white is the opening to go to the other part.

Structural Scoring: D+ FC'u Id 2.5
Holt Score: Fu 3 L2M(?) R–min DD = 1 DE = .5 DDXDE = .5
Aggression Scores: None
Primitive Modes of Relating: Boundary Disturbance, Womb Imagery, Engulfment
Defenses: Denial

9. Two women with light veils, like Arabian women, you can see only the eyes, standing in front of the large door, it's just open but you cannot go in.

E: (Rpt's S's response)
S: This is the woman with long cape and veils, with veils.
E: (?)
S: Because they're so tall standing in front all covered
E: (?)
S: You can not see the eyes, just a profile.

Structural Scoring: D+ Mp.FD– 2 H,Cg,Ay 2.5
Holt Score: F– 4 L2EV Ctr–L 1 R– = eth O–beh DD = 3 DE = –.5 DDXDE = –1.5
Aggression Scores: None
Primitive Modes of Relating: Boundary Disturbance, Womb Imagery
Defenses: Hypomanic Denial, Isolation, Intellectualization

(continued)

477

VII.

10. (V) A white house with a bad spirit, an evil spirit in the house. Around the house are clouds, good spirits guiding over the house where the bad spirits are trying to destroy the house. There's a lot of water by the house.

E: (Rpt's S's response)
S: This is the house, this is the water, and this is the evil spirit, the dark part above it are good spirits in the cloud, they protect the house from evil spirits.

Structural Scoring: WS+ Ma.FC'u Id, (H),Na,Cl,Hx 4.0 AB,AG, COP
Holt Score: Fu 4 2Ag2A SymI Rficn O–beh DD = 5 DE = +.5 DDXDE = +2.5
Aggression Scores: Aggressive Content, Aggressive Potential
Primitive Modes of Relating: Engulfment, Boundary Disturbance
Defenses: Splitting, Projective Identification

VIII.

11. Two rats, they are trying to climb a tree, a pine tree, they're very big, the rats. Under them are two other rats that cannot climb up. But are looking at them.

E: (Rpt's S's response)
S: This is the tree, pine tree, made like a pine tree, pointing, rat, feet, feet, trying to climb up. And other rats, just the head, like up. Both looking up.

Structural Scoring: W+ FMa–pu 2 A,Ad,Bt P 4.5
Holt Score: Fu 1 Ag2A R–an O–beh DD = 1 DE = 0 DDXDE = 0
Aggression Scores: None
Primitive Modes of Relating: None
Defenses: Devaluation, Projection

IX.

Rejection

X.

12. So strange . . . I see the face of a woman, the woman has a blue bra and two feather stoles.

E: (Rpt's S's response)
S: Here is the woman, her eyes, nose, and mouth, and bra that she wears, a small bra, and a feather stole, the pink is the feather stole, blue are the crabs that she's holding in her hands.

Structural Scoring: DdS+ Mp.FC– 2 Hd,Cg,A P 4.0 FAB1
Holt Score: F– 3 Ag2A, L2E–V Cac 2 R (an) O–beh min2 refl DD = 3 DE = –1 DDXDE = –3
Aggression Scores: None
Primitive Modes of Relating: None
Defenses: Devaluation

13. A man with a moustache.

E: (Rpt's S's response)
S: That's a mustache and this is his eyes, he looks surprised but he wants to be funny, just the face of a man.

Structural Scoring: DdSo Mp– Hd,Hx DR1
Holt Score: F– 2 Ctr A O–exp DD = 1 DE = –.5 DDXDE = –.5
Aggression Scores: None
Primitive Modes of Relating: None
Defenses: None

14. And I see two crabs.

E: (Rpt's S's response)
S: These are the crabs.

Structural Scoring: Do Fo 2 A P
Holt Score: Fo 1 Ag2A R (an) DD = 1 DE = 0 DDXDE = 1
Aggression Scores: None
Primitive Modes of Relating: None
Defenses: Repression

478

Sequence of Scores

Card	No.	Loc.	#	Determinant(s)	(2)	Content(s)	Pop Z	Special Scores
I	1	W+	1	Ma.mao		H, Cg, Na	4.0	
	2	WSo	1	Fu		(Hd)	1.0	MOR
II	3	W+	1	Ma.FCo	2	H, Cg, Ay, Hx	4.5	COP, AB
	4	D+		FMpo	2	A, Fd	P 3.0	DV
III	5	D+		Mp.Fro		H, Cg, Ay	P 4.0	DV
IV	6	W+	1	Fu		(H), Cg, An, Hx	P 4.0	AB, CON
V	7	Wo	1	FMao		A	P 1.0	
VI	8	D+		FC'u		Id	2.5	
	9	D+		Mp.FD−	2	H, Cg, Ay, Id	2.5	
VII	10	WS+	1	Ma.FC'u		(H), Na, Cl, Hx	4.0	AB, AG, COP
VIII	11	W+	1	FMa−pu	2	A, Ad, Bt	P 4.5	
X	12	DdS+		Mp.FC−	2	Hd, Cg, A	P 4.0	FAB
	13	DdSo		Mp−		Hd, Hx		
	14	Do		Fo	2	A	P	

Summary of Approach

I:W.WS	VI:D.D
II:W.D	VII:WS
III:D	VIII:W
IV:W	IX:*Rejection*
V:W	X:DdS.DdS.D

APPENDIX D
Rorschach Structural Summary

LOCATION FEATURES	DETERMINANTS		CONTENTS	S-CONSTELLATION
	BLENDS	SINGLE		NO..FV + VF + V + FD > 2

LOCATION FEATURES	BLENDS	SINGLE	CONTENTS	S-CONSTELLATION
			H = 4,0	NO..Col-Shd Bl>0
Zf = 12	M.m	M = 1	(H) = 2,0	YES..Ego<.31,>.44
ZSum = 39.0	M.FC	FM = 3	Hd = 2,0	NO..MOR>3
ZEst = 38.0	M.Fr	m = 0	(Hd) = 1,0	NO..Zd > ± 3.5
	M.FD	FC = 0	Hx = 0,4	NO..es>EA
W = 7	M.FC'	CF = 0	A = 4,1	NO..CF+C>FC
(Wv = 0)	M.FC	C = 0	(A) = 0,0	YES..X+%<.70
D = 5		Cn = 0	Ad = 0,1	YES..S>3
Dd = 2		FC' = 1	(Ad) = 0,0	NO..P<3 or >8
S = 4		C'F = 0	An = 0,1	NO..Pure H <2
		C' = 0	Art = 0,0	YES..R<17
DQ		FT = 0	Ay = 0,3	4.....TOTAL
..........(FQ-)		TF = 0	Bl = 0,0	
+ = 10 (2)		T = 0	Bt = 0,1	SPECIAL SCORINGS
o = 4 (1)		FV = 0	Cg = 0,6	Lv1 Lv2
v/+ = 0 (0)		VF = 0	Cl = 0,1	DV = 2x1 0x2
v = 0 (0)		V = 0	Ex = 0,0	INC = 0x2 0x4
		FY = 0	Fd = 0,1	DR = 0x3 0x6
		YF = 0	Fi = 0,0	FAB = 1x4 0x7
		Y = 0	Ge = 0,0	ALOG = 0x5
FORM QUALITY		Fr = 0	Hh = 0,0	CON = 1x7
		rF = 0	Ls = 0,0	SUM6 = 4
FQx FQf MQual SQx		FD = 0	Na = 0,2	WSUM6 = 13
+ = 0 0 0 0		F = 3	Sc = 0,0	
o = 6 1 3 0			Sx = 0,0	AB =3 CP = 0
u = 5 2 1 2			Xy = 0,0	AG =1 MOR = 1
− = 3 0 3 2			Id = 1,1	CFB =0 PER = 0
none = 0 − 0 0		(2) = 6		COP =2 PSV = 0

RATIOS, PERCENTAGES, AND DERIVATIONS						
R = 14	L = 0.27		FC:CF+C =2:0	COP = 2	AG = 1	
			Pure C =0	Food	= 1	
EB = 7:1.0	EA = 8.0	EBPer = 7.0	SumC':WSumC =2:1.0	Isolate/R	= 0.50	
eb = 4:2	es = 6	D = 0	Afr =0.40	H:(H)Hd(Hd)	= 4:5	
	Adj es = 6	Adj D = 0	S =4	(HHd):(AAd)	= 3:0	
			Blends:R =6:14	H+A:Hd + Ad	= 11:4	
FM = 3	C' = 2	T = 0	CP =0			
m = 1	V = 0	Y = 0				
			P = 7	Zf =12	3r+(2)/R = 0.64	
a:p = 6:6	Sum6 = 4	X+% = 0.43	Zd = +1.0	Fr+rF = 1	
Ma:Mp = 3:4	Lv2 = 0	F+% = 0.33	W:D:Dd =7:5:2	FD = 1	
2AB+Art+Ay = 9	WSum6 = 13	X-% = 0.21	W:M = 7:7	An + Xy = 1	
M− = 3	Mnone = 0	S-% = 0.67	DQ+ =10	MOR = 1	
		Xu% = 0.36	DQv =0		

SCZI = 2	DEPI = 4	CDI = 2	S-CON = 4	HVI = Yes	OBS = No

26

Baldur von Schirach, Hitler Youth Leader: Perversion of Boyish Idealism

Barry Ritzler
Long Island University

The Rorschach of Nazi Baldur von Schirach was chosen for comparing and integrating the Comprehensive System (Exner, 1993) and more content-oriented psychodynamic approaches (Lerner, 1991) because it is a relatively brief Rorschach with rich and complex responses. Von Schirach was the first leader of the Hitler Youth and later the Gauleiter of Vienna. This case study combines Rorschach interpretations and historical information (Craig, 1978; Davidson, 1966; Gilbert, 1947; Miale & Selzer, 1975; West, 1955; Zillmer, Harrower, Ritzler, & Archer, 1995) to explain von Schirach's behavior as a Nazi.

The von Schirach Rorschach is interpreted in accordance with the Comprehensive System cluster search routine (Exner, 1988). That is, his Structural Summary is used to order interpretive variable clusters according to their probable importance. Content interpretation is introduced only when the cluster search routine calls for it; that is, at the end of the Self-Perception and Interpersonal Perception clusters. Only responses that contain potentially meaningful projective material are interpreted; that is, in the Self-Perception cluster, movement responses, minus form quality responses, and responses with clearly identifiable embellishments are interpreted and only movement responses with pairs and human content responses for the Interpersonal Perception cluster.

BALDUR VON SCHIRACH, HITLER YOUTH LEADER

Baldur von Schirach's mother and grandmother were American, but he was pure German (Davidson, 1966). By the time he joined the Nazi party in 1925 at the age of 18, he already had been a member of the Young Germans' League for 8 years. He had joined this boys' organization because it fit his nature as a *schwaermerisch,* "a lad with sentimental longing for adventure linked to high pursuits and a love of poetry, tales of derring-do, and literary discussions that do not place too great a strain on one's intellectual capacities" (Davidson, 1966, p. 285).

As the son of the director of the National Theater in Weimar, von Schirach experienced the privilege and then the decline of upper-middle-class Germany. After the country's loss of World War I and the economic ruin that followed, the idealistic Baldur was primed to worship Hitler, the charismatic Führer who promised to restore German superiority.

von Schirach showed little restraint in his idealistic fervor and gave grand expression to it by organizing elaborate pageants that idolized the Nazi leader. He first met Hitler in 1926 when he prepared a special youth pageant to celebrate the Führer's visit to Weimar. Impressed by the celebration and by the "conventionally attractive young man, serious, plump, well mannered, and voluble, [who] spoke in a somewhat stilted, humorless style with solemn earnestness and in sentences that were studded with cliches" (Davidson, 1966, p. 286), Hitler invited von Schirach to Munich to serve the Party.

In the larger city, von Schirach continued to rise in the Nazi ranks until Hitler named him Reich youth leader of the National Socialist Party. He became particularly effective when he discovered that his pageants were more impressive when he wrote most of the spoken lines, but gave them to other youths to recite. His histrionic, ostentatious style was well-suited for composing and staging grand pageants, but he lacked the oratory skill and physical presence to be an inspirational speaker. His lines had the greatest impact when spoken by more handsome and verbally impressive members of the Hitler Youth.

Another problem existed for von Schirach. Although he was good at organizing and orchestrating, he was not a skilled administrator. His emotional, idealistic enthusiasm caused him to commit to grander and grander schemes while overlooking details of the everyday Hitler Youth administration. Also Goebbels, the Nazi Propaganda Minister, developed a jealous dislike for his closest rival as a director of grand Party ceremonies. The increasing disorganization of the Hitler Youth and Goebbel's criticisms eroded Hitler's esteem of von Schirach. As a result, von Schirach was recommissioned as Gauleiter of Vienna. Exposure to the culture and architectural beauty of Vienna, rather than dampening von Schirach's ardor for Hitler and the Nazi cause, further inspired him. Finally, however, Hitler denounced him for being too sentimental and sympathetic to non-Nazis and his days as a favorite were over. This happened on the occasion of a Hitler visit to Vienna when von Schirach and his wife expressed concern to the Führer that German soldiers had mistreated some of the citizens of Vienna.

Indeed, von Schirach was not a stereotypical sadistic, militaristic Nazi. Although an avowed anti-Semite who did nothing to lessen the horror of the Holocaust, he did not run the Hitler Youth as a military auxiliary. Although acknowledging that the children might eventually grow up to fight for the Führer, he resisted attempts by others to infuse early military training in the organization's activities. Instead, he sought to instill adoration and obedience to the Führer for the glorification of Germany and the Aryan ideals of the Third Reich.

At Nuremberg, von Schirach was described as a polite, uncritical admirer of the Fatherland whose defense was that he had no direct responsibility for the Nazi crimes against humanity (West, 1955). Indeed, the only direct tie between von Schirach and the Holocaust was some complicity in the deportation of Russian orphans to German work camps. Von Schirach had sanctioned the deportations, but had no hand in planning the actual fate of the children. However, von Schirach's major role in inspiring the youth of Germany to become blind followers of Hitler may have made up for the absence of sadism and aggression in his behavior–"he taught them for years that their highest duty was to say, 'You order, my Führer, we follow'" (Davidson, 1966, p. 308).

At Nuremberg, von Schirach was spared execution, but was sentenced to 20 years at Spandau prison. He remained, to the end, "the eternal boy scout, eager, idealistic when it came to Germans, sentimental, full of bad poetry and easy solutions" (Davidson, 1966, p. 582).

VON SCHIRACH'S RORSCHACH

Appendix A presents the modified verbatim Rorschach of Baldur von Schirach. Appendix B presents the Comprehensive System sequence of scores for the von Schirach protocol, and Appendix C contains von Schirach's Structural Summary. Coding was done by Barry Ritzler and an extensively trained research assistant.[1]

Agreement for the major scoring categories ranged from 98% on pairs to 82% on *Sum 6* Special Scores. Shading (87%) was the only other category with less than 90% interrater agreement.

INTERPRETATION

The Comprehensive System cluster search routine method of interpretation begins with the identification of a cluster search order that is most relevant for the protocol under consideration (Exner, 1988). An ordered table of key variables with associated cluster search orders is scanned for the most appropriate cluster order. For von Schirach's protocol, the first significant key variable is the Depression Index with a value of 7. The associated cluster search order is as follows:

---

[1]I wish to thank Michelle Smith-Kaskey for her coding of the von Schirach protocol.

Affect → Controls → Situation Stress → Self-Perception → Interpersonal Perception → Processing → Mediation → Ideation.

Affect

The highly significant *DEPI* indicates that von Schirach was either seriously depressed or very distressed emotionally. With a *DEPI* this elevated, the affective problem probably was to some extent chronic in nature even though there is an indication of a situational stress decompensation (see following).

The ambitent Erlebnistypus Balance (7:6.5) indicates that von Schirach's problem solving was inconsistently influenced by emotions; for instance, he might begin a decision process in response to a feeling and then abruptly shift to a more cerebral approach only to lean in the direction of his feelings when he was just on the verge of a final solution, thereby prolonging and complicating the process. The combination of serious emotional disruption (significant *DEPI*) and gross inconsistency in the use of emotions for problem solving (ambitent *EB*) makes it very likely that von Schirach found emotional situations to be quite taxing. In spite of this difficulty, there is much in the Structural Summary to substantiate that emotions for von Schirach were simultaneously disruptive and compelling. For instance, the evidence indicates that his expression of emotions was intense and loosely modulated (*FC:CF +* $C = 1:6$). Although such strong emotionality can be difficult to manage for the individual, it also can stir others to more intense emotional expression. Indeed, von Schirach made his mark in the Nazi party by inspiring young people to give enthusiastic support to the Nazi movement.

Information in the Affective cluster indicates that for von Schirach, emotional disruption often took the form of confusion (four color-shading blend responses) and intense affective pain (three shading-shading blend responses). This may have been particularly apparent at Nuremberg, where he was under considerable stress (*es* = 20), much of which was situational (*D* = –2 and *adjusted D* = 0) and emotional (*eb* = 6:14, much more than usually weighted on the Shading side). He was either lonely and/or experiencing a strong sense of emotional loss (*T* = 3) possibly because of the collapse of the Nazi party and the disillusionment he may have felt when the atrocities were revealed at the trial. He also probably was engaging in painful introspection (*V* = 1), either as a result of the public shame of Nuremberg or as an expression of a more long-standing personality characteristic. Interestingly, in spite of his strong tendency toward emotionality, part of his stress was due to efforts to hold back on his feelings (*C'* = 5). These efforts, however, were not very successful in limiting his intense emotionality (*SumC:SumC'* = 7:5).

Paradoxically, for all his emotional reactivity, von Schirach showed a marked tendency to avoid emotional stimuli (Affective Ratio = .42). This is an indication that he was aware of his problems with affect and tried to handle them by distancing himself from situations that were emotionally arousing. It might explain why he was drawn to the Nazi movement with its intense, but orchestrated emotional demonstrations. Hitler initially was impressed by von Schirach's ability to organize student rallies that enthusiastically provided early support for the Nazi movement. Always a good organizer of others' emotional displays, von Schirach preferred to observe his rallies from behind the scenes while others under his direction fanned the crowd's enthusiasm with their rhetoric. In films of Hitler Youth rallies, von Schirach seldom is seen, and when visible, he is standing passively in the background. Most of his feelings were channeled into highly romanticized bad poetry or the love of theater, another passion through which he could vicariously experience intense emotions being acted out by others. Also, idealization of the Party and glorifying in its successes might have been a way for von Schirach to compensate his tendency toward depression and emotional distress.

Capacity for Control and Stress Tolerance

As anticipated, von Schirach was not an impulsive, out of control individual. Despite his lack of a consistent problem-solving style, he had considerable resources ($EA = 13.5$) and was able to manage everyday stresses without becoming noticeably distressed. There was, however, much evidence of significant situational stress, both affective ($Y = 5$) and cognitive ($m = 4$). His elevated texture score ($T = 3$) suggests either chronic loneliness and/or recent traumatic loss. The fall of the Nazi movement constituted a major loss for von Schirach and it is likely that the elevated T signifies additional situational stress. In particular, the death of his idealized Führer and the defamation of the Nazi ideology must have been crushing blows to the emotionally dependent von Schirach.

Finally, the presence of a Vista response suggests that von Schirach also may have been experiencing an acute sense of public humiliation during the Nuremberg trials. If this is accurate, he is not typical of the Nuremberg Nazis, most of whom gave no Vista responses and publicly denied a sense of shame. Gilbert (1950) observed that von Schirach was one of the few Nuremberg prisoners to show genuine remorse.

Self-Perception Formal Score Interpretation

The Rorschach indicates below-average self-esteem for von Schirach (Egocentricity Ratio = .29). He was prone to excessive self-examination ($FD = 6$, $FV = 1$). Such ruminative introspection, when combined with an elevated Depression Index, suggests intense concern with personal adequacy. Von Schirach's enthusiasm for the Nazi movement likely served as a defense against a sense of inadequacy. Hence, when the war ended, von Schirach was distressed psychologically. It is important to note, however, that even though von

Schirach scored high on the Depression Index, he gave no Morbid responses. This suggests that even though he experienced serious depression, he maintained a superficially optimistic and positive attitude.

Self-Perception Content Analysis

At this point in the Comprehensive System cluster search routine method of interpretation, attention turns to content analysis of minus form quality, movement, and embellished responses. Out of von Schirach's 17 responses, 10 qualify as movement or minus (2, 3, 4, 6, 10, 11, 13, 15, 16, and 17). Responses 1, 7, 8, 12, and 14 were added for content analysis because of meaningful embellishments. Therefore, only Responses 5 and 12 were ineligible because of a lack of projective significance (Exner, 1988).

RESPONSE 1

Von Schirach at first projected emotional pain by immediately referring to "the painful gray tones," but compensates with a pollyannish attempt to brighten the mood by stating that, "If it was colored, I would have thought of a dancer." This shift is indicative of his use of gala performances to negate painful affect. He made reference to a performer (dancer) associated with a brighter mood (color). Then, by becoming preoccupied with the specks on the side of the card, he moved his attention completely away from the situation—a maneuver consistent with his behavior as the leader of the Hitler Youth.

RESPONSE 2

Von Schirach continued his focus on the positive by projecting a sense of himself as a happy, highly energetic, social individual. Nevertheless, devaluation ("grotesque") spoils the image and suggests an awkwardness and tenuousness in his defensive use of intense positive emotion. In the inquiry, he pulled back from the emotional intensity by emphasizing the ego aspects of the response ("clearly just the shape") and turning the color into an intellectualized abstraction ("the color gives the impression of gaiety").

RESPONSE 3

Von Schirach continued with a highly controlled, formal style ("men in coat-tail dress") while adding a subservient quality ("waiters"—perhaps a projection of his subservience to Hitler—see more in the Interpersonal Perception). Emotions were distanced further by making them ornaments (i.e., intellectualized art objects), putting them in the background ("behind them"), and making them part of an unreal fantasy (the reference to the Hoffman story). In the inquiry, this process continued as the waiters put a cloth over the pot because it's hot—another attempt to reduce the intensity of emotion. A sense of deterioration is added as he has the ornaments "falling down."

RESPONSE 4

Response 4 has implications for von Schirach's identification with the Nazi party. The "animal god" is suggestive of the idealized, animalistic character of the Nazi movement. Furthermore, the odd combinations of fur and a Rococo dance pantomime is similar to the grand, but oddly composed Nazi demonstrations von Schirach was so fond of orchestrating. The concurrence of the texture determinant in this response further suggests that von Schirach's grandiose idealization of the Nazi party had a soothing effect. Also, the image of a human covered by an animal skin during a ritualized pantomime dance is consistent with von Schirach's behind-the-scenes participation in Nazi ceremonies and his focus on appearances and superficiality. It should be noted here that the vagueness of the animal skin and the way it covers the human form lowers the levels of differentiation and articulation of the response, suggesting a regression in level of functioning associated with von Schirach's Nazi idealization.

RESPONSE 6

Falstaff, the jovial, convivial Shakespearian rogue, probably represents von Schirach's ego ideal. He enjoyed standing on the podium "cloaked" in his military finery as the Hitler Youth paraded (danced?) in front of him—a perfect cover for his underlying depression and sense of inadequacy. His rather pretentious intellectualizing (e.g., Rococo, Shakespeare) takes the form of comedy in this response. Often throughout the Rorschach, von Schirach's figures are associated with nonaggressive, often comedic activity. Unfortunately for von Schirach, his rather comical histrionics eventually caused him to lose favor with Hitler. Goebbels especially was highly critical of von Schirach, regarding him as ridiculous and lacking in substance (Craig, 1978). Goebbels, however, was wrong about the lack of depth. The quality of this response in terms of its scores and the creative content is well above average.

RESPONSE 10

Response 10 is the most obscure of von Schirach's responses that carry possible projective significance. Perhaps the sexual connotations of the card (his previous responses to VI were "fur," "a wooden *rod*," and "something feathery *behind*" [italics added]) created a need for him to retreat and erect a defensive wall. Nevertheless, von Schirach typically preserved something of the original primary process in this highly defensive response by making it "water *gushing* up [italics added]." It is easy to see how von Schirach's comfortable position in the upper echelon of the Nazi order enabled him to obtain vicarious gratification of primitive needs. Some authors (e.g., Gilbert, 1947) speculated about confusion in von Schirach's sexual identity. Although this response hardly confirms such a speculation, its stilted vagueness might be considered a "soft sign" of sexual uncertainty.

RESPONSE 11

Here, von Schirach projected a quality of seductive, but superficial social behavior, the implication of which is discussed more thoroughly in the next interpretive cluster, Interpersonal Perception. The degree of differentiation is lower than in previous human responses, possibly suggesting less empathy for the female object and/or partial regression in a sexualized situation.

RESPONSE 13

In this response, von Schirach may have been projecting some of the underlying tension of living near the top of the Nazi hierarchy. Frozen within the coat of arms (representing Nazi "royalty"?), the "grasping" animals are precariously "balanced on one foot." von Schirach eventually found out how precarious his position was as leader of the Hitler Youth when he was demoted to Gauleiter of Vienna. Also, this response signifies the precariousness of von Schirach's idealization.

RESPONSE 15

Amid the emotional implications of the difficult full-color Card IX, von Schirach hardened his self-projection into the alluring, but cold and textureless Chinese jade. Nevertheless, the fire inside continued to smolder. For all his social guardedness and intellectual aloofness, von Schirach never completely lost touch with his strong desires.

RESPONSE 16

Still struggling with Card IX color, von Schirach continued to keep himself hidden and distant behind the intellectualized smoke of his underlying desires. Even though he was a charismatic, even fiery individual given to histrionic expressions of emotion, his true feelings seldom may have been directly observable. For all his ostentatious displays of public fervor, the real person was not known to many.

RESPONSE 17

von Schirach's synthesizing style resulted in a chaotic *magnum opus* on Card X. He started out by immediately introducing the light (nonviolent) context of a fairy tale. Within that context, he again placed the themes of royalty (king's cape and crown and lions), comedy ("two blue devils running and laughing . . . waving a leaf"), and the seclusive connotation (sleeping mole). In this grand, but awkward response, von Schirach reiterated the self-perception apparent in earlier responses. He projected himself as pretentious, overintellectualized, histrionic, desirous of being admired from a distance, and prone to avoidance and simple denial of unpleasant affect. The overinclusiveness is particularly apparent here, and the only thing that kept it from being a more disturbed mess of unrelated figures was the rather immature intellectualization von Schirach placed on it at the beginning. Always the good Nazi organizer, he was capable of pulling together wildly disparate ideas into a grand synthesis that is attention-getting, but basically nonsensical. This response is the only one on a full-color card to include human content. It is one of the most immature in the protocol, suggesting von Schirach's difficulties in managing strong emotional impulses.

Interpersonal Perception Formal Score Interpretation

Von Schirach's two food responses suggest dependency—a finding not unusual in the Rorschachs of other Nazis (Zillmer et al., 1995). Apparently, finding a niche within the Nazi organization served to gratify dependency needs of Nazi Party members.

von Schirach also was vulnerable to intense loneliness ($T = 3$). With such propensities for dependency and loneliness, he was particularly vulnerable to manipulation through praise and promise of companionship—just the gratifications he received from no less than Hitler himself.

The pattern of two cooperative responses and zero aggression responses indicates that von Schirach was not the stereotypical sadistic, aggressive Nazi. Instead, he was probably perceived as likeable and cooperative. Nevertheless, his structural summary results (Isolation Index = .41 and Affective Ratio = .42) qualify him for the following Comprehensive System computer-derived interpretation:

> He appears to be socially isolated. He probably finds it difficult to create and/or sustain smooth or meaningful interpersonal relationships even though he tends to be interested in them. This is not surprising as other data suggest that he is somewhat emotionally withdrawn. This finding does not necessarily indicate some pathological kind of withdrawal, but there is a substantial probability of some sort of social maladjustment. (Exner, 1988)

Interpersonal Perception Content Analysis

In the Comprehensive System, a response qualifies for content analysis of interpersonal perception if it involves (a) movement and a pair and (b) human content. With these criteria, the following responses were selected for interpretation: 2, 3, 4, 6, 11, 13, 15, and 17. Content is interpreted only for its relevance to interpersonal perception.

RESPONSE 2

The response depicts a spirited, congenial interaction with much positive affect. It is quite likely that von Schirach frequently engaged in hearty, but superficial social exchange. The enthusiasm conveyed in this response may also account for why he was so successful as a inspirational leader. Nevertheless, the awkwardness ("grotesque"), defensiveness (clothing), and negativism (space) are not far beneath the surface. The intricate and highly cooperative nature of this response, however, suggests that von Schirach had the capacity for mature and possibly even altruistic socialization.

RESPONSE 3

Waiters in coat-tail dress are formal, subservient, and not as spontaneous as the hand-clapping dancing men of Response 2. In other words, von Schirach followed his exuberant gregariousness with a much more contained and distant demeanor that put a lid on his emotional intensity. The cooperativeness remains, however, as von Schirach, for all his histrionics and defensiveness, was always a team player. The cooperativeness of this response is somewhat muted here, indicating that in his servile orientation, von Schirach was inclined to function at a less mature and empathic level.

RESPONSE 4

There is no interaction in this response, but the image of a person portraying an animal god at a Rococo festival preserves some of the social nature of von Schirach's personality. Ritual celebrations of primitive desires were his special element—controlled, but intensely orchestrated demonstrations that enabled him to regress vicariously while maintaining a dominant position. Also, this particular texture response is typical of the surprisingly frequent use of texture by Nazis (Zillmer et al., 1995). That is, texture is combined with human content ("A dancer carrying an animal skin") in an odd, stilted context. The previous interpretation of the Nazi use of texture appears to pertain here: "Nazis, who have difficulty in finding and maintaining intimate relationships with significant others may use the Nazi comaraderie and *esprit de corps* to substitute for close contact with individuals" (Zillmer et al., 1995, p. 189). Indeed, von Schirach achieved his most intimate dyadic relationship by marrying the daughter of Hitler's photographer—a woman who, when she divorced him in 1950, complained that she never felt truly close to him primarily because he was disdainful and unaccepting of her feelings that he considered mundane and inferior to his intense, patriotic affect. There is only a hint of mutuality in the reference to a ritual, confirming the notion of an increased distance from intimacy projected in this response.

RESPONSE 6

Although von Schirach did not make it explicit, the situation in the last act of the *Merry Wives of Windsor* involving Falstaff is that the figures dancing around him are tormenting him and ridiculing him for his grandiose, but foolish attempts at seduction. It is tempting to speculate that with this response, von

Schirach was conveying his experience of the Nuremberg trials. Couched in his usual comedic hysteria, the response portrays him as a lusty, romantic figure laughing in the face of social censure and ridicule. When the world was identifying him as an evil object of intense hatred, he projected the image of a rakish clown, more entertaining than tragic. This response takes one more step away from cooperativeness in its portrayal of teasing and ridicule.

RESPONSE 11

Webster (1990) defines coquetry as "behavior . . . intended to attract mainly for the satisfaction of vanity" (p. 216). For all of von Schirach's interest in attention and admiration, he may have had little desire for true intimate contact. Instead, he may have sought to seduce others into admiring him and giving him attention without burdening him with demands for sincere affection. There is no interaction in this response, simply parallel activity.

RESPONSE 13

The two grasping, precariously perched bears are not interacting, but appear rather desperately engaged in their own self-preservation. This may well be the way von Schirach viewed himself and his fellow Nuremberg prisoners. Certainly, observers of the Nuremberg Nazis (e.g., Davidson, 1966; Gilbert, 1955; West, 1955) frequently remarked on the lack of mutual support and empathy among the notorious prisoners.

RESPONSE 15

The paired response of "Chinese dragon-like figures" on a jade vase for burning incense only hints at social warmth and interaction. People disguise themselves as Chinese dragons and burn incense at ritual ceremonies where true intimacy is replaced by spirited group celebrations and orgies. The notion of the Nazi demonstrations being von Schirach's favored mode of socialization is once again consistent with the apparent projected content of a response.

RESPONSE 17

In this final conglomeration of disparate figures engaged in loosely connected forms of activity, von Schirach showed how adept he could be at pulling together odd bedfellows. His social skills, however, ended with his organizing talents. Once an organization existed under his leadership, he had considerable difficulty in guiding its everyday activity. His failure in this regard probably had much to do with his ambitent problem-solving style, but may also have been a function of how wildly incompatible were the individual parts of any organization drawn together by von Schirach's flash-in-the-pan charismatic histrionics. There may be some mutuality in these figures dashing about, but it is difficult to isolate in the confusion of the response. This may reflect von Schirach's own confusion and loss of altruism when he found himself in the grand, but chaotic world of Nazi demonstrations.

THE COGNITIVE TRIAD

The final three Comprehensive System interpretive clusters constitute the Cognitive Triad—Information Processing, Cognitive Mediation, and Ideation. Much of what appears in these clusters already has been identified in the interpretive process, but new information will be briefly summarized in these areas of functioning that are relatively less critical to understanding von Schirach.

Information Processing

von Schirach, the busy organizer of Nazi pageants, clearly was an overincorporater ($Lambda = 0.00$, $Zf = 14$, $W{:}D = 12{:}4$, and $Zd = +4.5$) whose complex information processing undoubtedly enabled him to put together such grand displays of allegiance to Hitler. On the other hand, the nearly ceaseless effort he put into creating complexity probably interfered with his ability to attend to the simple details of everyday administration of the Hitler Youth organization. This is particularly true considering he is ambitent. Without a consistent approach to problem solving, complex processing may often lead to chaos and confusion.

Cognitive Mediation

In spite of von Schirach's tendency toward loosely organized and highly complex processing ($Lambda = 0.00$), he was quite conventional and accurate in his interpretation of reality ($X+\% = 76$, $X-\% = 6$). This probably accounts for why he was able to translate the Nazi party line into complex demonstrations. Ambitent individuals can perform well when their reality testing is good and when they are aided by sufficient external guidelines. Apparently, Nazi doctrine and Hitler's dogmatism provided von Schirach with the structure he needed to rise above his ambitent problem when devoting himself to the staging of Hitler Youth pageantry. The Nazi regime was notorious for its lack of consistent policies for simple daily administration. Some observers (e.g., Gilbert, 1955) speculated that Hitler intentionally avoided providing specific administrative guidelines to prevent any faction of the Nazi Party from becoming too powerful and independent of his dictatorship. von Schirach's organizational talents and his administrative ineptitude were a perfect example of the kind of leader Hitler allowed to prosper.

Ideation

Because he was ambitent, von Schirach probably was inconsistent and unpredictable in his decision making. Even though his reality testing was good, he could make some serious errors in judgement—for example, expressing concern to Hitler over the mistreatment of non-Nazis or, at the same dinner party, extolling the virtues of Vienna culture that Hitler had denounced as decadent.

The elevated m (4) score suggests that von Schirach was experiencing some confusion in thinking and problems with attention and concentration at Nuremberg. Considering the life-threatening circumstances at the war crimes trial, it is not surprising that this overincorporative, ambitent thinker was showing some decompensation while he was awaiting the verdict.

The Intellectualization Index, the final significant Comprehensive System variable (from the Ideation cluster), yields the following interpretive hypothesis based on the System's empirical validity:

> He uses intellectualization as a major defensive tactic in situations he perceives as affectively stressful. In effect, it is a pseudo-intellectual process that conceals and/or denies the presence of feelings and, as a result, tends to reduce the likelihood that feelings will be dealt with directly and/or realistically. People such as this are more vulnerable to disorganization during intense emotional experiences because the tactic becomes less effective as the magnitude of affective stimuli increases. (Exner, 1988)

Psychopathy?

As a final interpretive issue, the Nuremberg Nazis have been characterized essentially as "psychopaths"—antisocial, narcissistic, unfeeling, and caricatures of macho bluster (Miale & Selzer, 1975). Now that Gacono and Meloy (1994) have identified a set of indices in the Rorschachs of primary (severe) psychopaths, von Schirach's protocol can be put to the test: The Gacono and Meloy indices are $Y = 0$, $PER > 2$, $Fr + rF > 1$, $T = 0$, $EgoC > .45$, and "Good" $COP = 0$. von Schirach has $Y = 5$ (!), $PER = 0$, $Fr + rF = 0$, $T = 3$, $EgoC = .29$, and his COP responses have no "Bad" COP features (i.e., AG, $Sum6$ Special Scores, and Form Quality–). Clearly, von Schirach's Rorschach is not consistent with primary psychopathy (Hare, 1991).

Who (or what), then, was this man who was leader of the Hitler Youth? The Rorschach indicates that he was an individual of substantial, but not well-organized personality resources who struggled with intense emotions that both disturbed and stimulated him. He found in Hitler and the Nazi Party icons for his major defense of idealization that allowed him, by association, to compensate for strong feelings of inadequacy and emotional pain and confusion. His particular combination of strengths and frailties admirably suited the needs of an evil political movement that exploited his intense, aimless nature by providing him with a simplistic dogma and powerful bureaucratic structure to focus his intensity and give him direction. All else, including moral integrity and a universal regard for human life, fell outside the pale of Nazi fervor and nationalism. The very aimlessness and intense need that drew him to the Nazi movement made it impossible for him to escape from it or see his tragic role in it until it was too late. Truly, he was a perversion of boyish idealism.

REFERENCES

Craig, G. (1978). *Germany: 1866-1945*. New York: Oxford University Press.

Davidson, E. (1966). *The trial of the Germans*. New York: MacMillan.

Exner, J. (1993). *The Rorschach: A comprehensive system. Vol. 1: Basic Foundations* (3rd ed.). New York: Wiley.

Exner, J. (1988). *The Rorschach: A comprehensive system. Vol. 2: Interpretation* (2nd ed.). New York: Wiley.

Gacono, C., & Meloy, R. (1994). *The Rorschach assessment of aggressive and psychopathic personalities*. Hillsdale, NJ: Lawrence Erlbaum Associates.

Gilbert, G. (1955). *The Psychology of dictatorship*. New York: Ronald.

Gilbert, G. (1947). *Nuremberg diary*. New York: Signet.

Hare, R. (1991). *The Psychopathy Checklist–Revised manual*. Toronto: Multihealth Systems.

Lerner, P. (1991). *Psychoanalytic theory and the Rorschach*. Hillsdale, NJ: The Analytic Press.

Miale, F., & Selzer, M. (1975). *The Nuremberg mind: The psychology of the Nazi leaders*. New York: Quadrangle/New York Times.

Webster, D. (1990). *Webster's encyclopedic dictionary*. New York: Lexicon Publications.

West, R. (1955). *A train of powder*. New York: Viking.

Zillmer, E., Harrower, M., Ritzler, B., & Archer, R. (1995). *The quest for the Nazi personality*. Hillsdale, NJ: Lawrence Erlbaum Associates.

Balder von Schirach's Rorschach Protocol (Taken from Miale & Selzer, 1975)

Note: Additional responses occurred in the inquiry period of the von Schirach Rorschach. Also, some inappropriate inquiries were made by the examiner. In order to keep within proper procedures for the Comprehensive System all additional responses and the inappropriate inquiry material have been eliminated from consideration.

I

1. A bat

Inquiry: It's the painful gray tones, but it's mostly the shape and it's alive. If it was colored I would have thought of a dancer. The outside specks are only the mess from the airbrush; the white spaces just don't belong (W).

II

2. Two grotesque dancing men clapping hands with red turban and red boots, red waistband shimmering through . . . happy motif.

Inquiry: Clearly just the shape, but the color gives the impression of gaiety. I forgot to mention that they had white beards; yes, I saw that originally (W).

III

3. Caricature of two men in coattail dress holding a pot; waiters, maybe. Behind them on the wall are red ornaments and in the middle something like a butterfly ornament. Corner ornaments are like something similar falling down. Whole thing is like an illustration for an E.Th.A. Hoffman [author of fantasies] story. It's fantastic because they don't have human heads.

Inquiry: The pot is shiny, metallic, but they're putting a cloth over it, perhaps because it's hot; the waiters have white aprons with white strings around their waists and white ties and high collars (W).

IV

4. Fantastic animal god with powerful legs and slit eyes and a kind of widow's peak on his forehead. Gives impression of fur. Belongs to Rococo period. Dance pantomime in a Rococo festival.

Inquiry: Form is strong, but texture is also clear; it is soft, deep fur with animal skin on soles; probably a dancer carrying animal skin over him for festival dance (W).

V

5. First impression, like a bat.

Inquiry: The shape and darkness give impression of a bat, but the goat's feet don't correspond (W).

6. Two figures in Midsummer Night's Dream or Merry Wives of Windsor. . . . Shakespeare, in any case. [Shows he has Shakespeare book with him in cell.] The figures that dance around Falstaff in the last act of Merry Wives of Windsor.

Inquiry: Horns and fat central figure suggest Falstaff; rest are light wavy figures hidden behind his cloak . . . just vague forms (W).

VI

7. A wall decoration . . . a large animal fur.

Inquiry: Furry texture, probably tiger skin because of shading on legs (W).

8. Wooden rod or table leg.

Inquiry: Polished black wood.

9. Something feathery behind.

Inquiry: Gray tone (D).

(continued)

10. Part of a brick wall with gate or fountain in the middle; yes, a fountain in the distance with water gushing up . . . a definite scene in depth.

Inquiry: Definite vista; fieldstone wall because of mottled tones, like Maxfield Parrish; angle of perspective at bottom (lower portion of card D).

VII

11. Two women with coquettish hats looking back at each other.

Inquiry: (upper two-thirds D).

12. Impression of snow or sugar . . . texture of something baked with fancy icing.

Inquiry: From shading and texture; icing or snow has fallen on it (W).

VIII

13. Two animals standing on a mountain grasping the gray and blue parts, perhaps bears; gives strong impression of heraldry . . . animals on a coat of arms . . . pleasantly shaded colors, but no real construction.

Inquiry: They're balancing on one foot, holding on to coat of arms, climbing up (W).

IX

14. Orchid.

Inquiry: Shape and color equally; orange flower, green leaves, pink blossoms (W).

15. Something Oriental . . . Chinese dragonlike figures above and green jade . . . a Chinese vase for burning incense with smoke rising in the middle.

Inquiry: The brown is bronzelike and the green is jadelike, but there is no surface texture; just the color. (upper 2/3 D).

16. Mysterious animal with round head and slit eyes and green protectors before the face, blowing out red smoke . . . very artistic.

Inquiry: Brown suggests horns, center bulge the face with eye spaces; pink clouds on bottom are smoke (W).

X (Coded as a single response)

17. The whole thing is a page out of a fairytale book. Two mountains with two little animals on top, with big eyes and open mouths. Two blue devils running and laughing toward the mountain, waving a leaf. A mole on each side. Green dancers bending their backs, holding ornament with horns. Two yellow lions or dogs sitting, looking up. A king's cape and crown. A tree trunk behind the birdlike figures. Brown spots below are only decorative.

Inquiry: A fairy tale because of color; all are figures in the story. Just the shape for the mountain and animals. The color is cheerful even though they are devils. The moles are sleeping. I wouldn't have thought of a king's cape if it wasn't blue. (All other inquiry responses simply established shape and did not add to other coding decisions.)

APPENDIX B
Sequence of Scores

Card	No.	Loc.	#	Determinant(s)	(2)	Content(s)	Pop Z	Special Scores
I	1	Wo	1	FYo		A	P 1.0	
II	2	WS+	1	Ma.CF.FC'.FY+	2	H, Cg, Hx	4.5	AB, COP
III	3	WS+	1	Mp.CF.FD.mp.FC'+		(H), Cg, Art	P 5.5	COP
IV	4	W+	1	Ma.TF.FDo		H, Ad	4.0	AB
V	5	Wo	1	FYo		A	P 1.0	INC
	6	W+	1	Ma.FV–		H, Art, Cg	2.5	
VI	7	Wo	1	TFo		Ad, Art	P 2.5	
	8	Do	1	FC'.FYo		Hh		
	9	Ddo	22	FC'.FDo		Ad		
	10	D+	1	FD.FY.mao		Na, Fd		
VII	11	D+	1	Mpo	2	Hd, Cg	P 3.0	
	12	Wv	1	T		Na, Fd		
VIII	13	W+	1	FMp.CF.C'Fo	2	A, Ls, Art	P 4.5	
IX	14	Wo	1	FCo		Bt	5.5	
	15	D+	1	CF.mpu	2	Art, (A), Fi	2.5	
	16	WS+	1	CF.FD.Ma.mpu		Ad, Fd, Fi, Art	5.5	FAB
X	17	W+	1	CF.FMp.Ma.FD+	2	Art, Ls, A, (H)	5.5	

APPENDIX C
Structural Summary

RATIOS, PERCENTAGES, AND DERIVATIONS

R = 17	L = 0.00		FC:CF+C = 1:6	COP = 2	AG = 0
			C':WSumC = 5:6.5	Isolate/R	= 0.41
EB = 7:6.5	EA = 13.5	EBPer = N/A	Afr = 0.42	H:(H)Hd(Hd)	= 3:3
eb = 6:14	es = 20	D = –2	S = 3	(HHd):(AAd)	= 2:1
	Adj es = 13	Adj D = 0	Blends:R = 11:17	H+A:Hd + Ad	= 10:5
			CP = 0		

FM = 2	C' = 5	T = 3			
m = 4	V = 1	Y = 5			
			P = 6	Zf = 14	3r+(2)/R = 0.29
a:p	= 6:7	Sum6 = 2	X+% = 0.76	Zd = +4.5	Fr+rF = 0
Ma:Mp	= 5:2	Lv2 = 0	F+% = N/A	W:D:Dd = 12:4:1	FD = 6
2AB+Art+Ay	= 11	WSum6 = 6	X–% = 0.06	W:M = 12:7	An + Xy = 0
M–	= 1	Mnone = 0	S–% = 0.00	DQ+ = 10	MOR = 0
			Xu% = 0.12	DQv = 1	

SCZI = 0	DEPI = 7*	CDI = 2	S-CON = 6	HVI = No	OBS = No

27

He Says, She Says, They Say: The Consensus Rorschach

Leonard Handler
University of Tennessee

With few exceptions personality assessment instruments have focused on the individual rather than on the dyad. This has been true of the Rorschach as well; it has traditionally been viewed as an individual, intrapsychic instrument. Perhaps this is why the Consensus Rorschach (CR), which involves administration of the Rorschach to two or more people simultaneously, generated so little interest until the relatively recent emphasis on interpersonal and object relations psychoanalytic approaches and the increased popularity of marital and family therapy. The CR should not be considered a measure of personality, as we typically view the individual record, but rather as a measure of interpersonal relatedness.

In the CR technique two or more people are asked to arrive at a single set of agreed upon responses through some type of negotiation. Interpretation usually stresses either content or process, although traditional scoring is also possible (Aronow, Reznikoff, & Moreland, 1994). There are a number of variations in technique: (a) consensus protocols are obtained before or after the individual Rorschach; (b) the protocols are sometimes obtained without the standard individual administration; (c) the psychologist may or may not be present as a participant-observer; (d) all the cards may be given, or the patients may be given only one or two cards; (e) the test may be administered to a couple, or to an entire family or group; (f) the entire CR may be administered once, or it may be administered a number of times, to the same patient, with a variety of reference groups relevant to the patient's problem; (g) the time interval between test administrations may vary considerably from method to method, and there is "inadequate standardization . . . for determining when consensus has actually been achieved . . . whether or not [the examiner] subsequently elects to conduct an inquiry and how he goes about it" (Aronow & Reznikoff, 1976, p. 219); and (h) the number of responses may or may not be fixed by the examiner.

Two general approaches to CR administration are possible. The first approach, which is the more traditional one, involves giving each person the Rorschach, individually. The couple or group is then told that they will be asked to take the test again, this time arriving at one or more agreed-on responses. This procedure results in three scorable profiles that are then compared with each other. The focus here is on the dynamics of the individual patient and the "couple dynamics," family dynamics or group dynamics. It is rather difficult to record the interactions between husband and wife that lead to each interaction response. These transactions are a rich source of process data, but the time taken to record, transcribe, and analyze them is quite extensive. Instead, in this approach the dynamics are inferred by a comparison of the three protocols.

The second approach, described by Wynne (1968), Singer (1968, 1977), Singer and Wynne (1963, 1966, 1975), and Shapiro and Wild (1976), focuses on the interaction of the couple or among the group members rather than on scorable responses. The focus is on the process rather than the content of communications; the Rorschach is used here to identify and/or interpret the impact of a husband's, wife's, or other family member's verbal communication on others in the family. Singer (1977) viewed the Rorschach as a method of studying the stylistic features of an individual's communication, "an analog of those many occurrences in daily life in which two individuals attempt to establish a consensually shared view of reality" (p. 456). This approach was initially designed by Loveland (1967; Loveland, Wynne, & Singer, 1963) for research on relationships within families with a schizophrenic member. At first all 10 cards were used, but Loveland et al. found that data derived from more than one card were redundant. More recent research and case study examples using both approaches come primarily from foreign authors (e.g., Alanen & Kinnunen, 1975; Berg, 1980; Bos, 1974; Engel, 1978; Gentile, 1981; Nielsen, 1979; Shulman & Klein, 1982; Sokolova, 1985; Suzuki, 1972; Timsit & Gross, 1989; Wahlstrom, 1986, 1987; Wichstrom & Holte, 1991; Wichstrom, Holte, & Wynne, 1993; Willi, 1967, 1969, 1971, 1977, 1978–1979) and from dissertations (e.g., Crosby, 1983; Joseph, 1984).

HISTORY OF THE CONSENSUS RORSCHACH

The initial use of the CR, credited to W. H. Blanchard (1959, 1968), is rooted in group dynamics rather than in clinical work with couples. In 1954 Blanchard first observed significant differences between the individual and group behaviors of juvenile offenders. The psychological staff "were . . . struck by the discrepancy between the behavior of the youngsters . . . sitting across the desk from the examiner and the behavior of that same youth in the courtyard with others of his age" (Blanchard, 1968, p. 326). Observing the youths required many hours, but in the individual testing session, the youths were resistant, refractory, and defensive. For example, typical responses were: "It's an ink blot" and "I don't see nuthin'" (p. 327). The staff got the idea of giving the cards to the delinquent youths in a group when, in a staff meeting where the Rorschach was demonstrated to a group of social workers, "the spontaneity with which [they] revealed themselves" was noticed. Therefore, Blanchard began a similar procedure with the young offenders and "the richness and variety of responses were greatly increased" (p. 328).

During one specific week two groups of boys were examined because they had participated in a gang rape. Blanchard (1968) reported that in many respects the CR process was a reenactment of the gang rape experience. He stated, "It seemed clear that the struggle for dominance and the lines of resistance in the group behavior on the Rorschach took place in a manner similar to group performance in the life situation" (p. 330).

The CR has been administered in a wide variety of group situations—with therapy groups, among friends, and with families (Dudek, 1969; Levy & Epstein, 1964), even among school children in classrooms (Klopfer, 1969). Although the technique has come to be used a great deal with couples, it is unclear who the first person was to utilize it in this manner. Roman and Bauman (1960) reported on the use of the Rorschach with couples, which they called "interaction testing," initially designed to be used with several subtests of the Wechsler Adult Intelligence Scale. In this method (Bauman & Roman, 1966, 1968; Bauman, Roman, Borello, & Meltzer, 1967; Roman & Bauman, 1960), each joint response is scored according to the following system:

1. *Dominance*: The interaction response contains one member's individual response and not the other's response.
2. *Combination*: The elements of both members' responses are found in the interaction.
3. *Emergence*: The presence of a new percept in the interaction response.
4. *Reinforcement*: The same response is given by each individual and also by the husband and wife together.

The quality of the interaction response may be scored as +, –, or 0, compared with the individual protocol, depending on whether it is better, worse, or unchanged.

Cutter and Farberow (1968) administered a CR to five "groups," composed of an alcoholic patient, with three friends, three roommates, his wife, and a high–low status pair. They observed that the [approach] of the alcoholic with each group was different: "irresponsibility with friends, affective distance with roommates, a victim with his wife, and a parasite with the status pair" (p. 340). From the CR Cutter and Farberow could see how the patient related in the different settings: "With his friends he takes a relaxed, passive role of going along with [the] consensus. . . . With his roommates be becomes more active and attempts to dominate. . . . With his wife . . . he attempts to play a more dominant but inappropriately chivalrous role" (p. 373).

Dorr (1981) utilized a psychometrist, who administers the Rorschach individually to the husband and the wife; then he joins the couple for the consensus portion of the procedure. He asks each person to share their free associations to each card "and then, together, agree on what constitutes the 'best response'" (p. 550). They are asked to note which Rorschach card they like the best and which they like the least. These results are then placed on a chalkboard and discussed.

Perhaps one reason the CR has not been used more often is that it is quite time consuming. However, Aronow, Reznikoff, and Moreland (1994) used a procedure that takes less time; they administer the Rorschach to both people, simultaneously, by asking each person to "find three or four things that each blot may look like, and then agree on one thing that the blot looks like the most" (p. 159). The examiner remains in the room during the process and both husband and wife hear each others' individual associations (E. Aronow, personal communication, May 7, 1995). The procedure is continued until all 10 blots have been administered.

Although each approach has its merits and its disadvantages, I have chosen to describe a case in which the CR is used in the more traditional manner, so that both the scoring and the content of each Rorschach can be examined. This approach incorporates scores and ratios from the Comprehensive Scoring System, combined with psychodynamically oriented content analysis and the Roman and Bauman procedure. The emphasis is on the ways in which the interaction either enhances or detracts from the personalities, as they are portrayed in the individual records.

CASE HISTORY

Mr. and Mrs. Wilson sought treatment because their 11-year-old daughter was oppositional, especially with Mr. Wilson, her stepfather. It soon became obvious that the major problem was the couple's relationship and they decided to be evaluated together for possible marital therapy.

Mrs. Wilson is 36 years old and is college educated, with a major in biology. She was born in a small city in Oregon and has two older sisters, both close to her in age. Mrs. Wilson's parents divorced before she was 2 and she had little or no contact with her father thereafter. Mrs. Wilson believes her father was having an affair while he was married to her mother. Mrs. Wilson divorced her first husband after 5 years of marriage because he was frequently unfaithful. Life was quite difficult for her financially; she and her two children struggled quite a bit for 4 years, until she met and married Mr. Wilson.

Mr. Wilson, a 32-year-old high school graduate, was born and raised in a rural area of Michigan, the oldest of three brothers, each 2 years apart. The youngest brother was retarded, "caused scenes," and was quite difficult for the parents to handle. Mr. Wilson's parents argued a great deal and blamed each other for their problem child. His mother was suspicious of her husband's fidelity, and eventually the couple divorced when he was 15. His father was very strict, utilizing physical punishment frequently; he was also physically abusive to his wife. After 4 years of marriage, Mr. Wilson's first wife left him suddenly, without any apparent warning and divorced him; she wanted to "play and spend money," he stated, whereas he "wanted to be more responsible and save money."

Mr. Wilson felt that his current wife wanted only to be with the children and was too dedicated to being a mother instead of a wife. He complained that she was emotionally unresponsive to him; he felt isolated from the family because his wife accused him of not loving the children and being cruel to them. Mrs. Wilson reported that he was more loving to the child they had together, a daughter, age 5, born about 1 year after they married and who was reported to be more positively responsive to Mr. Wilson. He had thoughts of getting a divorce, but was reluctant to do so because he did not want to leave his younger daughter. He emphasized that he based his response to the children on their response to him: "I'm willing to *give* what I *get back*," he stated.

Mrs. Wilson felt her husband was much too strict, especially with her older daughter; he spanked her too often, even when she didn't deserve it, and he was harsh and coercive with her 12-year-old son, also a child from her former marriage. Mrs. Wilson stated that if her mother had remarried a man who ordered her and her sisters around, they would "kick him out." She was certain her children wanted to do the same. Mrs. Wilson feels she is letting her children down by not intervening in their conflicts with Mr. Wilson. The couple also argue because Mr. Wilson "likes having friends and going out." Mrs. Wilson refuses to get a babysitter, so he goes without her and she gets upset when he leaves. He complained that she is distant emotionally and sexually.

Several years ago Mr. Wilson became ill and was required to rest at home for some months. He felt his wife was not compassionate enough and she reports feeling quite guilty about that. Mrs. Wilson was reluctant to get help for her daughter, although her husband was pressuring her to do so, threatening to leave the family if she did not comply. When they discuss this problem Mr. Wilson becomes loud and loses his temper; his wife feels he becomes "too aggressive." In response, she becomes passive and refuses to discuss the issue any longer.

Mr. Wilson is a tall, thin, muscular man who was very concerned with his test performance and the examiner's opinion of him. He is employed as a graphic artist. He treated the examiner as a "buddy," but was sometimes quite overbearing, especially when relating his own opinions about child discipline. Mrs. Wilson, a tall, thin woman with short, dark hair, appeared friendly but rather childlike and innocent in her approach to the examiner, except when she discussed her husband, at which point she became bitter and cynical. She was quite passive and dependent on the examiner for guidance and direction.

See Appendix A for Mr. Wilson's Rorschach and Structural Summary; Appendix B for Mrs. Wilson's Rorschach and Structural Summary; and Appendix C for the Consensus Rorschach and Structural Summary.

RORSCHACH INTERPRETATION

Comprehensive System Scoring

The number of responses in the three records differs significantly: Mr. Wilson's record is longer than the typical record (32 R vs. 22–23 R), whereas Mrs. Wilson's record is shorter than average (17 R). The CR has even fewer responses than either person produced individually (13 R). Therefore we can hypothesize that with Mr. Wilson's cooperation, Mrs. Wilson exerts a significant controlling effect on her husband's productive activity, even more than she controls her own.

Mr. Wilson's Hypervigilance Index score is positive (7 out of a possible 8), whereas his wife's score is negative. Because the CR is also not positive for Hypervigilance, we may hypothesize that Mrs. Wilson's active interaction and control allow Mr. Wilson to be less vigilant in his approach to others, inviting him to feel safe and protected so he can abandon the hypervigilance defense when he is with his wife. Anything or anybody who interfaces with this "connection" will be seen as a potential danger, an intrusion into a dyadic relationship in which there is constriction, but comparative safety.

Mr. Wilson has five vague W responses in his record, compared with two for Mrs. Wilson, and zero for the CR. Again, we can see that Mrs. Wilson exerts a controlling, defining, and sharpening effect on her husband's perceptual world; she helps him to clarify what he sees and to organize his world. Developmental Quality (DQ) data reflect similar findings: Mr. Wilson's record contains five vague responses, where one or two are the norm, indicating a somewhat diffuse perceptual approach. Three of Mrs. Wilson's responses are vague, also indicating some diffuseness, but the CR contains no vague responses, indicating that the couple collaborate to be more focused and less diffuse than either is capable of being individually.

Compared with normative data for $X+\%$, $F+\%$, $X-\%$ and $Xu\%$, Mr. Wilson's scores are again more deviant, compared with Mrs. Wilson's scores; both his $X+\%$ (53%) and $F+\%$ (33%) are quite low, whereas his $X-\%$ (22%) and $Xu\%$ (25%) are quite high. Mrs. Wilson's $F+\%$ (80%) is higher than the norm, but her $X+\%$ (65%) is lower, although not extremely so. It is important to note the impact of R on $X+\%$ and $F+\%$; as R increases, they both go down and as R decreases, they both increase. Therefore, some of the differences in these variables among the three protocols are due to the differences in R. Nevertheless, these scores are quite extreme. Thus, Mr. Wilson's very low

$F+\%$ is an indication of the arbitrary, diffuse manner in which he approaches the world. His improvement with his wife's input is also striking; the joint score (71%) is double Mr. Wilson's score, although it is still somewhat lower than Mrs. Wilson's more normative score.

The couple did significantly better jointly on $X+$ (77%) than either of them did separately, achieving a score close to the norm. These findings indicate that in situations where emotions play a significant role the couple seem to collaborate productively to achieve a better reality-based focus than either is capable of individually. This is surprising considering the degree of disharmony they are experiencing. Perhaps their emotional disagreements are focused in only a few specific areas and do not extend throughout their relationship, or perhaps they utilize emotional disagreement to clarify and sharpen their own thinking. Similar results may be seen for $X-$, where the CR protocol contains about one third the $X-\%$ (8%), compared with Mr. Wilson's score (22%) and Mrs. Wilson's score (24%).

Mr. Wilson's *Lambda* score (.60) is within normal limits, as is his wife's score (.42). However, the *Lambda* for the CR is 1.14, which is above the .99 cutoff score indicated by Exner (1993) to be very high. On the CR the couple interacted to reduce stimulus situations to their most easily managed level; they agreed to narrow their approach to the world, oversimplifying complex stimulus demand situations. They do not see deeper implications of their joint marital problems and are therefore less effective in seeing complex or subtle aspects of their interaction. Therefore, they could not be expected to resolve their marital issues successfully. Exner (1993) described the high *Lambda* situation as one in which the simplification occurs as a defensive process:

> Significant elements of a field are viewed as having little importance when judged against the needs of the subject plus the perceived demands of the situation. As such those elements are afforded little or no attention in the formulation of responses. (p. 405)

It is no wonder that the couple go "round and round," each reiterating his or her point of view, in oversimplified terms; they focus primarily on the child-discipline issue, getting nowhere in the resolution of their marital difficulties. Their problems are far more complex than the child discipline issue, as is demonstrated in the continued analysis of the three protocols.

Both Mr. and Mrs. Wilson's $FC:CF + C$ ratios (4:3 and 3:1, respectively) are weighted more on the left side, as is the CR (2:0), which has a complete absence of right side responses. Although a number of other factors must be taken into account to determine the extent to which emotional discharge is modulated (e.g., D scores), Mrs. Wilson's ratio in favor of FC indicates well-controlled or modulated emotional expression, whereas Mr. Wilson's ratio indicates about equal emphasis on less well-modulated forms of emotional discharge and on more modulated emotional experience. Mrs. Wilson's influence in the CR is to modulate Mr. Wilson's emotionality, resulting in a significant reduction of emotion in their relationship, at a significant cost to their creative emotional life, especially for Mr. Wilson. Although his emotionality is somewhat better controlled in the CR, as is his focus on reality, his emotional control is probably imperfect, because it is less ego-syntonic. Emotional control is more typical for Mrs. Wilson, whose ratio is more similar to the CR ratio.

It is also important to consider the affective ratio (*Afr*) in deciding about responsiveness to emotional stimulation. Both Mr. Wilson's *Afr* (.39) and Mrs. Wilson's *Afr* (.31) are significantly lower than the norm (.69), but the ratio from the CR (.44) is only about 1 standard deviation below expectancy. Both Mr. and Mrs. Wilson individually demonstrate a marked effort to avoid emotional stimulation, but perhaps for different reasons. They both indicate discomfort with emotion and are socially constrained and isolated. Mr. Wilson attempts to avoid emotionality because he is probably quite aware that he has problems with its modulation and control, whereas Mrs. Wilson's overcontrol seems to be more characterological, as a stylistic element of her personality.

In both their individual *EB* scores and in their CR the couple are ambitent; their *M* values are about equally balanced with their color values, although the CR is more weighted toward *M* values, indicating a more introversive approach in this situation, focusing on the use of inner life to deal with basic gratification. Ambitent subjects are more vulnerable to difficulty in coping; because they have not developed a consistent coping style, they are less efficient and there is more vacillation (Exner, 1993). Thus, for both husband and wife emotions impact thinking, problem-solving, and decision-making activities in a rather inconsistent fashion.

Mrs. Wilson's Egocentricity Index score (.47) is high and not within normal limits; Mr. Wilson's score (.25) is low, whereas the CR Egocentricity Score (.54) is about 1.5 standard deviations above the norm. These findings indicate that together the couple are more egocentric than they are when functioning individually. Mrs. Wilson's record contains two reflections whereas Mr. Wilson's record has no reflections; the CR contains one reflection. The lower than average Egocentricity Index for Mr. Wilson indicates that he is significantly less self-focused than he should be. A lower than average Egocentricity Index indicates a lack of self-esteem, a sense of failure to meet one's expectations and desires for oneself, and is associated with depressive symptoms (Exner, 1993). The two reflection responses in Mrs. Wilson's short record suggest a narcissistic self-focus, making her involvement with self a significant problem for her husband, because this involvement is undoubtedly at the expense of her involvement with him. Her egocentric-narcissistic focus is brought through to the CR record, suggesting that it is a major aspect of the couple's interaction.

What stands out in the results for Special Scores is Mr. Wilson's 2 *MOR* responses, indicating some sense of feeling damaged. In the CR record there is an absence of *MOR*, again indicating the collaborative attempt to avoid negative affect and negative self-reflection and to concentrate on cooperative relationships. It is Mr. Wilson whose two *COP* scores are brought into the CR record, which suggests that Mr. and Mrs. Wilson utilize his cooperative efforts in their relationship. Although this finding does not fit with the history and the presenting problem, it is similar to several other such findings in their records, indicating that there are positive aspects to the couple's interaction.

Mr. Wilson's extremely high *PER* score (7) indicates an obsessive emphasis, because these scores indicate a need to be "overly precise in defending . . . self-image . . . and in fend[ing] off any potential challenge from the examiner, reflect[ing] a sort of defensive authoritarianism" (Exner, 1993, p. 526). A score of 3 suggests some tendency toward defensive authoritarianism in relationships that does not necessarily impair them, but indicates some security problems in situations that involve interpersonal challenge (Exner, 1993). Mrs. Wilson's score of 3 is certainly consistent with this interpretation; her husband has challenged her on a number of issues, such as their parenting disagreement. Mr. Wilson's score of 7 indicates that he is extremely insecure about his personal integrity; he feels challenged in many of his relationships, especially those with Mrs. Wilson. His defensive response to this perceived challenge is to become overtly authoritarian and argumentative, making him appear rigid, dogmatic, and inflexible. It is difficult to maintain a close relationship with him under these circumstances, because he seems to press others to be submissive to him to feel safe and unassailed. In their CR the *PER* scores drop to a minimum (1), again indicating that the couple do better together than each does separately. Although this is a good sign, it is inconsistent with the couple's report concerning child discipline. Perhaps this issue, which comes out of a feeling of emotional deprivation and intense nurturant need by Mr. Wilson, is relatively circumscribed in nature and the couple can collaborate more effectively in other areas.

In this regard it is important to examine the Coping Deficit Index (CDI) and the *D* and *Adjusted D* scores. Mrs. Wilson's record indicates the presence of a coping deficit (4 out of 5 positive signs), whereas Mr. Wilson's record does not (only 1 positive sign). The CR is also not positive for the presence of a coping deficit, although it contains 3 positive signs. Therefore, Mrs. Wilson's score seems to influence the interaction more so than Mr. Wilson's score. Although the interaction is effective in providing coping assistance for Mrs. Wilson, in combination with his wife he gives up a number of positive attributes in the service of the relationship, resulting in less adequate overall functioning for the couple. People with 4 or 5 indices positive for Coping Deficit are likely to have impoverished or unrewarding social relationships and difficulty contending with the typical demands of their social world, along with a history of limited interpersonal effectiveness and social ineptness, both related to depression (Exner, 1993). Mrs. Wilson's *D* and *Adjusted D* scores (−1 and 0, respectively) indicate that she is experiencing some feeling of being overloaded with life's demands, without adequate coping resources. Such individuals typically have trouble in new situations and they function best in predictable environments, becoming distracted and/or inefficient in their attempts to adapt in new situations. Mr. Wilson's *Adjusted D* of +2 indicates greater capacity for control and tolerance of stress. This finding is surprising because the focus of the family's complaint is Mr. Wilson's difficulty in dealing with the stress he experiences. Thus, the often cited observation concerning mutual deficits and problems for both spouses is also true here. In the CR record the *Adjusted D* score of 0 indicates a deficit in the interaction, compared with Mr. Wilson's superior score; as a couple they lose or give up Mr. Wilson's much better than average ability to tolerate stress.

Mrs. Wilson's *EA* score (4.5) is much lower than normal, whereas Mr. Wilson's score is somewhat above the norm (11.0); the *EA* of the CR record (3.0) is significantly lower than normal. Because *EA* is an index of accessible resources, "drawn on when necessary to formulate decisions and implement those decisions in deliberate behavioral activity" (Exner, 1993, p. 373), it appears that Mrs. Wilson's poverty of resources is brought through in the CR record. The couple functions as more impaired compared with Mr. Wilson's ability, but consistent with Mrs. Wilson's deficit; he gives up adequate coping and resource use and submits to his wife.

A high *Isolate/R* score indicates a desire to isolate oneself from relationships and withdraw. Mrs. Wilson's score (.47), significantly above the .20 norm, indicates a schizoid tendency. Mr. Wilson's score (.19) is essentially the normative score. The CR record score (.31) is somewhere between the two, but it is moderately elevated. These findings correspond with Mr. Wilson's complaint that his wife does not want to socialize or to go out with him. However, he collaborates with her to be more isolated. Her low *M* responsiveness (2) also suggests that she has a reduced interest and investment in people.

Although *AB* is a measure of intellectualization as a defensive process, it is important to note that this approach serves to neutralize the impact of the emotions, as a "naive form of denial" that distorts the true impact of a situation, "a pseudointellectual process that conceals and/or denies the presence of affect and, as a result, tends to reduce the likelihood that feelings will be dealt with directly and/or realistically" (Exner, 1993, p. 477). People who use this approach to manage emotions are more vulnerable to disorganization when they become intensely emotionally aroused. Mr. Wilson has 7 *AB* responses, a significantly high score; his wife's *AB* score is 0, as is the CR score. Thus, Mrs. Wilson does not resort to intellectualization as a defense and in the CR the couple avoid the defense as well.

Mr. Wilson's record contains 6 *M*, only one of which is a popular, indicating a high degree of imagination and an extensive use of fantasy, probably as a delaying tactic for impulse control and defensive withdrawal. Mr. Wilson's high *M* and *H* scores indicate that he is certainly interested in people, however much of this interest is not based in actual experience, but in fantasy. His *H:(H)* + *Hd* + *(Hd)* ratio is 4:11, well above the score for ambitents, suggesting that Mr. Wilson's self-image is largely based on imaginary rather than real experience, reflecting a significant degree of immaturity and a significantly distorted notion of self. The right side of the $H + A:Hd + Ad$ ratio (14:10) is much higher than it should be, suggesting a somewhat guarded and suspicious approach to others. His record contains a significant number of references to mythological beings (e.g., trolls, winged figures), indicating even further his regression from real-life issues to an emphasis on compensatory fantasy. The cartoon characters he sees seem like an attempt to distance himself from his impulses. The high number of H and (H) in his record (9), compared with M and the number of M that are associated with m, (H) and Hd indicate that he often resorts to fantasy rather than deal openly and directly in relationships; they are sometimes lived in his mind rather than lived out interpersonally.

Mr. and Mrs. Wilson's M responses are different, both in number and in quality. His 6 M responses emphasize mythology, whereas hers are more typical/popular. Piotrowski and Dudek (1956) indicated that people with dissimilar M responses are expected to be incompatible, because they cannot communicate with and understand each other on a deep level. They stated, "Marital mates with a difference of 3 or more in their sums of M . . . tend to manifest such disparate levels of psychological complexity that permanent and real understanding would be impossible between them" (p. 199). This is certainly the case with the Wilsons.

The 5 m responses in Mr. Wilson's record indicate that he feels forces are operating on him over which he has no control. He is probably experiencing his current life situation as one in which he is under severe stress and he experiences fear of disruption of controls. There is a sense of extreme helplessness present in this man, whereas his wife is experiencing helplessness to a much smaller degree (2 m). Thus, despite Mr. Wilson's attempts to utilize intellectualizing defenses maximally, they are not effective in helping him deal with the effects of the severe stress he is experiencing. The 5 m also represent the failure of repression, despite his attempts to distance himself from his impulses, which spill out into awareness as extreme subjective tension. He experiences himself as out of control and he feels the eruption of anger as dangerous and uncontrollable. However, the cause of the tension is experienced as external and he focuses instead on the press of situational factors. Mrs. Wilson's 2 m indicate that she, too, experiences her tension as external (her husband's aggressive discipline). On the CR the m response indicates that here their collaboration is an effective vehicle, other than in the "hot" area of child discipline; there is a "smoothing over" quality to the relationship, at least in this type of interactive situation. It remains to be seen in the content and process analysis whether this is accomplished through capitulation or through cooperation and collaboration. The 1 m in the CR protocol also indicates that the collaborative effort to inhibit, control, and dampen emotionality works well.

Mr. Wilson's record contains 3 blends that include *FY* responses, whereas Mrs. Wilson's record contains 1 *V* response and 2 *T* responses, but no *Y* responses. The CR protocol contains 1 *Y* response, but no *T* or *V* responses. Although Mr. and Mrs. Wilson's records contain only 1 *V,* the presence of even one such response is not positive. *V* represents an attempt to take distance in order to handle anxiety that is generated by self-focusing behavior, indicating that both Mr. and Mrs. Wilson experience, "discomfort, and possibly even pain . . . produced by . . . ruminative self-inspection which is focusing on *perceived* negative features of the self" (Exner, 1993, p. 387).

Y represents a painful absence of action, or a sense of paralysis, free-floating anxiety and stress-related helplessness. The *Y* findings for Mr. Wilson are quite consistent with the unusually high *m* finding. The *T* in Mrs. Wilson's record indicates need for closeness, whereas the absence of *T* in Mr. Wilson's record probably indicates the presence of a more guarded and/or distant approach to interpersonal relationships. However, it is important to consider the type of *T* response in order to determine how this underlying need is demonstrated in relationships. We return to this issue when we consider the individual responses.

In the CR record 1 *Y* response from Mr. Wilson's record was included, but his other 2 *Y* responses were discarded, indicating that the interaction has a salutary effect on Mr. Wilson; he seems willing to give up some or most of his painful anxiety. What replaces the *Y* scores in the CR record? *F*% increases, compared with the individual records; the CR record contains almost double Mrs. Wilson's *F*%, indicating that the couple resorts to simplification, ignoring the complexity of their stimulus world as a defensive response to conflict, focusing instead on obvious surface details.

Content Analysis

In this section I examine the content of the responses, card by card, for all three protocols.

Card I

Mr. Wilson's first response, spinning dancers, suggests that he is locked in a destabilizing relationship in which he feels out of control. Life events are moving too fast for him, producing a sense of heightened tension, causing him to experience the world as chaotic. Indeed, he sees the spinning person "holding onto someone else," indicating intense need to be grounded and cared for by someone on whom he can depend for nurturance. However, he believes there is no peaceful resolution. The process of engagement has a somewhat exhibitionistic, narcissistic flavor, which is enhanced in the next response, a winged, robed, mythological person, a powerful figure able to defy the gravity acting on him in the first response. This response is a defense against the chaos he feels about his relationships and may be seen from his scores for Card I (e.g., *2m; PER; (H)*). Mr. Wilson attempts to cope with these overwhelming feelings through overcompensation by resorting to an omnipotent and self-aggrandized stance with others (winged-person). This intellectualized attempt to find freedom and power, an ability to fly free and distance himself from his conflict, nevertheless contains an element of secrecy, where underlying inadequacies are hidden (robes) by assuming a powerful, but false self-stance. In this way he retreats from the problems of real life and does not deal with people directly and openly. Instead, he becomes authoritarian to avoid experiencing anxiety. Compared with the loss of secrecy in Response 1 ("something is coming out of their pockets"), the robe is successful in hiding what is underneath. In the third response Mr. Wilson sees a UFO "coming at you," perhaps indicating that he feels assailed by powerful, mysterious, and threatening forces. The last response, "a bug," indicates how he feels as a result and it is now possible to see what is underneath the self-aggrandizement and the attempts at omnipotence; he feels small and inadequate.

At first reading it appears as if there are two dancers in his first response, but a second reading suggests the presence of a third person, perhaps the older daughter, who is involved in the tension-filled, triangulated family relationship. Mr. Wilson appears to be attuned to these underlying issues; he recognizes that there are a host of problems related to this triangulation and he understands, on some level, that he has secrets he cannot keep from revealing. He attempts to stabilize himself through escape, using ideation and fantasy, but these defenses are not effective. He looks for control through a variety of obsessional defenses, but he continues to experience himself as fragile. He searches for some type of external order and clarity in his obsessive struggle to deal with the confusing complexity of his emotions. Mr. Wilson's view of the UFO "from above" suggests that despite his interest in people he will keep others at a distance by placing himself above them, to deal with the significant sense of inferiority and inadequacy he otherwise feels. The image is of a distant, powerful human being who has no clear identity and who travels alone in a somewhat empty world.

Mrs. Wilson's responses to Card I (moth; hat with horns) seem to convey that she is an unhappy, fragile woman with an underlying angry, somewhat aggressive stance to the world; her sense of power, obtained from a male, is used to bolster her more fragile sense of self. She has learned to take a stern, aggressive stance, but is more comfortable with indirect expression of her anger.

In the CR protocol the couple chose two responses from Mr. Wilson's record, somewhat abbreviated, and one response from Mrs. Wilson's record. Mr. Wilson's percept (mask) is merged with Mrs. Wilson's percept (helmet), both also abbreviated. They are much less productive together than Mr. Wilson was alone; their productivity matches Mrs. Wilson's productivity. More interesting than which percepts they chose is which percepts were omitted. Mrs. Wilson's fragile response (moth) and Mr. Wilson's fragile response (bug) were omitted, as well as the response that suggests that Mr. Wilson is threatened by forces he does not understand. The vague *W* responses, the *AB* and *PER* scores, and the mythological percept are all gone and there is now a *COP* score present. In their interaction they both agree that there are uncomfortable forces that are impairing them, but there is a better sense of control and well-being expressed. Yet the responses lack the imagination and creativity of Mr. Wilson's percepts and their number is reduced by half. There is certainly more control, balance, and cooperation, but these come at a great cost.

Card II

Mr. Wilson ignores the color until the last response, in which he expresses his emotion and sexual impulses with a great deal of power and force (torch with red fire shooting out). When he is initially emotionally stimulated, he hides his affect and sexuality (a mask with somebody behind it), continues on to caricature himself, and uses humor to hide his true emotions. He has trouble allowing himself to directly express human needs and desires (e.g., "a face," "a character from Walt Disney"; "two characters on their knees"). He attempts to deal with his needs for power, omnipotence, and emotional control through intellectualization (emblem), but the defense does not completely work. The force of the shooting fire and its glow both indicate his emotional lability and related sexual concerns, despite attempts to cognitively bind them. However, this approach, in which omnipotence, power, and control are used to deal with his overflowing emotionality is quite clever, as is his injection of the playful defense to hide his deeper needs (Disney character). Nevertheless, this defensive stance, in which he relies on external forms of adequacy, with a facade of bravado to hide underlying feelings of childlike dependence and passivity, is stimulated by a lurking recognition that such needs are unaccept-able to feel, or express. A summary of Card II might be: I am hiding the fact that I am childlike and seek nourishment and dependence as a child. I cannot accept those feelings, because they make me feel weak and inadequate. To compensate, I must use self-aggrandizing, omnipotent defenses, which run counter to my emotional and sexual needs.

In contrast, Mrs. Wilson begins with a typical response (people) after a significant delay, which implies color shock; she is compromised by the color and is negatively affected by it, indicating that she is very uncomfortable with her emotions. Her mention of the hats in the red area seems to represent her desire to control her emotions. Mrs. Wilson does not use the color in either of her two responses and her second response (sycamore bark) is one that appears cold and unempathic, symbolizing her feelings of fragility, as well as the lack of affection in her relationships. The awareness of painful, dysphoric affect is also represented in this percept; she feels separated from a safe, protected, and powerful environment and feels herself to be in a precarious position (the marriage?). There is a sense of detachment and isolation from others in this response; it reflects a temporary breach in reality testing, suggesting that she was experiencing strong, unpleasant, and disorganizing emotions.

In the CR record the number of responses is again reduced, and the couple collaborate on a response that is a good M, with playful affect, although it is rather childlike. Mr. Wilson's percept is agreed on, but the "characters" of his response become "people," from Mrs. Wilson's response. Thus, there is an improvement in the CR response, compared with Mrs. Wilson's rather painful and fragile "peeled sycamore bark" response. However, there is a loss of some creativity again and there is an attempt to control affect by mention of the hats from Mrs. Wilson's percept. Being together in a harmonious way requires that Mr. and Mrs. Wilson each must significantly compromise their typical approach, giving up much of their painful affect and allowing themselves to be somewhat playful in the presence of the other; but the cost, again, seems to be in the degree of productivity and creativity Mr. Wilson demonstrates on his own.

Card III

Mr. Wilson responds to this card in some positive and some negative ways. Certainly the smashed grasshopper indicates that he feels crushed by what he experiences as the unnatural, unyielding situation in his environment (the windshield). This is a significantly dysphoric response, from which he attempts to escape through immobilization (the "African characters" are not dancing, or even moving). He resorts to intellectualization (use of abstraction), and a more self-aggrandizing focus on surface omnipotence (tuxedo front). The ritual dance (Response 9) seems to be a description of the interaction Mr. Wilson experiences with his wife, with all its incongruities.

Mrs. Wilson's response is more typical, but she is uncertain about whether the people are wearing high heels or boots, perhaps suggesting some sexual identity confusion. She then gives a bony anatomy response, suggesting that she may be hiding hostile and aggressive impulses from herself, utilizing repression and reaction-formation. Thus, she would probably deny angry impulses but would display her anger in passive-aggressive ways. She is rigid and anxious in interpersonal relationships and is rather naive with regard to her own emotions. The mention that there is no backbone suggests that she feels a lack of emotional strength, especially in relation to her husband.

In the CR record Mr. Wilson's response is chosen, but with some important changes. Mrs. Wilson helps focus and direct him; the negative aspects of his responses (2– responses, 1 PER, 2 AB) are gone. In the CR the sexual identity of the "people" is significantly established (women) and there is a sexual response (breasts). When she is interacting with her husband, Mrs. Wilson's identity is clearly more feminine, but there is a lack of effort made toward intimacy, because there is no movement expressed in the human figures.

Card IV

At first Mr. Wilson's view of himself (and perhaps of his own father) as a mean and angry person who might aggressively attack seems satisfying to him ("It's a neat picture; I like that one"). However, he attempts to neutralize the impact of his forceful manner and angry ways and turns the animals into an abstract design on a headband, symbolizing attempts to control his rage through intellectualization. He really sees himself as more fragile (a leaf off an exotic plant), more needy, and more deprived. It is this weak, fragile, and needy view of self that is so frightening that it must be fended off by a return to a more defensive, aggressive stance (troll).

Mrs. Wilson's response seems to reflect her sense of insignificance in the face of male authority. Her attempts to defend herself do not work and she tries to distance herself from what she sees as an aggressive, overpowering authoritarian threat. The response chosen in the CR is not the powerless bug, nor the distancing response, but a character of meanness and aggressiveness (troll), a hostile, mythological being, often seen as a symbol of destructive instincts. Why did Mrs. Wilson allow the expression of Mr. Wilson's angry responses, when she states that she finds his anger troublesome? Perhaps her statement is not truly accurate, or the anger is muted because the troll is a devalued symbol, or perhaps it is "headed away" and is therefore not threatening. Although Mrs. Wilson complains of her husband's authoritarian manner, the couple agree to use more of his responses rather than hers. Is this because Mrs. Wilson is passive and/or frightened and therefore capitulates to her husband, or is it because she both desires and needs his creative and/or aggressive input because she is overcontrolled? Perhaps she depends on him to offer the emotionality and creativity she lacks.

Card V

Mr. Wilson seems to be responding to the darkness of the card and is probably aware of his depression, perhaps manifested by his anger (tentacles, pincers). Intense cognitive disturbance is indicated by the two *INCOM* scores; this card has caused him a significant degree of discomfort, from which he escapes with a hysteroid, exhibitionistic defense. While showing off, he nevertheless needs to hide some aspect of self, covering up (costume) the dysphoria, the confusion, and the discomforting combination of neediness, anger, and resentment.

Mrs. Wilson's rather ordinary response is the one chosen for the CR; it is unusual for her response to be chosen. What is new here is the distancing (looking down from the top) that was added through collaboration. They both distance themselves from their impulses and Mrs. Wilson again serves as the emotional stabilizer by facilitating Mr. Wilson's disengagement and distancing from affective involvement.

Card VI

Two of Mr. Wilson's 5 *m* responses occur on this card, one *F*– response (bug), the only passive movement response in the record, and one of the two *MOR* scores. It could be the content of, or the responses to Card V that caused such disturbance, or the content of and/or the responses to Card VI itself that was the problem. Mr. Wilson mentions the "dream catcher," an Indian object, said to catch evil spirits during sleep and prevent them from entering dreams, allowing only good dreams through. What evil spirits could attack? Is he speaking of his explosive anger, or is his response related to some aspect of sexuality, because Card VI often reflects sexual issues? He seems to be asking for a protective defense, a way of repressing uncomfortable thoughts and emotions. Mr. Wilson could be concerned about his masculinity, his sexual adequacy, or his sexual identity, and/or he could have some problem with sexual functioning. All these interpretations and others are possible. Whatever underlying feelings he has concerning his vulnerability make him feel terribly inadequate, because his next response was, "what it would look like if you stepped on a bug." All the cards, he says, remind him of a bug, meaning that he feels small, inadequate, and threatened all the time. His anger, although intense, is certainly muted in the next response (volcano) through intellectualizing and distancing defenses. There is a sense of impotence portrayed in these responses.

Mrs. Wilson responds with narcissistic disdain (reflection) and strong personal involvement on this card, probably distancing herself from any sexual interest. This is certainly consistent with the history given by him. Does Mrs. Wilson have a cool, intellectualized approach to sexuality, focused on her self-satisfaction rather than on mutuality? Does her description of cat tails, bushes, and so forth symbolize her awareness of a sexualized feeling, turned away from her husband? Her next response, "a bear skin with a big tail," indicates that she experiences the presence of male sexuality with some tension and discomfort (presence of m). In asking to draw a head on the bear skin she perhaps recognizes her discomfort and avoidance. Is she guilty and attempting to make repairs to her injured husband, or is she asking that she have more control over his sexual impulses and/or aggressiveness?

In the CR record Mr. Wilson's first response (hide) is utilized, with the addition of a description of the dark area as the backbone. This addition seems to focus on mutual need for compensatory strength and adequacy. The m tension is no longer present, but more diffuse anxiety seems reflected here (Y), suggesting that they both share a great deal of tension surrounding mutual sexual issues.

Card VII

Mr. Wilson's initial response is quite typical (a popular M), except that he sees "little girls" rather than women, suggesting a personal sense of immaturity as well as his view of women as childlike and immature. His reference to jester's masks indicates an attempt to ward off depressive affect and to present a happy false self.

Mrs. Wilson's first response (animal heads) and the significant delay in responding indicate that this card caused her extreme discomfort and confusion. Her percept (cross between an elephant and a horse) represents strong, aggressive instinctual forces in a card that ordinarily pulls for pleasant female percepts. She seems to be disavowing her femininity, which, however, fills her full of conflict. This response is followed by another that still reflects a high degree of emotional disturbance, despite attempts to gain distance (you're up, looking down). Again, there is a somewhat distorted view of an aggressive male animal (rottweiler) in the next response.

The first CR response is also a minus, again indicating a high degree of discomfort and disorganization in the couple's interaction. It is a new response, not given by either husband or wife, but it substitutes the younger daughter's legs, representing Mr. Wilson's source of affection, for part of Mrs. Wilson's rottweiler. The second CR response is Mr. Wilson's healthier individual response. Rather than two poor responses, there is only one, and the second response is at least improved and more appropriate; here the collaboration serves to at least partially ameliorate the discomfort and disorganized thinking that involves Mrs. Wilson's more direct expression of her strong underlying aggressive impulses. However, Mr. Wilson's assistance to his wife in controlling negative thoughts, feelings, and impulses is not as good as her efforts to do the same for him.

Card VIII

Mr. Wilson's first response indicates a great deal of creativity and excellent integrative ability. He again indicates how he goes about using compensatory intellectualizing and ego enhancing defenses, as he builds a percept from little animals (felt inadequacy) to a symbol on a knight's shield, indicating an underlying feeling of intense inadequacy and compensatory aggrandizing and narcissistic defenses in which he seeks strength, courage, and distinctiveness. He further enhances the percept with aggressive and phallic symbols (ram, tree). The shield protects him from his weak and inadequate feelings, as do the self-aggrandizing aspects of the response. However, such compensation is hardly enough; it does not last and the underlying inadequacy feelings quickly break through (face on a bug). The previous response and the one that follows serve to make him feel much better about himself, for the moment. He oscillates from a compensatory response to the view of himself as inadequate and thereby vulnerable to destruction at the hands of cruel, sadistic attackers. He again resorts to compensatory denial and aggrandizement (Indian headdress), indicating that these defenses work inadequately and sporadically. It will not take much to puncture this artificial stance; the result will be rage and aggressive attempts to dominate. He feels the examiner can see through him (magnified bug) and that these underlying feelings are readily apparent. The compensating oscillation to self-aggrandizement takes place once again, as indicated by his next percept, the African ceremonial headdress.

On this card Mrs. Wilson again resorts to a narcissistic stance, emphasizing her feelings of power and aggressiveness in this self-aggrandized response. Her description of the wax art of batik with a "crackly, wrinkled" surface suggests an emotional hardness and an underlying aggressive stance toward others, couched rather indirectly.

In the CR the more typical animals are seen, devoid of the anger and aggression (Mr. Wilson's animals, not Mrs. Wilson's cougars or tigers), but Mrs. Wilson's narcissistic stance is nevertheless included. Mr. Wilson goes along with her narcissism and self-aggrandizement, so long as the anger and aggressiveness are removed from the interaction. In this sense it is Mr. Wilson who modulates his wife's aggressiveness or the couple collaborate to have her respond less angrily or aggressively. However, as before, the responses appear less creative and original, indicating that the cost to the marriage is a loss of spontaneity and creativity.

Card IX

Mr. Wilson's response (exotic flower) seems to reflect an underlying passive and dependent orientation to the world, in sharp contrast to the active M responses he gives. He is uncomfortable with the feminine aspects of his personality and he modulates this stance with a more aggressive, phallic intrusiveness (stamen, cactus). He attempts to resolve this conflict by assuming an aggressive, independent, defensive stance and by hiding the more feminine part of his personality.

In the CR both Mr. and Mrs. Wilson's percepts are included, indicating that here Mr. Wilson feels it is safe to express his passive, dependent needs to his wife. However, he must tailor his responses and his expression of these needs very carefully. In the CR he omits the stamen, and the flower response is more clearly described. Mr. Wilson's CF and FC responses and Mrs. Wilson's FC response become one FC response and one F response; the color is no longer employed in the second CR response, when it was clearly expressed in Mrs. Wilson's response. She also omits the playful, childlike reference, "a girl with a pink hat," while Mr. Wilson omits the cartoon character. The couple seem to be saying that it is safe to communicate passive, dependent needs without Mr. Wilson's defensive, masculine sexualized stance. In addition, they collaborate to reduce playfulness and to control emotion more carefully.

For the sake of brevity the analysis of Card X is not included, because the themes are essentially a repetition of several other cards.

SUMMARY

The CR was quite useful in this case because it allowed the assessor and the potential therapist to obtain a unique and comprehensive view of this relationship, illuminating both its constructive and destructive elements. It is clear that the couple pay a significant emotional price in their marriage relationship. The problems in the relationship cause both Mr. and Mrs. Wilson to withdraw emotionally and physically. Mr. Wilson's response to the problems in their marriage is to become guarded, to live more in fantasy, and to resort to a variety of intellectualizing defenses to erect a strong false self to hide his intense neediness, the confusing feminine qualities in his personality, and an intense sense of inadequacy. To get along with each other Mr. and Mrs. Wilson must constrict their emotionality, which is a much easier task for Mrs. Wilson than it is for her husband. Mr. Wilson must give up creative exploration and resort extensively to fantasy. The couple compromise to constrict their lives, their interests, and their worldview to get along. This is a rather high price to pay for some small semblance of security offered by the marriage bond. Together the couple is significantly less productive, less emotional, and less creative than either person is apart, and much less so than Mr. Wilson is by himself. Together they exhibit poorer coping ability than Mr. Wilson is capable of himself and they appear to have exhausted their emotional resources. Yet, what is also missing in their CR is the very painful affect and the intense, precarious feeling that both have about themselves. This is especially true of Mr. Wilson, many of whose chaotic, tension-filled, and dysphoric responses disappear in the CR.

That Mrs. Wilson is cold, somewhat narcissistic, and indirectly controlling is rather obvious; that Mr. Wilson is obsessive, intellectualizing, and self-aggrandizing is also easy to see. Both of them seem difficult to live with and probably were difficult people before they ever met one another. Both have found some comfort in overinvolvement with their children—Mrs. Wilson with her two children from her former marriage and Mr. Wilson with the couple's new daughter. These children provide dynamic support for the couple, but each in a different manner. Mr. Wilson has substituted the positive emotional response he gets from the child for the nurturance he seeks and cannot find from his wife. Mrs. Wilson's style is to fuse with her children as a bulwark against a punitive father figure. Her deep-seated emotional hunger for a benign father is very difficult for Mrs. Wilson to fathom because she dislikes men and sees them as harsh and punishing.

Although there are certainly negative aspects to this relationship, there are also a number of positive findings that show up in the CR record, compared with the individual records. The couple demonstrate productive collaboration and a spark of playfulness in some of their joint responses. In some instances they combine their individual responses in the CR record to produce a response that is at least as good as their individual responses and sometimes better than either individual response. The couple do interact for mutual benefit: Together they avoid depressive affect; they interact to mediate Mrs. Wilson's coping deficit; and in their relationship Mr. Wilson often feels safe: His world is more clearly defined and balanced and his reality testing is better. In her collaboration with Mr. Wilson, Mrs. Wilson also copes better with the world. Thus, they provide some semblance of protection for each other; he helps her cope and she helps him to feel safer, with significantly less tension and possibly less destructive emotionality. However, neither Mr. or Mrs. Wilson seem to provide a loving, nourishing atmosphere for each other.

A therapist might want to facilitate both Mr. and Mrs. Wilson's dynamic understanding of their unempathic responses to each other, helping them to see how previous life issues have caused them to force extreme reactions in each other, especially concerning Mr. Wilson's punitive responses to Mrs. Wilson's children. The therapist might also highlight the positive aspects of the interaction as a couple, perhaps even utilizing their interaction on the Rorschach to illustrate both productive and unproductive interactions. I have found that such illustrations are experienced as productive, concrete examples for such couples, who often cannot fathom the intense relational nature of their unhappiness. Finally, the redundancy of findings for many elements in the Structural Summary, for the various cards in the content analysis, and also for both methods of interpretation compared with each other, help to reinforce the validity of interpretations made here. Nevertheless, it is important to compare these findings with additional test and interview data. A number of questions were raised in the analysis and a number of alternative hypotheses were considered. Typically, the examiner utilizes additional assessment and interview data to answer such questions and to choose appropriate alternatives.

ACKNOWLEDGMENTS

I thank Edward Aronow, John Exner, Barbara Handler, Mark Hilsenroth, and Paul Lerner, as well as Justin Padawer, Jay Moses, and Reva Herron for their very valuable assistance in the preparation of this chapter.

REFERENCES

Alanen, Y., & Kinnunen, P. (1975). Marriage and the development of schizophrenia. *Psychiatry*, *38*, 346–365.

Aronow, E., & Reznikoff, M. (1976). *Rorschach content interpretation*. New York: Grune & Stratton.

Aronow, E., Reznikoff, M., & Moreland, K. (1994). *The Rorschach technique*. Boston: Allyn & Bacon.

Bauman, G., & Roman, M. (1966). Interaction testing in the study of marital dominance. *Family Process*, *5*, 230–242.

Bauman, G., & Roman, M. (1968). Interaction product analysis in group and family diagnosis. *Journal of Projective Techniques and Personality Assessment*, *32*, 331–337.

Bauman, G., Roman, M., Borello, J., & Meltzer, B. (1967). Interaction testing in the measurement of marital intelligence. *Journal of Abnormal Psychology*, *72*, 489–495.

Berg, T. (1980). The "Couple's Rorschach" and the "Post-Rorschach": Two methods in marital diagnosis. *Tidsskrift for Norsk Psykologforening*, *17*, 333–345.

Blanchard, W. (1959). The group process in gang rape. *Journal of Social Psychology, 49*, 259–266.

Blanchard, W. (1968). The Consensus Rorschach: Background and development. *Journal of Projective Techniques and Personality Assessment, 32*, 327–330.

Bos, P. (1974). Family Rorschach: A method for detection of family dynamics. *Ceskoslovenska Psychiatrie, 70*, 167–173.

Cutter, F., & Farberow, N. (1968). Serial administration of Consensus Rorschachs to one patient. *Journal of Projective Techniques and Personality Assessment, 32*, 358–374.

Dorr, D. (1981). Conjoint psychological testing in marriage therapy: New wine in old skins. *Professional Psychology, 12*, 549–555.

Dudek, S. (1969). Interaction testing as a measure of therapeutic change in groups. *Journal of Projective Techniques and Personality Assessment, 33*, 127–137.

Engel, K. (1978). Testing cooperation in parents with children destined for home dialysis. *Psychotherapy and Psychosomatics, 30*(1), 28–36.

Exner, J. (1993). *The Rorschach: A comprehensive system: Vol. 1. Basic foundations* (3rd ed.). New York: Wiley.

Gentile, S. (1981). Ruling values of common Rorschach (Willi) calculated in a 50 couple sample. *Rivista di Psichiatria, 16*, 493–502.

Klopfer, W. (1969). Consensus Rorschach in the primary classroom. *Journal of Projective Techniques and Personality Assessment, 33*, 549–552.

Levy, J., & Epstein, N. (1964). An application of the Rorschach test in family investigation. *Family Process, 3*, 344–376.

Loveland, N. (1967). The relation Rorschach: A technique for studying interaction. *The Journal of Nervous and Mental Disease, 145*, 93–105.

Loveland, N., Wynne, L., & Singer, M. (1963). The family Rorschach: A new method for studying family interaction. *Family Process, 2*, 163, 187–215.

Nielsen, G. (1979). Rorschach for two. *Tidsskrift for Norsk Psykologforening, 16*, 417–423.

Piotrowski, Z., & Dudek, S. (1956). Research on human movement response in the Rorschach examinations of marital partners. In V. Eisenstein (Ed.), *Neurotic interaction in marriage* (pp. 192–207). New York: Basic Books.

Roman, M., & Bauman, G. (1960). Interaction testing: A technique for the psychological evaluation of small groups. In M. Harrower, P. Vorhaus, M. Roman, & G. Bauman (Eds.), *Creative variations is in the projective techniques* (pp. 93–138). Springfield, IL: Charles Thomas.

Shapiro, L., & Wild, C. (1976). The product of the Consensus Rorschach in families of male schizophrenics. *Family Process, 15*, 211–224.

Shulman, S., & Klein, M. (1982). The family and adolescence: A conceptual and experiential approach. *Journal of Adolescence, 5*, 219–234.

Singer, M. (1968). The Consensus Rorschach and family transaction. *Journal of Projective Techniques and Personality Assessment, 32*, 348–351.

Singer, M. (1977). The Rorschach as a transaction. In M. Rickers-Ovsiankina, (Ed.), *Rorschach psychology* (pp. 455–483). Huntington, NY: Krieger.

Singer, M., & Wynne, L. (1963). Thought disorders and family relations of schizophrenics. III. Methodology using projective techniques. *Archives of General Psychiatry, 12*, 187–200.

Singer, M., & Wynne, L. (1966). Principles for scoring communication defect and deviances in parents of schizophrenics: Rorschach and TAT scoring manuals. *Psychiatry, 29*, 260–288.

Singer, M., & Wynne, L. (1975). Principles for scoring communication defects and deviances in parents of schizophrenics: Rorschach and TAT scoring manuals. In P. Lerner (Ed.), *Handbook of Rorschach scales* (pp. 361–405). New York: International Universities Press.

Sokolova, Y. (1985, July–August). Modified Rorschach for studying disturbances in family interaction. *Voprosy Psikhologii, 4*, 145–150.

Suzuki, K. (1972). A study of families of schizophrenic patients: A study utilizing the family consensus Rorschach. *Journal of Mental Health, 46*(20), 1–40.

Timsit, M., & Gross, W. (1989). Identity and relationship in schizophrenic patients and their mothers revealed in a consensus Rorschach test. *Psychologie Medicale, 21,* 809–824.

Wahlstrom, J. (1986). Assessment of social influences on the cognitive-affective functioning in the Consensus Rorschach. *Psykologia, 21,* 408–413.

Wahlstrom, J. (1987). Consensus Rorschach interaction patterns of families with an asthmatic child. *Journal of Family Therapy, 9,* 265–280.

Wichstrom, L., & Holte, A. (1991). Maturity of personality and family communication. *Scandinavian Journal of Psychiatry, 32,* 372–383.

Wichstrom, L., Holte, A., & Wynne, L. (1993). Disqualifying family communication and anxiety in offspring at risk for psychopathology. *Acta Psychiatrica Scandinavica, 88,* 74–79.

Willi, J. (1967). The Combined Rorschach Test, a means of studying partner relations. *Psychotherapy and Psychosomatics, 15*(1), 69.

Willi, J. (1969). Joint Rorschach testing of partner relationships. *Family Process, 8,* 64–78.

Willi, J. (1971). Analysis of the structure of a marriage crisis with the help of the Joint Rorschach Test. *Psychotherapy and Psychosomatics, 19*(4), 193–225.

Willi, J. (1977). The utilization of the Joint Rorschach Test: A direct test of social interaction. *Psychologie Schweizererische Zeirschhrift fur Psychologie und ihre Anwendungen, 36,* 239–253.

Willi, J. (1978–1979). The Rorschach as a test of direct interaction in groups. *Bulletin de Psychologie, 32,* 279–282.

Wynne, L. (1968). Consensus Rorschach and related procedures for studying interpersonal patterns. *Journal of Projective Techniques and Personality Assessment, 32,* 352–356.

I. (8")

1. Looks like dancers, spinning around, dancing.

INQ: In the middle, holding on to someone else; it's abstract, blurred. Two dancers, one spinning the other around. (Dancers?) The hands are up. Whatever they have on, centrifugal force makes it look like that. We've been watching the Olympics. They could be skaters. (Spinning?) The line down the middle, like an axis. Everyone's pushed outward, like it's spinning. Maybe spinning too hard. Something is coming out of their pockets (Pt.points to little "dots" on the edge of card)

2. Looks Like a winged person. A Greek mythology character with its hands above its head, with wings spread out.

INQ: A person in the middle, with a robe and wings. (Greek mythology?) Because of the wings and the robes. It has a majestic look.

3. From the top, some kind of U.F.O. A spacecraft from Star Trek.

INQ: Wings (on the side) going backwards, coming at you, with the nose (bottom) at the front.

4. Or a bug. (Pt has a long discourse about a "guy who collected bugs," exotic bugs. He spoke too fast for the examiner to record it, however). (Bugs?) I make (he means create artistically) faces, abstractly. Ears, cheeks, nose.

II. (13.5")

5. ^ Looks like some kind of mask.

INQ: Looks like there's somebody behind it. (Pt points) nose, mouth, hair.

6. A face, a character from Walt Disney, with a beard.

INQ: Some kind of a character; nose (center top); mouth (2 lines in the center); hair around the sides

7. Two characters on their knees, with their hands together, playing patty cake on something.

INQ: The knees, feet (bottom side) hands (center top). (Pt points to details)

V8. An emblem—a company logo, a torch (white)

INQ: The white in the middle is a torch, with fire above it. (Torch ?) Statue of Liberty torch, red up on top. The shape of it. (Fire?) Red, and it shoots out at the top, glowing

III. (13")

9. It sounds nutty, but people dancing, again. Two characters doing some kind of ritual dance. African women. They have things in their lips, like in the National Geographic. It doesn't fit the characters, but they have high heels on, too.

INQ: They're dancing. Symmetricals. They're African because their necks look like in the National Geographic; the women put rings around their necks.

10. What it would look like if a grasshopper smashed itself up against a window. Kinda looks like a bug, too.

INQ: The grasshopper, it's in its mouth and eyes (Pt. points to areas; he means that what makes it look like a grasshopper, to him, is the mouth and eye areas).

11. People. Some kind of African characters. The head, neck, body

INQ: Head, beard, goatee, neck. The rest is abstract.

12. A bow tie; the front of a tuxedo. An abstract version of a tuxedo.

INQ: (Tuxedo?) Abstract. The way its shaped. (Bow tie?) The shape, the differences in color, the shading, the color.

IV. (10")

13. Looks like some kind of an animal, an abstract buffalo or something. Like a cross between a buffalo and horse, or warthog. It's a neat picture; I like that one. (Pt. indicates it is a design).

INQ: The ears (side) the dark place (in the middle) are eyes. Nostrils (lower center). An Indian might wear it (the design) on its head. (Pt. then lapsed into a long discussion about his job, making certain types of artwork).

V14. Looks like a leaf off an exotic plant. 3-dimensional; the leaf, curling.

INQ: The backside of a leaf (top, side). The shading is to give an effect, like its curled over.

15. Could be a troll; the whole body, big feet, little arms, sticking out. Fuzzy head, and tail. (Fuzzy?) The Outline

INQ: (Pt. talks about the Olympics opening ceremonies). Troll, heading away. Backbone, tail, large feet; not moving away, just pointing away.

V. (3")

16. Looks like a moth or a butterfly.

INQ: The shape, the tail, the tentacles. Symmetrical.

V17. Moth or butterfly with pincers

INQ: A cross between a butterfly and a crab. The pincers are like crab pincers.

18. Some kind of dancer; the character in the middle, in a costume in a play, spinning around, on tiptoes.

INQ: Tiptoes. In old movies. Some kind of a dancer, tiptoes and symmetrical-like movement.

VI. (8")

19. Some kind of something you see in an Indian's house; rug, hide, hanging up. Ornamental, with feathers. Something that's significant to them, like a round ring above their heads at bedtime.

INQ: Feathers and sticks; it means something like a dream catcher. I'm trying to make it look like a bird. (Hide?) the shape (Features?) the shape

20. What it would look like if you stepped on a bug. They all remind me of some kind of bug.

INQ: The shape

21. Almost looks like a clinical view or side view of a volcano, looking at it from the bottom, up.

INQ: The top of a volcano (top); earth's core (bottom), line coming up, lava coming up. A cut-away view; technical view, like you see in a school view. (Volcano?) From the shape, the darker part, a shaft coming up to it. (Earth's core?) The shading

VII. (13")

22. Two characters, two little girls, looking at each other, with their pony tails. I can't really visualize much in this one.

INQ: Hair, nose, little mouth. Ponytail, arms sticking out, part of the body.

23. Masks in a theater; Jester's masks; looks like they're balanced.

INQ: Nose, eye. They're looking outward. (Jester's masks?) The hats on the heads, like a jester would have. (Balanced?) Everything's balanced.

(continued)

VIII. (22")

24. Looks like some kind of little animals, climbing up the side of a hill or tree. Looks like some kind of a symbol for something, like the knights had on their shields, like a bear climbing a hill; ram at the bottom. I see the face at the bottom.

INQ: (bears?) feet, look like they're climbing; the shape makes it look like a furry animal. (Furry?) The shape. (Tree?) It's climbing up something. (Face of a ram?) The shape and the shading makes it look like a ram's horn, the nose. (Shield?) It's symmetrical.

25. Looks like the face on a bug, too. Put ink on a bug and pushed it against the wall.

INQ: Looks like a bug magnified 4000 times; the shape of it.

26. African ceremonial headdress.

INQ: The shape and the colors; bright; some kind of ceremonial outfit.

IX. (10")

27. Some kind of exotic flower, a flower bloom.

INQ: The colors, the symmetrical . . . .lots of flowers on the inside. The stamen (center line). We have cactuses, which bloom once every few years.

28. Looks like some kind of cartoon character with elephant ears and a green coat on.

INQ: (Pt. points) legs, coat on; elephant ears, trunk

X. (31")

29. I see characters in this, too; characters with robes on.

INQ: The red is the robe, head with headdress.

30. A face at the bottom, mustache, nose, eyes.

INQ: Real abstract, little mustache (green) with eyes (yellow). (Mustache?) curling up; I do them (Pt. means paints them) at work. A nose.

31. Looks like a three year old's rendition of some kind of a flower.

INQ: When Sandra goes into the greenhouse and what she would paint with watercolors. (Flower?) The stem, the colors.

32. Some kind of character; eyes, mouth, nose.

INQ: Eyes (yellow), outline of the face (pink). Mustache (blue), eyebrows (top of green).

(continued)

Card	No.	Loc.	#	Determinant(s)	(2)	Content(s)	Pop Z	Special Scores
I	1	W+	1	Ma.mao	2	H	4.0	AB, PER
	2	Wo	1	Mao		(H), Cg	1.0	
	3	Wo	1	ma.FDu		Sc	1.0	
	4	Wv	1	Fu		(Ad), Art		PER, AB
II	5	WSo	1	FDu		(Hd), Hd	4.5	
	6	WSo	1	F–		(Hd)	4.5	
	7	D+	6	Mao	2	(H)	3.0	COP
	8	DdSo	99	CF.mau		Fi, Art	4.5	
III	9	D+	9	Mao	2	H, Cg	3.0	COP
	10	Do	1	F–		Ad		MOR
	11	Do	1	Fo	2	H		AB
	12	DdSo	99	FC.FY–		Cg	4.5	AB
IV	13	Wo	1	FC'o		(A), Art, Cg	2.0	AB, PER, INC, DR
	14	Wv	1	FVo		Bt		
	15	Wo	1	Fo		(H)	P 2.0	PER
V	16	Wo	1	Fo	2	A	P 1.0	INC
	17	Wo	1	F–		(A)	1.0	INC
	18	Wo	1	Mao		H, Cg	1.0	
VI	19	Wo	1	mpo		Ad, Art	P 2.5	
	20	Wv	1	F–		A		MOR
	21	Wo	1	ma.FYu		Ls, Fi, Sc	2.5	
VII	22	D+	2	Mpo	2	Hd	P 3.0	
	23	Do	3	Fo	2	Cg		
VIII	24	W+	1	FMa.FYo		A, Na, Art	P 4.5	
	25	Wv	1	F–		Ad, Sc		
	26	Wo	1	FCu		Cg, Ay	4.5	
IX	27	Wo	1	CFo		Bt	5.5	PER
	28	Wo	1	FCu		(H), Cg	5.5	
X	29	Do	9	FCo	2	(H), Cg		
	30	DdSo	99	Fu		(Hd), Art		AB, PER
	31	Wv	1	CFo		Bt, Art		PER, AB
	32	DdSo	22	F–		(Hd)		

Summary of Approach

I:W.W.W.W	VI:W.W.W
II:WS.WS.D.DdS	VII:D.D
III:D.D.D.DdS	VIII:W.W.W
IV:W.W.W	IX:W.W
V:W.W.W	X:D.DdS.W.DdS

(continued)

Husband's Rorschach: Rorschach Structural Summary

LOCATION FEATURES	DETERMINANTS BLENDS	DETERMINANTS SINGLE	CONTENTS	S-CONSTELLATION
			H = 4,0	YES..FV + VF + V + FD > 2
			(H) = 5,0	YES..Col-Shd Bl>0
Zf = 21	M.m	M = 5	Hd = 1,1	YES..Ego<.31,>.44
ZSum = 65.0	m.FD	FM = 0	(Hd) = 4,0	NO..MOR>3
ZEst = 70.0	CF.m	m = 1	Hx = 0,0	YES..Zd > ± 3.5
	FC.FY	FC = 3	A = 3,0	NO..es>EA
W = 21	m.FY	CF = 2	(A) = 2,0	NO..CF+C>FC
(Wv = 5)	FM.FY	C = 0	Ad = 3,0	YES..X+%<.70
D = 7		Cn = 0	(Ad) = 1,0	YES..S>3
Dd = 4		FC' = 1	An = 0,0	NO..P<3 or >8
S = 6		C'F = 0	Art = 0,7	NO..Pure H <2
		C' = 0	Ay = 0,1	NO..R<17
		FT = 0	Bl = 0,0	6.....TOTAL
DQ		TF = 0	Bt = 3,0	
.........(FQ–)		T = 0	Cg = 3,6	SPECIAL SCORINGS

DQ	(FQ–)		SINGLE	CONTENTS		
+	= 5 (0)	FV = 1	Cl = 0,0		Lvl	Lv2
o	= 22 (5)	VF = 0	Ex = 0,0	DV	= 0x1	0x2
v/+	= 0 (0)	V = 0	Fd = 0,0	INC	= 3x2	0x4
v	= 5 (2)	FY = 0	Fi = 1,1	DR	= 1x3	0x6
		YF = 0	Ge = 0,0	FAB	= 0x4	0x7
		Y = 0	Hh = 0,0	ALOG	= 0x5	
FORM QUALITY		Fr = 0	Ls = 1,0	CON	= 0x7	
		rF = 0	Na = 0,1	SUM6	= 4	
		FD = 1	Sc = 1,2	WSUM6	= 9	

	FQx	FQf	MQual	SQx	SINGLE	CONTENTS		
+	= 0	0	0	0	F = 12	Sx = 0,0		
o	= 17	4	6	0		Xy = 0,0	AB =7	CP = 0
u	= 8	2	0	3		Id = 0,0	AG =0	MOR = 2
–	= 7	6	0	3			CFB =0	PER = 7
none	= 0	–	0	0	(2) = 8		COP =2	PSV = 0

RATIOS, PERCENTAGES, AND DERIVATIONS

R = 32	L = 0.60	FC:CF+C =4:3	COP = 2	AG = 0
		Pure C = 0	Food	= 0
EB = 6:5.0	EA = 11.0 EBPer = N/A	SumC':WSumC =1:5.0	Isolate/R	= 0.19
eb = 6:5	es = 11 D = 0	Afr = 0.39	H:(H)Hd(Hd)	= 4:11
	Adj es = 5 Adj D = +2	S = 6	(HHd):(AAd)	= 9:3
		Blends:R = 6:32	H+A:Hd + Ad	= 14:10
FM = 1 C' = 1 T = 0		CP = 0		
m = 5 V = 1 Y = 3				

		P = 5	Zf = 21	3r+(2)/R = 0.25
a:p = 10:2	Sum6 = 4	X+% = 0.53	Zd = –5.0	Fr+rF = 0
Ma:Mp = 5:1	Lv2 = 0	F+% = 0.33	W:D:Dd =21:7:4	FD = 2
2AB+Art+Ay = 22	WSum6 = 9	X–% = 0.22	W:M = 21:6	An + Xy = 0
M– = 0	Mnone = 0	S–% = 0.43	DQ+ = 5	MOR = 2
		Xu% = 0.25	DQv = 5	

SCZI = 0	DEPI = 5*	CDI = 1	S-CON = 6	HVI = Yes	OBS = No

I. (3")

1. That looks like a moth.

INQ: Little antennas, wings, body, and the white parts are designs on the wings. (Wings?) The shape

V2. Looks like a hat with horns on them, like Hagar the Horrible wears. I saw it on the Olympics the other day.

INQ: (Hat?) The bottom part, those horns, designs on them. (Horns?) The shape makes it look like animal horns.

II. (39")

3. Looks like two people, with their hands like this (shows) wearing hats of some sort. There are their knees and their toes.

INQ: (People?) Looks like people from their side, with their hands touching. Looks like feet and knees.

4. Reminds me of sycamore bark. It peels off into real thin layers; the color and it has a curly shape to it when it peels off; little curve shapes.

INQ: The texture, the way it's smeary looking. Two pieces.

III. (4")

5. That's two people with bowling balls. They're facing each other. They're wearing high heels or maybe they're cowboy boots.

INQ: (People?) The shape, a body shape; bending over.

6. Looks like bones; hip bones. The spine's not there. That could be part of the spine.

INQ: (Bones?) The way it comes out and then back in. That looks like part of a spine. I don't know what these things are (top red areas)

IV. (35")

7. Looks like some kind of bug.

INQ: (Bug?) Big beetle; looks like wings.

V8. Either that or an aerial photograph, where you can see the high and low parts. The white part, water; the gray would be land.

INQ: Dark places; kind of 3-D, where it's dark, then lighter.

V. (6")

9. Looks like another moth. I couldn't really see anything else in that one; it's such a good bug; moth.

INQ: The center part where the body would be. Antennas and wings. Looks like a luna moth. They're about that big. We've seen some at the house; they're beautiful.

VI. (20")

10. That looks like a pond with a reflection in it. The top part would be the real landscape; the bottom part looks like a reflection.

INQ: (Pond?) Because it's divided; tall trees, bushes, weeds, cat-tails. (Trees?) Its taller. The sun is going down between the trees, or coming up. (Sun?) The light spot. (Bushes?) Because they're smaller and a little more detailed.

V11. It also looks like a bear skin with a big tail. The skin is stretched out. These would be the arms, legs, back, long tail. The heads are missing. Can I draw a head in there?

(continued)

527

VII. (53")

12. These look like animal heads; eye, snout, legs. Going in opposite directions.

INQ: It's a cross between an elephant and a horse; the neck, front leg; this one would be going that way and the other going that way. The top has nothing to do with it.

13. It reminds one of the way my Rotweiler lays down. These are the legs and body. You're up, looking down.

INQ: Big, huge dog; makes his legs look like chicken legs; the hind leg; his head is off the picture. The rest is belly.

VIII. (5")

<14. Hmm. The pink looks like a cougar or tiger climbing on rocks. That's the real image and that's the reflection in the water.

INQ: head, four legs; three of them are on a rock; maybe he's walking! The ground line and a reflection in the water. (Rocks?) Four different colors look like four different big rocks. I don't see anything else.

15. I see batik; you take wax, paint it on fabric. You dye it, put wax on somewhere else and dye it again. It's beautiful.

INQ: Because its crackly looking like it's been wrinkled and the different colors where its been dyed. (Crackly, wrinkled?) The texture.

IX. (29")

V16. Looks like a monkey with a red hat on. Eyes, nose, and mouth. Her eyes; would be a girl with a pink hat.

INQ: Fur, shaggy hair on it's head (green). (Hat?) Because it's a different color, Round would be the top of his head; looks like its sitting on top. (Shaggy?) The Outline

X. (42")

17. That one's tricky. Flowers; different kinds of flowers. Maybe one tulip shape; these look like caterpillars—the green things, and these look like bugs. The flower shape is the big thing, with the bugs around it.

INQ: Flower, flower parts. These look like bugs. (Flower?) The stem; it's red, it's opened up. (Bugs?) The color; caterpillar green; shaped like caterpillars. This blue one looks like magnified spider mites. A bug that's grown out of control and got big.

(continued)

Card	No.	Loc.	#	Determinant(s)	(2)	Content(s)	Pop Z	Special Scores
I	1	WSo	1	Fo		A	3.5	
	2	Wo	1	Fo		Cg	1.0	PER
II	3	W+	1	Mao	2	H, Cg	4.5	
	4	Dv	6	FT–		Bt		
III	5	D+	1	Mao	2	H, Cg	P 3.0	
	6	Ddo	99	Fo		An		
IV	7	Wo	1	F–		A	2.0	
	8	Wv	1	VFu		Na, Sc		
V	9	Wo	1	Fo		A	1.0	PER
VI	10	W/	1	Fr.mao		Na	2.5	
	11	Wo	1	mao		Ad	2.5	DR
VII	12	Do	2	FMa–		(A)		INC
	13	Wo	1	FMp–		A	2.5	PER
VIII	14	W+	1	Fr.FMa.FCo		A, Na	P 4.5	
	15	Wv	1	CF.TFo		Art		
IX	16	W+	1	FCu		Ad, Cg	5.5	
X	17	W+	1	FCo		A, Bt	5.5	

Summary of Approach

I:WS.W	VI:W.W
II:W.D	VII:D.W
III:D.Dd	VIII:W.W
IV:W.W	IX:W
V:W	X:W

(continued)

Wife's Rorschach: Rorschach Structural Summary

LOCATION FEATURES	DETERMINANTS BLENDS	SINGLE	CONTENTS	S-CONSTELLATION
			H = 2,0	NO..FV + VF + V + FD > 2
Zf = 12	FR.m	M = 2	(H) = 0,0	YES..Col-Shd Bl>0
ZSum = 38.0	Fr.FM.FC	FM = 2	Hd = 0,0	YES..Ego<.31,>.44
ZEst = 38.0	CF.TF	m = 1	(Hd) = 0,0	NO..MOR>3
		FC = 2	Hx = 0,0	NO..Zd > ± 3.5
W = 13		CF = 0	A = 6,0	YES..es>EA
(Wv = 2)		C = 0	(A) = 1,0	NO..CF+C>FC
D = 3		Cn = 0	Ad = 2,0	YES..X+%<.70
Dd = 1		FC' = 0	(Ad) = 0,0	NO..S>3
S = 1		C'F = 0	An = 1,0	YES..P<3 or >8
		C' = 0	Art = 1,0	NO..Pure H <2
DQ		FT = 1	Ay = 0,0	NO..R<17
..........(FQ–)		TF = 0	Bl = 0,0	5.....TOTAL
+ = 5 (0)		T = 0	Bt = 1,1	SPECIAL SCORINGS

	FQx	FQf	MQual	SQx				Lvl	Lv2
o	= 8 (3)				FV = 0	Cg = 1,3	DV	= 0x1	0x2
v/+	= 1 (0)				VF = 1	Cl = 0,0	INC	= 1x2	0x4
v	= 3 (1)				V = 0	Ex = 0,0	DR	= 1x3	0x6
					FY = 0	Fd = 0,0	FAB	= 0x4	0x7
					YF = 0	Fi = 0,0	ALOG	= 0x5	
					Y = 0	Ge = 0,0	CON	= 0x7	
FORM QUALITY					Fr = 0	Hh = 0,0	SUM6	= 2	
					rF = 0	Ls = 0,0	WSUM6	= 5	
	FQx	FQf	MQual	SQx	FD = 0	Na = 2,1			
+	= 0	0	0	0	F = 5	Sc = 0,1			
o	= 11	4	2	1		Sx = 0,0	AB =0	CP = 0	
u	= 2	0	0	0		Xy = 0,0	AG =0	MOR = 0	
–	= 4	1	0	0		Id = 0,0	CFB =0	PER = 3	
none	= 0	–	0	0	(2) = 2		COP =0	PSV = 0	

RATIOS, PERCENTAGES, AND DERIVATIONS

R = 17	L = 0.42	FC:CF+C =3:1	COP = 0 AG = 0
		Pure C =0	Food = 0
EB = 2:2.5	EA = 4.5 EBPer = N/A	SumC':WSumC =0:2.5	Isolate/R = 0.47
eb = 5:3	es = 8 D = –1	Afr =0.31	H:(H)Hd(Hd) = 2:0
	Adj es = 7 Adj D = 0	S =1	(HHd):(AAd) = 0:1
		Blends:R =3:17	H+A:Hd + Ad = 9:2
FM = 3 C' = 0 T = 2		CP =0	
m = 2 V = 1 Y = 0			
		P = 2 Zf =12	3r+(2)/R = 0.47
a:p = 6:1 Sum6 = 2	X+% = 0.65 Zd = +0.0		Fr+rF = 2
Ma:Mp = 2:0 Lv2 = 0	F+% = 0.80 W:D:Dd =13:3:1		FD = 0
2AB+Art+Ay = 1 WSum6 = 5	X–% = 0.24 W:M = 13:2		An + Xy = 1
M– = 0 Mnone = 0	S–% = 0.00 DQ+ =5		MOR = 0
	Xu% = 0.12 DQv =3		

SCZI = 1	DEPI = 4	CDI = 4*	S-CON = 5	HVI = No	OBS = No

I.

    1. Dancers, spinning.

INQ: (Dancers?) Hands on top, toes, like a dancer would perform. (Spinning?) Because it's symmetrical; Things are flying out.

    V2. Helmet or mask

INQ: Shaped like a helmet, with horns sticking out.

II.

    3. Two people sitting, with hats, playing patty-cake.

INQ: (People?) The shape (Hats?) Sticking up playing patty-cake; hands are together.

III.

    4. Two women, African

INQ: (Women?) Lips protruding, long neck, breasts. (African?) Lips protruding.

IV.

    5. A troll

INQ: Shape. Walking away; from its back side (Walking?) No detail of the face; facing away. Not moving.

V.

    6. A Moth

INQ: The shape; head with antennas, tail. Looks like wings, like you're looking down on it from the top.

VI.

    7. The hide

INQ: The shape; the dark place would be the backbone. The color; shades of light and dark.

VII

    8. Sandra's legs (their daughter).

INQ: The shape.

    9. Two little girls, with ponytails

INQ: The shape of the head, ponytail, and hand.

VIII

    10. Some kind of animal; reflection in the water. An animal climbing on the rocks.

INQ: (Animal?) 4 legs, head, It looks like it's moving. (Water?) Looks like a reflection.

IX.

    11. A Flower

INQ: All the parts of a flower; the colors.

    V12. A Monkey

INQ: Eyes, shape, fur, cap (Pt.points); (Fur?) Because it's all fuzzy (points to outline). (Cap?) Because it's sitting on top of its head.

X.

    V13. A Flower

INQ: Stem, shape, and the colors.

(continued)

Consensus Rorschach: Sequence of Scores

Card	No.	Loc.	#	Determinant(s)	(2)	Content(s)	Pop Z	Special Scores
I	1	W+	1	Ma.mau	2	H	4.0	COP
	2	Wo	1	Fo		Cg	1.0	
II	3	W+	1	Mao	2	H, Cg	4.5	COP
III	4	Do	9	Fo	2	H, Sx	P	
IV	5	Wo	1	Fo		(H)	P 2.0	
V	6	Wo	1	Fo		A	1.0	
VI	7	Wo	1	FYo		Ad	P	
VII	8	Wo	1	Hd		Hd	2.5	PER
	9	Do	2	Fo	2	H	P	
VIII	10	W+	1	Fr.FMao		A, Na	P 4.5	
IX	11	Wo	1	FCo		Bt		
	12	W+	1	Fu		Ad, Cg	5.5	
X	13	Wo	1	FCo		Bt		

LOCATION	DETERMINANTS		CONTENTS	S-CONSTELLATION
FEATURES	BLENDS	SINGLE		NO..FV + VF + V + FD > 2

									S-CONSTELLATION

LOCATION FEATURES / **DETERMINANTS** (BLENDS / SINGLE) / **CONTENTS** / **S-CONSTELLATION**

				H	= 4,0	NO..Col-Shd Bl>0	
Zf	= 8	M.m	M = 1	(H)	= 1,0	YES..Ego<.31,>.44	
ZSum	= 25.0	Fr.FM	FM = 0	Hd	= 1,0	NO..MOR>3	
ZEst	= 24.0		m = 0	(Hd)	= 0,0	NO..Zd > ± 3.5	
			FC = 2	Hx	= 0,0	NO..es>EA	
W	= 11		CF = 0	A	= 2,0	NO..CF+C>FC	
(Wv	= 0)		C = 0	(A)	= 0,0	NO..X+%<.70	
D	= 2		Cn = 0	Ad	= 2,0	NO..S>3	
Dd	= 0		FC' = 0	(Ad)	= 0,0	NO..P<3 or >8	
S	= 0		C'F = 0	An	= 0,0	NO..Pure H <2	
			C' = 0	Art	= 0,0	YES..R<17	
	DQ		FT = 0	Ay	= 0,0	2.....TOTAL	
	..........(FQ–)		TF = 0	Bl	= 0,0		
+	= 4 (0)		T = 0	Bt	= 2,0	SPECIAL SCORINGS	
o	= 9 (0)		FV = 0	Cg	= 1,2	Lv1	Lv2
v/+	= 0 (0)		VF = 0	Cl	= 0,0	DV = 0x1	0x2
v	= 0 (0)		V = 0	Ex	= 0,0	INC = 0x2	0x4
			FY = 1	Fd	= 0,0	DR = 0x3	0x6
			YF = 0	Fi	= 0,0	FAB = 0x4	0x7
			Y = 0	Ge	= 0,0	ALOG = 0x5	
	FORM QUALITY		Fr = 0	Hh	= 0,0	CON = 0x7	
			rF = 0	Ls	= 0,0	SUM6 = 0	
	FQx FQf MQual SQx		FD = 0	Na	= 0,1	WSUM6 = 0	
+	= 0 0 0 0		F = 7	Sc	= 0,0		
o	= 10 5 1 0			Sx	= 0,1	AB =0 CP = 0	
u	= 2 1 1 0			Xy	= 0,0	AG =0 MOR = 0	
–	= 1 1 0 0			Id	= 0,0	CFB =0 PER = 1	
none	= 0 – 0 0	(2) = 4				COP =2 PSV = 0	

RATIOS, PERCENTAGES, AND DERIVATIONS

R = 13	L = 1.17		FC:CF+C = 2:0	COP = 2	AG = 0
			Pure C = 0	Food	= 0
EB = 2:1.0	EA = 3.0	EBPer = N/A	SumC':WSumC =0:1.0	Isolate/R	= 0.31
eb = 2:1	es = 3	D = 0	Afr =0.44	H:(H)Hd(Hd)	= 4:2
	Adj es = 3	Adj D = 0	S =0	(HHd):(AAd)	= 1:0
			Blends:R =2:13	H+A:Hd + Ad	= 7:3
FM = 1	C' = 0 T = 0		CP =0		
m = 1	V = 0 Y = 1				
			P = 5 Zf =8	3r+(2)/R = 0.54	
a:p	= 4:0	Sum6 = 0	X+% = 0.77 Zd =+1.0	Fr+rF = 1	
Ma:Mp	= 2:0	Lv2 = 0	F+% = 0.71 W:D:Dd =11:2:0	FD = 0	
2AB+Art+Ay	= 0	WSum6 = 0	X-% = 0.08 W:M = 11:2	An + Xy = 0	
M–	= 0	Mnone = 0	S-% = 0.00 DQ+ =3	MOR = 0	
			Xu% = 0.15 DQv =3		

SCZI = 0	DEPI = 2	CDI = 3	S-CON = 2	HVI = No	OBS = No

28

The Neuropsychology of the Rorschach: An M.D. With M.B.D.

Susan C. Colligan
Rorschach Workshops and John Muir Medical Center

The task demands of the Rorschach Inkblot Method (RIM; Weiner, 1995) invoke a complex set of psychological and neuropsychological operations (Acklin, 1994; Colligan & Exner, 1985). Rorschach himself (1942/1981) was intrigued by this process and posited that it involved perception rather than imagination.

Rorschach described the different type of responding given by "most organic cases (senile dements, paretics), epileptics, many schizophrenics, most manics, almost all the feeble-minded subjects, and even many normals, who are not aware of the assimilative effort. These subjects do not interpret the pictures, they name them" (1942/1981, p. 17). They fail the "as . . . if" aspects of the task and remain concrete. In utilizing the inkblots to differentiate between patients with organic brain disease and those without, Rorschach reported that, "the test cannot be used to probe into the content of the subconscious" (p. 123). The ensuing debate regarding the inkblots as a stimulus to fantasy—versus the inkblots as a perceptual-cognitive, problem-solving task—might have been delimited if he had lived long enough to complete more research.

The RIM has found itself purported to be representative of many schools and philosophies (dynamic, analytic, and perceptual-cognitive), but the question remains: Can the RIM be useful in assessing the interplay and/or interaction between the neurological and psychological issues that may be simultaneously present in a person? What is the impact of neurological injury on psychological functioning (as in patients with traumatic brain injury, who as a group present with a very specific set of premorbid characteristics)? Conversely, what are the influences of personality on the neurological process? I present a case that suggests how the RIM might be uniquely suited to differentiate these complex issues and arrive at an appropriate diagnostic formulation and treatment/intervention targets.

Goldfried, Stricker, and Weiner (1971) addressed this issue:

It is possible, but not necessary, to become involved in a metaphysical discussion of the mind–body problem and the implied dualism of a distinction between functional and organic illness. We can grant that there are physiological processes underlying all behavior and still recognize that a large number of behaviors which are considered pathological are also regarded as being functional in origin. Other symptoms, however, can be traced initially to an impairment in the central nervous system and are considered organic in origin. *This distinction is of importance in that the approach to treatment should, in part, depend upon the proper identification of the cause of the difficulty* [italics added]. (p. 26)

More recently, Zillmer and Perry (1996) posited a relative independence between neuropsychological and personality assessment measures and the Minnesota Multiphasic Personality Inventory (MMPI) and the RIM. They recommended an "integrationist perspective" approach as we attempt to delineate the neuropsychology of personality. Basic to any approach is the understanding that behavior and personality are a product of brain functioning. In other words, does the mind live in the brain?

TO BE OR NOT TO BE (ORGANIC)

Dr. W. is a left-dominant, English-speaking, married, 43-year-old White male, who was a U.S. Navy Lieutenant Commander physician/surgeon on active duty at a Naval hospital. He was completing a residency in a surgery specialty when he was noted to have some difficulties in the completion of some of his duties. He was referred by his department head, a senior Naval officer and surgeon, for a neurological workup. The neurologist referred Dr. W. to me with the following consultation note: "43 year old physician with long-standing memory and organizational difficulties → ? progressive, but are interfering with vocational activities. Exam indicates subtle evidence of both organic problems and depression." As one aspect of "expert diagnostic consultation" (Weiner, 1972) has to do with answering the right question, it is apparent that this neurologist was very savvy and knew how to formulate the referral issue.

Dr. W. was described by his Director of Training as a nice, but somewhat odd guy with "adequate" surgical skills but good medical skills. He had one or two friends in his department and was close with only one other surgeon. He had been married 8 years and had two stepchildren, but no biological offspring. He was actively involved in gun collecting and primarily spent time alone with his dog and his wife (who traveled frequently due to her job). There was no history of drug/alcohol or psychiatric problems, nor traumatic brain injury.

Dr. W. had an interesting, if indirect, route to his chosen specialty. He was born and raised in an intact family in California and had enlisted in the U.S. Navy as a weapons specialist and was assigned to a battleship. After completing his enlistment, he attended a university as a mathematics major on the G.I. Bill. After graduation he decided to pursue medical school, which he did. He was commissioned as an officer and entered a surgical residency with a specialty in Ear/Nose/Throat. It was during his training that he came into contact with two senior staff physicians with whom he clashed. His difficulty in completing tasks, evidence of memory problems, and lackluster surgical skills culminated in the referral to the neurologist for what was considered a "fitness for duty" evaluation. Dr. W. was beginning the final phase of his training and plans were being formulated for his reassignment. At his next duty station, he would be expected to function independently as a surgeon and questions were raised regarding his ability to do this. However, there were also some unspoken political issues and pressures. Dr. W.'s department head was known not to like Dr. W. personally, and there was "scuttlebutt"[1] that he was attempting to rid himself and the U.S. Navy of Dr. W. Also, both the neurologist and I knew Dr. W. and we were both junior in rank to both the referring Officer and the patient.

I formulated an assessment plan and Dr. W. was administered the Wechsler Adult Intelligence Scale–Revised (WAIS–R), the Rorschach Inkblot Test (Comprehensive System), the MMPI, the Halstead–Reitan Test Battery and selected neuropsychological tests, the Shipley Hartford Scale, and the Wechsler Memory Scale I.

RESULTS

Appendix A is the Rorschach protocol; Appendix B is the Sequence of Scores; and Appendix C is the Structural Summary, generated by Rorschach Interpretation Assistance Program, Version 3.1 (Exner & Ona, 1995). Appendix D is the summary data from the Halstead–Reitan and Appendix E presents test scores.

DISCUSSION

Mental Status

Dr. W. is a very intelligent, personable, and verbally facile person who was cooperative throughout the evaluation and testing. He presented in a self-effacing, somewhat deprecating manner, and admits to memory problems that he describes as the result of poor organizational abilities. His self-description is that of an "absent-minded professor," which appears to be a compensatory tactic. Despite this covering of identity, he was appropriately concerned regarding the situation he was in, and he approached the assessment in such a

---

[1]Scuttlebutt = rumor, gossip started around a drinking fountain on a ship or at a naval or marine installation.

way that the results are considered an accurate reflection of his psychological and neuropsychological functioning. Dr. W. exhibited mildly dysphoric mood and flat affect, but was not suicidal. He was concerned about his problems at work, the completion of his residency, and the uncertainty of the future. Although he denied marital conflicts, his marriage was also in the midst of some crisis, as he separated from his wife and subsequently divorced within 1 year of the evaluation. There was no evidence of thought disorder, hallucinations, or homicidal ideation.

INTERPRETATION

Psychostructural Data

The Comprehensive System (Exner, 1986a, 1993) protocol, sequence of scores, and Structural Summary are listed in Appendices A, B, and C. The Rorschach Interpretation Assistance Program, Version 3.1 (Exner & Ona, 1995) generated a valid and interpretable record (Responses = 23 and *Lambda* = 0.77). The protocol was positive for the Depression Index (*DEPI* = 5). Dr. W.'s capacity for control is summarized first. The cluster of variables related to affect follows. However, due to the neurological aspects of the case, I next address the three clusters known as the Cognitive Triad (Processing, Mediation, and Ideation) and then return to self-perception and interpersonal perception.

Additional experimental scores that focus on aggressive drives and content as discussed by Gacono and Meloy (1994) are also scored.[2]

Capacity for Control and Stress Tolerance

This subject is in a state of chronic overload, probably due to fewer resources available from which to plan and implement decisions. The overload is created by the presence of more internally irritating experiences than he can easily contend with. This is highly unusual because this is a very intelligent person (*FS IQ* = 120) who has been through medical and surgical training. As most psychologists know, intellectual resources are not necessarily psychological resources, and as a result, a clear tendency for impulsiveness exists.

The elevation in the *CDI* is not expected in a practicing physician. The highest percentage of positive indices are found among inadequate personalities, alcohol and substance abusers, and adjudicated character disorders (Exner, 1993). This suggests a considerable disorganization may be occurring. However, the *CDI* clearly appears to be a measure found in people who have

---

[2]Aggressive Content (*AgC*); Aggressive Potential (*AgPot*); Aggressive Past (*AgPast*).

coping limitations and/or difficulties, especially in the interpersonal arena. The *CDI* is not another depression measure, but its presence is often found among depressed patients and is frequently found among patients with affective disorders who are not positive on the Depression Index.

Dr. W. exhibits constricted affect (C' = 3) that results in some internal irritation. This elevation is often seen in depressed patients and may explain his limited affective expression (*WtSumC* = 0.5). This shutting down may be congruent with Dr. W.'s style, exacerbated by his position in the U.S. Naval hierarchy (in a training program and junior to his department head).

Affect

Dr. W.'s personality organization tends to give rise to frequent and intense experiences of depression. These experiences tend to predispose him to the kinds of emotional turmoil that can easily interfere with psychological operations, and in general make it difficult to maintain effective patterns of adjustment.

Dr. W. has a pervasively ideational problem-solving style (*EB* = 6:0.5) in which feelings are kept at bay. Although he may be willing to display feelings, he is quite concerned about modulating them. He is not very flexible about the use of this style and persists in setting emotions aside, even when an emotive, trial-and-error approach would be more effective. He tends to experience discomfort because he holds in feelings that he would prefer to express openly. There is limited psychological complexity (*Blends* = 3) and two of his blends include *M* (*M.FC'* and *M.m*).

COGNITIVE TRIAD

The Cognitive Triad is composed of three clusters that provide data about how a person handles information in a purposeful and deliberate way. These three clusters of Processing, Mediation, and Ideation are each related to cognition, are interpreted together, and are part of a looping and nonlinear system (Erdberg, 1994). This Triad provides Rorschach data about how a person handles information as he or she solves the perceptual-cognitive task of the RIM. Rorschach (1942/1981) clearly stated his view that the inkblots measure physiological functions (perception) and it may be postulated that the Cognitive Triad is the arena in which we might glean, via the RIM, a look at one aspect of a person's neuropsychological functioning.

With our present knowledge, there are no RIM patterns specific to, or diagnostic of, any discrete neurologic entity. Aita, Reitan, and Ruth (1947) attempted to corroborate Piotrowski's 10 organic signs with war veterans. Other groups have been studied, including severe head injury patients (Ellis

& Zahn, 1985), learning-disabled children (Acklin, 1990); and Perry, Potterat, and Auslander (1995) worked with Alzheimer patients in studying the perseverative responses on the RIM. These studies have generally been with small groups, without control groups, and do not provide normative guidelines. However, we do use some specific variables and other RIM data that can be extremely useful in discerning a patient's adaptation to their condition and/or situation, their psychological needs, their sense of self as damaged or injured as they manage the course of their condition, and comorbid conditions that may affect the manifestation of the neurological condition, such as depression or anxiety (Weiner, 1995).

For example, Zd, a measure of information processing, was found to be low (< -3.0) in the protocols of children who were diagnosed as "hyperactive." An elevation in *Lambda* ($L > .99$) is often found in protocols collected from closed head injury patients. Also, an increase in mechanistic perseverations ($PSV > 1$) is found in neurologically involved patients who are severely impaired (Exner, 1993). Although these variables are not specific to these conditions, they are sensitive to them and may provide a guideline for evaluation of a protocol (either present or absent).

The RIM can also be used very effectively to assess potential for treatment and/or treatment compliance and to assess the unique ability of a person to participate in their own recovery and rehabilitation (Exner, 1994). When the RIM is considered a perceptual-cognitive problem-solving task, it can serve as a microcosm of the person in the real-world situation and how they handle information, and may have advantages over self-report data.

Information Processing

Here is where one can see the *cognitive* aspects of Dr. W.'s interpersonal problems. Although he is willing to process the complexities of a stimulus field and the quality of his processing is adequate, some of his processing is conservative and not very thorough. This likely reflects a defensive withdrawal from social competitiveness. Because Dr. W.'s intellectual level is above average, this is probably the result of a negative self-image. His tendency to deal with less complex and easily managed stimuli is common among those who feel uncomfortable about their decision-making capabilities. This irregular approach to processing is common among children and is a major liability for a surgeon in its potential for a reduced quality of input.

Cognitive Mediation

Dr. W. is less oriented to translating inputs as conventionally as most people. Therefore, he formulates his behaviors with less concern about social acceptability and is strongly individualistic. This presents, and has presented, problems for Dr. W. because the military does not value individualism and actually honors effort and ideas committed to the "greater good."

Ideation

It is here that Dr. W.'s cognitive deficits and his emotional state have a decidedly devastating impact. His thinking is disturbed, but there is no evidence of schizophrenic thought disorder (from the RIM, Schizophrenic Index = 0), history, behavior, mental status examination, or follow-up information. There are similarities between some variables and ratios on Dr. W.'s record and that observed in a schizotypal population (Exner, 1986b). This disturbed thinking is often marked by flawed judgment and inconsistent decision making. Dr. W.'s tendency to rely on internal evaluations in making judgments is particularly detrimental because of his flawed thinking. Also he is highly inflexible in his style of coping and persists in this ideational set when his emotions might assist him in his problem solving. There is also a rigidity in his approach to values and ideas. These two aspects of his ideation have placed him on a collision course with the military power structure. His ideation deficits are discussed more fully when the neuropsychological data are presented.

Self-Perception

Dr. W.'s estimate of his personal worth tends to be more negative than should be the case, given his intellectual and academic achievements. His self-image tends to be based on imaginary rather than real experience and may produce a distorted and immature internal picture. This limited awareness will sometimes lead to ineffective decision making that has created another potential for interpersonal difficulties. Dr. W. attempts to deal with issues in an overintellectualized way that tends to ignore reality and is negative and/or distorted.

Interpersonal Perception and Relations

Dr. W. is less socially mature than might be expected, and he is prone to experience frequent difficulties in the interpersonal sphere. He maintains superficial relationships at best, and is regarded by others as distant, inept, or helpless in dealing with others. He prefers a more passive role in relationships and likes to avoid responsibility for decision making. His expectations concerning needs for closeness are more conservative than most people.

Summary

Dr. W. appears to be prone to frequent episodes of depression or emotional turmoil. A chronic state of stimulus overload exists that impairs his capacity for control and makes him quite vulnerable to impulsiveness and/or disorganization. He tends to be less concerned with issues of social acceptability than most people. Consequently, many of his behaviors will be more idiosyncratic. He uses a basic ideational approach to problem solving and decision making in which he prefers to think things through before initiating any behavior. His thinking is often marked by flawed logic or faulty judgment and becomes easily disorganized. He seems to control his emotions reasonably well. He is a rather negative and angry person. He tends to regard himself less favorably when he compares himself to others. His conception of himself is not well-developed and is probably distorted. He is the type of person who is prone to experience frequent difficulties when interacting with the environment, and these difficulties often extend into the interpersonal sphere. As a result, his relationships tend to be more superficial and less easily sustained. He is cautious about interpersonal relations and does not usually anticipate being close to others. He usually likes to avoid responsibility for decisions and takes a more passive role when interacting with others.

Content and Sequence Summary

Mentioning a scoring dilemma is appropriate here as we discuss the content interpretation. A conservative scoring strategy was maintained by this examiner, and in rescoring Dr. W.'s record, I would have enjoyed the opportunity to ask another inquiry question to clarify two responses (Responses 14 and 19). These were "almost" shading responses. Fischer (1994) eloquently addressed this issue and suggested that the "scoring dilemma" may reflect the client's dilemma in contending with the Rorschach task demands. Despite the lack of a question, the patient neither rubbed the card nor specified a shading determinant. In fact, on Card VI, the card with "pull" toward a texture (T) response, Dr. W. avoids the texture and produces a T-less response. Congruent with Fischer's premise, this backing away from T responses is similar to his dealings in his real (noninkblot) world.

This does not appear to be a protocol produced by a patient with organic brain syndrome. There are no perseveration responses, the *Lambda* is not elevated, and there is not a preponderance of strained reasoning ($ALOG$).

Utilizing the 10 Piotrowski signs of brain damage (Goldfried et al., 1971), Dr. W.'s record has only one ($F\% < 70$) of the nine signs that are compatible with, although not identical to, those of the Comprehensive System.

There are many RIM issues here that are important and relevant, but I focus on the immaturity, sense of vulnerability and resultant anxiety, and the level of self-deprecation and inadequacy experienced and expressed by Dr. W. His first response says something about his problem-solving strategy, and he begins his very conservative detail approach (D) to the Rorschach "problem." There is an immaturity and confusion regarding sexual identity and a passive wish for soothing. The preponderance of animal contents in playful activities instead of mature human contents further underscores Dr. W.'s arrested development.

The sense of vulnerability is seen in the rabbit (Response 12), who is "hanging up or jumping—one of the two," the beetle who has a hard cover but soft interior (Response 2), a torso with "legs too short" (Response 20), and a Ku Klux Klan hood (Response 22). Even Dr. W.'s last response of Card X, the crayfish (Response 23), has a protective covering.

Self-depreciation and helplessness is extant throughout the record: The older edentulous face (Response 6) with drooping nose, the bony anatomy response of grey matter in the spinal cord (Response 8), and a bobcat hide up on a barn (Response 15) all suggest a self-image that is tragically defective. He feels helpless throughout with, "no feet seen," "legs too short" (Response 20), and a body "too small to fit the head" (Response 19). In one response (22), "you don't see the rest of the face." What does he do with these disturbing and disorganizing feelings? He intellectualizes and experiences significant emotional disruption, including depression, anxiety, and aggression. There are many sexual and phallic issues that I leave to the reader to develop further hypotheses.

MMPI

The MMPI (1943/1967) was administered and found to be reliable and valid. Greene's (1980) interpretive guidelines were used to evaluate the inventory. There were elevations only on Scale 2 (Depression: T-score $= 78$) and Scale 0 (Social Introversion T-score $= 73$). These results are consistent with the RIM.

Patients with high-point pairs 2–0 often exhibit chronic levels of depression along with their social introversion. They display feelings of inadequacy, shyness, and isolation in social situations, and these features reflect their interpersonal ineptitude. Although there is a reactive component to the dysphoria, the depression is generally chronic and the passivity and sense of inadequacy produce little motivation to change.

To differentiate the level of a patient's personality organization, many choices are available. In this volume, we are utilizing the RIM to assist in this differentiation (Acklin, 1992) drawn from the developmental object relations theory of Kernberg (1976). Dr. W. appears to be predominantly functioning at the neurotic level of organization with concomitant conflicts about self and others. There is no major evidence of psychotic or borderline personality organization, defenses, or bizarre thought disorder. The neuropsychological data describe some aspects of Dr. W.'s unusual thinking.

Neuropsychological Findings

Dr. W. is left-handed (or more technically correct, non-right-handed; Lezak, 1995) and as a surgeon is often required to function in an ambidextrous way. Both of these factors add to the complexity of the interpretation of the findings, especially the implications of the lateralization results.

Intellectual Functioning

Dr. W. presents an intriguing WAIS–R profile. His Verbal IQ is in the superior range, but the performance IQ (55th percentile), albeit "average," shows a 26-point difference from the Verbal IQ, a statistically significant finding. One would expect a surgeon to be as "fluent" manually as Dr. W. is verbally. Utilizing the age and IQ-corrected Halstead Russell Neuropsychological Evaluation System by Russell and Starkey (1993), mental speed (Digit Symbol), planning, and attention span reveal the most impairment.

It is possible that Dr. W. is able to verbally mediate in a compensatory way, but not enough to easily function in his current situation. Lezak (1995) also reported on a tendency for right-handers to perform better than left-handers on visuospatial tasks due to the more diffuse hemispheric mediation in left-handers.

Neuropsychological Performance

Utilizing the interpretive guidelines of Jarvis and Barth (1994) with regard to level of performance, none of his performances were below the average range. However, when compared to persons with his occupation and education level, several of his scores suggest impairment. On manual tasks Dr. W. does not demonstrate the expected 10% superiority of his dominant left hand.

Memory results are also contradictory because his Wechsler Memory Quotient (WMQ) is in the superior range (despite his self-report of memory problems), but his TPT–memory and localization are in the borderline impairment range. These latter tests have a strong motor component, whereas the WMQ is based primarily on verbal memory.

His excellent performance on the Category Test argues against the presence of significant, widespread, and/or deteriorating cortical dysfunction. The deficits in Trails-A, Digit Symbol, lack of left-hand superiority on manual tasks, attention-concentration impairments and visual-spatial deficits on the WAIS–R and in drawing tasks, and intact aphasia screening test, all suggest mildly lateralized deficits to the right cerebral hemisphere. Subcortical involvement may also explain some of the findings, including some of the depressive aspects.

Summary and Recommendations

It was felt that the preponderance of evidence argued against any progressive organic impairment. However, as mentioned earlier, there is the possibility of mild deficits that were more developmental and may have contributed to his interpersonal befuddlement (Small, 1973). These mild cognitive deficits can be seen in depressed patients (Kaszniak & Christenson, 1994) who complain of memory and other cognitive problems, such as concentration. Compelling evidence from the RIM, MMPI, and clinical interview suggested that the disruptive aspects of Dr. W.'s emotional state contributed to a disorganization of his ability to attend, concentrate, and process information accurately. Depression could account for some, but not all of his performance variability.

Tasks requiring verbal skills were generally better than tasks with a motor component. Memory, as assessed by the WMQ and TPT Memory, was in the intact and/or superior range despite the reported complaints by the patient. This may have been due to the purposeful effort put forth by Dr. W. for his "performance" that overrode the "hypothetical limited capacity attentional system" (Kaszniak & Christenson, 1994). He does well when compared to most adults, but as a surgeon, his findings are unexpected. His generalized mild deficits in information processing are exhibited in both neuropsychological testing and on the RIM, especially the Cognitive Triad. He will likely continue to have problems in grasping spatial aspects of relationships with implications for his surgery skills. Compensatory verbal mediation will help but only partially. He can "talk the talk" but has trouble "walking the walk" (W. Lynch, personal communication, March 15, 1995).

Based on these findings, I referred Dr. W. for psychiatric evaluation and treatment and consideration for medication. I specifically requested assistance from the Department Head of Psychiatry who was a senior officer for two reasons: enhanced prestige in case "mano à mano" conflict occurred, and to add credibility to the consultation in view of Dr. W.'s general lack of motivation and psychological curiosity. Due to the "macho" environment in which we existed, and as a junior female officer, I felt he needed the enhanced "horse power" of a senior male. Perhaps there was some devaluation in our interaction of which I was only minimally aware. He agreed to this, was evaluated, and was placed on an antidepressant and continued in psychotherapy for a brief period of time.

As a result of the neurological and neuropsychological consultations, the Medical Board was dropped. Dr. W. was allowed to complete his residency and was transferred to another U.S. Naval hospital, where he performed competently throughout his 3-year assignment. Unfortunately, he was passed over for promotion due to the negative fitness reports he had compiled while in his residency, and he then left the U.S. Navy to begin competing in the civilian sector.

EPILOGUE

Not surprisingly, Dr. W. had continuing interpersonal difficulties and "misunderstandings" in civilian medicine. In one situation, he and the hospital he worked at "squared off" and entered the legal arena regarding issues related to Dr. W.'s educational time. He then went to a practice in the "Heartland" and left there after interpersonal difficulties. A few years ago, he was hired by a Veteran Affairs Medical Center and has since performed well. As readers are aware, some systems work better than others for certain personality types.

Despite the previously noted problems caused by his characterological deficits and weaknesses, there is good news related to the question of a progressive brain syndrome. At 10 years, Dr. W. is doing well cognitively, does not report any memory deficits, and seems to have found a niche where he fits and has performed well, although with decreased demands. He has not remarried, maintains a friendship with his wife, and remains in contact with his surgeon friend from the time of this consultation. Weapons remain a major interest, and one should consider the phallic aspects of this given Dr. W.'s self-denegrating and impotent view of himself. I do not have information regarding his depressive state other than his ongoing interpersonal problems.

For me, the case of Dr. W. suggests the value of utilizing both neuropsychological and personality data, specifically the RIM, to provide the assessment expert with a complete data set. The RIM Cognitive Triad provided information processing data not spuriously affected by lateralization issues; it also provided information related to some of the concentration and other processing problems. More importantly, it provided critical information related to the levels of personality development and the impact of the neuropsychological deficits on the person. Rourke, Bakker, Fisk, and Strang (1983) noted: "Current theories of behavior have come to recognize that behavior can only be explained as an interaction between capacity and experience" (p. 2).

ACKNOWLEDGMENTS

I thank Bill Lynch for his help with the neuropsychological preparation of this chapter and Robert Westerfield for his expert computer assistance.

REFERENCES

Acklin, M. W. (1990). Personality dimensions in two types of learning-disabled children: A Rorschach study. *Journal of Personality Assessment, 54,* 67–77.

Acklin, M. W. (1992). Psychodiagnosis of personality structure: Psychotic personality organization. *Journal of Personality Assessment, 58,* 454–463.

Acklin, M. W. (1994). Some contributions of cognitive science to the Rorschach test. *Rorschachiana, 19,* 129–145.

Aita, J., Reitan, R., & Ruth, J. (1947). Rorschach's test as a diagnostic aid in brain injury. *American Journal of Psychiatry, 103,* 770–779.

Colligan, S. C., & Exner, J. E., Jr. (1985). Responses of schizophrenics and nonpatients to a tachistoscopic presentation of the Rorschach. *Journal of Personality Assessment, 49,* 129–136.

Ellis, D., & Zahn, B. (1985). Psychological functioning after severe closed head injury. *Journal of Personality Assessment, 49,* 125–128.

Erdberg, P. (1994, March). *The Rorschach and neurological findings.* Presentation to the Northern California Neuropsychology Forum.

Exner, J. E., Jr. (1986a). *The Rorschach: A comprehensive system: Vol. 1. Basic foundations* (2nd ed.). New York: Wiley.

Exner, J. E., Jr. (1986b). Some Rorschach data comparing schizophrenics with borderline and schizotypal personality disorders. *Journal of Personality Assessment, 50,* 455–471.

Exner, J. E., Jr. (1993). *The Rorschach: A comprehensive system: Vol 1. Basic foundations* (3rd ed.). New York: Wiley.

Exner, J. E., Jr. (1994). Rorschach and the study of the individual. *Rorschachiana, 19,* 7–23.

Exner, J. E., Jr., & Ona, N. (1995). *A Rorschach workbook for the comprehensive system* (4th ed.). Asheville, NC: Rorschach Workshops.

Fischer, C. T. (1994). Rorschach scoring questions as access to dynamics. *Journal of Personality Assessment, 62,* 515–524.

Gacono, C. B., & Meloy, J. R. (1994). *The Rorschach assessment of aggressive and psychopathic personalities.* Hillsdale, NJ: Lawrence Erlbaum Associates.

Goldfried, M., Stricker, G., & Weiner, S. (1971). *Rorschach handbook of clinical and research applications.* Englewood Cliffs, NJ: Prentice-Hall.

Greene, R. L. (1980). *The MMPI: An interpretive manual.* New York: Grune & Stratton.

Hathaway, S. R., & McKinley, J. C. (1967). *Minnesota multiphasic personality inventory.* Minnapolis: University of Minnesota Press. (Original work published 1943)

Jarvis, P. E., & Barth, J. T. (1994). *Halstead–Reitan test battery: An interpretive guide* (2nd ed.). Odessa, FL: Psychological Assessment Resources.

Kaszniak, A. W., & Christenson, G. D. (1994). Differential diagnosis of dementia and depression. In M. Storandt & G. R. VandenBos (Eds.), *Neuropsychological assessment of dementia and depression in older adults: A clinician's guide* (pp. 81–117). Washington, DC: American Psychological Association.

Kernberg, O. (1976). *Object relations theory and clinical psychoanalysis.* New York: Aronson.

Lezak, M. D. (1995). *Neuropsychological assessment* (3rd ed.). New York: Oxford University Press.

Perry, W., Potterat, E., & Auslander, L. (1995, March). *A neuropsychological approach to assessing perseverative responses on the Rorschach.* Society for Personality Assessment Meeting, Atlanta, GA.

Rorschach, H. (1981). *Psycho-diagnostics: A diagnostic test based on perception* (9th ed.). Berg: Hans Huber Verlag. (Original work published 1942)

Rourke, B. P., Bakker, D. J., Fisk, J. L., & Strang, J. D. (1983). *Child neuropsychology: An introduction to theory, research, and clinical practice.* New York: Guilford.

Russell, E. W., & Starkey, R. I. (1993). *Halstead–Russell neuropsychological evaluation system.* Los Angeles: Western Psychological Services.

Small, L. (1973). *Neuropsychodiagnosis in psychotherapy.* New York: Brunner-Mazel.

Weiner, I. B. (1972). Does psychodiagnosis have a future? *Journal of Personality Assessment, 34,* 534–546.

Weiner, I. B. (1995). Speaking Rorschach: Let not theory come between us. *Rorschachiana, 20,* 1–7.

Zillmer, E., & Perry, W. (1996). Neuropsychology and personality assessment. *Assessment, 3,* 205–363.

I 5"

1) It looks like somebody with a long nose . . . like a jocular mode . . . a smile and the way the eyebrows are arched. A beer-belly. Oddly enough a breast and penis.

Structural Score: Do 2 Mpo H,Sx INC
Aggression Score: None (See Footnote 2)

E: Prompts

2) I suppose you would say it looks like an insect . . . the horns of a beetle. The side part doesn't go along with it.

S: Do you want me to go on?

E: It's up to you.

Structural Score: Do 4 Fo A INC
Aggression Score: AgC

3) If you squint it looks like a devil's face . . . neck, horns, and you can't see the whole mouth.

Structural Score: DdSo99 Mpu (Hd), Hx 3.5
Aggression Score: AgC

II 8"

4) It looks like two elephants looking up-ward . . . trunks upward on midline. One leg is raised.

Structural Scoring: D+1 FMpo 2 A P 3.0
Aggression Score: None

5) It could be a dog or bear balancing something on his nose because there are two of them.

Structural Scoring: D+1 FMp.FC'o 2 A,Id P 3.0 ALOG,PER
Aggression Score: None

6) You might see a face along the back. Older . . . edentulous due to prominence of chin and drooping nose.

Structural Scoring: Ddo 99 Fu Hd MOR
Aggression Score: None

E: Repeats S's response (RR)
S: Here's the face, the breast with nipple, penis-circumcised.
E: What part of the inkblot are you using?
S: (Pts) From here over

E: RR
S: The horns at the very top. It has a blunt head and thorax area.

E: RR
S: The mouth, horns, & neck
E: (?)
S: First off it looks like horns. Expression. Eyes look sinister

E: RR
S: There's one leg bent at the knee. Trunk's going up. Ears back here . . . Not exactly elephant ears.

E: RR
S: The ink blot is darker here and it could be the end of the profile and you are left with this—whatever you're balancing.
E: (?)
S: Fact that it has a muzzle. Head is longer than a muzzle. That, to me, is what dogs look like. Has same profile as my dog.

E: RR
S: Right there.

III 30"

7) It looks like two individuals facing each other . . . It's like they're bent at the waist. This could be a formal—like a tuxedo and stiff starch . . . sticking up or a woman's profile with breast and the hands down like they're holding onto something . . . like a child's turn-table. Wearing Italian shoes or woman's high heels.

E: RR
S: The individual is bent at the waist . . . like centrifugal force. . . . Arms are bent. Sometimes on older tuxedo, they have wide lapels.
E: (?)
S: Fact that it's uniformly dark—black. Cuffs on it.

Structural Scoring: D+ 9 Mp.FC′+ 2 H,Id,Cg P 3.0
Aggression Score: None

S: When I look at these things I see essentially one thing. Everything looks paired. It's artificial to break it down.

8) The center part of that looks like the grey matter in the spinal cord.

E: RR
S: Red part right there.
E: (?)
S: That's almost exactly what grey matter looks like on cross-section.

Structural Scoring: Do 3 Fu An
Aggression Score: None

9) This part looks like an esophagus coming down to the stomach. The stomach's backward on this side.

E: RR
S: It's what it's attached to. It's a long tube attached to fundus of stomach

Structural Scoring: D+ Fu An 3.0
Aggression Score: None

IV 7"

10) What immediately comes to mind is a turkey . . . It's long and hangs down and the wattle coming off here. Could be a vulture as well as a turkey.

E: RR
S: This part here (points)
E: (?)
S: The shape of the bill. Profile of head in combination with bill.

Structural Scoring: Do 4 Fo Ad
Aggression Score: None

11) I can see two faces up here on the back of the turkey. I wouldn't associate it riding the turkey. It's just there.

E: RR
S: It looks like the top of the head coming to the noseum. Nose has upward tilt. Lips and chin.

Structural Scoring: Ddo 21 Fo 2 Hd DV
Aggression Score: None

V 5"

12) The center part looks like a rabbit with the head and legs hanging down. It's either hanging up or jumping—one of the two.

E: RR
S: Think of the rabbit having large part around mouth and large ears.

Structural Scoring: Do 1 FMpo A
Aggression Score: None

13) If you look at the whole thing, it looks like a moth. A moth has a wide antennae off the back.

E: RR
S: The wings, body, and antennae. Some kind of moths have something off back-end. I don't know what you call it.

Structural Scoring: Wo 1 Fo A 1.0
Aggression Score: None

(continued)

549

14) On the sides I think I can see a face. Hair is not very long. Nose is straight along dorsum.

E: RR
S: Top of head, nose, mouth, possibly a mustache. Similar to profile up here (Response #11).

Structural Scoring: Ddo 99 Fo Hd
Aggression Score: None
VI 15"

15) It looks like a bobcat hide up on a barn. It has four legs, head looks like a cat's head with whiskers up front and the pattern of the inkblot itself suggests an animal. No tail.

E: RR
S: The whole thing. No tail. You can see spots on it here that make it look like an animal.

Structural Scoring: Wo 1 FYo Ad P 2.5
Aggression Score: None
VII 2"

16) Two girls looking at each other. They have pony tails going up and not down by gravity. Hair, short turned up nose. One on right has puckered lips. Other one doesn't for some reason. Arms are back there and woman's profile—Down to breasts and then cut-off.

E: RR
S: There's the whole head with pony tail. Puckered lips. Not symmetrical. Short nose.

Structural Scoring: D+ 2 Mp.mpo 2 Hd P 3.0
Aggression Score: None
VIII 35"

17) Most immediate thing I saw was shape of an animal. Either a bear or a wolverine.

E: RR
S: This right here. The part that's a rose color.
E: (?)
S: Four legs, leaning forward off right rear leg. Other leg reaching forward.

Structural Scoring: Do 1 FMpo A P
Aggression Score: AgC

S: Central part just doesn't look like anything. It doesn't bring anything out in particular.

IX 40"

18) The central part looks like an animal's head and those look like nostrils there. Not very full. I don't see any eyes or ears.

E: RR
S: Light green color. Looks like a horse's head. No eyes or ears (outlines).

Structural Scoring: DSo 8 FCu Ad 5.0 INC
Aggression Score: None

<

19) This to me looks like some sort of reptile. Perhaps a dinosaur . . . a head. The body is too small to fit the head.

E: RR
S: The eye right there. Shape of mouth. Too full to be a crocodile or alligator . . . Skin looks leathery.

Structural Scoring: Ddo 28 F– A
Aggression Score: None

<

20) This thing here looks like a torso. Proportions fit a baby but head looks like an adult. Sitting down on rear-end with legs out. No feet seen. Legs too short.

Structural Scoring: Ddo 99 Mpo H MOR
Aggression Score: None

X 30"

21) This looks like two crayfish talking to each other. They don't look like real crayfish but like Lewis Carroll's drawing. They look like they're talking earnestly about something.

Structural Scoring: D+ 8 Mpu Art,A 4.5 FABCOM,COP
Aggression Score: None

22) This part here looks like a hood . . . Ku Klux Klan, maybe . . . White with eye-holes. You don't see the rest of the face.

Structural Scoring: DdSo 22 FC'– (Hd) 6.0
Aggression Score: AgC

23) That could be a crayfish, also. The way the legs are and one claw. This looks more literal and that one more like the picture I'd seen in a book before.

Structural Scoring: Ddo 99 Fo A
Aggression Score: None

E: RR
S: Head there. Trunk underneath it with legs sticking out. Rudimentary arms.

E: RR
S: Well, just the shape. Looks like a head, comes over. Head & eyes & antennae. Looks like eyes might be what you see on a cat with vertical pupil.

E: RR
S: Just the white part that comes up here. That's reaching some but usually I see more on the first one. More defects on later one.

E: RR
S: Right there. The claw would be the green part.

Sequence of Scores

Card	No.	Loc.	#	Determinant(s)	(2)	Content(s)	Pop Z	Special Scores
I	1	Do	2	Mpo		H, Sx		INC
	2	Do	4	Fo		A		INC
	3	DdSo	99	Mpu		(Hd), Hx	3.5	
II	4	D+	1	FMpo	2	A	P 3.0	
	5	D+	1	FMp.FC'o	2	A, Id	P 3.0	ALOG, PER
	6	Ddo	99	Fu		Hd		MOR
III	7	D+	9	Mp.FC'+	2	H, Id, Cg	P 3.0	
	8	Do	3	Fu		An		
	9	D+	2	Fu		An	3.0	
IV	10	Do	4	Fo		Ad		
	11	Ddo	21	Fo	2	Hd		DV
V	12	Do	7	FMpo		A		
	13	Wo	1	Fo		A	1.0	
	14	Ddo	99	Fo		Hd		
VI	15	Wo	1	FYo		Ad	P 2.5	
VII	16	D+	2	Mp.mpo	2	Hd	P 3.0	
VIII	17	Do	1	FMpo		A	P	
IX	18	DSo	8	FCu		Ad	5.0	INC
	19	Ddo	28	F−		A		
	20	Ddo	99	Mpo		H		MOR
X	21	D+	8	Mpu		Art, A	4.5	FAB, COP
	22	DdSo	22	FC−		(Hd)	6.0	
	23	Ddo	99	Fo		A		

Summary of Approach

I:D.D.DdS	VI:W
II:D.D.Dd	VII:D
III:D.D.D	VIII:D
IV:D.Dd	IX:DS.Dd.Dd
V:D.W.Dd	X:D.DdS.Dd

Rorschach Structural Summary

LOCATION	DETERMINANTS		CONTENTS	S-CONSTELLATION
FEATURES	BLENDS	SINGLE		NO..FV + VF + V + FD > 2
			H = 3,0	NO..Col-Shd Bl>0
Zf = 11	FM.FC'	M = 4	(H) = 0,0	YES..Ego<.31,>.44
ZSum = 37.5	M.FC'	FM = 3	Hd = 4,0	NO..MOR>3
ZEst = 34.5	M.m	m = 0	(Hd) = 2,0	NO..Zd > ± 3.5
		FC = 1	Hx = 0,1	YES..es>EA
W = 2		CF = 0	A = 8,1	NO..CF+C>FC
(Wv = 0)		C = 0	(A) = 0,0	YES..X+%<.70
D = 13		Cn = 0	Ad = 3,0	NO..S>3
Dd = 8		FC' = 1	(Ad) = 0,0	NO..P<3 or >8
S = 3		C'F = 0	An = 2,0	NO..Pure H <2
		C' = 0	Art = 1,0	NO..R<17
DQ		FT = 0	Ay = 0,0	3.....TOTAL
..........(FQ–)		TF = 0	Bl = 0,0	
+ = 6 (0)		T = 0	Bt = 0,0	SPECIAL SCORINGS
o = 17 (2)		FV = 0	Cg = 0,1	Lv1 Lv2
v/+ = 0 (0)		VF = 0	Cl = 0,0	DV = 1x1 0x2
v = 0 (0)		V = 0	Ex = 0,0	INC = 3x2 0x4
		FY = 1	Fd = 0,0	DR = 0x3 0x6
		YF = C	Fi = 0,0	FAB = 1x4 0x7
		Y = 0	Ge = 0,0	ALOG = 1x5
FORM QUALITY		Fr = 0	Hh = 0,0	CON = 0x7
		rF = 0	Ls = 0,0	SUM6 = 6
FQx FQf MQual SQx		FD = 0	Na = 0,0	WSUM6 = 16
+ = 1 0 1 0		F = 10	Sc = 0,0	
o = 14 6 3 0			Sx = 0,1	AB =0 CP = 0
u = 6 3 2 2			Xy = 0,0	AG =0 MOR = 2
– = 2 1 0 1			Id = 0,2	CFB =0 PER = 1
none = 0 – 0 0		(2) = 5		COP =1 PSV = 0

RATIOS, PERCENTAGES, AND DERIVATIONS

R = 23	L = 0.77		FC:CF+C =1:0	COP = 1	AG = 0
			Pure C =0	Food	= 0
EB = 6:0.5	EA = 6.5	EBPer = 6.0	SumC':WSumC =3:0.5	Isolate/R	= 0.00
eb = 5:4	es = 9	D = 0	Afr =0.44	H:(H)Hd(Hd)	= 3:6
	Adj es = 9	Adj D = 0	S =3	(HHd):(AAd)	= 2:0
			Blends:R =3:23	H+A:Hd + Ad	= 12:9
FM = 4	C' = 3 T = 0		CP =0		
m = 1	V = 0 Y = 1				
		P = 6	Zf =11	3r+(2)/R = 0.22	
a:p = 0:11	Sum6 = 6	X+% = 0.65	Zd = +3.0	Fr+rF = 0	
Ma:Mp = 0:6	Lv2 = 0	F+% = 0.60	W:D:Dd =2:13:8	FD = 0	
2AB+Art+Ay = 1	WSum6 = 16	X–% = 0.09	W:M = 2:6	An + Xy = 2	
M– = 0	Mnone = 0	S–% = 0.50	DQ+ =6	MOR = 2	
		Xu% = 0.26	DQv =0		

SCZI = 0	DEPI = 5*	CDI = 3	S-CON = 3	HVI = No	OBS = No

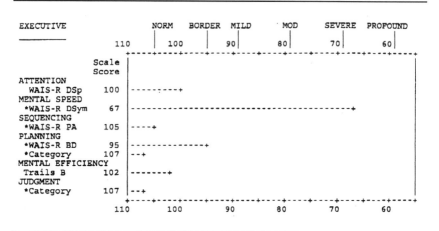

```
EXECUTIVE                       NORM   BORDER  MILD     MOD      SEVERE  PROFOUND
_____                  110  |  100   |    90|      80|       70|       60|
                    Scale       +----+----+----+----+----+----+----+----+----+----+----+
                    Score       |
ATTENTION
  WAIS-R DSp        100         |----------+
MENTAL SPEED
  *WAIS-R DSym       67         |-----------------------------------------------+
SEQUENCING
  *WAIS-R PA        105         |----+
PLANNING
  *WAIS-R BD         95         |--------------+
  *Category         107         |--+
MENTAL EFFICIENCY
  Trails B          102         |-------+
JUDGMENT
  *Category         107         |--+
                                +----+----+----+----+----+----+----+----+----+----+----+
                           110      100       90       80       70       60
```

Note. * indicates the test may appear more than once in Profiles.

Data Summary Form: Results of Neuropsychological Examination

Case Number: _____ Age: __43__ Sex: __M__ Education: __20+(M.D.)__ Handedness: __Left__

Name: __Dr. W__ Employment: _____ Date of Testing: _____

WAIS-R

VIQ	1 2 8
PIQ	1 0 2
FS IQ	1 2 0

Scaled Scores

Information	1 6
Comprehension	1 5
Digit Span	1 2
Arithmetic	1 4
Similarities	1 2
Vocabulary	1 6
Picture Arrangement	1 2
Picture Completion	1 0
Block Design	1 0
Object Assembly	1 0
Digit Symbol	6

MINNESOTA MULTIPHASIC PERSONALITY INVENTORY

T Scores

?	0
L	4 3
F	6 2
K	4 8
Hs	4 7
D	7 8
Hy	5 3
Pd	5 3
Mf	6 3
Pa	5 9
Pt	6 4
Sc	6 5
Ma	4 0
Si	7 3

IMPAIRMENT INDEX ☐ . ☐ *

CATEGORY TEST (Booklet) 1 5 *

TACTUAL PERFORMANCE TEST

Time _____ # of Blks. In

	Time	# of Blks. In
Dominant hand:	5 . 3	ALL
Nondomin. hand:	5 . 9	ALL
Both hands:	2 . 1	ALL
Total Time:	1 3 . 3	*
Memory:		3 *
Localization:		4 *

TRAIL MAKING TEST

Part A: 3 6 seconds ☐ errors

Part B: 4 6 seconds ☐ errors

SEASHORE RHYTHM TEST (correct)

Raw Score: ☐ *

SPEECH-SOUNDS PERCEPTION TEST

Errors: ☐ *

FINGER OSCILLATION TEST

Dominant hand: 5 1 . 4 *

Nondominant hand: 5 2 . 4

STRENGTH OF GRIP

Dominant hand: 5 4 kilograms

Nondominant hand: 5 5 kilograms

REITAN-KLØVE TACTILE FORM RECOGNITION TEST

	Errors	Seconds
Dominant hand:	☐	☐
Nondominant hand:	☐	☐

SENSORY SUPPRESSIONS

Dominant: 0

Nondominant: R L 0

FTNW 2 3

FINAGN 0 0

APHASIA SIGNS: none

Beyond Personality Assessment: The Use of the Rorschach as a Neuropsychological Instrument in Patients With Amnestic Disorders

William Perry
University of California, San Diego

Eric G. Potterat
California School of Professional Psychology, San Diego

The role of memory is critical in one's ability to function in everyday life. It is through memory that we develop an appreciation for our surroundings, plan for the future, and are able to protect ourselves from potentially harmful elements in our environment. Memory is also fundamental in our ability to integrate past experience into present behavior (Hartmann, 1951). Hartmann (1939) described memory as an autonomous ego function and stated that it developed independent of intrapsychic conflicts. Thus, memory is critical to understanding personality and yet is often not included in the psychodiagnostician's assessment, that is, until it fails. Memory failure can consist of momentary lapses or distinct types of permanent disturbances due to cerebral impairment. Neuropsychologists have been very successful in gaining an understanding of memory (Squire, 1987) and the primary memory disorders, referred to as *amnestic disorders*, that result from brain disease. In contrast, research in the area of memory has lagged in the field of psychodiagnostics and personality assessment. One reason for this apparent lack of interest on the part of psychodiagnosticians is that memory is considered a brain function and under the purview of neuropsychologists. In turn, the personality or emotional changes that usually occur following brain damage have only recently been explored by neuropsychologists, except in cases where the change is directly attributable to damage to a specific anatomical site. Consequently, two independent traditions have developed using an independent set of assessment instruments. A renewed interest in integrating the traditions of

557

psychodiagnostic and neuropsychological assessment has emerged (Zillmer & Perry, 1996), and has provided the opportunity to reexamine the role of traditional personality tests with neurologically impaired individuals.

In this vein, we examine two cases of persons with amnestic disorders. The first case is of a patient diagnosed with Dementia of the Alzheimer's Type (DAT), the prototypic progressive cortical dementia. The second case is that of a patient with Wernicke–Korsakoff Syndrome, an amnestic disorder secondary to hemorrhagic lesions of the diencephalic region. In both cases, a neuropsychological approach to the Rorschach provides the major source for the assessment. The goal of this chapter is to illustrate how a traditional personality assessment instrument can be used to characterize brain functioning. We present an argument that the Rorschach inkblot test can be considered a neuropsychological instrument as well as a personality assessment test, particularly when the protocol results are interpreted from "a conceptual frame of reference that takes brain function as its point of departure" (Lezak, 1995, p. 18).

THE INTERFACE BETWEEN NEUROPSYCHOLOGICAL AND PERSONALITY ASSESSMENT

The fields of neuropsychology and personality assessment both involve the study of behavior. The primary goal of neuropsychology is to understand the behavioral expression of brain dysfunction. Lezak (1995) stated that neuropsychological and personality assessment rely on "many of the same techniques, assumptions, and theories" (p. 18). However, she explained that what makes a test neuropsychological is if "the questions that prompted it, the central issues, the findings, or the inferences drawn from them, ultimately relate to brain function" (p. 18). Until recently, most neuropsychological tests have been developed to assess a circumscribed cognitive function and utilize an "achievement" approach to analyze the subject's performance. In other words, tests are administered to patients and scored on the basis of whether or not they passed or failed; and then their total performance is compared against a predetermined criteria (e.g., the Halstead–Reitan Battery; Reitan & Wolfson, 1985). The achievement or actuarial approach has come under some strong criticism. Werner (1937) was the first to argue that relying strictly on the final answer, without attending to the processes used to arrive at that answer, may distort the results of an evaluation. He suggested that a subject may be able to perform a task meeting a certain criterion level, but may use a highly aberrant strategy indicative of some type of brain pathology.

In place of the achievement approach, a "process" orientation is patient-centered and monitors the patient's problem-solving behavior with emphasis on the strategies and types of errors that a subject displays (Kaplan, 1988). Kaplan (1988) stated that the process analysis captures the most neuropsychological meaning from a sample of behaviors. The process approach then examines qualitative aspects of behavior according to cognitive-based and operationally defined indicators. In turn, these indicators are quantified and can be subjected to statistical analyses. A number of tests have been developed based on the process approach, such as the California Verbal Learning Test (Delis, Kramer, Kaplan, & Ober, 1987), a comprehensive verbal learning and memory assessment instrument, as well as new objective scoring systems applied to established tests (e.g., the Wechsler Adult Intelligence Scale–Revised [WAIS–R; Wechsler, 1981] as a neuropsychological instrument; Kaplan, Fein, Morris, & Delis, 1991).

THE RORSCHACH AS A NEUROPSYCHOLOGICAL INSTRUMENT

The use of traditional personality assessment instruments, such as the Rorschach, to understand brain functioning is not a new concept. In the case of the Rorschach test, Rorschach (1921/1942) himself believed that his technique could definitively differentiate between normal individuals and "organics." This belief was supported by the traditional neuropsychiatrists of his time, such as Bleuler, who encouraged Rorschach to pursue his technique. Piotrowski, under the tutelage of Goldstein, continued the study of the application of the Rorschach in aiding in neuropsychiatric diagnoses (Piotrowski, 1937). Benton and Reitan, both pioneers of clinical neuropsychology, also studied the Rorschach early in their careers (Aita, Reitan, & Ruth, 1947; Benton, 1945). However, the utility of using the Rorschach in diagnosing neurological disease was called into question, and due to the failure of the early use of the Rorschach to correctly distinguish between mild or moderate brain injured subjects from nonpatients, the fields of personality assessment and neuropsychology parted company and developed into separate traditions (Aita et al., 1947). For neuropsychologists, the developments in neuroscience have allowed for exciting advances in the assessment of brain–behavior relationships, whereas personality assessment branched out to the investigation of assessing nonorganically impaired individuals.

Exner (1993) reframed the Rorschach as a problem-solving test, and in so doing provided a foundation for the Rorschach to be used as a neuropsychological instrument. He postulated that numerous operations occur in the process of answering the question, "what might this be?" He suggested that when posed with the inkblot the subject initiates a series of cognitive steps that include "scanning, coding, classifying, comparing, discarding, and selecting" (Exner, 1990, p. 5). Similarly, for the purpose of understanding the neuropsychological operations involved in providing a Rorschach percept, we can examine each of these steps and generate explanatory hypotheses regarding a person's impaired performance. A starting point would be to determine whether the subject understands the Rorschach task and if he or she can sustain this understanding over the duration of the 10 Rorschach cards. Failure to comprehend the assignment of creating a percept from the inkblot may reveal deficits in attention, orientation, and short-term memory. Once embracing the task, we can assess the subject's cognitive facility to scan the entire blot. For example, feature detection and visual scanning is mediated by the frontal eye fields (Broadmann area 8) and act in cooperation with the dorsolateral prefrontal cortex, particularly when memory is involved (Goldman-Rakic, 1991; McDowell, Clementz, & Wixted, 1996). Deficits to these areas might lead to an inefficient search of the visual field. Luria (1980) suggested that two visual search strategies are often observed in patients with frontal lobe damage. The first strategy is a random or chaotic search strategy, whereas the second is a strategy in which the subject is "stuck" and extrapolates from one critical element to the entire visual field.

Perceptual organizational abilities are also differentiated between the two hemispheres and can influence Rorschach responses. Delis, Kiefner, and Fridlund (1988) determined hemispheric differences in hierarchical analysis. Their work has demonstrated that the left hemisphere of most right-handed people is specialized for detection and interpretation of small bits of detail, whereas the right hemisphere is superior for processing the global or gestalt. Damage to either hemisphere would impair a person's ability to identify the Rorschach stimuli and integrate a coherent response. Specifically, we would speculate that damage to the posterior area of the left hemisphere would render an individual unable to process the fine details of the Rorschach inkblot, resulting in an exaggerated preference for producing whole responses (W). Offering solely whole responses is not uncommon for many individuals with and without brain disease and does not necessarily mean that the left hemisphere is impaired. In cases, however, where the pathology of the left hemisphere is known, we would expect an inability on the part of the person to offer anything but a whole response. Furthermore, on those cards that are most difficult to integrate into a single whole response (e.g., Cards IX and X), we would expect clear examples of perceptual disturbance manifesting as poor form. In contrast, an individual with right hemisphere damage would not offer an integrated whole response, but instead, would extrapolate a response based on small details. For example, a 56-year-old, right-handed man with a stroke to the posterior portion of the right hemisphere produced a Rorschach protocol of 13 responses. Among his responses, he produced 11 Dd responses, and all 13 responses received form quality minus (FQ–) scores. Additionally, on inspection of his responses during the inquiry phase, it was observed that he had generated his responses almost exclusively from the right side of the inkblot, revealing a condition known as *hemineglect*.

The coding, classifying, comparing, discarding, and selecting of a response can all be regarded as components of information processing and require intact cerebral functioning. Because the Rorschach stimulus is a complex field of images, colors, hues, textures, and associations, the corresponding cerebral cortex activated to process the stimulus includes a vast ensemble of neurons. Fuster (1989) presented a hierarchical processing framework for understanding how a sensation becomes a perception. He suggested that on a neuronal level there is a network made up of two broad categories. The first is comprised of neurons that "participate in the discrimination and analysis of the physical attributes of the stimulus" (Fuster, 1989, p. 168). The second "contains neurons representing attributes that the stimulus has acquired by experience" (Fuster, 1989, p. 168). Based on a hierarchical processing schema, the simple features of the stimulus are processed at the lower stages, whereas the complex features are processed at higher stages. Electrophysiological data have provided evidence that these two processing stages occur in parallel (Fuster, 1989). It is during the processing of the complex features of the stimulus (Rorschach) that the coding, classifying, comparing, and discarding of the response transpires. Whereas sensory processing is mainly represented in the posterior cortex, the final organization and execution of the behavior (the delivery of a response) involves the frontal cortex.

There is considerable evidence from neuropsychological and neurophysiological research to support a complex interconnected system involving posterior cortex fibers projecting to the frontal cortex, as well as fibers originating from the frontal cortex descending through subcortical regions and looping back via the thalamus to the frontal lobe (Cummings & Benson, 1992; DeLong & Georgopolus, 1981; Swerdlow & Kolb, 1987). Thus, it is the frontal cortex that serves as the mediator for the integration of primary sensory processing and the formation of a complex behavior, such as producing a Rorschach percept. This is particularly significant when assessing neuropsychiatric disorders, because these disorders are thought to reflect impairment of the frontal-subcortical circuits (Swerdlow & Kolb, 1987). Moreover, the Rorschach being an abstract problem-solving task is likely to activate these frontal-subcortical circuits because "any disturbance in thought and behavior must have its expression via frontal functions" (Malloy & Duffy, 1994, p. 203). Thus, the more disruption to the frontal-subcortical circuit, the more impairment should be expressed during Rorschach performance. With extensive damage, characteristic responses would include a low number of responses with few blends, few movement responses, few content categories, and a high *lambda*. These Rorschach test characteristics are similar to the signs that Piotrowski (1937) identified as being pathognomonic of cortical-subcortical damaged patients.

What role then does memory have in this analysis? Most complex behaviors are inextricably anchored in past experience. All deliberate behaviors involve some previous exposure to a stimulus or to some association to a stimulus. On Card I, when we perceive a bat, we know that it, in fact, is not a bat and does not look like a "good" bat at all. We do, however, make an association based on past experience that bats resemble this percept, which is consistent with the Rorschach instructions to create versus identify (Oberholzer, 1931; Peterson & Schilling, 1983; Schafer, 1954). In humans, memory is distributed throughout the brain so that no single center exists. The posterior cortical areas are devoted to the representation of images and constructs of the external world, whereas the hippocampus, a deep structure within the temporal lobe, is critical for the consolidation of present experiences with previous experiences (Kolb & Whishaw, 1990). The frontal lobe is also critical for memory functioning. Patients with frontal lobe impairment have a tendency not to organize information efficiently and therefore tend to have problems with storage and retrieval of information, which is fundamental for adequate memory functioning (Stuss & Benson, 1987). Impaired encoding and retrieval strategies may lead to numerous deficits including perseverative responses. For example, Perry, Potterat, Auslander, Kaplan, and Jeste (1996) developed a new scale for assessing linguistic and perseveration errors from Rorschach responses. Adapted from the work of Barr, Bilder, Goldberg, Kaplan, and Mukherjee (1989), this scale is based on a neuropsychological framework and identifies paraphasic errors, word finding difficulties, and awkward and stilted speech. Three types of perseverative errors are also coded. The categories of perseveration are based in part on a taxonomy developed by Sandson and Albert (1984), consisting of types of perseverations that are distinct at the levels of cognitive process and neuroanatomy. The first type, *phonemic perseveration* is coded for a repetition of phonemic or morphemic quality of a previous response. The second type, *stuck-in-set perseveration,* refers to the compulsive use of a framework or strategy from a previous response and is characteristic of patients with dorsolateral prefrontal cortex lesions. Finally, *thematic perseveration* is coded for the reappearance of a content or theme, whether or not it is appropriate to the blot. Thematic perseveration involves abnormal recall of items from short-term memory and is characteristic of aphasic patients, such as those with DAT and patients with left hemisphere lesions (Sandson & Albert, 1984). In their initial study, Perry et al. (1996) used the scale to characterize the Rorschach protocols of patients diagnosed with DAT. In that study, DAT patients demonstrated a propensity to commit thematic perseverations. In a subsequent study, Perry and Braff (1995) demonstrated that schizophrenia patients who are purported to have a putative deficit of the dorsolateral prefrontal cortex produced a significantly high number of stuck-in-set perseveration in their Rorschach protocols, again supporting the use of their scale.

Collectively, their work illustrates how a neuropsychological approach to understanding Rorschach responses can provide rich data regarding the way an individual approaches the Rorschach problem. Although the present scale is not used to differentiate "organics" from "nonorganics" in the manner of Piotrowski (1937), some of the neuropsychological processes highlighted here have heritage in "Piotrowski's signs." The advantages of using the present neuropsychological approach to the Rorschach for understanding brain–behavior relationships in general, and memory in particular, may best be illustrated by examining the following two cases in detail.

DAT

DAT is a progressive cortical disease that is characterized by the presence of neurofibrillary tangles and senile plaques concentrated in the associative areas of the parietal, temporal, and frontal lobes (Lezak, 1995). Memory disturbance (amnesia), language deficits (aphasia), and visuospatial impairments are the cardinal neurocognitive signs of DAT (Cummings & Benson, 1992). Disturbances of calculation (dyscalculia), failure to recognize the symbolic meaning of a stimulus (agnosia), the inability to perform a purposeful act (apraxia), and loss of abstraction emerge as the dementia advances. Motor and sensory abnormalities do not appear until late in the disease.

The memory impairment of DAT is characterized by an impaired ability to encode new material and difficulty recalling information due to the rapid loss of information from short-term memory storage. Priming, category cueing, and recognition tasks do not facilitate recall (Salmon, Shimamura, Butters, & Smith, 1988). The language deficits of DAT are characterized by word finding difficulties, circumlocution, and the occurrence of paraphasic errors. As the illness progresses, language comprehension and the ability to converse become impaired. Visuospatial impairments usually appear in the form of patients getting lost in familiar surroundings. Visuoconstructional abilities, such as simple drawing tests, are often used to reveal the significant impairment these patients experience. Finally, behavior of DAT patients is hallmarked by indifference. Personality, however, is not markedly changed during the early phases of the illness, but profound impairment in the ability to think abstractly, plan, initiate, sequence, monitor, and cease behavior influences their interpersonal skills.

CASE 1: DAT PATIENT "P. R."

P. R. was a 71-year-old, right-handed, White male with 12 years of education who worked in a grocery store that he owned. He was referred to a neurologist by his general physician because he was having increased difficulty finding his way home from his store, even though he had traveled the same path for 27 years. His wife noted that over the past 3 years he had become more forgetful and was now having difficulty filling out order forms for his business. She also reported that he was experiencing difficulties with recalling the names of common day-to-day items.

On neurological examination he was found to be in excellent general medical health. An electroencephalogram (EEG) and computer tomography (CT) scan were completed to rule out a stroke or mass. The results of the CT revealed cerebral atrophy consistent with DAT. P. R. was referred for a neuropsychological screening that included the Mini Mental Status Exam

(Folstein, Folstein, & McHugh, 1975), the Dementia Rating Scale (Mattis, 1988), and the Rorschach Inkblot Test. On the Mini Mental Status Exam, his score of 23 out of a possible 30 indicates significantly impaired cognitive functioning. On the Dementia Rating Scale, his score of 125 out of 144 places him at the 90th percentile when compared to a sample of DAT patients, suggesting that he is moderately impaired (Mattis, 1988).

P. R. was administered the Rorschach test according to the Comprehensive System instructions (Exner, 1986; see Appendix A). On the Rorschach, P. R. offered 14 responses ($R = 14$), comprised entirely of pure F responses (*Lambda* = 14.00). Exner (1986) suggested that low R on the Rorschach is a sign of defensiveness or distancing from the task at hand. Alternatively, we have found that low R and high *lambda* is common in brain-damaged patients and is probably a nonspecific sign of cerebral impairment. Furthermore, in this record, the reduction in the total number of content categories used to formulate the 14 responses (3) and the absence of movement responses (see Appendix B), which require abstract reasoning, is commensurate with the specific type of aphasia (impairment in the use of language for communication) observed in DAT. The linguistic error scoring method of Perry et al. (1996) adds further support to the detection of aphasia and anomia in P. R.'s protocol. Clear evidence of word finding problems can be observed in three responses (1, 3, and 12). Two other responses (6 and 10) illustrate a more subtle form of word finding problem, referred to as superordinate categorization (i.e., the naming of an object without providing defining characteristics). On Card V, Response 7, P. R. illustrates an example of a paraphasic error ("eartlers"). Cummings and Benson (1992) reported that paraphasic errors are typically observed in conjunction with anomia in DAT, but as the disease progresses the paraphasic error becomes less related to the target word and approaches a neologism.

P. R.'s Rorschach protocol (Appendices B and C) also included eight form quality minus responses ($X-\% = .57$). Exner (1986) suggested that when $X-$ is elevated that "the subject is having some difficulty in translating perceptual inputs appropriately" (p. 368). This is further supported in the lack of Popular responses ($P = 2$) and the use of areas that encompass large segments of the blot, resulting in an overreliance on whole or common details when formulating a response ($W = 6$ and $D = 7$). Collectively, these results reflect the visuospatial difficulties that are one of the hallmark signs of DAT. Furthermore, his Rorschach record reveals many of the signs that Piotrowski (1937) identified as characteristic of "organic cases."

The memory disturbance of DAT is characterized by poor encoding strategies, rapid forgetting, and the inability to benefit from category cueing. During novel reasoning tasks, such as the Rorschach, the production of a topic-oriented discourse that communicates the complex notion requires the ability to be flexible and to change cognitive sets as the environment (inkblot) changes. When an individual cannot adapt to the changing of environments, cannot encode new information, and cannot benefit from visual or semantic cues in retrieving information, there is a tendency to perseverate. Perseveration, or the inability to change sets, results in a decline of themes. For example, in P. R.'s protocol, themes involving dogs, ears, and faces appear in 50% of the responses (3, 4, 6, 8, 9, 10, and 11). Additionally, he commits a phonemic perseveration when discussing ears in Response 6 and then in Response 7 introducing "eartlers." Sandson and Albert (1984) suggested that thematic perseveration involves an abnormal recall from short-term memory. Finally, evidence of a mechanical perseveration (Exner, 1986) can be observed in Response 12. Thus, themes intrude in a repetitive fashion into the discourse that results in the classic perseveration of DAT patients.

WERNICKE–KORSAKOFF SYNDROME

Wernicke–Korsakoff Syndrome is a nondementing amnestic disorder hallmarked by lesions of the midbrain, principally the thalamus, mamillary bodies, and limbic structures (Brust, 1993). In addition, a profound loss of gray matter is often noted in the orbitofrontal and mesiotemporal cortex (Jernigan, Schafer, Butters, & Cermak, 1991). Although the etiology remains obscure, considerable evidence suggests that malabsorption of thiamine (Vitamin B1), secondary to chronic alcohol use and poor diet, is the primary cause of this disease (Butters & Cermak, 1980).

The disease often emerges as an encephalopathy with oculomotor disturbance, ataxia (gait disturbance), and mental confusion and disorientation. Left untreated, the disease develops into the classic Wernicke–Korsakoff Syndrome, with anterograde and retrograde amnesia, profound visuospatial and executive functioning impairment and, at times, the presence of confabulation. Although memory impairment includes both anterograde and retrograde amnesia, the anterograde deficits are most readily apparent, for

> patients with a full-blown Korsakoff's Syndrome live in a time zone of about three to five minutes, having little or no ready access to events or learning tasks in which they participated prior to the space allowed by their memory deficits. (Lezak, 1995, p. 256)

Although their performance on well-structured, overlearned tasks typically remains intact, performance on timed, spatial organization tests, as well as tests requiring hypothesis generation and problem solving, is usually impaired (Laine & Butters, 1982).

CASE 2: WERNICKE–KORSAKOFF PATIENT "S. H."

S. H. was a 62-year-old, right-handed, White male with 16 years of education who was brought to the hospital by the police for an evaluation. They responded to a report of a man who was wandering aimlessly, trying to use his own personal key to gain entry into various motels in which he was not a resident. The police noted that the man, S. H., was unable to respond to their questions in a coherent fashion and was profoundly emaciated and appeared to be intoxicated. S. H. was brought to the hospital emergency room for evaluation and was assessed as confused and psychotic. On examination of his mental status, he was oriented only to his name, and demonstrated confabulation, anterograde amnesia, and retrograde amnesia for information for the past 3 years. He was admitted to the hospital and a psychiatric workup, which included a series of blood tests, a Magnetic Resonance Imaging (MRI) scan, neuropsychological testing, and the gathering of history, was initiated.

A review of S. H.'s old medical records revealed that he had been married three times and had been a heavy drinker since his teenage years. When he was 17 years old, he dropped out of high school and joined the armed forces. Records indicated that he had received his General Education Degree while in the service and that his IQ was tested to be 138. When his military obligation came to an end, he earned a college degree in literature from a well-known university. Following college, he owned a bar and returned to drinking heavily, averaging one case of beer along with a fifth of whiskey weekly. During this time, he spent 4 years in jail for robbing a bank. The circumstances surrounding his criminal activity are unknown; however, it is clear that, after his release, he returned to drinking heavily. Little other information is known about him after this time.

While in the psychiatric unit, S. H. was unable to locate his own room, was confused, disorganized and disoriented, and required assistance in maintaining his personal hygiene. He was polite and cooperative, however, and did not evidence problems with his speech. The hospital notes indicated that he was amnestic and had a tendency to confabulate when he could not answer questions readily. For example, he stated to a staff member who questioned his absence from a group that, "I went fishing this morning and they were not biting very good"; and he reported another time that, "I just woke up and got bit by a 15 foot rattle snake . . . he's lucky I don't have my gun."

On the neuropsychological testing he achieved a Verbal IQ Score of 108 and performed normally on many tests. His most impaired performances, however, were on memory tests and executive functioning tests, such as the Wisconsin Card Sorting Test (Berg, 1948), on which he committed a significant number of perseverative responses. His EEG indicated abnormal intermittent bursts of slow wave activity, with greater amplitude in the frontal lobe, consistent with encephalopathy. His MRI scan showed diffuse cerebral atrophy, most pronounced in the frontal and midbrain regions. Based on his extensive evaluation, the neuropsychologists, psychiatrists, and psychologists concurred that his diagnosis was most consistent with Wernicke–Korsakoff Syndrome. Once his diagnosis was established, S. H. was administered the Rorschach test according to the Comprehensive System (Exner, 1986).

By inspecting his responses (see Appendix D), a number of areas can be highlighted that characterize his neurocognitive functioning, particularly when comparing his performance to P. R., the patient with DAT. The most striking feature of S. H.'s Rorschach performance is the absence of an inquiry to his responses. In initiating the inquiry phase of the test, S. H. was read his responses verbatim. He, being amnestic of his free associations to the blots, insisted that he did not make those responses, became agitated and refused to continue with the testing. Thus, his response to our inquiry is evidence of his anterograde amnesia and illustrates the extremely short time span in which information can remain stored. This is in sharp contrast to P. R., who could recollect his responses during the inquiry phase. Consequently, we were unable to score S. H.'s protocol and were left to speculate as to the location and the determinants that he used to create his responses. Based on this experience, we have since modified our administration procedure and inquire directly following the free associations to each card. This modified approach follows the method of Rapaport, Gill, and Schafer (1945–1946).

As was indicated in the description of S. H.'s presenting illness, he was prone to confusion and disorganization, which gave way to bizarre behavior. On the more structured neuropsychological tests, which assess language, perceptual, and motor skills, S. H. could follow the directions and demonstrated the skills needed to perform the tasks, whereas during the Rorschach, an abstract problem-solving test, the nature and extent of his confused state was most clearly revealed. His responses illustrate the fluidity of his thinking and the primitive and disturbing nature of his logic when the structure of the test environment is removed. Furthermore, his propensity for confabulation is illuminated in almost every response; however, in this context it does not serve to integrate his environment but rather reveals his strained efforts to make sense of his environment. His response to Card IV can serve as an example of the fluidity of his response process and his ineffective attempt to communicate what he sees to the examiner. He stated, "It looks like a giant ancient cow. They're gone now." Thus, instead of explaining what he sees, the percept merely disappears. His perceptual difficulties are also apparent in that his responses to all but Card VII would result in at least one form quality minus score. These results are consistent with the findings of Oscar-Berman and Samuel (1977), who reported that Korsakoff's patients' perceptual problems may be due to impaired encoding (i.e., a partial analysis of complex visual stimuli).

In contrast to the aphasia observed in P. R.'s protocol, S. H.'s output is fluent and lengthy and no word finding difficulties are present. On the other hand, among his 18 responses, several examples of paraphasic errors (Responses 15 and 16), and one example of awkward and inappropriate speech (Response 9), can be observed. Perry and Braff (1995) demonstrated, using factor analysis, that awkward and inappropriate speech loaded with cognitive special scores on the Rorschach, which suggested a relationship to thought disturbance rather than language difficulties.

To further assess S. H.'s memory, we turn to the perseveration-executive functioning error classification method (Perry et al., 1996). Scoring S. H.'s protocol revealed five examples of perseveration (Responses 6, 8, 11, 13, and 14). However, unlike the numerous thematic perseverations observed in P. R.'s record, four of the five perseverations were of the stuck-in-set variety, suggesting cognitive inflexibility in the process of generating a response. It has been suggested that all forms of perseveration involve impaired frontal cortex mediated executive-functioning, resulting in an increase in the number of perseverations across every domain of behavior and cognition (Bilder & Goldberg, 1987). Stuck-in-set perseverations, however, are characteristic of individuals with frontal lobe pathology, whereas thematic perseverations are most common in aphasic subjects and DAT patients (Sandson & Albert, 1984). Thus, the results of S. H.'s Rorschach are consistent with the neuroradiology report of cerebral atrophy to the frontal region.

Although S. H.'s protocol clearly evidences his underlying organic impairment, the content of his responses reveals the essence of his personality. Hartmann (1924) stated that "the memory disorder of the Korsakoff's syndrome is organically founded . . . but there is also a functional factor and that only its interaction with the organic-cerebral factor yields the total psychological picture of the Korsakoff's syndrome" (p. 368). We concur.

SUMMARY AND CONCLUSION

This chapter marks an initial attempt to provide guidelines for using the Rorschach as a clinical neuropsychological instrument. We offer a very basic interpretation of the Rorschach protocols of two individuals with amnestic disorders. Although both individuals present with severe memory problems, the nature of their amnesia, the degree of associated neurocognitive deficits, and the neuroanatomical sites of their pathology are extremely different. The Rorschach, used as an abstract problem-solving test, can help characterize the distinct nature of these two very different processes, as well as the unique psychological features of the individuals who are inflicted with these diseases. Thus, the Rorschach may provide unique advantages over other neurocognitive tests. With additional studies comparing the Rorschach test to more traditional neuropsychological assessment tests, we believe that the Rorschach can become a valuable instrument to clinical neuropsychologists and personality diagnosticians alike.

ACKNOWLEDGMENT

We thank Joyce Sprock and Andrea M. Potterat for their assistance in chapter preparation.

REFERENCES

Aita, J., Reitan, R., & Ruth, J. (1947). Rorschach's test as a diagnostic aid in brain injury. *American Journal of Psychiatry, 103,* 770–779.

Barr, W. B., Bilder, R. M., Goldberg, E., Kaplan, E., & Mukherjee, S. (1989). The neuropsychology of schizophrenic speech. *Journal of Communication Disorders, 22,* 327–349.

Benton, A. L. (1945). Rorschach performance with suspected malingerers. *Journal of Abnormal and Social Psychology, 40,* 94–96.

Berg, E. A. (1948). A simple objective treatment for measuring flexibility in thinking. *Journal of General Psychology, 39,* 15–22.

Bilder, R., & Goldberg, E. (1987). Motor perseverations in schizophrenia. *Archives of Clinical Neuropsychology, 2,* 195–214.

Brust, J. C. M. (1993). *Neurological aspects of substance abuse.* Boston: Butterworth-Heinemann.

Butters, N., & Cermak, L. S. (1980). *Alcoholic Korsakoff's syndrome.* New York: Academic.

Cummings, J. L., & Benson, F. D. (1992). *Dementia: A clinical approach* (2nd ed.). Boston: Butterworth-Heinemann.

Delis, D. C., Kiefner, M. G., & Fridlund, A. J. (1988). Visuospatial dysfunction following unilateral brain damage: Dissociations in hierarchical and hemispatial analysis. *Journal of Clinical and Experimental Neuropsychology, 10,* 421–431.

Delis, D. C., Kramer, J. H., Kaplan, E., & Ober, B. A. (1987). *California Verbal Learning Test: Adult version.* San Antonio, TX: Psychological Corporation.

DeLong, M. P., & Georgopolus, A. P. (1981). Motor functions of the basal ganglia. In V. B. Brooks (Ed.), *Handbook of physiology: Vol. II* (pp. 1017–1061). Bethesda, MD: American Physiological Society.

Exner, J. E., Jr. (1986). *The Rorschach: A comprehensive system: Vol. 1. Basic foundations* (2nd ed.). New York: Wiley.

Exner, J. E., Jr. (1990). *A Rorschach workbook for the comprehensive system* (3rd ed.). Asheville, NC: Rorschach Workshops.

Exner, J. E., Jr. (1993). *The Rorschach: A comprehensive system: Vol. 1. Basic foundations* (3rd ed.). New York: Wiley.

Folstein, M. F., Folstein, S. E., & McHugh, P. R. (1975). Mini-mental state. *Journal of Psychiatric Research, 12,* 189–198.

Fuster, J. M. (1989). *The prefrontal cortex: Anatomy, physiology, and neuropsychology of the frontal lobe.* New York: Raven.

Goldman-Rakic, P. S. (1991). Prefrontal cortex dysfunction in schizophrenia: The relevance of working memory. In B. J. Carroll & J. E. Barrett (Eds.), *Psychopathology and the brain* (pp. 1–21). New York: Raven.

Hartmann, H. (1924). On parapraxes in the Korsakoff psychosis. In H. Hartmann (Ed.), *Essays on ego psychology* (pp. 350–368). New York: International Universities Press.

Hartmann, H. (1939). *Ego psychology and the problem of adaptation.* New York: International Universities Press.

Hartmann, H. (1951). Technical implications of ego psychology. In H. Hartmann (Ed.), *Essays on ego psychology* (pp. 142–154). New York: International Universities Press.

Jernigan, T. L., Schafer, K., Butters, N., & Cermak, L. S. (1991). Magnetic resonance imaging of alcoholic Korsakoff patients. *Neuropsychopharmacology, 4,* 175–186.

Kaplan, E. (1988). A process approach to neuropsychological assessment. In T. Boll & B. K. Bryant (Eds.), *Clinical neuropsychology and brain function: Research, measurement, and practice* (pp. 125–167). Washington, DC: American Psychological Association.

Kaplan, E., Fein, D., Morris, R., & Delis, D. (1991). *WAIS–R as a neuropsychological instrument.* San Antonio, TX: Psychological Corporation.

Kolb, B., & Whishaw, I. Q. (1990). *Fundamentals of human neuropsychology* (3rd ed.). New York: Freeman.

Laine, M., & Butters, N. (1982). A preliminary study of the problem-solving strategies of detoxified long-term alcoholics. *Drug and Alcohol Dependence, 10,* 235–242.

Lezak, M. D. (1995). *Neuropsychological assessment* (3rd ed.). New York: Oxford University Press.

Luria, A. R. (1980). *Higher cortical functions in man*. New York: Basic Books.

Malloy, P., & Duffy, J. (1994). The frontal lobes in neuropsychiatric disorders. In F. Boller & J. Grafman (Eds.), *Handbook of neuropsychology* (Vol. 9, pp. 203–230). New York: Oxford University Press.

Mattis, S. (1988). *Dementia rating scale*. Odessa, FL: Psychological Assessment Resources.

McDowell, J., Clementz, B., & Wixted, J. T. (1996). Timing and amplitude of saccades during predictive saccadic tracking in schizophrenia. *Psychophysiology, 33*, 93–101.

Oberholzer, E. (1931). Zur differentialdiagnose psychischer Folgezustande nach Schadeltraumen mittels des Rorschachschen Formdeutversuchs [Regarding the differential psychiatric sequelae following head trauma using the Rorschach test]. *Journal of Neurology, 136*, 596–629.

Oscar-Berman, M., & Samuel, I. (1977). Stimulus preference and memory factors in Korsakoff's Syndrome. *Neuropsychologia, 15*, 99–106.

Perry, W., & Braff, D. L. (1995). A qualitative assessment of perseverative responses of schizophrenia patients. *Biological Psychiatry, 37*(9), 635.

Perry, W., Potterat, E. G., Auslander, L., Kaplan, E., & Jeste, D. (1996). A neuropsychological approach to the Rorschach in patients with dementia of the Alzheimer type. *Assessment, 3*, 351–361.

Peterson, C. A., & Schilling, K. M. (1983). Card pull in projective testing. *Journal of Personality Assessment, 47*, 265–275.

Piotrowski, Z. (1937). The Rorschach ink-blot method in organic disturbances of the central nervous system. *Journal of Nervous and Mental Disease, 86*, 525–537.

Rapaport, D., Gill, M., & Schafer, R. (1945–1946). *Diagnostic psychological testing* (Vols. 1 & 2). Chicago: Yearbook Publishers.

Reitan, R. M., & Wolfson, D. (1985). *The Halstead–Reitan Neuropsychological Test Battery: Theory and clinical interpretation*. Tucson, AZ: Neuropsychology Press.

Rorschach, H. (1942). *Psychodiagnostics*. New York: Grune & Stratton. (Original work published 1921)

Salmon, D. P., Shimamura, A. P., Butters, N., & Smith, S. (1988). Lexical and semantic priming deficits in patients with Alzheimer's disease. *Journal of Clinical and Experimental Neuropsychology, 10*, 477–494.

Sandson, J., & Albert, M. L. (1984). Varieties of perseveration. *Neuropsychologia, 22*, 715–732.

Schafer, R. (1954). *Psychoanalytic interpretation in Rorschach testing*. New York: Grone & Stratton.

Squire, L. R. (1987). *Memory and brain*. New York: Oxford University Press.

Stuss, D. T., & Benson, D. F. (1986). *The frontal lobes*. New York: Raven.

Swerdlow, N. R., & Kolb, G. F. (1987). Dopamine, schizophrenia, mania, and depression: Toward a unified hypothesis of cortico-striato-palido-thalamic function. *Behavioral and Brain Sciences, 10*, 197–245.

Wechsler, D. (1981). *Wechsler Adult Intelligence Scale–Revised*. New York: The Psychological Corporation.

Werner, H. (1937). Process and achievement: A basic problem of education and developmental psychology. *Harvard Educational Review, 7*, 353–368.

Zillmer, E., & Perry, W. (1996). The neuropsychology of personality. *Assessment, 3*, 205–363.

I.

1) It is a face of a thing. I don't know what . . . maybe with fur and a nose.

E: (Rpts S's response)
S: Here is the face and the nose.
E: (fur?)
S: I don't know [subject points to the edges].

2) It looks like a dog's ear.

E: (Rpts S's response)
S: Right here.
E: (?)
S: I don't know.

II.

3) A dog face . . . maybe a cat, I don't know.

E: (Rpts S's response)
S: I can't remember. Maybe this part with the open part, the face part.
E: (?)
S: I don't know.

III.

4) I can't make it out. I don't know. Maybe a dog's head.

E: (Rpts S's response)
S: I don't know, it looks like a dog. This is the mouth.

5) This looks like a fish

E: (Rpts S's response)
S: This is the head. What kind fish is this?

IV.

6) I don't know what this is. It looks like two animals. I don't know what kind.

E: (Rpts S's response)
S: Here and here. Here are the ears . . . they look like dogs.

V.

7) I can't figure this out. I'm really failing. A boy bat.

E: (Rpts S's response)
S: Here are the eartlers. Here it is [subject points to the outside form . . . outlines].

VI.

8) Another bat.

E: (Rpts S's response)
S: I don't know. It is big. [circles with finger]
E: (?)
S: I don't know.

VII.

9) I see ears here.

E: (Rpts S's response)
S: Long ones pointing up.
E: (?)
S: I don't know. That's it.

10) Maybe a face.

E: (Rpts S's response)
S: This part is the face.
E: (?)
S: [subject non-responsive]

(continued)

VIII.

11) A face of an animal.

E: (Rpts S's response)
S: Here are the ears and the nose.
E: (?)
S: [subject non-responsive]

IX.

12) A face of an animal.

E: (Rpts S's response)
S: The ears and the nose are here. What is this called? [points to his own face] I don't know, cheeks I guess.

X.

13) A spider.

E: (Rpts S's response)
S: It just looks like one.

14) Two flies.

E: (Rpts S's response)
S: It looks like one here and here.
E: (?)
S: They just look like flies.

Sequence of Scores

Card	No.	Loc.	#	Determinant(s)	(2)	Content(s)	Pop Z	Special Scores
I	1	Wo	1	Fo		Ad	1.0	
	2	Do	7	F–		Ad		
II	3	WSo	1	F–		Ad	4.5	
III	4	Ddo	32	F–		Ad		
	5	Do	5	Fo		A		
IV	6	Do	6	Fo	2	A		
V	7	Wo	1	Fo		A	P 1.0	DV2
VI	8	Wo	1	F–		A	2.5	
VII	9	Do	2	F–	2	Hd		
	10	Do	9	Fo		Hd		
VIII	11	Wo	1	F–		Ad	4.5	
IX	12	Wo	1	F–		Ad	5.5	
X	13	Do	1	Fo		A	P	
	14	Do	7	F–	2	A		

Summary of Approach

I:W.D	VI:W
II:WS	VII:D.D
III:Dd.D	VIII:W
IV:D	IX:W
V:W	X:D.D

APPENDIX C
Rorschach Structural Summary

LOCATION FEATURES	DETERMINANTS	CONTENTS	S-CONSTELLATION

DETERMINANTS — BLENDS / SINGLE

S-CONSTELLATION

- NO..FV + VF + V + FD > 2
- NO..Col-Shd Bl>0
- YES..Ego<.31,>.44
- NO..MOR>3
- NO..Zd > ± 3.5
- NO..es>EA
- NO..CF+C>FC
- YES..X+%<.70
- NO..S>3
- YES..P<3 or >8
- YES..Pure H <2
- YES..R<17
- 5.....TOTAL

LOCATION FEATURES

Zf	= 6	
ZSum	= 19.0	
ZEst	= 17.0	
W	= 6	
(Wv	= 0)	
D	= 7	
Dd	= 1	
S	= 1	

DETERMINANTS — SINGLE

			CONTENTS	
M	= 0	H	= 0,0	
FM	= 0	(H)	= 0,0	
m	= 0	Hd	= 2,0	
FC	= 0	(Hd)	= 0,0	
CF	= 0	Hx	= 0,0	
C	= 0	A	= 6,0	
Cn	= 0	(A)	= 0,0	
FC'	= 0	Ad	= 6,0	
C'F	= 0	(Ad)	= 0,0	
C'	= 0	An	= 0,0	
FT	= 0	Art	= 0,0	
TF	= 0	Ay	= 0,0	
T	= 0	Bl	= 0,0	
FV	= 0	Bt	= 0,0	
VF	= 0	Cg	= 0,0	
V	= 0	Cl	= 0,0	
FY	= 0	Ex	= 0,0	
YF	= 0	Fd	= 0,0	
Y	= 0	Fi	= 0,0	
Fr	= 0	Ge	= 0,0	
rF	= 0	Hh	= 0,0	
FD	= 0	Ls	= 0,0	
F	= 14	Na	= 0,0	
		Sc	= 0,0	
		Sx	= 0,0	
		Xy	= 0,0	
		Id	= 0,0	
(2)	= 3			

DQ

.........(FQ–)

+	= 0	(0)
o	= 14	(8)
v/+	= 0	(0)
v	= 0	(0)

FORM QUALITY

	FQx	FQf	MQual	SQx
+	= 0	0	0	0
o	= 6	6	0	0
u	= 0	0	0	0
−	= 8	8	0	1
none	= 0	–	0	0

SPECIAL SCORINGS

	Lvl	Lv2
DV	= 0x1	1x2
INC	= 0x2	0x4
DR	= 0x3	0x6
FAB	= 0x4	0x7
ALOG	= 0x5	
CON	= 0x7	
SUM6	= 1	
WSUM6	= 2	

AB	=0	CP	= 0
AG	=0	MOR	= 0
CFB	=0	PER	= 0
COP	=0	PSV	= 0

RATIOS, PERCENTAGES, AND DERIVATIONS

R = 14	L = 14.00	FC:CF+C =0:0	COP = 0 AG = 0
		Pure C =0	Food = 0
EB = 0:0.0	EA = 0.0 EBPer = N/A	Afr =0.40	Isolate/R = 0.00
eb = 0:0	es = 0 D = 0	S =1	H:(H)Hd(Hd) = 0:2
	Adj es = 0 Adj D = 0	Blends:R =0:14	(HHd):(AAd) = 0:0
		CP =0	H+A:Hd + Ad = 6:8

FM = 0	C' = 0	T = 0	
m = 0	V = 0	Y = 0	

				P = 2	Zf =6		3r+(2)/R = 0.21
a:p	= 0:0	Sum6	= 1	X+% = 0.43	Zd =+2.0		Fr+rF = 0
Ma:Mp	= 0:0	Lv2	= 1	F+% = 0.43	W:D:Dd =6:7:1		FD = 0
2AB+Art+Ay	= 0	WSum6	= 2	X–% = 0.57	W:M = 6:0		An + Xy = 0
M–	= 0	Mnone	= 0	S–% = 0.13	DQ+ =0		MOR = 0
				Xu% = 0.00	DQv =0		

SCZI = 4*	DEPI = 3	CDI = 4*	S-CON = 5	HVI = No	OBS = No

Free Association

I

1) It could be a two-headed dragon.

2) A turtle sitting on top of two seals.

3) It could be a three-fingered witch.

II

4) It could be two poodles kissing under a tree.

5) It could be Jerry Lewis here on the bottom.

III

6) It looks like poodles, two poodles with lamps here. The lamps look like rabbits and these are a couple of birds flying by in the background . . . all one picture.

IV

7) It looks like a giant ancient cow. They're gone now. She just laid a baby right here.

V

8) It looks like a giant bat.

9) It looks like the facial characteristics of a varmet, a facial creature of some sort.

VI

10) It looks like the cross-section of a sea pod and it's getting ready to spring forward out of the earth.

11) It could be a god damned vagina with a giant clit on it.

VII

12) It looks like two dolls looking at each other.

13) It looks like a girl looking at herself in the mirror.

VIII

14) It looks like two giant otters. They are breaking the water with their necks and they are biting a giant frog. There is the water right here and they are standing on their two-headed mama down here.

IX

15) I've seen a critter like this under a microscope one time. It is some kind of microbe. It's splitting now. That is how they gestate.

X

16) It looks like a fish feed. Cut in half and unfolded. It is a dichotomy; the same on both sides. Here are the two crabs with green fish right here and here. He has it in his runney.

17) There is a worm here with it's reflection here.

18) This is a lung right here. I have my Ph.D. in psychology. I know what a lung looks like.

Author Index

577

Subject Index